The Portable
WALT WHITMAN

The Portable
WALT
WHITMAN

SELECTED AND WITH NOTES
BY MARK VAN DOREN

Revised by Malcolm Cowley
With a Chronology and a Bibliographical
Check List by Gay Wilson Allen

THE VIKING PRESS
New York

First published in 1945 by The Viking Press
40 West 23rd Street, New York, N.Y. 10010

Chronology and Bibliographical Check List
from *Walt Whitman* (revised edition), by Gay Wilson Allen.
Copyright © 1969 by Wayne State University Press,
Detroit, Michigan 48202.
Reprinted by permission.
Portable is a registered Trademark of
Viking Penguin, Inc.

Printed and Bound in the United States of America

Library of Congress Cataloging-in-Publication Data

Whitman, Walt, 1819–1892.
The portable Walt Whitman.

Bibliography: p.
I. Van Doren, Mark, 1894–1972. II. Cowley,
Malcolm, 1898–   .   III. Allen, Gay Wilson,
        1903–   .   IV. Title.
[PS3203.V3   1985]   811'.3   85-13614
ISBN: 0-517-478595

h g f e d c b a

Contents

DEMOCRATIC VISTAS

SPECIMEN DAYS

Introduction

BY MARK VAN DOREN

There still is something legendary about Walt Whitman—about the man himself, and about the one book, *Leaves of Grass*, for which he is so famous. This is not strange in view of the fact that *Leaves of Grass*, which made Emerson rub his eyes, still produces that effect on anyone who reads it well. It remains amazing, and so we look for wonders in the man. Nor is there any lack of them at hand. Whitman himself saw to that, as have a series of disciples whose constant burden has been the all but Messianic nature of their master. Whitman was certainly a remarkable man, or he could not have written his book. But for him to say, as he did in the poem "So Long!":

> Camerado! This is no book;
> Who touches this, touches a man

was to suggest something that can never quite be true. It was to suggest that *Leaves of Grass* had not been written at all; that it was the miracle of a man becoming, and becoming easily, the same thing as his words—whereas they can be distinguished and they should be, in the interest of both the man and the words. The man will then emerge as the artist he was, and the words—in this case the poems—will be disembarrassed of legends which never were relevant to the question of their intrinsic worth. Their worth as poetry is great. It is greater than some disciples of Whitman ever suspected, for they had only their god in view. *Leaves of Grass* can afford to be read for and by itself. And so can the best prose of Whitman, concerning which more will be said in the proper place.

The legend of the man was largely self-created. It was Whitman himself who wrote, over no signature, this account of the author of *Leaves of Grass* in an early review: "An American bard at last! One of the roughs, large, proud, affectionate, eating, drinking, and breeding, his costume manly and free, his face sunburnt and bearded, his posture strong and erect, his voice bringing hope and prophecy to the generous races of young and old. . . . If health were not his distinguishing attribute, this poet would be the very harlot of persons. Right and left he flings his arms, drawing men and women with undeniable love to his close embrace, loving the clasp of their hands, the touch of their neck and breasts, and the sound of their voices. All else seems to burn up under his fierce affection for persons." Such a man would of course be one who "steps into literature, talking like a man unaware that there was ever hitherto such a production as a book, or such a being as a writer. . . . He must recreate poetry with the elements always at hand. He must imbue it with himself as he is, disorderly, fleshly, and sensual, a lover of things, yet a lover of men and women above the whole of the other objects of the universe."

The legend these sentences were creating was the legend of a man who became a book by the simple process of overflowing into it. And the legend stuck. For it was interesting in itself, and there were those who in later days would repeat it, just as there were—and are—those who consider it a special glory to cease being critical as soon as Whitman's poetry heaves in sight. Such persons take everything in *Leaves of Grass* at its face value. They take it, that is, as bible and as autobiography. But it is poetry, at which a lonely artist labored with originality and tenacity.

A lonely artist. Whitman was that, because he was a lonely man. The legend of the large, proud, affectionate tough who hugged all America like a bear does not appear to be the truth. If Whitman was this way, it was in his imagination and by his desire, a fact which illuminates his book but does not help us to write his life. It is not merely a matter of his having wanted to be this way, and of having pretended that he was; the legend was not created to deceive us, or to aggrandize himself. The legend was legitimate, for it expressed Whitman's own failure to distinguish between the artist in himself and the person. Perhaps the distinction is never a clear one, nor is it assumed that anyone can say in Whitman's case just where it should be drawn. But there are fascinating discrepancies between the record and the legend, and to name some of them is in the long run to define Whitman's imagination a little more sharply than even he ever succeeded in doing, much as he was occupied with the subject of himself. He was probably too much occupied with that subject to be altogether clear about it. Among the mysteries of human personality this is one to which, in the nature of things, he could not give his full attention.

He was born in 1819 at West Hills, in the town of Huntington, Long Island, of poorly educated parents in whom Dutch and English blood was dominant. His father, Walter Whitman, whose name the son kept until 1855 when he abbreviated it, was a farmer and a carpenter; his mother he has more to say about—indeed, the two were always very close, and many of the Whitman letters which survive are addressed to her. Whitman never ceased to be glad that he had been born where he was, or to be proud that there had been Quakers among his ancestors on both sides. The opening pages of his *Specimen Days*, reprinted in the present volume, are devoted to his earliest environment, as well as to that one which surrounded him when in his fourth year the family moved to Brooklyn. Brooklyn and New York, together with rural and seaside "Paumanok," his name for fish-shaped Long Island, provided him with all the environment he was ever to need. Travel added others, but this one was the source of his thoughts and feelings; nor were his feelings about the city any less powerful than those he remembered having had along the shore when, on vacations and visits to the first world of his life, he would "race up and down the hard sand, and declaim Homer or Shakespeare to the turf and sea-gulls by the hour." The streets of Brooklyn and Manhattan, and the ferry which ran between, were equally exciting to him. New York he was always to celebrate as a sea of shoulders and faces, a tossing universe of souls that teemed as the sea did with fathomless wonders.

He went to the public schools of Brooklyn, but only until his thirteenth, or possibly his eleventh, year. After that he had to educate himself, and soon he was doing so in newspaper and printing offices. Newspapers became his trade, which he followed as office boy, printer's devil, journeyman compositor, reporter, book reviewer, and editor. For a while he taught school in Long Island villages, but the main record is of many dozen editorial dens where he drudged and wrote undistinguished pieces, whether of prose or of verse, between the years of his early manhood and the great year of 1855 when at thirty-six he burst upon the world in an entirely new identity as the author of *Leaves of Grass*. The unconventional writer of that book had in all of his previous works been conventional. There is no resemblance between the early and the mature poet in Whitman, nor can the ideas for which he is famous be traced back and found in his newspaper columns. Even as the editor of the *Brooklyn Eagle* (1846–48) he was no more than intelligent and liberal. The peculiar passions of his soul were so far only latent. The temperance novel, *Franklin Evans*, which he published in 1842 was routine for its time—bombastic and sentimental both. But so was everything else he did, though his editorials in the *Eagle* represented the routine at its best. The man—or the poet—who was to emerge in *Leaves of Grass* was slow in coming, and came only after a seven-year period about which his biographers know least, as is immemorially the case with prophets, self-appointed or otherwise. The reading he had done, and the plays and operas he had seen with such avidity on Broadway—these too he was to digest again and convert into the special materials his imagination was now to nourish itself with.

In 1848, when Whitman suddenly picked up and went to New Orleans, he was for all practical purposes a failure—a journalist who had never kept a job, a writer without a name. He was in addition a man who had lived in many boarding houses and tramped many streets. He does not seem in fact to have been the high-hearted rover among crowds, the mythical embracer of multitudes, who appears as the "I" in *Leaves of Grass*. Neither is there any evidence that he thought especially well of himself, that he felt himself to be the "proud, noble, vigorous" person whom he was to describe seven years later in an anonymous review of his own poems. The contrary was probably the case. He went to New Orleans to take another job, on the *Crescent;* and he returned a few months later to take still others in Brooklyn again. All this was nothing to boast about, and in those days Whitman did not boast.

But he was now on the threshold of his great days, and it is here that he more or less disappears from his biographers. Some of them think that New Orleans changed him, and indeed there is a legend that he loved a woman there, and that this made all the difference; there is even the further legend that he had children by her, now and later, and that this proved him the normal male he otherwise might be taken to have missed being. But in the present state of our knowledge all of this must be set down as pure legend—except that it remains possible to wonder whether a change of scene had worked some kind of magic in his mind. If so, however, there had to be in him the mind to receive the magic. Such a mind had always been there, of course. But other things could have moved it now toward an awakened state. Biographers speculate concerning a mystical experience around the year 1850. There was one, but the nature of it cannot be known. It could have been, for instance, an experience of illumination following upon his reading of Emerson, which was certainly important for him at some time or other. Emerson was the most potent writer of the age, and men responded to him in proportion to their own power. Whitman liked later on to suggest that Emerson had never been his intellectual creditor, but the trouble he took to deny discipleship may in itself be a sign that the discipleship was there. His preface to the first edition of *Leaves of Grass*, reproduced as the first selection in the present volume, will be evidence enough for some readers that Emerson had worked a revolution in Whitman's mind.

What Emerson had done for others was to fill them with a sense of their individual importance, and to convince them that as citizens of a New World they were under obligation to make a fresh start in the life of man—which here was to be a new life in the sense that henceforth each man was to be both average and extraordinary, both a democrat and a prince, both an artisan and a philosopher. Emerson was and is a very exciting writer. So is Whitman, and the one fact may be the result of the other. It may have been Emerson, that is, who recovered for Whitman his self-respect, and not only recovered it but inflated it to the point where he could describe himself, in still another anonymous review, as "of pure American breed, large and lusty ... a naïve, masculine, contemplative, sensual, imperious person," Emerson had recommended that everyone be all of that—without the special emphasis, to be sure, which Whitman was to place upon "sensual."

Whatever the cause, Whitman changed between 1848 and 1855 from a commonplace man to one of the most remarkable men we know; to be more precise, he changed into a person who understood how to talk as if he were Adam reborn. Reborn or not, he was now in one stroke the complete figure of his own legend. The first edition of *Leaves of Grass*, printed in Brooklyn in 1855 at the author's expense, was a failure with the public, which mostly abused and ignored it. But one copy had been sent to Emerson in Concord, and the letter of acknowledgment which came must in itself have paid Whitman for all his trouble. "I am not blind," said Emerson, "to the worth of the wonderful gift of *Leaves of Grass*. I find it the most extraordinary piece of wit and wisdom that America has yet contributed. I am very happy in reading it, as great power makes us happy. . . . I give you joy of your free and brave thought. I have great joy in it. I find incomparable things, said incomparably well, as they must be. . . . I greet you at the beginning of a great career, which yet must have had a long foreground, for such a start." Better praise has never been bestowed upon the book in equal space.

But the book was only at the beginning of its career, which henceforth was Whitman's career also. The first edition contained but twelve poems besides the preface. The rest of Whitman's life revolved about the succeeding editions, the first of which came the next year, in 1856, and the second in 1860. The edition of 1860 was more successful than either of its predecessors had been, though it was more shocking to those who could be shocked. Its two new sections, "Children of Adam" and "Calamus," explored the extremes of "amativeness," by which Whitman, adopting the phrenological language of his day, meant the love of men and women, and "adhesive-

ness," by which he meant the love or comradeship of men for
men. The "Calamus" poems were the first expression Whitman
had given, at least in *Leaves of Grass*, to the furtive, yearning
aspect of his soul; they no longer luxuriated in images of mating, but spoke instead of the distance that separates lovers—
even the distance of death, which makes love finally beautiful.
If the more athletic and affirmative poems had been difficult
to understand and believe, these were puzzling in another
sense; they hinted abnormality and confessed an all but incurable sadness.

Many further editions, rewritten and rearranged, were to
follow until Whitman's death in 1892, but meanwhile came the
Civil War, an episode of prime importance in Whitman's story.
He did not witness the war at first hand until the end of 1862,
when he went to Virginia to see his brother George, who had
been wounded. But now he was witness to such suffering as
he had never encountered before; and the rest of the war years
he spent in Washington, going among the wounded in the hospitals there, carrying sweets and writing paper, comforting those
whom he could with conversation, and assisting now and then
with dressings and operations. His prose book, *Memoranda
During the War* (1875), now included in *Specimen Days,* is
the best record we have of these years, and on any score is one
of his most interesting works. But the richest fruit of the war
was the volume of poems which he called *Drum-Taps* (1865),
and which when it was absorbed into the ever-growing *Leaves
of Grass* contributed to it his masterpiece in any form, "When
Lilacs Last in the Dooryard Bloom'd."

In 1865 Whitman was given a position in the Department of
the Interior, but it was soon taken away from him because, it
was said, Secretary Harlan disapproved of *Leaves of Grass*.
Although he was given another place in the Attorney General's
office, the indignation felt by his friends over his dismissal came
to a head in the publication of a pamphlet by William Douglas
O'Connor. The title of this pamphlet, *The Good Gray Poet,*
became attached to Whitman himself, and he carried it to
his grave. O'Connor's book in praise of Whitman was but the
first of several that were to appear during his lifetime, as his
reputation, already established in both the United States and

England, steadily grew. Half of the next book about him, *Notes on Walt Whitman as Poet and Person,* by John Burroughs (1867), was written by the subject himself; but from that point on, though he never ceased to assist his fame when he could, he did not need to depend upon his own efforts. Fame came of its free will, from Europe and America, along with many visitors.

His visitors found him in Camden, New Jersey, whither he had gone from Washington in 1873 because of a paralytic stroke from which he never fully recovered. He could still write, and did; and he could enjoy his friendships in leisure, along with the natural world which *Specimen Days* (1882) shows him enjoying with a delicious serenity. His last days were somewhat overwhelmed by the disciples who gathered about him and took down every word he spoke. He had said important things in *Democratic Vistas* (1871) and in the other books of his which have been named; but now his most unimportant remark was mistaken for a footnote to gospel. On the whole he basked in this adoration, though he was always more sensible than his Boswells were; and as late as 1888, in "A Backward Glance O'er Travel'd Roads," the preface to *November Boughs,* he composed a valuable new statement, not only about *Leaves of Grass* in retrospect, but about religion and literature in general. His final position is considerably different from the first one of 1855. He mellowed with time, learning to recognize the validity of many things he had begun by scorning.

With his death his reputation grew still greater, and it has ever continued to increase. The adulation of his coterie proved both a hindrance and a help in the process of making his name the universal thing it is at present. If his fame is immense at last, the reason is the residue of his works themselves rather than any program of interested praise. By now Whitman has proved that he can make his own way in the world. Indeed he has done so, though it is true that he has not become the prophet of the proletariat he seems to have assumed he was destined to become. He is probably too sophisticated a writer for that. He is certainly a difficult poet, and it may be that he will always seem a strange one. But it is now in order to speak of his works themselves, and to explain the principles upon which the present selection has been made.

The emphasis in the selection has of course been placed upon *Leaves of Grass*. But the prose in which Whitman explained and justified his poetry is in itself so interesting that two pieces of it have been placed before and after: the famous "Preface" of 1855, and the riper, reminiscent "Backward Glance O'er Travel'd Roads" of 1888. The remainder of the volume is devoted to the two principal prose works of Whitman: *Democratic Vistas and Specimen Days*, both reproduced entire. Whitman is less widely known for his prose than for his verse, but his prose has its own unique and careless power, and it is necessary to any reader's full understanding of him.

Leaves of Grass went through many forms before Whitman put the finishing touches on it in his declining years. The first edition, as has been said, contained only twelve poems: "Song of Myself," "A Song for Occupations," "To Think of Time," "The Sleepers," "I Sing the Body Electric," "Faces," "Now List to My Morning's Romanza," "Europe," "A Boston Ballad," "There Was a Child Went Forth," "Who Learns My Lesson Complete?" and "Great Are the Myths." They did not bear these titles; they bore none at all, except that the title of the volume preceded each of the first six. And they were much changed in later editions. Whitman was always rewriting *Leaves of Grass*, as well as extending its bulk. Also, he could never rest content with its arrangement. He liked to classify his poems, as Wordsworth did. His classifications are interesting, but they are not always intelligible. The best arrangement for the reader is that of time; the order in the selection which follows is chronological, at least within the limits of our knowledge on the point.

The second edition of 1856 contained thirty-two poems, including "Song of the Broad-Axe," "Crossing Brooklyn Ferry," and "Song of the Open Road." The third edition of 1860 was greatly enlarged, among other things by the inclusion, in a section called "Enfans d'Adam" (later called, more sensibly, "Children of Adam"), of such poems as "From Pent-up Aching Rivers"—poems which Emerson, when Whitman visited him in Boston, is said gently to have suggested were both too numerous and too fleshly in their frankness. There was also the section which ever since that date has born the name "Calamus"; its masterpiece is probably "I Saw in Louisiana a Live-Oak Growing," though in many another short poem concerning "manly love" Whitman came very near the perfection of this celebrated lyric. The outstanding contribution of the third edition, however, was "Out of the Cradle Endlessly Rocking," which had made its first appearance in the New York *Saturday Press* in 1859. Its only rival among all of Whitman's poems is "When Lilacs Last in the Dooryard Bloom'd," which distinguished the fourth edition of 1867, when *Leaves of Grass* absorbed the volume of Civil War poems, *Drum-Taps*, published in 1865. The fifth edition of 1871 contained "Passage to India," the last of Whitman's major poems. Subsequent editions in 1872, 1876, 1881, 1882, 1884, 1888, 1889, and 1891–92 saw the processes continuing of revision, rearrangement, and new composition.

The whole of *Leaves of Grass* naturally has great interest, but the work gains with most readers when it is cut. Much of it is repetition, and much of it is bad. The present selection aims at the best of it only, yet on a scale generous enough to exhibit Whitman as the great poet he is—great in terms of the personality he creates, the ideas he expresses, and the art he practices. After each poem to be found here, the date of its first publication is printed so that the reader may follow Whitman's progress through the editions to which he gave so much care.

The personality he creates and parades is sometimes assertive, sometimes furtive. The asserter of himself is better known —the rough specimen, the rediscovered Adam, the lusty fellow who says near the end of "Song of Myself":

Do I contradict myself?
Very well then . . . . I contradict myself;
I am large . . . . I contain multitudes.

I too am not a bit tamed . . . . I too am untranslatable,
I sound my barbaric yawp over the roofs of the world.

This fellow insists that he is "representative"—Emerson's word —rather than unique. He is an individual speaking for all individuals if they only knew what they might become; if he seems outrageous, he seems to say, that is only because the nature which is in him no less than in other men is always outrageous when met head on. He is human force, and human timidity had better get out of the way.

But this same fellow has another side; he can be longing, defeated, unsure of himself, and most delicately tentative in the confession of his private state. Thus speaks the poet of "Calamus," though he appears elsewhere too. And he is not necessarily inconsistent with the other man. The bridge between them is probably such poems as "There Was a Child Went Forth," in which Whitman develops the image of an individual soul uniting itself with all other souls on earth—of things as well as of persons—through the magic of identification. The child "becomes" what he sees; and as he does so he desires to see other things which he can become; he keeps on looking, keeps on taking the world in, till he has it all. In himself he is nobody, but in the end he is everything. "Salut au Monde!" continues the theme to a wearisome degree, and is therefore excluded here, but it is an announcement of how

Within me latitude widens, longitude lengthens,

and it is an exhaustive record of how

My spirit has pass'd in compassion and determination around
the whole earth.

The ideas of Whitman are clustered in the first place about an entity which he calls The New World. He was eventually to celebrate, in "Passage to India" and other poems, the claims which the old world, the world to the East, still has upon us. But most of the time he is intoxicated with America.

Having studied the mocking-bird's tones, and the mountain-
hawk's,
And heard at dusk the unrival'd one, the hermit thrush from
the swamp-cedars,
Solitary, singing in the West, I strike up for a New World.

So he concludes the first section of "Starting from Paumanok"; and in a hundred passages he writes of the miraculous fresh life which These States have before them.

It is the democratic life, the life of great average individuals, persons lyric with self-reliance, careless of history, and free at last of Europe's ancient agonies, of her indecisions. It is the life that Emerson had recommended, though many of its lineaments are peculiar to this poet who now is writing as if no one ever wrote before. It is a life which few if any actual persons live—Whitman is always aware of that, as for instance in the long poem "As I Sat Alone by Blue Ontario's Shore," where he warns his American readers:

I am he who walks the States with a barb'd tongue, questioning
        everyone I meet;
Who are you, that wanted only to be told what you knew
        before?
Who are you, that wanted only a book to join you in your
        nonsense?

He is never a flatterer of his people, whose manners and whose minds he blisters with many an unmerciful remark, in verse, in prose. The life he praises is still to be lived; or it can be imagined as existing now if details are not scrutinized.

Here is what moves in magnificent masses, careless of partic-
        ulars.

And indeed it can be more than imagined in contemporary America. It tends to be actual in those "powerful uneducated persons" whose greatness Whitman is more than willing to assume. He asserts it with all his might, dismissing as he does so the feeble thing which passes for education in seminaries and colleges. Such an education enervates and tames the citizen. Whitman would release that same citizen, whoever he is, into a larger world where education would go under its own power, with no one but America for schoolmistress. The citizen's opportunity is to become the unlimited Emersonian individual, all soul and body, all earth and heaven in one depository of flesh. Let there be no more heroes; or rather, let every individual be a hero, let the average man become divine.

I swear I begin to see the meaning of these things!
It is not the earth, it is not America, who is so great,
It is I who am great, or to be great—it is you up there, or
     any one;
It is to walk rapidly through civilizations, governments,
     theories,
Through poems, pageants, shows, to form great individuals.

Underneath all, individuals!
I swear nothing is good to me now that ignores individuals,
The American compact is altogether with individuals,
The only government is that which makes minute of indi-
     viduals,
The whole theory of the universe is directed to one single indi-
     vidual—namely to You.

That again is from the poem "As I Sat Alone by Blue Ontario's
Shore," a poem valuable chiefly for these lines and for the four
others quoted above.

And the thing that binds individuals together is love.
Whitman is a great love poet because love is necessary to his
understanding of the universe, as it must be for anyone who
tries to see into the heart of creation. Also, love was necessary
to *him*. He may have missed it in its more familiar manifesta-
tions, as his biography suggests, and as "Calamus" says. But
men who miss it are likely to be men with a special sense of its
unique price. So at any rate with Whitman, who explores its
mysteries on many levels.

     Who goes there! hankering, gross, mystical, nude?

Thus, in "Song of Myself," speaks the Whitman whom most
readers know, the semibarbarous, semiangelic singer of
sexual delight. No one has ever been franker than he concerning this delight, or more savage in insisting that it be given
expression in its own terms, regardless of who will shrink from
the result. When its own terms are brutal, then the poet must
be brutal to match them, though he will be as tender too as
desire in another aspect knows how to be. But Whitman goes
farther than this. In certain sections of "Song of Myself" he

explores the terrors and inversions of sex as well as its sunny places. No reality of love was alien to his interest, which he kept always at a pitch of intensity rare in the records of the theme.

The sign that he approached the limit of the theme is its inseparableness in his best poems from the theme of death. Death is the subject of his masterpieces, "Out of the Cradle Endlessly Rocking" and "When Lilacs Last in the Dooryard Bloom'd." The fact may appear strange to one who thinks of Whitman as a poet dedicated to life. But in all great poetry love and life have been stated in terms of death, so that the dedication in Whitman's case need not be suspect.

> And I will show that whatever happens to anybody, it may be
> turn'd to beautiful results—and I will show that nothing
> can happen more beautiful than death.

Heavenly death—it is a common phrase on Whitman's lips, and he means it literally. For it is through death that he sees, as he believes, into the heart of creation—where of course life also is, as sister and bride. At the center of the universe love and death lie down together. Any great love plunges to this point in its career, as any great death—like that of Lincoln— becomes a carol announcing the union. Whitman is mystically certain about all this, which is why, together with the reason that he is already a magnificent poet, he reaches in his best poems the height that he does. Not many other poets would be at home there.

It was difficult for him to accept death, and it was even more difficult for him to love it. The record of his success is written in the chronology of the poems, from "This Compost" on. The true mystic does not see easily what at last he sees. For Whitman there was the advantage that from the beginning he had announced he would accept everything. All is beautiful and good, he says; and so death should be. But the vision came hard—another sign of its reality. So for that matter may have come the vision of all as beautiful and good. Whitman's constant asseveration of this may have been to keep his courage up. He contemplates ugly things—ulcers, monsters, and the carnage of battle—with a fierceness of attention which testifies to his resolution that he will love them in spite of everything. The "everything" in his case was a natural fastidiousness surpassing that of most men. It was much to conquer. But he conquered it as he had conquered his first fear of death.

For I do not see one imperfection in the universe;
And I do not see one cause or result lamentable at last in the universe.

O setting sun! though the time has come,
I still warble under you, if none else does, unmitigated adoration.

Whitman's art as a poet is a matter of some mystery. There are those who say that he had no art, or if he did that it was bad in the sense that nobody else can learn it. But those who admit the existence in him of a potent artist, crafty as well as inspired, are often at a loss to say what they mean. As with any good poet, of course, there are effects in him which cannot be explained. Nor should one desire to explain his power with phrases. It is a fresh power, an originating power, and as such is as strange as the equivalent thing in Shakespeare, Homer, Dante, or any other master of the great thing suddenly said. Such a way with words is never to be understood. It is miraculous, and must be let alone; nor can any poet who lacks it hope for fame. In *Leaves of Grass* it riots in the first lines of poems:

I celebrate myself.

There was a child went forth every day.

Weapon shapely, naked, wan.

Afoot and light-hearted I take to the open road.

A woman waits for me.

Out of the cradle endlessly rocking.

I hear America singing.

A noiseless patient spider.

But it riots everywhere—"O, night of the large few stars!"—
"I am he that walks with the tender and growing night"—
"Which let us go forth in the bold day and write."

But a poet needs more than this miraculous power. He must
also be an architect of poems, if only so that a fine line may
become still finer by benefit of context. Here Whitman fails
quite as often as he succeeds. His best poems are organized with
a superb subtlety—not only the two masterpieces which have
been mentioned, but many an evanescent lyric over which it
might have been supposed he had forgotten to linger with a
craftsman's care. Two perfect instances are "I Saw in Louisiana
a Live-Oak Growing" and "A Noiseless Patient Spider."
Their form is flawless, as doubtless befits the importance each
subject had for Whitman—comradeship in the one case, sepa-
rateness in the other. A great many of Whitman's poems,
however, both short and long, are without discoverable organization. He is notorious for his resort to the catalogue of
details. Now and then he succeeds with it, but more often, as
certainly in "Salut au Monde!," he drones on to dreary lengths,
inviting parody. Hence the pages and pages in *Leaves of Grass*
which few persons read, or at any rate read again. Whitman
had the illusion, common to prophetic natures, that everything
he said must be right because he said it. Poetry has a special
way of exposing the error, for it demands its own kind of
rightness, regardless of any other. Whitman did not regularly
take the trouble to be right as a poet. He has paid the penalty.

He would have said that he was an orator also. He studied
oratory as an art, and imagined himself a god of the platform.
But even the arts of eloquence have their obligation to form.
The man on the rostrum must build his discourse as well as
stud it with splendid sayings. Whitman too often let the whole
matter go with a phrase. It was grand, but it was not enough.

The prose of a good poet is likely to be good prose.
Whitman's has the defect of his verse—it tends to be careless,
to rely upon improvisation, to pile itself up; but it also has its
moments, and in general it is better than at first glance, or on
first hearing, it seems. The bear moves with his own grace, and
gets there sooner than we expected he would. So the prose
of Whitman, bad as it undoubtedly is through long stretches

of dashes and expletives, and approximations rather than revelations of his thought, has its fascinations and cannot be ignored.

Democratic Vistas (1871) is in a certain sense unrepresentative of its author. For it seeks to be a treatise, and Whitman had no gift for ordering ideas. It is of the greatest interest because of what it manages to get said—it is a powerful indictment of the shortcomings of American democracy in Whitman's time, as well as an eloquent reminder of what democracy at its best is supposed to mean, and for this reason it will always occupy a position near the center of his work. But superficially it is less attractive reading than *Specimen Days* (1882), which rambles as Whitman liked to ramble, with neither form nor direction for a finish line. Writing its pages in full confidence that an audience existed for any reminiscences he saw fit to furnish, he traveled comfortably among his memories and impressions, or worked in passages from the notes he inveterately kept on what he thought and observed. The result is an undressed book but a real one; and in its Civil War section it is matchless reporting.

So much for the two prose books which are represented in the following pages, though more will be said about them in their places. But Whitman wrote a vast deal else in prose, and something should be said about his range of subject matter. One subject which he could never leave alone was Shakespeare. As a critic of other poets he is always worth reading—as witness him on Poe, Longfellow, Bryant—but he was particularly taken by the greatest of them all. He does not seem to have known this, for he spent much time accusing Shakespeare of not having been a democrat—of being, in fact, "feudal," and hence not for "us." But it is clear that Shakespeare had infected him with the charm no man can withstand, the charm which inheres in the accurate knowledge of other men, no matter in what perspective of theory we choose to see them. Shakespeare, in other words, had life; and Whitman was never able to resist life. His admiration for Shakespeare shines through every indictment he draws, and often for the same reason that he felt bound to praise Carlyle. Carlyle was scornful of democracy (as Shakespeare, for all we know, would not have been if he had understood the term), but Whitman values him precisely for that reason. Carlyle is the critic he has been looking for, and he can overlook the premises of the criticism in view of the fact that such a good surgeon is at hand. As Shakespeare had shown what near-gods men may be if they can, so Carlyle has "an intuition of the absolute balance, in time and space, of the whole of this multifarious, mad chaos of fraud, frivolity, hoggishness—this revel of fools, and incredible make-believe and general unsettledness, we call the *world*.... His rude, rasping, taunting, contradictory tones—what ones are more wanted amid the supple, polish'd, money-worshipping, Jesus-and-Judas-equalizing, suffrage-sovereignty echoes of current America?" That is Whitman speaking, not Carlyle.

It may be, however, that none of Whitman's prose is more important than his prefaces to *Leaves of Grass*. For in those prefaces he is trying to pursue his thought to the end—his thought not only about poetry but about the life he would like to see lived. As for poetry, he saw no enemy to it in the science which like each of his contemporaries he troubled himself to understand as well as he could. Science in his opinion was making over the world. Very well, the world needed to be made over. What was his own poetry doing but making it over too? There could be a partnership between these revolutionary agencies, provided science agreed with poetry that the lives of all should be affected. "To have great poets, there must be great audiences too." So certainly with science. To have great philosophers there must be great people. Whitman always came back to the people, and to their potential greatness.

A good many letters of Whitman survive, but they are of little or no literary interest. This is a sample of those to Peter Doyle, the young horse-car conductor to whom he became attached in Washington: "It is splendid today—I have been over all day working, quite busy—and have just got home, and had my dinner—it is now about 4. It is quite pleasant riding here in Brooklyn—we have large open cars, in good weather it is real lively—I quite enjoy it—Pete, give my respects to Mr. and Mrs. Nash, and to your cousin—also to Jenny Murphy —not forgetting the boys on the road—also Wash Milburn— God bless you—and goodbye for this time, my own dear loving

boy. Walt." And this is a sample of those to his mother:
"Mother I send a couple of papers same time with this—they
are not much, but will do just for a change;—poor old Uncle
John—he is failing then at last—I suppose George is well &
having good times—I see him every day as I have his picture
tacked up on the door of my desk in front—Goodbye dearest
mother & take care of yourself, & don't work too hard. Walt."
The correspondence with Doyle is silly, and though the same
thing cannot be said of Whitman's letters to his mother, yet it is
obvious that they served no other purpose than a private one,
and there is no point in considering them as public possessions.

Whitman's reputation is best served by those who concentrate upon his best work: *Leaves of Grass* and its prefaces, and
the two prose works by which he expected to be remembered.
They alone are enough to justify the praise he is everywhere
given. It is proper praise for one who looked and said:

I see a great round wonder rolling through the air.

A Note on the New Edition

BY MALCOLM COWLEY

This is a somewhat revised, enlarged, and completely reset edition of a book that first appeared in 1945. Mark Van Doren's fine biographical and critical introduction stands here without change after all those years; it was not written for the moment. His editorial scheme for the book also stands unchanged, as having proved the best for a one-volume Whitman. Particularly sound was his notion of choosing the best poems from *Leaves of Grass*—something he did with a poet's discriminating taste —and printing them in chronological order. He also selected the essential prose works: *Democratic Vistas, Specimen Days,* the preface to the First edition, and "A Backward Glance O'er Travel'd Roads." The development of Whitman scholarship over thirty-odd years has confirmed the judgments he made in 1945.

The same development, however, has made it advisable to change the Whitman texts that Van Doren followed, especially for *Leaves of Grass*. During Whitman's lifetime there were nine editions of the *Leaves*, each (through the Seventh, 1881–82) incorporating revisions and rearrangements, and all adding new poems. There were only twelve poems in the First edition (1855); there were 389 in the Ninth edition (1891–92), widely known as the Deathbed; and thirteen others, called "Old Age Echoes," were added posthumously in the Inclusive edition of 1897. As for Whitman's revisions, they were usually improvements over earlier versions, but there are exceptions to the rule. It is now widely felt that the twelve poems of the

First edition—including the greatest, "Song of Myself"—are fresher, bolder, more personal, more unified as Whitman first printed them.

All this explains the procedure followed in this new edition of *The Portable Walt Whitman*. Poems from the First edition —there are seven of them here—are printed in the 1855 text; and the Preface to *Leaves of Grass* also follows that text. For poems that first appeared in 1856 and later years, the text followed scrupulously is that of the 1891–92 or Deathbed edition, the last one that Whitman supervised. A few admired poems have been added to Van Doren's first selection; among them are "As I Ebb'd with the Ocean of Life," "Prayer of Columbus" (the last of his greater poems), and "Good-bye My Fancy!" Two poems have been omitted, in spite of their containing some eloquent lines. One is "Who Learns My Lesson Complete?" which Whitman kept revising, but never, apparently, to his own satisfaction, and the other is "Great Are the Myths," which the poet himself omitted after 1876. There are one hundred poems in the present selection, as against the original ninety-seven, and they are the lasting heart of *Leaves of Grass*.

Fewer changes had to be made in the text of Whitman's prose works, but one of them is an important addition. *Specimen Days* is now reprinted complete. Van Doren had wished to include the full text of it in his 1945 edition, but the book was being printed in wartime, when paper was hard to come by, and so he had to save pages by making a selection of the best passages. It was a rich selection, as good as could be made, but the complete book is even better. There is also space in this revised edition for two new features that will be appreciated by students and teachers. These are a Whitman chronology and a bibliographical check list, both of them contributed by our friend Gay Wilson Allen, author of the standard Whitman biography.

I say "our friend" because Mark Van Doren and I shared an admiration for Allen's scholarly work. As with the other changes in the original Portable, this addition was discussed with Mark and met with his entire approval. Work on this new edition was substantially completed before his death, which was a loss to the world of letters and a personal loss for me, as it was for I cannot say how many others.

1973

Chronology

BY GAY WILSON ALLEN

1819   Born May 31 at West Hills, near Huntington, Long Island, New York.

1823   Whitman family moved to Brooklyn.

1830(?)–34 Learning printing trade.

1835   Printer in New York City until great fire August 12.

1836–38   Summer of 1836 begins teaching school at East Norwich, Long Island; by winter of 1837–38 had taught at Hempstead, Babylon, Long Swamp, and Smithtown.

1838–39   Edits newspaper, the *Long Islander*, at Huntington, about twelve months; works on newspaper at Jamaica, the *Long Island Democrat*; contributes "Sun-Down Papers from the Desk of a Schoolmaster" while teaching school at Little Bay Side (near Jamaica).

1840–41   In late summer and autumn 1840 electioneers for Van Buren; then teaches school at Trimming Square, Woodbury, Dix Hills, and Whitestone.

1841   Goes to New York City in May as printer in *New World* office and begins writing for the *Democratic Review*.

1842   For about two months in spring edits a daily newspaper, the *New York Aurora*; edits the *Evening Tattler* for a few months.

1845–46   In August returns to Brooklyn, writes for *Long Island Star* from September 1845 until March 1846.

1846–48   From March 1846 until late January 1848 editor of *Brooklyn Daily Eagle;* in February 1848, trip to New Orleans via railroad, stagecoach, and steamboat; employed on *New Orleans Crescent* from March 5 to May 25; returns by boat via Mississippi, Great Lakes, and Hudson River.

1848–49   From September 9, 1848, to September 11, 1849, editor of *Brooklyn Freeman,* a "Free Soil" newspaper.

1850–54   Operates printing office and stationery store; does free-lance writing for newspapers; mainly a building contractor and real estate speculator.

1855   Early July, *Leaves of Grass* printed by Rome Brothers in Brooklyn; father dies July 11.

1856   Second edition of *Leaves of Grass* printed in summer. "The Eighteenth Presidency" written; copies survive only in proof sheets.

1857–59   From spring of 1857 to mid-summer of 1859, editor of *Brooklyn Times.*

1860   March 1860, in Boston to see new edition of *Leaves of Grass* through the press, published in May by Thayer and Eldridge; June 16, Japanese "ambassadors" parade on Broadway and Whitman writes "The Errand-Bearers" (A Broadway Pageant"); frequents Pfaff's restaurant.

1861   April 12, Fort Sumter fired upon by Confederate batteries—beginning of Civil War.

1862   In December goes to Fredericksburg, scene of recent battle in which George Whitman was wounded, stays in camp about two weeks; remains in Washington, D.C., working part time in Paymaster's Office, visiting soldiers in hospitals.

1863–64   Hospital visits in Washington continue until mid-June 1864; returns to Brooklyn because of ill health.

1865   January 24, appointed clerk in Department of Interior and returns to Washington.
           March 4, second inauguration of President Lincoln witnessed by Whitman. While he is visiting his

family in Brooklyn, Lincoln assassinated April 14. George recently released from Confederate prison. May, *Drum-Taps* printed.

Discharged from position in Department of Interior by Secretary James Harlan on June 30; re-employed next day in Attorney General's Office. *Sequel to Drum-Taps,* containing "When Lilacs Last in the Dooryard Bloom'd," printed in September.

1866   In January, William D. O'Connor's *Good Gray Poet* published by Bunce & Harrington, New York City.

1867   Publication of first biography of Whitman, John Burroughs' *Notes on Walt Whitman as Poet and Person;* William Rossetti publishes article on Whitman's poetry in *London Chronicle,* July 6.

Fourth edition of *Leaves of Grass* printed.

"Democracy" (part of *Democratic Vistas*) in December *Galaxy.*

1868   William Rossetti's selected English edition (slightly expurgated) of *Poems of Walt Whitman;* wider recognition in England.

"Personalism" (part of *Democratic Vistas*) in May *Galaxy.*

Second issue of Fourth edition of *Leaves of Grass* with *Drum-Taps* and *Sequel* added.

1870   July 15, beginning of Franco-Prussian War; Whitman very depressed for personal reasons.

1871   Fifth edition of *Leaves of Grass,* containing "Passage to India."

September 3, Mrs. Anne Gilchrist's first love letter to Whitman.

1872   "As a Strong Bird on Pinions Free" read at Dartmouth College Commencement, June 26.

"After All Not to Create Only" ("Song of the Exposition") read at National Industrial Exposition in New York, September 7.

Quarrel with O'Connor and end of friendship.

Swinburne's attack in "Under the Microscope."

1873	Paralytic stroke night of January 23, 1873.
	Death of poet's mother, May 23, in Camden, New Jersey; unable to work, has to live with brother George in Camden.
1874	Publication of "Song of the Redwood-Tree" and "Prayer of Columbus."
1875	Centennial edition of *Leaves of Grass* and *Two Rivulets* printed (dated 1876).
1876	Controversy in British and American press over America's neglect of Whitman.
	In spring, begins visits to Stafford Farm.
	In September, Mrs. Gilchrist arrives in United States.
1879	First lecture on Lincoln, April 14, Philadelphia.
	Trip to West (Colorado), September 1879 to January 1880.
1880	Summer, trip to London, Ontario, to visit Dr. R. M. Bucke.
1881	Lincoln lecture given in Boston in April.
	James R. Osgood, Boston, publishes *Leaves of Grass*.
1882	In spring, District Attorney threatens prosecution and Osgood gives up *Leaves of Grass;* publication resumed by Rees Welsh and Co., of Philadelphia, which also publishes *Specimen Days and Collect*. Both books transferred to David McKay, Philadelphia.
1883	Dr. R. M. Bucke publishes *Walt Whitman,* a biography on which the poet had assisted.
1884	Buys house on Mickle Street in Camden, New Jersey.
1887	Lincoln lecture given in New York.
	Sculptured by Sidney Morse; painted by Herbert Gilchrist, J. W. Alexander, and Thomas Eakins.
1888	Horace Traubel raises funds for doctors and nurses. *November Boughs* printed.
1889	Birthday dinner, proceedings published as *Camden's Compliments*.

1890   Letter from John Addington Symonds provokes poet to claim six unacknowledged children.

1891   *Good-Bye, My Fancy* printed.

1892   Ninth edition of *Leaves of Grass*.
        Death of poet March 26; buried in Harleigh Cemetery, Camden, New Jersey.

LEAVES OF GRASS 1850–1891

SELECTIONS

EDITOR'S NOTE TO
PREFACE TO LEAVES OF GRASS

The long preface which Whitman placed before the first issue
of *Leaves of Grass* in 1855 was a manifesto, not an apology.
It does not refer to the poems that follow except through an
occasional use, without quotation marks, of phrases which the
reader will find in them when he goes on. Modern literature
is full of manifestoes, but few have been written with a purer
sense of dedication than Whitman felt here. One sign of this
is the epigrammatic brilliance of his style, a brilliance encountered nowhere else in his prose. The sentences are short and
powerful because they abridge a genuine vision. The vision is
traceable to Emerson, as the style is, but the whole effect is
nevertheless in a high sense original. This preface is one of
Whitman's finest works.

"The United States themselves are essentially the greatest
poem." "There is that indescribable freshness and unconscious-
ness about an illiterate person that humbles and mocks the
power of the noblest expressive genius." "The greatest poet
... is a seer ... he is individual ... he is complete in himself
... the others are as good as he, only he sees it and they do
not." Each of these sentences has implications that volumes
could develop, and particularly the third of them has; it is
one of the best definitions of the poet, of the great person, ever
made. "The art of art ... is simplicity." "Men and women and
the earth and all upon it are simply to be taken as they are."
"Every man shall be his own priest." "The known universe
has one complete lover and that is the greatest poet." So the
sentences run—each one quiet, each one startling. The last of
all has gained pathos with time. "The proof of a poet is that
his country absorbs him as affectionately as he has absorbed
it." America has never absorbed Whitman in the way he hoped

it would, in the way, for instance, that it has absorbed Long-fellow. For all his devotion to the people, he has not become in the technical sense of the term a popular poet. The blame, it is true, does not lie entirely with him.

Preface to Leaves of Grass
1855

America does not repel the past or what it has produced under its forms or amid other politics or the idea of castes or the old religions . . . accepts the lesson with calmness . . . is not so impatient as has been supposed that the slough still sticks to opinions and manners and literature while the life which served its requirements has passed into the new life of the new forms . . . perceives that the corpse is slowly borne from the eating and sleeping rooms of the house . . . perceives that it waits a little while in the door . . . that it was fittest for its days . . . that its action has descended to the stalwart and wellshaped heir who approaches . . . and that he shall be fittest for his days.

The Americans of all nations at any time upon the earth have probably the fullest poetical nature. The United States themselves are essentially the greatest poem. In the history of the earth hitherto the largest and most stirring appear tame and orderly to their ampler largeness and stir. Here at last is something in the doings of man that corresponds with the broadcast doings of the day and night. Here is not merely a nation but a teeming nation of nations. Here is action untied from strings necessarily blind to particulars and details magnificently moving in vast masses. Here is the hospitality which forever indicates heroes. . . . Here are the roughs and beards and space and ruggedness and nonchalance that the soul loves. Here the performance disdaining the trivial unapproached in the tremendous audacity of its crowds and groupings and the push of its perspective spreads with crampless and flowing breadth and showers its prolific and splendid extravagance. One sees it must indeed own the riches of the summer and winter, and need never be bankrupt while corn grows from the ground or the orchards drop apples or the bays contain fish or men beget children upon women.

Other states indicate themselves in their deputies ... but the genius of the United States is not best or most in its executives or legislatures, nor in its ambassadors or authors or colleges or churches or parlors, nor even in its newspapers or inventors ... but always most in the common people. Their manners speech dress friendships—the freshness and candor of their physiognomy—the picturesque looseness of their carriage ... their deathless attachment to freedom—their aversion to anything indecorous or soft or mean—the practical acknowledgment of the citizens of one state by the citizens of all other states—the fierceness of their roused resentment— their curiosity and welcome of novelty—their self-esteem and wonderful sympathy—their susceptibility to a slight—the air they have of persons who never knew how it felt to stand in the presence of superiors—the fluency of their speech—their delight in music, the sure symptom of manly tenderness and native elegance of soul ... their good temper and openhandedness—the terrible significance of their elections—the President's taking off his hat to them not they to him—these too are unrhymed poetry. It awaits the gigantic and generous treatment worthy of it.

The largeness of nature of the nation were monstrous without a corresponding largeness and generosity of the spirit of the citizen. Not nature nor swarming states nor streets and steamships nor prosperous business nor farms nor capital nor learning may suffice for the ideal of man ... nor suffice the poet. No reminiscences may suffice either. A live nation can always cut a deep mark and can have the best authority the cheapest ... namely from its own soul. This is the sum of the profitable uses of individuals or states and of present action and grandeur and of the subjects of poets.—As if it were necessary to trot back generation after generation to the eastern records! As if the beauty and sacredness of the demonstrable must fall behind that of the mythical! As if men do not make their mark out of any times! As if the opening of the western

continent by discovery and what has transpired since in North
and South America were less than the small theatre of the
antique or the aimless sleepwalking of the middle ages! The
pride of the United States leaves the wealth and finesse of the
cities and all returns of commerce and agriculture and all the
magnitude of geography or shows of exterior victory to enjoy
the breed of fullsized men or one fullsized man unconquerable
and simple.

The American poets are to enclose old and new for America
is the race of races. Of them a bard is to be commensurate
with a people. To him the other continents arrive as contributions ... he gives them reception for their sake and his own
sake. His spirit responds to his country's spirit ... he incarnates
its geography and natural life and rivers and lakes. Mississippi
with annual freshets and changing chutes, Missouri and Columbia and Ohio and Saint Lawrence with the falls and beautiful masculine Hudson, do not embouchure where they spend
themselves more than they embouchure into him. The blue
breadth over the inland sea of Virginia and Maryland and the
sea off Massachusetts and Maine and over Manhattan bay and
over Champlain and Erie and over Ontario and Huron and
Michigan and Superior, and over the Texan and Mexican
and Floridian and Cuban seas and over the seas off California
and Oregon, is not tallied by the blue breadth of the waters
below more than the breadth of above and below is tallied by
him. When the long Atlantic coast stretches longer and the
Pacific coast stretches longer he easily stretches with them
north or south. He spans between them also from east to west
and reflects what is between them. On him rise solid growths
that offset the growths of pine and cedar and hemlock and
liveoak and locust and chestnut and cypress and hickory and
limetree and cottonwood and tuliptree and cactus and wildvine
and tamarind and persimmon ... and tangles as tangled as any
canebrake or swamp ... and forests coated with transparent
ice and icicles hanging from the boughs and crackling in the
wind ... and sides and peaks of mountains ... and pasturage
sweet and free as savannah or upland or prairie ... with flights
and songs and screams that answer those of the wildpigeon

and highhold and orchard-oriole and coot and surf-duck and redshouldered-hawk and fish-hawk and white-ibis and indian-hen and cat-owl and water-pheasant and qua-bird and pied-sheldrake and blackbird and mockingbird and buzzard and condor and night-heron and eagle. To him the hereditary countenance descends both mother's and father's. To him enter the essences of the real things and past and present events—of the enormous diversity of temperature and agriculture and mines—the tribes of red aborigines—the weatherbeaten vessels entering new ports or making landings or rocky coasts—the first settlements north or south—the rapid stature and muscle —the haughty defiance of '76, and the war and peace and formation of the constitution . . . the union always surrounded by blatherers and always calm and impregnable—the perpetual coming of immigrants—the wharfhem'd cities and superior marine—the unsurveyed interior—the loghouses and clearings and wild animals and hunters and trappers . . . the free commerce—the fisheries and whaling and gold-digging—the endless gestation of new states—the convening of Congress every December, the members duly coming up from all climates and the uttermost parts . . . the noble character of the young mechanics and for all free American workmen and workwomen . . . the general ardor and friendliness and enterprise—the perfect equality of the female with the male . . . the large amativeness —the fluid movement of the population—the factories and mercantile life and laborsaving machinery—the Yankee swap —the New-York firemen and the target excursion—the southern plantation life—the character of the northeast and of the northwest and southwest—slavery and the tremulous spreading of hands to protect it, and the stern opposition to it which shall never cease till it ceases or the speaking of tongues and the moving of lips cease. For such the expression of the American poet is to be transcendent and new. It is to be indirect and not direct or descriptive or epic. Its quality goes through these to much more. Let the age and wars of other nations be chanted and their eras and characters be illustrated and that finish the verse. Not so the great psalm of the republic. Here the theme is creative and has vista. Here comes one among the wellbeloved stonecutters and plans with decision and science and sees the solid and beautiful forms of the future where there are now no solid forms.

Of all nations the United States with veins full of poetical stuff most need poets and will doubtless have the greatest and use them the greatest. Their Presidents shall not be their common referee so much as their poets shall. Of all mankind the great poet is the equable man. Not in him but off from him things are grotesque or eccentric or fail of their sanity. Nothing out of its place is good and nothing in its place is bad. He bestows on every object or quality its fit proportions neither more nor less. He is the arbiter of the diverse and he is the key. He is the equalizer of his age and land . . . he supplies what wants supplying and checks what wants checking. If peace is the routine out of him speaks the spirit of peace, large, rich, thrifty, building vast and populous cities, encouraging agriculture and the arts and commerce—lighting the study of man, the soul, immortality—federal, state or municipal government, marriage, health, freetrade, intertravel by land and sea . . . nothing too close, nothing too far off . . . the stars not too far off. In war he is the most deadly force of the war. Who recruits him recruits horse and foot . . . he fetches parks of artillery the best that engineer ever knew. If the time becomes slothful and heavy he knows how to arouse it . . . he can make every word he speaks draw blood. Whatever stagnates in the flat of custom or obedience or legislation he never stagnates. Obedience does not master him, he masters it. High up out of reach he stands turning a concentrated light . . . he turns the pivot with his finger . . . he baffles the swiftest runners as he stands and easily overtakes and envelops them. The time straying toward infidelity and confections and persiflage he withholds by his steady faith . . . he spreads out his dishes . . . he offers the sweet firmfibred meat that grows men and women. His brain is the ultimate brain. He is no arguer . . . he is judgment. He judges not as the judge judges but as the sun falling around a helpless thing. As he sees the farthest he has the most faith. His thoughts are the hymns of the praise of things. In the talk on the soul and eternity and God off his equal plane he is silent. He sees eternity less like a play with a prologue and denouement . . . he sees eternity in men and women . . . . he does

not see men and women as dreams or dots. Faith is the antiseptic of the soul ... it pervades the common people and
preserves them ... they never give up believing and expecting
and trusting. There is that indescribable freshness and un-
consciousness about an illiterate person that humbles and
mocks the power of the noblest expressive genius. The poet
sees for a certainty how one not a great artist may be just as
sacred and perfect as the greatest artist.... The power to
destroy or remould is freely used by him but never the power
of attack. What is past is past. If he does not expose superior
models and prove himself by every step he takes he is not
what is wanted. The presence of the greatest poet conquers ...
not parleying or struggling or any prepared attempts. Now he
has passed that way see after him! there is not left any vestige
of despair or misanthropy or cunning or exclusiveness or the
ignominy of a nativity or color or delusion of hell or the
necessity of hell ... and no man thenceforward shall be degraded for ignorance or weakness or sin.

The greatest poet hardly knows pettiness or triviality. If he
breathes into any thing that was before thought small it dilates
with the grandeur and life of the universe. He is a seer ... he
is individual ... he is complete in himself ... the others are
as good as he, only he sees it and they do not. He is not one
of the chorus ... he does not stop for any regulations ... he
is the president of regulation. What the eyesight does to the
rest he does to the rest. Who knows the curious mystery of
the eyesight? The other senses corroborate themselves, but this
is removed from any proof but its own and foreruns the
identities of the spiritual world. A single glance of it mocks
all the investigations of man and all the instruments and books
of the earth and all reasoning. What is marvellous? what is
unlikely? what is impossible or baseless or vague? after you
have once just opened the space of a peachpit and given
audience to far and near and to the sunset and had all things
enter with electric swiftness softly and duly without confusion
or jostling or jam.

The land and sea, the animals fishes and birds, the sky of
heaven and the orbs, the forests mountains and rivers, are not
small themes ... but folks expect of the poet to indicate more

than the beauty and dignity which always attach to dumb real objects... they expect him to indicate the path between reality and their souls. Men and women perceive the beauty well enough ... probably as well as he. The passionate tenacity of hunters, woodmen, early risers, cultivators of gardens and orchards and fields, the love of healthy women for the manly form, seafaring persons, drivers of horses, the passion for light and the open air, all is an old varied sign of the unfailing perception of beauty and of a residence of the poetic in out-door people. They can never be assisted by poets to perceive ... some may but they never can. The poetic quality is not marshalled in rhyme or uniformity or abstract addresses to things nor in melancholy complaints or good precepts, but is the life of these and much else and is in the soul. The profit of rhyme is that it drops seeds of a sweeter and more luxuriant rhyme, and of uniformity that it conveys itself into its own roots in the ground out of sight. The rhyme and uniformity of perfect poems show the free growth of metrical laws and bud from them as unerringly and loosely as lilacs or roses on a bush, and take shapes as compact as the shapes of chest-nuts and oranges and melons and pears, and shed the perfume impalpable to form. The fluency and ornaments of the finest poems or music or orations or recitations are not independent but dependent. All beauty comes from beautiful blood and a beautiful brain. If the greatnesses are in conjunction in a man or woman it is enough ... the fact will prevail through the universe ... but the gaggery and gilt of a million years will not prevail. Who troubles himself about his ornaments or fluency is lost. This is what you shall do: Love the earth and sun and the animals, despise riches, give alms to every one that asks, stand up for the stupid and crazy, devote your in-come and labor to others, hate tyrants, argue not concerning God, have patience and indulgence toward the people, take off your hat to nothing known or unknown or to any man or number of men, go freely with powerful uneducated persons and with the young and with the mothers of families, read these leaves in the open air every season of every year of your life, re-examine all you have been told at school or church or in any book, dismiss whatever insults your own soul, and your

very flesh shall be a great poem and have the richest fluency
not only in its words but in the silent lines of its lips and face
and between the lashes of your eyes and in every motion and
joint of your body.... The poet shall not spend his time in
unneeded work. He shall know that the ground is always ready
ploughed and manured ... others may not know it but he
shall. He shall go directly to the creation. His trust shall
master the trust of everything he touches ... and shall master
all attachment.

The known universe has one complete lover and that is the
greatest poet. He consumes an eternal passion and is indifferent
which chance happens and which possible contingency of fortune or misfortune and persuades daily and hourly his delicious
pay. What balks or breaks others is fuel for his burning progress
to contact and amorous joy. Other proportions of the reception of pleasure dwindle to nothing to his proportions. All
expected from heaven or from the highest he is rapport with
in the sight of the daybreak or a scene of the winter woods
or the presence of children playing or with his arm round
the neck of a man or woman. His love above all love has
leisure and expanse ... he leaves room ahead of himself. He
is no irresolute or suspicious lover ... he is sure ... he scorns
intervals. His experience and the showers and thrills are not
for nothing. Nothing can jar him ... suffering and darkness
cannot—death and fear cannot. To him complaint and jealousy
and envy are corpses buried and rotten in the earth ... he saw
them buried. The sea is not surer of the shore or the shore
of the sea than he is of the fruition of his love and all perfection
and beauty.

The fruition of beauty is no chance of hit or miss ... it is
inevitable as life ... it is exact and plumb as gravitation. From
the eyesight proceeds another eyesight and from the hearing
proceeds another hearing and from the voice proceeds another
voice eternally curious of the harmony of things with man.
To these respond perfections not only in the committees that
were supposed to stand for the rest but in the rest themselves
just the same. These understand the law of perfection in masses
and floods ... that its finish is to each for itself and onward
from itself ... that it is profuse and impartial ... that there is

not a minute of the light or dark nor an acre of the earth or sea without it—nor any direction of the sky nor any trade or employment nor any turn of events. This is the reason that about the proper expression of beauty there is precision and balance ... one part does not need to be thrust above another. The best singer is not the one who has the most lithe and powerful organ ... the pleasure of poems is not in them that take the handsomest measure and similes and sound.

Without effort and without exposing in the least how it is done the greatest poet brings the spirit of any or all events and passions and scenes and persons some more and some less to bear on your individual character as you hear or read. To do this well is to compete with the laws that pursue and follow time. What is the purpose must surely be there and the clue of it must be there ... and the faintest indication is the indication of the best and then becomes the clearest indication. Past and present and future are not disjoined but joined. The greatest poet forms the consistence of what is to be from what has been and is. He drags the dead out of their coffins and stands them again on their feet ... he says to the past, Rise and walk before me that I may realize you. He learns the lesson ... he places himself where the future becomes present. The greatest poet does not only dazzle his rays over character and scenes and passions ... he finally ascends and finishes all ... he exhibits the pinnacles that no man can tell what they are for or what is beyond ... he glows a moment on the extremest verge. He is most wonderful in his last half-hidden smile or frown ... by that flash of the moment of parting the one that sees it shall be encouraged or terrified afterwards for many years. The greatest poet does not moralize or make applications of morals ... he knows the soul. The soul has that measureless pride which consists in never acknowledging any lessons but its own. But it has sympathy as measureless as its pride and the one balances the other and neither can stretch too far while it stretches in company with the other. The inmost secrets of art sleep with the twain. The greatest poet has lain close betwixt both and they are vital in his style and thoughts.

The art of art, the glory of expression and the sunshine of the light of letters is simplicity. Nothing is better than simplicity ... nothing can make up for excess or for the lack of definiteness. To carry on the heave of impulse and pierce intellectual depths and give all subjects their articulations are powers neither common nor very uncommon. But to speak in literature with the perfect rectitude and insouciance of the movements of animals and the unimpeachableness of the sentiment of trees in the woods and grass by the roadside is the flawless triumph of art. If you have looked on him who has achieved it you have looked on one of the masters of the artists of all nations and times. You shall not contemplate the flight of the graygull over the bay or the mettlesome action of the blood horse or the tall leaning of sunflowers on their stalk or the appearance of the sun journeying through heaven or the appearance of the moon afterward with any more satisfaction than you shall contemplate him. The greatest poet has less a marked style and is more the channel of thoughts and things without increase or diminution, and is the free channel of himself. He swears to his art, I will not be meddlesome, I will not have in my writing any elegance or effect or originality to hang in the way between me and the rest like curtains. I will have nothing hang in the way, not the richest curtains. What I tell I tell for precisely what it is. Let who may exalt or startle or fascinate or soothe I will have purposes as health or heat or snow has and be as regardless of observation. What I experience or portray shall go from my composition without a shred of my composition. You shall stand by my side and look in the mirror with me.

The old red blood and stainless gentility of great poets will be proved by their unconstraint. A heroic person walks at his ease through and out of that custom or precedent or authority that suits him not. Of the traits of the brotherhood of writers savans musicians inventors and artists nothing is finer than silent defiance advancing from new free forms. In the need of poems philosophy politics mechanism science behaviour, the craft of art, an appropriate native grand-opera, shipcraft, or any craft, he is greatest forever and forever who contributes the greatest original practical example. The cleanest expression is that which finds no sphere worthy of itself and makes one.

The messages of great poets to each man and woman are,

Come to us on equal terms, Only then can you understand us,
We are no better than you, What we enclose you enclose,
What we enjoy you may enjoy. Did you suppose there could
be only one Supreme? We affirm there can be unnumbered
Supremes, and that one does not countervail another any more
than one eyesight countervails another . . . and that men can be
good or grand only of the consciousness of their supremacy
within them. What do you think is the grandeur of storms
and dismemberments and the deadliest battles and wrecks and
the wildest fury of the elements and the power of the sea and
the motion of nature and of the throes of human desires and
dignity and hate and love? It is that something in the soul
which says, Rage on, Whirl on, I tread master here and everywhere, Master of the spasms of the sky and of the shatter of
the sea, Master of nature and passion and death, And of all
terror and all pain.

The American bards shall be marked for generosity and
affection and for encouraging competitors . . . They shall be
kosmos . . . without monopoly or secrecy . . . glad to pass any
thing to any one . . . hungry for equals night and day. They
shall not be careful of riches and privilege . . . they shall be
riches and privilege . . . they shall perceive who the most affluent man is. The most affluent man is he that confronts all the
shows he sees by equivalents out of the stronger wealth of
himself. The American bard shall delineate no class of persons
nor one or two out of the strata of interests nor love most nor
truth most nor the soul most nor the body most . . . and not
be for the eastern states more than the western or the northern
states more than the southern.

Exact science and its practical movements are no checks on
the greatest poet but always his encouragement and support.
The outset and remembrance are there . . . there the arms that
lifted him first and brace him best . . . there he returns after all
his goings and comings. The sailor and traveller . . . the anatomist chemist astronomer geologist phrenologist spiritualist
mathematician historian and lexicographer are not poets, but
they are the lawgivers of poets and their construction underlies
the structure of every perfect poem. No matter what rises or
is uttered they sent the seed of the conception of it . . . of them

and by them stand the visible proofs of souls ... always of their fatherstuff must be begotten the sinewy races of bards. If there shall be love and content between the father and the son and if the greatness of the son is the exuding of the greatness of the father there shall be love between the poet and the man of demonstrable science. In the beauty of poems are the tuft and final applause of science.

Great is the faith of the flush of knowledge and of the investigation of the depths of qualities and things. Cleaving and circling here swells the soul of the poet yet is president of itself always. The depths are fathomless and therefore calm. The innocence and nakedness are resumed ... they are neither modest nor immodest. The whole theory of the special and supernatural and all that was twined with it or educed out of it departs as a dream. What has ever happened ... what happens and whatever may or shall happen, the vital laws enclose all ... they are sufficient for any case and for all cases ... none to be hurried or retarded ... any miracle of affairs or persons inadmissible in the vast clear scheme where every motion and every spear of grass and the frames and spirits of men and women and all that concerns them are unspeakably perfect miracles all referring to all and each distinct and in its place. It is also not consistent with the reality of the soul to admit that there is anything in the known universe more divine than men and women.

Men and women and the earth and all upon it are simply to be taken as they are, and the investigation of their past and present and future shall be unintermitted and shall be done with perfect candor. Upon this basis philosophy speculates ever looking toward the poet, ever regarding the eternal tendencies of all toward happiness never inconsistent with what is clear to the senses and to the soul. For the eternal tendencies of all toward happiness make the only point of sane philosophy. Whatever comprehends less than that ... whatever is less than the laws of light and of astronomical motion ... or less than the laws that follow the thief the liar the glutton and the drunkard through this life and doubtless afterward ... or less than vast stretches of time or the slow formation of density or the patient upheaving of strata—is of no account. Whatever

would put God in a poem or system of philosophy as contending against some being or influence is also of no account. Sanity
and ensemble characterise the great master ... spoilt in one
principle all is spoilt. The great master has nothing to do with
miracles. He sees health for himself in being one of the mass
... he sees the hiatus in singular eminence. To the perfect shape
comes common ground. To be under the general law is great
for that is to correspond with it. The master knows that he is
unspeakably great and that all are unspeakably great ... that
nothing for instance is greater than to conceive children and
bring them up well ... that to be is just as great as to perceive or tell.

   In the make of the great masters the idea of political liberty
is indispensable. Liberty takes the adherence of heroes wherever men and women exist ... but never takes any adherence
or welcome from the rest more than from poets. They are the
voice and exposition of liberty. They out of ages are worthy
the grand idea ... to them it is confided and they must sustain
it. Nothing has precedence of it and nothing can warp or
degrade it. The attitude of great poets is to cheer up slaves and
horrify despots. The turn of their necks, the sound of their
feet, the motions of their wrists, are full of hazard to the one
and hope to the other. Come nigh them awhile and though they
neither speak or advise you shall learn the faithful American
lesson. Liberty is poorly served by men whose good intent is
quelled from one failure or two failures or any number of
failures, or from the casual indifference or ingratitude of the
people, or from the sharp show of the tushes of power, or the
bringing to bear soldiers and cannon or any penal statutes.
Liberty relies upon itself, invites no one, promises nothing, sits
in calmness and light, is positive and composed, and knows
no discouragement. The battle rages with many a loud alarm
and frequent advance and retreat ... the enemy triumphs ...
the prison, the handcuffs, the iron necklace and anklet, the
scaffold, garrot and leadballs do their work ... the cause is
asleep ... the strong throats are choked with their own blood
.. the young men drop their eyelashes toward the ground
when they pass each other ... and is liberty gone out of that
place? No never. When liberty goes it is not the first to go

nor the second or third to go...it waits for all the rest to go
...it is the last... When the memories of the old martyrs are
faded utterly away...when the large names of patriots are
laughed at in the public halls from the lips of the orators...
when the boys are no more christened after the same but
christened after tyrants and traitors instead...when the laws
of the free are grudgingly permitted and laws for informers
and bloodmoney are sweet to the taste of the people...when
I and you walk abroad upon the earth stung with compassion
at the sight of numberless brothers answering our equal friendship and calling no man master—and when we are elated with
noble joy at the sight of slaves...when the soul retires in the
cool communion of the night and surveys its experience and
has much extasy over the word and deed that put back a helpless innocent person into the gripe of the gripers or into any
cruel inferiority...when those in all parts of these states who
could easier realize the true American character but do not
yet—when the swarms of cringers, suckers, doughfaces, lice
of politics, planners of sly involutions for their own preferment
to city offices or state legislatures or the judiciary or congress
or the presidency, obtain a response of love and natural deference from the people whether they get the offices or no...
when it is better to be a bound booby and rogue in office at a
high salary than the poorest free mechanic or farmer with his
hat unmoved from his head and firm eyes and a candid and
generous heart...and when servility by town or state or the
federal government or any oppression on a large scale or small
scale can be tried on without its own punishment following duly
after in exact proportion against the smallest chance of escape
...or rather when all life and all the souls of men and women
are discharged from any part of the earth—then only shall the
instinct of liberty be discharged from that part of the earth.

As the attributes of the poets of the kosmos concentre in the
real body and soul and in the pleasure of things they possess
the superiority of genuineness over all fiction and romance.
As they emit themselves facts are showered over with light...
the daylight is lit with more volatile light...also the deep
between the setting and rising sun goes deeper many fold. Each

precise object or condition or combination or process exhibits
a beauty ... the multiplication table its—old age its—the carpenter's trade its—the grand-opera its ... the hugehulled clean-
shaped New-York clipper at sea under steam or full sail
gleams with unmatched beauty ... the American circles and
large harmonies of government gleam with theirs ... and the
commonest definite intentions and actions with theirs. The
poets of the kosmos advance through all interpositions and
coverings and turmoils and stratagems to first principles. They
are of use ... they dissolve poverty from its need and riches
from its conceit. You large proprietor they say shall not realize
or perceive more than any one else. The owner of the library is
not he who holds a legal title to it having bought and paid for it.
Any one and every one is owner of the library who can read
the same through all the varieties of tongues and subjects and
styles, and in whom they enter with ease and take residence and
force toward paternity and maternity, and make supple and
powerful and rich and large .... These American states strong
and healthy and accomplished shall receive no pleasure from
violations of natural models and must not permit them. In
paintings or mouldings or carvings in mineral or wood, or in
the illustrations of books or newspapers, or in any comic or
tragic prints, or in the patterns of woven stuffs or any thing
to beautify rooms or furniture or costumes, or to put upon
cornices or monuments or on the prows or sterns of ships, or
to put anywhere before the human eye indoors or out, that
which distorts honest shapes or which creates unearthly beings
or places or contingencies is a nuisance and revolt. Of the
human form especially it is so great it must never be made
ridiculous. Of ornaments to a work nothing outre can be
allowed ... but those ornaments can be allowed that conform
to the perfect facts of the open air and that flow out of the
nature of the work and come irrepressibly from it and are
necessary to the completion of the work. Most works are most
beautiful without ornament. .... Exaggerations will be revenged
in human physiology. Clean and vigorous children are jetted
and conceived only in those communities where the models
of natural forms are public every day ... Great genius and the

people of these states must never be demeaned to romances.
As soon as histories are properly told there is no more need
of romances.

The great poets are also to be known by the absence in them
of tricks and by the justification of perfect personal candor.
Then folks echo a new cheap joy and divine voice leaping from
their brains: How beautiful is candor! All faults may be
forgiven of him who has perfect candor. Henceforth let no
man of us lie, for we have seen that openness wins the inner
and outer world and that there is no single exception, and that
never since our earth gathered itself in a mass have deceit or
subterfuge or prevarication attracted its smallest particle or the
faintest tinge of a shade—and that through the enveloping
wealth and rank of a state or the whole republic of states a
sneak or sly person shall be discovered and despised . . . and
that the soul has never been once fooled and never can be
fooled . . . and thrift without the loving nod of the soul is only
a fœtid puff . . . and there never grew up in any of the continents of the globe nor upon any planet or satellite or star, nor
upon the asteroids, nor in any part of ethereal space, nor in the
midst of density, nor under the fluid wet of the sea, nor in
that condition which precedes the birth of babes, nor at any
time during the changes of life, nor in that condition that
follows what we term death, nor in any stretch of abeyance
or action afterward of vitality, nor in any process of formation or reformation anywhere, a being whose instinct hated
the truth.

Extreme caution or prudence, the soundest organic health,
large hope and comparison and fondness for women and children, large alimentiveness and destructiveness and causality,
with a perfect sense of the oneness of nature and the propriety
of the same spirit applied to human affairs . . . these are called
up of the float of the brain of the world to be parts of the
greatest poet from his birth out of his mother's womb and from
her birth out of her mother's. Caution seldom goes far enough.
It has been thought that the prudent citizen was the citizen who
applied himself to solid gains and did well for himself and his
family and completed a lawful life without debt or crime. The
greatest poet sees and admits these economies as he sees the

economies of food and sleep, but has higher notions of prudence than to think he gives much when he gives a few slight attentions at the latch of the gate. The premises of the prudence of life are not the hospitality of it or the ripeness and harvest of it. Beyond the independence of a little sum laid aside for burial-money, and of a few clapboards around and shingles overhead on a lot of American soil owned, and the easy dollars that supply the year's plain clothing and meals, the melancholy prudence of the abandonment of such a great being as a man is to the toss and pallor of years of moneymaking with all their scorching days and icy nights and all their stifling deceits and underhanded dodgings, or infinitesimals of parlors, or shameless stuffing while others starve . . . and all the loss of the bloom and odor of the earth and of the flowers and atmosphere and of the sea and of the true taste of the women and men you pass or have to do with in youth or middle age, and the issuing sickness and desperate revolt at the close of a life without elevation or naivete, and the ghastly chatter of a death without serenity or majesty, is the great fraud upon modern civilization and forethought, blotching the surface and system which civilization undeniably drafts, and moistening with tears the immense features it spreads and spreads with such velocity before the reached kisses of the soul . . . Still the right explanation remains to be made about prudence. The prudence of the mere wealth and respectability of the most esteemed life appears too faint for the eye to observe at all when little and large alike drop quietly aside at the thought of the prudence suitable for immortality. What is wisdom that fills the thinness of a year or seventy or eighty years to wisdom spaced out by ages and coming back at a certain time with strong reinforcements and rich presents and the clear faces of wedding-guests as far as you can look in every direction running gaily toward you? Only the soul is of itself . . . all else has reference to what ensues. All that a person does or thinks is of consequence. Not a move can a man or woman make that affects him or her in a day or a month or any part of the direct lifetime or the hour of death but the same affects him or her onward afterward through the indirect lifetime. The indirect is always as great and real as the direct. The spirit receives from the body just as much as

it gives to the body. Not one name of word or deed . . . not
of venereal sores or discolorations . . . not the privacy of the
onanist . . . not of the putrid veins of gluttons or rumdrinkers
. . . not peculation or cunning or betrayal or murder . . . no
serpentine poison of those that seduce women . . . not the foolish
yielding of women . . . not prostitution . . . not of any depravity
of young men . . . not of the attainment of gain by discreditable
means . . . not any nastiness of appetite . . . not any harshness
of officers to men or judges to prisoners or fathers to sons or
sons to fathers or husbands to wives or bosses to their boys
. . . not of greedy looks or malignant wishes . . . nor any of the
wiles practised by people upon themselves . . . ever is or ever
can be stamped on the programme but it is duly realized and
returned, and that returned in further performances . . . and
they returned again. Nor can the push of charity or personal
force ever be any thing else than the profoundest reason, whether it brings arguments to hand or no. No specification is necessary . . . to add or subtract or divide is in vain. Little or big,
learned or unlearned, white or black, legal or illegal, sick or
well, from the first inspiration down the windpipe to the last
expiration out of it, all that a male or female does that is
vigorous and benevolent and clean is so much sure profit to
him or her in the unshakable order of the universe and through
the whole scope of it forever. If the savage or felon is wise
it is well . . . if the greatest poet or savan is wise it is simply
the same . . . if the President or chief justice is wise it is the
same . . . if the young mechanic or farmer is wise it is no more
or less . . . if the prostitute is wise it is no more nor less. The
interest will come round . . . all will come round. All the best
actions of war and peace . . . all help given to relatives and
strangers and the poor and old and sorrowful and young children and widows and the sick, and to all shunned persons . . .
all furtherance of fugitives and of the escape of slaves . . . all
the self-denial that stood steady and aloof on wrecks and saw
others take the seats of the boats . . . all offering of substance
or life for the good old cause, or for a friend's sake or opinion's
sake . . . all pains of enthusiasts scoffed at by their neighbors
. . . all the vast sweet love and precious suffering of mothers . . .
all honest men baffled in strifes recorded or unrecorded . . .

all the grandeur and good of the few ancient nations whose
fragments of annals we inherit ... and all the good of the
hundreds of far mightier and more ancient nations unknown
to us by name or date or location ... all that was ever manfully
begun, whether it succeeded or not ... all that has at any time
been well suggested out of the divine heart of man or by the
divinity of his mouth or by the shaping of his great hands ...
and all that is well thought or done this day on any part of the
surface of the globe ... or on any of the wandering stars or
fixed stars by those there as we are here ... or that is henceforth
to be well thought or done by you whoever you are, or by any
one—these singly and wholly inured at their time and inure
now and will inure always to the identities from which they
sprung or shall spring ... Did you guess any of them lived
only its moment? The world does not so exist ... no parts
palpable or impalpable so exist ... no result exists now without
being from its long antecedent result, and that from its antecedent, and so backward without the farthest mentionable spot
coming a bit nearer the beginning than any other spot ... Whatever satisfies the soul is truth. The prudence of the greatest
poet answers at last the craving and glut of the soul, is not
contemptuous of less ways of prudence if they conform to its
ways, puts off nothing, permits no let-up for its own case or
any case, has no particular sabbath or judgment-day, divides
not the living from the dead or the righteous from the unright-
eous, is satisfied with the present, matches every thought or act
by its correlative, knows no possible forgiveness or deputed
atonement ... knows that the young man who composedly
periled his life and lost it has done exceeding well for himself,
while the man who has not periled his life and retains it to
old age in riches and ease has perhaps achieved nothing for
himself worth mentioning ... and that only that person has
no great prudence to learn who has learnt to prefer real long-
lived things, and favors body and soul the same, and perceives
the indirect assuredly following the direct, and what evil or
good he does leaping onward and waiting to meet him again
—and who in his spirit in any emergency whatever neither
hurries or avoids death.

The direct trial of him who would be the greatest poet is

today. If he does not flood himself with the immediate age as with vast oceanic tides ... and if he does not attract his own land body and soul to himself and hang on its neck with incomparable love and plunge his semitic muscle into its merits and demerits ... and if he be not himself the age transfigured ... and if to him is not opened the eternity which gives similitude to all periods and locations and processes and animate and inanimate forms, and which is the bond of time, and rises up from its inconceivable vagueness and infiniteness in the swimming shape of today, and is held by the ductile anchors of life, and makes the present spot the passage from what was to what shall be, and commits itself to the representation of this wave of an hour and this one of the sixty beautiful children of the wave—let him merge in the general run and wait his development ... Still the final test of poems or any character or work remains. The prescient poet projects himself centuries ahead and judges performer or performance after the changes of time. Does it live through them? Does it still hold on untired? Will the same style and the direction of genius to similar points be satisfactory now? Has no new discovery in science or arrival at superior planes of thought and judgment and behaviour fixed him or his so that either can be looked down upon? Have the marches of tens and hundreds and thousands of years made willing detours to the right hand and the left hand for his sake? Is he beloved long and long after he is buried? Does the young man think often of him? and the young woman think often of him? and do the middleaged and the old think of him?

A great poem is for ages and ages in common and for all degrees and complexions and all departments and sects and for a woman as much as a man and a man as much as a woman. A great poem is no finish to a man or woman but rather a beginning. Has any one fancied he could sit at last under some due authority and rest satisfied with explanations and realize and be content and full? To no such terminus does the greatest poet bring ... he brings neither cessation or sheltered fatness and ease. The touch of him tells in action. Whom he takes he takes with firm sure grasp into live regions previously unattained ... thenceforward is no rest ... they see the space and ineffable sheen that turn the old spots and lights into dead vacuums. The companion of him beholds the birth and progress of stars and learns one of the meanings. Now there shall be a man cohered out of tumult and chaos ... the elder encourages the younger and shows him how ... they two shall launch off fearlessly together till the new world fits an orbit for itself and looks unabashed on the lesser orbits of the stars and sweeps through the ceaseless rings and shall never be quiet again.

There will soon be no more priests. Their work is done. They may wait awhile ... perhaps a generation or two ... dropping off by degrees. A superior breed shall take their place ... the gangs of kosmos and prophets en masse shall take their place. A new order shall arise and they shall be the priests of man, and every man shall be his own priest. The churches built under their umbrage shall be the churches of men and women. Through the divinity of themselves shall the kosmos and the new breed of poets be interpreters of men and women and of all events and things. They shall find their inspiration in real objects today, symptoms of the past and future. ... They shall not deign to defend immortality or God or the perfection of things or liberty or the exquisite beauty and reality of the soul. They shall arise in America and be responded to from the remainder of the earth.

The English language befriends the grand American expression ... it is brawny enough and limber and full enough. On the tough stock of a race who through all change of circumstances was never without the idea of political liberty, which is the animus of all liberty, it has attracted the terms of daintier and gayer and subtler and more elegant tongues. It is the powerful language of resistance ... it is the dialect of common sense. It is the speech of the proud and melancholy races and of all who aspire. It is the chosen tongue to express growth faith self-esteem freedom justice equality friendliness amplitude prudence decision and courage. It is the medium that shall well nigh express the inexpressible.

No great literature nor any like style of behaviour or oratory or social intercourse or household arrangements or public institutions or the treatment by bosses of employed people, nor executive detail or detail of the army or navy, nor spirit of legislation or courts or police or tuition or architecture or songs or amusements or the costumes of young men, can long elude the jealous and passionate instinct of American standards. Whether or no the sign appears from the mouths of the people, it throbs a live interrogation in every freeman's and freewoman's heart after that which passes by or this built to remain. Is it uniform with my country? Are its disposals without ignominious distinctions? Is it for the evergrowing communes of brothers and lovers, large, well-united, proud beyond the old models, generous beyond all models? Is it something grown fresh out of the fields or drawn from the sea for use to me today here? I know that what answers for me an American must answer for any individual or nation that serves for a part of my materials. Does this answer? or is it without reference to universal needs? or sprung of the needs of the less developed society of special ranks? or old needs of pleasure overlaid by modern science and forms? Does this acknowledge liberty with audible and absolute acknowledgement, and set slavery at nought for life and death? Will it help breed one goodshaped and wellhung man, and a woman to be his perfect and independent mate? Does it improve manners? Is it for the nursing of the young of the republic? Does it solve readily with the sweet milk of the nipples of the breasts of the mother of many children? Has it too the old ever-fresh forbearance and impartiality? Does it look with the same love on the last born and on those hardening toward stature, and on the errant, and on those who disdain all strength of assault outside of their own?

The poems distilled from other poems will probably pass away. The coward will surely pass away. The expectation of the vital and great can only be satisfied by the demeanor of the vital and great.

The swarms of the polished deprecating and reflectors and the polite float off and leave no remembrance. America prepares with composure and goodwill for the visitors that have sent word. It is not intellect that is to be their warrant and welcome. The talented, the artist, the ingenious, the editor, the statesman, the erudite ... they are not unappreciated ... they fall in their place and do their work. The soul of the nation also does its work. No disguise can pass on it . . . no disguise can conceal from it. It rejects none, it permits all. Only toward as good as itself and toward the like of itself will it advance half-way. An individual is as superb as a nation when he has the qualities which make a superb nation. The soul of the largest and wealthiest and proudest nation may well go half-way to meet that of its poets. The signs are effectual. There is no fear of mistake. If the one is true the other is true. The proof of a poet is that his country absorbs him as affectionately as he has absorbed it.

EDITOR'S NOTE TO
LEAVES OF GRASS

Leaves of Grass is the central item in all of Whitman's work. It is the one book upon which he lavished constant care, molding it ever more affectionately into the shape he desired that it should have after his death. The various arrangements he made of its poems never yielded an altogether satisfactory result; but then no poet has succeeded at this impossible task. The poems are the thing, and they still speak for themselves in a powerful voice. The arrangement of the following selection is chronological, on the theory that time's arrangement is the most revealing. The dates printed at the end of the poems will guide the reader through the first edition of 1855, the "Children of Adam" and the "Calamus" sections of 1860, the Civil War pieces of 1865, and the various annexes to *Leaves of Grass* thereafter.

The one criterion of choice has been excellence as the editor understands excellence. Certain of the longer poems—notably "Salut au Monde!" "As I Sat Alone by Blue Ontario's Shore," and "Starting from Paumanok"—have been omitted because of stretches in them which did not seem to balance the few lines worth saving; these lines have, as a matter of fact, been saved by quotation in the Introduction, which also suggests a reason for the failure of the stretches. The other major pieces are here—"Song of Myself," "A Song for Occupations," "I Sing the Body Electric," "Song of the Broad-Axe," "Crossing Brooklyn Ferry," "Song of the Open Road," "Out of the Cradle Endlessly Rocking," "When Lilacs Last in the Dooryard Bloom'd," "Proud Music of the Storm," "Prayer of Columbus," and "Passage to India." Not that it is a complete list, or that the word "major" is to be taken as meaning anything but "long." Whitman's short poems have perhaps equal greatness when they are good, as they so often are. The best of them are likely to be found over the dates 1860 and 1865—that is, in the sections to which Whitman gave the names "Calamus" and "Drum-Taps." The vignettes of war in "Drum-Taps" are unrivaled for the things they do, and "Calamus" is still unique in the world's poetry. But in other places too Whitman will be found both brief and brilliant. In 1868 he published "A Noiseless Patient Spider"; in 1874, "The Ox-Tamer" and "The Dalliance of the Eagles"; and in 1891, the year before he died, "Good-bye My Fancy!" which is a brief and moving afterword to his poetic career.

The First Edition
1855

[Europe: *The 72d and 73d Years of These States*]

Suddenly out of its stale and drowsy lair, the lair of slaves,
Like lightning Europe le'pt forth .... half startled at itself,
Its feet upon the ashes and the rags .... Its hands tight
    to the throats of kings.

O hope and faith! O aching close of lives! O many
    a sickened heart!
Turn back unto this day, and make yourselves afresh.

And you, paid to defile the People .... you liars mark:
Not for numberless agonies, murders, lusts,
For court thieving in its manifold mean forms,
Worming from his simplicity the poor man's wages;
For many a promise sworn by royal lips, and broken, and
    laughed at in the breaking,
Then in their power not for all these did the blows strike of
    personal revenge .. or the heads of the nobles fall;
The People scorned the ferocity of kings.

But the sweetness of mercy brewed bitter destruction,
    and the frightened rulers come back:
Each comes in state with his train .... hangman, priest and
    tax-gatherer .... soldier, lawyer, jailer and sycophant.

Yet behind all, lo, a Shape,
Vague as the night, draped interminably, head front
    and form in scarlet folds,

Whose face and eyes none may see,
Out of its robes only this .... the red robes, lifted
    by the arm,
One finger pointed high over the top, like the head of
    a snake appears.

Meanwhile corpses lie in new-made graves .... bloody
    corpses of young men:
The rope of the gibbet hangs heavily .... the bullets of
    princes are flying .... the creatures of power laugh aloud,
And all these things bear fruits .... and they are good.

Those corpses of young men,
Those martyrs that hang from the gibbets ... those hearts
    pierced by the gray lead,
Cold and motionless as they seem .. live elsewhere with
    unslaughter'd vitality.

They live in other young men, O kings,
They live in brothers, again ready to defy you:
They were purified by death .... they were taught and exalted.

Not a grave of the murdered for freedom but grows
    seed for freedom .... in its turn to bear seed,
Which the winds carry afar and re-sow, and the rains and
    the snows nourish.

Not a disembodied spirit can the weapons of tyrants let loose,
But it stalks invisibly over the earth .. whispering
    counseling cautioning.

Liberty let others despair of you .... I never despair of you.

Is the house shut? Is the master away?
Nevertheless be ready .... be not weary of watching,
He will soon return .... his messengers come anon.

[1850]

[Song of Myself]

[1]

I celebrate myself,
And what I assume you shall assume,
For every atom belonging to me as good belongs to you.

I loafe and invite my soul,
I lean and loafe at my ease .... observing a spear of
    summer grass.

[2]

Houses and rooms are full of perfumes .... the shelves are
    crowded with perfumes,
I breathe the fragrance myself, and know it and like it,
The distillation would intoxicate me also, but I shall
    not let it.

The atmosphere is not a perfume .... it has no taste of the
    distillation .... it is odorless,
It is for my mouth forever .... I am in love with it,
I will go to the bank by the wood and become undisguised
    and naked,
I am mad for it to be in contact with me.

The smoke of my own breath,
Echoes, ripples, and buzzed whispers .... loveroot,
    silkthread, crotch and vine,
My respiration and inspiration .... the beating of my heart
    .... the passing of blood and air through my lungs,
The sniff of green leaves and dry leaves, and of the shore
    and darkcolored sea-rocks, and of hay in the barn,
The sound of the belched words of my voice .... words
    loosed to the eddies of the wind,
A few light kisses .... a few embraces .... a reaching
    around of arms,
The play of shine and shade on the trees as the supple
    boughs wag,

The delight alone or in the rush of the streets, or along the
      fields and hillsides,
The feeling of health .... the full-noon trill .... the song
      of me rising from bed and meeting the sun.

Have you reckoned a thousand acres much? Have you
      reckoned the earth much?
Have you practiced so long to learn to read?
Have you felt so proud to get at the meaning of poems?

Stop this day and night with me and you shall possess the
      origin of all poems,
You shall possess the good of the earth and sun ....
      there are millions of suns left,
You shall no longer take things at second or third hand ....
      nor look through the eyes of the dead .... nor feed
      on the spectres in books,
You shall not look through my eyes either, nor take things
      from me,
You shall listen to all sides and filter them from yourself.

[3]

I have heard what the talkers were talking .... the
      talk of the beginning and the end,
But I do not talk of the beginning or the end.

There was never any more inception than there is now,
Nor any more youth or age than there is now;
And will never be any more perfection than there is now,
Nor any more heaven or hell than there is now.

Urge and urge and urge,
Always the procreant urge of the world.

Out of the dimness opposite equals advance .... Always
      substance and increase,
Always a knit of identity .... always distinction ....
      always a breed of life.

To elaborate is no avail .... Learned and unlearned feel
    that it is so.

Sure as the most certain sure .... plumb in the uprights,
    well entretied, braced in the beams,
Stout as a horse, affectionate, haughty, electrical,
I and this mystery here we stand.

Clear and sweet is my soul .... and clear and sweet
    is all that is not my soul.

Lack one lacks both .... and the unseen is proved
    by the seen,
Till that becomes unseen and receives proof in its turn.

Showing the best and dividing it from the worst,
    age vexes age,
Knowing the perfect fitness and equanimity of things, while
    they discuss I am silent, and go bathe and admire myself.

Welcome is every organ and attribute of me, and of any
    man hearty and clean,
Not an inch nor a particle of an inch is vile, and none
    shall be less familiar than the rest.

I am satisfied .... I see, dance, laugh, sing;
As God comes a loving bedfellow and sleeps at my side all
    night and close on the peep of the day,
And leaves for me baskets covered with white towels
    bulging the house with their plenty,
Shall I postpone my acceptation and realization and
    scream at my eyes,
That they turn from gazing after and down the road,
And forthwith cipher and show me to a cent,
Exactly the contents of one, and exactly the contents of
    two, and which is ahead?

[4]

Trippers and askers surround me,
People I meet .... the effect upon me of my early life ....
    of the ward and city I live in .... of the nation,
The latest news .... discoveries, inventions, societies ....
    authors old and new,
My dinner, dress, associates, looks, business, compliments,
    dues,
The real or fancied indifference of some man or woman
    I love,
The sickness of one of my folks—or of myself .... or
    ill-doing .... or loss or lack of money .... or
    depressions or exaltations,
They come to me days and nights and go from me again,
But they are not the Me myself.

Apart from the pulling and hauling stands what I am,
Stands amused, complacent, compassionating, idle, unitary,
Looks down, is erect, bends an arm on an impalpable
    certain rest,
Looks with its sidecurved head curious what will come next,
Both in and out of the game, and watching and wondering
    at it.

Backward I see in my own days where I sweated through fog
    with linguists and contenders,
I have no mockings or arguments .... I witness and wait.

[5]

I believe in you my soul .... the other I am must not abase
    itself to you,
And you must not be abased to the other

Loafe with me on the grass .... loose the stop from your
    throat,
Not words, not music or rhyme I want .... not custom or
    lecture, not even the best,
Only the lull I like, the hum of your valved voice.

I mind how we lay in June, such a transparent summer
      morning;
You settled your head athwart my hips and gently turned
      over upon me,
And parted the shirt from my bosom-bone, and plunged
      your tongue to my barestript heart,
And reached till you felt my beard, and reached till you held
      my feet.

Swiftly arose and spread around me the peace and joy and
      knowledge that pass all the art and argument of
      the earth;
And I know that the hand of God is the elderhand of my own,
And I know that the spirit of God is the eldest brother
      of my own,
And that all the men ever born are also my brothers . . . .
      and the women my sisters and lovers,
And that a kelson of the creation is love;
And limitless are leaves stiff or drooping in the fields,
And brown ants in the little wells beneath them,
And mossy scabs of the wormfence, and heaped stones,
      and elder and mullen and pokeweed.

[6]
A child said, What is the grass? fetching it to me with full
      hands;
How could I answer the child? . . . . I do not know what it is
      any more than he.

I guess it must be the flag of my disposition, out of hopeful
      green stuff woven.

Or I guess it is the handkerchief of the Lord,
A scented gift and remembrancer designedly dropped,
Bearing the owner's name someway in the corners, that we
      may see and remark, and say Whose?

Or I guess the grass is itself a child . . . . the produced babe
      of the vegetation.

Or I guess it is a uniform hieroglyphic,
And it means, Sprouting alike in broad zones and narrow
   zones,
Growing among black folks as among white,
Kanuck, Tuckahoe, Congressman, Cuff, I give them the
   same, I receive them the same.
And now it seems to me the beautiful uncut hair of graves.

Tenderly will I use you curling grass,
It may be you transpire from the breasts of young men,
It may be if I had known them I would have loved them;
It may be you are from old people and from women, and
   from offspring taken soon out of their mothers' laps,
And here you are the mothers' laps.

This grass is very dark to be from the white heads of
   old mothers,
Darker than the colorless beards of old men,
Dark to come from under the faint red roofs of mouths.

O I perceive after all so many uttering tongues!
And I perceive they do not come from the roofs of mouths
   for nothing.

I wish I could translate the hints about the dead young men
   and women,
And the hints about old men and mothers, and the offspring
   taken soon out of their laps.

What do you think has become of the young and old men?
And what do you think has become of the women and
   children?

They are alive and well somewhere;
The smallest sprout shows there is really no death,
And if ever there was it led forward life, and does not wait
   at the end to arrest it,
And ceased the moment life appeared.

All goes onward and outward .... and nothing collapses,
And to die is different from what any one supposed, and
    luckier.

[7]

Has any one supposed it lucky to be born?
I hasten to inform him or her it is just as lucky to die,
    and I know it.

I pass death with the dying, and birth with the new-washed
    babe .... and am not contained between my hat
    and boots,
And peruse manifold objects, no two alike, and every one
    good,
The earth good, and the stars good, and their adjuncts
    all good.

I am not an earth nor an adjunct of an earth,
I am the mate and companion of people, all just as immortal
    and fathomless as myself;
They do not know how immortal, but I know.

Every kind for itself and its own .... for me mine male
    and female,
For me all that have been boys and that love women,
For mé the man that is proud and feels how it stings to be
    slighted,
For me the sweetheart and the old maid .... for me mothers
    and the mothers of mothers,
For me lips that have smiled, eyes that have shed tears,
For me children and the begetters of children.

Who need be afraid of the merge?
Undrape .... you are not guilty to me, nor stale nor
    discarded,
I see through the broadcloth and gingham whether or no,
And am around, tenacious, acquisitive, tireless .... and can
    never be shaken away.

[8]

The little one sleeps in its cradle,
I lift the gauze and look a long time, and silently brush away
    flies with my hand.

The youngster and the redfaced girl turn aside up the
    bushy hill,
I peeringly view them from the top.

The suicide sprawls on the bloody floor of the bedroom,
It is so .... I witnessed the corpse .... there the pistol had
    fallen.

The blab of the pave .... the tires of carts and sluff of
    bootsoles and talk of the promenaders,
The heavy omnibus, the driver with his interrogating thumb,
    the clank of the shod horses on the granite floor,
The carnival of sleighs, the clinking and shouted jokes and
    pelts of snowballs;
The hurrahs for popular favorites .... the fury of roused
    mobs,
The flap of the curtained litter—the sick man inside,
    borne to the hospital,
The meeting of enemies, the sudden oath, the blows and fall,
The excited crowd—the policeman with his star quickly
    working his passage to the centre of the crowd;
The impassive stones that receive and return so many echoes,
The souls moving along .... are they invisible while the
    least atom of the stones is visible?
What groans of overfed or half-starved who fall on the flags
    sunstruck or in fits,
What exclamations of women taken suddenly, who hurry
    home and give birth to babes,
What living and buried speech is always vibrating here ....
    what howls restrained by decorum,
Arrests of criminals, slights, adulterous offers made,
    acceptances, rejections with convex lips,
I mind them or the resonance of them .... I come again
    and again.

[9]

The big doors of the country-barn stand open and ready,
The dried grass of the harvest-time loads the slow-drawn
    wagon.
The clear light plays on the brown gray and green
    intertinged,
The armfuls are packed to the sagging mow:
I am there .... I help .... I came stretched atop of the load,
I felt its soft jolts .... one leg reclined on the other,
I jump from the crossbeams, and seize the clover and
    timothy,
And roll head over heels, and tangle my hair full of wisps.

[10]

Alone far in the wilds and mountains I hunt,
Wandering amazed at my own lightness and glee,
In the late afternoon choosing a safe spot to pass the night,
Kindling a fire and broiling the freshkilled game,
Soundly falling asleep on the gathered leaves, my dog and
    gun by my side.

The Yankee clipper is under her three skysails .... she cuts
    the sparkle and scud,
My eyes settle the land .... I bend at her prow or shout
    joyously from the deck.

The boatmen and clamdiggers arose early and stopped for me,
I tucked my trowser-ends in my boots and went and had a
    good time,
You should have been with us that day round the
    chowder-kettle.

I saw the marriage of the trapper in the open air in the
    far-west .... the bride was a red girl,
Her father and his friends sat near by crosslegged and
    dumbly smoking .... they had moccasins to their feet
    and large thick blankets hanging from their shoulders;
On a bank lounged the trapper .... he was dressed mostly
    in skins .... his luxuriant beard and curls protected
    his neck,

One hand rested on his rifle . . . . the other hand held firmly
the wrist of the red girl,
She had long eyelashes . . . . her head was bare . . . . her coarse
straight locks descended upon her voluptuous limbs
and reached to her feet.

The runaway slave came to my house and stopped outside,
I heard his motions crackling the twigs of the woodpile,
Through the swung half-door of the kitchen I saw him
limpsey and weak,
And went where he sat on a log, and led him in and
assured him,
And brought water and filled a tub for his sweated body and
bruised feet,
And gave him a room that entered from my own, and
gave him some coarse clean clothes,
And remember perfectly well his revolving eyes and his
awkwardness,
And remember putting plasters on the galls of his neck and
ankles;
He staid with me a week before he was recuperated and
passed north,
I had him sit next me at table . . . . my firelock leaned in the
corner.

[11]

Twenty-eight young men bathe by the shore,
Twenty-eight young men, and all so friendly,
Twenty-eight years of womanly life, and all so lonesome.

She owns the fine house by the rise of the bank.
She hides handsome and richly drest aft the blinds of the
window.

Which of the young men does she like the best?
Ah the homeliest of them is beautiful to her.

Where are you off to, lady? for I see you,
You splash in the water there, yet stay stock still in your
room.

Dancing and laughing along the beach came the twenty-ninth
    bather,
The rest did not see her, but she saw them and loved them.

The beards of the young men glistened with wet, it ran from
    their long hair,
Little streams passed all over their bodies.

An unseen hand also passed over their bodies,
It descended tremblingly from their temples ribs.

The young men float on their backs, their white bellies swell
    to the sun .... they do not ask who seizes fast to them,
They do not know who puffs and declines with pendant
    and bending arch,
They do not think whom they souse with spray.

[12]
The butcher-boy puts off his killing clothes, or sharpens his
    knife at the stall in the market,
I loiter enjoying his repartee and his shuffle and breakdown.

Blacksmiths with grimed and hairy chests environ the anvil,
Each has his main-sledge .... they are all out .... there is
    a great heat in the fire.

From the cinder-strewed threshold I follow their movements,
The lithe sheer of their waists plays even with their
    massive arms,
Overhand the hammers roll—overhand so slow—overhand
    so sure,
They do not hasten, each man hits in his place.

[13]
The negro holds firmly the reins of his four horses .... the
    block swags underneath on its tied-over chain,
The negro that drives the huge dray of the stoneyard ....
    steady and tall he stands poised on one leg on
    the stringpiece,

His blue shirt exposes his ample neck and breast and
    loosens over his hipband,
His glance is calm and commanding....he tosses the
    slouch of his hat away from his forehead,
The sun falls on his crispy hair and moustache....falls on
    The black of his polish'd and perfect limbs.

I behold the picturesque giant and love him....and I do
    not stop there,
I go with the team also.

In me the caresser of life wherever moving....backward
    as well as forward slueing,
To niches aside and junior bending.

Oxen that rattle the yoke or halt in the shade, what is
    that you express in your eyes?
It seems to me more than all the print I have read in my life.

My tread scares the wood-drake and wood-duck on my
    distant and daylong ramble,
They rise together, they slowly circle around.
....I believe in those winged purposes,
And acknowledge the red yellow and white playing
    within me,
And consider the green and violet and the tufted crown
    intentional;
And do not call the tortoise unworthy because she is
    not something else,
And the mocking bird in the swamp never studied the
    gamut, yet trills pretty well to me,
And the look of the bay mare shames silliness out of me.

[14]

The wild gander leads his flock through the cool night,
Ya-honk! he says, and sounds it down to me like an
    invitation;
The pert may suppose it meaningless, but I listen closer,
I find its purpose and place up there toward the
    November sky.

The sharphoofed moose of the north, the cat on the
    housesill, the chickadee, the prairie-dog,
The litter of the grunting sow as they tug at her teats,
The brood of the turkeyhen, and she with her halfspread
    wings,
I see in them and myself the same old law.

The press of my foot to the earth springs a hundred
    affections,
They scorn the best I can do to relate them.

I am enamoured of growing outdoors,
Of men that live among cattle or taste of the ocean or woods,
Of the builders and steerers of ships, of the wielders of
    axes and mauls, of the drivers of horses,
I can eat and sleep with them week in and week out.

What is commonest and cheapest and nearest and
    easiest is Me,
Me going in for my chances, spending for vast returns,
Adorning myself to bestow myself on the first that will
    take me,
Not asking the sky to come down to my goodwill,
Scattering it freely forever.

[15]
The pure contralto sings in the organloft,
The carpenter dresses his plank ....the tongue of his
    foreplane whistles its wild ascending lisp,
The married and unmarried children ride home to their
    thanksgiving dinner,
The pilot seizes the king-pin, he heaves down with a
    strong arm,
The mate stands braced in the whaleboat, lance and
    harpoon are ready,
The duck-shooter walks by silent and cautious stretches,
The deacons are ordained with crossed hands at the altar,

The spinning-girl retreats and advances to the hum of the
     big wheel,
The farmer stops by the bars of a Sunday and looks at
     the oats and rye,
The lunatic is carried at last to the asylum a confirmed case,
He will never sleep any more as he did in the cot in his
     mother's bedroom;
The jour printer with gray head and gaunt jaws works
     at his case,
He turns his quid of tobacco, his eyes get blurred with
     the manuscript;
The malformed limbs are tied to the anatomist's table,
What is removed drops horribly in a pail;
The quadroon girl is sold at the stand . . . . the drunkard nods
     by the barroom stove,
The machinist rolls up his sleeves . . . . the policeman
     travels his beat . . . . the gatekeeper marks who pass,
The young fellow drives the express-wagon . . . . I love
     him though I do not know him;
The half-breed straps on his light boots to compete
     in the race,
The western turkey-shooting draws old and young . . . .
     some lean on their rifles, some sit on logs,
Out from the crowd steps the marksman and takes his
     position and levels his piece;
The groups of newly-come immigrants cover the wharf
     or levee,
The woollypates hoe in the sugarfield, the overseer
     views them from his saddle;
The bugle calls in the ballroom, the gentlemen run for their
     partners, the dancers bow to each other;
The youth lies awake in the cedar-roofed garret and
     harks to the musical rain,
The Wolverine sets traps on the creek that helps fill
     the Huron,
The reformer ascends the platform, he spouts with his
     mouth and nose,
The company returns from its excursion, the darkey
     brings up the rear and bears the well-riddled target,

The squaw wrapt in her yellow-hemmed cloth is
    offering moccasins and beadbags for sale,
The connoisseur peers along the exhibition-gallery with
    halfshut eyes bent sideways,
The deckhands make fast the steamboat, the plank is
    thrown for the shoregoing passengers,
The young sister holds out the skein, the elder sister winds it
    off in a ball and stops now and then for the knots,
The one-year wife is recovering and happy, a week
    ago she bore her first child,
The cleanhaired Yankee girl works with her sewing-machine
    or in the factory or mill,
The nine months' gone is in the parturition chamber, her
    faintness and pains are advancing;
The pavingman leans on his twohanded rammer—
    the reporter's lead flies swiftly over the notebook—
    the signpainter is lettering with red and gold,
The canal-boy trots on the towpath—the bookkeeper
    counts at his desk—the shoemaker waxes his thread,
The conductor beats time for the band and all the
    performers follow him,
The child is baptised—the convert is making the first
    professions,
The regatta is spread on the bay . . . . how the white
    sails sparkle!
The drover watches his drove, he sings out to them
    that would stray,
The pedlar sweats with his pack on his back—the
    purchaser higgles about the odd cent,
The camera and plate are prepared, the lady must sit
    for her daguerreotype,
The bride unrumples her white dress, the minutehand
    of the clock moves slowly,
The opium eater reclines with rigid head and
    just-opened lips,
The prostitute draggles her shawl, her bonnet bobs
    on her tipsy and pimpled neck,
The crowd laugh at her blackguard oaths, the men jeer
    and wink to each other,

(Miserable! I do not laugh at your oaths nor jeer you,)
The President holds a cabinet council, he is surrounded
    by the great secretaries,
On the piazza walk five friendly matrons with twined arms;
The crew of the fish-smack pack repeated layers of
    halibut in the hold,
The Missourian crosses the plains toting his wares and
    his cattle,
The fare-collector goes through the train—he gives
    notice by the jingling of loose change,
The floormen are laying the floor—the tinners are tinning
    the roof—the masons are calling for mortar,
In single file each shouldering his hod pass onward
    the laborers;
Seasons pursuing each other the indescribable crowd
    is gathered . . . . it is the Fourth of July . . . . what salutes
    of cannon and small arms!
Seasons pursuing each other the plougher ploughs and
    the mower mows and the winter grain falls in the ground;
Off on the lakes the pikefisher watches and waits by the
    hole in the frozen surface,
The stumps stand thick round the clearing, the squatter
    strikes deep with his axe,
The flatboatmen make fast toward dusk near the
    cottonwood or pekantrees,
The coon-seekers go now through the regions of the
    Red river, or through those drained by the Tennessee,
    or through those of the Arkansas,
The torches shine in the dark that hangs on the
    Chattahoochee or Altamahaw;
Patriarchs sit at supper with sons and grandsons and
    great grandsons around them,
In walls of adobie, in canvas tents, rest hunters and
    trappers after their day's sport.
The city sleeps and the country sleeps,
The living sleep for their time . . . . the dead sleep for
    their time,
The old husband sleeps by his wife and the young
    husband sleeps by his wife;

And these one and all tend inward to me, and I tend
    outward to them,
And such as it is to be of these more or less I am.

[*16*]

I am of old and young, of the foolish as much as the wise,
Regardless of others, ever regardful of others,
Maternal as well as paternal, a child as well as a man,
Stuffed with the stuff that is coarse, and stuffed with
    the stuff that is fine,
One of the great nations, the nation of many nations—
    the smallest the same and the largest the same,
A southerner soon as a northerner, a planter nonchalant
    and hospitable,
A Yankee bound my own way . . . . ready for trade . . . .
    my joints the limberest joints on earth and the
    sternest joints on earth,
A Kentuckian walking the vale of the Elkhorn in my
    deerskin leggings,
A boatman over the lakes or bays or along coasts . . . .
    a Hoosier, a Badger, a Buckeye,
A Louisianian or Georgian, a poke-easy from sandhills
    and pines,
At home on Canadian snowshoes or up in the bush,
    or with fishermen off Newfoundland,
At home in the fleet of iceboats, sailing with the rest
    and tacking,
At home on the hills of Vermont or in the woods of
    Maine or the Texan ranch,
Comrade of Californians . . . . comrade of free
    northwesterners, loving their big proportions,
Comrade of raftsmen and coalmen—comrade of all who
    shake hands and welcome to drink and meat;
A learner with the simplest, a teacher of the thoughtfulest,
A novice beginning experient of myriads of seasons,
Of every hue and trade and rank, of every caste
    and religion,
Not merely of the New World but of Africa Europe or
    Asia . . . . a wandering savage,

A farmer, mechanic, or artist . . . . a gentleman, sailor,
    lover or quaker,
A prisoner, fancy-man, rowdy, lawyer, physician or priest.

I resist anything better than my own diversity,
And breathe the air and leave plenty after me,
And am not stuck up, and am in my place.

The moth and the fisheggs are in their place,
The suns I see and the suns I cannot see are in their place.
The palpable is in its place and the impalpable is in its place.

   [*17*]

These are the thoughts of all men in all ages and lands,
    they are not original with me,
If they are not yours as much as mine they are nothing
    or next to nothing,
If they do not enclose everything they are next to nothing,
If they are not the riddle and the untying of the riddle
    they are nothing,
If they are not just as close as they are distant they
    are nothing.

This is the grass that grows wherever the land is and the
    water is,
This is the common air that bathes the globe.

This is the breath of laws and songs and behaviour,
This is the tasteless water of souls . . . . this is the true
    sustenance,
It is for the illiterate . . . . it is for the judges of the
    supreme court . . . . it is for the federal capitol and
    the state capitols,
It is for the admirable communes of literary men and
    composers and singers and lecturers and engineers
    and savans,
It is for the endless races of working people and
    farmers and seamen.

[*18*]

This is the trill of a thousand clear cornets and scream
    of the octave flute and strike of triangles.

I play not a march for victors only .... I play great
    marches for conquered and slain persons.

Have you heard that it was good to gain the day?
I also say it is good to fall .... battles are lost in the same
    spirit in which they are won.

I sound triumphal drums for the dead .... I fling through
    my embouchures the loudest and gayest music to them,
Vivas to those who have failed, and to those whose
    war-vessels sank in the sea, and those themselves
    who sank in the sea,
And to all generals that lost engagements, and all
    overcome heroes, and the numberless unknown heroes
    equal to the greatest heroes known.

[*19*]

This is the meal pleasantly set .... this is the meat and
    drink for natural hunger,
It is for the wicked just the same as the righteous ....
    I make appointments with all,
I will not have a single person slighted or left away,
The keptwoman and sponger and thief are hereby invited
    .... the heavy-lipped slave is invited .... the
    venerealee is invited,
There shall be no difference between them and the rest.

This is the press of a bashful hand .... this is the float
    and odor of hair,
This is the touch of my lips to yours .... this is the
    murmur of yearning,
This is the far-off depth and height reflecting my own face,
This is the thoughtful merge of myself and the outlet again.

Do you guess I have some intricate purpose?
Well I have .... for the April rain has, and the mica
    on the side of a rock has.

Do you take it I would astonish?
Does the daylight astonish? or the early redstart twittering
    through the woods?
Do I astonish more than they?

This hour I tell things in confidence,
I might not tell everybody but I will tell you.

   [20]
Who goes there! hankering, gross, mystical, nude?
How is it I extract strength from the beef I eat?

What is a man anyhow? What am I? and what are you?
All I mark as my own you shall offset it with your own,
Else it were time lost listening to me.

I do not snivel that snivel the world over,
That months are vacuums and the ground but wallow
    and filth,
That life is a suck and a sell, and nothing remains at the
    end but threadbare crape and tears.

Whimpering and truckling fold with powders for
    invalids .... conformity goes to the fourth-removed,
I cock my hat as I please indoors or out.

Shall I pray? Shall I venerate and be ceremonious?
I have pried through the strata and analyzed to a hair,
And counselled with doctors and calculated close
    and found no sweeter fat than sticks to my own bones.

In all people I see myself, none more and not one a
    barleycorn less,
And the good or bad I say of myself I say of them.

And I know I am solid and sound,
To me the converging objects of the universe
    perpetually flow,
All are written to me, and I must get what the writing
    means.

And I know I am deathless,
I know this orbit of mine cannot be swept by a
    carpenter's compass,
I know I shall not pass like a child's carlacue cut with a
    burnt stick at night.

I know I am august,
I do not trouble my spirit to vindicate itself or be
    understood,
I see that the elementary laws never apologize,
I reckon I behave no prouder than the level I plant my
    house by after all.

I exist as I am, that is enough,
If no other in the world be aware I sit content,
And if each and all be aware I sit content.

One world is aware, and by far the largest to me, and
    that is myself,
And whether I come to my own today or in ten thousand
    or ten million years,
I can cheerfully take it now, or with equal cheerfulness
    I can wait.

My foothold is tenoned and mortised in granite,
I laugh at what you call dissolution,
And I know the amplitude of time.

[21]
I am the poet of the body,
And I am the poet of the soul.

The pleasures of heaven are with me, and the pains of
    hell are with me,
The first I graft and increase upon myself .... the latter I
    translate into a new tongue.

I am the poet of the woman the same as the man,
And I say it is as great to be a woman as to be a man,
And I say there is nothing greater than the mother of men.

I chant a new chant of dilation or pride,
We have had ducking and deprecating about enough,
I show that size is only development.

Have you outstript the rest? Are you the President?
It is a trifle .... they will more than arrive there every one,
    and still pass on.

I am he that walks with the tender and growing night;
I call to the earth and sea half-held by the night.

Press close barebosomed night! Press close magnetic
    nourishing night!
Night of south winds! Night of the large few stars!
Still nodding night! Mad naked summer night!

Smile O voluptuous coolbreathed earth!
Earth of the slumbering and liquid trees!
Earth of departed sunset! Earth of the mountains misty-topt!
Earth of the vitreous pour of the full moon just
    tinged with blue!
Earth of shine and dark mottling the tide of the river!
Earth of the limpid gray of clouds brighter and clearer
    for my sake!
Far-swooping elbowed earth! Rich apple-blossomed earth!
Smile, for your lover comes!

Prodigal! you have given me love! .... therefore I
    to you give love!
O unspeakable passionate love!

Thruster holding me tight and that I hold tight!
We hurt each other as the bridegroom and the bride hurt
    each other.

[22]
You sea! I resign myself to you also . . . . I guess
    what you mean,
I behold from the beach your crooked inviting fingers,
I believe you refuse to go back without feeling of me;
We must have a turn together . . . . I undress . . . . hurry me
    out of sight of the land,
Cushion me soft . . . . rock me in billowy drowse,
Dash me with amorous wet . . . . I can repay you.

Sea of stretched ground-swells!
Sea breathing broad and convulsive breaths!
Sea of the brine of life! Sea of unshovelled and
    always-ready graves!
Howler and scooper of storms! Capricious and dainty sea!
I am integral with you . . . . I too am of one phase and
    of all phases.

Partaker of influx and efflux . . . . extoller of hate and
    conciliation,
Extoller of amies and those that sleep in each others' arms.

I am he attesting sympathy;
Shall I make my list of things in the house and skip
    the house that supports them?

I am the poet of commonsense and of the demonstrable
    and of immortality;
And am not the poet of goodness only . . . . I do not
    decline to be the poet of wickedness also.

Washes and razors for foofoos . . . . for me freckles and
    a bristling beard.

What blurt is it about virtue and about vice?
Evil propels me, and reform of evil propels me ....
    I stand indifferent,
My gait is no faultfinder's or rejector's gait,
I moisten the roots of all that has grown.

Did you fear some scrofula out of the unflagging pregnancy?
Did you guess the celestial laws are yet to be worked
    over and rectified?

I step up to say that what we do is right and what we
    affirm is right .... and some is only the ore of right,
Witnesses of us .... one side a balance and the antipodal
    side a balance,
Soft doctrine as steady help as stable doctrine,
Thoughts and deeds of the present our rouse and early start.

This minute that comes to me over the past decillions,
There is no better than it and now.

What behaved well in the past or behaves well today
    is not such a wonder,
The wonder is always and always how there can be a mean
    man or an infidel.

[23]
Endless unfolding of words of ages!
And mine a word of the modern .... a word en masse.

A word of the faith that never balks,
One time as good as another time .... here or
    henceforward it is all the same to me.

A word of reality .... materialism first and last imbuing.

Hurrah for positive science! Long live exact demonstration!
Fetch stonecrop and mix it with cedar and branches of lilac;

This is the lexicographer or chemist .... this made a
    grammar of the old cartouches,
These mariners put the ship through dangerous
    unknown seas,
This is the geologist, and this works with the scalpel,
    and this is a mathematician.

Gentlemen I receive you, and attach and clasp hands
    with you,
The facts are useful and real .... they are not my
    dwelling .... I enter by them to an area of the dwelling.

I am less the reminder of property or qualities, and more
    the reminder of life,
And go on the square for my own sake and for other's sake,
And make short account of neuters and geldings, and
    favor men and women fully equipped,
And beat the gong of revolt, and stop with fugitives
    and them that plot and conspire.

[24]

Walt Whitman, an American, one of the roughs, a kosmos,
Disorderly fleshy and sensual .... eating drinking and
    breeding,
No sentimentalist .... no stander above men and women or
    apart from them .... no more modest than immodest.

Unscrew the locks from the doors!
Unscrew the doors themselves from their jambs!

Whoever degrades another degrades me .... and whatever
    is done or said returns at last to me,
And whatever I do or say I also return.

Through me the afflatus surging and surging .... through
    me the current and index.

I speak the password primeval .... I give the sign of
    democracy;

By God! I will accept nothing which all cannot have
    their counterpart of on the same terms.

Through me many long dumb voices,
Voices of the interminable generations of slaves,
Voices of prostitutes and of deformed persons,
Voices of the diseased and despairing, and of thieves
    and dwarfs,
Voices of cycles of preparation and accretion,
And of the threads that connect the stars—and of wombs,
    and of the fatherstuff,
And of the rights of them the others are down upon,
Of the trivial and flat and foolish and despised,
Of fog in the air and beetles rolling balls of dung.

Through me forbidden voices,
Voices of sexes and lusts .... voices veiled, and I remove
    the veil,
Voices indecent by me clarified and transfigured.

I do not press my finger across my mouth,
I keep as delicate around the bowels as around the
    head and heart,
Copulation is no more rank to me than death is.

I believe in the flesh and the appetites,
Seeing hearing and feeling are miracles, and each part
    and tag of me is a miracle.

Divine am I inside and out, and I make holy whatever
    I touch or am touched from;
The scent of these arm-pits is aroma finer than prayer,
This head is more than churches or bibles or creeds.

If I worship any particular thing it shall be some of the
    spread of my body;
Translucent mould of me it shall be you,
Shaded ledges and rests, firm masculine coulter,
    it shall be you,

Whatever goes to the tilth of me it shall be you,
You my rich blood, your milky stream pale strippings
    of my life;
Breast that presses against other breasts it shall be you.
My brain it shall be your occult convolutions,
Root of washed sweet-flag, timorous pond-snipe, nest
    of guarded duplicate eggs, it shall be you,
Mixed tussled hay of head and beard and brawn
    it shall be you,
Trickling sap of maple, fibre of manly wheat, it shall be you;
Sun so generous it shall be you,
Vapors lighting and shading my face it shall be you,
You sweaty brooks and dews it shall be you.
Winds whose soft-tickling genitals rub against me
    it shall be you,
Broad muscular fields, branches of liveoak, loving
    lounger in my winding paths, it shall be you,
Hands I have taken, face I have kissed, mortal I have
    ever touched, it shall be you.

I dote on myself .... there is that lot of me, and all
    so luscious,
Each moment and whatever happens thrills me with joy.

I cannot tell how my ankles bend .... nor whence
    the cause of my faintest wish,
Nor the cause of the friendship I emit .... nor the cause
    of the friendship I take again.

To walk up my stoop is unaccountable .... I pause to
    consider if it really be,
That I eat and drink is spectacle enough for the great
    authors and schools,
A morning-glory at my window satisfies me more than the
    metaphysics of books.

To behold the daybreak!
The little light fades the immense and diaphanous shadows,
The air tastes good to my palate.

Hefts of the moving world at innocent gambols,
    silently rising, freshly exuding,
Scooting obliquely high and low.

Something I cannot see puts upward libidinous prongs,
Seas of bright juice suffuse heaven.

The earth by the sky staid with .... the daily close of
    their junction,
The heaved challenge from the east that moment
    over my head,
The mocking taunt, See then whether you shall be master!

[25]

Dazzling and tremendous how quick the sunrise would
    kill me,
If I could not now and always send sunrise out of me.

We also ascend dazzling and tremendous as the sun,
We found our own my soul in the calm and cool of
    the daybreak.

My voice goes after what my eyes cannot reach,
With the twirl of my tongue I encompass worlds and
    volumes of worlds.

Speech is the twin of my vision .... it is unequal to
    measure itself.

It provokes me forever,
It says sarcastically, Walt, you understand enough ....
    why don't you let it out then?

Come now I will not be tantalized.. . you conceive
    too much of articulation.

Do you not know how the buds beneath are folded?
Waiting in gloom protected by frost,

The dirt receding before my prophetical screams,
I underlying causes to balance them at last,
My knowledge my live parts . . . . it keeping tally with the
    meaning of things,
Happiness . . . . which whoever hears me let him or her
    set out in search of this day.

My final merit I refuse you . . . . I refuse putting from
    me the best I am.

Encompass worlds but never try to encompass me,
I crowd your noisiest talk by looking toward you.

Writing and talk do not prove me,
I carry the plenum of proof and every thing else in my face,
With the hush of my lips I confound the topmost skeptic.

[26]
I think I will do nothing for a long time but listen,
And accrue what I hear into myself . . . . and let sounds
    contribute toward me.

I hear the bravuras of birds . . . . the bustle of growing
    wheat . . . . gossip of flames . . . . clack of sticks
    cooking my meals.

I hear the sound of the human voice . . . . a sound I love,
I hear all sounds as they are tuned to their uses . . . .
    sounds of the city and sounds out of the city . . . .
    sounds of the day and night;
Talkative young ones to those that like them . . . . the
    recitative of fish-pedlars and fruit-pedlars . . . . the
    loud laugh of workpeople at their meals,
The angry base of disjointed friendship . . . . the faint
    tones of the sick,
The judge with hands tight to the desk, his shaky lips
    pronouncing a death-sentence,
The heave'e'yo of stevedores unlading ships by the
    wharves . . . . the refrain of the anchor-lifters;

The ring of alarm-bells .... the cry of fire .... the
    whirr of swift-streaking engines and hose-carts with
    premonitory tinkles and colored lights,
The steam-whistle .... the solid roll of the train of
    approaching cars;
The slow-march played at night at the head of the
    association,
They go to guard some corpse .... the flag-tops are
    draped with black muslin.

I hear the violincello or man's heart complaint,
And hear the keyed cornet or else the echo of sunset.

I hear the chorus .... it is a grand-opera .... this indeed
    is music!

A tenor large and fresh as the creation fills me,
The orbic flex of his mouth is pouring and filling me full.

I hear the trained soprano .... she convulses me like
    the climax of my love-grip;
The orchestra whirls me wider than Uranus flies,
It wrenches unnamable ardors from my breast,
It throbs me to gulps of the farthest down horror,
It sails me .... I dab with bare feet .... they are licked
    by the indolent waves,
I am exposed .... cut by bitter and poisoned hail,
Steeped amid honeyed morphine .... my windpipe
    squeezed in the fakes of death,
Let up again to feel the puzzle of puzzles,
And that we call Being.

[27]

To be in any form, what is that?
If nothing lay more developed the quahaug and its callous
    shell were enough.

Mine is no callous shell,
I have instant conductors all over me whether I pass or stop,
They seize every object and lead it harmlessly through me.

I merely stir, press, feel with my fingers, and am happy,
To touch my person to some one else's is about as much as
    I can stand.

   [28]

Is this then a touch? .... quivering me to a new identity,
Flames and ether making a rush for my veins,
Treacherous tip of me reaching and crowding to help them,
My flesh and blood playing out lightning, to strike what
    is hardly different from myself,
On all sides prurient provokers stiffening my limbs,
Straining the udder of my heart for its withheld drip,
Behaving licentious towards me, taking no denial,
Depriving me of my best as for a purpose,
Unbuttoning my clothes and holding me by the bare waist,
Deluding my confusion with the calm of the sunlight
    and pasture fields,
Immodestly sliding the fellow-senses away,
They bribed to swap off with touch, and go and graze
    at the edges of me,
No consideration, no regard for my draining strength or
    my anger,
Fetching the rest of the herd around to enjoy them awhile,
Then all uniting to stand on a headland and worry me.

The sentries desert every other part of me,
They have left me helpless to a red marauder,
They all come to the headland to witness and assist
    against me.

I am given up by traitors;
I talk wildly .... I have lost my wits .... I and nobody else
    am the greatest traitor,
I went myself first to the headland .   . my own hands
    carried me there.

You villain touch! what are you doing? .... my breath
    is tight in its throat;
Unclench your floodgates! you are too much for me.

[*29*]

Blind loving wrestling touch! Sheathed hooded
    sharptoothed touch!
Did it make you ache so leaving me?

Parting tracked by arriving .... perpetual payment of the
    perpetual loan,
Rich showering rain, and recompense richer afterward.

Sprouts take and accumulate .... stand by the curb
    prolific and vital,
Landscapes projected masculine full-sized and golden.

[*30*]

All truths wait in all things,
They neither hasten their own delivery nor resist it,
They do not need the obstetric forceps of the surgeon,
The insignificant is as big to me as any,
What is less or more than a touch?

Logic and sermons never convince,
The damp of the night drives deeper into my soul.

Only what proves itself to every man and woman is so,
Only what nobody denies is so.

A minute and a drop of me settle my brain;
I believe the soggy clods shall become lovers and lamps,
And a compend of compends is the meat of a man or
    woman,
And a summit and flower there is the feeling they have
    for each other,
And they are to branch boundlessly out of that lesson
    until it becomes omnific,
And until every one shall delight us, and we them.

[*31*]

I believe a leaf of grass is no less than the journeywork of
    the stars,

And the pismire is equally perfect, and a grain of sand,
    and the egg of the wren,
And the tree-toad is a chef-d'œuvre for the highest,
And the running blackberry would adorn the parlors of
    heaven,
And the narrowest hinge in my hand puts to scorn all
    machinery,
And the cow crunching with depressed head surpasses
    any statue,
And a mouse is miracle enough to stagger sextillions of
    infidels,
And I could come every afternoon of my life to look at the
    farmer's girl boiling her iron tea-kettle and baking
    shortcake.

I find I incorporate gneiss and coal and long-threaded moss
    and fruits and grains and esculent roots,
And am stucco'd with quadrupeds and birds all over,
And have distanced what is behind me for good reasons,
And call any thing close again when I desire it.

In vain the speeding or shyness,
In vain the plutonic rocks send their old heat against my
    approach,
In vain the mastodon retreats beneath its own powdered bones,
In vain objects stand leagues off and assume manifold shapes,
In vain the ocean settling in hollows and the great monsters
    lying low,
In vain the buzzard houses herself with the sky,
In vain the snake slides through the creepers and logs,
In vain the elk takes to the inner passes of the woods,
In vain the razorbilled auk sails far north to Labrador,
I follow quickly .... I ascend to the nest in the fissure of
    the cliff.

[32]
I think I could turn and live awhile with the animals ....
    they are so placid and self-contained,
I stand and look at them sometimes half the day long.

They do not sweat and whine about their condition,
They do not lie awake in the dark and weep for their sins,
They do not make me sick discussing their duty to God,
Not one is dissatisfied .... not one is demented with the
    mania of owning things,
Not one kneels to another nor to his kind that lived
    thousands of years ago,
Not one is respectable or industrious over the whole earth.

So they show their relations to me and I accept them;
They bring me tokens of myself .... they evince them plainly
    in their possession.

I do not know where they got those tokens,
I must have passed that way untold times ago and
    negligently dropt them,
Myself moving forward then and now and forever,
Gathering and showing more always and with velocity,
Infinite and omnigenous and the like of these among them;
Not too exclusive toward the reachers of my remembrancers,
Picking out here one that shall be my amie,
Choosing to go with him on brotherly terms.

A gigantic beauty of a stallion, fresh and responsive to my
    caresses,
Head high in the forehead and wide between the ears,
Limbs glossy and supple, tail dusting the ground,
Eyes well apart and full of sparkling wickedness .... ears
    finely cut and flexibly moving.

His nostrils dilate .... my heels embrace him   ... his well
    built limbs tremble with pleasure .... we speed
    around and return.

I but use you a moment and then I resign you stallion ....
    and do not need your paces, and outgallop them,
And myself as I stand or sit pass faster than you.

[33]

Swift wind! Space! My Soul! Now I know it is true what I
    guessed at;
What I guessed when I loafed on the grass,
What I guessed while I lay alone in my bed .... and again as I
    walked the beach under the paling stars of the morning.

My ties and ballasts leave me .... I travel .... I sail ....
    my elbows rest in the sea-gaps,
I skirt the sierras .... my palms cover continents,
I am afoot with my vision.

By the city's quadrangular houses .... in log-huts, or
    camping with lumbermen,
Along the ruts of the turnpike .... along the dry gulch and
    rivulet bed,
Hoeing my onion-patch, and rows of carrots and parsnips
    .... crossing savannas .... trailing in forests,
Prospecting .... gold-digging .... girdling the trees of
    a new purchase,
Scorched ankle-deep by the hot sand .... hauling my boat
    down the shallow river;
Where the panther walks to and fro on a limb overhead
    .... where the buck turns furiously at the hunter,
Where the rattlesnake suns his flabby length on a rock ....
    where the otter is feeding on fish,
Where the alligator in his tough pimples sleeps by the bayou,
Where the black bear is searching for roots or honey ....
    where the beaver pats the mud with his paddle-tail;
Over the growing sugar .... over the cottonplant .... over
    the rice in its low moist field;
Over the sharp-peaked farmhouse with its scalloped scum
    and slender shoots from the gutters;
Over the western persimmon .... over the longleaved
    corn and the delicate blue-flowered flax;
Over the white and brown buckwheat, a hummer and
    a buzzer there with the rest,

Over the dusky green of the rye as it ripples and shades in
    the breeze;
Scaling mountains .... pulling myself cautiously up ....
    holding on by low scragged limbs,
Walking the path worn in the grass and beat through the
    leaves of the brush;
Where the quail is whistling betwixt the woods and the
    wheatlot,
Where the bat flies in the July eve .... where the great
    goldbug drops through the dark;
Where the flails keep time on the barn floor,
Where the brook puts out of the roots of the old tree and
    flows to the meadow,
Where cattle stand and shake away flies with the tremulous
    shuddering of their hides,
Where the cheese-cloth hangs in the kitchen, and andirons
    straddle the hearth-slab, and cobwebs fall in festoons
    from the rafters;
Where triphammers crash .... where the press is whirling
    its cylinders;
Wherever the human heart beats with terrible throes
    out of its ribs;
Where the pear-shaped balloon is floating aloft ....
    floating in it myself and looking composedly down;
Where the life-car is drawn on the slipnoose .... where the
    heat hatches pale-green eggs in the dented sand,
Where the she-whale swims with her calves and never
    forsakes them,
Where the steamship trails hindways its long pennant of
    smoke,
Where the ground-shark's fin cuts like a black chip
    out of the water,
Where the half-burned brig is riding on unknown currents,
Where shells grow to her slimy deck, and the dead are
    corrupting below;
Where the striped and starred flag is borne at the head of the
    regiments;
Approaching Manhattan, up by the long-stretching island,

Under Niagara, the cataract falling like a veil over my
    countenance;

Upon a door-step .... upon the horse-block of hard wood
    outside,

Upon the race-course, or enjoying pic-nics or jigs or a
    good game of base-ball,

At he-festivals with blackguard jibes and ironical license
    and bull-dances and drinking and laughter,

At the cider-mill, tasting the sweet of the brown sqush
    .... sucking the juice through a straw,

At apple-peelings, wanting kisses for all the red fruit I find,

At musters and beach-parties and friendly bees and
    huskings and house-raisings;

Where the mockingbird sounds his delicious gurgles, and
    cackles and screams and weeps,

Where the hay-rick stands in the barnyard, and the
    dry-stalks are scattered, and the brood cow waits
    in the hovel,

Where the bull advances to do his masculine work, and the
    stud to the mare, and the cock is treading the hen,

Where the heifers browse, and the geese nip their food
    with short jerks;

Where the sundown shadows lengthen over the limitless
    and lonesome prairie,

Where the herds of buffalo make a crawling spread of
    the square miles far and near;

Where the hummingbird shimmers .... where the neck
    of the longlived swan is curving and winding;

Where the laughing-gull scoots by the slappy shore and
    laughs her near-human laugh;

Where beehives range on a gray bench in the garden
    half-hid by the high weeds;

Where the band-necked partridges roost in a ring on the
    ground with their heads out;

Where burial coaches enter the arched gates of a cemetery;

Where winter wolves bark amid wastes of snow and icicled
    trees;

Where the yellow-crowned heron comes to the edge of the
    marsh at night and feeds upon small crabs;

Where the splash of swimmers and divers cools the
    warm noon;
Where the katydid works her chromatic reed on the
    walnut-tree over the well;
Through patches of citrons and cucumbers with silver-wired
    leaves,
Through the salt-lick or orange glade . . . . or under conical firs;
Through the gymnasium . . . . through the curtained
    saloon . . . . through the office or public hall;
Pleased with the native and pleased with the foreign . . . .
    pleased with the new and old,
Pleased with women, the homely as well as the handsome,
Pleased with the quakeress as she puts off her bonnet and
    talks melodiously,
Pleased with the primitive tunes of the choir of the
    whitewashed church,
Pleased with the earnest words of the sweating Methodist
    preacher, or any preacher . . . . looking seriously
    at the camp-meeting;
Looking in at the shop-windows in Broadway the whole
    forenoon . . . . pressing the flesh of my nose to the
    thick plate-glass,
Wandering the same afternoon with my face turned up
    to the clouds;
My right and left arms round the sides of two friends and
    I in the middle;
Coming home with the bearded and dark-cheeked bush-boy
    . . . . riding behind him at the drape of the day;
Far from the settlements studying the print of animals'
    feet, or the moccasin print;
By the cot in the hospital reaching lemonade to a
    feverish patient,
By the coffined corpse when all is still, examining with
    a candle;
Voyaging to every port to dicker and adventure;
Hurrying with the modern crowd, as eager and fickle as any,
Hot toward one I hate, ready in my madness to knife him;
Solitary at midnight in my back yard, my thoughts gone
    from me a long while,

Walking the old hills of Judea with the beautiful gentle
      god by my side;
Speeding through space .... speeding through heaven and
      the stars,
Speeding amid the seven satellites and the broad ring and
      the diameter of eighty thousand miles,
Speeding with tailed meteors .... throwing fire-balls
      like the rest,
Carrying the crescent child that carries its own full mother
      in its belly:
Storming enjoying planning loving cautioning,
Backing and filling, appearing and disappearing,
I tread day and night such roads.

I visit the orchards of God and look at the spheric product,
And look at quintillions ripened, and look at quintillions
      green.

I fly the flight of the fluid and swallowing soul,
My course runs below the soundings of plummets.

I help myself to material and immaterial,
No guard can shut me off, no law can prevent me.

I anchor my ship for a little while only,
My messengers continually cruise away or bring their
      returns to me.

I go hunting polar furs and the seal .... leaping chasms
      with a pike-pointed staff .... clinging to topples of
      brittle and blue.

I ascend to the foretruck .... I take my place late at night
      in the crow's nest .... we sail through the arctic sea
      .... it is plenty light enough,
Through the clear atmosphere I stretch around on the
      wonderful beauty,

The enormous masses of ice pass me and I pass them ....
    the scenery is plain in all directions,
The white-topped mountains point up in the distance ....
    I fling out my fancies toward them;
We are about approaching some great battlefield in which
    we are soon to be engaged,
We pass the colossal outposts of the encampment ....
    we pass with still feet and caution;
Or we are entering by the suburbs some vast and ruined
    city .... the blocks and fallen architecture more
    than all the living cities of the globe.

I am a free companion .... I bivouac by invading watchfires.

I turn the bridegroom out of bed and stay with the bride
    myself,
And tighten her all night to my thighs and lips.

My voice is the wife's voice, the screech by the rail of
    the stairs,
They fetch my man's body up dripping and drowned.

I understand the large hearts of heroes,
The courage of present times and all times;
How the skipper saw the crowded and rudderless wreck
    of the steamship, and death chasing it up and down
    the storm,
How he knuckled tight and gave not back one inch, and was
    faithful of days and faithful of nights,
And chalked in large letters on a board, Be of good cheer,
    We will not desert you;
How he saved the drifting company at last,
How the lank loose-gowned women looked when boated
    from the side of their prepared graves,
How the silent old-faced infants, and the lifted sick, and
    the sharplipped unshaved men;
All this I swallow and it tastes good .... I like it well,
    and it becomes mine,
I am the man .... I suffered .... I was there.

The disdain and calmness of martyrs,
The mother condemned for a witch and burnt with dry
     wood, and her children gazing on;
The hounded slave that flags in the race and leans by the
     fence, blowing and covered with sweat,
The twinges that sting like needles his legs and neck,
The murderous buckshot and the bullets,
All these I feel or am.

I am the hounded slave . . . . I wince at the bite of the dogs,
Hell and despair are upon me . . . . crack and again crack
     the marksmen,
I clutch the rails of the fence . . . . my gore dribs thinned
     with the ooze of my skin,
I fall on the weeds and stones,
The riders spur their unwilling horses and haul close,
They taunt my dizzy ears . . . . they beat me violently
     over the head with their whip-stocks.

Agonies are one of my changes of garments;
I do not ask the wounded person how he feels . . . . I myself
     become the wounded person,
My hurt turns livid upon me as I lean on a cane and observe.

I am the mashed fireman with breastbone broken . . . .
     tumbling walls buried me in their debris,
Heat and smoke I inspired . . . . I heard the yelling shouts
     of my comrades,
I heard the distant click of their picks and shovels;
They have cleared the beams away . . . . they tenderly
     lift me forth.

I lie in the night air in my red shirt . . . . the pervading
     hush is for my sake,
Painless after all I lie, exhausted but not so unhappy,
White and beautiful are the faces around me . . . . the
     heads are bared of their fire-caps,
The kneeling crowd fades with the light of the torches.

Distant and dead resuscitate,
They show as the dial or move as the hands of me .... and
    I am the clock myself.

I am an old artillerist, and tell of some fort's bombardment
    .... and am there again.

Again the reveille of drummers .... again the attacking
    cannon and mortars and howitzers,
Again the attacked send their cannon responsive.

I take part .... I see and hear the whole,
The cries and curses and roar .... the plaudits for well
    aimed shots,
The ambulanza slowly passing and trailing its red drip,
Workmen searching after damages and to make
    indispensable repairs,
The fall of grenades through the rent roof .... the fan-shaped
    explosion,
The whizz of limbs heads stone wood and iron high in
    the air.

Again gurgles the mouth of my dying general .... he
    furiously waves with his hand,
He gasps through the clot .... Mind not me .... mind ....
    the entrenchments.

[34]
I tell not the fall of Alamo .... not one escaped to tell
    the fall of Alamo,
The hundred and fifty are dumb yet at Alamo.

Hear now the tale of a jetblack sunrise,
Hear of the murder in cold blood of four hundred and twelve
    young men.

Retreating they had formed in a hollow square with their
    baggage for breastworks,

Nine hundred lives out of the surrounding enemy's nine
    times their number was the price they took in advance,
Their colonel was wounded and their ammunition gone,
They treated for an honorable capitulation, received
    writing and seal, gave up their arms, and marched back
    prisoners of war.

They were the glory of the race of rangers,
Matchless with a horse, a rifle, a song, a supper or a courtship,
Large, turbulent, brave, handsome, generous, proud and
    affectionate,
Bearded, sunburnt, dressed in the free costume of hunters,
Not a single one over thirty years of age.

The second Sunday morning they were brought out in
    squads and massacred .... it was beautiful early
    summer,
The work commenced about five o'clock and was over
    by eight.

None obeyed the command to kneel,
Some made a mad and helpless rush .... some stood stark
    and straight,
A few fell at once, shot in the temple or heart .... the living
    and dead lay together,
The maimed and mangled dug in the dirt .... the
    new-comers saw them there;
Some half-killed attempted to crawl away,
These were dispatched with bayonets or battered with the
    blunts of muskets;
A youth not seventeen years old seized his assassin till
    two more came to release him,
The three were all torn, and covered with the boy's blood.

At eleven o'clock began the burning of the bodies;
And that is the tale of the murder of the four hundred
    and twelve young men,
And that was a jetblack sunrise.

[35]

Did you read in the seabooks of the oldfashioned
        frigate-fight?
Did you learn who won by the light of the moon and stars?

Our foe was no skulk in his ship, I tell you,
His was the English pluck, and there is no tougher or truer,
        and never was, and never will be;
Along the lowered eve he came, horribly raking us.

We closed with him .... the yards entangled .... the cannon
        touched,
My captain lashed fast with his own hands.

We had received some eighteen-pound shots under the
        water,
On our lower-gun-deck two large pieces had burst at the first
        fire, killing all around and blowing up overhead.

Ten o'clock at night, and the full moon shining and the
        leaks on the gain, and five feet of water reported,
The master-at-arms loosing the prisoners confined in the
        after-hold to give them a chance for themselves.

The transit to and from the magazine was now stopped
        by the sentinels,
They saw so many strange faces they did not know whom
        to trust.

Our frigate was afire .... the other asked if we demanded
        quarters? if our colors were struck and the fighting done?

I laughed content when I heard the voice of my little
        captain,
We have not struck, he composedly cried, We have just
        begun our part of the fighting.

Only three guns were in use,
One was directed by the captain himself against the enemy's
    mainmast,
Two well-served with grape and canister silenced his
    musketry and cleared his decks. .

The tops alone seconded the fire of this little battery,
    especially the maintop,
They all held out bravely during the whole of the action.

Not a moment's cease,
The leaks gained fast on the pumps .... the fire eat
    toward the powder-magazine,
One of the pumps was shot away .... it was generally
    thought we were sinking.

Serene stood the little captain,
He was not hurried .... his voice was neither high nor low,
His eyes gave more light to us than our battle-lanterns.

Toward twelve at night, there in the beams of the moon
    they surrendered to us.

[36]
Stretched and still lay the midnight,
Two great hulls motionless on the breast of the darkness,
Our vessel riddled and slowly sinking .... preparations
    to pass to the one we had conquered,
The captain on the quarter deck coldly giving his
    orders through a countenance white as a sheet,
Near by the corpse of the child that served in the cabin,
The dead face of an old salt with long white hair and
    carefully curled whiskers,
The flames spite of all that could be done flickering
    aloft and below,
The husky voices of the two or three officers yet
    fit for duty,
Formless stacks of bodies and bodies by themselves ....
    dabs of flesh upon the masts and spars,

The cut of cordage and dangle of rigging . . . . the slight
    shock of the soothe of waves,
Black and impassive guns, and litter of powder-parcells, and
    the strong scent,
Delicate sniffs of the seabreeze . . . . smells of sedgy
    grass and fields by the shore . . . . death-messages given
    in charge to survivors,
The hiss of the surgeon's knife and the gnawing teeth
    of his saw,
The wheeze, the cluck, the swash of falling blood . . . . the
    short wild scream, the long dull tapering groan,
These so . . . . these irretrievable.

[37]
O Christ! My fit is mastering me!
What the rebel said gaily adjusting his throat to
    the rope-noose,
What the savage at the stump, his eye-sockets empty,
    his mouth spirting whoops and defiance,
What stills the traveler come to the vault at Mount Vernon,
What sobers the Brooklyn boy as he looks down the shores
    of the Wallabout and remembers the prison ships,
What burnt the gums of the redcoat at Saratoga when
    he surrendered his brigades,
These become mine and me every one, and they are
    but little,
I become as much more as I like.

I become any presence or truth of humanity here,
And see myself in prison shaped like another man,
And feel the dull unintermitted pain.

For me the keepers of convicts shoulder their carbines
    and keep watch,
It is I let out in the morning and barred at night.

Not a mutineer walks handcuffed to the jail, but I am
    handcuffed to him and walk by his side,
I am less the jolly one there, and more the silent one
    with sweat on my twitching lips.

Not a youngster is taken for larceny, but I go too and am
    tried and sentenced.

Not a cholera patient lies at the last gasp, but I also
    lie at the last gasp,
My face is ash-colored, my sinews gnarl . . . . away from
    me people retreat.

Askers embody themselves in me, and I am embodied
    in them,
I project my hat and sit shamefaced and beg.

I rise extatic through all, and sweep with the true gravitation,
The whirling and whirling is elemental within me.

    [38]
Somehow I have been stunned. Stand back!
Give me a little time beyond my cuffed head and slumbers
    and dreams and gaping,
I discover myself on a verge of the usual mistake.

That I could forget the mockers and insults!
That I could forget the trickling tears and the blows of the
    bludgeons and hammers!
That I could look with a separate look on my own
    crucifixion and bloody crowning!

I remember . . . . I resume the overstaid fraction,
The grave of rock multiplies what has been confided to it
    . . . . or to any graves,
The corpses rise . . . . the gashes heal . . . . the fastenings
    roll away.

I troop forth replenished with supreme power, one of an
    average unending procession,
We walk the roads of Ohio and Massachusetts and
    Virginia and Wisconsin and New York and New Orleans

and Texas and Montreal and San Francisco and
   Charleston and Savannah and Mexico,
Inland and by the seacoast and boundary lines .... and we
   pass the boundary lines.

Our swift ordinances are on their way over the whole earth,
The blossoms we wear in our hats are the growth of
   two thousand years.

Eleves I salute you,
I see the approach of your numberless gangs .... I see
   you understand yourselves and me,
And know that they who have eyes are divine, and the
   blind and lame are equally divine,
And that my steps drag behind yours yet go before them,
And are aware how I am with you no more than I am
   with everybody.

[39]
The friendly and flowing savage .... Who is he?
Is he waiting for civilization or past it and mastering it?

Is he some southwesterner raised outdoors? Is he Canadian?
Is he from the Mississippi country? or from Iowa, Oregon
   or California? or from the mountain? or prairie
   life or bush-life? or from the sea?

Wherever he goes men and women accept and desire him,
They desire he should like them and touch them and
   speak to them and stay with them.

Behaviour lawless as snow-flakes .... words simple as
   grass .... uncombed head and laughter and naivete;
Slowstepping feet and the common features, and the
   common modes and emanations,
They descend in new forms from the tips of his fingers,
They are wafted with the odor of his body or breath ....
   they fly out of the glance of his eyes.

[*40*]

Flaunt of the sunshine I need not your bask .... lie over,
You light surfaces only .... I force the surfaces and
    the depths also.

Earth! you seem to look for something at my hands,
Say old topknot! what do you want?

Man or woman! I might tell how I like you, but cannot,
And might tell what it is in me and what it is in you,
    but cannot,
And might tell the pinings I have .... the pulse of my
    nights and days.

Behold I do not give lectures or a little charity,
What I give I give out of myself.

You there, impotent, loose in the knees, open your
    scarfed chops till I blow grit within you,
Spread your palms and lift the flaps of your pockets,
I am not to be denied .... I compel .... I have stores plenty
    and to spare,
And any thing I have I bestow.

I do not ask who you are .... that is not important to me,
You can do nothing and be nothing but what I will
    infold you.

To a drudge of the cottonfields or emptier of privies
    I lean .... on his right cheek I put the family kiss,
And in my soul I swear I never will deny him.

On women fit for conception I start bigger and
    nimbler babes,
This day I am jetting the stuff of far more arrogant republics.

To any one dying .... thither I speed and twist the knob of
    the door,
Turn the bedclothes toward the foot of the bed,
Let the physician and the priest go home.

I seize the descending man . . . . I raise him with
     resistless will.

O despairer, here is my neck,
By God! you shall not go down! Hang your whole weight
     upon me.

I dilate you with tremendous breath . . . . I buoy you up;
Every room of the house do I fill with an armed force
     . . . . lovers of me bafflers of graves:
Sleep! I and they keep guard all night;
Not doubt, not decease shall dare to lay finger upon you,
I have embraced you, and henceforth possess you
     to myself,
And when you rise in the morning you will find what I tell
     you is so.

[41]

I am he bringing help for the sick as they pant on their backs,
And for strong upright men I bring yet more needed help.

I heard what was said of the universe,
Heard it and heard of several thousand years;
It is middling well as far as it goes . . . . but is that all?

Magnifying and applying come I,
Outbidding at the start the old cautious hucksters,
The most they offer for mankind and eternity less than a
     spirt of my own seminal wet,
Taking myself the exact dimensions of Jehovah and laying
     them away,
Lithographing Kronos and Zeus his son, and Hercules
     his grandson,
Buying drafts of Osiris and Isis and Belus and Brahma
     and Adonai,
In my portfolio placing Manito loose, and Allah on a
     leaf, and the crucifix engraved,
With Odin, and the hideous-faced Mexitli, and all idols
     and images,

Honestly taking them all for what they are worth, and not
    a cent more,
Admitting they were alive and did the work of their day,
Admitting they bore mites as for unfledged birds
    who have now to rise and fly and sing for themselves,
Accepting the rough deific sketches to fill out better
    in myself . . . . bestowing them freely on each man
    and woman I see,
Discovering as much or more in a framer framing a house,
Putting higher claims for him there with his rolled-up
    sleeves, driving the mallet and chisel;
Not objecting to special revelations . . . . considering a
    curl of smoke or a hair on the back of my hand as
    curious as any revelation;
Those ahold of fire-engines and hook-and-ladder ropes
    more to me than the gods of the antique wars,
Minding their voices peal through the crash of destruction,
Their brawny limbs passing safe over charred laths . . . . their
    white foreheads whole and unhurt out of the flames;
By the mechanic's wife with her babe at her nipple
    interceding for every person born;
Three scythes at harvest whizzing in a row from three
    lusty angels with shirts bagged out at their waists;
The snag-toothed hostler with red hair redeeming sins past
    and to come,
Selling all he possesses and traveling on foot to fee
    lawyers for his brother and sit by him while he is
    tried for forgery:
What was strewn in the amplest strewing the square rod
    about me, and not filling the square rod then;
The bull and the bug never worshipped half enough,
Dung and dirt more admirable than was dreamed,
The supernatural of no account . . . . myself waiting my
    time to be one of the supremes,
The day getting ready for me when I shall do as much good
    as the best, and be as prodigious,
Guessing when I am it will not tickle me much to receive
    puffs out of pulpit or print;
By my life-lumps! becoming already a creator!

Putting myself here and now to the ambushed womb
    of the shadows!

[42]
. . . . A call in the midst of the crowd,
My own voice, orotund sweeping and final.

Come my children,
Come my boys and girls, and my women and household
    and intimates,
Now the performer launches his nerve . . . . he has passed
    his prelude on the reeds within.

Easily written loosefingered chords! I feel the thrum
    of their climax and close.

My head evolves on my neck,
Music rolls, but not from the organ . . . . folks are around
    me, but they are no household of mine.

Ever the hard and unsunk ground,
Ever the eaters and drinkers . . . . ever the upward and
    downward sun . . . . ever the air and the ceaseless tides,
Ever myself and my neighbors, refreshing and wicked
    and real,
Ever the old inexplicable query . . . . ever that thorned
    thumb—that breath of itches and thirsts,
Ever the vexer's hoot! hoot! till we find where the sly
    one hides and bring him forth;
Ever love . . . . ever the sobbing liquid of life,
Ever the bandage under the chin . . . . ever the trestles
    of death.

Here and there with dimes on the eyes walking,
To feed the greed of the belly the brains liberally spooning,
Tickets buying or taking or selling, but in to the feast
    never once going;
Many sweating and ploughing and thrashing, and then the
    chaff for payment receiving,

A few idly owning, and they the wheat continually
    claiming.

This is the city .... and I am one of the citizens;
Whatever interests the rest interests me .... politics,
    churches, newspapers, schools,
Benevolent societies, improvements, banks, tariffs,
    steamships, factories, markets,
Stocks and stores and real estate and personal estate.

They who piddle and patter here in collars and tailed
    coats .... I am aware who they are .... and that they
    are not worms or fleas,
I acknowledge the duplicates of myself under all the
    scrape-lipped and pipe-legged concealments.

The weakest and shallowest is deathless with me,
What I do and say the same waits for them,
Every thought that flounders in me the same flounders
    in them.

I know perfectly well my own egotism,
And know my omnivorous words, and cannot say any less,
And would fetch you whoever you are flush with myself.

My words are words of a questioning, and to indicate
    reality;
This printed and bound book .... but the printer and the
    printing-office boy?
The marriage estate and settlement .... but the body
    and mind of the bridegroom? also those of the bride?
The panorama of the sea .... but the sea itself?
The well-taken photographs .... but your wife or friend
    close and solid in your arms?
The fleet of ships of the line and all the modern
    improvements .... but the craft and pluck of the
    admiral?
The dishes and fare and furniture .... but the host and
    hostess, and the look out of their eyes?

The sky up there.... yet here or next door or across
    the way?
The saints and sages in history.... but you yourself?
Sermons and creeds and theology.... but the human
    brain, and what is called reason, and what is called
    love, and what is called life?

[43]

I do not despise you priests;
My faith is the greatest of faiths and the least of faiths,
Enclosing all worship ancient and modern, and all
    between ancient and modern,
Believing I shall come again upon the earth after
    five thousand years,
Waiting responses from oracles.... honoring the gods....
    saluting the sun,
Making a fetish of the first rock or stump.... powowing
    with sticks in the circle of obis,
Helping the lama or brahmin as he trims the lamps
    of the idols,
Dancing yet through the streets in a phallic procession
    .... rapt and austere in the woods, a gymnosophist,
Drinking mead from the skull-up.... to shasta and
    vedas admirant.... minding the koran,
Walking the teokallis, spotted with gore from the stone
    and knife—beating the serpent-skin drum;
Accepting the gospels, accepting him that was crucified,
    knowing assuredly that he is divine,
To the mass kneeling—to the puritan's prayer rising—
    sitting patiently in a pew,
Ranting and frothing in my insane crisis—waiting dead-like
    till my spirit arouses me;
Looking forth on pavement and land, and outside of
    pavement and land,
Belonging to the winders of the circuit of circuits.

One of that centripetal and centrifugal gang,
I turn and talk like a man leaving charges before a journey.

Down-hearted doubters, dull and excluded,
Frivolous sullen moping angry affected disheartened
    atheistical,
I know every one of you, and know the unspoken
    interrogatories,
By experience I know them.

How the flukes splash!
How they contort rapid as lightning, with spasms and spouts
    of blood!

Be at peace bloody flukes of doubters and sullen mopers,
I take my place among you as much as among any;
The past is the push of you and me and all precisely the same,
And the day and night are for you and me and all,
And what is yet untried and afterward is for you and me
    and all.

I do not know what is untried and afterward,
But I know it is sure and alive and sufficient.

Each who passes is considered, and each who stops is
    considered, and not a single one can it fail.

It cannot fail the young man who died and was buried,
Nor the young woman who died and was put by his side,
Nor the little child that peeped in at the door and then drew
    back and was never seen again,
Nor the old man who has lived without purpose, and feels
    it with bitterness worse than gall,
Nor him in the poorhouse tubercled by rum and the bad
    disorder,
Nor the numberless slaughtered and wrecked .... nor the
    brutish koboo, called the ordure of humanity,
Nor the sacs merely floating with open mouths for food
    to slip in,

Nor any thing in the earth, or down in the oldest graves
    of the earth,
Nor any thing in the myriads of spheres, nor one of the
    myriads of myriads that inhabit them,
Nor the present, nor the least wisp that is known.

[44]
It is time to explain myself .... let us stand up.

What is known I strip away .... I launch all men and
    women forward with me into the unknown.

The clock indicates the moment .... but what does
    eternity indicate?

Eternity lies in bottomless reservoirs .... its buckets are
    rising forever and ever,
They pour and they pour and they exhale away.

We have thus far exhausted trillions of winters and summers;
There are trillions ahead, and trillions ahead of them.

Births have brought us richness and variety,
And other births will bring us richness and variety.

I do not call one greater and one smaller,
That which fills its period and place is equal to any.

Were mankind murderous or jealous upon you my brother
    or my sister?
I am sorry for you .... they are not murderous or jealous
    upon me;
All has been gentle with me .... I keep no account with
    lamentation;
What have I to do with lamentation?

I am an acme of things accomplished, and I an encloser
    of things to be.

My feet strike an apex of the apices of the stairs,
On every step bunches of ages, and larger bunches between
    the steps,
All below duly traveled—and still I mount and mount.

Rise after rise bow the phantoms behind me,
Afar down I see the huge first Nothing, the vapor from
    the nostrils of death,
I know I was even there . . . . I waited unseen and always,
And slept while God carried me through the lethargic mist,
And took my time . . . . and took no hurt from the fœtid
    carbon.

Long I was hugged close . . . . long and long.

Immense have been the preparations for me,
Faithful and friendly the arms that have helped me.

Cycles ferried my cradle, rowing and rowing like cheerful
    boatmen;
For room to me stars kept aside in their own rings,
They sent influences to look after what was to hold me.

Before I was born out of my mother generations guided me,
My embryo has never been torpid . . . . nothing could
    overlay it;
For it the nebula cohered to an orb . . . . the long slow
    strata piled to rest it on . . . . vast vegetables gave it
    sustenance,
Monstrous sauroids transported it in their mouths and
    deposited it with care.

All forces have been steadily employed to complete and
    delight me,
Now I stand on this spot with my soul.

[45]

Span of youth! Ever-pushed elasticity! Manhood balanced
    and florid and full!

My lovers suffocate me!
Crowding my lips, and thick in the pores of my skin,
Jostling me through streets and public halls .... coming
    naked to me at night,
Crying by day Ahoy from the rocks of the river ....
    swinging and chirping over my head,
Calling my name from flowerbeds or vines or tangled
    underbrush,
Or while I swim in the bath .... or drink from the pump
    at the corner .... or the curtain is down at the opera
    .... or I glimpse at a woman's face in the railroad car;
Lighting on every moment of my life,
Bussing my body with soft and balsamic busses,
Noiselessly passing handfuls out of their hearts and giving
    them to be mine.

Old age superbly rising! Ineffable grace of dying days!

Every condition promulges not only itself .... it promulges
    what grows after and out of itself,
And the dark hush promulges as much as any.

I open my scuttle at night and see the far-sprinkled systems,
And all I see, multiplied as high as I can cipher, edge but
    the rim of the farther systems.

Wider and wider they spread, expanding and always
    expanding,
Outward and outward and forever outward.

My sun has his sun, and round him obediently wheels,
He joins with his partners a group of superior circuit,
And greater sets follow, making specks of the greatest inside
    them.

There is no stoppage, and never can be stoppage;
If I and you and the worlds and all beneath or upon their
    surfaces, and all the palpable life, were this moment

reduced back to a pallid float, it would not avail
in the long run,
We should surely bring up again where we now stand,
And as surely go as much farther, and then farther and
farther.

A few quadrillions of eras, a few octillions of cubic leagues,
do not hazard the span, or make it impatient,
They are but parts .... any thing is but a part.

See ever so far .... there is limitless space outside of that,
Count ever so much .... there is limitless time around that.

Our rendezvous is fitly appointed .... God will be there
and wait till we come.

[46]
I know I have the best of time and space—and that I was
never measured, and never will be measured.

I tramp a perpetual journey,
My signs are a rain-proof coat and good shoes and a staff
cut from the woods;
No friend of mine takes his ease in my chair,
I have no chair, nor church nor philosophy;
I lead no man to a dinner-table or library or exchange,
But each man and each woman of you I lead upon a knoll,
My left hand hooks you round the waist,
My right hand points to landscapes of continents, and
a plain public road.

Not I, not any one else can travel that road for you,
You must travel it for yourself.

It is not far .... it is within reach,
Perhaps you have been on it since you were born, and
did not know,
Perhaps it is every where on water and on land.

Shoulder your duds, and I will mine, and let us hasten forth;
Wonderful cities and free nations we shall fetch as we go.

If you tire, give me both burdens, and rest the chuff
    of your hand on my hip,
And in due time you shall repay the same service to me;
For after we start we never lie by again.

This day before dawn I ascended a hill and looked at the
    crowded heaven,
And I said to my spirit, When we become the enfolders of
    those orbs and the pleasure and knowledge of every
    thing in them, shall we be filled and satisfied then?
And my spirit said No, we level that lift to pass and
    continue beyond.

You are also asking me questions, and I hear you;
I answer that I cannot answer .... you must find out for
    yourself.

Sit awhile wayfarer,
Here are biscuits to eat and here is milk to drink,
But as soon as you sleep and renew yourself in sweet
    clothes I will certainly kiss you with my goodbye kiss
    and open the gate for your egress hence.

Long enough have you dreamed contemptible dreams,
Now I wash the gum from your eyes,
You must habit yourself to the dazzle of the light and of
    every moment of your life.

Long have you timidly waded, holding a plank by the shore,
Now I will you to be a bold swimmer,
To jump off in the midst of the sea, and rise again and nod
    to me and shout, and laughingly dash with your hair.

[47]
I am the teacher of athletes,
He that by me spreads a wider breast than my own proves
    the width of my own,
He most honors my style who learns under it to destroy
    the teacher.

The boy I love, the same becomes a man not through
    derived power but in his own right,
Wicked, rather than virtuous out of conformity or fear,
Fond of his sweetheart, relishing well his steak,
Unrequited love or a slight cutting him worse than a
    wound cuts,
First rate to ride, to fight, to hit the bull's eye, to sail a skiff,
    to sing a song or play on the banjo,
Preferring scars and faces pitted with smallpox over all
    latherers and those that keep out of the sun.

I teach straying from me, yet who can stray from me?
I follow you whoever you are from the present hour;
My words itch at your ears till you understand them.

I do not say these things for a dollar, or to fill up the time
    while I wait for a boat;
It is you talking just as much as myself . . . . I act as the
    tongue of you,
It was tied in your mouth . . . . in mine it begins to
    be loosened.

I swear I will never mention love or death inside a house,
And I swear I never will translate myself at all, only to
    him or her who privately stays with me in the open air.

If you would understand me go to the heights or
    water-shore,
The nearest gnat is an explanation and a drop or the
    motion of waves a key,
The maul the oar and the handsaw second my words.

No shuttered room or school can commune with me,
But roughs and little children better than they.

The young mechanic is closest to me . . . . he knows
    me pretty well,
The woodman that takes his axe and jug with him shall
    take me with him all day,

The farmboy ploughing in the field feels good at the
    sound of my voice,
In vessels that sail my words must sail . . . . I go with
    fishermen and seamen, and love them,
My face rubs to the hunter's face when he lies down alone
    in his blanket,
The driver thinking of me does not mind the jolt of
    his wagon,
The young mother and old mother shall comprehend me,
The girl and the wife rest the needle a moment and
    forget where they are,
They and all would resume what I have told them.

[48]

I have said that the soul is not more than the body,
And I have said that the body is not more than the soul,
And nothing, not God, is greater to one than one's-self is,
And whoever walks a furlong without sympathy walks
    to his own funeral, dressed in his shroud,
And I or you pocketless of a dime may purchase the
    pick of the earth,
And to glance with an eye or show a bean in its pod
    confounds the learning of all times,
And there is no trade or employment but the young man
    following it may become a hero,
And there is no object so soft but it makes a hub for
    the wheeled universe,
And any man or woman shall stand cool and supercilious
    before a million universes.

And I call to mankind, Be not curious about God,
For I who am curious about each am not curious about God,
No array of terms can say how much I am at peace
    about God and about death.

I hear and behold God in every object, yet I understand
    God not in the least,
Nor do I understand who there can be more wonderful
    than myself.

Why should I wish to see God better than this day?
I see something of God each hour of the twenty-four, and
    each moment then,
In the faces of men and women I see God, and in my
    own face in the glass;
I find letters from God dropped in the street, and every one
    is signed by God's name,
And I leave them where they are, for I know that others
    will punctually come forever and ever.

[49]
And as to you death, and you bitter hug of mortality . . . .
    it is idle to try to alarm me.

To his work without flinching the accoucheur comes,
I see the elderhand pressing receiving supporting,
I recline by the sills of the exquisite flexible doors . . . . and
    mark the outlet, and mark the relief and escape.

And as to you corpse I think you are good manure, but that
    does not offend me,
I smell the white roses sweetscented and growing,
I reach to the leafy lips . . . . I reach to the polished breasts
    of melons.

And as to you life, I reckon you are the leavings of many
    deaths,
No doubt I have died myself ten thousand times before.

I hear you whispering there O stars of heaven,
O suns . . . . O grass of graves . . . . O perpetual transfers
    and promotions . . . . if you do not say anything
    how can I say anything?

Of the turbid pool that lies in the autumn forest,
Of the moon that descends the steeps of the soughing
    twilight,

Toss, sparkles of day and dusk . . . . toss on the black stems
    that decay in the muck,
Toss to the moaning gibberish of the dry limbs.

I ascend from the moon . . . . I ascend from the night,
And perceive of the ghastly glitter the sunbeams reflected,
And debouch to the steady and central from the offspring
    great or small.

[50]

There is that in me . . . . I do not know what it is . . . . but
    I know it is in me.

Wrenched and sweaty . . . . calm and cool then my body
    becomes;
I sleep . . . . I sleep long.

I do not know it . . . . it is without name . . . . it is a word
    unsaid,
It is not in any dictionary or utterance or symbol.

Something it swings on more than the earth I swing on,
To it the creation is the friend whose embracing awakes me.

Perhaps I might tell more . . . . Outlines! I plead for my
    brothers and sisters.

Do you see O my brothers and sisters?
It is not chaos or death . . . . it is form and union and plan
    . . . . it is eternal life . . . . it is happiness.

[51]

The past and present wilt . . . . I have filled them and emptied
    them,
And proceed to fill my next fold of the future.

Listener up there! Here you . . . . what have you to confide
    to me?

Look in my face while I snuff the sidle of evening,
Talk honestly, for no one else hears you, and I stay only
     a minute longer.

Do I contradict myself?
Very well then . . . . I contradict myself;
I am large . . . . I contain multitudes.

I concentrate toward them that are nigh . . . . I wait on the
     door-slab.
Who has done his day's work and will soonest be through
     with his supper?
Who wishes to walk with me?

Will you speak before I am gone? Will you prove already
     too late?

     [52]
The spotted hawk swoops by and accuses me . . . . he
     complains of my gab and my loitering.

I too am not a bit tamed . . . . I too am untranslatable,
I sound my barbaric yawp over the roofs of the world.

The last scud of day holds back for me,
It flings my likeness after the rest and true as any on the
     shadowed wilds,
It coaxes me to the vapor and the dusk.

I depart as air . . . . I shake my white locks at the runaway
     sun,
I effuse my flesh in eddies and drift it in lacy jags.

I bequeath myself to the dirt to grow from the grass I love,
If you want me again look for me under your bootsoles.

You will hardly know who I am or what I mean,
But I shall be good health to you nevertheless,
And filter and fibre your blood.

Failing to fetch me at first keep encouraged,
Missing me one place search another,
I stop some where waiting for you.

[1855]

[*A Song for Occupations*]

[*1*]

Come closer to me,
Push close my lovers and take the best I possess,
Yield closer and closer and give me the best you possess.

This is unfinished business with me .... how is it with you?
I was chilled with the cold types and cylinder and wet paper
between us.

I pass so poorly with paper and types .... I must pass
with the contact of bodies and souls.

I do not thank you for liking me as I am, and liking the
touch of me .... I know that it is good for you to do so.

Were all educations practical and ornamental well
displayed out of me, what would it amount to?
Were I as the head teacher or charitable proprietor or wise
statesman, what would it amount to?
Were I to you as the boss employing and paying you,
would that satisfy you?

The learned and virtuous and benevolent, and the usual
terms;
A man like me, and never the usual terms.

Neither a servant nor a master am I,
I take no sooner a large price than a small price .... I will

have my own whoever enjoys me,
I will be even with you, and you shall be even with me.

If you are a workman or workwoman I stand as nigh as
    the nighest that works in the same shop,
If you bestow gifts on your brother or dearest friend,
    I demand as good as your brother or dearest friend,
If your lover or husband or wife is welcome by day or
    night, I must be personally as welcome;
If you have become degraded or ill, then I will become
    so for your sake;
If you remember your foolish and outlawed deeds, do you
    think I cannot remember my foolish and outlawed
    deeds?
If you carouse at the table I say I will carouse at the
    opposite side of the table;
If you meet some stranger in the street and love him or
    her, do I not often meet strangers in the street and
    love them?
If you see a good deal remarkable in me I see just as much
    remarkable in you.

Why what have you thought of yourself?
Is it you then that thought yourself less?
Is it you that thought the President greater than you? or the
    rich better off than you? or the educated wiser than
    you?

Because you are greasy or pimpled—or that you was once
    drunk, or a thief, or diseased, or rheumatic, or a
    prostitute—or are so now—or from frivolity or
    impotence—or that you are no scholar, and never
    saw your name in print . . . . do you give in that you
    are any less immortal?

[2]

Souls of men and women! it is not you I call unseen,
    unheard, untouchable and untouching;
It is not you I go argue pro and con about, and to settle
    whether you are alive or no;

I own publicly who you are, if nobody else owns .... and
    see and hear you, and what you give and take;
What is there you cannot give and take?

I see not merely that you are polite or whitefaced ....
    married or single .... citizens of old states or citizens
    of new states .... eminent in some profession .... a
    lady or gentleman in a parlor .... or dressed in the
    jail uniform .... or pulpit uniform,
Not only the free Utahan, Kansian, or Arkansian .... not
    only the free Cuban .... not merely the slave ....
    not Mexican native, or Flatfoot, or negro from Africa,
Iroquois eating the warflesh—fishtearer in his lair of
    rocks and sand .... Esquimaux in the dark cold
    snowhouse .... Chinese with his transverse eyes ....
    Bedowee—or wandering nomad—or tabounschik
    at the head of his droves,
Grown, half-grown, and babe—of this country and every
    country, indoors and outdoors I see .... and all else
    is behind or through them.

The wife—and she is not one jot less than the husband,
The daughter—and she is just as good as the son,
The mother—and she is every bit as much as the father.

Offspring of those not rich—boys apprenticed to trades,
Young fellows working on farms and old fellows working
    on farms;
The naive .... the simple and hardy .... he going to the
    polls to vote .... he who has a good time, and he
    who has a bad time;
Mechanics, southerners, new arrivals, sailors, mano'warsmen,
    merchantmen, coasters,
All these I see .... but nigher and farther the same I see;
None shall escape me, and none shall wish to escape me.

I bring what you much need, yet always have,
I bring not money or amours or dress or eating .... but
    I bring as good;

And send no agent or medium .... and offer no
    representative of value—but offer the value itself.

There is something that comes home to one now and
    perpetually,
It is not what is printed or preached or discussed .... it
    eludes discussion and print,
It is not to be put in a book .... it is not in this book,
It is for you whoever you are .... it is no farther from you
    than your hearing and sight are from you,
It is hinted by nearest and commonest and readiest ....
    it is not them, though it is endlessly provoked by
    them .... What is there ready and near you now?

You may read in many languages and read nothing about it;
You may read the President's message and read nothing
    about it there;
Nothing in the reports from the state department or
    treasury department .... or in the daily papers, or
    the weekly papers,
Or in the census returns or assessors' returns or prices
    current or any accounts of stock.

    [3]

The sun and stars that float in the open air .... the
    appleshaped earth and we upon it .... surely the
    drift of them is something grand;
I do not know what it is except that it is grand, and that it is
    happiness,
And that the enclosing purport of us here is not a
    speculation, or bon-mot or reconnoissance,
And that it is not something which by luck may turn out
    well for us, and without luck must be a failure for us,
And not something which may yet be retracted in a certain
    contingency.

The light and shade—the curious sense of body and
    identity—the greed that with perfect complaisance
    devours all things—the endless pride and outstretching
    of man—unspeakable joys and sorrows,

The wonder every one sees in every one else he sees . . . .
    and the wonders that fill each minute of time forever
    and each acre of surface and space forever,
Have you reckoned them as mainly for a trade or
    farmwork? or for the profits of a store? or to achieve
    yourself a position? or to fill a gentleman's leisure
    or a lady's leisure?

Have you reckoned the landscape took substance and
    form that it might be painted in a picture?
Or men and women that they might be written of,
    and songs sung?
Or the attraction of gravity and the great laws and
    harmonious combinations and the fluids of the air
    as subjects for the savans?
Or the brown land and the blue sea for maps and charts?
Or the stars to be put in constellations and named fancy
    names?
Or that the growth of seeds is for agricultural tables
    or agriculture itself?

Old institutions . . . . these arts libraries legends collections
    —and the practice handed along in manufactures
    . . . . will we rate them so high?
Will we rate our prudence and business so high? . . . .
    I have no objection,
I rate them as high as the highest . . . . but a child born of a
    woman and man I rate beyond all rate.

We thought our Union grand and our Constitution grand;
I do not say they are not grand and good—for they are,
I am this day just as much in love with them as you,
But I am eternally in love with you and with all my fellows
    upon the earth.

We consider the bibles and religions divine . . . . I do not
    say they are not divine,
I say they have all grown out of you and may grow
    out of you still,

It is not they who give the life .... it is you who give the life;
Leaves are not more shed from the trees or trees from
    the earth than they are shed out of you.

[4]

The sum of all known value and respect I add up in
    you whoever you are;
The President is up there in the White House for you ....
    it is not you who are here for him,
The Secretaries act in their bureaus for you .... not you
    here for them,
The Congress convenes every December for you,
Laws, courts, the forming of states, the charters of cities,
    the going and coming of commerce and mails are
    all for you.

All doctrines, all politics and civilization exurge from you,
All sculpture and monuments and anything inscribed
    anywhere are tallied in you,
The gist of histories and statistics as far back as the
    records reach is in you this hour—and myths and
    tales the same;
If you were not breathing and walking here where
    would they all be?
The most renowned poems would be ashes .... orations
    and plays would be vacuums.

All architecture is what you do to it when you look upon it;
Did you think it was in the white or gray stone? or the
    lines of the arches and cornices?

All music is what awakens from you when you are
    reminded by the instruments,
It is not the violins and the cornets .... it is not the oboe
    nor the beating drums—nor the notes of the baritone
    singer singing his sweet romanza .... nor those of
    the men's chorus, nor those of the women's chorus,
It is nearer and farther than they.

[5]

Will the whole come back then?
Can each see the signs of the best by a look in the
    lookingglass? Is there nothing greater or more?
Does all sit there with you and here with me?

The old forever new things .... you foolish child! ....
    the closest simplest things—this moment with you,
Your person and every particle that relates to your
    person,
The pulses of your brain waiting their chance and
    encouragement at every deed or sight;
Anything you do in public by day, and anything you do
    in secret betweendays,
What is called right and what is called wrong ....
    what you behold or touch .... what causes your
    anger or wonder,
The anklechain of the slave, the bed of the bedhouse,
    the cards of the gambler, the plates of the forger;
What is seen or learned in the street, or intuitively learned,
What is learned in the public school—spelling, reading,
    writing and ciphering .... the blackboard and the
    teacher's diagrams:
The panes of the windows and all that appears through
    them .... the going forth in the morning and the aimless
    spending of the day;
(What is it that you made money? what is it that you
    got what you wanted?)
The usual routine .... the workshop, factory, yard,
    office, store, or desk;
The jaunt of hunting or fishing, or the life of hunting or
    fishing,
Pasturelife, foddering, milking and herding, and all
    the personnel and usages;
The plum-orchard and apple-orchard .... gardening ....
    seedlings, cuttings, flowers and vines,
Grains and manures .. marl, clay, loam .. the subsoil
    plough .. the shovel and pick and rake and hoe ..
    irrigation and draining;

The currycomb .. the horse-cloth .. the halter and
    bridle and bits .. the very wisps of straw,
The barn and barn-yard .. the bins and mangers ..
    the mows and racks:
Manufacturers .. commerce .. engineering .. the building
    of cities, and every trade carried on there ... and the
    implements of every trade,
The anvil and tongs and hammer .. the axe and wedge .. the
    square and mitre and jointer and smoothingplane;
The plumbob and trowel and level .. the wall-scaffold, and
    the work of walls and ceilings .. or any mason-work:
The ship's compass .. the sailor's tarpaulin .. the stays
    and lanyards, and the ground-tackle for anchoring or
    mooring,
The sloop's tiller .. the pilot's wheel and bell .. the
    yatch or fishsmack .. the great gay-pennanted
    three-hundred-foot steamboat under full headway,
    with her proud fat breasts and her delicate
    swift-flashing paddles,
The trail and line and hooks and sinkers .. the seine, and
    hauling the seine;
Smallarms and rifles .... the powder and shot and caps and
    wadding .... the ordnance for war .... the carriages:
Everyday objects .... the housechairs, the carpet, the
    bed and the counterpane of the bed, and him or her
    sleeping at night, and the wind blowing, and the
    indefinite noises:
The snowstorm or rainstorm .... the tow-trowsers ....
    the lodgehut in the woods, and the still-hunt:
City and country .. fireplace and candle .. gaslight and
    heater and aqueduct;
The message of the governor, mayor, or chief of police ....
    the dishes of breakfast or dinner or supper;
The bunkroom, the fire-engine, the string-team, and the
    car or truck behind;
The paper I write on or you write on .. and every word
    we write .. and every cross and twirl of the pen .. and
    the curious way we write what we think .... yet
    very faintly;

The directory, the detector, the ledger .... the books
    in ranks or the bookshelves .... the clock attached
    to the wall,
The ring on your finger .. the lady's wristlet .. the
    hammers of stonebreakers or coppersmiths .. the
    druggist's vials and jars;
The etui of surgical instruments, and the etui of oculist's
    or aurist's instruments, or dentist's instruments;
Glassblowing, grinding of wheat and corn .. casting, and
    what is cast .. tinroofing, shingledressing,
Shipcarpentering, flagging of sidewalks by flaggers ..
    dockbuilding, fishcuring, ferrying;
The pump, the piledriver, the great derrick .. the coalkiln
    and brickkiln,
Ironworks or whiteleadworks .. the sugarhouse ..
    steam-saws, and the great mills and factories;
The cottonbale .. the stevedore's hook .. the saw and
    buck of the sawyer .. the screen of the coalscreener
    .. the mould of the moulder .. the workingknife of
    the butcher;
The cylinder press .. the handpress .. the frisket and
    tympan .. the compositor's stick and rule,
The implements for daguerreotyping .... the tools of the
    rigger or grappler or sailmaker or blockmaker,
Goods of guttapercha or papiermache .... colors and
    brushes .... glaziers' implements,
The veneer and gluepot .. the confectioner's ornaments ..
    the decanter and glasses .. the shears and flatiron;
The awl and kneestrap .. the pint measure and quart
    measure .. the counter and stool .. the writingpen of
    quill or metal;
Billiards and tenpins .... the ladders and hanging ropes
    of the gymnasium, and the manly exercises;
The designs for wallpapers or oilcloths or carpets .... the
    fancies for goods for women .... the bookbinder's
    stamps;
Leatherdressing, coachmaking, boilermaking, ropetwisting,
    distilling, signpainting, limeburning, coopering,
    cottonpicking,

The walkingbeam of the steam-engine . . the throttle and
    governors, and the up and down rods,
Stavemachines and planingmachines . . . . the cart of the
    carman . . the omnibus . . the ponderous dray;
The snowplough and two engines pushing it . . . . the
    ride in the express train of only one car . . . . the swift
    go through a howling storm:
The bearhunt or coonhunt . . . . the bonfire of shavings in the
    open lot in the city . . the crowd of children watching;
The blows of the fighting-man . . the upper cut and
    one-two-three;
The shopwindows . . . . the coffins in the sexton's wareroom
    . . . . the fruit on the fruitstand . . . . the beef on the
    butcher's stall,
The bread and cakes in the bakery . . . . the white and red
    pork in the pork-store;
The milliner's ribbons . . the dressmaker's patterns . . . .
    the tea-table . . the homemade sweetmeats:
The column of wants in the one-cent paper . . the news by
    telegraph . . . . the amusements and operas and shows:
The cotton and woolen and linen you wear . . . . the money
    you make and spend;
Your room and bedroom . . . . your piano-forte . . . .
    the stove and cookpans,
The house you live in . . . . the rent . . . . the other tenants
    . . . . the deposit in the savings-bank . . . . the trade
    at the grocery,
The pay on Saturday night . . . . the going home, and
    the purchases;
In them the heft of the heaviest . . . . in them far more than
    you estimated, and far less also,
In them, not yourself . . . . you and your soul enclose all
    things, regardless of estimation,
In them your themes and hints and provokers . . if not,
    the whole earth has no themes or hints or provokers,
    and never had.

I do not affirm what you see beyond is futile . . . . I do
    not advise you to stop,

I do not say leadings you thought great are not great,
But I say that none lead to greater or sadder or happier
than those lead to.

[6]
Will you seek afar off? You surely come back at last,
In things best known to you finding the best or as good
as the best,
In folks nearest to you finding also the sweetest and
strongest and lovingest,
Happiness not in another place, but this place .. not for
another hour, but this hour,
Man in the first you see or touch .... always in your
friend or brother or nighest neighbor .... Woman in
your mother or lover or wife,
And all else thus far known giving place to men and women.

When the psalm sings instead of the singer,
When the script preaches instead of the preacher,
When the pulpit descends and goes instead of the carver
that carved the supporting desk,
When the sacred vessels or the bits of the eucharist, or
the lath and plast, procreate as effectually as the young
silversmiths or bakers, or the masons in their overalls,
When a university course convinces like a slumbering
woman and child convince,
When the minted gold in the vault smiles like the
nightwatchman's daughter,
When warrantee deeds loafe in chairs opposite and
are my friendly companions,
I intend to reach them my hand and make as much of them
as I do of men and women.

[1855]

[To Think of Time]

[1]

To think of time . . . . to think through the retrospection,
To think of today . . and the ages continued henceforward.

Have you guessed you yourself would not continue? Have
     you dreaded those earth-beetles?
Have you feared the future would be nothing to you?

Is today nothing? Is the beginningless past nothing?
If the future is nothing they are just as surely nothing.

To think that the sun rose in the east . . . . that men and
     women were flexible and real and alive . . . . that
     every thing was real and alive;
To think that you and I did not see feel think nor
     bear our part,
To think that we are now here and bear our part.

[2]

Not a day passes . . not a minute or second without an
     accouchement;
Not a day passes . . not a minute or second without a corpse.

When the dull nights are over, and the dull days also,
When the soreness of lying so much in bed is over,
When the physician, after long putting off, gives the
     silent and terrible look for an answer,
When the children come hurried and weeping, and the
     brothers and sisters have been sent for,
When medicines stand unused on the shelf, and the
     camphor-smell has pervaded the rooms,
When the faithful hand of the living does not desert the
     hand of the dying,
When the twitching lips press lightly on the forehead
     of the dying,

When the breath ceases and the pulse of the heart ceases,
Then the corpse-limbs stretch on the bed, and the living
    look upon them,
They are palpable as the living are palpable.

The living look upon the corpse with their eyesight,
But without eyesight lingers a different living and
    looks curiously on the corpse.

   [3]

To think that the rivers will come to flow, and the snow fall,
    and fruits ripen . . and act upon others as upon us
    now . . . . yet not act upon us;
To think of all these wonders of city and country . . and
    others taking great interest in them . . and we taking
    small interest in them.

To think how eager we are in building our houses,
To think others shall be just as eager . . and we quite
    indifferent.

I see one building the house that serves him a few years
    . . . . or seventy or eighty years at most;
I see one building the house that serves him longer than that.

Slowmoving and black lines creep over the whole earth
    . . . . they never cease . . . . they are the burial lines,
He that was President was buried, and he that is now
    President shall surely be buried.

   [4]

Cold dash of waves at the ferrywharf,
Posh and ice in the river . . . . half-frozen mud in the streets,
A gray discouraged sky overhead . . . . the short last
    daylight of December,
A hearse and stages . . . . other vehicles give place,
The funeral of an old stagedriver . . . . the cortege mostly
    drivers.

Rapid the trot to the cemetery,
Duly rattles the deathbell .... the gate is passed .... the
    grave is halted at .... the living alight ....
    the hearse uncloses,
The coffin is lowered and settled .... the whip is laid on
    the coffin,
The earth is swiftly shovelled in .... a minute .. no one
    moves or speaks .... it is done,
He is decently put away .... is there anything more?

He was a goodfellow,
Freemouthed, quicktempered, not badlooking, able to take
    his own part,
Witty, sensitive to a slight, ready with life or death for
    a friend,
Fond of women, .. played some .. eat hearty and drank
    hearty,
Had known what it was to be flush .. grew lowspirited
    toward the last .. sickened .. was helped by a
    contribution,
Died aged forty-one years .. and that was his funeral.

Thumb extended or finger uplifted,
Apron, cape, gloves, strap .... wetweather clothes ....
    whip carefully chosen .... boss, spotter, starter,
    and hostler,
Somebody loafing on you, or you loafing on somebody ....
    headway .... man before and man behind,
Good day's work or bad day's work .... pet stock or mean
    stock .... first out or last out .... turning in at night,
To think that these are so much and so nigh to other
    drivers .... and he there takes no interest in them.

[5]
The markets, the government, the workingman's wages
    .... to think what account they are through our
    nights and days;
To think that other workingmen will make just as great
    account of them .. yet we make little or no account.

The vulgar and the refined . . . . what you call sin and
    what you call goodness . . to think how wide a
    difference;
To think the difference will still continue to others,
    yet we lie beyond the difference.

To think how much pleasure there is!
Have you pleasure from looking at the sky? Have you
    pleasure from poems?
Do you enjoy yourself in the city? or engaged in business?
    or planning a nomination and election? or with your
    wife and family?
Or with your mother and sisters? or in womanly housework?
    or the beautiful maternal cares?

These also flow onward to others . . . . you and I flow onward;
But in due time you and I shall take less interest in them.

Your farm and profits and crops . . . . to think how
    engrossed you are;
To think there will still be farms and profits and crops
    . . yet for you of what avail?

[6]
What will be will be well—for what is is well,
To take interest is well, and not to take interest shall be
    well.

The sky continues beautiful . . . . the pleasure of men with
    women shall never be sated . . nor the pleasure of
    women with men . . nor the pleasure from poems;
The domestic joys, the daily housework or business, the
    building of houses—they are not phantasms . . they
    have weight and form and location;
The farms and profits and crops . . the markets and wages
    and government . . they also are not phantasms;
The difference between sin and goodness is no apparition;
The earth is not an echo . . . . man and his life and all the
    things of his life are well-considered.

You are not thrown to the winds .. you gather certainly
    and safely around yourself,
Yourself! Yourself! Yourself forever and ever!

[7]
It is not to diffuse you that you were born of your mother
    and father—it is to identify you,
It is not that you should be undecided, but that you
    should be decided;
Something long preparing and formless is arrived and
    formed in you,
You are thenceforth secure, whatever comes or goes.

The threads that were spun are gathered .... the weft
    crosses the warp .... the pattern is systematic.

The preparations have every one been justified;
The orchestra have tuned their instruments sufficiently ....
    the baton has given the signal.

The guest that was coming .... he waited long for reasons
    .... he is now housed,
He is one of those who are beautiful and happy .... he is
    one of those that to look upon and be with is enough.

The law of the past cannot be eluded,
The law of the present and future cannot be eluded,
The law of the living cannot be eluded .... it is eternal,
The law of promotion and transformation cannot be eluded,
The law of heroes and good-doers cannot be eluded,
The law of drunkards and informers and mean persons
    cannot be eluded.

[8]
Slowmoving and black lines go ceaselessly over the earth,
Northerner goes carried and southerner goes carried ...
    and they on the Atlantic side and they on the

Pacific, and they between, and all through the
    Mississippi country . . . . and all over the earth.

The great masters and kosmos are well as they go . . . . the
    heroes and good-doers are well,
The known leaders and inventors and the rich owners
    and pious and distinguished may be well,
But there is more account than that . . . . there is strict
    account of all.

The interminable hordes of the ignorant and wicked are
    not nothing,
The barbarians of Africa and Asia are not nothing,
The common people of Europe are not nothing . . . . the
    American aborigines are not nothing,
A zambo or a foreheadless Crowfoot or a Camanche is not
    nothing,
The infected in the immigrant hospital are not nothing
    . . . . the murderer or mean person is not nothing,
The perpetual succession of shallow people are not
    nothing as they go,
The prostitute is not nothing . . . . the mocker of religion
    is not nothing as he goes.

I shall go with the rest . . . . we have satisfaction:
I have dreamed that we are not to be changed so much
    . . . . nor the law of us changed;
I have dreamed that heroes and good-doers shall be under
    the present and past law,
And that murderers and drunkards and liars shall be
    under the present and past law;
For I have dreamed that the law they are under now
    is enough.

And I have dreamed that the satisfaction is not so much
    changed . . . . and that there is no life without
    satisfaction;

What is the earth? what are body and soul without
      satisfaction?

I shall go with the rest,
We cannot be stopped at a given point . . . . that is no
      satisfaction;
To show us a good thing or a few good things for a space of
      time—that is no satisfaction;
We must have the indestructible breed of the best,
      regardless of time.

If otherwise, all these things came but to ashes of dung;
If maggots and rats ended us, then suspicion and treachery
      and death.

Do you suspect death? If I were to suspect death I should
      die now,
Do you think I could walk pleasantly and well-suited
      toward annihilation?

Pleasantly and well-suited I walk,
Whither I walk I cannot define, but I know it is good,
The whole universe indicates that it is good,
The past and the present indicate that it is good.

How beautiful and perfect are the animals! How perfect
      is my soul!
How perfect the earth, and the minutest thing upon it!
What is called good is perfect, and what is called
      sin is just as perfect;
The vegetables and minerals are perfect . . and the
      imponderable fluids are perfect;
Slowly and surely they have passed on to this, and slowly
      and surely they will yet pass on.

O my soul! if I realize you I have satisfaction,
Animals and vegetables! if I realize you I have satisfaction,
Laws of the earth and air! if I realize you I have
      satisfaction.

I cannot define my satisfaction .. yet it is so,
I cannot define my life .. yet it is so.

[9]
I swear I see now that every thing has an eternal soul!
The trees have, rooted in the ground .... the weeds of
    the sea have .... the animals.

I swear I think there is nothing but immortality!
That the exquisite scheme is for it, and the nebulous
    float is for it, and the cohering is for it,
And all preparation is for it .. and identity is for it ..
    and life and death are for it.

[1855]

[*The Sleepers*]

[1]
I wander all night in my vision,
Stepping with light feet .... swiftly and noiselessly stepping
    and stopping,
Bending with open eyes over the shut eyes of sleepers;
Wandering and confused .... lost to myself .... ill-assorted
    .... contradictory,
Pausing and gazing and bending and stopping.

How solemn they look there, stretched and still;
How quiet they breathe, the little children in their cradles.

The wretched features of ennuyees, the white features
    of corpses, the livid faces of drunkards, the sick-gray
    faces of onanists,
The gashed bodies on battlefields, the insane in their
    strong-doored rooms, the sacred idiots,

The newborn emerging from gates and the dying
        emerging from gates,
The night pervades them and enfolds them.

The married couple sleep calmly in their bed, he with
        his palm on the hip of the wife, and she with her
        palm on the hip of the husband,
The sisters sleep lovingly side by side in their bed,
The men sleep lovingly side by side in theirs,
And the mother sleeps with her little child carefully
        wrapped.

The blind sleep, and the deaf and dumb sleep,
The prisoner sleeps well in the prison . . . . the runaway
        son sleeps,
The murderer that is to be hung next day . . . .
        how does he sleep?
And the murdered person . . . . how does he sleep?

The female that loves unrequited sleeps,
And the male that loves unrequited sleeps;
The head of the moneymaker that plotted all day sleeps,
And the enraged and treacherous dispositions sleep.

I stand with drooping eyes by the worstsuffering and restless,
I pass my hands soothingly to and fro a few inches from
        them;
The restless sink in their beds . . . . they fitfully sleep.

The earth recedes from me into the night,
I saw that it was beautiful . . . . and I see that what is not
        the earth is beautiful.

I go from bedside to bedside . . . . I sleep close with
        the other sleepers, each in turn;
I dream in my dream all the dreams of the other dreamers,
And I become the other dreamers.

I am a dance . . . . Play up there! the fit is whirling me fast.

I am the everlaughing.... it is new moon and twilight,
I see the hiding of douceurs.... I see nimble ghosts
    whichever way I look,
Cache and cache again deep in the ground and sea, and
    where it is neither ground or sea.

Well do they do their jobs, those journeymen divine,
Only from me can they hide nothing and would not
    if they could;
I reckon I am their boss, and they make me a pet besides,
And surround me, and lead me and run ahead when I walk,
And lift their cunning covers and signify me with
    stretched arms, and resume the way;
Onward we move, a gay gang of blackguards with
    mirthshouting music and wildflapping pennants of joy.

I am the actor and the actress.... the voter .. the politician,
The emigrant and the exile .. the criminal that stood
    in the box,
He who has been famous, and he who shall be famous
    after today,
The stammerer.... the wellformed person .. the wasted or
    feeble person.

I am she who adorned herself and folded her hair
    expectantly,
My truant lover has come and it is dark.

Double yourself and receive me darkness,
Receive me and my lover too .... he will not let me go
    without him.

I roll myself upon you as upon a bed .... I resign myself
    to the dusk.

He whom I call answers me and takes the place of
    my lover,
He rises with me silently from the bed.

Darkness you are gentler than my lover .... his flesh was
     sweaty and panting,
I feel the hot moisture yet that he left me.

My hands are spread forth .. I pass them in all directions,
I would sound up the shadowy shore to which you are
     journeying.

Be careful, darkness .... already, what was it touched me?
I thought my lover had gone .... else darkness and he are one,
I hear the heart-beat .... I follow .. I fade away.

O hotcheeked and blushing! O foolish hectic!
O for pity's sake, no one must see me now! .... my
     clothes were stolen while I was abed,
Now I am thrust forth, where shall I run?

Pier that I saw dimly last night when I looked from the
     windows,
Pier out from the main, let me catch myself with you and
     stay .... I will not chafe you;
I feel ashamed to go naked about the world,
And am curious to know where my feet stand .... and
     what is this flooding me, childhood or manhood ....
     and the hunger that crosses the bridge between.

The cloth laps a first sweet eating and drinking,
Laps life-swelling yolks .... laps ear of rose-corn, milky
     and just ripened:
The white teeth stay, and the boss-tooth advances in
     darkness,
And liquor is spilled on lips and bosoms by touching
     glasses, and the best liquor afterward.

[2]
I descend my western course .... my sinews are flaccid,
Perfume and youth course through me, and I am their wake.

It is my face yellow and wrinkled instead of the old
    woman's,
I sit low in a strawbottom chair and carefully darn my
    grandson's stockings.

It is I too .... the sleepless widow looking out on the winter
    midnight,
I see the sparkles of starshine on the icy and pallid earth.

A shroud I see—and I am the shroud .... I wrap a
    body and lie in the coffin;
It is dark here underground .... it is not evil or pain
    here .... it is blank here, for reasons.

It seems to me that everything in the light and air ought
    to be happy;
Whoever is not in his coffin and the dark grave, let him
    know he has enough.

[3]

I see a beautiful gigantic swimmer swimming naked through
    the eddies of the sea,
His brown hair lies close and even to his head .... he
    strikes out with courageous arms .... he urges
    himself with his legs.

I see his white body .... I see his undaunted eyes;
I hate the swift-running eddies that would dash him
    headforemost on the rocks.

What are you doing you ruffianly red-trickled waves?
Will you kill the courageous giant? Will you kill him
    in the prime of his middle age?

Steady and long he struggles;
He is baffled and banged and bruised .... he holds out
    while his strength holds out,

The slapping eddies are spotted with his blood .... they
      bear him away .... they roll him and swing him
      and turn him:
His beautiful body is borne in the circling eddies ....
      it is continually bruised on rocks,
Swiftly and out of sight is borne the brave corpse.

[4]
I turn but do not extricate myself;
Confused .... a pastreading .... another, but with darkness
      yet.

The beach is cut by the razory ice-wind .... the wreck-guns
      sounds,
The tempest lulls and the moon comes floundering
      through the drifts.

I look where the ship helplessly heads end on .... I hear
      the burst as she strikes .. I hear the howls of dismay
      .... they grow fainter and fainter.

I cannot aid with my wringing fingers;
I can but rush to the surf and let it drench me and freeze
      upon me.

I search with the crowd .... not one of the company is
      washed to us alive;
In the morning I help pick up the dead and lay them in
      rows in a barn.

[5]
Now of the old war-days .. the defeat at Brooklyn;
Washington stands inside the lines .. he stands on the
      entrenched hills amid a crowd of officers,
His face is cold and damp .... he cannot repress the weeping
      drops .... he lifts the glass perpetually to his eyes
      .... the color is blanched from his cheeks,
He sees the slaughter of the southern braves confided to
      him by their parents.

The same at last and at last when peace is declared,
He stands in the room of the old tavern .... the wellbeloved
    soldiers all pass through.

The officers speechless and slow draw near in their turns,
The chief encircles their necks with his arm and kisses
    them on the cheek,
He kisses lightly the wet cheeks one after another ....
    he shakes hands and bids goodbye to the army.

[6]
Now I tell what my mother told me today as we sat
    at dinner together,
Of when she was a nearly grown girl living home with her
    parents on the old homestead.

A red squaw came one breakfastime to the old homestead,
On her back she carried a bundle of rushes for
    rushbottoming chairs;
Her hair straight shiny coarse black and profuse
    halfenveloped her face,
Her step was free and elastic .... her voice sounded
    exquisitely as she spoke.

My mother looked in delight and amazement at the stranger,
She looked at the beauty of her tallborne face and full
    and pliant limbs,
The more she looked upon her she loved her,
Never before had she seen such wonderful beauty and
    purity;
She made her sit on a bench by the jamb of the fireplace
    .... she cooked food for her,
She had no work to give her but she gave her remembrance
    and fondness.

The red squaw staid all the forenoon, and toward the
    middle of the afternoon she went away;
O my mother was loth to have her go away,

All the week she thought of her .... she watched for her
    many a month,
She remembered her many a winter and many a summer,
But the red squaw never came nor was heard of there again.

Now Lucifer was not dead .... or if he was I am his
    sorrowful terrible heir;
I have been wronged .... I am oppressed .... I hate
    him that oppresses me,
I will either destroy him, or he shall release me.

Damn him! how he does defile me,
How he informs against my brother and sister and takes
    pay for their blood,
How he laughs when I look down the bend after the
    steamboat that carries away my woman.

Now the vast dusk bulk that is the whale's bulk .... it seems
    mine,
Warily, sportsman! though I lie so sleepy and sluggish,
    my tap is death.

[7]

A show of the summer softness .... a contract of something
    unseen .... an amour of the light and air;
I am jealous and overwhelmed with friendliness,
And will go gallivant with the light and the air myself,
And have an unseen something to be in contact with
    them also.

O love and summer! you are in the dreams and in me,
Autumn and winter are in the dreams .... the farmer
    goes with his thrift,
The droves and crops increase .... the barns are wellfilled.

Elements merge in the night .... ships make tacks in
    the dreams .... the sailor sails .... the exile
    returns home,

The fugitive returns unharmed . . . . the immigrant is back
    beyond months and years;
The poor Irishman lives in the simple house of his
    childhood, with the wellknown neighbors and faces,
They warmly welcome him . . . . he is barefoot again
    . . . . he forgets he is welloff;
The Dutchman voyages home, and the Scotchman and
    Welchman voyage home . . and the native of the
    Mediterranean voyages home;
To every port of England and France and Spain enter
    wellfilled ships;
The Swiss foots it toward his hills . . . . the Prussian goes
    his way, and the Hungarian his way, and the Pole
    goes his way,
The Swede returns, and the Dane and Norwegian return.

The homeward bound and the outward bound,
The beautiful lost swimmer, the ennuyee, the onanist,
    the feamle that loves unrequited, the moneymaker,
The actor and actress . . those through with their parts
    and those waiting to commence,
The affectionate boy, the husband and wife, the voter,
    the nominee that is chosen and the nominee that
    has failed,
The great already known, and the great anytime after
    to day,
The stammerer, the sick, the perfectformed, the homely,
The criminal that stood in the box, the judge that sat and
    sentenced him, the fluent lawyers, the jury, the audience,
The laugher and weeper, the dancer, the midnight widow,
    the red squaw,
The consumptive, the erysipalite, the idiot, he that is
    wronged,
The antipodes, and every one between this and them
    in the dark,
I swear they are averaged now . . . . one is no better than
    the other,
The night and sleep have likened them and restored them.

I swear they are all beautiful,

Every one that sleeps is beautiful .... every thing in the
    dim night is beautiful,
The wildest and bloodiest is over and all is peace.

Peace is always beautiful,
The myth of heaven indicates peace and night.

The myth of heaven indicates the soul;
The soul is always beautiful .... it appears more or it
    appears less .... it comes or lags behind,
It comes from its embowered garden and looks pleasantly
    on itself and encloses the world;
Perfect and clean the genitals previously jetting, and perfect
    and clean the womb cohering,
The head wellgrown and proportioned and plumb, and
    the bowels and joints proportioned and plumb.

The soul is always beautiful,
The universe is duly in order .... every thing is in its place,
What is arrived is in its place, and what waits is in
    its place;
The twisted skull waits .... the watery or rotten blood
    waits,
The child of the glutton or venerealee waits long, and the
    child of the drunkard waits long, and the drunkard
    himself waits long,
The sleepers that lived and died wait .... the far advanced
    are to go on in their turns, and the far behind are
    to go on in their turns,
The diverse shall be no less diverse, but they shall flow
    and unite .... they unite now.

[8]

The sleepers are very beautiful as they lie unclothed,
They flow hand in hand over the whole earth from east to
    west as they lie unclothed;
The Asiatic and African are hand in hand .. the
    European and American are hand in hand,
Learned and unlearned are hand in hand .. and male
    and female are hand in hand;

The bare arm of the girl crosses the bare breast of her
    lover .... they press close without lust .... his lips
    press her neck,
The father holds his grown or ungrown son in his arms with
    measureless love .... and the son holds the father
    in his arms with measureless love,
The white hair of the mother shines on the white wrist
    of the daughter,
The breath of the boy goes with the breath of the man
    .... friend is inarmed by friend,
The scholar kisses the teacher and the teacher kisses
    the scholar .... the wronged is made right,
The call of the slave is one with the master's call .. and
    the master salutes the slave,
The felon steps forth from the prison .... the insane
    becomes sane .... the suffering of sick persons
    is relieved,
The sweatings and fevers stop .. the throat that was
    unsound is sound .. the lungs of the consumptive are
    resumed .. the poor distressed head is free,
The joints of the rheumatic move as smoothly as ever,
    and smoother than ever,
Stiflings and passages open .... the paralysed become
    supple,
The swelled and convulsed and congested awake to
    themselves in condition,
They pass the invigoration of the night and the chemistry
    of the night and awake.

I too pass from the night;
I stay awhile away O night, but I return to you again
    and love you;
Why should I be afraid to trust myself to you?
I am not afraid .... I have been well brought forward by
    you;
I love the rich running day, but I do not desert her in
    whom I lay so long :
I know not how I came of you, and I know not where I go
    with you .... but I know I came well and shall go well.

I will stop only a time with the night . . . . and rise betimes.

I will duly pass the day O my mother and duly return to you;
Not you will yield forth the dawn again more surely
    than you will yield forth me again,
Not the womb yields the babe in its time more surely than
    I shall be yielded from you in my time.

[1855]

[*I Sing the Body Electric*]

[*1*]

The bodies of men and women engirth me, and I engirth
    them,
They will not let me off nor I them till I go with them and
    respond to them and love them.

Was it dreamed whether those who corrupted their
    own live bodies could conceal themselves?
And whether those who defiled the living were as bad as
    they who defiled the dead?

[*2*]

The expression of the body of man or woman balks account,
The male is perfect and that of the female is perfect.

The expression of a wellmade man appears not only in
    his face,
It is in his limbs and joints also . . . . it is curiously
    in the joints of his hips and wrists,
It is in his walk . . the carriage of his neck . . the flex of
    his waist and knees . . . . dress does not hide him,
The strong sweet supple quality he has strikes through the
    cotton and flannel;
To see him pass conveys as much as the best poem . .
    perhaps more,

You linger to see his back and the back of his neck
    and shoulderside.

The sprawl and fulness of babes .... the bosoms and
    heads of women .... the folds of their dress ....
    their style as we pass in the street .... the contour of
    their shape downwards;
The swimmer naked in the swimmingbath .. seen as
    he swims through the salt transparent greenshine, or
    lies on his back and rolls silently with the heave
    of the water;
Framers bare-armed framing a house .. hoisting the
    beams in their places .. or using the mallet and
    mortising-chisel,
The bending forward and backward of rowers in
    rowboats .... the horseman in his saddle;
Girls and mothers and housekeepers in all their
    exquisite offices,
The group of laborers seated at noontime with their open
    dinner-kettles, and their wives waiting,
The female soothing a child .... the farmer's daughter
    in the garden or cowyard,
The woodman rapidly swinging his axe in the woods
    .... the young fellow hoeing corn .... the sleighdriver
    guiding his six horses through the crowd,
The wrestle of wrestlers .... two apprentice-boys,
    quite grown, lusty, goodnatured, nativeborn, out on
    the vacant lot at sun-down after work,
The coats vests and caps thrown down .. the embrace
    of love and resistance,
The upperhold and underhold—the hair rumpled over and
    blinding the eyes;
The march of firemen in their own costumes—the play
    of the masculine muscle through cleansetting trowsers
    and waistbands,
The slow return from the fire .... the pause when
    the bell strikes suddenly again—the listening on the alert,
The natural perfect and varied attitudes .... the bent
    head, the curved neck, the counting:

Suchlike I love .... I loosen myself and pass freely ....
    and am at the mother's breast with the little child,
And swim with the swimmer, and wrestle with
    wrestlers, and march in line with the firemen, and
    pause and listen and count.

[3]

I knew a man .... he was a common farmer .... he was
    the father of five sons .... and in them were the fathers
    of sons .... and in them were the fathers of sons.

This man was of wonderful vigor and calmness
    and beauty of person;
The shape of his head, the richness and breadth of his
    manners, the pale yellow and white of his hair
    and beard, the immeasurable meaning of his black eyes,
These I used to go and visit him to see .... He was wise also,
He was six feet tall .... he was over eighty years old ....
    his sons were massive clean bearded tanfaced
    and handsome,
They and his daughters loved him ... all who saw him
    loved him ... they did not love him by allowance ...
    they loved him with personal love;
He drank water only .... the blood showed like scarlet
    through the clear brown skin of his face;
He was a frequent gunner and fisher ... he sailed his
    boat himself ... he had a fine one presented to him
    by a shipjoiner .... he had fowling pieces, presented to
    him by men that loved him;
When he went with his five sons and many grandsons
    to hunt or fish you would pick him out as the most
    beautiful and vigorous of the gang,
You would wish long and long to be with him ....
    you would wish to sit by him in the boat that you and
    he might touch each other.

[4]

I have perceived that to be with those I like is enough,
To stop in company with the rest at evening is enough,

To be surrounded by beautiful curious breathing laughing
    flesh is enough,
To pass among them .. to touch any one .... to rest
    my arm ever so lightly round his or her neck for a
    moment .... what is this then?
I do not ask any more delight .... I swim in it as in a sea.

There is something in staying close to men and women
    and looking on them and in the contact and odor
    of them that pleases the soul well,
All things please the soul, but these please the soul well.

[5]

This is the female form,
A divine nimbus exhales from it from head to foot,
It attracts with fierce undeniable attraction,
I am drawn by its breath as if I were no more than a helpless
    vapor .... all falls aside but myself and it,
Books, art, religion, time .. the visible and solid earth ..
    the atmosphere and the fringed clouds .. what was
    expected of heaven or feared of hell are now consumed,
Mad filaments, ungovernable shoots play out of it .. the
    response likewise ungovernable,
Hair, bosom, hips, bend of legs, negligent falling
    hands—all diffused .... mine too diffused,
Ebb stung by the flow, and flow stung by the ebb ....
    loveflesh swelling and deliciously aching,
Limitless limpid jets of love hot and enormous ....
    quivering jelly of love .... white-blow and delirious
    juice,
Bridegroom-night of love working surely and softly
    into the prostrate dawn,
Undulating into the willing and yielding day,
Lost in the cleave of the clasping and sweetfleshed day.

This is the nucleus ... after the child is born of
    woman the man is born of woman,
This is the bath of birth ... this is the merge of small and
    large and the outlet again.

Be not ashamed women .. your privilege encloses the
      rest .. it is the exit of the rest,
You are the gates of the body and you are the gates
      of the soul.

The female contains all qualities and tempers them
      .... she is in her place .... she moves with perfect
      balance,
She is all things duly veiled .... she is both passive
      and active .... she is to conceive daughters as well as
      sons and sons as well as daughters.

As I see my soul reflected in nature .... as I see through
      a mist one with inexpressible completeness and beauty
      .... see the bent head and arms folded over the
      breast .... the female I see,
  see the bearer of the great fruit which is immortality
      .... the good thereof is not tasted by roues, and
      never can be.

[6]

The male is not less the soul, nor more .... he too is
      in his place,
He too is all qualities .... he is action and power ....
      the flush of the known universe is in him,
Scorn becomes him well and appetite and defiance
      become him well,
The fiercest largest passions .. bliss that is utmost and
      sorrow that is utmost become him well .... pride is
      for him,
The fullspread pride of man is calming and excellent
      to the soul;
Knowledge becomes him .... he likes it always ....
      he brings everything to the test of himself,
Whatever the survey .. whatever the sea and the sail,
      he strikes soundings at last only here,
Where else does he strike soundings except here?

The man's body is sacred and the woman's body is sacred
     . . . . it is no matter who,
Is it a slave? Is it one of the dullfaced immigrants
     just landed on the wharf?

Each belongs here or anywhere just as much as the welloff
     . . . . just as much as you,
Each has his or her place in the procession.

All is a procession,
The universe is a procession with measured and beautiful
     motion.

Do you know so much that you call the slave or the
     dullfaced ignorant?
Do you suppose you have a right to a good sight . . . and
     he or she has no right to a sight?
Do you think matter has cohered together from its
     diffused float, and the soil is on the surface and water
     runs and vegetation sprouts for you . . and not for
     him and her?

[7]
A slave at auction!
I help the auctioneer . . . . the sloven does not half know
     his business.

Gentlemen look on this curious creature,
Whatever the bids of the bidders they cannot be high
     enough for him,
For him the globe lay preparing quintillions of years without
     one animal or plant,
For him the revolving cycles truly and steadily rolled.

In that head the allbaffling brain,
In it and below it the making of the attributes of heroes.

Examine these limbs, red black or white .... they are
        very cunning in tendon and nerve;
They shall be stript that you may see them.

Exquisite senses, lifelit eyes, pluck, volition,
Flakes of breastmuscle, pliant backbone and neck, flesh
        not flabby, goodsized arms and legs,
And wonders within there yet.

Within there runs his blood .... the same old blood ....
        the same red running blood;
There swells and jets his heart .... There all passions and
        desires .. all reachings and aspirations:
Do you think they are not there because they are not
        expressed in parlors and lecture-rooms ?

This is not only one man .... he is the father of those
        who shall be fathers in their turns,
In him the start of populous states and rich republics,
Of him countless immortal lives with countless embodiments
        and enjoyments.

How do you know who shall come from the offspring of
        his offspring through the centuries?
Who might you find you have come from yourself if you
        could trace back through the centuries?

[8]
A woman at auction,
She too is not only herself .... she is the teeming mother
        of mothers,
She is the bearer of them that shall grow and be mates
        to the mothers.

Her daughters or their daughters' daughters .. who
        knows who shall mate with them?
Who knows through the centuries what heroes may come
        from them?

In them and of them natal love . . . . in them the divine
      mystery . . . . the same old beautiful mystery.

Have you ever loved a woman?
Your mother . . . . is she living? . . . . Have you been
      much with her? and has she been much with you?
Do you not see that these are exactly the same to all in all
      nations and times all over the earth?

If life and the soul are sacred the human body is sacred;
And the glory and sweet of a man is the token of manhood
      untainted,
And in man or woman a clean strong firmfibred body
      is beautiful as the most beautiful face.

Have you seen the fool that corrupted his own live body?
      or the fool that corrupted her own live body?
For they do not conceal themselves, and cannot conceal
      themselves.

Who degrades or defiles the living human body is cursed,
Who degrades or defiles the body of the dead is not
      more cursed.

                                        [1855]

[*There Was a Child Went Forth*]

There was a child went forth every day,
And the first object he looked upon and received with
      wonder or pity or love or dread, that object
      he became,
And that object became part of him for the day or a certain
      part of the day . . . . or for many years or stretching
      cycles of years.

The early lilacs became part of this child,
And grass, and white and red morningglories, and white
and red clover, and the song of the phœbe-bird,
And the March-born lambs, and the sow's pink-faint litter,
and the mare's foal, and the cow's calf, and the
noisy brood of the barnyard or by the mire of the
pondside .. and the fish suspending themselves so
curiously below there .. and the beautiful curious
liquid .. and the water-plants with their graceful flat
heads .. all became part of him.

And the field-sprouts of April and May became part of him
.... wintergrain sprouts, and those of the light-yellow
corn, and of the esculent roots of the garden,
And the appletrees covered with blossoms, and the fruit
afterward .... and woodberries .. and the commonest
weeds by the road;
And the old drunkard staggering home from the outhouse
of the tavern whence he had lately risen,
And the schoolmistress that passed on her way to the
school .. and the friendly boys that passed .. and
the quarrelsome boys .. and the tidy and freshcheeked
girls .. and the barefoot negro boy and girl,
And all the changes of city and country wherever he went.

His own parents .. he that had propelled the fatherstuff
at night, and fathered him .. and she that conceived
him in her womb and birthed him .... they gave
this child more of themselves than that,
They gave him afterward every day .... they and of them
became part of him.

The mother at home quietly placing the dishes on the
suppertable,
The mother with mild words .... clean her cap and
gown .... a wholesome odor falling off her person and
clothes as she walks by:
The father, strong, selfsufficient, manly, mean, angered,
unjust,

The blow, the quick loud word, the tight bargain, the crafty
    lure,

The family usages, the language, the company, the
    furniture . . . . the yearning and swelling heart,

Affection that will not be gainsayed . . . . The sense of
    what is real . . . . the thought if after all it should
    prove unreal,

The doubts of daytime and the doubts of nighttime . . .
    the curious whether and how,

Whether that which appears so is so . . . . Or is it all
    flashes and specks?

Men and women crowding fast in the streets . . if they
    are not flashes and specks what are they?

The streets themselves, and the facades of houses . . . .
    the goods in the windows,

Vehicles . . teams . . the tiered wharves, and the huge
    crossing at the ferries;

The village on the highland seen from afar at sunset . . . .
    the river between,

Shadows . . aureola and mist . . light falling on roofs and
    gables of white or brown, three miles off,

The schooner near by sleepily dropping down the tide . .
    the little boat slacktowed astern,

The hurrying tumbling waves and quickbroken crests
    and slapping;

The strata of colored clouds . . . . the long bar of
    maroontint away solitary by itself . . . . the spread
    of purity it lies motionless in,

The horizon's edge, the flying seacrow, the fragrance of
    saltmarsh and shoremud;

These became part of that child who went forth every day,
    and who now goes and will always go forth every day,

And these become of him or her that peruses them now.

[1855]

Song of the Broad-Axe

1

Weapon shapely, naked, wan,
Head from the mother's bowels drawn,
Wooded flesh and metal bone, limb only one and lip
    only one,
Gray-blue leaf by red-heat grown, helve produced from
    a little seed sown,
Resting the grass amid and upon,
To be lean'd and to lean on.

Strong shapes and attributes of strong shapes, masculine
    trades, sights and sounds,
Long varied train of an emblem, dabs of music,
Fingers of the organist skipping staccato over the keys
    of the great organ.

2

Welcome are all earth's lands, each for its kind,
Welcome are lands of pine and oak,
Welcome are lands of the lemon and fig,
Welcome are lands of gold,
Welcome are lands of wheat and maize, welcome those of
    the grape,
Welcome are lands of sugar and rice,
Welcome the cotton-lands, welcome those of the white
    potato and sweet potato,
Welcome are mountains, flats, sands, forests, prairies,
Welcome the rich borders of rivers, table-lands, openings,
Welcome the measureless grazing-lands, welcome the
    teeming soil of orchards, flax, honey, hemp;
Welcome just as much the other more hard-faced lands,
Lands rich as lands of gold or wheat and fruit lands,
Lands of mines, lands of the manly and rugged ores,

Lands of coal, copper, lead, tin, zinc,
Lands of iron—lands of the make of the axe.

   3

The log at the wood-pile, the axe supported by it,
The sylvan hut, the vine over the doorway, the space clear'd
        for a garden,
The irregular tapping of rain down on the leaves after the
        storm is lull'd,
The wailing and moaning at intervals, the thought of the sea,
The thought of ships struck in the storm and put on their
        beam ends, and the cutting away of masts,
The sentiment of the huge timbers of old-fashion'd
        houses and barns.
The remember'd print or narrative, the voyage at a
        venture of men, families, goods,
The disembarkation, the founding of a new city,
The voyage of those who sought a New England and
        found it, the outset anywhere,
The settlements of the Arkansas, Colorado, Ottawa,
        Willamette,
The slow progress, the scant fare, the axe, rifle, saddle-bags;
The beauty of all adventurous and daring persons,
The beauty of wood-boys and wood-men with their clear
        untrimm'd faces,
The beauty of independence, departure, actions that rely
        on themselves,
The American contempt for statutes and ceremonies,
        the boundless impatience of restraint,
The loose drift of character, the inkling through random
        types, the solidification;
The butcher in the slaughter-house, the hands aboard
        schooners and sloops, the raftsman, the pioneer,
Lumbermen in their winter camp, daybreak in the
        woods, stripes of snow on the limbs of trees,
        the occasional snapping,
The glad clear sound of one's own voice, the merry song,
        the natural life of the woods, the strong day's work,

The blazing fire at night, the sweet taste of supper, the talk,
    the bed of hemlock-boughs and the bear-skin;
The house-builder at work in cities or anywhere,
The preparatory jointing, squaring sawing, mortising,
The hoist-up of beams, the push of them in their places,
    laying them regular,
Setting the studs by their tenons in the mortises according
    as they were prepared,
The blows of mallets and hammers, the attitudes of
    the men, their curv'd limbs,
Bending, standing, astride the beams, driving in pins,
    holding on by posts and braces,
The hook'd arm over the plate, the other arm wielding
    the axe,
The floor-men forcing the planks close to be nail'd,
Their postures bringing their weapons downward on the
    bearers,
The echoes resounding through the vacant building;
The huge storehouse carried up in the city well under way,
The six framing-men, two in the middle and two at
    each end, carefully bearing on their shoulders
    a heavy stick for a cross-beam,
The crowded line of masons with trowels in their
    right hands rapidly laying the long side-wall,
    two hundred feet from front to rear,
The flexible rise and fall of backs, the continual click
    of the trowels striking the bricks,
The bricks one after another each laid so workmanlike
    in its place, and set with a knock of the trowel-handle,
The piles of materials, the mortar on the mortar-boards,
    and the steady replenishing by the hod-men;
Spar-makers in the spar-yard, the swarming row of
    well-grown apprentices,
The swing of their axes on the square-hew'd log shaping
    it toward the shape of a mast,
The brisk short crackle of the steel driven slantingly into
    the pipe,
The butter-color'd chips flying off in great flakes and slivers,

The limber motion of brawny young arms and hips
    in easy costumes,
The constructor of wharves, bridges, piers, bulk-heads,
    floats, stays against the sea;
The city fireman, the fire that suddenly bursts forth in the
    close-pack'd square,
The arriving engines, the hoarse shouts, the nimble stepping
    and daring,
The strong command through the fire-trumpets, the falling in
    line, the rise and fall of the arms forcing the water,
The slender, spasmic, blue-white jets, the bringing to
    bear of the hooks and ladders and their execution,
The crash and cut away of connecting wood-work, or
    through floors if the fire smoulders under them,
The crowd with their lit faces watching, the glare and
    dense shadows;
The forger at his forge-furnace and the user of iron after him,
The maker of the axe large and small, and the welder
    and temperer,
The chooser breathing his breath on the cold steel and trying
    the edge with his thumb,
The one who clean-shapes the handle and sets it firmly
    in the socket;
The shadowy processions of the portraits of the past
    users also,
The primal patient mechanics, the architects and engineers,
The far-off Assyrian edifice and Mizra edifice,
The Roman lictors preceding the consuls,
The antique European warrior with his axe in combat,
The uplifted arm, the clatter of blows on the helmeted head,
The death-howl, the limpsy tumbling body, the rush
    of friend and foe thither,
The siege of revolted lieges determin'd for liberty,
The summons to surrender, the battering at castle gates,
    the truce and parley,
The sack of an old city in its time,
The bursting in of mercenaries and bigots tumultuously and
    disorderly,

Roar, flames, blood, drunkenness, madness,
Goods freely rifled from houses and temples, screams
      of women in the gripe of brigands,
Craft and thievery of camp-followers, men running,
      old persons despairing,
The hell of war, the cruelties of creeds,
The list of all executive deeds and words just or unjust,
The power of personality just or unjust.

4

Muscle and pluck forever!
What invigorates life invigorates death,
And the dead advance as much as the living advance,
And the future is no more uncertain than the present,
For the roughness of the earth and of man encloses as
      much as the delicatesse of the earth and of man,
And nothing endures but personal qualities.

What do you think endures?
Do you think a great city endures?
Or a teeming manufacturing state? or a prepared
      constitution? or the best built steamships?
Or hotels of granite and iron? or any chef-d'œuvres of
      engineering, forts, armaments?
Away! these are not to be cherish'd for themselves,
They fill their hour, the dancers dance, the musicians play
      for them,
The show passes, all does well enough of course,
All does very well till one flash of defiance.

A great city is that which has the greatest men and women,
If it be a few ragged huts it is still the greatest city in the
      whole world.

5

The place where a great city stands is not the place of
      stretch'd wharves, docks, manufactures, deposits of
      produce merely,

Nor the place of ceaseless salutes of new-comers or the
      anchor-lifters of the departing,
Nor the place of the tallest and costliest buildings or
      shops selling goods from the rest of the earth,
Nor the place of the best libraries and schools, nor the place
      where money is plentiest,
Nor the place of the most numerous population.

Where the city stands with the brawniest breed of orators
      and bards,
Where the city stands that is belov'd by these, and loves
      them in return and understands them,
Where no monuments exist to heroes but in the
      common words and deeds,
Where thrift is in its place, and prudence is in its place,
Where the men and women think lightly of the laws,
Where the slave ceases, and the master of slaves ceases,
Where the populace rise at once against the never-ending
      audacity of elected persons,
Where fierce men and women pour forth as the sea to the
      whistle of death pours its sweeping and unript waves,
Where outside authority enters always after the precedence
      of inside authority,
Where the citizen is always the head and ideal, and
      President, Mayor, Governor and what not, are
      agents for pay,
Where children are taught to be laws to themselves, and
      to depend on themselves,
Where equanimity is illustrated in affairs,
Where speculations on the soul are encouraged,
Where women walk in public processions in the streets
      the same as the men,
Where they enter the public assembly and take places
      the same as the men;
Where the city of the faithfulest friends stands,
Where the city of the cleanliness of the sexes stands,
Where the city of the healthiest fathers stands,
Where the city of the best-bodied mothers stands,
There the great city stands.

6

How beggarly appear arguments before a defiant deed!
How the floridness of the materials of cities shrivels before
    a man's or woman's look!

All waits or goes by default till a strong being appears;
A strong being is the proof of the race and of the
    ability of the universe,
When he or she appears materials are overaw'd,
The dispute on the soul stops,
The old customs and phrases are confronted, turn'd back,
    or laid away.

What is your money-making now? what can it do now?
What is your respectability now?
What are your theology, tuition, society, traditions,
    statute-books, now?
Where are your jibes of being now?
Where are your cavils about the soul now?

7

A sterile landscape covers the ore, there is as good as the
    best for all the forbidding appearance.
There is the mine, there are the miners,
The forge-furnace is there, the melt is accomplish'd,
    the hammersmen are at hand with their tongs
    and hammers,
What always served and always serves is at hand.

Than this nothing has better served, it has served all,
Served the fluent-tongued and subtle-sensed Greek, and
    long ere the Greek,
Served in building the buildings that last longer than any,
Served the Hebrew, the Persian, the most ancient
    Hindustanee,
Served the mound-raiser on the Mississippi, served those
    whose relics remain in Central America,
Served Albic temples in woods or on plains, with unhewn
    pillars and the druids,

Served the artificial clefts, vast, high, silent, on the
    snow-cover'd hills of Scandinavia,
Served those who time out of mind made on the granite
    walls rough sketches of the sun, moon, stars, ships,
    ocean waves,
Served the paths of the irruptions of the Goths, served the
    pastoral tribes and nomads,
Served the long distant Kelt, served the hardy pirates of
    the Baltic,
Served before any of those the venerable and harmless
    men of Ethiopia,
Served the making of helms for the galleys of pleasure
    and the making of those for war,
Served all great works on land and all great works on the sea,
For the mediæval ages and before the mediæval ages,
Served not the living only then as now, but served the dead.

8

I see the European headsman,
He stands mask'd, clothed in red, with huge legs and
    strong naked arms,
And leans on a ponderous axe.

(Whom have you slaughter'd lately European headsman?
Whose is that blood upon you so wet and sticky?)

I see the clear sunset of the martyrs,
I see from the scaffolds the descending ghosts,
Ghosts of dead lords, uncrown'd ladies, impeach'd
    ministers, rejected kings,
Rivals, traitors, poisoners, disgraced chieftains and the rest.

I see those who in any land have died for the good cause,
The seed is spare, nevertheless the crop shall never run out,
(Mind you O foreign kings, O priests, the crop shall
    never run out.)

I see the blood wash'd entirely away from the axe,
Both blade and helve are clean,

They spirt no more the blood of European nobles, they
    clasp no more the necks of queens.

I see the headsman withdraw and become useless,
I see the scaffold untrodden and mouldy, I see no
    longer any axe upon it,
I see the mighty and friendly emblem of the power of my
    own race, the newest, largest race.

9

(America! I do not vaunt my love for you,
I have what I have.)

The axe leaps!
The solid forest gives fluid utterances,
They tumble forth, they rise and form,
Hut, tent, landing, survey,
Flail, plough, pick, crowbar, spade,
Shingle, rail, prop, wainscot, jamb, lath, panel, gable,
Citadel, ceiling, saloon, academy, organ, exhibition-house,
    library,
Cornice, trellis, pilaster, balcony, window, turret, porch,
Hoe, rake, pitchfork, pencil, wagon, staff, saw,
    jack-plane, mallet, wedge, rounce,
Chair, tub, hoop, table, wicket, vane, sash, floor,
Work-box, chest, string'd instrument, boat, frame, and
    what not,
Capitols of States, and capitol of the nation of States,
Long stately rows in avenues, hospitals for orphans or for
    the poor or sick,
Manhattan steamboats and clippers taking the measure of
    all seas.

The shapes arise!
Shapes of the using of axes anyhow, and the users and
    all that neighbors them,
Cutters down of wood and haulers of it to the
    Penobscot or Kennebec,
Dwellers in cabins among the Californian mountains
    or by the little lakes, or on the Columbia,

Dwellers south on the banks of the Gila or Rio Grande,
    friendly gatherings, the characters and fun,
Dwellers along the St. Lawrence, or north in Kanada, or
      down by the Yellowstone, dwellers on coasts
      and off coasts,
Seal-fishers, whalers, arctic seamen breaking passages
    through the ice.

The shapes arise!
Shapes of factories, arsenals, foundries, markets,
Shapes of the two-threaded tracks of railroads,
Shapes of the sleepers of bridges, vast frameworks, girders,
    arches,
Shapes of the fleets of barges, tows, lake and canal craft,
    river craft,
Ship-yards and dry-docks along the Eastern and
      Western seas, and in many a bay and by-place,
The live-oak kelsons, the pine planks, the spars, the
    hackmatack-roots for knees,
The ships themselves on their ways, the tiers of scaffolds,
    the workmen busy outside and inside,
The tools lying around, the great auger and little auger,
    the adze, bolt, line, square, gouge, and bead-plane.

10

The shapes arise!
The shape measur'd, saw'd, jack'd, join'd, stain'd,
The coffin-shape for the dead to lie within in his shroud,
The shape got out in posts, in the bedstead posts, in the
    posts of the bride's bed,
The shape of the little trough, the shape of the rockers
    beneath, the shape of the babe's cradle,
The shape of the floor-planks, the floor-planks for
    dancers' feet,
The shape of the planks of the family home, the home
    of the friendly parents and children,
The shape of the roof of the home of the happy young man
    and woman, the roof over the well-married young
    man and woman,

The roof over the supper joyously cook'd by the
    chaste wife, and joyously eaten by the chaste husband,
    content after his day's work.

The shapes arise!
The shape of the prisoner's place in the court-room,
    and of him or her seated in the place,
The shape of the liquor-bar lean'd against by the
    young rum-drinker and the old rum-drinker,
The shape of the shamed and angry stairs trod by
    sneaking footsteps,
The shape of the sly settee, and the adulterous
    unwholesome couple,
The shape of the gambling-board with its devilish
    winnings and losings,
The shape of the step-ladder for the convicted and
    sentenced murderer, the murderer with haggard
    face and pinion'd arms,
The sheriff at hand with his deputies, the silent and
    white-lipp'd crowd, the dangling of the rope.

The shapes arise!
Shapes of doors giving many exits and entrances,
The door passing the dissever'd friend flush'd and in haste,
The door that admits good news and bad news,
The door whence the son left home confident and puff'd up,
The door he enter'd again from a long and scandalous
    absence, diseas'd, broken down, without innocence,
    without means.

11

Her shape arises,
She less guarded than ever, yet more guarded than ever,
The gross and soil'd she moves among do not make her
    gross and soil'd,
She knows the thoughts as she passes, nothing is
    conceal'd from her,
She is none the less considerate or friendly therefor,

She is the best belov'd, it is without exception, she has
    no reason to fear and she does not fear,
Oaths, quarrels, hiccupp'd songs, smutty expressions,
    are idle to her as she passes,
She is silent, she is possess'd of herself, they do not offend her,
She receives them as the laws of Nature receive them,
    she is strong,
She too is a law of Nature—there is no law stronger than
    she is.

12

The main shapes arise!
Shapes of Democracy total, result of centuries,
Shapes ever projecting other shapes,
Shapes of turbulent manly cities,
Shapes of the friends and home-givers of the whole earth,
Shapes bracing the earth and braced with the whole earth.

[1856]

This Compost

1

Something startles me where I thought I was safest,
I withdraw from the still woods I loved,
I will not go now on the pastures to walk,
I will not strip the clothes from my body to meet my lover
    the sea,
I will not touch my flesh to the earth as to other flesh
    to renew me.

O how can it be that the ground itself does not sicken?
How can you be alive you growths of spring?
How can you furnish health you blood of herbs, roots,
    orchards, grain?
Are they not continually putting distemper'd corpses
    within you?
Is not every continent work'd over and over with sour dead?

Where have you disposed of their carcasses?
Those drunkards and gluttons of so many generations?
Where have you drawn off all the foul liquid and meat?
I do not see any of it upon you to-day, or perhaps
    I am deceiv'd,
I will run a furrow with my plough, I will press my
    spade through the sod and turn it up underneath,
I am sure I shall expose some of the foul meat.

2

Behold this compost! behold it well!
Perhaps every mite has once form'd part of a sick
    person—yet behold!
The grass of spring covers the prairies,
The bean bursts noiselessly through the mould in the garden,
The delicate spear of the onion pierces upward,
The apple-buds cluster together on the apple-branches,
The resurrection of the wheat appears with pale visage
    out of its graves,
The tinge awakes over the willow-tree and the mulberry-tree,
The he-birds carol mornings and evenings while the
    she-birds sit on their nests,
The young of poultry break through the hatch'd eggs,
The new-born of animals appear, the calf is dropt from
    the cow, the colt from the mare,
Out of its little hill faithfully rise the potato's dark green
    leaves,
Out of its hill rises the yellow maize-stalk, the lilacs
    bloom in the dooryards,
The summer growth is innocent and disdainful
    above all those strata of sour dead.

What chemistry!
That the winds are really not infectious,
That this is no cheat, this transparent green-wash
    of the sea which is so amorous after me,
That it is safe to allow it to lick my naked body all over
    with its tongues,

That it will not endanger me with the fevers that have
    deposited themselves in it,
That all is clean forever and forever,
That the cool drink from the well tastes so good,
That blackberries are so flavorous and juicy,
That the fruits of the apple-orchard and the orange-orchard,
    that melons, grapes, peaches, plums, will none
    of them poison me,
That when I recline on the grass I do not catch any disease,
Though probably every spear of grass rises out of what
    was once a catching disease.

Now I am terrified at the Earth, it is that calm and patient,
It grows such sweet things out of such corruptions,
It turns harmless and stainless on its axis, with such
    endless successions of diseas'd corpses,
It distills such exquisite winds out of such infused fetor,
It renews with such unwitting looks its prodigal,
    annual, sumptuous crops,
It gives such divine materials to men, and accepts
    such leavings from them at last.

[1856]

Crossing Brooklyn Ferry

1

Flood-tide below me! I see you face to face!
Clouds of the west—sun there half an hour high—I see you
    also face to face.

Crowds of men and women attired in the usual costumes,
    how curious you are to me!
On the ferry-boats the hundreds and hundreds that
    cross, returning home, are more curious to me
    than you suppose,

And you that shall cross from shore to shore years hence
　　are more to me, and more in my meditations, than you
　　might suppose.

2

The impalpable sustenance of me from all things at all
　　hours of the day,
The simple, compact, well-join'd scheme, myself
　　disintegrated, every one disintegrated yet part of
　　the scheme,
The similitudes of the past and those of the future,
The glories strung like beads on my smallest sights and
　　hearings, on the walk in the street and the passage
　　over the river,
The current rushing so swiftly and swimming with me
　　far away,
The others that are to follow me, the ties between
　　me and them,
The certainty of others, the life, love, sight, hearing of
　　others.

Others will enter the gates of the ferry and cross from shore
　　to shore,
Others will watch the run of the flood-tide,
Others will see the shipping of Manhattan north and west,
　　and the heights of Brooklyn to the south and east,
Others will see the islands large and small;
Fifty years hence, others will see them as they cross,
　　the sun half an hour high,
A hundred years hence, or ever so many hundred years
　　hence, others will see them,
Will enjoy the sunset, the pouring-in of the flood-tide,
　　the falling-back to the sea of the ebb-tide.

3

It avails not, time nor place—distance avails not,
I am with you, you men and women of a generation,
　　or ever so many generations hence,

Just as you feel when you look on the river and sky,
    so I felt,
Just as any of you is one of a living crowd, I was
    one of a crowd,
Just as you are refresh'd by the gladness of the river and the
    bright flow, I was refresh'd,
Just as you stand and lean on the rail, yet hurry with the
    swift current, I stood yet was hurried,
Just as you look on the numberless masts of ships
    and the thick-stemm'd pipes of steamboats, I look'd.

I too many and many a time cross'd the river of old,
Watched the Twelfth-month sea-gulls, saw them high
    in the air floating with motionless wings, oscillating
    their bodies,
Saw how the glistening yellow lit up parts of their
    bodies and left the rest in strong shadow,
Saw the slow-wheeling circles and the gradual edging
    toward the south,
Saw the reflection of the summer sky in the water,
Had my eyes dazzled by the shimmering track of beams,
Look'd at the fine centrifugal spokes of light round the
    shape of my head in the sunlit water,
Look'd on the haze on the hills southward and
    south-westward,
Look'd on the vapor as it flew in fleeces tinged with violet,
Look'd toward the lower bay to notice the vessels arriving,
Saw their approach, saw aboard those that were near me,
Saw the white sails of schooners and sloops, saw the
    ships at anchor,
The sailors at work in the rigging or out astride the spars,
The round masts, the swinging motion of the hulls, the
    slender serpentine pennants,
The large and small steamers in motion, the pilots in
    their pilot-houses,
The white wake left by the passage, the quick tremulous
    whirl of the wheels,
The flags of all nations, the falling of them at sunset,

The scallop-edged waves in the twilight, the ladled cups,
    the frolicsome crests and glistening,
The stretch afar growing dimmer and dimmer, the gray
    walls of the granite storehouses by the docks,
On the river the shadowy group, the big steam-tug
    closely flank'd on each side by the barges, the hay-boat,
    the belated lighter,
On the neighboring shore the fires from the foundry
    chimneys burning high and glaringly into the night,
Casting their flicker of black contrasted with wild
    red and yellow light over the tops of houses, and
    down into the clefts of streets.

4

These and all else were to me the same as they are to you,
I loved well those cities, loved well the stately and rapid river,
The men and women I saw were all near to me,
Others the same—others who look back on me because
    I look'd forward to them,
(The time will come, though I stop here to-day and to-night.)

5

What is it then between us?
What is the count of the scores or hundreds of years
    between us?

Whatever it is, it avails not—distance avails not,
    and place avails not,
I too lived, Brooklyn of ample hills was mine,
I too walk'd the streets of Manhattan island, and bathed
    in the waters around it,
I too felt the curious abrupt questionings stir within me,
In the day among crowds of people sometimes they came
    upon me,
In my walks home late at night or as I lay in my bed
    they came upon me,
I too had been struck from the float forever held in solution,
I too had receiv'd identity by my body,

That I was I knew was of my body, and what I should
    be I knew I should be of my body.

6

It is not upon you alone the dark patches fall,
The dark threw its patches down upon me also,
The best I had done seem'd to me blank and suspicious,
My great thoughts as I supposed them, were they not
    in reality meagre?
Nor is it you alone who know what it is to be evil,
I am he who knew what it was to be evil,
I too knitted the old knot of contrariety,
Blabb'd, blush'd, resented, lied, stole, grudg'd,
Had guile, anger, lust, hot wishes I dared not speak,
Was wayward, vain, greedy, shallow, sly, cowardly, malignant,
The wolf, the snake, the hog, not wanting in me,
The cheating look, the frivolous word, the adulterous
    wish, not wanting,
Refusals, hates, postponements, meanness, laziness, none
    of these wanting,
Was one with the rest, the days and haps of the rest,
Was call'd by my nighest name by clear loud voices of
    young men as they saw me approaching or passing,
Felt their arms on my neck as I stood, or the negligent
    leaning of their flesh against me as I sat,
Saw many I loved in the street or ferry-boat or public
    assembly, yet never told them a word,
Lived the same life with the rest, the same old laughing,
    gnawing, sleeping,
Play'd the part that still looks back on the actor or actress,
The same old role, the role that is what we make it,
    as great as we like,
Or as small as we like, or both great and small.

7

Closer yet I approach you,
What thought you have of me now, I had as much of you—
    I laid in my stores in advance,
I consider'd long and seriously of you before you were born.

Who was to know what should come home to me?
Who knows but I am enjoying this?
Who knows, for all the distance, but I am as good as
    looking at you now, for all you cannot see me?

8

Ah, what can ever be more stately and admirable to me
    than mast-hemm'd Manhattan?
River and sunset and scallop-edg'd waves of flood-tide?
The sea-gulls oscillating their bodies, the hay-boat
    in the twilight, and the belated lighter?
What gods can exceed these that clasp me by the hand, and
    with voices I love call me promptly and loudly by
    my nighest name as I approach?
What is more subtle than this which ties me to the
    woman or man that looks in my face?
Which fuses me into you now, and pours my meaning
    into you?

We understand then do we not?
What I promis'd without mentioning it, have you not
    accepted?
What the study could not teach—what the preaching
    could not accomplish is accomplish'd, is it not?

9

Flow on, river! flow with the flood-tide, and ebb with
    the ebb-tide!
Frolic on, crested and scallop-edg'd waves!
Gorgeous clouds of the sunset! drench with your splendor
    me, or the men and women generations after me!
Cross from shore to shore, countless crowds of passengers!
Stand up, tall masts of Mannahatta! stand up, beautiful
    hills of Brooklyn!
Throb, baffled and curious brain! throw out questions
    and answers!
Suspend here and everywhere, eternal float of solution!

Gaze, loving and thirsting eyes, in the house or street or
    public assembly!
Sound out, voices of young men? loudly and musically
    call me by my nighest name!
Live, old life! play the part that looks back on the
    actor or actress!
Play the old role, the role that is great or small according
    as one makes it!
Consider, you who peruse me, whether I may not in
    unknown ways be looking upon you;
Be firm, rail over the river, to support those who lean idly,
    yet haste with the hasting current;
Fly on, sea-birds! fly sideways, or wheel in large circles
    high in the air;
Receive the summer sky, you water, and faithfully hold it
    till all downcast eyes have time to take it from you!

Diverge, fine spokes of light, from the shape of my head,
    or any one's head, in the sunlit water!
Come on, ships from the lower bay! pass up or down,
    white-sail'd schooners, sloops, lighters!
Flaunt away, flags of all nations! be duly lower'd at sunset!
Burn high your fires, foundry chimneys! cast black
    shadows at nightfall! cast red and yellow light over
    the tops of the houses!
Appearances, now or henceforth, indicate what you are,
You necessary film, continue to envelop the soul,
About my body for me, and your body for you, be
    hung our divinest aromas,
Thrive, cities—bring your freight, bring your shows, ample
    and sufficient rivers,
Expand, being than which none else is perhaps more
    spiritual,
Keep your places, objects than which none else is
    more lasting.

You have waited, you always wait, you dumb, beautiful
    ministers,

We receive you with free sense at last, and are insatiate
      henceforward,
Not you any more shall be able to foil us, or withhold
      yourselves from us,
We use you, and do not cast you aside—we plant
      you permanently within us,
We fathom you not—we love you—there is perfection
      in you also,
You furnish your parts toward eternity,
Great or small, you furnish your parts toward the soul.

[1856]

Song of the Open Road

1

Afoot and light-hearted I take to the open road,
Healthy, free, the world before me,
The long brown path before me leading wherever I choose.

Henceforth I ask not good-fortune, I myself am good-fortune,
Henceforth I whimper no more, postpone no more, need
      nothing,
Done with indoor complaints, libraries, querulous criticisms,
Strong and content I travel the open road.

The earth, that is sufficient,
I do not want the constellations any nearer,
I know they are very well where they are,
I know they suffice for those who belong to them.

(Still here I carry my old delicious burdens,
I carry them, men and women, I carry them with me
      wherever I go,
I swear it is impossible for me to get rid of them,
I am fill'd with them, and I will fill them in return.)

2

You road I enter upon and look around, I believe you are
    not all that is here,
I believe that much unseen is also here.

Here the profound lesson of reception, nor preference
    nor denial,
The black with his woolly head, the felon, the diseas'd,
    the illiterate person, are not denied;
The birth, the hasting after the physician, the beggar's
    tramp, the drunkard's stagger, the laughing party of
    mechanics,
The escaped youth, the rich person's carriage, the fop,
    the eloping couple,
The early market-man, the hearse, the moving of furniture
    into the town, the return back from the town,
They pass, I also pass, any thing passes, none can be
    interdicted,
None but are accepted, none but shall be dear to me.

3

You air that serves me with breath to speak!
You objects that call from diffusion my meanings and
    give them shape!
You light that wraps me and all things in delicate
    equable showers!
You paths worn in the irregular hollows by the roadsides!
I believe you are latent with nuseen existences, you are
    so dear to me.

You flagg'd walks of the cities! you strong curbs at
    the edges!
You ferries! you planks and posts of wharves! you
    timber-lined sides! you distant ships!
You rows of houses! you window-pierc'd façades! you roofs!
You porches and entrances! you copings and iron guards!
You windows whose transparent shells might expose
    so much!

You doors and ascending steps! you arches!
You gray stones of interminable pavements! you trodden
    crossings!
From all that has touch'd you I believe you have
    imparted to yourselves, and now would impart the
    same secretly to me,
From the living and the dead you have peopled
    your impassive surfaces, and the spirits thereof would
    be evident and amicable with me.

4

The earth expanding right hand and left hand,
The picture alive, every part in its best light,
The music falling in where it is wanted, and stopping where
    it is not wanted,
The cheerful voice of the public road, the gay fresh
    sentiment of the road.

O highway I travel, do you say to me *Do not leave me?*
Do you say *Venture not—if you leave me you are lost?*
Do you say *I am already prepared, I am well-beaten
    and undenied, adhere to me?*

O public road, I say back I am not afraid to leave you,
    yet I love you,
You express me better than I can express myself,
You shall be more to me than my poem.

I think heroic deeds were all conceiv'd in the open air, and
    all free poems also,
I think I could stop here myself and do miracles,
I think whatever I shall meet on the road I shall like,
    and whoever beholds me shall like me,
I think whoever I see must be happy.

5

From this hour I ordain myself loos'd of limits and
    imaginary lines,
Going where I list, my own master total and absolute,
Listening to others, considering well what they say,

Pausing, searching, receiving, contemplating,
Gently, but with undeniable will, divesting myself of the
    holds that would hold me.

I inhale great draughts of space,
The east and the west are mine, and the north and
    the south are mine.

I am larger, better than I thought,
I did not know I held so much goodness.

All seems beautiful to me,
I can repeat over to men and women You have done such
    good to me I would do the same to you,
I will recruit for myself and you as I go,
I will scatter myself among men and women as I go,
I will toss a new gladness and roughness among them,
Whoever denies me it shall not trouble me,
Whoever accepts me he or she shall be blessed and shall
    bless me.

6

Now if a thousand perfect men were to appear it would not
    amaze me,
Now if a thousand beautiful forms of women appear'd
    it would not astonish me.

Now I see the secret of the making of the best persons,
It is to grow in the open air and to eat and sleep with
    the earth.

Here a great personal deed has room,
(Such a deed seizes upon the hearts of the whole race of men,
Its effusion of strength and will overwhelms law and
    mocks all authority and all argument against it.)

Here is the test of wisdom,
Wisdom is not finally tested in schools,
Wisdom cannot be pass'd from one having it to
    another not having it,

Wisdom is of the soul, is not susceptible of proof, is its
    own proof,
Applies to all stages and objects and qualities and is content,
Is the certainty of the reality and immortality of things, and
    the excellence of things;
Something there is in the float of the sight of things
    that provokes it out of the soul.

Now I re-examine philosophies and religions,
They may prove well in lecture-rooms, yet not prove
    at all under the spacious clouds and along the landscape
    and flowing currents.

Here is realization,
Here is a man tallied—he realizes here what he has in him,
The past, the future, majesty, love—if they are vacant
    of you, you are vacant of them.

Only the kernel of every object nourishes;
Where is he who tears off the husks for you and me?
Where is he that undoes stratagems and envelopes
    for you and me?

Here is adhesiveness, it is not previously fashion'd, it is
    apropos;
Do you know what it is as you pass to be loved by strangers?
Do you know the talk of those turning eye-balls?

7

Here is the efflux of the soul,
The efflux of the soul comes from within through
    embower'd gates, ever provoking questions,
These yearnings why are they? these thoughts in the
    darkness why are they?
Why are there men and women that while they are nigh
    me the sunlight expands my blood?
Why when they leave me do my pennants of joy sink
    flat and lank?
Why are there trees I never walk under but large and
    melodious thoughts descend upon me?

(I think they hang there winter and summer on
   those trees and always drop fruit as I pass;)
What is it I interchange so suddenly with strangers?
What with some driver as I ride on the seat by his side?
What with some fisherman drawing his seine by the
   shore as I walk by and pause?
What gives me to be free to a woman's and man's
   good-will? what gives them to be free to mine?

8

The efflux of the soul is happiness, here is happiness,
I think it pervades the open air, waiting at all times,
Now it flows unto us, we are rightly charged.

Here rises the fluid and attaching character,
The fluid and attaching character is the freshness and
   sweetness of man and woman,
(The herbs of the morning sprout no fresher and sweeter
   every day out of the roots of themselves, than it sprouts
   fresh and sweet continually out of itself.)

Toward the fluid and attaching character exudes the sweat
   of the love of young and old,
From it falls distill'd the charm that mocks beauty and
   attainments,
Toward it heaves the shuddering longing ache of contact.

9

Allons! whoever you are come travel with me!
Traveling with me you find what never tires.

The earth never tires,
The earth is rude, silent, incomprehensible at first, Nature
   is rude and incomprehensible at first,
Be not discouraged, keep on, there are divine things
   well envelop'd,
I swear to you there are divine things more beautiful
   than words can tell.

Allons! we must not stop here,
However sweet these laid-up stores, however convenient
    this dwelling we cannot remain here,
However shelter'd this port and however calm these
    waters we must not anchor here,
However welcome the hospitality that surrounds us
    we are permitted to receive it but a little while.

10

Allons! the inducements shall be greater,
We will sail pathless and wild seas,
We will go where winds blow, waves dash, and the Yankee
    clipper speeds by under full sail.

Allons! with power, liberty, the earth, the elements,
Health, defiance, gayety, self-esteem, curiosity;
Allons! from all formules!
From your formules, O bat-eyed and materialistic priests.

The stale cadaver blocks up the passage—the burial waits
    no longer.

Allons! yet take warning!
He traveling with me needs the best blood, thews, endurance,
None may come to the trial till he or she bring courage
    and health,
Come not here if you have already spent the best of yourself,
Only those may come who come in sweet and determin'd
    bodies,
No diseas'd person, no rum drinker or venereal taint
    is permitted here.

(I and mine do not convince by arguments, similes, rhymes,
We convince by our presence.)

11

Listen! I will be honest with you,
I do not offer the old smooth prizes, but offer rough
    new prizes,

These are the days that must happen to you:
You shall not heap up what is call'd riches,
You shall scatter with lavish hand all that you earn or
    achieve,
You but arrive at the city to which you were destin'd,
        you hardly settle yourself to satisfaction before
        you are call'd by an irresistible call to depart,
You shall be treated to the ironical smiles and mockings
        of those who remain behind you,
What beckonings of love you receive you shall only answer
        with passionate kisses of parting,
You shall not allow the hold of those who spread their
        reach'd hands toward you.

12

Allons! after the great Companions, and to belong to
    them!
They too are on the road—they are the swift and majestic
        men—they are the greatest women,
Enjoyers of calms of seas and storms of seas,
Sailors of many a ship, walkers of many a mile of land,
Habituès of many distant countries, habituès of far-distant
        dwellings,
Trusters of men and women, observers of cities, solitary
        toilers,
Pausers and contemplators of tufts, blossoms, shells
        of the shore,
Dancers at wedding-dances, kissers of brides, tender
        helpers of children, bearers of children,
Soldiers of revolts, standers by gaping graves,
        lowerers-down of coffins,
Journeyers over consecutive seasons, over the years,
        the curious years each emerging from that
        which preceded it,
Journeyers as with companions, namely their own diverse
        phases,
Forth-steppers from the latent unrealized baby-days,
Journeyers gayly with their own youth, journeyers with
        their bearded and well-grain'd manhood,

Journeyers with their womanhood, ample, unsurpass'd,
content,
Journeyers with their own sublime old age of manhood
or womanhood,
Old age, calm, expanded, broad with the haughty breadth
of the universe,
Old age, flowing free with the delicious near-by freedom
of death.

13

Allons! to that which is endless as it was beginningless,
To undergo much, tramps of days, rests of nights,
To merge all in the travel they tend to, and the days
and nights they tend to,
Again to merge them in the start of superior journeys,
To see nothing anywhere but what you may reach it and
pass it,
To conceive no time, however distant, but what you
may reach it and pass it,
To look up or down no road but it stretches and waits for
you, however long but it stretches and waits for you,
To see no being, not God's or any, but you also go thither,
To see no possession but you may possess it, enjoying
all without labor or purchase, abstracting the feast
yet not abstracting one particle of it,
To take the best of the farmer's farm and the rich
man's elegant villa, and the chaste blessings of the
well-married couple, and the fruits of orchards
and flowers of gardens,
To take to your use out of the compact cities as you pass
through,
To carry buildings and streets with you afterward
wherever you go,
To gather the minds of men out of their brains as you
encounter them, to gather the love out of their hearts,
To take your lovers on the road with you, for all that
you leave them behind you,
To know the universe itself as a road, as many roads, as
roads for traveling souls.

All parts away for the progress of souls,
All religion, all solid things, arts, governments—all that
     was or is apparent upon this globe or any globe,
     falls into niches and corners before the procession
     of souls along the grand roads of the universe.

Of the progress of the souls of men and women along
     the grand roads of the universe, all other progress is the
     needed emblem and sustenance.

Forever alive, forever forward,
Stately, solemn, sad, withdrawn, baffled, mad, turbulent,
     feeble, dissatisfied,
Desperate, proud, fond, sick, accepted by men, rejected
     by men,
They go! they go! I know that they go, but I know
     not where they go,
But I know that they go toward the best—toward
     something great.

Whoever you are, come forth! or man or woman come forth!
You must not stay sleeping and dallying there in the house,
     though you built it, or though it has been built for you.

Out of the dark confinement! out from behind the screen!
It is useless to protest, I know all and expose it.

Behold through you as bad as the rest,
Through the laughter, dancing, dining, supping, of people,
Inside of dresses and ornaments, inside of those wash'd
     and trimm'd faces,
Behold a secret silent loathing and despair.

No husband, no wife, no friend, trusted to hear the
     confession,
Another self, a duplicate of every one, skulking and
     hiding it goes,
Formless and wordless through the streets of the cities,
     polite and bland in the parlors,

In the cars of railroads, in steamboats, in the public
 assembly,
Home to the houses of men and women, at the table,
 in the bedroom, everywhere,
Smartly attired, countenance smiling, form upright, death
 under the breast-bones, hell under the skull-bones,
Under the broadcloth and gloves, under the ribbons and
 artificial flowers,
Keeping fair with the customs, speaking not a syllable
 of itself,
Speaking of any thing else but never of itself.

14

Allons! through struggles and wars!
The goal that was named cannot be countermanded.

Have the past struggles succeeded?
What has succeeded? yourself? your nation? Nature?
Now understand me well—it is provided in the essence
 of things that from any fruition of success, no
 matter what, shall come forth something to make
 a greater struggle necessary.

My call is the call of battle, I nourish active rebellion,
He going with me must go well arm'd,
He going with me goes often with spare diet, poverty,
 angry enemies, desertions.

15

Allons! the road is before us!
It is safe—I have tried it—my own feet have tried
 it well—be not detain'd!
Let the paper remain on the desk unwritten, and the
 book on the self unopen'd!
Let the tools remain in the workshop! let the
 money remain unearn'd!
Let the school stand! mind not the cry of the teacher!
Let the preacher preach in his pulpit! let the lawyer
 plead in the court, and the judge expound the law.

Camerado, I give you my hand!
I give you my love more precious than money,
I give you myself before preaching or law;
Will you give me yourself? will you come travel with me?
Shall we stick by each other as long as we live?

[1856]

A Woman Waits for Me

A woman waits for me, she contains all, nothing is lacking,
Yet all were lacking if sex were lacking, or if the moisture
    of the right man were lacking.

Sex contains all, bodies, souls,
Meanings, proofs, purities, delicacies, results, promulgations,
Songs, commands, health, pride, the maternal mystery,
    the seminal milk,
All hopes, benefactions, bestowals, all the passions,
    loves, beauties, delights of the earth,
All the governments, judges, gods, follow'd persons of
    the earth,
These are contain'd in sex as parts of itself and justifications
    of itself.

Without shame the man I like knows and avows the
    deliciousness of his sex,
Without shame the woman I like knows and avows hers.

Now I will dismiss myself from impassive women,
I will go stay with her who waits for me, and with those
    women that are warm-blooded and sufficient for me,
I see that they understand me and do not deny me,
I see that they are worthy of me, I will be the robust
    husband of those women.

They are not one jot less than I am,
They are tann'd in the face by shining suns and blowing
     winds,
Their flesh has the old divine suppleness and strength,
They know how to swim, row, ride, wrestle, shoot, run,
     strike, retreat, advance, resist, defend themselves,
They are ultimate in their own right—they are calm,
     clear, well-possess'd of themselves.

I draw you close to me, you women,
I cannot let you go, I would do you good,
I am for you, and you are for me, not only for our own sake,
     but for others' sakes,
Envelop'd in you sleep greater heroes and bards,
They refuse to awake at the touch of any man but me.

It is I, you women, I make my way,
I am stern, acrid, large, undissuadable, but I love you,
I do not hurt you any more than is necessary for you,
I pour the stuff to start sons and daughters fit for these
     States, I press with slow rude muscle,
I brace myself effectually, I listen to no entreaties,
I dare not withdraw till I deposit what has so long
     accumulated within me.

Through you I drain the pent-up rivers of myself,
In you I wrap a thousand onward years,
On you I graft the grafts of the best-beloved of me and
     America,
The drops I distil upon you shall grow fierce and
     athletic girls, new artists, musicians, and singers,
The babes I beget upon you are to beget babes in their turn,
I shall demand perfect men and women out of my
     love-spendings,
I shall expect them to interpenetrate with others,
     as I and you interpenetrate now,
I shall count on the fruits of the gushing showers of them,
     as I count on the fruits of the gushing showers
     I give now,

I shall look for loving crops from the birth, life, death,
    immortality, I plant so lovingly now.

                                            [1856]

On the Beach at Night Alone

On the beach at night alone,
As the old mother sways her to and fro singing her
    husky song,
As I watch the bright stars shining, I think a thought of
    the clef of the universes and of the future.

A vast similitude interlocks all,
All spheres, grown, ungrown, small, large, suns, moons,
    planets,
All distances of place however wide,
All distances of time, all inanimate forms,
All souls, all living bodies though they be ever so different,
    or in different worlds,
All gaseous, watery, vegetable, mineral processes, the
    fishes, the brutes,
All nations, colors, barbarisms, civilizations, languages,
All identities that have existed or may exist on this
    globe or any globe,
All lives and deaths, all of the past, present, future,
This vast similitude spans them, and always has spann'd,
And shall forever span them and compactly hold and
    enclose them.

                                            [1856]

To a Foil'd European Revolutionaire

Courage yet, my brother or my sister!
Keep on—Liberty is to be subserv'd whatever occurs;

That is nothing that is quell'd by one or two failures, or
     any number of failures,
Or by the indifference or ingratitude of the people,
     or by any unfaithfulness,
Or the show of the tushes of power, soldiers, cannon,
     penal statutes.

What we believe in waits latent forever through
     all the continents,
Invites no one, promises nothing, sits in calmness and light,
     is positive and composed, knows no discouragement,
Waiting patiently, waiting its time.

(Not songs of loyalty alone are these,
But songs of insurrection also,
For I am the sworn poet of every dauntless rebel the
     world over,
And he going with me leaves peace and routine behind him,
And stakes his life to be lost at any moment.)

The battle rages with many a loud alarm and frequent
     advance and retreat,
The infidel triumphs, or supposes he triumphs,
The prison, scaffold, garroté, handcuffs, iron necklace
     and leadballs do their work,
The named and unnamed heroes pass to other spheres,
The great speakers and writers are exiled, they lie sick
     in distant lands,
The cause is asleep, the strongest throats are choked
     with their own blood,
The young men droop their eyelashes toward the ground
     when they meet;
But for all this Liberty has not gone out of the place,
     nor the infidel enter'd into full possession.

When liberty goes out of a place it is not the first to
     go, nor the second or third to go,
It waits for all the rest to go, it is the last.

When there are no more memories of heroes and martyrs,
And when all life and all the souls of men and women
    are discharged from any part of the earth,
Then only shall liberty or the idea of liberty be discharged
     from that part of the earth,
And the infidel come into full possession.

Then courage European revolter, revoltress!
For till all ceases neither must you cease.

I do not know what you are for, (I do not know what
    I am for myself, nor what any thing is for,)
But I will search carefully for it even in being foil'd,
In defeat, poverty, misconception, imprisonment—for they
     too are great.

Did we think victory great?
So it is—but now it seems to me, when it cannot be
     help'd, that defeat is great,
And that death and dismay are great.

                                [1856]

Out of the Cradle Endlessly Rocking

Out of the cradle endlessly rocking,
Out of the mocking-bird's throat, the musical shuttle,
Out of the Ninth-month midnight,
Over the sterile sands and the fields beyond, where the child
    leaving his bed wander'd alone, bareheaded, barefoot,
Down from the shower'd halo,
Up from the mystic play of shadows twining and twisting
    as if they were alive,
Out from the patches of briers and blackberries,
From the memories of the bird that chanted to me,

From your memories sad brother, from the fitful risings
    and fallings I heard,
From under that yellow half-moon late-risen and
    swollen as if with tears,
From those beginning notes of yearning and love there
    in the mist,
From the thousand responses of my heart never to cease,
From the myriad thence-arous'd words,
From the word stronger and more delicious than any,
From such as now they start the scene revisiting,
As a flock, twittering, rising, or overhead passing,
Borne hither, ere all eludes me, hurriedly,
A man, yet by these tears a little boy again,
Throwing myself on the sand, confronting the waves,
I, chanter of pains and joys, uniter of here and hereafter,
Taking all hints to use them, but swiftly leaping
    beyond them,
A reminiscence sing.

Once Paumanok,
When the lilac-scent was in the air and Fifth-month
    grass was growing,
Up this seashore in some briers,
Two feather'd guests from Alabama, two together,
And their nest, and four light-green eggs spotted
    with brown,
And every day the he-bird to and fro near at hand,
And every day the she-bird crouch'd on her nest, silent,
    with bright eyes,
And every day I, a curious boy, never too close,
    never disturbing them,
Cautiously peering, absorbing, translating.

Shine! shine! shine!
Pour down your warmth, great sun!
While we bask, we two together.

Two together!
Winds blow south, or winds blow north,

Day come white, or night come black,
Home, or rivers and mountains from home,
Singing all time, minding no time,
While we two keep together.

Till of a sudden,
May-be kill'd, unknown to her mate,
One forenoon the she-bird crouch'd not on the nest,
Nor return'd that afternoon, nor the next,
Nor ever appear'd again.

And thenceforward all summer in the sound of the sea,
And at night under the full of the moon in calmer weather,
Over the hoarse surging of the sea,
Or flitting from brier to brier by day,
I saw, I heard at intervals the remaining one, the he-bird,
The solitary guest from Alabama.

Blow! blow! blow!
Blow up sea-winds along Paumanok's shore;
I wait and I wait till you blow my mate to me.

Yes, when the stars glisten'd,
All night long on the prong of a moss-scallop'd stake,
Down almost amid the slapping waves,
Sat the lone singer wonderful causing tears.

He call'd on his mate,
He pour'd forth the meanings which I of all men know.

Yes my brother I know,
The rest might not, but I have treasur'd every note,
For more than once dimly down to the beach gliding,
Silent, avoiding the moonbeams, blending myself with the
    shadows,
Recalling now the obscure shapes, the echoes, the
    sounds and sights after their sorts,
The white arms out in the breakers tirelessly tossing,

I, with bare feet, a child, the wind wafting my hair,
Listen'd long and long.

Listen'd to keep, to sing, now translating the notes,
Following you my brother

Soothe! soothe! soothe!
Close on its wave soothes the wave behind,
And again another behind embracing and lapping, every
    one close,
But my love soothes not me, not me.

Low hangs the moon, it rose late,
It is lagging—O I think it is heavy with love, with love.

O madly the sea pushes upon the land,
With love, with love.

O night! do I not see my love fluttering out among the
    breakers?
What is that little black thing I see there in the white?

Loud! loud! loud!
Loud I call to you, my love!

High and clear I shoot my voice over the waves,
Surely you must know who is here, is here,
You must know who I am, my love.

Low-hanging moon!
What is that dusky spot in your brown yellow?
O it is the shape, the shape of my mate!
O moon do not keep her from me any longer.

Land! land! O land!
Whichever way I turn, O I think you could give me
    my mate back again if you only would,
For I am almost sure I see her dimly whichever way I look.

O rising stars!
Perhaps the one I want so much will rise, will rise
        with some of you.

O throat! O trembling throat!
Sound clearer through the atmosphere!
Pierce the woods, the earth,
Somewhere listening to catch you must be the one I want.

Shake out carols!
Solitary here, the night's carols!
Carols of lonesome love! death's carols!
Carols under that lagging, yellow, waning moon!
O under that moon where she droops almost down
        into the sea!
O reckless despairing carols.

But soft! sink low!
Soft! let me just murmur,
And do you wait a moment you husky-nois'd sea,
For somewhere I believe I heard my mate responding to me,
So faint, I must be still, be still to listen,
But not altogether still, for then she might not come
        immediately to me.

Hither my love!
Here I am! here!
With this just-sustain'd note I announce myself to you,
This gentle call is for you my love, for you.

Do not be decoy'd elsewhere,
That is the whistle of the wind, it is not my voice,
That is the fluttering, the fluttering of the spray,
Those are the shadows of leaves.

O darkness! O in vain!
O I am very sick and sorrowful.

O brown halo in the sky near the moon, drooping upon
    the sea!
O troubled reflection in the sea!
O throat! O throbbing heart!
And I singing uselessly, uselessly all the night.

O past! O happy life! O songs of joy!
In the air, in the woods, over fields,
Loved! loved! loved! loved! loved!
But my mate no more, no more with me!
We two together no more.

The aria sinking,
All else continuing, the stars shining,
The winds blowing, the notes of the bird continuous
    echoing,
With angry moans the fierce old mother incessantly
    moaning,
On the sands of Paumanok's shore gray and rustling,
The yellow half-moon enlarged, sagging down, drooping,
    the face of the sea almost touching,
The boy ecstatic, with his bare feet the waves, with
    his hair the atmosphere dallying,
The love in the heart long pent, now loose, now at
    last tumultuously bursting,
The aria's meaning, the ears, the soul, swiftly depositing,
The strange tears down the cheeks coursing,
The colloquy there, the trio, each uttering,
The undertone, the savage old mother incessantly crying,
To the boy's soul's questions sullenly timing, some drown'd
    secret hissing,
To the outsetting bard.

Demon or bird! (said the boy's soul,)
Is it indeed toward your mate you sing? or is it really to me?
For I, that was a child, my tongue's use sleeping,
    now I have heard you,
Now in a moment I know what I am for, I awake,

And already a thousand singers, a thousand songs, clearer,
    louder and more sorrowful than yours,
A thousand warbling echoes have started to life
    within me, never to die.

O you singer solitary, singing by yourself, projecting me,
O solitary me listening, never more shall I cease
    perpetuating you,
Never more shall I escape, never more the reverberations,
Never more the cries of unsatisfied love be absent from me,
Never again leave me to be the peaceful child I was
    before what there in the night,
By the sea under the yellow and sagging moon,
The messenger there arous'd, the fire, the sweet hell within,
The unknown want, the destiny of me.

O give me the clew! (it lurks in the night here somewhere,)
O if I am to have so much, let me have more!

A word then, (for I will conquer it,)
The word final, superior to all,
Subtle, sent up—what is it?— I listen;
Are you whispering it, and have been all the time,
    you sea-waves?
Is that it from your liquid rims and wet sands?

Whereto answering, the sea,
Delaying not, hurrying not,
Whisper'd me through the night, and very plainly
    before daybreak,
Lisp'd to me the low and delicious word death,
And again death, death, death, death,
Hissing melodious, neither like the bird nor like my
    arous'd child's heart,
But edging near as privately for me rustling at my feet,
Creeping thence steadily up to my ears and laving
    me softly all over,
Death, death, death, death, death.

Which I do not forget,
But fuse the song of my dusky demon and brother,
That he sang to me in the moonlight on Paumanok's
　　　gray beach,
With the thousand responsive songs at random,
My own songs awaked from that hour,
And with them the key, the word up from the waves,
The word of the sweetest song and all songs,
That strong and delicious word which, creeping to my feet,
(Or like some old crone rocking the cradle, swathed
　　　in sweet garments, bending aside,)
The sea whisper'd me.

[1859]

As I Ebb'd with the Ocean of Life

1

As I ebb'd with the ocean of life,
As I wended the shores I know,
As I walk'd where the ripples continually wash you
　　　Paumanok,
Where they rustle up hoarse and sibilant,
Where the fierce old mother endlessly cries for her
　　　castaways,
I musing late in the autumn day, gazing off southward,
Held by this electric self out of the pride of which I
　　　utter poems,
Was seiz'd by the spirit that trails in the lines underfoot,
The rim, the sediment that stands for all the water and
　　　all the land of the globe.

Fascinated, my eyes reverting from the south, dropt,
　　　to follow those slender windrows,
Chaff, straw, splinters of wood, weeds, and the sea-gluten,
Scum, scales from shining rocks, leaves of salt-lettuce,
　　　left by the tide,

Miles walking, the sound of breaking waves the
    other side of me,
Paumanok there and then as I thought the old thought
    of likenesses,
These you presented to me you fish-shaped island,
As I wended the shores I know,
As I walk'd with that electric self seeking types.

2

As I wend to the shores I know not,
As I list to the dirge, the voices of men and women wreck'd,
As I inhale the impalpable breezes that set in upon me,
As the ocean so mysterious rolls toward me closer and closer,
I too but signify at the utmost a little wash'd-up drift,
A few sands and dead leaves to gather,
Gather, and merge myself as part of the sands and drift.

O baffled, balk'd, bent to the very earth,
Oppress'd with myself that I have dared to open my mouth,
Aware now that amid all that blab whose echoes recoil upon
    me I have not once had the least idea who or what I am,
But that before all my arrogant poems the real Me stands
    yet untouch'd, untold, altogether unreach'd,
Withdrawn far, mocking me with mock-congratulatory
    signs and bows,
With peals of distant ironical laughter at every word
    I have written,
Pointing in silence to these songs, and then to the
    sand beneath.

I perceive I have not really understood any thing not a
    single object, and that no man ever can,
Nature here in sight of the sea taking advantage of me
    to dart upon me and sting me,
Because I have dared to open my mouth to sing at all.

3

You oceans both, I close with you,
We murmur alike reproachfully rolling sands and drift,
    knowing not why,

These little shreds indeed standing for you and me
    and all.

You friable shore with trails of debris,
You fish-shaped island, I take what is underfoot,
What is yours is mine my father.

I too Paumanok,
I too have bubbled up, floated the measureless float,
    and been wash'd on your shores,
I too am but a trail of drift and debris,
I too leave little wrecks upon you, you fish-shaped island.

I throw myself upon your breast my father,
I cling to you so that you cannot unloose me,
I hold you so firm till you answer me something.

Kiss me my father,
Touch me with your lips as I touch those I love,
Breathe to me while I hold you close the secret of the
    murmuring I envy.

4

Ebb, ocean of life, (the flow will return,)
Cease not your moaning you fierce old mother,
Endlessly cry for your castaways, but fear not, deny not me,
Rustle not up so hoarse and angry against my feet as
    I touch you or gather from you.

I mean tenderly by you and all,
I gather for myself and for this phantom looking down
    where we lead, and following me and mine.

Me and mine, loose windrows, little corpses,
Froth, snowy white, and bubbles,
(See, from my dead lips the ooze exuding at last,
See, the prismatic colors glistening and rolling,)
Tufts of straw, sands, fragments,

Buoy'd hither from many moods, one contradicting another,
From the storm, the long calm, the darkness, the swell,
Musing, pondering, a breath, a briny tear, a dab of
    liquid or soil,
Up just as much out of fathomless workings fermented
    and thrown,
A limp blossom or two, torn, just as much over waves
    floating, drifted at random,
Just as much for us that sobbing dirge of Nature,
Just as much whence we come that blare of the
    cloud-trumpets,
We, capricious, brought hither we know not whence,
    spread out before you,
You up there walking or sitting,
Whoever you are, we too lie in drifts at your feet.

[1860]

Me Imperturbe

Me imperturbe, standing at ease in Nature,
Master of all or mistress of all, aplomb in the midst of
    irrational things,
Imbued as they, passive, receptive, silent as they,
Finding my occupation, poverty, notoriety, foibles, crimes,
    less important than I thought,
Me toward the Mexican sea, or in the Mannahatta or
    the Tennessee, or far north or inland,
A river man, or a man of the woods, or of any farm-life
    of these States or of the coast, or the lakes or Kanada,
Me wherever my life is lived, O to be self-balanced for
    contingencies,
To confront night, storms, hunger, ridicule, accidents,
    rebuffs, as the trees and animals do.

[1860]

I Hear America Singing

I hear America singing, the varied carols I hear,
Those of mechanics, each one singing his as it should be
    blithe and strong,
The carpenter singing his as he measures his plank or beam,
The mason singing his as he makes ready for work, or
    leaves off work,
The boatman singing what belongs to him in his boat,
    the deckhand singing on the steamboat deck,
The shoemaker singing as he sits on his bench, the hatter
    singing as he stands,
The wood-cutter's song, the ploughboy's on his way in the
    morning, or at noon intermission or at sundown,
The delicious singing of the mother, or of the young wife
    at work, or of the girl sewing or washing,
Each singing what belongs to him or her and to none else,
The day what belongs to the day—at night the party of
    young fellows, robust, friendly,
Singing with open mouths their strong melodious songs.

[1860]

Poets to Come

Poets to come! orators, singers, musicians to come!
Not to-day is to justify me and answer what I am for,
But you, a new brood, native, athletic, continental, greater
    than before known,
Arouse! for you must justify me.

I myself but write one or two indicative words for the future,
I but advance a moment only to wheel and hurry back
    in the darkness.

I am a man who, sauntering along without fully stopping,
    turns a casual look upon you and then averts his face,

Leaving it to you to prove and define it,
Expecting the main things from you.

[1860]

From Pent-up Aching Rivers

From pent-up aching rivers,
From that of myself without which I were nothing,
From what I am determin'd to make illustrious, even
          if I stand sole among men,
From my own voice resonant, singing the phallus,
Singing the song of procreation,
Singing the need of superb children and therein superb
          grown people,
Singing the muscular urge and the blending,
Singing the bedfellow's song, (O resistless yearning!
O for any and each the body correlative attracting!
O for you whoever you are your correlative body! O it,
          more than all else, you delighting!)
From the hungry gnaw that eats me night and day,
From native moments, from bashful pains, singing them,
Seeking something yet unfound though I have diligently
          sought it many a long year,
Singing the true song of the soul fitful at random,
Renascent with grossest Nature or among animals,
Of that, of them and what goes with them my poems
          informing,
Of the smell of apples and lemons, of the pairing of birds,
Of the wet of woods, of the lapping of waves,
Of the mad pushes of waves upon the land, I them chanting,
The overture lightly sounding, the strain anticipating,
The welcome nearness, the sight of the perfect body,
The swimmer swimming naked in the bath, or motionless
          on his back lying and floating,
The female form approaching, I pensive, love-flesh
          tremulous aching,

The divine list for myself or you or for any one making,
The face, the limbs, the index from head to foot, and
    what it arouses,
The mystic deliria, the madness amorous, the utter
    abandonment,
(Hark close and still what I now whisper to you,
I love you, O you entirely possess me,
O that you and I escape from the rest and go utterly off,
    free and lawless,
Two hawks in the air, two fishes swimming in the sea not
    more lawless than we;)
The furious storm through me careering, I passionately
    trembling,
The oath of the inseparableness of two together, of the
    woman that loves me and whom I love more
    than my life, that oath swearing,
(O I willingly stake all for you,
O let me be lost if it must be so!
O you and I! what is it to us what the rest do or think?
What is all else to us? only that we enjoy each other and
    exhaust each other if it must be so;)
From the master, the pilot I yield the vessel to,
The general commanding me, commanding all, from
    him permission taking,
From time the programme hastening, (I have loiter'd
    too long as it is,)
From sex, from the warp and from the woof,
From privacy, from frequent repinings alone,
From plenty of persons near and yet the right person
    not near,
From the soft sliding of hands over me and thrusting of
    fingers through my hair and beard,
From the long sustain'd kiss upon the mouth or bosom,
From the close pressure that makes me or any man
    drunk, fainting with excess,
From what the divine husband knows, from the work of
    fatherhood,
From exultation, victory and relief, from the bedfellow's
    embrace in the night,

From the act-poems of eyes, hands, hips and bosoms,
From the cling of the trembling arm,
From the bending curve and the clinch,
From side by side the pliant coverlet off-throwing,
From the one so unwilling to have me leave, and me
    just as unwilling to leave,
(Yet a moment O tender waiter, and I return,)
From the hour of shining stars and dropping dews,
From the night a moment I emerging flitting out,
Celebrate you act divine and you children prepared for,
And you stalwart loins.

[1860]

Native Moments

Native moments—when you come upon me—ah you are
    here now,
Give me now libidinous joys only,
Give me the drench of my passions, give me life coarse
    and rank,
To-day I go consort with Nature's darlings, to-night too,
I am for those who believe in loose delights, I share
    the midnight orgies of young men,
I dance with the dancers and drink with the drinkers,
The echoes ring with our indecent calls, I pick out some low
    person for my dearest friend,
He shall be lawless, rude, illiterate, he shall be one condemn'd
    by others for deeds done,
I will play a part no longer, why should I exile myself
    from my companions?
O you shunn'd persons, I at least do not shun you,
I come forthwith in your midst, I will be your poet,
I will be more to you than to any of the rest.

[1860]

Once I Pass'd through a Populous City

Once I pass'd through a populous city imprinting my brain
    for future use with its shows, architecture, customs,
    traditions,
Yet now of all that city I remember only a woman I casually
    met there who detain'd me for love of me,
Day by day and night by night we were together—all else has
    long been forgotten by me,
I remember I say only that woman who passionately clung
    to me,
Again we wander, we love, we separate again,
Again she holds me by the hand, I must not go,
I see her close beside me with silent lips sad and tremulous.

[1860]

Facing West from California's Shores

Facing west from California's shores,
Inquiring, tireless, seeking what is yet unfound,
I, a child, very old, over waves, towards the house of maternity,
    the land of migrations, look afar,
Look off the shores of my Western sea, the circle almost circled;
For starting westward from Hindustan, from the vales of
    Kashmere,
From Asia, from the north, from the God, the sage, and the
    hero,
From the south, from the flowery peninsulas and the spice
    islands,
Long having wander'd since, round the earth having wander'd,
Now I face home again, very pleas'd and joyous,
(But where is what I started for so long ago?
And why is it yet unfound?)

[1860]

As Adam Early in the Morning

As Adam early in the morning,
Walking forth from the bower refresh'd with sleep,
Behold me where I pass, hear my voice, approach,
Touch me, touch the palm of your hand to my body as I pass,
Be not afraid of my body.

[1861]

Calamus

In Paths Untrodden

In paths untrodden,
In the growth by margins of pond-waters,
Escaped from the life that exhibits itself,
From all the standards hitherto publish'd, from the pleasures,
    profits, conformities,
Which too long I was offering to feed my soul,
Clear to me now standards not yet publish'd, clear to me
    that my soul,
That the soul of the man I speak for rejoices in comrades,
Here by myself away from the clank of the world,
Tallying and talk'd to here by tongues aromatic,
No longer abash'd, (for in this secluded spot I can
    respond as I would not dare elsewhere,)
Strong upon me the life that does not exhibit itself,
    yet contains all the rest,
Resolv'd to sing no songs to-day but those of manly
    attachment,
Projecting them along that substantial life,
Bequeathing hence types of athletic love,
Afternoon this delicious Ninth-month in my forty-first year,
I proceed for all who are or have been young men,
To tell the secret of my nights and days,
To celebrate the need of comrades.

[1860]

Scented Herbage of My Breast

Scented herbage of my breast,
Leaves from you I glean, I write, to be perused best
    afterwards,
Tomb-leaves, body-leaves growing up above me above death,
Perennial roots, tall leaves, O the winter shall not freeze
    you delicate leaves,
Every year shall you bloom again, out from where you
    retired you shall emerge again;
O I do not know whether many passing by will discover
    you or inhale your faint odor, but I believe a few will;
O slender leaves! O blossoms of my blood! I permit you
    to tell in your own way of the heart that is under you,
O I do not know what you mean there underneath
    yourselves, you are not happiness,
You are often more bitter than I can bear, you burn
    and sting me,
Yet you are beautiful to me you faint tinged roots,
    you make me think of death,
Death is beautiful from you, (what indeed is finally
    beautiful except death and love?)
O I think it is not for life I am chanting here my chant
    of lovers, I think it must be for death,
For how calm, how solemn it grows to ascend to the
    atmosphere of lovers,
Death or life I am then indifferent, my soul declines
    to prefer,
(I am not sure but the high soul of lovers welcomes
    death most,)
Indeed O death, I think now these leaves mean precisely
    the same as you mean,
Grow up taller sweet leaves that I may see! grow up out of
    my breast!
Spring away from the conceal'd heart there!
Do not fold yourself so in your pink-tinged roots timid
    leaves!

Do not remain down there so ashamed, herbage of my
      breast!
Come I am determin'd to unbare this broad breast of
      mine, I have long enough stifled and choked;
Emblematic and capricious blades I leave you,
      now you serve me not,
I will say what I have to say by itself,
I will sound myself and comrades only, I will never
      again utter a call only their call,
I will raise with it immortal reverberations through the
      States,
I will give an example to lovers to take permanent shape and
      will through the States,
Through me shall the words be said to make death
      exhilarating,
Give me your tone therefore O death, that I may accord
      with it,
Give me yourself, for I see that you belong to me now
      above all, and are folded inseparably together, you
      love and death are,
Nor will I allow you to balk me any more with what
      I was calling life,
For now it is convey'd to me that you are the purports
      essential,
That you hide in these shifting forms of life, for reasons,
      and that they are mainly for you,
That you beyond them come forth to remain, the real
      reality,
That behind the mask of materials you patiently wait,
      no matter how long,
That you will one day perhaps take control of all,
That you will perhaps dissipate this entire show of
      appearance,
That may-be you are what it is all for, but it does not
      last so very long,
But you will last very long.

[1860]

Whoever You Are Holding Me Now in Hand

Whoever you are holding me now in hand,
Without one thing all will be useless,
I give you fair warning before you attempt me further,
I am not what you supposed, but far different.

Who is he that would become my follower?
Who would sign himself a candidate for my affections?

The way is suspicious, the result uncertain, perhaps
    destructive,
You would have to give up all else, I alone would expect
    to be your sole and exclusive standard,
Your novitiate would even then be long and exhausting,
The whole past theory of your life and all conformity to the
    lives around you would have to be abandon'd,
Therefore release me now before troubling yourself any
    further, let go your hand from my shoulders,
Put me down and depart on your way.

Or else by stealth in some wood for trial,
Or back of a rock in the open air,
(For in any roof'd room of a house I emerge not, nor in
    company,
And in libraries I lie as one dumb, a gawk, or unborn,
    or dead,)
But just possibly with you on a high hill, first watching
    lest any person for miles around approach unawares,
Or possibly with you sailing at sea, or on the beach of
    the sea or some quiet island,
Here to put your lips upon mine I permit you,
With the comrade's long-dwelling kiss or the new
    husband's kiss,
For I am the new husband and I am the comrade.

Or if you will, thrusting me beneath your clothing,
Where I may feel the throbs of your heart or rest upon
    your hip,

Carry me when you go forth over land or sea;
For thus merely touching you is enough, is best,
And thus touching you would I silently sleep and be
    carried eternally.

But these leaves conning you con at peril,
For these leaves and me you will not understand,
They will elude you at first and still more afterward, I will
    certainly elude you,
Even while you should think you had unquestionably
    caught me, behold!
Already you see I have escaped from you.

For it is not for what I have put into it that I have
    written this book,
Nor is it by reading it you will acquire it,
Nor do those know me best who admire me and
    vauntingly praise me,
Nor will the candidates for my love (unless at most
    a very few) prove victorious,
Nor will my poems do good only, they will do just as much
    evil, perhaps more,
For all is useless without that which you may guess at
    many times and not hit, that which I hinted at;
Therefore release me and depart on your way.

[1860]

For You O Democracy

Come, I will make the continent indissoluble,
I will make the most splendid race the sun ever shone upon,
I will make divine magnetic lands,
        With the love of comrades,
            With the life-long love of comrades.

I will plant companionship thick as trees along all the
    rivers of America, and along the shores of the great
    lakes, and all over the prairies,
I will make inseparable cities with their arms about
    each other's necks,
        By the love of comrades,
          By the manly love of comrades.

For you these from me, O Democracy, to serve you
    ma femme!
For you, for you I am trilling these songs.

                                      [1860]

These I Singing in Spring

These I singing in spring collect for lovers,
(For who but I should understand lovers and all their
    sorrow and joy?
And who but I should be the poet of comrades?)
Collecting I traverse the garden the world, but soon I pass
    the gates,
Now along the pond-side, now wading in a little,
    fearing not the wet,
Now by the post-and-rail fences where the old stones
    thrown there, pick'd from the fields, have accumulated,
(Wild-flowers and vines and weeds come up through the
    stones and partly cover them, beyond these I pass,)
Far, far in the forest, or sauntering later in summer,
    before I think where I go,
Solitary, smelling the earthy smell, stopping now
    and then in the silence,
Alone I had thought, yet soon a troop gathers around me,
Some walk by my side and some behind, and some
    embrace my arms or neck,

They the spirits of dear friends dead or alive, thicker
    they come, a great crowd, and I in the middle,
Collecting, dispensing, singing, there I wander with them,
Plucking something for tokens, tossing toward whoever
    is near me,
Here, lilac, with a branch of pine,
Here, out of my pocket, some moss which I pull'd off
    a live-oak in Florida as it hung trailing down,
Here, some pinks and laurel leaves, and a handful of sage,
And here what I now draw from the water, wading
    in the pond-side,
(O here I last saw him that tenderly loves me, and returns
    again never to separate from me,
And this, O this shall henceforth be the token of
    comrades, this calamus-root shall,
Interchange it youths with each other! let none render
    it back!)
And twigs of maple and a bunch of wild orange
    and chestnut,
And stems of currants and plum-blows, and the
    aromatic cedar,
These I compass'd around by a thick cloud of spirits,
Wandering, point to or touch as I pass, or throw them
    loosely from me,
Indicating to each one what he shall have, giving
    something to each;
But what I drew from the water by the pond-side, that
    I reserve,
I will give of it, but only to them that love as I myself
    am capable of loving.

[1860]

Of the Terrible Doubt of Appearances

Of the terrible doubt of appearances,
Of the uncertainty after all, that we may be deluded,

That may-be reliance and hope are but speculations after all,
     after all,
That may-be identity beyond the grave is a beautiful
     fable only,
May-be the things I perceive, the animals, plants, men,
     hills, shining and flowing waters,
The skies of day and night, colors, densities, forms, may-be
     these are (as doubtless they are) only apparitions,
     and the real something has yet to be known,
(How often they dart out of themselves as if to
     confound me and mock me!
How often I think neither I know, nor any man knows,
     aught of them,)
May-be seeming to me what they are (as doubtless they
     indeed but seem) as from my present point of view,
     and might prove (as of course they would) nought
     of what they appear, or nought anyhow, from
     entirely changed points of view;
To me these and the like of these are curiously answer'd
     by my lovers, my dear friends,
When he whom I love travels with me or sits a long
     while holding me by the hand,
When the subtle air, the impalpable, the sense that words
     and reason hold not, surround us and pervade us,
Then I am charged with untold and untellable wisdom,
     I am silent, I require nothing further,
I cannot answer the question of appearances or that of
     identity beyond the grave,
But I walk or sit indifferent, I am satisfied,
He ahold of my hand has completely satisfied me.

[1860]

Recorders Ages Hence

Recorders ages hence,
Come, I will take you down underneath this impassive
     exterior, I will tell you what to say of me,

Publish my name and hang up my picture as that of the
    tenderest lover,
The friend the lover's portrait, of whom his friend
    his lover was fondest,
Who was not proud of his songs, but of the measureless
    ocean of love within him, and freely pour'd it forth,
Who often walk'd lonesome walks thinking of his dear
    friends, his lovers,
Who pensive away from one he lov'd often lay sleepless
    and dissatisfied at night,
Who knew too well the sick, sick dread lest the one he
    lov'd might secretly be indifferent to him,
Whose happiest days were far away through fields, in
    woods, on hills, he and another wandering hand
    in hand, they twain apart from other men,
Who oft as he saunter'd the streets curv'd with his
    arm the shoulder of his friend, while the arm of his
    friend rested upon him also.

[1860]

When I Heard at the Close of the Day

When I heard at the close of the day how my name
    had been receiv'd with plaudits in the capitol, still it was
    not a happy night for me that follow'd,
And else when I carous'd, or when my plans were
    accomplish'd still I was not happy,
But the day when I rose at dawn from the bed of
    perfect health, refresh'd, singing, inhaling the ripe
    breath of autumn,
When I saw the full moon in the west grow pale and
    disappear in the morning light,
When I wander'd alone over the beach, and undressing
    bathed, laughing with the cool waters, and saw
    the sun rise,

And when I thought how my dear friend my lover was
    on his way coming, O then I was happy,
O then each breath tasted sweeter, and all that day my food
    nourish'd me more, and the beautiful day pass'd well,
And the next came with equal joy, and with the
    next at evening came my friend,
And that night while all was still I heard the waters roll
    slowly continually up the shores,
I heard the hissing rustle of the liquid and sands as
    directed to me whispering to congratulate me,
For the one I love most lay sleeping by me under the same
    cover in the cool night,
In the stillness in the autumn moonbeams his face was
    inclined toward me,
And his arm lay lightly around my breast—and that night
    I was happy.

[1860]

Roots and Leaves Themselves Alone

Roots and leaves themselves alone are these,
Scents brought to me and women from the wild woods
    and pond-side,
Breast-sorrel and pinks of love, fingers that wind around
    tighter than vines,
Gushes from the throats of birds hid in the foliage of
    trees as the sun is risen,
Breezes of land and love set from living shores to you
    on the living sea, to you O sailors!
Frost-mellow'd berries and Third-month twigs offer'd
    fresh to young persons wandering out in the fields
    when the winter breaks up,
Love-buds put before you and within you whoever
    you are,
Buds to be unfolded on the old terms,

If you bring the warmth of the sun to them they will
    open and bring form, color, perfume, to you,
If you become the aliment and the wet they will become
    flowers, fruits, tall branches and trees.

[1860]

Of Him I Love Day and Night

Of him I love day and night I dream'd I heard he was dead,
And I dream'd I went where they had buried him
    I love, but he was not in that place,
And I dream'd I wander'd searching among burial-places
    to find him,
And I found that every place was a burial-place;
The houses full of life were equally full of death, (this
    house is now),
The streets, the shipping, the places of amusement, the
    Chicago, Boston, Philadelphia, the Mannahatta, were
    as full of the dead as of the living,
And fuller, O vastly fuller of the dead than of the living;
And what I dream'd I will henceforth tell to every
    person and age,
And I stand henceforth bound to what I dream'd,
And now I am willing to disregard burial-places and
    dispense with them,
And if the memorials of the dead were put up indifferently
    everywhere, even in the room where I eat or sleep,
    I should be satisfied,
And if the corpse of any one I love, or if my own corpse,
    be duly render'd to powder and pour'd in the sea,
    I shall be satisfied,
Or if it be distributed to the winds I shall be satisfied.

[1860]

I Saw in Louisiana a Live-Oak Growing

I saw in Louisiana a live-oak growing,
All alone stood it and the moss hung down from the
    branches,
Without any companion it grew there uttering joyous
    leaves of dark green,
And its look, rude, unbending, lusty, made me think
    of myself,
But I wonder'd how it could utter joyous leaves standing
    alone there without its friend near, for I knew
    I could not,
And I broke off a twig with a certain number of leaves
    upon it, and twined around it a little moss,
And brought it away, and I have placed it in sight
    in my room,
It is not needed to remind me as of my own dear friends,
(For I believe lately I think of little else than of them,)
Yet it remains to me a curious token, it makes me think
    of manly love;
For all that, and though the live-oak glistens there in
    Louisiana solitary in a wide flat space,
Uttering joyous leaves all its life without a friend
    a lover near,
I know very well I could not.

[1860]

I Hear It Was Charged against Me

I hear it was charged against me that I sought to destroy
    institutions,
But really I am neither for nor against institutions,
(What indeed have I in common with them? or what
    with the destruction of them?)

Only I will establish in the Mannahatta and in every city
    of these States inland and seaboard,
And in the fields and woods, and above every keel little
    or large that dents the water,
Without edifices or rules or trustees or any argument,
The institution of the dear love of comrades.

[1860]

Here the Frailest Leaves of Me

Here the frailest leaves of me and yet my strongest lasting,
Here I shade and hide my thoughts, I myself do not
    expose them,
And yet they expose me more than all my other poems.

[1860]

Sometimes with One I Love

Sometimes with one I love I fill myself with rage for
    fear I effuse unreturn'd love,
But now I think there is no unreturn'd love, the pay is
    certain one way or another,
(I loved a certain person ardently and my love was
    not return'd,
Yet out of that I have written these songs.)

[1860]

Among the Multitude

Among the men and women the multitude,
I perceive one picking me out by secret and divine signs,

Acknowledging none else, not parent, wife, husband,
    brother, child, any nearer than I am,
Some are baffled, but that one is not—that one knows me.

Ah lover and perfect equal,
I meant that you should discover me so by faint indirections,
And I when I meet you mean to discover you by the
    like in you.

[1860]

That Shadow My Likeness

That shadow my likeness that goes to and fro seeking
    a livelihood, chattering, chaffering,
How often I find myself standing and looking at it where
    it flits,
How often I question and doubt whether that is really me;
But among my lovers and caroling these songs,
O I never doubt whether that is really me.

[1860]

The World below the Brine

The world below the brine,
Forests at the bottom of the sea, the branches and leaves,
Sea-lettuce, vast lichens, strange flowers and seeds, the
    thick tangle, openings, and pink turf,
Different colors, pale gray and green, purple, white, and
    gold, the play of light through the water,
Dumb swimmers there among the rocks, coral, gluten,
    grass, rushes, and the aliment of the swimmers,
Sluggish existences grazing there suspended, or slowly
    crawling close to the bottom,
The sperm-whale at the surface blowing air and spray,
    or disporting with his flukes,
The leaden-eyed shark, the walrus, the turtle, the hairy
    sea-leopard, and the sting-ray,
Passions there, wars, pursuits, tribes, sight in those
    ocean-depths, breathing that thick-breathing air, as
    so many do,
The change thence to the sight here, and to the subtle
    air breathed by beings like us who walk this sphere,
The change onward from ours to that of beings who
    walk other spheres.

[1860]

I Sit and Look Out

I sit and look out upon all the sorrows of the world, and
    upon all oppression and shame,
I hear secret convulsive sobs from young men at anguish
    with themselves, remorseful after deeds done,
I see in low life the mother misused by her children, dying,
    neglected, gaunt, desperate,
I see the wife misused by her husband, I see the treacherous
    seducer of young women,

I mark the ranklings of jealousy and unrequited love
      attempted to be hid, I see these sights on the earth,
I see the workings of battle, pestilence, tyranny, I see
      martyrs and prisoners,
I observe a famine at sea, I observe the sailors casting lots
      who shall be kill'd to preserve the lives of the rest,
I observe the slights and degradations cast by arrogant
      persons upon laborers, the poor, and upon
      negroes, and the like;
All these—all the meanness and agony without end
      I sitting look out upon,
See, hear, and am silent.

[1860]

To Him That Was Crucified

My spirit to yours dear brother,
Do not mind because many sounding your name do not
      understand you,
I do not sound your name, but I understand you,
I specify you with joy O my comrade to salute you, and
      to salute those who are with you, before and
      since, and those to come also,
That we all labor together transmitting the same charge
      and succession,
We few equals indifferent of lands, indifferent of times,
We, enclosers of all continents, all castes, allowers of
      all theologies,
Compassionaters, perceivers, rapport of men,
We walk silent among disputes and assertions, but reject
      not the disputers nor any thing that is asserted,
We hear the bawling and din, we are reach'd at by divisions,
      jealousies, recriminations on every side,
They close peremptorily upon us to surround us, my
      comrade,

Yet we walk unheld, free, the whole earth over,
    journeying up and down till we make our ineffaceable
    mark upon time and the diverse eras,
Till we saturate time and eras, that the men and women
    of races, ages to come, may prove brethren and
    lovers as we are.

                                               [1860]

You Felons on Trial in Courts

You felons on trial in courts,
You convicts in prison-cells, you sentenced assassins
    chain'd and handcuff'd with iron,
Who am I too that I am not on trial or in prison?
Me ruthless and devilish as any, that my wrists are not
    chain'd with iron, or my ankles with iron?

You prostitutes flaunting over the trottoirs or obscene
    in your rooms,
Who am I that I should call you more obscene than myself?
O culpable! I acknowledge—I exposé!
(O admirers, praise not me—compliment not me—
    you make me wince,
I see what you do not—I know what you do not.)
Inside these breast-bones I lie smutch'd and choked,
Beneath this face that appears so impassive hell's tides
    continually run,
Lusts and wickedness are acceptable to me,
I walk with delinquents with passionate love,
I feel I am of them—I belong to those convicts and
    prostitutes myself,
And henceforth I will not deny them—for how can I
    deny myself?

                                               [1860]

To a Common Prostitute

Be composed—be at ease with me—I am Walt Whitman,
    liberal and lusty as Nature,
Not till the sun excludes you do I exclude you,
Not till the waters refuse to glisten for you and the leaves
    to rustle for you, do my words refuse to glisten
    and rustle for you.

My girl I appoint with you an appointment, and I charge you
    that you make preparation to be worthy to meet me,
And I charge you that you be patient and perfect till I come.

Till then I salute you with a significant look that you
    do not forget me.

[1860]

O Magnet-South

O magnet-South! O glistening perfumed South! my South!
O quick mettle, rich blood, impulse and love! good
    and evil! O all dear to me!
O dear to me my birth-things—all moving things and the
    trees where I was born—the grains, plants, rivers,
Dear to me my own slow sluggish rivers where they flow
    distant, over flats of silvery sands or through swamps,
Dear to me the Roanoke, the Savannah, the Altamahaw,
    the Pedee, the Tombigbee, the Santee, the Coosa
    and the Sabine,
O pensive, far away wandering, I return with my soul
    to haunt their banks again,
Again in Florida I float on transparent lakes, I float
    on the Okeechobee, I cross the hummock-land or
    through pleasant openings or dense forests,
I see the parrots in the woods. I see the papaw-tree and
    the blossoming titi;
Again, sailing in my coaster on deck, I coast off Georgia,
    I coast up the Carolinas,

I see where the live-oak is growing, I see where the
  yellow-pine, the scented bay-tree, the lemon and
  orange, the cypress, the graceful palmetto,
I pass rude sea-headlands and enter Pamlico sound through an
  inlet, and dart my vision inland;
O the cotton plant! the growing fields of rice, sugar, hemp!
The cactus guarded with thorns, the laurel-tree with
  large white flowers,
The range afar, the richness and barrenness, the old woods
  charged with mistletoe and trailing moss,
The piney odor and the gloom, the awful natural stillness,
  (here in these dense swamps the freebooter carries
  his gun, and the fugitive has his conceal'd hut;)
O the strange fascination of these half-known
  half-impassable swamps, infested by reptiles,
  resounding with the bellow of the alligator, the sad
  noises of the night-owl and the wild-cat, and the
  whirr of the rattlesnake,
The mocking-bird, the American mimic, singing all the
  forenoon, singing through the moon-lit night,
The humming-bird, the wild turkey, the raccoon,
  the opossum;
A Kentucky corn-field, the tall, graceful, long-leav'd corn,
  slender, flapping, bright green, with tassels, with
  beautiful ears each well-sheath'd in its husk;
O my heart! O tender and fierce pangs, I can stand them
  not, I will depart;
O to be a Virginian where I grew up! O to be a Carolinian!
O longings irrepressible! O I will go back to old
  Tennessee and never wander more.

[1860]

Mannahatta

I was asking for something specific and perfect for my city,
Whereupon lo! upsprang the aboriginal name.

Now I see what there is in a name, a word, liquid, sane,
      unruly, musical, self-sufficient,
I see that the word of my city is that word from of old,
Because I see that word nested in nests of water-bays,
      superb,
Rich, hemm'd thick all around with sailships and
      steamships, an island sixteen miles long, solid-founded,
Numberless crowded streets, high growths of iron, slender,
      strong, light, splendidly uprising toward clear skies,
Tides swift and ample, well-loved by me, toward sundown,
The flowing sea-currents, the little islands, larger
      adjoining islands, the heights, the villas,
The countless masts, the white shore-steamers, the lighters,
      the ferry-boats, the black sea-steamers well-model'd,
The down-town streets, the jobbers' houses of business,
      the houses of business of the ship-merchants and
      money-brokers, the river-streets,
Immigrants arriving, fifteen or twenty thousand in a week,
The carts hauling goods, the manly race of drivers of
      horses, the brown-faced sailors,
The summer air, the bright sun shining, and the sailing
      clouds aloft,
The winter snows, the sleigh-bells, the broken ice in the river,
      passing along up or down with the flood-tide or ebb-tide,
The mechanics of the city, the masters, well-form'd,
      beautiful-faced, looking you straight in the eyes,
Trottoirs throng'd, vehicles, Broadway, the women, the
      shops and shows,
A million people—manners free and superb—open
      voices—hospitality—the most courageous and friendly
      young men,
City of hurried and sparkling waters! city of spires
      and masts!
City nested in bays! my city!

All Is Truth

O me, man of slack faith so long,
Standing aloof, denying portions so long,
Only aware to-day of compact all-diffused truth,
Discovering to-day there is no lie or form of lie,
        and can be none, but grows as inevitably upon itself
        as the truth does upon itself,
Or as any law of the earth or any natural production
        of the earth does.

(This is curious and may not be realized immediately, but
        it must be realized,
I feel in myself that I represent falsehoods equally with
        the rest,
And that the universe does.)

Where has fail'd a perfect return indifferent of lies or
        the truth?
Is it upon the ground, or in water or fire? or in the
        spirit of man? or in the meat and blood?

Meditating among liars and retreating sternly into myself,
        I see that there are really no liars or lies after all,
And that nothing fails its perfect return, and that what
        are called lies are perfect returns,
And that each thing exactly represents itself and what has
        preceded it,
And that the truth includes all, and is compact just as
        much as space is compact,
And that there is no flaw or vacuum in the amount of
        the truth—but that all is truth without exception;
And henceforth I will go celebrate any thing I see or am,
And sing and laugh and deny nothing.

                                                    [1860]

I Heard You Solemn-Sweet Pipes of the Organ

I heard you solemn-sweet pipes of the organ as last Sunday
    morn I pass'd the church,
Winds of autumn, as I walk'd the woods at dusk I heard
    your long-stretch'd sighs up above so mournful,
I heard the perfect Italian tenor singing at the opera, I
    heard the soprano in the midst of the quartet singing;
Heart of my love! you too I heard murmuring low through
    one of the wrists around my head,
Heard the pulse of you when all was still ringing little
    bells last night under my ear.

[1861]

The Ship Starting

Lo, the unbounded sea,
On its breast a ship starting, spreading all sails, carrying
    even her moonsails,
The pennant is flying aloft as she speeds she speeds so
    stately—below emulous waves press forward,
They surround the ship with shining curving motions
    and foam.

[1865]

Out of the Rolling Ocean the Crowd

Out of the rolling ocean the crowd came a drop gently to me,
Whispering *I love you, before long I die,*
I have travel'd a long way merely to look on you to
    touch you,
For I could not die till I once look'd on you,
For I fear'd I might afterward lose you.

Now we have met, we have look'd, we are safe,
Return in peace to the ocean my love,
I too am part of that ocean my love, we are not so
        much separated,
Behold the great roundure, the cohesion of all, how perfect!
But as for me, for you, the irresistible sea is to separate us,
As for an hour carrying us diverse, yet cannot carry us
        diverse forever;
Be not impatient—a little space—know you I salute
        the air, the ocean and the land,
Every day at sundown for your dear sake my love.

                                                [1865]

Pioneers! O Pioneers!

    Come my tan-faced children,
Follow well in order, get your weapons ready,
Have you your pistols? have you your sharp-edged axes?
        Pioneers! O pioneers!

    For we cannot tarry here,
We must march my darlings, we must bear the brunt of
            danger,
We the youthful sinewy races, all the rest on us depend,
        Pioneers! O pioneers!

    O you youths, Western youths,
So impatient, full of action, full of manly pride and
            friendship,
Plain I see you Western youths, see you tramping with
        the foremost,
        Pioneers! O pioneers!

    Have the elder races halted?
Do they droop and end their lesson, wearied over there
        beyond the seas?

We take up the task eternal, and the burden and the lesson,
    Pioneers! O pioneers!

    All the past we leave behind,
We debouch upon a newer mightier world, varied world,
Fresh and strong the world we seize, world of labor and
        the march,
    Pioneers! O pioneers!

    We detachments steady throwing,
Down the edges, through the passes, up the mountains
        steep,
Conquering, holding, daring, venturing as we go the
        unknown ways,
    Pioneers! O pioneers!

    We primeval forests felling,
We the rivers stemming, vexing we and piercing deep the
        mines within,
We the surface broad surveying, we the virgin soil upheaving,
    Pioneers! O pioneers!

    Colorado men are we,
From the peaks gigantic, from the great sierras and the high
        plateaus,
From the mine and from the gully, from the hunting trail
        we come,
    Pioneers! O pioneers!

    From Nebraska, from Arkansas,
Central inland race are we, from Missouri, with the
        continental blood intervein'd,
All the hands of comrades clasping, all the Southern,
        all the Northern,
    Pioneers! O pioneers!

    O resistless restless race!
O beloved race in all! O my breast aches with tender love
        for all!

O I mourn and yet exult, I am rapt with love for all,
 Pioneers! O pioneers!

 Raise the mighty mother mistress,
Waving high the delicate mistress, over all the starry
  mistress, (bend your heads all,)
Raise the fang'd and warlike mistress, stern, impassive,
  weapon'd mistress,
 Pioneers! O pioneers!

 See my children, resolute children,
By those swarms upon our rear we must never yield
  or falter,
Ages back in ghostly millions frowning there behind us
  urging,
 Pioneers! O pioneers!

 On and on the compact ranks,
With accessions ever waiting, with the places of the dead
  quickly fill'd,
Through the battle, through defeat, moving yet and never
  stopping,
 Pioneers! O pioneers!

 O to die advancing on!
Are there some of us to droop and die? has the hour come?
Then upon the march we fittest die, soon and sure the
  gap is fill'd,
 Pioneers! O pioneers!

 All the pulses of the world,
Falling in they beat for us, with the Western movement
  beat,
Holding single or together, steady moving to the front,
  all for us,
 Pioneers! O pioneers!

 Life's involv'd and varied pageants,
All the forms and shows, all the workmen at their work,

All the seamen and the landsmen, all the masters with
      their slaves,
      Pioneers! O pioneers!

      All the hapless silent lovers,
All the prisoners in the prisons, all the righteous and the
      wicked,
All the joyous, all the sorrowing, all the living, all the
      dying,
      Pioneers! O pioneers!

      I too with my soul and body,
We, a curious trio, picking, wandering on our way,
Through these shores amid the shadows, with the
      apparitions pressing,
      Pioneers! O pioneers!

      Lo, the darting bowling orb!
Lo, the brother orbs around, all the clustering suns and
      planets,
All the dazzling days, all the mystic nights with dreams,
      Pioneers! O pioneers!

      These are of us, they are with us,
All for primal needed work, while the followers there in
      embryo wait behind,
We to-day's procession heading, we the route for travel
      clearing,
      Pioneers! O pioneers!

      O you daughters of the West!
O you young and elder daughters! O you mothers and
      you wives!
Never must you be divided, in our ranks you move united,
      Pioneers! O pioneers!

      Minstrels latent on the prairies!
(Shrouded bards of other lands, you may rest, you have
      done your work,)

Soon I hear you coming warbling, soon you rise and
        tramp amid us,
    Pioneers! O pioneers!

    Not for delectations sweet,
Not the cushion and the slipper, not the peaceful and the
        studious,
Not the riches safe and palling, not for us the tame
        enjoyment,
    Pioneers! O pioneers!

    Do the feasters gluttonous feast?
Do the corpulent sleepers sleep? have they lock'd and
        bolted doors?
Still be ours the diet hard, and the blanket on the ground,
    Pioneers! O pioneers!

    Has the night descended?
Was the road of late so toilsome? did we stop discouraged
        nodding on our way?
Yet a passing hour I yield you in your tracks to pause
        oblivious,
    Pioneers! O pioneers!

    Till with sound of trumpet,
Far, far off the daybreak call—hark! how loud and clear
        I hear it wind,
Swift! to the head of the army!—swift! spring to your places,
    Pioneers! O pioneers!

[1865]

When I Heard the Learn'd Astronomer

When I heard the learn'd astronomer,
When the proofs, the figures, were ranged in columns
    before me,

When I was shown the charts and diagrams, to add, divide,
    and measure them,
When I sitting heard the astronomer where he lectured
    with much applause in the lecture-room,
How soon unaccountable I became tired and sick,
Till rising and gliding out I wander'd off by myself,
In the mystical moist night-air, and from time to time,
Look'd up in perfect silence at the stars.

[1865]

A Farm Picture

Through the ample open door of the peaceful country barn,
A sunlit pasture field with cattle and horses feeding,
And haze and vista, and the far horizon fading away.

[1865]

Drum-Taps

Beat! Beat! Drums!

Beat! beat! drums!—blow! bugles! blow!
Through the windows—through doors—burst like a ruthless
    force,
Into the solemn church, and scatter the congregation,
Into the school where the scholar is studying;
Leave not the bridegroom quiet—no happiness must he
    have now with his bride,
Nor the peaceful farmer any peace, ploughing his field
    or gathering his grain,
So fierce you whirr and pound you drums—so shrill you
    bugles blow.

Beat! beat! drums!—blow! bugles! blow!
Over the traffic of cities—over the rumble of wheels in the
    streets;
Are beds prepared for sleepers at night in the houses?
    no sleepers must sleep in those beds,
No bargainers' bargains by day—no brokers or
    speculators—would they continue?
Would the talkers be talking? would the singer attempt
    to sing?
Would the lawyer rise in the court to state his case before the
    judge?
Then rattle quicker, heavier drums—you bugles wilder blow.

Beat! beat! drums!—blow! bugles! blow!
Make no parley—stop for no expostulation,
Mind not the timid—mind not the weeper or prayer,

Mind not the old man beseeching the young man,
Let not the child's voice be heard, nor the mother's
    entreaties,
Make even the trestles to shake the dead where they lie
    awaiting the hearses,
So strong you thump O terrible drums—so loud you
    bugles blow.

[1861]

City of Ships

City of ships!
(O the black ships! O the fierce ships!
O the beautiful sharp-bow'd steam-ships and sail-ships!)
City of the world! (for all races are here,
All the lands of the earth make contributions here;)
City of the sea! city of hurried and glittering tides!
City whose gleeful tides continually rush or recede,
    whirling in and out with eddies and foam!
City of wharves and stores—city of tall façades of marble
    and iron!
Proud and passionate city—mettlesome, mad, extravagant
    city!
Spring up O city—not for peace alone, but be indeed
    yourself, warlike!
Fear not—submit to no models but your own O city!
Behold me—incarnate me as I have incarnated you!
I have rejected nothing you offer'd me—whom you adopted
    I have adopted,
Good or bad I never question you—I love all—
    I do not condemn any thing,
I chant and celebrate all that is yours—yet peace no more,
In peace I chanted peace, but now the drum of war is mine,
War, red war is my song through your streets, O city!

[1865]

Cavalry Crossing a Ford

A line in long array where they wind betwixt green islands,
They take a serpentine course, their arms flash in the sun—
  hark to the musical clank,
Behold the silvery river, in it the splashing horses loitering
  stop to drink,
Behold the brown-faced men, each group, each person
  a picture, the negligent rest on the saddles,
Some emerge on the opposite bank, others are just
  entering the ford—while,
Scarlet and blue and snowy white,
The guidon flags flutter gayly in the wind.

              [1865]

Bivouac on a Mountain Side

I see before me now a traveling army halting,
Below a fertile valley spread, with barns and the
  orchards of summer,
Behind, the terraced sides of a mountain, abrupt, in
  places rising high,
Broken, with rocks, with clinging cedars, with tall shapes
  dingily seen,
The numerous camp-fires scatter'd near and far, some
  away up on the mountain,
The shadowy forms of men and horses, looming, large-sized,
  flickering,
And over all the sky—the sky! far, far out of reach,
  studded, breaking out, the eternal stars.

              [1865]

An Army Corps on the March

With its cloud of skirmishers in advance,
With now the sound of a single shot snapping like a whip,
    and now an irregular volley,
The swarming ranks press on and on, the dense brigades
    press on,
Glittering dimly, toiling under the sun—the dust-cover'd
    men,
In columns rise and fall to the undulations of the ground,
With artillery interspers'd—the wheels rumble, the
    horses sweat,
As the army corps advances.

[1865–66]

By the Bivouac's Fitful Flame

By the bivouac s fitful flame,
A procession winding around me, solemn and sweet and
    slow—but first I note,
The tents of the sleeping army, the fields' and woods'
    dim outline,
The darkness lit by spots of kindled fire, the silence,
Like a phantom far or near an occasional figure moving,
The shrubs and trees, (as I lift my eyes they seem to be
    stealthily watching me,)
While wind in procession thoughts, O tender and wondrous
    thoughts,
Of life and death, of home and the past and loved, and
    of those that are far away;
A solemn and slow procession there as I sit on the ground,
By the bivouac's fitful flame.

[1865]

Come Up from the Fields Father

Come up from the fields father, here's a letter from
    our Pete,
And come to the front door mother, here's a letter from
    thy dear son.

Lo, 'tis autumn,
Lo, where the trees, deeper green, yellower and redder,
Cool and sweeten Ohio's villages with leaves fluttering in the
    moderate wind,
Where apples ripe in the orchards hang and grapes on
    the trellis'd vines,
(Smell you the smell of the grapes on the vines?
Smell you the buckwheat where the bees were lately
    buzzing?)

Above all, lo, the sky so calm, so transparent after the
    rain, and with wondrous clouds,
Below too, all calm, all vital and beautiful, and the farm
    prospers well.

Down in the fields all prospers well,
But now from the fields come father, come at the
    daughter's call,
And come to the entry mother, to the front door come
    right away.

Fast as she can she hurries, something ominous, her steps
    trembling,
She does not tarry to smooth her hair nor adjust her cap.

Open the envelope quickly,
O this is not our son's writing, yet his name is sign'd,
O a strange hand writes for our dear son, O stricken
    mother's soul!
All swims before her eyes, flashes with black, she catches
    the main words only,
Sentences broken, *gunshot wound in the breast, cavalry
    skirmish, taken to hospital,*
At present low, but will soon be better.

Ah now the single figure to me,
Amid all teeming and wealthy Ohio with all its cities and
     farms,
Sickly white in the face and dull in the head, very faint,
By the jamb of a door leans.

Grieve not so, dear mother, (the just-grown daughter
     speaks through her sobs,
The little sisters huddle around speechless and dismay'd,)
*See, dearest mother, the letter says Pete will soon be
     better.*

Alas poor boy, he will never be better, (nor may-be
     needs to be better, that brave and simple soul,)
While they stand at home at the door he is dead already,
The only son is dead.

But the mother needs to be better,
She with thin form presently drest in black,
By day her meals untouch'd then at night fitfully sleeping,
     often waking,
In the midnight waking, weeping, longing with one deep
     longing,
O that she might withdraw unnoticed, silent from life
     escape and withdraw,
To follow, to seek, to be with her dear dead son.

                                                              [1865]

Vigil Strange I Kept on the Field One Night

Vigil strange I kept on the field one night;
When you my son and my comrade dropt at my side
     that day,
One look I but gave which your dear eyes return'd with
     a look I shall never forget,

One touch of your hand to mine O boy, reach'd up as
    you lay on the ground,
Then onward I sped in the battle, the even-contested battle,
Till late in the night reliev'd to the place at last again
    I made my way,
Found you in death so cold dear comrade, found your
    body son of responding kisses, (never again
    on earth responding,)
Bared your face in the starlight, curious the scene, cool
    blew the moderate night-wind,
Long there and then in vigil I stood, dimly around me
    the battle-field spreading,
Vigil wondrous and vigil sweet there in the fragrant
    silent night,
But not a tear fell, not even a long-drawn sigh, long, long
    I gazed,
Then on the earth partially reclining sat by your side
    leaning my chin in my hands,
Passing sweet hours, immortal and mystic hours with
    you dearest comrade—not a tear, not a word,
Vigil of silence, love and death, vigil for you my son
    and my soldier,
As onward silently stars aloft, eastward new ones upward
    stole,
Vigil final for you brave boy, (I could not save you,
    swift was your death,
I faithfully loved you and cared for you living, I think
    we shall surely meet again,)
Till at latest lingering of the night, indeed just as the
    dawn appear'd,
My comrade I wrapt in his blanket, envelop'd well his form,
Folded the blanket well, tucking it carefully over head
    and carefully under feet,
And there and then and bathed by the rising sun, my son
    in his grave, in his rude-dug grave I deposited,
Ending my vigil strange with that, vigil of night and
    battle-field dim,
Vigil for boy of responding kisses, (never again on earth
    responding,)

Vigil for comrade swiftly slain, vigil I never forget,
    how as day brighten'd,
I rose from the chill ground and folded my soldier
    well in his blanket,
And buried him where he fell.

[1865]

A March in the Ranks Hard-Prest,
and the Road Unknown

A march in the ranks hard-prest, and the road unknown,
A route through a heavy wood with muffled steps in
    the darkness,
Our army foil'd with loss severe, and the sullen remnant
    retreating,
Till after midnight glimmer upon us the lights of a
    dim-lighted building,
We come to an open space in the woods, and halt by
    the dim-lighted building,
'Tis a large old church at the crossing roads, now an
    impromptu hospital,
Entering but for a minute I see a sight beyond all the
    pictures and poems ever made,
Shadows of deepest, deepest black, just lit by moving candles
    and lamps,
And by one great pitchy torch stationary with wild red
    flame and clouds of smoke,
By these, crowds, groups of forms vaguely I see on the
    floor, some in the pews laid down,
At my feet more distinctly a soldier, a mere lad,
    in danger of bleeding to death, (he is shot in the
    abdomen,)
I stanch the blood temporarily, (the youngster's face is
    white as a lily,)
Then before I depart I sweep my eyes o'er the scene
    fain to absorb it all,

Faces, varieties, postures beyond description, most in
    obscurity, some of them dead,
Surgeons operating, attendants holding lights, the smell of
    ether, the odor of blood,
The crowd, O the crowd of the bloody forms, the yard
    outside also fill'd,
Some on the bare ground, some on planks or stretchers,
    some in the death-spasm sweating,
An occasional scream or cry, the doctor's shouted
    orders or calls,
The glisten of the little steel instruments catching the
    glint of the torches,
These I resume as I chant, I see again the forms, I smell
    the odor,
Then hear outside the orders given, *Fall in, my men, fall in;*
But first I bend to the dying lad, his eyes open, a half-smile
    gives he me,
Then the eyes close, calmly close, and I speed forth
    to the darkness,
Resuming, marching, ever in darkness marching,
    on in the ranks,
The unknown road still marching.

[1865]

A Sight in Camp in the Daybreak Gray and Dim

A sight in camp in the daybreak gray and dim,
As from my tent I emerge so early sleepless,
As slow I walk in the cool fresh air the path near by the
    hospital tent,
Three forms I see on stretchers lying, brought out there
    untended lying,
Over each the blanket spread, ample brownish woolen
    blanket,
Gray and heavy blanket, folding, covering all.

Curious I halt and silent stand,
Then with light fingers I from the face of the nearest
     the first just lift the blanket;
Who are you elderly man so gaunt and grim, with well-gray'd
     hair, and flesh all sunken about the eyes?
Who are you my dear comrade?

Then to the second I step—and who are you my child
     and darling?
Who are you sweet boy with cheeks yet blooming?

Then to the third—a face nor child nor old, very calm,
     as of beautiful yellow-white ivory;
Young man I think I know you—I think this face is
     the face of the Christ himself,
Dead and divine and brother of all, and here again he lies.

                                              [1865]

As Toilsome I Wander'd Virginia's Woods

As toilsome I wander'd Virginia's woods,
To the music of rustling leaves kick'd by my feet, (for 'twas
     autumn,)
I mark'd at the foot of a tree the grave of a soldier;
Mortally wounded he and buried on the retreat, (easily
     all could I understand,)
The halt of a mid-day hour, when up! no time to lose—
     yet this sign left,
On a tablet scrawl'd and nail'd on the tree by the grave,
Bold, cautious, true, and my loving comrade.

Long, long I muse, then on my way go wandering,
Many a changeful season to follow, and many a scene of life,
Yet at times through changeful season and scene, abrupt,
     alone, or in the crowded street,

Comes before me the unknown soldier's grave, comes
    the inscription rude in Virginia's woods,
Bold, cautious, true, and my loving comrade.

[1865]

The Wound-Dresser

1

An old man bending I come among new faces,
Years looking backward resuming in answer to children,
Come tell us old man, as from young men and
    maidens that love me,
(Arous'd and angry, I'd thought to beat the alarum, and
    urge relentless war,
But soon my fingers fail'd me, my face droop'd and
    I resign'd myself,
To sit by the wounded and soothe them, or silently watch
    the dead;)
Years hence of these scenes, of these furious passions,
    these chances,
Of unsurpass'd heroes, (was one side so brave? the other
    was equally brave;)
Now be witness again, paint the mightiest armies of earth,
Of those armies so rapid so wondrous what saw
    you to tell us?
What stays with you latest and deepest? of curious panics,
Of hard-fought engagements or sieges tremendous
    what deepest remains?

2

O maidens and young men I love and that love me,
What you ask of my days those the strangest and sudden
    your talking recalls,
Soldier alert I arrive after a long march cover'd with
    sweat and dust,

In the nick of time I come, plunge in the fight, loudly
    shout in the rush of successful charge,
Enter the captur'd works—yet lo, like a swift-running river
    they fade,
Pass and are gone they fade—I dwell not on soldiers'
    perils or soldiers' joys,
(Both I remember well—many the hardships, few the
    joys, yet I was content.)

But in silence, in dreams' projections,
While the world of gain and appearance and mirth
    goes on,
So soon what is over forgotten, and waves wash the
    imprints off the sand,
With hinged knees returning I enter the doors, (while for
    you up there,
Whoever you are, follow without noise and be of
    strong heart.)

Bearing the bandages, water and sponge,
Straight and swift to my wounded I go,
Where they lie on the ground after the battle brought in,
Where their priceless blood reddens the grass the ground,
Or to the rows of the hospital tent, or under the
    roof'd hospital,
To the long rows of cots up and down each side I return,
To each and all one after another I draw near, not
    one do I miss,
An attendant follows holding a tray, he carries a refuse pail,
Soon to be fill'd with clotted rags and blood, emptied,
    and fill'd again.

I onward go, I stop,
With hinged knees and steady hand to dress wounds,
I am firm with each, the pangs are sharp yet unavoidable,
One turns to me his appealing eyes—poor boy! I never
    knew you,
Yet I think I could not refuse this moment to die for
    you, if that would save you.

3

On, on I go, (open doors of time! open hospital doors!)
The crush'd head I dress, (poor crazed hand tear not
    the bandage away,)
The neck of the cavalry-man with the bullet through
    and through I examine,
Hard the breathing rattles, quite glazed already the eye,
    yet life struggles hard,
(Come sweet death! be persuaded O beautiful death!
In mercy come quickly.)

From the stump of the arm, the amputated hand,
I undo the clotted lint, remove the slough, wash off the
    matter and blood,
Back on his pillow the soldier bends with curv'd neck
    and side-falling head,
His eyes are closed, his face is pale, he dares not look on
    the bloody stump,
And has not yet look'd on it.

I dress a wound in the side, deep, deep,
But a day or two more, for see the frame all wasted
    and sinking,
And the yellow-blue countenance see.

I dress the perforated shoulder, the foot with the
    bullet-wound,
Cleanse the one with a gnawing and putrid gangrene,
    so sickening, so offensive,
While the attendant stands behind aside me holding the
    tray and pail.

I am faithful, I do not give out,
The fractur'd thigh, the knee, the wound in the abdomen,
These and more I dress with impassive hand, (yet deep
    in my breast a fire, a burning flame.)

4

Thus in silence in dreams' projections,
Returning, resuming, I thread my way through the
    hospitals,

The hurt and wounded I pacify with soothing hand,
I sit by the restless all the dark night, some are so young,
Some suffer so much, I recall the experience sweet and sad,
 (Many a soldier's loving arms about this neck have
       cross'd and rested,
Many a soldier's kiss dwells on these bearded lips.)

[1865]

Give Me the Splendid Silent Sun

1

Give me the splendid silent sun with all his beams
       full-dazzling,
Give me juicy autumnal fruit ripe and red from the
       orchard,
Give me a field where the unmow'd grass grows,
Give me an arbor, give me the trellis'd grape,
Give me fresh corn and wheat, give me serene-moving
       animals teaching content,
Give me nights perfectly quiet as on high plateaus west
       of the Mississippi, and I looking up at the stars,
Give me odorous at sunrise a garden of beautiful
       flowers where I can walk undisturb'd,
Give me for marriage a sweet-breath'd woman of
       whom I should never tire,
Give me a perfect child, give me away aside from the noise
       of the world a rural domestic life,
Give me to warble spontaneous songs recluse by myself,
       for my own ears only,
Give me solitude, give me Nature, give me again
       O Nature your primal sanities!

These demanding to have them, (tired with ceaseless
       excitement, and rack'd by the war-strife,)
These to procure incessantly asking, rising in cries
       from my heart,

While yet incessantly asking still I adhere to my city,
Day upon day and year upon year O city, walking
    your streets,
Where you hold me enchain'd a certain time refusing to
    give me up,
Yet giving to make me glutted, enrich'd of soul, you
    give me forever faces;
(O I see what I sought to escape, confronting, reversing
    my cries,
I see my own soul trampling down what it ask'd for.)

    2

Keep your splendid silent sun,
Keep your woods O Nature, and the quiet places
    by the woods,
Keep your fields of clover and timothy, and your
    corn-fields and orchards,
Keep the blossoming buckwheat fields where the
    Ninth-month bees hum;
Give me faces and streets—give me these phantoms
    incessant and endless along the trottoirs!
Give me interminable eyes—give me women—give me
    comrades and lovers by the thousand!
Let me see new ones every day—let me hold new
    ones by the hand every day!
Give me such shows—give me the streets of Manhattan!
Give me Broadway, with the soldiers marching—
    give me the sound of the trumpets and drums!
(The soldiers in companies or regiments—some starting
    away, flush'd and reckless,
Some, their time up, returning with thinn'd ranks,
    young, yet very old, worn, marching, noticing nothing;)
Give me the shores and wharves heavy-fringed with
    black ships!
O such for me! O an intense life, full to repletion
    and varied!
The life of the theatre, bar-room, huge hotel, for me!
The saloon of the steamer! the crowded excursion for me!
    the torchlight procession!

The dense brigade bound for the war, with high
    piled military wagons following;
People, endless, streaming, with strong voices,
    passions, pageants,
Manhattan streets with their powerful throbs, with
    beating drums as now,
The endless and noisy chorus, the rustle and clank of
    muskets, (even the sight of the wounded,)
Manhattan crowds, with their turbulent musical chorus!
Manhattan faces and eyes forever for me.

[1865]

Over the Carnage Rose Prophetic a Voice

Over the carnage rose prophetic a voice,
Be not dishearten'd, affection shall solve the problems
    of freedom yet,
Those who love each other shall become invincible,
They shall yet make Columbia victorious.

Sons of the Mother of All, you shall yet be victorious,
You shall yet laugh to scorn the attacks of all the
    remainder of the earth.

No danger shall balk Columbia's lovers,
If need be a thousand shall sternly immolate themselves
    for one.

One from Massachusetts shall be a Missourian's comrade,
From Maine and from hot Carolina, and another an
    Oregonese, shall be friends triune,
More precious to each other than all the riches of the earth.

To Michigan, Florida perfumes shall tenderly come,
Not the perfumes of flowers, but sweeter, and wafted
    beyond death.

It shall be customary in the houses and streets to see
    manly affection,
The most dauntless and rude shall touch face to face lightly,
The dependence of Liberty shall be lovers,
The continuance of Equality shall be comrades.

These shall tie you and band you stronger
    than hoops of iron,
I, ecstatic, O partners! O lands! with the love
    of lovers tie you.

(Were you looking to be held together by lawyers?
Or by an agreement on a paper? or by arms?
Nay, nor the world, nor any living thing, will so cohere.)

                                        [1860]

I Saw Old General at Bay

I saw old General at bay,
(Old as he was, his gray eyes yet shone out in battle
    like stars,)
His small force was now completely hemm'd in,
    in his works,
He call'd for volunteers to run the enemy's lines, a
    desperate emergency,
I saw a hundred and more step forth from the ranks,
    but two or three were selected,
I saw them receive their orders aside, they listen'd with
    care, the adjutant was very grave,
I saw them depart with cheerfulness, freely risking
    their lives.

                                          [1865]

Look Down Fair Moon

Look down fair moon and bathe this scene,
Pour softly down night's nimbus floods on faces ghastly,
    swollen, purple,
On the dead on their backs with arms toss'd wide,
Pour down your unstinted nimbus sacred moon.

[1865]

Reconciliation

Word over all, beautiful as the sky,
Beautiful that war and all its deeds of carnage must
    in time be utterly lost,
That the hands of the sisters Death and Night incessantly
    softly wash again, and ever again, this soil'd world;
For my enemy is dead, a man divine as myself is dead,
I look where he lies white-faced and still in the
    coffin—I draw near,
Bend down and touch lightly with my lips the white face
    in the coffin.

[1865-66]

To a Certain Civilian

Did you ask dulcet rhymes from me?
Did you seek the civilian's peaceful and languishing rhymes?
Did you find what I sang erewhile so hard to follow?
Why I was not singing erewhile for you to follow,
    to understand—nor am I now;
(I have been born of the same as the war was born,
The drum-corps' rattle is ever to me sweet music, I love
    well the martial dirge,

With slow wail and convulsive throb leading the
    officer's funeral;)
What to such as you anyhow such a poet as I? therefore
    leave my works,
And go lull yourself with what you can understand,
    and with piano-tunes,
For I lull nobody, and you will never understand me.

[1865]

When Lilacs Last in the Dooryard Bloom'd

1

When lilacs last in the dooryard bloom'd,
And the great star early droop'd in the western sky in the
    night,
I mourn'd, and yet shall mourn with ever-returning spring,

Ever-returning spring, trinity sure to me you bring,
Lilac blooming perennial and drooping star.in the west,
And thought of him I love.

2

O powerful western fallen star!
O shades of night—O moody, tearful night!
O great star disappear'd—O the black murk that hides
    the star!
O cruel hands that hold me powerless—O helpless soul
    of me!
O harsh surrounding cloud that will not free my soul.

3

In the dooryard fronting an old farm-house near the
    white-wash'd palings,
Stands the lilac-bush tall-growing with heart-shaped leaves
    of rich green,
With many a pointed blossom rising delicate, with the
    perfume strong I love,
With every leaf a miracle—and from this bush in the
    dooryard,
With delicate-color'd blossoms and heart-shaped leaves of
    rich green,
A sprig with its flower I break.

4

In the swamp in secluded recesses,
A shy and hidden bird is warbling a song.

Solitary the thrush,
The hermit withdrawn to himself, avoiding the settlements,
Sings by himself a song.

Song of the bleeding throat,
Death's outlet song of life, (for well dear brother I know,
If thou wast not granted to sing thou would'st surely die.)

5

Over the breast of the spring, the land, amid cities,
Amid lanes and through old woods, where lately the violets
    peep'd from the ground, spotting the gray debris,
Amid the grass in the fields each side of the lanes, passing
    the endless grass,
Passing the yellow-spear'd wheat, every grain from its
    shroud in the dark-brown fields uprisen,
Passing the apple-tree blows of white and pink in the
    orchards,
Carrying a corpse to where it shall rest in the grave,
Night and day journeys a coffin.

6

Coffin that passes through lanes and streets,
Through day and night with the great cloud darkening
    the land,
With the pomp of the inloop'd flags with the cities draped
    in black,
With the show of the States themselves as of crape-veil'd
    women standing,
With processions long and winding and the flambeaus
    of the night,
With the countless torches lit, with the silent sea of faces
    and the unbared heads,
With the waiting depot, the arriving coffin, and the sombre
    faces,
With dirges through the night, with the thousand voices
    rising strong and solemn,
With all the mournful voices of the dirges pour'd around
    the coffin,

The dim-lit churches and the shuddering organs—where
    amid these you journey,
With the tolling tolling bells' perpetual clang,
Here, coffin that slowly passes,
I give you my sprig of lilac.

7

(Nor for you, for one alone,
Blossoms and branches green to coffins all I bring,
For fresh as the morning, thus would I chant a song for you
    O sane and sacred death.

All over bouquets of roses,
O death, I cover you over with roses and early lilies,
But mostly and now the lilac that blooms the first,
Copious I break, I break the sprigs from the bushes,
With loaded arms I come, pouring for you,
For you and the coffins all of you O death.)

8

O western orb sailing the heaven,
Now I know what you must have meant as a month since I
    walk'd,
As I walk'd in silence the transparent shadowy night,
As I saw you had something to tell as you bent to me night
    after night,
As you droop'd from the sky low down as if to my side,
    (while the other stars all look'd on,)
As we wander'd together the solemn night, (for something
    I know not what kept me from sleep,)
As the night advanced, and I saw on the rim of the west
    how full you were of woe,
As I stood on the rising ground in the breeze in the cool
    transparent night,
As I watch'd where you pass'd and was lost in the
    netherward black of the night,
As my soul in its trouble dissatisfied sank, as where you
    sad orb,
Concluded, dropt in the night, and was gone.

9

Sing on there in the swamp,
O singer bashful and tender, I hear your notes, I hear
     your call,
I hear, I come presently, I understand you,
But a moment I linger, for the lustrous star has detain'd me,
The star my departing comrade holds and detains me.

10

O how shall I warble myself for the dead one there I loved?
And how shall I deck my song for the large sweet soul
     that has gone?
And what shall my perfume be for the grave of him I love?

Sea-winds blown from east and west,
Blown from the Eastern sea and blown from the Western
     sea, till there on the prairies meeting,
These and with these and the breath of my chant,
I'll perfume the grave of him I love.

11

O what shall I hang on the chamber walls?
And what shall the pictures be that I hang on the walls,
To adorn the burial-house of him I love?

Pictures of growing spring and farms and homes,
With the Fourth-month eve at sundown, and the gray
     smoke lucid and bright,
With floods of the yellow gold of the gorgeous, indolent,
     sinking sun, burning, expanding the air,
With the fresh sweet herbage under foot, and the pale green
     leaves of the trees prolific,
In the distance the flowing glaze, the breast of the river,
     with a wind-dapple here and there,
With ranging hills on the banks, with many a line against
     the sky, and shadows,
And the city at hand with dwellings so dense, and stacks of
     chimneys,
And all the scenes of life and the workshops, and the
     workmen homeward returning.

12

Lo, body and soul—this land,
My own Manhattan with spires, and the sparkling and
    hurrying tides, and the ships,
The varied and ample land, the South and the North in the
    light, Ohio's shores and flashing Missouri,
And ever the far-spreading prairies cover'd with grass
    and corn.

Lo, the most excellent sun so calm and haughty,
The violet and purple morn with just-felt breezes,
The gentle soft-born measureless light,
The miracle spreading bathing all, the fulfill'd noon,
The coming eve delicious, the welcome night and the stars,
Over my cities shining all, enveloping man and land.

13

Sing on, sing on you gray-brown bird,
Sing from the swamps, the recesses, pour your chant from
    the bushes,
Limitless out of the dusk, out of the cedars and pines.

Sing on dearest brother, warble your reedy song,
Loud human song, with voice of uttermost woe,

O liquid and free and tender!
O wild and loose to my soul—O wondrous singer!
You only I hear—yet the star holds me, (but will soon
    depart,)
Yet the lilac with mastering odor holds me.

14

Now while I sat in the day and look'd forth,
In the close of the day with its light and the fields of spring,
    and the farmers preparing their crops,
In the large unconscious scenery of my land with its lakes
    and forests,
In the heavenly aerial beauty, (after the perturb'd winds
    and the storms,)

Under the arching heavens of the afternoon swift passing,
    and the voices of children and women,
The many-moving sea-tides, and I saw the ships how they
    sail'd,
And the summer approaching with richness, and the fields
    all busy with labor,
And the infinite separate houses, how they all went on,
    each with its meals and minutia of daily usages,
And the streets how their throbbings throbb'd, and the
    cities pent—lo, then and there,
Falling upon them all and among them all, enveloping me
    with the rest,
Appear'd the cloud, appear'd the long black trail,
And I knew death, its thought, and the sacred knowledge
    of death.

Then with the knowledge of death as walking one side of me,
And the thought of death close-walking the other side of me,
And I in the middle as with companions, and as holding
    the hands of companions,
I fled forth to the hiding receiving night that talks not,
Down to the shores of the water, the path by the swamp
    in the dimness,
To the solemn shadowy cedars and ghostly pines so still.

And the singer so shy to the rest receiv'd me,
The gray-brown bird I know receiv'd us comrades three,
And he sang the carol of death, and a verse for him I love.

From deep secluded recesses,
From the fragrant cedars and the ghostly pines so still,
Came the carol of the bird.

And the charm of the carol rapt me,
As I held as if by their hands my comrades in the night,
And the voice of my spirit tallied the song of the bird.

Come lovely and soothing death,
Undulate round the world, serenely arriving, arriving,

WHEN LILACS LAST IN THE DOORYARD BLOOM'D   241

In the day, in the night, to all, to each,
Sooner or later delicate death.

Prais'd be the fathomless universe,
For life and joy, and for objects and knowledge curious,
And for love, sweet love—but praise! praise! praise!
For the sure-enwinding arms of cool-enfolding death.

Dark mother always gliding near with soft feet,
Have none chanted for thee a chant of fullest welcome?
Then I chant it for thee, I glorify thee above all,
I bring thee a song that when thou must indeed come,
*   come unfalteringly.*

Approach strong deliveress,
When it is so, when thou hast taken them I joyously sing
*   the dead,*
Lost in the loving floating ocean of thee,
Laved in the flood of thy bliss O death.

From me to thee glad serenades,
Dances for thee I propose saluting thee, adornments and
*   feastings for thee,*
And the sights of the open landscape and the high-spread
*   sky are fitting,*
And life and the fields, and the huge and thoughtful night.

The night in silence under many a star,
The ocean shore and the husky whispering wave whose
*   voice I know,*
And the soul turning to thee O vast and well-veil'd death,
And the body gratefully nestling close to thee.

Over the tree-tops I float thee a song,
Over the rising and sinking waves, over the myriad fields
*   and the prairies wide,*
Over the dense-pack'd cities all and the teeming wharves
*   and ways,*
I float this carol with joy, with joy to thee O death.

15

To the tally of my soul,
Loud and strong kept up the gray-brown bird,
With pure deliberate notes spreading filling the night.

Loud in the pines and cedars dim,
Clear in the freshness moist and the swamp-perfume,
And I with my comrades there in the night.

While my sight that was bound in my eyes unclosed,
As to long panoramas of visions.

And I saw askant the armies,
I saw as in noiseless dreams hundreds of battle-flags,
Borne through the smoke of the battles and pierc'd with
        missiles I saw them,
And carried hither and yon through the smoke, and torn
        and bloody,
And at last but a few shreds left on the staffs, (and all in
        silence,)
And the staffs all splinter'd and broken.

I saw battle-corpses, myriads of them,
And the white skeletons of young men, I saw them,
I saw the debris and debris of all the slain soldiers of the war,
But I saw they were not as was thought,
They themselves were fully at rest, they suffer'd not,
The living remain'd and suffer'd, the mother suffer'd,
And the wife and the child and the musing comrade suffer'd,
And the armies that remain'd suffer'd.

16

Passing the visions, passing the night,
Passing, unloosing the hold of my comrades' hands,
Passing the song of the hermit bird and the tallying song
        of my soul,
Victorious song, death's outlet song, yet varying
        ever-altering song,

As low and wailing, yet clear the notes, rising and falling,
 flooding the night,
Sadly sinking and fainting, as warning and warning, and
 yet again bursting with joy,
Covering the earth and filling the spread of the heaven,
As that powerful psalm in the night I heard from recesses,
Passing, I leave thee lilac with heart-shaped leaves,
I leave thee there in the door-yard, blooming, returning
 with spring.

I cease from my song for thee,
From my gaze on thee in the west, fronting the west,
 communing with thee,
O comrade lustrous with silver face in the night.

Yet each to keep and all, retrievements out of the night,
The song, the wondrous chant of the gray-brown bird,
And the tallying chant, the echo arous'd in my soul,
With the lustrous and drooping star with the countenance
 full of woe,
With the holders holding my hand nearing the call of
 the bird,
Comrades mine and I in the midst, and their memory ever
 to keep, for the dead I loved so well,
For the sweetest, wisest soul of all my days and lands—and
 this for his dear sake,
Lilac and star and bird twined with the chant of my soul,
There in the fragrant pines and the cedars dusk and dim.

[1865-66]

O Captain! My Captain!

O Captain! my Captain! our fearful trip is done,
The ship has weather'd every rack, the prize we sought
 is won,
The port is near, the bells I hear, the people all exulting,

While follow eyes the steady keel, the vessel grim and daring;
    But O heart! heart! heart!
        O the bleeding drops of red,
           Where on the deck my Captain lies,
              Fallen cold and dead.

O Captain! my Captain! rise up and hear the bells;
Rise up—for you the flag is flung—for you the bugle trills,
For you bouquets and ribbon'd wreaths—for you the
    shores a-crowding,
For you they call, the swaying mass, their eager faces turning;
        Here Captain! dear father!
           This arm beneath your head!
             It is some dream that on the deck,
              You've fallen cold and dead.

My Captain does not answer, his lips are pale and still,
My father does not feel my arm, he has no pulse nor will,
The ship is anchor'd safe and sound, its voyage closed
    and done,
From fearful trip the victor ship comes in with object won;
        Exult O shores, and ring O bells!
           But I with mournful tread,
             Walk the deck my Captain lies,
              Fallen cold and dead.

                            [1865-66]

Old War-Dreams

In midnight sleep of many a face of anguish,
Of the look at first of the mortally wounded, (of that
    indescribable look,)
Of the dead on their backs with arms extended wide,
    I dream, I dream, I dream.

Of scenes of Nature, fields and mountains,
Of skies so beauteous after a storm, and at night the moon
    so unearthly bright,
Shining sweetly, shining down, where we dig the trenches
    and gather the heaps,
    I dream, I dream, I dream.

Long have they pass'd, faces and trenches and fields,
Where through the carnage I moved with a callous
    composure, or away from the fallen,
Onward I sped at the time—but now of their forms at night,
    I dream, I dream, I dream.

[1865-66]

Years of the Modern

Years of the modern! years of the unperform'd!
Your horizon rises, I see it parting away for more august
    dramas,
I see not America only, not only Liberty's nation but other
    nations preparing,
I see tremendous entrances and exits, new combinations,
    the solidarity of races,
I see that force advancing with irresistible power on the
    world's stage,
(Have the old forces, the old wars, played their parts? are
    the acts suitable to them closed?)
I see Freedom, completely arm'd and victorious and very
    haughty, with Law on one side and Peace on the other,
A stupendous trio all issuing forth against the idea of caste;
What historic denouements are these we so rapidly
    approach?
I see men marching and countermarching by swift millions,
I see the frontiers and boundaries of the old aristocracies
    broken,

I see the landmarks of European kings removed,
I see this day the People beginning their landmarks, (all
    others give way;)
Never were such sharp questions ask'd as this day,
Never was average man, his soul, more energetic, more
    like a God,
Lo, how he urges and urges, leaving the masses no rest!
His daring foot is on land and sea everywhere, he colonizes
    the Pacific, the archipelagoes,
With the steamship, the electric telegraph, the newspaper,
    the wholesale engines of war,
With these and the world-spreading factories he interlinks
    all geography, all lands;
What whispers are these O lands, running ahead of you,
    passing under the seas?
Are all nations communing? is there going to be
    but one heart to the globe?
Is humanity forming en-masse for lo, tyrants tremble,
    crowns grow dim,
The earth, restive, confronts a new era, perhaps a general
    divine war,
No one knows what will happen next, such portents fill the
    days and nights;
Years prophetical! the space ahead as I walk, as I vainly
    try to pierce it, is full of phantoms,
Unborn deeds, things soon to be, project their shapes
    around me,
This incredible rush and heat, this strange ecstatic fever of
    dreams O years!
Your dreams O years, how they penetrate through me!
    (I know not whether I sleep or wake;)
The perform'd America and Europe grow dim, retiring in
    shadow behind me,
The unperform'd, more gigantic than ever, advance,
    advance upon me.

[1865]

Ashes of Soldiers

Ashes of soldiers South or North,
As I muse retrospective murmuring a chant in thought,
The war resumes, again to my sense your shapes,
And again the advance of the armies.

Noiseless as mists and vapors,
From their graves in the trenches ascending,
From cemeteries all through Virginia and Tennessee,
From every point of the compass out of the countless graves,
In wafted clouds, in myriads large, or squads of twos or
    threes or single ones they come,
And silently gather round me.

Now sound no note O trumpeters,
Not at the head of my cavalry parading on spirited horses,
With sabres drawn and glistening, and carbines by their thighs,
    (ah my brave horsemen!
My handsome tan-faced horsemen! what life, what joy and
    pride,
With all the perils were yours.)

Nor you drummers, neither at reveillé at dawn,
Nor the long roll alarming the camp, nor even the muffled beat
    for a burial,
Nothing from you this time O drummers bearing my warlike
    drums.

But aside from these and the marts of wealth and the crowded
    promenade,
Admitting around me comrades close unseen by the rest and
    voiceless,
The slain elate and alive again, the dust and debris alive,
I chant this chant of my silent soul in the name of all dead
    soldiers.

Faces so pale with wondrous eyes, very dear, gather closer yet,
Draw close, but speak not.

Phantoms of countless lost,
Invisible to the rest henceforth become my companions,
Follow me ever—desert me not while I live.

Sweet are the blooming cheeks of the living—sweet are the
    musical voices sounding,
But sweet, ah sweet, are the dead with their silent eyes.

Dearest comrades, all is over and long gone,
But love is not over— and what love, O comrades!
Perfume from battle-fields rising, up from the fœtor arising.

Perfume therefore my chant, O love, immortal love,
Give me to bathe the memories of all dead soldiers,
Shroud them, embalm them, cover them all over with tender
    pride.

Perfume all—make all wholesome,
Make these ashes to nourish and blossom,
O love, solve all, fructify all with the last chemistry.

Give me exhaustless, make me a fountain,
That I exhale love from me wherever I go like a moist
    perennial dew,
For the ashes of all dead soldiers South or North.

[1865]

Pensive on Her Dead Gazing

Pensive on her dead gazing I heard the Mother of All,
Desperate on the torn bodies, on the forms covering the
    battle-fields gazing,
(As the last gun ceased, but the scent of the powder-smoke
    linger'd,)
As she call'd to her earth with mournful voice while she
    stalk'd,

Absorb them well O my earth, she cried, I charge you
    lose not my sons, lose not an atom,
And you streams absorb them well, taking their dear blood,
And you local spots, and you airs that swim above lightly
    impalpable,
And all you essences of soil and growth, and you my
    rivers' depths,
And you mountain sides, and the woods where my
    dear children's blood trickling redden'd,
And your trees down in your roots to bequeath to all
    future trees,
My dead absorb or South or North—my young men's bodies
    absorb, and their precious precious blood,
Which holding in trust for me faithfully back again give me
    many a year hence,
In unseen essence and odor of surface and grass, centuries
    hence,
In blowing airs from the fields back again give me my
    darlings, give my immortal heroes,
Exhale me them centuries hence, breathe me their breath,
    let not an atom be lost,
O years and graves! O air and soil! O my dead,
    an aroma sweet!
Exhale them perennial sweet death, years, centuries hence.

[1865]

Shut Not Your Doors

Shut not your doors to me proud libraries,
For that which was lacking on all your well-fill'd shelves,
    yet needed most, I bring,
Forth from the war emerging, a book I have made,
The words of my book nothing, the drift of it every thing,
A book separate, not link'd with the rest nor felt by the
    intellect,
But you ye untold latencies will thrill to every page.

[1865]

Chanting the Square Deific

1

Chanting the square deific, out of the One advancing,
    out of the sides,
Out of the old and new, out of the square entirely divine,
Solid, four-sided, (all the sides needed,) from this side
    Jehovah am I,
Old Brahm I, and I Saturnius am;
Not Time affects me—I am Time, old, modern as any,
Unpersuadable, relentless, executing righteous judgments,
As the Earth, the Father, the brown old Kronos, with laws,
Aged beyond computation, yet ever new, ever with those
    mighty laws rolling,
Relentless I forgive no man—whoever sins dies—I will
    have that man's life;
Therefore let none expect mercy—have the seasons,
    gravitation, the appointed days, mercy? no more
    have I,
But as the seasons and gravitation, and as all the appointed
    days that forgive not,
I dispense from this side judgments inexorable without
    the least remorse.

2

Consolator most mild, the promis'd one advancing,
With gentle hand extended, the mightier God am I,
Foretold by prophets and poets in their most rapt
    prophecies and poems,
From this side, lo! the Lord Christ gazes—lo! Hermes
    I—lo! mine is Hercules' face,
All sorrow, labor, suffering, I, tallying it, absorb in myself,
Many times have I been rejected, taunted, put in prison,
    and crucified, and many times shall be again,
All the world have I given up for my dear brothers' and
    sisters' sake, for the soul's sake,
Wending my way through the homes of men, rich or
    poor, with the kiss of affection,

For I am affection, I am the cheer-bringing God,
    with hope and all-enclosing charity,
With indulgent words as to children, with fresh and
    sane words, mine only,
Young and strong I pass knowing well I am destin'd
    myself to an early death;
But my charity has no death—my wisdom dies not, neither
    early nor late,
And my sweet love bequeath'd here and elsewhere
    never dies.

    3

Aloof, dissatisfied, plotting revolt,
Comrade of criminals, brother of slaves,
Crafty, despised, a drudge, ignorant,
With sudra face and worn brow, black, but in the depths
    of my heart, proud as any,
Lifted now and always against whoever scorning assumes
    to rule me,
Morose, full of guile, full of reminiscences, brooding,
    with many wiles,
(Though it was thought I was baffled and dispel'd,
    and my wiles done, but that will never be,)
Defiant, I, Satan, still live, still utter words, in new
    lands duly appearing, (and old ones also,)
Permanent here from my side, warlike, equal with any,
    real as any,
Nor time nor change shall ever change me or my words.

    4

Santa Spirita, breather, life,
Beyond the light, lighter than light,
Beyond the flames of hell, joyous, leaping easily above hell,
Beyond Paradise, perfumed solely with mine own perfume,
Including all life on earth, touching, including God,
    including Saviour and Satan,
Beyond the flames of hell, joyous, leaping easily above hell,
    what were God?)

Essence of forms, life of the real identities, permanent,
    positive, (namely the unseen),
Life of the great round world, the sun and stars, and of man,
    I, the general soul,
Here the square finishing, the solid, I the most solid,
Breathe my breath also through these songs.

                                           [1865–66]

One's-Self I Sing

One's-Self I sing, a simple separate person,
Yet utter the word Democratic, the word En-Masse.

Of physiology from top to toe I sing,
Not physiognomy alone nor brain alone is worthy for
    the Muse, I say the Form complete is worthier far,
The Female equally with the Male I sing.

Of Life immense in passion, pulse, and power,
Cheerful, for freest action form'd under the laws divine,
The Modern Man I sing.

                                           [1867]

Tears

Tears! tears! tears!
In the night, in solitude, tears,
On the white shore dripping, dripping, suck'd in by the sand,
Tears, not a star shining, all dark and desolate,
Moist tears from the eyes of a muffled head;
O who is that ghost? that form in the dark, with tears?
What shapeless lump is that, bent, crouch'd there on
    the sand?

Streaming tears, sobbing tears, throes, choked with
    wild cries;
O storm, embodied, rising, careering with swift steps
    along the beach!
O wild and dismal night storm, with wind—O belching and
    desperate!
O shade so sedate and decorous by day, with calm
    countenance and regulated pace,
But away at night as you fly, none looking—O then the
    unloosen'd ocean,
Of tears! tears! tears!

[1867]

Aboard at a Ship's Helm

Aboard at a ship's helm,
A young steersman steering with care.

Through fog on a sea-coast dolefully ringing,
An ocean-bell—O a warning bell, rock'd by the waves.

O you give good notice indeed, you bell by the sea-reefs
    ringing,
Ringing, ringing, to warn the ship from its wreck-place.

For as on the alert O steersman, you mind the loud
    admonition,
The bows turn, the freighted ship tacking speeds away
    under her gray sails,
The beautiful and noble ship with all her precious wealth
    speeds away gayly and safe.

But O the ship, the immortal ship! O ship aboard the ship!
Ship of the body, ship of the soul, voyaging, voyaging,
    voyaging.

[1867]

The Runner

On a flat road runs the well-train'd runner,
He is lean and sinewy with muscular legs,
He is thinly clothed, he leans forward as he runs,
With lightly closed fists and arms partially rais'd.

[1867]

A Noiseless Patient Spider

A noiseless patient spider,
I mark'd where on a little promontory it stood isolated,
Mark'd how to explore the vacant vast surrounding,
It launch'd forth filament, filament, filament, out of itself,
Ever unreeling them, ever tirelessly speeding them.

And you O my soul where you stand,
Surrounded, detached, in measureless oceans of space,
Ceaselessly musing, venturing, throwing, seeking the
    spheres to connect them,
Till the bridge you will need be form'd, till the ductile
    anchor hold,
Till the gossamer thread you fling catch somewhere,
    O my soul.

[1868]

The Last Invocation

At the last, tenderly,
From the walls of the powerful fortress'd house,
From the clasp of the knitted locks, from the keep of the
    well-closed doors,
Let me be wafted.

Let me glide noiselessly forth;
With the key of softness unlock the locks—with a whisper,
Set ope the doors O soul.

Tenderly—be not impatient,
(Strong is your hold O mortal flesh,
Strong is your hold O love.)

[1868]

Proud Music of the Storm

1

Proud music of the storm,
Blast that careers so free, whistling across the prairies,
Strong hum of forest tree-tops—wind of the mountains,
Personified dim shapes—you hidden orchestras,
You serenades of phantoms with instruments alert,
Blending with Nature's rhythmus all the tongues of nations;
You chords left as by vast composers—you choruses,
You formless, free, religious dances—you from the Orient,
You undertone of rivers, roar of pouring cataracts,
You sounds from distant guns with galloping cavalry,
Echoes of camps with all the different bugle-calls,
Trooping tumultuous, filling the midnight late, bending me
    powerless,
Entering my lonesome slumber-chamber, why have you
    seiz'd me?

2

Come forward O my soul, and let the rest retire,
Listen, lose not, it is toward thee they tend,
Parting the midnight, entering my slumber-chamber,
For thee they sing and dance O soul.

A festival song,
The duet of the bridegroom and the bride, a marriage-march,

With lips of love, and hearts of lovers fill'd to the brim
    with love,
The red-flush'd cheeks and perfumes, the cortege swarming
    full of friendly faces young and old,
To flutes' clear notes and sounding harps' cantabile.

Now loud approaching drums,
Victoria! see'st thou in powder-smoke the banners torn
    but flying? the rout of the baffled?
Hearest those shouts of a conquering army?

(Ah soul, the sobs of women, the wounded groaning in agony,
The hiss and crackle of flames, the blacken'd ruins, the
    embers of cities,
The dirge and desolation of mankind.)

Now airs antique and mediæval fill me,
I see and hear old harpers with their harps at Welsh festivals,
I hear the minnesingers singing their lays of love,
I hear the minstrels, gleemen, troubadours, of the middle
    ages.

Now the great organ sounds,
Tremulous, while underneath, (as the hid footholds of
    the earth,
On which arising rest, and leaping forth depend,
All shapes of beauty, grace and strength, all hues
    we know,
Green blades of grass and warbling birds, children that
    gambol and play, the clouds of heaven above,)
The strong base stands, and its pulsations intermits not,
Bathing, supporting, merging all the rest, maternity of
    all the rest,
And with it every instrument in multitudes,
The players playing, all the world's musicians,
The solemn hymns and masses rousing adoration,
All passionate heart-chants, sorrowful appeals,
The measureless sweet vocalists of ages,
And for their solvent setting earth's own diapason,

Of winds and woods and mighty ocean waves,
A new composite orchestra, binder of years and climes,
　　ten-fold renewer,
As of the far-back days the poets tell, the Paradiso,
The straying thence, the separation long, but now the
　　wandering done,
The journey done, the journeyman come home,
And man and art with Nature fused again.

Tutti! for earth and heaven;
(The Almighty leader now for once has signal'd with
　　his wand.)

The manly strophe of the husbands of the world,
And all the wives responding.

The tongues of violins,
(I think O tongues ye tell this heart, that cannot tell itself,
This brooding yearning heart, that cannot tell itself.)

3

Ah from a little child,
Thou knowest soul how to me all sounds became music,
My mother's voice in lullaby or hymn,
(The voice, O tender voices, memory's loving voices,
Last miracle of all, O dearest mother's, sister's, voices;)
The rain, the growing corn, the breeze among the
　　long-leav'd corn,
The measur'd sea-surf beating on the sand,
The twittering bird, the hawk's sharp scream,
The wild-fowl's notes at night as flying low migrating north
　　or south,
The psalm in the country church or mid the clustering trees,
　　the open air camp-meeting,
The fiddler in the tavern, the glee, the long-strung
　　sailor-song,
The lowing cattle, bleating sheep, the crowing cock at dawn.

All songs of current lands come sounding round me,
The German airs of friendship, wine and love,

Irish ballads, merry jigs and dances, English warbles,
Chansons of France, Scotch tunes, and o'er the rest,
Italia's peerless compositions.

Across the stage with pallor on her face, yet lurid passion,
Stalks Norma brandishing the dagger in her hand.

I see poor crazed Lucia's eyes' unnatural gleam,
Her hair down her back falls loose and dishevel'd.

I see where Ernani walking the bridal garden,
Amid the scent of night-roses, radiant, holding his bride
     by the hand,
Hears the infernal call, the death-pledge of the horn.

To crossing swords and gray hairs bared to heaven,
The clear electric base and baritone of the world,
The trombone duo, Libertad forever!
From Spanish chestnut trees' dense shade,
By old and heavy convent walls a wailing song,
Song of lost love, the torch of youth and life quench'd
     in despair,
Song of the dying swan, Fernando's heart is breaking.

Awaking from her woes at last retriev'd Amina sings,
Copious as stars and glad as morning light the torrents
     of her joy.

(The teeming lady comes,
The lustrious orb, Venus contralto, the blooming mother,
Sister of loftiest gods, Alboni's self I hear.)

        4

I hear those odes, symphonies, operas,
I hear in the *William Tell* the music of an arous'd
     and angry people.
I hear Meyerbeer's *Huguenots*, the *Prophet*, or *Robert*,
Gounod's *Faust*, or Mozart's *Don Juan*.

I hear the dance-music of all nations,
The waltz, some delicious measure, lapsing, bathing
    me in bliss,
The bolero to tinkling guitars and clattering castanets.

I see religious dances old and new,
I hear the sound of the Hebrew lyre,
I see the crusaders marching bearing the cross on high,
    to the martial clang of cymbals,
I hear dervishes monotonously chanting, interspers'd,
    with frantic shouts, as they spin around turning always
    towards Mecca,
I see the rapt religious dances of the Persians and the Arabs,
Again, at Eleusis, home of Ceres, I see the modern
    Greeks dancing,
I hear them clapping their hands as they bend their bodies,
I hear the metrical shuffling of their feet.

I see again the wild old Corybantian dance, the
    performers wounding each other,
I see the Roman youth to the shrill sound of flageolets
    throwing and catching their weapons,
As they fall on their knees and rise again.

I hear from the Mussulman mosque the muezzin calling,
I see the worshippers within, nor form nor sermon,
    argument nor word,
But silent, strange, devout, rais'd, glowing heads,
    ecstatic faces.

I hear the Egyptian harp of many strings,
The primitive chants of the Nile boatmen,
The sacred imperial hymns of China,
To the delicate sounds of the king, (the stricken wood
    and stone,)
Or to Hindu flutes and the fretting twang of the vina,
A band of bayaderes.

5

Now Asia, Africa leave me, Europe seizing inflates me,
To organs huge and bands I hear as from vast
    concourses of voices,
Luther's strong hymn *Eine feste Burg ist unser Gott*,
Rossini's *Stabat Mater dolorosa*,
Or floating in some high cathedral dim with gorgeous
    color'd windows,
The passionate *Agnus Dei* or *Gloria in Excelsis*.

Composers! mighty maestros!
And you, sweet singers of old lands, soprani, tenori, bassi!
To you a new bard caroling in the West,
Obeisant sends his love.

(Such led to thee O soul,
All senses, shows and objects, lead to thee,
But now it seems to me sound leads o'er all the rest.)

I hear the annual singing of the children in
    St. Paul's cathedral,
Or, under the high roof of some colossal hall, the
    symphonies, oratorios of Beethoven, Handel, or Haydn,
The *Creation* in billows of godhood laves me.

Give me to hold all sounds, (I madly struggling cry,)
Fill me with all the voices of the universe,
Endow me with their throbbings, Nature's also,
The tempests, waters, winds, operas and chants, marches
    and dances,
Utter, pour in, for I would take them all!

6

Then I woke softly,
And pausing, questioning awhile the music of my dream,
And questioning all those reminiscences, the tempest
    in its fury,
And all the songs of sopranos and tenors,
And those rapt oriental dances of religious fervor,

And the sweet varied instruments, and the diapason
    of organs,
And all the artless plaints of love and grief and death,
I said to my silent curious soul out of the bed of
    the slumber-chamber,
Come, for I have found the clew I sought so long,
Let us go forth refresh'd amid the day,
Cheerfully tallying life, walking the world, the real,
Nourish'd henceforth by our celestial dream.

And I said, moreover,
Haply what thou hast heard O soul was not the sound
    of winds,
Nor dream of raging storm, nor sea-hawk's flapping
    wings nor harsh scream,
Nor vocalism of sun-bright Italy,
Nor German organ majestic, nor vast concourse of
    voices, nor layers of harmonies,
Nor strophes of husbands and wives, nor sound of
    marching soldiers,
Nor flutes, nor harps, nor the bugle-calls of camps,
But to a new rhythmus fitted for thee,
Poems bridging the way from Life to Death, vaguely wafted
    in night air, uncaught, unwritten,
Which let us go forth in the bold day and write.

[1869]

The Base of All Metaphysics

And now gentlemen,
A word I give to remain in your memories and minds,
As base and finalè too for all metaphysics.

(So to the students the old professor,
At the close of his crowded course.)

Having studied the new and antique, the Greek and Germanic
    systems,

Kant having studied and stated, Fichte and Schelling and Hegel,
Stated the lore of Plato, and Socrates greater than Plato,
And greater than Socrates sought and stated, Christ divine
    having studied long,
I see reminiscent to-day those Greek and Germanic systems,
See the philosophies all, Christian churches and tenets see,
Yet underneath Socrates clearly see, and underneath
    Christ the divine I see,
The dear love of man for his comrade, the attraction of friend
    to friend,
Of the well-married husband and wife, of children and parents,
Of city for city and land for land.

[1871]

Song of the Exposition

1

(Ah little recks the laborer,
How near his work is holding him to God,
The loving Laborer through space and time.)

After all not to create only, or found only,
But to bring perhaps from afar what is already founded,
To give it our own identity, average, limitless, free,
To fill the gross the torpid bulk with vital religious fire,
Not to repel or destroy so much as accept, fuse, rehabilitate,
To obey as well as command, to follow more than to lead,
These also are the lessons of our New World;
While how little the New after all, how much the Old,
    Old World!

Long and long has the grass been growing,
Long and long has the rain been falling,
Long has the globe been rolling round.

2

Come Muse migrate from Greece and Ionia,
Cross out please those immensely overpaid accounts,

That matter of Troy and Achilles' wrath, and Æneas',
    Odysseus' wanderings,
Placard "Removed" and "To Let" on the rocks of
    your snowy Parnassus,
Repeat at Jerusalem, place the notice high on Jaffa's gate
    and on Mount Moriah,
The same on the walls of your German, French and
    Spanish castles, and Italian collections,
For know a better, fresher, busier sphere, a wide, untried
    domain awaits, demands you.

3

Responsive to our summons,
Or rather to her long-nurs'd inclination,
Join'd with an irresistible, natural gravitation,
She comes! I hear the rustling of her gown,
I scent the odor of her breath's delicious fragrance,
I mark her step divine, her curious eyes a-turning, rolling,
Upon this very scene.

The dame of dames! can I believe then,
Those ancient temples, sculptures classic, could none
    of them retain her?
Nor shades of Virgil and Dante, nor myriad memories,
    poems, old associations, magnetize and hold on to her?
But that she's left them all—and here?

Yes, if you will allow me to say so,
I, my friends, if you do not, can plainly see her,
The same undying soul of earth's, activity's, beauty's,
    heroism's expression,
Out from her evolutions hither come, ended the strata
    of her former themes,
Hidden and cover'd by to-day's, foundation of to-day's,
Ended, deceas'd through time, her voice by
    Castaly's fountain,
Silent the broken-lipp'd Sphynx in Egypt, silent all those
    century-baffling tombs,

Ended for aye the epics of Asia's, Europe's helmeted
    warriors, ended the primitive call of the muses,
Calliope's call forever closed, Clio, Melpomene, Thalia dead,
Ended the stately rhythmus of Una and Oriana, ended
    the quest of the holy Graal,
Jerusalem a handful of ashes blown by the wind, extinct,
The Crusaders' streams of shadowy midnight troops
    sped with the sunrise,
Amadis, Tancred, utterly gone, Charlemagne, Roland,
    Oliver gone,
Palmerin, ogre, departed, vanish'd the turrets that Usk
    from its waters reflected,
Arthur vanish'd with all his knights, Merlin and Lancelot and
    Galahad, all gone, dissolv'd utterly like an exhalation;
Pass'd! pass'd! for us, forever pass'd, that once so
    mighty world, now void, inanimate, phantom world,
Embroider'd, dazzling, foreign world, with all its gorgeous
    legends, myths,
Its kings and castles proud, its priests and warlike
    lords and courtly dames,
Pass'd to its charnel vault, coffin'd with crown and armor on,
Blazon'd with Shakspere's purple page,
And dirged by Tennyson's sweet sad rhyme.

I say I see, my friends, if you do not, the illustrious emigré,
    (having it is true in her day, although the same,
    changed, journey'd considerable,)
Making directly for this rendezvous, vigorously clearing
    a path for herself, striding through the confusion,
By thud of machinery and shrill steam-whistle undismay'd,
Bluff'd not a bit by drain-pipe, gasometers,
    artificial fertilizers,
Smiling and pleas'd with palpable intent to stay,
She's here, install'd amid the kitchen ware!

4

But hold—don't I forget my manners?
To introduce the stranger, (what else indeed do I live
    to chant for?) to thee Columbia;

In liberty's name welcome immortal! clasp hands,
And ever henceforth sisters dear be both.

Fear not O Muse! truly new ways and days receive,
    surround you,
I candidly confess a queer, queer race, of novel fashion,
And yet the same old human race, the same within, without,
Faces and hearts the same, feelings the same, yearnings
    the same,
The same old love, beauty and use the same.

5

We do not blame thee elder World, nor really separate
    ourselves from thee,
(Would the son separate himself from the father?)
Looking back on thee, seeing thee to thy duties,
    grandeurs, through past ages bending, building,
We build to ours to-day.

Mightier than Egypt's tombs,
Fairer than Grecia's, Roma's temples,
Prouder than Milan's statued, spired cathedral,
More picturesque than Rhenish castle-keeps,
We plan even now to raise, beyond them all,
Thy great cathedral sacred industry, no tomb,
A keep for life for practical invention.

As in a waking vision,
E'en while I chant I see it rise, I scan and prophesy
    outside and in,
Its manifold ensemble.

Around a palace, loftier, fairer, ampler than any yet,
Earth's modern wonder, history's seven outstripping,
High rising tier on tier with glass and iron façades,
Gladdening the sun and sky, enhued in cheerfulest hues,
Bronze, lilac, robin's-egg, marine and crimson,
Over whose golden roof shall flaunt, beneath thy
    banner Freedom,

The banners of the States and flags of every land,
A brood of lofty, fair, but lesser palaces shall cluster.

Somewhere within their walls shall all that forwards
    perfect human life be started,
Tried, taught, advanced, visibly exhibited.

Not only all the world of works, trade, products,
But all the workmen of the world here to be represented.

Here shall you trace in flowing operation,
In every state of practical, busy movement, the rills
    of civilization,
Materials here under your eye shall change their
    shape as if by magic,
The cotton shall be pick'd almost in the very field,
Shall be dried, clean'd, ginn'd, baled, spun into thread and
    cloth before you,
You shall see hands at work at all the old processes
    and all the new ones,
You shall see the various grains and how flour is
    made and then bread baked by the bakers,
You shall see the crude ores of California and Nevada
    passing on and on till they become bullion,
You shall watch how the printer sets type, and learn what
    a composing-stick is,
You shall mark in amazement the Hoe press whirling its
    cylinders, shedding the printed leaves steady and fast,
The photograph, model, watch, pin, nail, shall be
    created before you.

In large calm halls, a stately museum shall teach you the
    infinite lessons of minerals,
In another, woods, plants, vegetation shall be illustrated—
    in another animals, animal life and development.

One stately house shall be the music house,
Others for other arts—learning, the sciences, shall
    all be here,
None shall be slighted, none but shall here be honor'd,
    help'd, exampled.

6

(This, this and these, America, shall be *your* pyramids
    and obelisks,
Your Alexandrian Pharos, gardens of Babylon,
Your temple at Olympia.)

The male and female many laboring not,
Shall ever here confront the laboring many,
With precious benefits to both, glory to all,
To thee America, and thee eternal Muse.

And here shall ye inhabit powerful Matrons!
In your vast state vaster than all the old,
Echoed through long, long centuries to come,
To sound of different, prouder songs, with stronger themes,
Practical, peaceful life, the people's life, the
    People themselves,
Lifted, illumin'd, bathed in peace—elate, secure in peace.

7

Away with themes of war! away with war itself!
Hence from my shuddering sight to never more
    return that show of blacken'd, mutilated corpses!
That hell unpent and raid of blood, fit for wild tigers or
    for lop-tongued wolves, not reasoning men,
And in its stead speed industry's campaigns,
With thy undaunted armies, engineering,
Thy pennants labor, loosen'd to the breeze,
Thy bugles sounding loud and clear.

Away with old romance!
Away with novels, plots and plays of foreign courts,
Away with love-verses sugar'd in rhyme, the intrigues,
    amours of idlers,
Fitted for only banquets of the night where dancers
    to late music slide,
The unhealthy pleasures, extravagant dissipations
    of the few,
With perfumes, heat and wine, beneath the dazzling
    chandeliers.

To you ye reverent sane sisters,
I raise a voice for far superber themes for poets and for art,
To exalt the present and the real,
To teach the average man the glory of his daily
    walk and trade,
To sing in songs how exercise and chemical life are never
    to be baffled,
To manual work for each and all, to plough, hoe, dig,
To plant and tend the tree, the berry, vegetables, flowers,
For every man to see to it that he really do something,
    for every woman too;
To use the hammer and the saw, (rip, or cross-cut,)
To cultivate a turn for carpentering, plastering, painting,
To work as tailor, tailoress, nurse, hostler, porter,
To invent a little, something ingenious, to aid the
    washing, cooking, cleaning,
And hold it no disgrace to take a hand at them themselves.

I say I bring thee Muse to-day and here,
All occupations, duties broad and close,
Toil, healthy toil and sweat, endless, without cessation,
The old, old practical burdens, interests, joys,
The family, parentage, childhood, husband and wife,
The house-comforts, the house itself and all its belongings,
Food and its preservation, chemistry applied to it,
Whatever forms the average, strong, complete, sweet-blooded
    man or woman, the perfect longeve personality,
And helps its present life to health and happiness, and
    shapes its soul,
For the eternal real life to come.

With latest connections, works, the inter-transportation
    of the world,
Steam-power, the great express lines, gas, petroleum,
These triumphs of our time, the Atlantic's delicate cable,
The Pacific railroad, the Suez canal, the Mont Cenis and
    Gothard and Hoosac tunnels, the Brooklyn bridge,

This earth all spann'd with iron rails, with lines of
    steamships threading every sea,
Our own rondure, the current globe I bring.

8

And thou America,
Thy offspring towering e'er so high, yet higher Thee
    above all towering,
With Victory on thy left, and at thy right hand Law;
Thou Union holding all, fusing, absorbing, tolerating all,
Thee, ever thee, I sing.

Thou, also thou, a World,
With all thy wide geographies, manifold, different, distant,
Rounded by thee in one—one common orbic language,
One common indivisible destiny for All.

And by the spells which ye vouchsafe to those
    your ministers in earnest,
I here personify and call my themes, to make them pass
    before ye.

Behold, America! (and thou, ineffable guest and sister!)
For thee come trooping up thy waters and thy lands;
Behold! thy fields and farms, thy far-off woods
    and mountains,
As in procession coming.

Behold, the sea itself,
And on its limitless, heaving breast, the ships;
See, where their white sails, bellying in the wind, speckle
    the green and blue,
See, the steamers coming and going, steaming in or out
    of port,
See, dusky and undulating, the long pennants of smoke.

Behold, in Oregon, far in the north and west,
Or in Maine, far in the north and east, thy cheerful axemen,
Wielding all day their axes.

Behold, on the lakes, thy pilots at their wheels, thy oarsmen,
How the ash writhes under those muscular arms!

There by the furnace, and there by the anvil,
Behold thy sturdy blacksmiths swinging their sledges,
Overhand so steady, overhand they turn and fall with
    joyous clank,
Like a tumult of laughter.

Mark the spirit of invention everywhere, thy rapid patents,
Thy continual workshops, foundries, risen or rising,
See, from their chimneys how the tall flame-fires stream.

Mark, thy interminable farms, North, South,
Thy wealthy daughter-states, Eastern and Western,
The varied products of Ohio, Pennsylvania, Missouri,
    Georgia, Texas, and the rest,
Thy limitless crops, grass, wheat, sugar, oil, corn, rice,
    hemp, hops,
Thy barns all fill'd, the endless freight-train and the bulging
    storehouse,
The grapes that ripen on thy vines, the apples in thy
    orchards,
Thy incalculable lumber, beef, pork, potatoes, thy coal,
    thy gold and silver,
The inexhaustible iron in thy mines.

All thine O sacred Union!
Ships, farms, shops, barns, factories, mines,
City and State, North, South, item and aggregate,
We dedicate, dread Mother, all to thee!

Protectress absolute, thou! bulwark of all!
For well we know that while thou givest each and all,
    (generous as God,)
Without thee neither all nor each, nor land, home,
Nor ship, nor mine, nor any here this day secure,
Nor aught, nor any day secure.

9

And thou, the Emblem waving over all!
Delicate beauty, a word to thee, (it may be salutary,)
Remember thou hast not always been as here to-day so
    comfortably ensovereign'd,
In other scenes than these have I observ'd thee flag,
Not quite so trim and whole and freshly blooming in
    folds of stainless silk,
But I have seen thee bunting, to tatters torn upon thy
    splinter'd staff,
Or clutch'd to some young color-bearer's breast with
    desperate hands,
Savagely struggled for, for life or death, fought over long,
'Mid cannons' thunder-crash and many a curse and groan
    and yell, and rifle-volleys cracking sharp,
And moving masses as wild demons surging, and lives as
    nothing risk'd,
For thy mere remnant grimed with dirt and smoke and
    sopp'd in blood,
For sake of that, my beauty, and that thou might'st dally
    as now secure up there,
Many a good man have I seen go under.

Now here and these and hence in peace, all thine O Flag!
And here and hence for thee, O universal Muse! and thou
    for them!
And here and hence O Union, all the work and workmen
    thine!
None separate from thee—henceforth One only, we and thou,
(For the blood of the children, what is it, only the blood
    maternal?
And lives and works, what are they all at last, except the
    roads to faith and death?)

While we rehearse our measureless wealth, it is for thee,
    dear Mother,
We own it all and several to-day indissoluble in thee;
Think not our chant, our show, merely for products gross or
    lucre—it is for thee, the soul in thee, electric, spiritual!

Our farms, inventions, crops, we own in thee! cities and
        States in thee!
Our freedom all in thee! our very lives in thee!

                                                    [1871]

On the Beach at Night

On the beach at night,
Stands a child with her father,
Watching the east, the autumn sky.

Up through the darkness,
While ravening clouds, the burial clouds, in black masses
        spreading,
Lower sullen and fast athwart and down the sky,
Amid a transparent clear belt of ether yet left in the east,
Ascends large and calm the lord-star Jupiter,
And nigh at hand, only a very little above,
Swim the delicate sisters the Pleiades.

From the beach the child holding the hand of her father,
Those burial-clouds that lower victorious soon to devour all,
Watching, silently weeps.

Weep not, child,
Weep not, my darling,
With these kisses let me remove your tears,
The ravening clouds shall not long be victorious,
They shall not long possess the sky, they devour the stars
        only in apparition,
Jupiter shall emerge, be patient, watch again another night,
        the Pleiades shall emerge,
They are immortal, all those stars both silvery and golden
        shall shine out again,
The great stars and the little ones shall shine out again,
        they endure,

The vast immortal suns and the long-enduring pensive
    moons shall again shine.

Then dearest child mournest thou only for Jupiter?
Considerest thou alone the burial of the stars?

Something there is,
(With my lips soothing thee, adding I whisper,
I give thee the first suggestion, the problem and indirection,)
Something there is more immortal even than the stars,
(Many the burials, many the days and nights, passing away,)
Something that shall endure longer even than lustrous
    Jupiter,
Longer than sun or any revolving satellite,
Or the radiant sisters the Pleiades.

[1871]

Ethiopia Saluting the Colors

Who are you dusky woman, so ancient hardly human,
With your woolly-white and turban'd head, and bare
    bony feet?
Why rising by the roadside here, do you the colors greet?

('Tis while our army lines Carolina's sands and pines,
Forth from thy hovel door thou Ethiopia com'st to me,
As under doughty Sherman I march toward the sea.)

Me master years a hundred since from my parents sunder'd,
A little child, they caught me as the savage beast is caught,
Then hither me across the sea the cruel slaver brought.

No further does she say, but lingering all the day,
Her high-borne turban'd head she wags, and rolls her
    darkling eye,
And courtesies to the regiments, the guidons moving by.

What is it fateful woman, so blear, hardly human?
Why wag your head with turban bound, yellow, red and
    green?
Are the things so strange and marvelous you see or have
    seen?

[1871]

Sparkles from the Wheel

Where the city's ceaseless crowd moves on the livelong day,
Withdrawn I join a group of children watching, I pause
    aside with them.

By the curb toward the edge of the flagging,
A knife-grinder works at his wheel sharpening a great knife,
Bending over he carefully holds it to the stone, by foot
    and knee,
With measur'd tread he turns rapidly, as he presses with
    light but firm hand,
Forth issue then in copious golden jets,
Sparkles from the wheel.

The scene and all its belongings, how they seize
    and affect me,
The sad sharp-chinn'd old man with worn clothes and
    broad shoulder-band of leather,
Myself effusing and fluid, a phantom curiously floating,
    now here absorb'd and arrested,
The group, (an unminded point set in a vast surrounding,)
The attentive, quiet children, the loud, proud, restive base
    of the streets,
The low hoarse purr of the whirling stone, the light-press'd
    blade,
Diffusing, dropping, sideways-darting, in tiny showers of
    gold,
Sparkles from the wheel.

[1871]

Passage to India

1

Singing my days,
Singing the great achievements of the present,
Singing the strong light works of engineers,
Our modern wonders, (the antique ponderous Seven
    outvied,)
In the Old World the east the Suez canal,
The New by its mighty railroad spann'd,
The seas inlaid with eloquent gentle wires;
Yet first to sound, and ever sound, the cry with thee O soul,
The Past! the Past! the Past!

The Past—the dark unfathom'd retrospect!
The teeming gulf—the sleepers and the shadows!
The past—the infinite greatness of the past!
For what is the present after all but a growth out of the past?
(As a projectile form'd, impell'd, passing a certain line, still
    keeps on,
So the present, utterly form'd, impell'd by the past.)

2

Passage O soul to India!
Eclaircise the myths Asiatic, the primitive fables.

Not you alone proud truths of the world,
Nor you alone ye facts of modern science,
But myths and fables of eld, Asia's, Africa's fables,
The far-darting beams of the spirit, the unloos'd dreams,
The deep diving bibles and legends,
The daring plots of the poets, the elder religions;
O you temples fairer than lilies pour'd over by the rising sun!
O you fables spurning the known, eluding the hold of the
    known, mounting to heaven!
You lofty and dazzling towers, pinnacled, red as roses,
    burnish'd with gold!
Towers of fables immortal fashion'd from mortal dreams!

You too I welcome and fully the same as the rest!
You too with joy I sing.

Passage to India!
Lo, soul, seest thou not God's purpose from the first?
The earth to be spann'd, connected by network,
The races, neighbors, to marry and be given in marriage,
The oceans to be cross'd, the distant brought near,
The lands to be welded together.

A worship new I sing,
You captains, voyagers, explorers, yours,
You engineers, you architects, machinists, yours,
You, not for trade or transportation only,
But in God's name, and for thy sake O soul.

3

Passage to India!
Lo soul for thee of tableaus twain,
I see in one the Suez canal initiated, open'd,
I see the procession of steamships, the Empress Eugenie's
      leading the van,
I mark from on deck the strange landscape, the pure sky,
      the level sand in the distance,
I pass swiftly the picturesque groups, the workmen gather'd,
The gigantic dredging machines.

In one again, different, (yet thine, all thine, O soul, the
      same,)
I see over my own continent the Pacific railroad surmounting
      every barrier,
I see continual trains of cars winding along the Platte
      carrying freight and passengers,
I hear the locomotives rushing and roaring, and the shrill
      steam-whistle,
I hear the echoes reverberate through the grandest scenery
      in the world,
I cross the Laramie plains, I note the rocks in grotesque
      shapes, the buttes,

I see the plentiful larkspur and wild onions, the barren,
    colorless, sage-deserts,
I see in glimpses afar or towering immediately above me the
    great mountains, I see the Wind river and the
    Wahsatch mountains,
I see the Monument mountain and the Eagle's Nest, I pass
    the Promontory, I ascend the Nevadas,
I scan the noble Elk mountain and wind around its base,
I see the Humboldt range, I thread the valley and cross the
    river,
I see the clear waters of lake Tahoe, I see forests of majestic
    pines,
Or crossing the great desert, the alkaline plains, I behold
    enchanting mirages of waters and meadows,
Marking through these and after all, in duplicate slender
    lines,
Bridging the three or four thousand miles of land travel,
Tying the Eastern to the Western sea,
The road between Europe and Asia.

(Ah Genoese thy dream! thy dream!
Centuries after thou art laid in thy grave,
The shore thou foundest verifies thy dream.)

4

Passage to India!
Struggles of many a captain, tales of many a sailor dead,
Over my mood stealing and spreading they come,
Like clouds and cloudlets in the unreach'd sky.

Along all history, down the slopes,
As a rivulet running, sinking now, and now again to the
    surface rising,
A ceaseless thought, a varied train—lo, soul, to thee, thy
    sight, they rise,
The plans, the voyages again, the expeditions;
Again Vasco da Gama sails forth,
Again the knowledge gain'd, the mariner's compass,
Lands found and nations born, thou born America,

For purpose vast, man's long probation fill'd,
Thou rondure of the world at last accomplish'd.

5

O vast Rondure, swimming in space,
Cover'd all over with visible power and beauty,
Alternate light and day and the teeming spiritual darkness,
Unspeakable high processions of sun and moon and
    countless stars above,
Below, the manifold grass and waters, animals, mountains,
    trees,
With inscrutable purpose, some hidden prophetic intention,
Now first it seems my thought begins to span thee.

Down from the gardens of Asia descending radiating,
Adam and Eve appear, then their myriad progeny after
    them,
Wandering, yearning, curious, with restless explorations,
With questionings, baffled, formless, feverish, with
    never-happy hearts,
With that sad incessant refrain, *Wherefore unsatisfied soul?*
    and *Whither O mocking life?*

Ah who shall soothe these feverish children?
Who justify these restless explorations?
Who speak the secret of impassive earth?
Who bind it to us? what is this separate Nature so unnatural?
What is this earth to our affections? (unloving earth,
    without a throb to answer ours,
Cold earth, the place of graves.)

Yet soul be sure the first intent remains, and shall be
    carried out,
Perhaps even now the time has arrived.

After the seas are all cross'd (as they seem already cross'd,)
After the great captains and engineers have accomplish'd
    their work,

After the noble inventors, after the scientists, the chemist,
    the geologist, ethnologist,
Finally shall come the poet worthy that name,
The true son of God shall come singing his songs.

Then not your deeds only O voyagers, O scientists and
    inventors, shall be justified,
All these hearts as of fretted children shall be sooth'd,
All affection shall be fully responded to, the secret shall be
    told,
All these separations and gaps shall be taken up and hook'd
    and link'd together,
The whole earth, this cold, impassive, voiceless earth, shall
    be completely justified,
Trinitas divine shall be gloriously accomplish'd and
    compacted by the true son of God, the poet,
(He shall indeed pass the straits and conquer the mountains,
He shall double the cape of Good Hope to some purpose,)
Nature and Man shall be disjoin'd and diffused no more,
The true son of God shall absolutely fuse them.

6

Year at whose wide-flung door I sing!
Year of the purpose accomplish'd!
Year of the marriage of continents, climates and oceans!
(No mere doge of Venice now wedding the Adriatic,)
I see O year in you the vast terraqueous globe given and
    giving all,
Europe to Asia, Africa join'd, and they to the New World,
The lands, geographies, dancing before you, holding a
    festival garland,
As brides and bridegrooms hand in hand.

Passage to India!
Cooling airs from Caucasus far, soothing cradle of man,
The river Euphrates flowing, the past lit up again.

Lo soul, the retrospect brought forward,
The old, most populous, wealthiest of earth's lands,

The streams of the Indus and the Ganges and their many
  affluents,
(I my shores of America walking to-day behold, resuming
  all,)
The tale of Alexander on his warlike marches suddenly
  dying,
On one side China and on the other side Persia and Arabia,
To the south the great seas and the bay of Bengal,
The flowing literatures, tremendous epics, religions, castes,
Old occult Brahma interminably far back, the tender and
  junior Buddha,
Central and southern empires and all their belongings,
  possessors,
The wars of Tamerlane, the reign of Aurungzebe,
The traders, rulers, explorers, Moslems, Venetians,
  Byzantium, the Arabs, Portuguese,
The first travelers famous yet, Marco Polo, Batouta the
  Moor,
Doubts to be solv'd, the map incognita, blanks to be fill'd,
The foot of man unstay'd, the hands never at rest,
Thyself O soul that will not brook a challenge.

The mediæval navigators rise before me,
The world of 1492, with its awaken'd enterprise,
Something swelling in humanity now like the sap of the
  earth in spring,
The sunset splendor of chivalry declining.

And who art thou sad shade?
Gigantic, visionary, thyself a visionary,
With majestic limbs and pious beaming eyes,
Spreading around with every look of thine a golden world,
Enhuing it with gorgeous hues.

As the chief histrion,
Down to the footlights walks in some great scena,
Dominating the rest I see the Admiral himself,
(History's type of courage, action, faith,)
Behold him sail from Palos leading his little fleet,

His voyage behold, his return, his great fame,
His misfortunes, calumniators, behold him a prisoner,
    chain'd,
Behold his dejection, poverty, death.

(Curious in time I stand, noting the efforts of heroes,
Is the deferment long? bitter the slander, poverty, death?
Lies the seed unreck'd for centuries in the ground? lo, to
    God's due occasion,
Uprising in the night, it sprouts, blooms,
And fills the earth with use and beauty.)

7

Passage indeed O soul to primal thought,
Not lands and seas alone, thy own clear freshness,
The young maturity of brood and bloom,
To realms of budding bibles.

O soul, repressless, I with thee and thou with me,
Thy circumnavigation of the world begin,
Of man, the voyage of his mind's return,
To reason's early paradise,
Back, back to wisdom's birth, to innocent intuitions,
Again with fair creation.

8

O we can wait no longer,
We too take ship O soul,
Joyous we too launch out on trackless seas,
Fearless for unknown shores on waves of ecstasy to sail,
Amid the wafting winds, (thou pressing me to thee, I thee
    to me, O soul,)
Caroling free, singing our song of God,
Chanting our chant of pleasant exploration.

With laugh and many a kiss,
(Let others deprecate, let others weep for sin, remorse,
    humiliation,)
O soul thou pleasest me, I thee.

Ah more than any priest O soul we too believe in God,
But with the mystery of God we dare not dally.

O soul thou pleasest me, I thee,
Sailing these seas or on the hills, or waking in the night,
Thoughts, silent thoughts, of Time and Space and Death,
    like waters flowing,
Bear me indeed as through the regions infinite,
Whose air I breathe, whose ripples hear, lave me all over,
Bathe me O God in thee, mounting to thee,
I and my soul to range in range of thee.

O Thou transcendent,
Nameless, the fibre and the breath,
Light of the light, shedding forth universes, thou centre of
    them,
Thou mightier centre of the true, the good, the loving,
Thou moral, spiritual fountain—affection's source—thou
    reservoir,
(O pensive soul of me—O thirst unsatisfied—waitest not
    there?
Waitest not haply for us somewhere there the Comrade
    perfect?)
Thou pulse—thou motive of the stars, suns, systems,
That, circling, move in order, safe, harmonious,
Athwart the shapeless vastnesses of space,
How should I think, how breathe a single breath, how
    speak, if, out of myself,
I could not launch, to those, superior universes?

Swiftly I shrivel at the thought of God,
At Nature and its wonders, Time and Space and Death,
But that I, turning, call to thee O soul, thou actual Me,
And lo, thou gently masterest the orbs,
Thou matest Time, smilest content at Death,
And fillest, swellest full the vastnesses of Space.

Greater than stars or suns,
Bounding O soul thou journeyest forth;

What love than thine and ours could wider amplify?
What aspirations, wishes, outvie thine and ours O soul?
What dreams of the ideal? what plans of purity, perfection,
    strength?
What cheerful willingness for others' sake to give up all?
For others' sake to suffer all?

Reckoning ahead O soul, when thou, the time achiev'd,
The seas all cross'd, weather'd the capes, the voyage done,
Surrounded, copest, frontest God, yieldest, the aim attain'd,
As fill'd with friendship, love complete, the Elder Brother
    found,
The Younger melts in fondness in his arms.

9

Passage to more than India!
Are thy wings plumed indeed for such far flights?
O soul, voyagest thou indeed on voyages like those?
Disportest thou on waters such as those?
Soundest below the Sanscrit and the Vedas?
Then have thy bent unleash'd.

Passage to you, your shores, ye aged fierce enigmas!
Passage to you, to mastership of you, ye strangling problems!
You, strew'd with the wrecks of skeletons, that, living,
    never reach'd you.

Passage to more than India!
O secret of the earth and sky!
Of you O waters of the sea! O winding creeks and rivers!
Of you O woods and fields! of you strong mountains of
    my land!
Of you O prairies! of you gray rocks!
O morning red! O clouds! O rain and snows!
O day and night, passage to you!

O sun and moon and all you stars! Sirius and Jupiter!
Passage to you!

Passage, immediate passage! the blood burns in my veins!
Away O soul! hoist instantly the anchor!
Cut the hawsers—haul out—shake out every sail!
Have we not stood here like trees in the ground long enough?
Have we not grovel'd here long enough, eating and drinking
    like mere brutes?
Have we not darken'd and dazed ourselves with books
    long enough?

Sail forth—steer for the deep waters only,
Reckless O soul, exploring, I with thee, and thou with me,
For we are bound where mariner has not yet dared to go,
And we will risk the ship, ourselves and all.

O my brave soul!
O farther farther sail!
O daring joy, but safe! are they not all the seas of God?
O farther, farther, farther sail!

[1871]

The Mystic Trumpeter

1

Hark, some wild trumpeter, some strange musician,
Hovering unseen in air, vibrates capricious tunes to-night.

I hear thee trumpeter, listening alert I catch thy notes,
Now pouring, whirling like a tempest round me,
Now low, subdued, now in the distance lost.

2

Come nearer bodiless one, haply in thee resounds
Some dead composer, haply thy pensive life
Was fill'd with aspirations high, unform'd ideals,
Waves, oceans musical, chaotically surging,

That now ecstatic ghost, close to me bending, thy cornet
    echoing, pealing,
Gives out to no one's ears but mine, but freely gives to mine,
That I may thee translate.

3

Blow trumpeter free and clear, I follow thee,
While at thy liquid prelude, glad, serene,
The fretting world, the streets, the noisy hours of day
    withdraw,
A holy calm descends like dew upon me,
I walk in cool refreshing night the walks of Paradise,
I scent the grass, the moist air and the roses;
Thy song expands my numb'd imbonded spirit, thou
    freest, launchest me,
Floating and basking upon heaven's lake.

4

Blow again trumpeter! and for my sensuous eyes,
Bring the old pageants, show the feudal world.

What charm thy music works! thou makest pass before me,
Ladies and cavaliers long dead, barons are in their castle
    halls, the troubadours are singing,
Arm'd knights go forth to redress wrongs, some in quest
    of the holy Graal;
I see the tournament, I see the contestants incased in
    heavy armor seated on stately champing horses,
I hear the shouts, the sounds of blows and smiting steel;
I see the Crusaders' tumultuous armies—hark, how the
    cymbals clang,
Lo, where the monks walk in advance, bearing the
    cross on high.

5

Blow again trumpeter! and for thy theme,
Take now the enclosing theme of all, the solvent and
    the setting,
Love, that is pulse of all, the sustenance and the pang,

The heart of man and woman all for love,
No other theme but love—knitting, enclosing, all-diffusing
    love.

O how the immortal phantoms crowd around me!
I see the vast alembic ever working, I see and know
    the flames that heat the world,
The glow, the blush, the beating hearts of lovers,
So blissful happy some, and some so silent, dark, and
    nigh to death;
Love, that is all the earth to lovers—love, that mocks
    time and space,
Love, that is day and night—love, that is sun and moon
    and stars,
Love, that is crimson, sumptuous, sick with perfume,
No other words but words of love, no other thought but love.

6

Blow again trumpeter—conjure war's alarums.

Swift to thy spell a shuddering hum like distant thunder
    rolls,
Lo, where the arm'd men hasten—lo, mid the clouds of
    dust the glint of bayonets,
I see the grime-faced cannoneers, I mark the rosy flash
    amid the smoke, I hear the cracking of the guns;
Nor war alone—thy fearful music-song, wild player,
    brings every sight of fear,
The deeds of ruthless brigands, rapine, murder—I hear
    the cries for help!
I see ships foundering at sea, I behold on deck and below
    deck the terrible tableaus.

7

O trumpeter, methinks I am myself the instrument thou
    playest,
Thou melt'st my heart, my brain—thou movest, drawest,
    changest them at will;
And now thy sullen notes send darkness through me,

Thou takest away all cheering light, all hope,
I see the enslaved, the overthrown, the hurt, the opprest
    of the whole earth,
I feel the measureless shame and humiliation of my
    race, it becomes all mine,
Mine too the revenges of humanity, the wrongs of ages,
    baffled feuds and hatreds,
Utter defeat upon me weighs—all lost—the foe victorious,
(Yet 'mid the ruins Pride colossal stands unshaken
    to the last,
Endurance, resolution to the last.)

8

Now trumpeter for thy close,
Vouchsafe a higher strain than any yet,
Sing to my soul, renew its languishing faith and hope,
Rouse up my slow belief, give me some vision of the future,
Give me for once its prophecy and joy.

O glad, exculting, culminating song!
A vigor more than earth's is in thy notes,
Marches of victory—man disenthral'd—the conqueror at last,
Hymns to the universal God from universal man—all joy!
A reborn race appears—a perfect world, all joy!
Women and men in wisdom innocence and health—all joy!
Riotous laughing bacchanals fill'd with joy!
War, sorrow, suffering gone—the rank earth purged—
    nothing but joy left!
The ocean fill'd with joy—the atmosphere all joy!
Joy! joy! in freedom, worship, love! joy in the ecstasy of life!
Enough to merely be! enough to breathe!
Joy! joy! all over joy!

[1872]

Prayer of Columbus

A batter'd, wreck'd old man,
Thrown on this savage shore, far, far from home,

Pent by the sea and dark rebellious brows, twelve dreary
    months,
Sore, stiff with many toils, sicken'd and nigh to death,
I take my way along the island's edge,
Venting a heavy heart.

I am too full of woe!
Haply I may not live another day;
I cannot rest O God, I cannot eat or drink or sleep,
Till I put forth myself, my prayer, once more to Thee,
Breathe, bathe myself one more in Thee, commune with
    Thee,
Report myself once more to Thee.

Thou knowest my years entire, my life,
My long and crowded life of active work, not adoration
    merely;
Thou knowest the prayers and vigils of my youth,
Thou knowest my manhood's solemn and visionary
    meditations,
Thou knowest how before I commenced I devoted all
    to come to Thee,
Thou knowest I have in age ratified all those vows and
    strictly kept them,
Thou knowest I have not once lost nor faith nor ecstasy
    in Thee,
In shackles, prison'd, in disgrace, repining not,
Accepting all from Thee, as duly come from Thee.

All my emprises have been fill'd with Thee,
My speculations, plans, begun and carried on in thoughts
    of Thee,
Sailing the deep or journeying the land for Thee;
Intentions, purports, aspirations mine, leaving results to
    Thee.

O I am sure they really came from Thee,
The urge, the ardor, the unconquerable will,
The potent, felt, interior command, stronger than words,

A message from the Heavens whispering to me even
    in sleep,
These sped me on.

By me and these the work so far accomplish'd,
By me earth's elder cloy'd and stifled lands uncloy'd,
    unloos'd,
By me the hemispheres rounded and tied, the unknown to
    the known.

The end I know not, it is all in Thee,
Or small or great I know not—haply what broad fields,
    what lands,
Haply the brutish measureless human undergrowth I know,
Transplanted there may rise to stature, knowledge worthy
    Thee,
Haply the swords I know may there indeed be turn'd to
    reaping-tools,
Haply the lifeless cross I know, Europe's dead cross,
    may bud and blossom there.

One effort more, my altar this bleak sand;
That Thou O God my life hast lighted,
With ray of light, steady, ineffable, vouchsafed of Thee,
Light rare untellable, lighting the very light,
Beyond all signs, descriptions, languages;
For that O God, be it my latest word, here on my knees,
Old, poor, and paralyzed, I thank Thee.

My terminus near,
The clouds already closing in upon me,
The voyage balk'd the course disputed, lost,
I yield my ships to Thee.

My hands, my limbs grow nerveless,
My brain feels rack'd, bewilder'd,
Let the old timbers part, I will not part,
I will cling fast to Thee, O God, though the waves buffet me,
Thee, Thee at least I know.

Is it the prophet's thought I speak, or am I raving?
What do I know of life? what of myself?
I know not even my own work past or present,
Dim ever-shifting guesses of it spread before me,
Of newer better worlds, their mighty parturition,
Mocking, perplexing me.

And these things I see suddenly, what mean they?
As if some miracle, some hand divine unseal'd my eyes,
Shadowy vast shapes smile through the air and sky,
And on the distant waves sail countless ships,
And anthems in new tongues I hear saluting me.

[1874]

After the Sea-Ship

After the sea-ship, after the whistling winds,
After the white-gray sails taut to their spars and ropes,
Below, a myriad myriad waves hastening, lifting up their
    necks,
Tending in ceaseless flow toward the track of the ship,
Waves of the ocean bubbling and gurgling, blithely prying,
Waves, undulating waves, liquid, uneven, emulous waves,
Toward that whirling current, laughing and buoyant,
    with curves,
Where the great vessel sailing and tacking displaced the
    surface,
Larger and smaller waves in the spread of the ocean
    yearnfully flowing,
The wake of the sea-ship after she passes, flashing and
    frolicsome under the sun,
A motley procession with many a fleck of foam and many
    fragments,
Following the stately and rapid ship, in the wage following.

[1874]

The Ox-Tamer

In a far-away northern county in the placid pastoral region,
Lives my farmer friend, the theme of my recitative, a
    famous tamer of oxen,
There they bring him the three-year-olds and the four-year-
    olds to break them,
He will take the wildest steer in the world and break him
    and tame him,
He will go fearless without any whip where the young
    bullock chafes up and down the yard,
The bullock's head tosses restless high in the air with
    raging eyes,
Yet see you! how soon his rage subsides—how soon this
    tamer tames him;
See you! on the farms hereabout a hundred oxen young
    and old, and he is the man who has tamed them,
They all know him, all are affectionate to him;
See you! some are such beautiful animals, so lofty looking;
Some are buff-color'd, some mottled, one has a white line
    running along his back, some are brindled,
Some have wide flaring horns (a good sign)—see you the
    bright hides,
See, the two with stars on their foreheads—see, the round
    bodies and broad backs,
How straight and square they stand on their legs—what fine
    sagacious eyes!
How they watch their tamer—they wish him near them—
    how they turn to look after him!
What yearning expression! how uneasy they are when he
    moves away from them;
Now I marvel what it can be he appears to them, (books,
    politics, poems, depart—all else departs,)
I confess I envy only his fascination—my silent, illiterate
    friend,
Whom a hundred oxen love there in his life on farms,
In the northern county far, in the placid pastoral region.

[1874]

To the Man-of-War-Bird

Thou who hast slept all night upon the storm,
Waking renew'd on thy prodigious pinions,
(Burst the wild storm? above it thou ascended'st,
And rested on the sky, thy slave that cradled thee,)
Now a blue point, far, far in heaven floating,
As to the light emerging here on deck I watch thee,
(Myself a speck, a point on the world's floating vast.)

Far, far at sea,
After the night's fierce drifts have strewn the shore with
     wrecks,
With re-appearing day as now so happy and serene,
The rosy and elastic dawn, the flashing sun,
The limpid spread of air cerulean,
Thou also re-appearest.

Thou born to maetch the gale, (thou art all wings,)
To cope with heaven and earth and sea and hurricane,
Thou ship of air that never furl'st thy sails,
Days, even weeks untired and onward, through spaces,
     realms gyrating,
That sport'st amid the lightning-flash and thunder-cloud,
In them, in thy experiences, had'st thou my soul,
What joys! what joys were thine!

                                                [1876]

The Dalliance of the Eagles

Skirting the river road, (my forenoon walk, my rest,)
Skyward in air a sudden muffled sound, the dalliance of
     the eagles,
The rushing amorous contact high in space together,
The clinching interlocking claws, a living, fierce,
     gyrating wheel,

Four beating wings, two beaks, a swirling mass tight
    grappling,
In tumbling turning clustering loops, straight downward
    falling,
Till o'er the river pois'd, the twain yet one, a moment's lull,
A motionless still balance in the air, then parting, talons
    loosing,
Upward again on slow-firm pinions slanting, their separate
    diverse flight,
She hers, he his, pursuing.

[1880]

Good-bye My Fancy!

Good-bye my Fancy!
Farewell dear mate, dear love!
I'm going away, I know not where,
Or to what fortune, or whether I may ever see you again,
So Good-bye my Fancy.

Now for my last—let me look back a moment;
The slower fainter ticking of the clock is in me,
Exit, nightfall, and soon the heart-thud stopping.

Long have we lived, joy'd, caress'd together;
Delightful!—now separation—Good-bye my Fancy.

Yet let me not be too hasty,
Long indeed have we lived, slept, filter'd, become really
    blended into one;
Then if we die we die together, (yes, we'll remain one,)
If we go anywhere we'll go together to meet what happens,
May-be we'll be better off and blither, and learn something,
May-be it is yourself now really ushering me to the
    true songs, (who knows?)

May-be it is you the mortal knob really undoing, turning—
    so now finally,
Good-bye—and hail! my Fancy.

[1891]

Whitman's last preface to *Leaves of Grass*, included with other
prose in an edition of that work which he planned as a cele-
bration of his seventieth year, is second in importance only to
the first of 1855. The epigrams are missing, for the vision is
dispersed. "So here I sit gossiping in the early candlelight of
old age—I and mybook—casting backward glances over our
travel'd road." The septuagenarian remembers all the opposition his book has met, and grants that from a worldly point
of view it has been "worse than a failure." But "friends and
upholders" have been at his side, and "unstopp'd and unwarp'd by any influence outside the soul within me, I have
had my say entirely my own way, and put it unerringly on
record—the value thereof to be decided by time." He is less
sanguine than his friends about the decision time will make.
He assumes that it will take at least a hundred years for audiences to emerge with the capacity to understand the "experimental" nature of *Leaves of Grass*, which he now would rather
not call literature at all. It is experiment and prophecy. The
assertive individual of 1855 has grown tentative.

And he has modified his scorn of older poetries than his.
Once he had dismissed them as irrelevant, as good only for
their different times. Now he speaks of "their indescribable
preciousness as heirlooms for America," and insists that if he
had not in the first place been worshipful of "their colossal
grandeur and beauty of form and spirit" he could never have
written *Leaves of Grass*. The New World still needs a new
poetry—he does not relinquish this point—but it must be as
sure as Homer, Dante, and Shakespeare were that it has a
firm hold on "the last majesty" of man. The New World he
sees about him actually threatens that majesty. The prime need,
then, is for rededication to the cause of man's soul. Thus in
his critical thinking Whitman comes full circle. He is an older
and wiser man, but in essence he has not changed. He has
merely, and nobly, made the adjustments which truth had told
him were necessary.

A Backward Glance
O'er Travel'd Roads
1888

Perhaps the best of songs heard, or of any and all true love, or life's fairest episodes or sailors', soldiers' trying scenes on land or sea, is the *résumé* of them, or any of them, long afterwards, looking at the actualities away back past, with all their practical excitations gone. How the soul loves to float amid such reminiscences!

So here I sit gossiping in the early candlelight of old age— I and my book—casting backward glances over our travel'd road. After completing, as it were, the journey—(a varied jaunt of years, with many halts and gaps of intervals—or some lengthen'd ship-voyage, wherein more than once the last hour had apparently arrived, and we seem'd certainly going down —yet reaching port in a sufficient way through all discomfitures at last)—After completing my poems, I am curious to review them in the light of their own (at the time unconscious, or mostly unconscious) intentions, with certain unfoldings of the thirty years they seek to embody. These lines, therefore, will probably blend the weft of first purposes and speculations, with the warp of that experience afterwards, always bringing strange developments.

Result of seven or eight stages and struggles extending through nearly thirty years, (as I nigh my three-score-and-ten I live largely on memory,) I look upon *Leaves of Grass*, now finish'd to the end of its opportunities and powers, as my definitive *carte visite* to the coming generations of the New

World,[1] if I may assume to say so. That I have not gain'd the acceptance of my own time, but have fallen back on fond dreams of the future—anticipations—("still lives the song, though Regnar dies")—That from a worldly and business point of view *Leaves of Grass* has been worse than a failure—that public criticism on the book and myself as author of it yet shows mark'd anger and contempt more than anything else— ("I find a solid line of enemies to you everywhere,"—letter from W. S. K., Boston, May 28, 1884)—And that solely for publishing it I have been the object of two or three pretty serious special official buffetings—is all probably no more than I ought to have expected. I had my choice when I commenc'd. I bid neither for soft eulogies, big money returns, nor the approbation of existing schools and conventions. As fulfill'd or partially fulfill'd, the best comfort of the whole business (after a small band of the dearest friends and upholders ever vouchsafed to man or cause—doubtless all the more faithful and uncompromising—this little phalanx!—for being so few) is that, unstopp'd and unwarp'd by any influence outside the soul within me, I have had my say entirely my own way, and put it unerringly on record—the value thereof to be decided by time.

In calculating that decision, William O'Connor and Dr. Bucke are far more peremptory than I am. Behind all else that can be said, I consider *Leaves of Grass* and its theory experimental—as, in the deepest sense, I consider our American republic itself to be, with its theory. (I think I have at least enough philosophy not to be too absolutely certain of anything, or any results.) In the second place, the volume is a *sortie*— whether to prove triumphant, and conquer its field of aim and escape and construction, nothing less than a hundred years from now can fully answer. I consider the point that I have positively gain'd a hearing, to far more than make up for any and all other lacks and withholdings. Essentially, *that* was from the first, and has remain'd throughout, the main object.

[1]When Champollion, on his deathbed, handed to the printer the revised proof of his *Egyptian Grammar*, he said gayly, "Be careful of this—it is my *carte de visite* to posterity."

Now it seems to be achiev'd, I am certainly contented to waive any otherwise momentous drawbacks, as of little account. Candidly and dispassionately reviewing all my intentions, I feel that they were creditable—and I accept the result, whatever it may be.

After continued personal ambition and effort, as a young fellow, to enter with the rest into competition for the usual rewards, business, political, literary, etc.—to take part in the great *mêlée*, both for victory's prize itself and to do some good —After years of those aims and pursuits, I found myself remaining possess'd, at the age of thirty-one to thirty-three, with a special desire and conviction. Or rather, to be quite exact, a desire that had been flitting through my previous life, or hovering on the flanks, mostly indefinite hitherto, had steadily advanced to the front, defined itself, and finally dominated everything else. This was a feeling or ambition to articulate and faithfully express in literary or poetic form, and uncompromisingly, my own physical, emotional, moral, intellectual, and æsthetic Personality, in the midst of, and tallying, the momentous spirit and facts of its immediate days, and of current America—and to exploit that Personality, identified with place and date, in a far more candid and comprehensive sense than any hitherto poem or book.

Perhaps this is in brief, or suggests, all I have sought to do. Given the Nineteenth Century, with the United States, and what they furnish as area and points of view, *Leaves of Grass* is, or seeks to be, simply a faithful and doubtless self-will'd record. In the midst of all, it gives one man's—the author's—identity, ardors, observations, faiths, and thoughts, color'd hardly at all with any decided coloring from other faiths or other identities. Plenty of songs had been sung—beautiful, matchless songs— adjusted to other lands than these—another spirit and stage of evolution; but I would sing, and leave out or put in, quite solely with reference to America and today. Modern science and democracy seem'd to be throwing out their challenge to poetry to put them in its statements in contradistinction to the songs and myths of the past. As I see it now (perhaps too late,) I have unwittingly taken up that challenge and made an attempt at such statements—which I certainly would not assume to do now, knowing more clearly what it means.

For grounds for *Leaves of Grass*, as a poem, I abandon'd the conventional themes, which do not appear in it: none of the stock ornamentation, or choice plots of love or war, or high, exceptional personages of Old-World song; nothing, as I may say, for beauty's sake—no legend, or myth, or romance, nor euphemism, nor rhyme. But the broadest average of humanity and its identities in the now ripening Nineteenth Century, and especially in each of their countless examples and practical occupations in the United States today.

One main contrast of the ideas behind every page of my verses, compared with establish'd poems, is their different relative attitude toward God, toward the objective universe, and still more (by reflection, confession, assumption, &c.) the quite changed attitude of the ego, the one chanting or talking, toward himself and toward his fellow-humanity. It is certainly time for America, above all, to begin this readjustment in the scope and basic point of view of verse; for everything else has changed. As I write, I see in an article on Wordsworth, in one of the current English magazines, the lines, "A few weeks ago an eminent French critic said that, owing to the special tendency to science and to its all-devouring force, poetry would cease to be read in fifty years." But I anticipate the very contrary. Only a firmer, vastly broader, new area begins to exist—nay, is already form'd—to which the poetic genius must emigrate. Whatever may have been the case in years gone by, the true use for the imaginative faculty of modern times is to give ultimate vivification to facts, to science, and to common lives, endowing them with glows and glories and final illustriousness which belong to every real thing, and to real things only. Without that ultimate vivification—which the poet or other artist alone can give—reality would seem incomplete, and science, democracy, and life itself, finally in vain.

Few appreciate the moral revolutions of our age, which have been profounder far than the material or inventive or war-produced ones. The Nineteenth Century, now well toward its close (and ripening into fruit the seeds of the two preceding centuries[2])—the uprisings of national masses and shiftings of boundary lines—the historical and other prominent facts of the United States—the war of attempted Secession—the stormy rush and haste of nebulous forces—never can future years witness more excitement and din of action—never completer change of army front along the whole line, the whole civilized world. For all these new and evolutionary facts, meanings, purposes, new poetic messages, new forms and expressions, are inevitable.

My Book and I—what a period we have presumed to span! those thirty years from 1850 to '80—and America in them! Proud, proud indeed may we be, if we have cull'd enough of that period in its own spirit to worthily waft a few live breaths of it to the future!

Let me not dare, here or anywhere, for my own purposes, or any purposes, to attempt the definition of Poetry, nor answer the question what it is. Like Religion, Love, Nature, while those terms are indispensable, and we all give a sufficiently accurate meaning to them, in my opinion no definition that has ever been made sufficiently encloses the name Poetry; nor can any rule or convention ever so absolutely obtain but some great exception may arise and disregard and overturn it.

Also it must be carefully remember'd that first-class literature does not shine by any luminosity of its own; nor do its poems. They grow of circumstances, and are evolutionary. The actual living light is always curiously from elsewhere—follows unaccountable sources, and is lunar and relative at the best. There are, I know, certain controlling themes that seem endlessly appropriated to the poets—as war, in the past—in the Bible, religious rapture and adoration—always love, beauty, some fine plot, or pensive or other emotion. But, strange as it may sound at first, I will say there is something striking far deeper and

---

[2]The ferment and germination even of the United States today, dating back to, and in my opinion mainly founded on, the Elizabethan age in English history, the age of Francis Bacon and Shakespeare. Indeed, when we pursue it, what growth or advent is there that does not date back, back, until lost—perhaps its most tantalizing clues lost —in the receded horizons of the past?

towering far higher than those themes for the best elements of modern song.

Just as all the old imaginative works rest, after their kind, on long trains of presuppositions, often entirely unmention'd by themselves, yet supplying the most important bases of them, and without which they could have had no reason for being, so *Leaves of Grass,* before a line was written, presupposed something different from any other, and, as it stands, is the result of such presupposition. I should say, indeed, it were useless to attempt reading the book without first carefully tallying that preparatory background and quality in the mind. Think of the United States today—the facts of these thirty-eight or forty empires solder'd in one—sixty or seventy millions of equals with their lives, their passions, their future—these incalculable, modern, American, seething multitudes around us, of which we are inseparable parts! Think, in comparison, of the petty environage and limited area of the poets of past or present Europe, no matter how great their genius. Think of the absence and ignorance in all cases hitherto, of the multitudinousness, vitality, and the unprecedented stimulants of today and here. It almost seems as if a poetry with cosmic and dynamic features of magnitude and limitlessness suitable to the human soul were never possible before. It is certain that a poetry of absolute faith and equality for the use of the democratic masses never was.

In estimating first-class song, a sufficient Nationality, or, on the other hand, what may be call'd the negative and lack of it, (as in Goethe's case, it sometimes seems to me,) is often, if not always, the first element. One needs only a little penetration to see, at more or less removes, the material facts of their country and radius, with the coloring of the moods of humanity at the time, and its gloomy or hopeful prospects, behind all poets and each poet, and forming their birthmarks. I know very well that my *Leaves* could not possibly have emerged or been fashion'd or completed, from any other era than the latter half of the Nineteenth Century, nor any other land than democratic America, and from the absolute triumph of the National Union arms.

And whether my friends claim it for me or not, I know well enough, too, that in respect to pictorial talent, dramatic situations, and especially in verbal melody and all the conventional technique of poetry, not only the divine works that today stand ahead in the world's reading but dozens more, transcend (some of them immeasurably transcend) all I have done, or could do. But it seem'd to me, as the objects in Nature, the themes of estheticism, and all special exploitations of the mind and soul, involve not only their own inherent quality, but the quality, just as inherent and important, of *their point of view*[3] the time had come to reflect all themes and things, old and new, in the lights thrown on them by the advent of America and democracy—to chant those themes through the utterance of one, not only the grateful and reverent legatee of the past, but the born child of the New World—to illustrate all through the genesis and ensemble of today; and that such illustration and ensemble are the chief demands of America's prospective imaginative literature. Not to carry out, in the approved style, some choice plot of fortune or misfortune, or fancy, or fine thoughts, or incidents, or courtesies—all of which has been done overwhelmingly and well, probably never to be excell'd—but that while in such aesthetic presentation of objects, passions, plots, thoughts, etc., our lands and days do not want, and probably will never have, anything better than they already possess from the bequests of the past, it still remains to be said that there is even toward all those a subjective and contemporary point of view appropriate to ourselves alone, and to our new genius and environments, different from anything hitherto; and that such conception of current or gone-by life and art is for us the only means of their assimilation consistent with the Western world.

Indeed, and anyhow, to put it specifically, has not the time arrived when, (if it must be plainly said, for democratic America's sake, if for no other) there must imperatively come a readjustment of the whole theory and nature of Poetry? The question is important, and I may turn the argument over and repeat it: Does not the best thought of our day and Republic

---

[3]According to Immanuel Kant, the last essential reality, giving shape and significance to all the rest.

conceive of a birth and spirit of song superior to anything past
or present? To the effectual and moral consolidation of our
lands (already, as materially establish'd, the greatest factors in
known history, and far, far greater through what they prelude
and necessitate, and are to be in future)—to conform with and
build on the concrete realities and theories of the universe
furnish'd by science, and henceforth the only irrefragable basis
for anything, verse included—to root both influences in the
emotional and imaginative action of the modern time, and
dominate all that precedes or opposes them—is not either a
radical advance and step forward, or a new verteber of the
best song indispensable?

The New World receives with joy the poems of the antique,
with European feudalism's rich fund of epics, plays, ballads—
seeks not in the least to deaden or displace those voices from
our ear and area—holds them indeed as indispensable studies,
influences, records, comparisons. But though the dawn-dazzle
of the sun of literature is in those poems for us of today—
though perhaps the best parts of current character in nations,
social groups, or any man's or woman's individuality, Old
World or New, are from them—and though if I were ask'd to
name the most precious bequest to current American civilization from all the hitherto ages, I am not sure but I would name
those old and less old songs ferried hither from east and west
—some serious words and debits remain; some acrid considerations demand a hearing. Of the great poems receiv'd from
abroad and from the ages, and today enveloping and penetrating America, is there one that is consistent with these United
States, or essentially applicable to them as they are and are to
be? Is there one whose underlying basis is not a denial and
insult to democracy? What a comment it forms, anyhow, on
this era of literary fulfillment, with the splendid day-rise of
science and resuscitation of history, that our chief religious and
poetical works are not our own, nor adapted to our light, but
have been furnish'd by far-back ages out of their arriere and
darkness, or, at most, twilight dimness! What is there in those
works that so imperiously and scronfully dominates all our
advanced civilization, and culture?

Even Shakespeare, who so suffuses current letters and

art (which indeed have in most degrees grown out of him,) belongs essentially to the buried past. Only he holds the proud distinction for certain important phases of that past, of being the loftiest of the singers life has yet given voice to. All, however, relate to and rest upon conditions, standards, politics, sociologies, ranges of belief, that have been quite eliminated from the Eastern hemisphere, and never existed at all in the Western. As authoritative types of song they belong in America just about as much as the persons and institutes they depict. True, it may be said, the emotional, moral, and aesthetic natures of humanity have not radically changed—that in these the old poems apply to our times and all times, irrespective of date; and that they are of incalculable value as pictures of the past. I willingly make those admissions and to their fullest extent; then advance the points herewith as of serious, even paramount importance.

I have indeed put on record elsewhere my reverence and eulogy for those never-to-be-excell'd poetic bequests, and their indescribable preciousness as heirlooms for America. Another and separate point must now be candidly stated. If I had not stood before those poems with uncover'd head, fully aware of their colossal grandeur and beauty of form and spirit, I could not have written *Leaves of Grass*. My verdict and conclusions as illustrated in its pages are arrived at through the temper and inculcation of the old works as much as through anything else—perhaps more than through anything else. As America fully and fairly construed is the legitimate result and evolutionary outcome of the past, so I would dare to claim for my verse. Without stopping to qualify the averment, the Old World has had the poems of myths, fictions, feudalism, conquest, caste, dynastic wars, and splendid exceptional characters and affairs, which have been great; but the New World needs the poems of realities and science and of the democratic average and basic equality, which shall be greater. In the center of all, and object of all, stands the Human Being, toward whose heroic and spiritual evolution poems and everything directly or indirectly tend, Old World or New.

Continuing the subject, my friends have more than once suggested—or may be the garrulity of advancing age is possessing me—some further embryonic facts of *Leaves of Grass*, and especially how I enter'd upon them. Dr. Bucke has, in his volume, already fully and fairly described the preparation of my poetic field, with the particular and general plowing, planting, seeding, and occupation of the ground, till everything was fertilized, rooted, and ready to start its own way for good or bad. Not till after this, did I attempt any serious acquaintance with poetic literature. Along in my sixteenth year I had become the possessor of a stout, well-cramm'd one-thousand-page octavo volume (I have it yet,) containing Walter Scott's poetry entire—an inexhaustible mine and treasury of poetic forage (especially the endless forests and jungles of notes)—has been so to me for fifty years, and remains so to this day.[4]

Later, at intervals, summers and falls, I used to go off, sometimes for a week at a stretch, down in the country, or to Long Island's seashores—there, in the presence of outdoor influences, I went over thoroughly the Old and New Testaments, and absorb'd (probably to better advantage for me than in any library or indoor room—it makes such difference *where* you read,) Shakespeare, Ossian, the best translated versions I could get of Homer, Aeschylus, Sophocles, the old German Nibelungen, the ancient Hindu poems, and one or two other masterpieces, Dante's among them. As it happen'd, I read the latter mostly in an old wood. The *Iliad* (Buckley's prose version) I read first thoroughly on the peninsula of Orient, northeast end of Long Island, in a shelter'd hollow of rocks and sand, with the sea on each side. (I have wonder'd since why I was not overwhelm'd by those mighty masters. Likely because I read them, as described, in the full presence of Nature, under the sun, with the far-spreading landscape and vistas, or the sea rolling in.)

[4]Sir Walter Scott's *Complete Poems;* especially including Border Minstrelsy; then Sir Tristrem; Lay of the Last Minstrel; Ballads from the German; Marmion; Lady of the Lake; Vision of Don Roderick; Lord of the Isles; Rokeby; Bridal of Triermain; Field of Waterloo; Harold the Dauntless; all the Dramas; various Introductions, endless interesting Notes and Essays on Poetry, Romance, etc.

Lockhart's 1833 (or '34) edition with Scott's latest and copious revisions and annotations. (All the poems were thoroughly read by me, but the ballads of the Border Minstrelsy over and over again.)

Toward the last I had among much else look'd over Edgar Poe's poems—of which I was not an admirer, tho' I always saw that beyond their limited range of melody (like perpetual chimes of music bells, ringing from lower *b* flat up to *g*) they were melodious expressions, and perhaps never-excell'd ones, for certain pronounc'd phases of human morbidity. (The Poetic area is very spacious—has room for all—has so many mansions!) But I was repaid in Poe's prose by the idea that (at any rate for our occasions, our day) there can be no such thing as a long poem. The same thought had been haunting my mind before, but Poe's argument, though short, work'd the sum and proved it to me.

Another point had an early settlement, clearing the ground greatly. I saw, from the time my enterprise and questionings positively shaped themselves (how best can I express my own distinctive era and surroundings, America, Democracy?) that the trunk and center whence the answer was to radiate, and to which all should return from straying however far a distance, must be an identical body and soul, a personality—which personality, after many considerations and ponderings I deliberately settled should be myself—indeed could not be any other. I also felt strongly (whether I have shown it or not) that to the true and full estimate of the Present both the Past and the Future are main considerations.

These, however, and much more might have gone on and come to naught (almost positively would have come to naught,) if a sudden, vast, terrible, direct and indirect stimulus for new and national declamatory expression had not been given to me. It is certain, I say, that, although I had made a start before, only from the occurrence of the Secession War, and what it show'd me as by flashes of lightning, with the emotional depths it sounded and arous'd (of course, I don't mean in my own heart only, I saw it just as plainly in others, in millions)—that only from the strong flare and provocation of that war's sights and scenes the final reasons-for-being of an autochthonic and passionate song definitely came forth.

I went down to the war fields in Virginia (end of 1862), lived thenceforward in camp—saw great battles and the days and nights afterward—partook of all the fluctuations, gloom, despair, hopes again arous'd, courage evoked—death readily risk'd—*the cause,* too—along and filling those agonistic and lurid following years, 1863-'64-'65—the real parturition years (more than 1776-'83) of this henceforth homogeneous Union. Without those three or four years and the experiences they gave, *Leaves of Grass* would not now be existing.

But I set out with the intention also of indicating or hinting some point-characteristics which I since see (though I did not then, at least not definitely) were bases and object-urgings toward those *Leaves* from the first. The word I myself put primarily for the description of them as they stand at last, is the word Suggestiveness. I round and finish little, if anything; and could not, consistently with my scheme. The reader will always have his or her part to do, just as much as I have had mine. I seek less to state or display any theme or thought, and more to bring you, reader, into the atmosphere of the theme or thought—there to pursue your own flight. Another impetus-word is Comradeship as for all lands, and in a more commanding and acknowledg'd sense than hitherto. Other word signs would be Good Cheer, Content, and Hope.

The chief trait of any given poet is always the spirit he brings to the observation of Humanity and Nature—the mood out of which he contemplates his subjects. What kind of temper and what amount of faith report these things? Up to how recent a date is the song carried? what the equipment, and special raciness of the singer—what his tinge of coloring? The last value of artistic expressers, past and present—Greek aesthetes, Shakespeare—or in our own day Tennyson, Victor Hugo, Carlyle, Emerson—is certainly involv'd in such questions. I say the profoundest service that poems or any other writings can do for their reader is not merely to satisfy the intellect, or supply something polish'd and interesting, nor even to depict great passions, or persons or events, but to fill him with vigorous and clean manliness, religiousness, and give him *good heart* as a radical possession and habit. The educated world seems to have been growing more and more ennuyed for ages, leaving to our time the inheritance of it all. Fortunately there is the original inexhaustible fund of buoyance, normally resident in the race, forever eligible to be appeal'd to and relied on.

As for native American individuality, though certain to come, and on a large scale, the distinctive and ideal type of Western character (as consistent with the operative political and even moneymaking features of United States' humanity in the Nineteenth Century as chosen knights, gentlemen and warriors were the ideals of the centuries of European feudalism) it has not yet appear'd. I have allow'd the stress of my poems from beginning to end to bear upon American individuality and assist it—not only because that is a great lesson in Nature, amid all her generalizing laws, but as counterpoise to the leveling tendencies of Democracy—and for other reasons. Defiant of ostensible literary and other conventions, I avowedly chant "the great pride of man in himself," and permit it to be more or less a *motif* of nearly all my verse. I think this pride indispensable to an American. I think it not inconsistent with obedience, humility, deference, and self-questioning.

Democracy has been so retarded and jeopardized by powerful personalities, that its first instincts are fain to clip, conform, bring in stragglers, and reduce everything to a dead level. While the ambitious thought of my song is to help the forming of a great aggregate Nation, it is, perhaps, altogether through the forming of myriads of fully develop'd and enclosing individuals. Welcome as are equality's and fraternity's doctrines and popular education, a certain liability accompanies them all, as we see. That primal and interior something in man, in his soul's abysms, coloring all, and, by exceptional fruitions, giving the last majesty to him—something continually touch'd upon and attain'd by the old poems and ballads of feudalism, and often the principal foundation of them—modern science and democracy appear to be endangering, perhaps eliminating. But that forms an appearance only; the reality is quiet different. The new influences, upon the whole, are surely preparing the way for grander individualities than ever. Today and here personal force is behind everything, just the same. The times and depictions from the *Iliad* to Shakespeare inclusive can happily never again be realized—but the elements of courageous and lofty manhood are unchanged.

Without yielding an inch the workingman and working-woman were to be in my pages from first to last. The ranges of heroism and loftiness with which Greek and feudal poets endow'd their god-like or lordly born characters—indeed prouder and better based and with fuller ranges than those— I was to endow the democratic averages of America. I was to show that we, here and today, are eligible to the grandest and the best—more eligible now than any times of old were. I will also want my utterances (I said to myself before beginning) to be in spirit the poems of the morning. (They have been founded and mainly written in the sunny forenoon and early midday of my life.) I will want them to be the poems of women entirely as much as men. I have wish'd to put the complete Union of the States in my songs without any preference or partiality whatever. Henceforth, if they live and are read, it must be just as much South as North—just as much along the Pacific as Atlantic—in the valley of the Mississippi, in Canada, up in Maine, down in Texas, and on the shores of Puget Sound.

From another point of view Leaves of Grass is avowedly the song of Sex and Amativeness, and even Animality—though meanings that do not usually go along with those words are behind all, and will duly emerge; and all are sought to be lifted into a different light and atmosphere. Of this feature, intention-ally palpable in a few lines, I shall only say the espousing principle of those lines so gives breath of life to my whole scheme that the bulk of the pieces might as well have been left unwritten were those lines omitted. Difficult as it will be, it has become, in my opinion, imperative to achieve a shifted attitude from superior men and women toward the thought and fact of sexuality, as an element in character, personality, the emotions, and a theme in literature. I am not going to argue the question by itself; it does not stand by itself. The vitality of it is altogether in its relations, bearings, significance—like the clef of a symphony. At last analogy the lines I allude to, and the spirit in which they are spoken, permeate all Leaves of Grass, and the work must stand or fall with them, as the human body and soul must remain as an entirety.

Universal as are certain facts and symptoms of communities or individuals all times, there is nothing so rare in modern conventions and poetry as their normal recognizance. Literature is always calling in the doctor for consultation and confession, and always giving evasions and swathing suppressions in place of that "heroic nudity"[5] on which only a genuine diagnosis of serious cases can be built. And in respect to editions of *Leaves of Grass* in time to come (if there should be such) I take occasion now to confirm those lines with the settled convictions and deliberate renewals of thirty years, and to hereby prohibit, as far as word of mine can do so, any elision of them.

Then still a purpose enclosing all, and over and beneath all. Ever since what might be call'd thought, or the budding of thought, fairly began in my youthful mind, I had had a desire to attempt some worthy record of that entire faith and acceptance ("to justify the ways of God to man" is Milton's well-known and ambitious phrase) which is the foundation of moral America. I felt it all as positively then in my young days as I do now in my old ones; to formulate a poem whose every thought or fact should directly or indirectly be or connive at an implicit belief in the wisdom, health, mystery, beauty of every process, every concrete object, every human or other existence, not only consider'd from the point of view of all, but of each.

While I cannot understand it or argue it out, I fully believe in a clue and purpose in Nature, entire and several; and that invisible spiritual results, just as real and definite as the visible, eventuate all concrete life and all materialism, through Time. My book ought to emanate buoyancy and gladness legitimately enough, for it was grown out of those elements, and has been the comfort of my life since it was originally commenced.

One main genesis-motive of the *Leaves* was my conviction (just as strong today as ever) that the crowning growth of the United States is to be spiritual and heroic. To help start and favor that growth—or even to call attention to it, or the need of it—is the beginning, middle and final purpose of the poems. (In fact, when really cipher'd out and summ'd to the last, plowing up in earnest the interminable average fallows of humanity—

[5]*Nineteenth Century,* July 1883.

not "good government" merely, in the common sense—is the justification and main purpose of these United States.)

Isolated advantages in any rank or grace or fortune—the direct or indirect threads of all the poetry of the past—are in my opinion distasteful to the republican genius, and offer no foundation for its fitting verse. Establish'd poems, I know, have the very great advantage of chanting the already perform'd, so full of glories, reminiscences dear to the minds of men. But my volume is a candidate for the future. "All original art," says Taine, anyhow, "is self-regulated, and no original art can be regulated from without; it carries its own counterpoise, and does not receive it from elsewhere—lives on its own blood"—a solace to my frequent bruises and sulky vanity.

As the present is perhaps mainly an attempt at personal statement or illustration, I will allow myself as further help to extract the following anecdote from a book, *Annals of Old Painters*, conn'd by me in youth. Reubens, the Flemish painter, in one of his wanderings through the galleries of old convents, came across a singular work. After looking at it thoughtfully for a good while, and listening to the criticisms of his suite of students, he said to the latter, in answer to their questions, (as to what school the work implied or belong'd,) "I do not believe the artist, unknown and perhaps no longer living, who has given the world this legacy, ever belong'd to any school, or ever painted anything but this one picture, which is a personal affair —a piece out of a man's life."

Leaves of Grass indeed (I cannot too often reiterate) has mainly been the outcropping of my own emotional and other personal nature—an attempt, from first to last, to put a *Person*, a human being (myself, in the latter half of the Nineteenth Century, in America,) freely, fully and truly on record. I could not find any similar personal record in current literature that satisfied me. But it is not on *Leaves of Grass* distinctively as *literature*, or a specimen thereof, that I feel to dwell, or advance claims. No one will get at my verses who insist upon viewing them as a literary performance, or attempt at such performance, or as aiming mainly toward art or aestheticism.

I say no land or people or circumstances ever existed so

needing a race of singers and poems differing from all others, and rigidly their own, as the land and people and circumstances of our United States need such singers and poems today, and for the future. Still further, as long as the States continue to absorb and be dominated by the poetry of the Old World, and remain unsupplied with autochthonous song, to express, vitalize and give color to and define their material and political success, and minister to them distinctively, so long will they stop short of first-class Nationality and remain defective.

In the free evening of my day I give to you, reader, the foregoing garrulous talk, thoughts, reminiscences,

> As idly drifting down the ebb,
> Such ripples, half-caught voices, echo from the shore.

Concluding with two items for the imaginative genius of the West, when it worthily rises—First, what Herder taught to the young Goethe, that really great poetry is always (like the Homeric or Biblical canticles) the result of a national spirit, and not the privilege of a polish'd and select few; Second, that the strongest and sweetest songs yet remain to be sung.

DEMOCRATIC VISTAS

EDITOR'S NOTE TO
DEMOCRATIC VISTAS

Democratic Vistas (1871) was not the effort of a single moment. In 1867 and 1868 Whitman had written essays on democracy and the individual—the two pole themes of his thought about American society. These were now absorbed into a pamphlet whose partial inspiration at least was Carlyle's attack upon that society in *Shooting Niagara*. Here, as later in *Specimen Days*, Whitman answered Carlyle in principle but admitted in detail that the savage critic across the sea was right. *Democratic Vistas* itself is savage. In a single paragraph Whitman diagnoses the "deep disease" of America as "hollowness of heart." Hypocrisy, superciliousness, deceit, depravity, corruption, and flippancy are among the terms he flings at a people whose manners have disillusioned him. The prophet of 1855 has sobered down. He has not lost his faith in the future, but the future is the only thing that gives him hope. Neither has he lost faith in his theory of democracy, which for him is still the theory of America. It is simply that he must imagine a golden age to come rather than hail one that is here. For none is here among the "vulgarians of his time." "I can conceive," he says, "a community . . . in which, on a sufficient scale, the perfect personalities without noise meet; say in some pleasant western settlement or town." That is the best he can do. The great poetry he had predicted has not arrived. There are only "piano songs and tinkling rhymes," there are only dandies and dapper gentlemen "whimpering and crying about something, chasing one aborted conceit after another, and forever occupied in dyspeptic amours with dyspeptic women." We must have, he says, "great poems of death." He had written two such poems in "Out of the Cradle Endlessly Rocking" and "When Lilacs Last in the Dooryard Bloom'd," and it is interesting to see that he recognized the profundity of their subject.

No book of Whitman's is more honest than this one, and only *Leaves of Grass* is more important. *Democratic Vistas* is a tragic utterance, perhaps a turgid one to ears accustomed only to the lyric optimism of which Whitman also was capable. It was a hard book for Whitman to feel and write, and it has been found a hard book to read. But it is a necessary book, not only for the notes it provides on the disillusionment that followed the Civil War, but for the criticism it gives of a society which always can benefit, as any live society can, from chastisement by its best lovers.

Democratic Vistas
1871

As the greatest lessons of Nature through the universe are perhaps the lessons of variety and freedom, the same present the
greatest lessons also in New World politics and progress. If a
man were asked, for instance, the distinctive points contrasting
modern European and American political and other life with
the old Asiatic cultus, as lingering-bequeathed yet in China and
Turkey, he might find the amount of them in John Stuart Mill's
profound essay on Liberty in the future, where he demands two
main constituents, or sub-strata, for a truly grand nationality—
1st, a large variety of character—and 2nd, full play for human
nature to expand itself in numberless and even conflicting directions—(seems to be for general humanity much like the influences that make up, in their limitless field, that perennial
health-action of the air we call the weather—an infinite number
of currents and forces, and contributions, and temperatures,
and cross purposes, whose ceaseless play of counterpart upon
counterpart brings constant restoration and vitality). With this
thought—and not for itself alone, but all it necessitates, and
draws after it—let me begin my speculations.

America, filling the present with greatest deeds and problems, cheerfully accepting the past, including feudalism (as,
indeed, the present is but the legitimate birth of the past, including feudalism), counts, as I reckon, for her justification and
success (for who, as yet, dare claim success?) almost entirely
on the future. Nor is that hope unwarranted. Today, ahead,
though dimly yet, we see, in vistas, a copious, sane, gigantic
offspring. For our New World I consider far less important for
what it has done, or what it is, than for results to come. Sole
among nationalities, these States have assumed the task to put

in forms of lasting power and practicality, on areas of amplitude rivaling the operations of the physical kosmos, the moral political speculations of ages, long, long deferred, the democratic republican principle, and the theory of development and perfection by voluntary standards, and self-reliance. Who else, indeed, except the United States, in history, so far, have accepted in unwitting faith, and, as we now see, stand, act upon, and go security for, these things?

But preluding no longer, let me strike the keynote of the following strain. First premising that, though the passages of it have been written at widely different times (it is, in fact, a collection of memoranda, perhaps for future designers, comprehenders), and though it may be open to the charge of one part contradicting another—for there are opposite sides to the great question of democracy, as to every great question—I feel the parts harmoniously blended in my own realization and convictions, and present them to be read only in such oneness, each page and each claim and assertion modified and tempered by the others. Bear in mind, too, that they are not the result of studying up in political economy, but of the ordinary sense, observing, wandering among men, these States, these stirring years of war and peace. I will not gloss over the appalling dangers of universal suffrage in the United States. In fact, it is to admit and face these dangers I am writing. To him or her within whose thought rages the battle, advancing, retreating, between democracy's convictions, aspirations, and the people's crudeness, vice, caprices, I mainly write this essay. I shall use the words America and democracy as convertible terms. Not an ordinary one is the issue. The United States are destined either to surmount the gorgeous history of feudalism, or else prove the most tremendous failure of time. Not the least doubtful am I on any prospects of their material success. The triumphant future of their business, geographic and productive departments, on larger scales and in more varieties than ever, is certain. In those respects the republic must soon (if she does not already) outstrip all examples hitherto afforded, and dominate the world.[1]

[1] "From a territorial area of less than nine hundred thousand square miles, the Union has expanded into over four millions and a half—

Admitting all this, with the priceless value of our political institutions, general suffrage (and fully acknowledging the latest, widest opening of the doors), I say that, far deeper than these, what finally and only is to make of our Western world a nationality superior to any hither known, and outtopping the past, must be vigorous, yet unsuspected Literatures, perfect personalities and sociologies, original, transcendental, and expressing (what, in highest sense, are not yet expressed at all) democracy and the modern. With these, and out of these, I

---

fifteen times larger than that of Great Britain and France combined—with a shore-line, including Alaska, equal to the entire circumference of the earth, and with a domain within these lines far wider than that of the Romans in their proudest days of conquest and renown. With a river, lake, and coastwise commerce estimated at over two thousand millions of dollars per year; with a railway traffic of four to six thousand millions per year, and the annual domestic exchanges of the country running up to nearly ten thousand millions per year; with over two thousand millions of dollars invested in manufacturing, mechanical, and mining industry; with over five hundred millions of acres of land in actual occupancy, wiht their appurtenances, at over seven thousand millions of dollars, and producing annually crops valued at over three thousand millions of dollars; with a realm which, if the density of Belgium's population were possible, would be vast enough to include all the present inhabitants of the world; and with equal rights guaranteed to even the poorest and humblest of our forty millions of people—we can, with a manly pride akin to that which distinguished the palmiest days of Rome, claim," etc., etc., etc.—Vice-President Colfax's Speech, July 4, 1870.
Later—*London Times (Weekly),* June 23, '82.
"The wonderful wealth-producing power of the United States defies and sets at naught the grave drawbacks of a mischievous protective tariff, and has already obliterated, almost wholly, the traces of the greatest of modern civil wars. What is especially remarkable in the present development of American energy and success is its wide and equable distribution. North and south, east and west, on the shores of the Atlantic and the Pacific, along the chain of the great lakes, in the valley of the Mississippi, and on the coasts of the Gulf of Mexico, the creation of wealth and the increase of population are signally exhibited. It is quite true, as has been shown by the recent apportionment of population in the House of Representatives, that some sections of the Union have advanced, relatively to the rest, in an extraordinary and unexpected degree. But this does not imply that the States which have gained no additional representatives or have actually lost some have been stationary or have receded. The fact is that the present tide of prosperity has risen so high that it has overflowed all barriers, and has filled up the backwaters, and established something like an approach to uniform success."

promulgate new races of Teachers, and of perfect Women, indispensable to endow the birth-stock of a New World. For feudalism, caste, the ecclesiastic traditions, though palpably retreating from political institutions, still hold essentially, by their spirit, even in this country, entire possession of the more important fields, indeed the very subsoil, of education, and of social standards and literature.

I say that democracy can never prove itself beyond cavil, until it founds and luxuriantly grows its own forms of art, poems, schools, theology, displacing all that exists, or that has been produced anywhere in the past, under opposite influences. It is curious to me that while so many voices, pens, minds, in the press, lecture rooms, in our Congress, etc., are discussing intellectual topics, pecuniary dangers, legislative problems, the suffrage, tariff and labor questions, and the various business and benevolent needs of America, with propositions, remedies, often worth deep attention, there is one need, a hiatus the profoundest, that no eye seems to perceive, no voice to state. Our fundamental want today in the United States, with closest, amplest reference to present conditions, and to the future, is of a class, and the clear idea of a class, of native authors, literatures, far different, far higher in grade, than any yet known, sacerdotal, modern, fit to cope with our occasions, lands, permeating the whole mass of American mentality, taste, belief, breathing into it a new breath of life, giving it decision, affecting politics far more than the popular superficial suffrage, with results inside and underneath the elections of Presidents or Congresses—radiating, begetting appropriate teachers, schools, manners, and, as its grandest result, accomplishing (what neither the schools nor the churches and their clergy have hitherto accomplished, and without which this nation will no more stand, permanently, soundly, than a house will stand without a sub-stratum), a religious and moral character beneath the political and productive and intellectual bases of the States. For know you not, dear, earnest reader, that the people of our land may all read and write, and may all possess the right to vote— and yet the main things may be entirely lacking?—(and this to suggest them).

Viewed, today, from a point of view sufficiently over-arching,

the problem of humanity all over the civilized world is social
and religious, and is to be finally met and treated by literature.
The priest departs, the divine literatus comes. Never was anything more wanted than, today, and here in the States, the poet
of the modern is wanted, or the great literatus of the modern.
At all times, perhaps, the central point in any nation, and that
whence it is itself really swayed the most, and whence it sways
others, is its national literature, especially its archetypal poems.
Above all previous lands, a great original literature is surely to
become the justification and reliance (in some respects the sole
reliance of American democracy).

Few are aware how the great literature penetrates all, gives
hue to all, shapes aggregates and individuals, and, after subtle
ways, with irresistible power, constructs, sustains, demolishes
at will. Why tower, in reminiscence, above all the nations of
the earth, two special lands, petty in themselves, yet inexpressibly gigantic, beautiful, columnar? Immortal Judah lives, and
Greece immortal lives, in a couple of poems.

Nearer than this. It is not generally realized, but it is true, as
the genius of Greece, and all the sociology, personality, politics,
and religion of those wonderful states, resided in their literature
or aesthetics, that what was afterwards the main support of
European chivalry, the feudal, ecclesiastical, dynastic world
over there—forming its osseous structure, holding it together
for hundreds, thousands of years, preserving its flesh and
bloom, giving it form, decision, rounding it out, and so saturat-
ing it in the conscious and unconscious blood, breed, belief,
and intuitions of men, that it still prevails powerful to this day,
in defiance of the mighty changes of time—was its literature,
permeating to the very marrow, especially that major part, its
enchanting songs, ballads, and poems.[2]

[2]See, for hereditaments, specimens, Walter Scott's Border Minstrelsy,
Percy's collection, Ellis's early English Metrical Romances, the European continental poems of Walter of Aquitania, and the Nibelungen,
of pagan stock, but monkish-feudal redaction; the history of the
Troubadours, by Fauriel; even the far-back cumbrous old Hindu
epics, as indicating the Asian eggs out of which European chivalry
was hatched; Ticknor's chapters on the Cid, and on the Spanish
poems and poets of Calderon's time. Then always, and, of course, as
the superbest poetic culmination-expression of feudalism, the Shakes-
pearean dramas, in the attitudes, dialogue, characters, etc., of the

To the ostent of the senses and eyes, I know, the influences which stamp the world's history are wards, uprisings or downfalls of dynasties, changeful movement of trade, important inventions, navigation, military or civil governments, advent of powerful personalities, conquerors, etc. These of course play their part; yet, it may be, a single new thought, imagination, abstract principle, even literary style, fit for the time, put in shape by some great literatus, and projected among mankind, may duly cause changes, growths, removals, greater than the longest and bloodiest war, or the most stupendous merely political, dynastic, or commercial overturn.

In short, as though it may not be realized, it is strictly true, that a few first-class poets, philosophs, and authors have substantially settled and given status to the entire religion, education, law, sociology, etc., of the hitherto civilized world, by tingeing and often creating the atmospheres out of which they have arisen, such also must stamp, and more than ever stamp, the interior and real democratic construction of this American continent, today, and days to come. Remember also this fact of difference, that, while through the antique and throguh the medieval ages, highest thoughts and ideals realized themselves, and their expression made its way by other arts, as much as, or even more than by, technical literature (not open to the mass of persons, or even to the majority of eminent persons), such literature in our day and for current purposes is not only more eligible than all the other arts put together, but has become the only general means of morally influencing the world. Painting, sculpture, and the dramatic theatre, it would seem, no longer play an indispensable or even important part in the workings and mediumship of intellect, utility, or even high aesthetics. Architecture remains, doubtless with capacities, and a real future. Then music, the combiner, nothing more spiritual, nothing more sensuous, a god, yet completely human, advances, prevails, holds highest place; supplying in certain wants and quarters what nothing else could supply. Yet in the civilization of today it is undeniable that, over all the arts, literature domi-

---

princes, lords, and gentlemen, the pervading atmosphere, the implied and expressed standard of manners, the high port and proud stomach, the regal embroidery of style, etc.

nates, serves beyond all—shapes the character of church and school—or, at any rate, is capable of doing so. Including the literature of science, its scope is indeed unparalleled.

Before proceeding further, it were perhaps well to discriminate on certain points. Literature tills its crops in many fields, and some may flourish, while others lag. What I say in these Vistas has its main bearing on imaginative literature, especially poetry, the stock of all. In the department of science, and the speciality of journalism, there appear, in these States, promises, perhaps fulfillments, of highest earnestness, reality and life. These, of course, are modern. But in the region of imaginative, spinal and essential attributes, something equivalent to creation is, for our age and lands, imperatively demanded. For not only is it not enough that the new blood, new frame of democracy shall be vivified and held together merely by political means, superficial suffrage, legislation, etc., but it is clear to me that, unless it goes deeper, gets at least as firm and as warm a hold in men's hearts, emotions and belief, as, in their days, feudalism or ecclesiasticism, and inaugurates its own perennial sources, welling from the center forever, its strength will be defective, its growth doubtful, and its main charm wanting. I suggest, therefore, the possibility, should some two or three really original American poets (perhaps artists or lecturers) arise, mounting the horizon like planets, stars of the first magnitude, that, from their eminence, fusing contributions, races, far localities, etc., together, they would give more compaction and more moral identity (the quality today most needed) to these States, than all its Constitutions, legislative and judicial ties, and all its hitherto political, warlike, or materialistic experiences. As, for instance, there could hardly happen anything that would more serve the States, with all their variety of origins, their diverse climes, cities, standards, etc., than possessing an aggregate of heroes, characters, exploits, sufferings, prosperity or misfortune, glory or disgrace, common to all, typical of it all—no less, but even greater would it be to possess the aggregation of a cluster of mighty poets, artists, teachers, fit for us, national expressers, comprehending and effusing for the men and women of the States, what is universal, native, common to all, inland and seaboard, northern and southern. The

historians say of ancient Greece, with her ever-jealous autono-
mies, cities and states, that the only positive unity she ever
owned or received, was the sad unity of a common subjection,
at the last, to foreign conquerors. Subjection, aggregation of
that sort, is impossible to America; but the fear of conflicting
and irreconcilable interiors, and the lack of a common skeleton,
knitting all close, continually haunts me. Or, if it does not,
nothing is plainer than the need, a long period to come, of a
fusion of the States into the only reliable identity, the moral
and artistic one. For, I say, the true nationality of the States,
the genuine union, when we come to a mortal crisis, is, and is
to be, after all, neither the written law, nor (as is generally
supposed) either self-interest, or common pecuniary or material
objects—but the fervid and tremendous Idea, melting everything else with resistless heat, and solving all lesser and definite
distinctions in vast, indefinite, spiritual, emotional power.

It may be claimed (and I admit the weight of the claim) that
common and general worldly prosperity, and a populace well-
to-do, and with all life's material comforts, is the main thing,
and is enough. It may be argued that our republic is, in performance, really enacting today the grandest arts, poems, etc., by
beating up the wilderness into fertile farms, and in her railroads, ships, machinery, etc. And it may be asked, Are these
not better, indeed, for America, than any utterances even of
greatest rhapsode, artist, or literatus?

I too hail those achievements with pride and joy: then answer
that the soul of man will not with such only—nay, not with
such at all—be finally satisfied; but needs what (standing on
these and on all things, as the feet stand on the ground) is
addressed to the loftiest, to itself alone.

Out of such considerations, such truths, arises for treatment
in these Vistas the important question of character, of an
American stock-personality, with literatures and arts for outlets
and return-expressions, and, of course, to correspond, within
outlines common to all. To these, the main affair, the thinkers
of the United States, in general so acute, have either given
feeblest attention, or have remained, and remain, in a state
of somnolence.

For my part, I would alarm and caution even the political

and business reader, and to the utmost extent, against the prevailing delusion that the establishment of free political institutions, and plentiful intellectual smartness, with general good order, physical plenty, industry, etc. (desirable and precious advantages as they all are), do, of themselves, determine and yield to our experiment of democracy the fruitage of success. With such advantages at present fully, or almost fully, possessed—the Union just issued, victorious, from the struggle with the only foes it need ever fear (namely, those within itself, the interior ones), and with unprecedented materialistic advancement—society, in these States, is cankered, crude, superstitious and rotten. Political, or law-made society is, and private, or voluntary society, is also. In any vigor, the element of the moral conscience, the most important, the verteber to State or man, seems to me either entirely lacking, or seriously enfeebled or ungrown.

I say we had best look our times and lands searchingly in the face, like a physician diagnosing some deep disease. Never was there, perhaps, more hollowness at heart than at present, and here in the United States. Genuine belief seems to have left us. The underlying principles of the States are not honestly believed in (for all this hectic glow, and these melodramatic screamings), nor is humanity itself believed in. What penetrating eye does not everywhere see through the mask? The spectacle is appalling. We live in an atmosphere of hypocrisy throughout. The men believe not in the women, nor the women in the men. A scornful superciliousness rules in literature. The aim of all the *littérateurs* is to find something to make fun of. A lot of churches, sects, etc., the most dismal phantasms I know, usurp the name of religion. Conversation is a mass of badinage. From deceit in the spirit, the mother of all false deeds, the offspring is already incalculable. An acute and candid person, in the revenue department in Washington, who is led by the course of his employment to regularly visit the cities, north, south, and west, to investigate frauds, has talked much with me about his discoveries. The depravity of the business classes of our country is not less than has been supposed, but infinitely greater. The official services of America, national, state, and municipal, in all their branches and departments,

except the judiciary, are saturated in corruption, bribery, falsehood, maladministration; and the judiciary is tainted. The great
cities reek with respectable as much as non-respectable robbery
and scoundrelism. In fashionable life, flippancy, tepid amours,
weak infidelism, small aims, or no aims at all, only to kill time.
In business (this all-devouring modern word, business), the
one sole object is, by any means, pecuniary gain. The magician's serpent in the fable ate up all the other serpents; and
moneymaking is our magician's serpent, remaining today sole
master of the field. The best class we show, is but a mob of
fashionably dressed speculators and vulgarians. True, indeed,
behind this fantastic farce, enacted on the visible stage of
society, solid things and stupendous labors are to be discovered,
existing crudely and going on in the background, to advance
and tell themselves in time. Yet the truths are none the less
terrible. I say that our New World democracy, however great
a success in uplifting the masses out of their sloughs, in materialistic development, products, and in a certain highly decep-
tive superficial popular intellectuality, is, so far, an almost
complete failure in its social aspects, and in really grand religious, moral, literary, and aesthetic results. In vain do we march
with unprecedented strides to empire so colossal, outvying the
antique, beyond Alexander's, beyond the proudest sway of
Rome. In vain have we annexed Texas, California, Alaska, and
reach north for Canada and south for Cuba. It is as if we were
somehow being endowed with a vast and more and more
thoroughly appointed body, and then left with little or no soul.

Let me illustrate further, as I write, with current observations, localities, etc. The subject is important, and will bear
repetition. After an absence, I am now again (September 1870)
in New York City and Brooklyn, on a few weeks' vacation.
The splendor, picturesqueness, and oceanic amplitude and rush
of these great cities, the unsurpassed situation, rivers and bay,
sparkling sea-tides, costly and lofty new buildings, façades of
marble and iron, of original grandeur and elegance of design,
with the masses of gay color, the preponderance of white and
blue, the flags flying, the endless ships, the tumultuous streets,
Broadway, the heavy, low, musical roar, hardly ever intermitted, even at night; the jobbers' houses, the rich shops, the

wharves, the great Central Park, and the Brooklyn Park of hills (as I wander among them this beautiful fall weather, musing, watching, absorbing)—the assemblages of the citizens in their groups, conversations, trades, evening amusements, or along the by-quarters—these, I say, and the like of these, completely satisfy my senses of power, fullness, motion, etc., and give me, through such senses and appetites, and through my aesthetic conscience, a continued exaltation and absolute fulfillment. Always and more and more, as I cross the East and North rivers, the ferries, or with the pilots in their pilot-houses, or pass an hour in Wall Street, or the Gold Exchange, I realize (if we must admit such partialisms) that not Nature alone is great in her fields of freedom and the open air, in her storms, the shows of night and day, the mountains, forests, sea—but in the artificial, the work of man too is equally great —in this profusion of teeming humanity—in these ingenuities, streets, goods, houses, ships—these hurrying, feverish, electric crowds and men, their complicated business genius (not least among the geniuses), and all this mighty, many-threaded wealth and industry concentrated here.

But sternly discarding, shutting our eyes to the glow and grandeur of the general superficial effect, coming down to what is of the only real importance, Personalities, and examining minutely, we question, we ask, Are there, indeed, *men* here worthy the name? Are there athletes? Are there perfect women, to match the generous material luxuriance? Is there a pervading atmosphere of beautiful manners? Are there crops of fine youths, and majestic old persons? Are there arts worthy freedom and a rich people? Is there a great moral and religious civilization—the only justification of a great material one? Confess that to severe eyes, using the moral microscope upon humanity, a sort of dry and flat Sahara appears, these cities, crowded with petty grotesques, malformations, phantoms, playing meaningless antics. Confess that everywhere, in shop, street, church, theatre, barroom, official chair, are pervading flippancy and vulgarity, low cunning, infidelity—everywhere the youth puny, impudent, foppish, prematurely ripe—everywhere an abnormal libidinousness, unhealthy forms, male, female, painted, padded, dyed, chignoned, muddy complexions, bad blood, the capacity for good motherhood decreasing or deceased, shallow notions of beauty, with a range of manners, or rather lack of manners (considering the advantages enjoyed), probably the meanest to be seen in the world.[3]

Of all this, and these lamentable conditions, to breathe into them the breath recuperative of same and heroic life, I say a new-founded literature, not merely to copy and reflect existing surfaces, or pander to what is called taste—not only to amuse, pass away time, celebrate the beautiful, the refined, the past, or exhibit technical, rhythmic, or grammatical dexterity—but a literature underlying life, religious, consistent with science, handling the elements and forces with competent power, teaching and training men—and, as perhaps the most precious of its results, achieving the entire redemption of woman out of these incredible holds and webs of silliness, millinery, and every kind of dyspeptic depletion—and thus insuring to the States a strong and sweet Female Race, a race of perfect Mothers— is what is needed.

And now, in the full conception of these facts and points, and all that they infer, pro and con—with yet unshaken faith in the elements of the American masses, the composites, of both sexes, and even considered as individuals—and ever recognizing in them the broadest bases of the best literary and aesthetic appreciation—I proceed with my speculations, Vistas.

First, let us see what we can make out of a brief, general, sentimental consideration of political democracy, and whence it has arisen, with regard to some of its current features, as

---

[3]Of these rapidly sketched hiatuses, the two which seems to be most serious are, for one, the condition, absence, or perhaps the singular abeyance, of moral conscientious fiber all through American society; and, for another, the appalling depletion of women in their powers of sane athletic maternity, their crowning attribute, and ever making the woman, in loftiest spheres, superior to the man.

I have sometimes thought, indeed, that the sole avenue and means of a reconstructed sociology depended, primarily, on a new birth, elevation, expansion, invigoration of woman, affording, for races to come (as the conditions that antedate birth are indispensable), a perfect motherhood. Great, great, indeed, far greater than they know, is the sphere of women. But doubtless the question of such new sociology all goes together, includes many varied and complex influences and premises, and the man as well as the woman, and the woman as well as the man.

an aggregate, and as the basic structure of our future literature and authorship. We shall, it is true, quickly and continually find the origin idea of the singleness of man, individualism, asserting itself, and cropping forth, even from the opposite ideas. But the mass, or lump character, for imperative reasons, is to be ever carefully weighed, borne in mind, and provided for. Only from it, and from its proper regulation and potency, comes the other, comes the chance of individualism. The two are contradictory, but our task is to reconcile them.[4]

The political history of the past may be summed up as having grown out of what underlies the words, order, safety, caste, and especially out of the need of some prompt deciding authority, and of cohesion at all cost. Leaping time, we come to the period within the memory of people now living, when, as from some lair where they had slumbered long, accumulating wrath, sprang up and are yet active (1790, and on even to the present, 1870), those noisy eructations, destructive iconoclasms, a fierce sense of wrongs, amid which moves the form, well known in modern history, in the Old World, stained with much blood, and marked by savage reactionary clamors and demands. These bear, mostly, as on one inclosing point of need.

For after the rest is said—after the many time-honored and really true things for subordination, experience, rights of property, etc., have been listened to and acquiesced in—after the valuable and well-settled statement of our duties and relations in society is thoroughly conned over and exhausted—it remains to bring forward and modify everything else with the idea of that Something a man is (last precious consolation of the drudging poor), standing apart from all else, divine in his own right, and a woman in hers, sole and untouchable by any canons of authority, or any rule derived from precedent, state-

[4]The question hinted here is one which time only can answer. Must not the virtue of modern Individualism, continually enlarging, usurping all, seriously affect, perhaps keep down entirely, in America, the like of the ancient virtue of Patriotism, the fervid and absorbing love of general country? I have no doubt myself that the two will merge, and will mutually profit and brace each other, and that from them a greater product, a third, will arise. But I feel that at present they and their oppositions form a serious problem and paradox in the United States.

safety, the acts of legislatures, or even from what is called religion, modesty, or art. The radiation of this truth is the key of the most significant doing of our immediately preceding three centuries, and has been the political genesis and life of America. Advancing visibly, it still more advances invisibly. Underneath the fluctuations of the expressions of society, as well as the movements of the politics of the leading nations of the world, we see steadily pressing ahead and strengthening itself, even in the midst of immense tendencies toward aggregation, this image of completeness in separation, of individual personal dignity, of a single person, either male or female, characterized in the main, not from extrinsic acquirements or position, but in the pride of himself or herself alone; and, as an eventual conclusion and summing up (or else the entire scheme of things is aimless, a cheat, a crash), the simple idea that the last, best dependence is to be upon humanity itself, and its own inherent, normal, full-grown qualities without any superstitious support whatever. This idea of perfect individualism it is indeed that deepest tinges and gives character to the idea of the aggregate. For it is mainly or altogether to serve independent separatism that we favor a strong generalization, consolidation. As it is to give the best vitality and freedom to the rights of the States (every bit as important as the right of nationality, the union), that we insist on the identity of the Union at all hazards.

The purpose of democracy—supplanting old belief in the necessary absoluteness of established dynastic rulership, temporal, ecclesiastical, and scholastic, as furnishing the only security against chaos, crime, and ignorance—is, through many transmigrations and amid endless ridicules, arguments, and ostensible failures, to illustrate, at all hazards, this doctrine or theory that man, properly trained in sanest, highest freedom, may and must become a law, and series of laws, unto himself, surrounding and providing for, not only his own personal control, but all his relations to other individuals, and to the State; and that, while other theories, as in the past histories of nations, have proved wise enough, and indispensable perhaps for their conditions, *this*, as matters now stand in our civilized world, is the only scheme worth working from, as warranting results like those of Nature's laws, reliable, when once established, to carry on themselves.

The argument of the matter is extensive, and, we admit, by no means all on one side. What we shall offer will be far, far from sufficient. But while leaving unsaid much that should properly even prepare the way for the treatment of this many-sided question of political liberty, equality, or republicanism —leaving the whole history and consideration of the feudal plan and its products, embodying humanity, its politics and civilization, through the retrospect of past time (which plan and products, indeed, make up all of the past, and a large part of the present)—leaving unanswered, at least by any specific and local answer, many a well-wrought argument and instance, and many a conscientious declamatory cry and warning—as, very lately, from an eminent and venerable person abroad[5]— things, problems, full of doubt, dread, suspense (not new to me, but old occupiers of many an anxious hour in city's din, or night's silence), we still may give a page or so, whose drift is opportune. Time alone can finally answer these things. But as a substitute in passing, let us, even if fragmentarily, throw forth a short direct or indirect suggestion of the premises of that other plan, in the new spirit, under the new forms, started here in our America.

As to the political section of Democracy, which introduces and breaks ground for further and vaster sections, few probably are the minds, even in these republican States, that fully comprehend the aptness of that phrase, "the government of the people, by the people, for the people," which we inherit from the lips of Abraham Lincoln; a formula whose verbal shape is homely wit, but whose scope includes both the totality and all minutiæ of the lesson.

[5]*Shooting Niagara.*—I was at first roused to much anger and abuse by this essay from Mr. Carlyle, so insulting to the theory of America— but happening to think afterwards how I had more than once been in the like mood, during which his essay was evidently cast, and seen persons and things in the same light (indeed, some might say there are signs of the same feeling in these Vistas)—I have since read it again, not only as a study, expressing as it does certain judgments from the highest feudal point of view, but have read it with respect as coming from an earnest soul, and as contributing certain sharp-cutting metallic grains, which, if not gold or silver, may be good, hard, honest iron.

The People! Like our huge earth itself, which, to ordinary scansion, is full of vulgar contradictions and offense, man, viewed in the lump, displeases, and is a constant puzzle and affront to the merely educated classes. The rare, cosmical, artist-mind, lit with the Infinite, alone confronts his manifold and oceanic qualities—but taste, intelligence and culture (so-called), have been against the masses, and remain so. There is plenty of glamour about the most damnable crimes and hoggish meannesses, special and general, of the feudal and dynastic world over there, with its *personnel* of lords and queens and courts, so well dressed and so handsome. But the People are ungrammatical, untidy, and their sins gaunt and ill bred.

Literature, strictly considered, has never recognized the People, and, whatever may be said, does not today. Speaking generally, the tendencies of literature, as hitherto pursued, have been to make mostly critical and querulous men. It seems as if, so far, there were some natural repugnance between a literary and professional life, and the rude rank spirit of the democracies. There is, in later literature, a treatment of benevolence, a charity business, rife enough it is true; but I know nothing more rare, even in this country, than a fit scientific estimate and reverent appreciation of the People—of their measureless wealth of latent power and capacity, their vast, artistic contrasts of lights and shades—with, in America, their entire reliability in emergencies, and a certain breadth of historic grandeur, of peace or war, far surpassing all the vaunted samples of book-heroes, or any *haut ton* coteries, in all the records of the world.

The movements of the late Secession War, and their results, to any sense that studies well and comprehends them, show that popular democracy, whatever its faults and dangers, practically justifies itself beyond the proudest claims and wildest hopes of its enthusiasts. Probably no future age can know, but I well know, how the gist of this fiercest and most resolute of the world's warlike contentions resided exclusively in the unnamed, unknown rank and file; and how the brunt of its labor of death was, to all essential purposes, volunteered. The People, of their own choice, fighting, dying for their own idea, insolently attacked by the secession-slave-power, and its very

existence imperiled. Descending to detail, entering any of the
armies, and mixing with the private soldiers, we see and have
seen august spectacles. We have seen the alacrity with which
the American-born populace, the peaceablest and most good-
natured race in the world, and the most personally independent
and intelligent, and the least fitted to submit to the irksomeness
and exasperation of regimental discipline, sprang, at the first
tap of the drum, to arms—not for gain, nor even glory, nor
to repel invasion—but for an emblem, a mere abstraction—
for the life, *the safety of the flag*. We have seen the unequaled
docility and obedience of these soldiers. We have seen them
tried long and long by hopelessness, mismanagement, and by
defeat; have seen the incredible slaughter toward or through
which the armies (as at first Fredericksburg, and afterward at
the Wilderness), still unhesitatingly obey'd orders to advance.
We have seen them in trench, or crouching behind breastwork,
or tramping in deep mud, or amid pouring rain or thick-falling
snow, or under forced marches in hottest summer (as on the
road to get to Gettysburg)—vast suffocating swarms, divisions,
corps, with every single man so grimed and black with sweat
and dust, his own mother would not have known him—his
clothes all dirty, stained and torn, with sour, accumulated sweat
for perfume—many a comrade, perhaps a brother, sun-struck,
staggering out, dying, by the roadside, of exhaustion—yet the
great bulk bearing steadily on, cheery enough, hollow-bellied
from hunger, but sinewy with unconquerable resolution.

We have seen this race proved by wholesale, by drearier, yet
more fearful tests—the wound, the amputation, the shattered
face or limb, the slow hot fever, long impatient anchorage in
bed, and all the forms of maiming, operation, and disease. Alas!
America have we seen, though only in her early youth, already
to hospital brought. There have we watched these soldiers,
many of them only boys in years—marked their decorum,
their religious nature and fortitude, and their sweet affection.
Wholesale, truly. For at the front, and through the camps,
in countless tents, stood the regimental, brigade, and division
hospitals; while everywhere amid the land, in or near cities,
rose clusters of huge, whitewashed, crowded, one-story wooden
barracks; and there ruled agony with bitter scourge, yet seldom

brought a cry; and there stalked death by day and night along the narrow aisles between the rows of cots, or by the blankets on the ground, and touched lightly many a poor sufferer, often with blessed, welcome touch.

I know not whether I shall be understood, but I realize that it is finally from what I learned personally mixing in such scenes that I am now penning these pages. One night in the gloomiest period of the war, in the Patent Office hospital in Washington city, as I stood by the bedside of a Pennsylvania soldier, who lay, conscious of quick approaching death, yet perfectly calm, and with noble, spiritual manner, the veteran surgeon, turning aside, said to me, that though he had witnessed many, many deaths of soldiers, and had been a worker at Bull Run, Antietam, Fredericksburg, etc., he had not seen yet the first case of man or boy that met the approach of dissolution with cowardly qualms or terror. My own observation fully bears out the remark.

What have we here, if not, towering above all talk and argument, the plentifully supplied, last-needed proof of democracy, in its personalities? Curiously enough, too, the proof on this point comes, I should say, every bit as much from the south, as from the north. Although I have spoken only of the latter, yet I deliberately include all. Grand, common stock! to me the accomplished and convincing growth, prophetic of the future; proof undeniable to sharpest sense, of perfect beauty, tenderness and pluck, that never feudal lord, nor Greek, nor Roman breed, yet rivaled. Let no tongue ever speak in disparagement of the American races, north or south, to one who has been through the war in the great army hospitals.

Meantime, general humanity (for to that we return, as, for our purposes, what it really is, to bear in mind), has always, in every department, been full of perverse maleficence, and is so yet. In downcast hours the soul thinks it always will be —but soon recovers from such sickly moods. I myself see clearly enough the crude, defective streaks in all the strata of the common people; the specimens and vast collections of the ignorant, the credulous, the unfit and uncouth, the incapable, and the very low and poor. The eminent person just mentioned sneeringly asks whether we expect to elevate and improve a nation's politics by absorbing such morbid collections and qualities therein. The point is a formidable one, and there will doubtless always be numbers of solid and reflective citizens who will never get over it. Our answer is general, and is involved in the scope and letter of this essay. We believe the ulterior object of political and all other government (having, of course, provided for the police, the safety of life, property, and for the basic statute and common law, and their administration, always first in order), to be among the rest, not merely to rule, to repress disorder, etc., but to develop, to open up to cultivation, to encourage the possibilities of all beneficent and manly outcroppage, and of that aspiration for independence, and the pride and self-respect latent in all characters. (Or, if there be exceptions, we cannot, fixing our eyes on them alone, make theirs the rule for all.)

I say the mission of government, henceforth, in civilized lands, is not repression alone, and not authority alone, not even of law, nor by that favorite standard of the eminent writer, the rule of the best men, the born heroes and captains of the race (as if such ever, or one time out of a hundered, get into the big places, elective or dynastic)—but higher than the highest arbitrary rule, to train communities through all their grades, beginning with individuals and ending there again, to rule themselves. What Christ appeared for in the moral-spiritual field for human-kind, namely, that in respect to the absolute soul, there is in the possession of such by each single individual, something so transcendent, so incapable of gradations (like life), that, to that extent, it places all beings on a common level, utterly regardless of the distinctions of intellect, virtue, station, or any height or lowliness whatever—is tallied in like manner, in this other field, by democracy's rule that men, the nation, as a common aggregate of living identities, affording in each a separate and complete subject for freedom, wordly thrift and happiness, and for a fair chance for growth, and for protection in citizenship, etc., must, to the political extent of the suffrage or vote, if no further, be placed, in each and in the whole, on one broad, primary, universal, common platform.

The purpose is not altogether direct; perhaps it is more indirect. For it is not that democracy is of exhaustive account in itself. Perhaps, indeed, it is (like Nature), of no account in itself. It is that, as we see, it is the best, perhaps only, fit and full means, formulater, general caller-forth, trainer, for the million, not for grand material personalities only, but for immortal souls. To be a voter with the rest is not much; and this, like every institute, will have its imperfections. But to become an enfranchised man, and now, impediments removed, to stand and start without humiliation, and equal with the rest; to commence, or have the road cleared to commence, the grand experiment of development, whose end (perhaps requiring several generations), may be the forming of a full-grown man or woman—that *is* something. To ballast the State is also secured, and in our times is to be secured, in no other way.

We do not (at any rate I do not), put it either on the ground that the People, the masses, even the best of them, are, in their latent or exhibited qualities, essentially sensible and good—nor on the ground of their rights; but that good or bad, rights or no rights, the democratic formula is the only safe and pre-servative one for coming times. We endow the masses with the suffrage for their own sake, no doubt; then, perhaps still more, from another point of view, for community's sake. Leaving the rest to the sentimentalists, we present freedom as sufficient in its scientific aspect, cold as ice, reasoning, deductive, clear and passionless as crystal.

Democracy too is law, and of the strictest, amplest kind. Many suppose (and often in its own ranks the error), that it means a throwing aside of law, and running riot. But, briefly, it is the superior law, not alone that of physical force, the body, which, adding to, it supersedes with that of the spirit. Law is the unshakable order of the universe forever; and the law over all, and law of laws, is the law of successions; that of the superior law, in time, gradually supplanting and overwhelming the inferior one. (While, for myself, I would cheerfully agree —first convenanting that the formative tendencies shall be ad-ministered in favor, or at least not against it, and that this reservation be closely construed—that until the individual or community show due signs, or be so minor and fractional as not to endanger the State, the condition of authoritative tute-lage may continue, and self-government must abide its time.)

Nor is the aesthetic point, always an important one, without fascination for highest aiming souls. The common ambition strains for elevations, to become some privileged exclusive. The master sees greatness and health in being part of the mass; nothing will do as well as common ground. Would you have in yourself the divine, vast, general law? Then merge yourself in it.

And, topping democracy, this most alluring record, that it alone can bind, and ever seeks to bind, all nations, all men, of however various and distant lands, into a brotherhood, a family. It is the old, yet ever-modern dream of earth, out of her eldest and her youngest, her fond philosophers and poets. Not that half only, individualism, which isolates. There is another half, which is adhesiveness or love, that fuses, ties, and aggregates, making the races comrades, and fraternizing all. Both are to be vitalized by religion (sole worthiest elevator of man or State), breathing into the proud, material tissues, the breath of life. For I say at the core of democracy, finally, is the religious element. All the religions, old and new, are there. Nor may the scheme step forth, clothed in resplendent beauty and command, till these, bearing the best, the latest fruit, the spiritual, shall fully appear.

A portion of our pages we might indite with reference toward Europe, especially the British part of it, more than our own land, perhaps not absolutely needed for the home reader. But the whole question hangs together, and fastens and links all peoples. The liberalist of today has this advantage over antique or medieval times, that his doctrine seeks not only to individualize but to universalize. The great word Solidarity has arisen. Of all dangers to a nation, as things exist in our day, there can be no greater one than having certain portions of the people set off from the rest by a line drawn—they not privileged as others, but degraded, humiliated, made of no account. Much quackery teems, of course, even on democracy's side, yet does not really affect the orbic quality of the matter. To work in, if we may so term it, and justify God, His divine aggregate, the People (or, the veritable horned and sharp-tailed Devil, *His* aggregate, if there be who convulsively insist upon it)—this, I say, is what democracy is for; and this is what our America means, and is doing—may I not say, has done? If not, she means nothing more, and does nothing more, than any other land. And, as by virtue of its cosmical, antiseptic power, Nature's stomach is fully strong enough not only to digest the morbific matter always presented, not to be turned aside, and perhaps, indeed, intuitively gravitating thither—but even to change such contributions into nutriment for highest use and life—so American democracy's. That is the lesson we, these days, send over to European lands by every western breeze.

And truly, whatever may be said, in the way of abstract argument, for or against the theory of a wider democratizing of institutions in any civilized country, much trouble might well be saved to all European lands by recognizing this palpable fact (for a palpable fact it is), that some form of such democratizing is about the only resource now left. *That*, or chronic dissatisfaction continued, mutterings which grow annually louder and louder, till, in due course, and pretty swiftly in most cases, the inevitable crisis crash, dynastic ruin. Anything worthy to be called statesmanship in the Old World, I should say, among the advanced students, adepts, or men of any brains, does not debate today whether to hold on, attempting to lean back and monarchize, or to look forward and democratize —but *how*, and in what degree and part, most prudently to democratize.

The eager and often inconsiderate appeals of reformers and revolutionists are indispensable, to counterbalance the inertness and fossilism making so large a part of human institutions. The latter will always take care of themselves—the danger being that they rapidly tend to ossify us. The former is to be treated with indulgence, and even with respect. As circulations to air, so is agitation and a plentiful degree of speculative license to political and moral sanity. Indirectly, but surely, goodness, virtue, law (of the very best), follow freedom. These, to democracy, are what the keel is to the ship, or saltness to the ocean.

The true gravitation-hold of liberalism in the United States will be a more universal ownership of property, general homesteads, general comfort—a vast, intertwining reticulation of wealth. As the human frame, or, indeed, any object in this manifold universe, is best kept together by the simple miracle of its own cohesion, and the necessity, exercise, and profit there-of, so a great and varied nationality, occupying millions of square miles, were firmest held and knit by the principle of the safety and endurance of the aggregate of its middling property owners. So that, from another point of view, ungracious as it may sound, and a paradox after what we have been saying, democracy looks with suspicious, ill-satisfied eye upon the very poor, the ignorant, and on those out of business. She asks for men and women with occupations, well-off, owners of houses and acres, and with cash in the bank—and with some cravings for literature, too; and must have them, and hastens to make them. Luckly, the seed is already well sown, and has taken ineradicable root.[6]

Huge and mighty are our days, our republican lands—and most in their rapid shiftings, their changes, all in the interest of the cause. As I write this particular passage (November 1868), the din of disputation rages around me. Acrid the temper of the parties, vital the pending questions. Congress convenes; the President sends his message; reconstruction is still in abeyance; the nomination and the contest for the twenty-first Presidentiad draw close, with loudest threat and bustle. Of these, and all the like of these, the eventuations I know not; but well I know that behind them, and whatever their eventuations, the vital things remain safe and certain, and all the needed work goes on. Time, with soon or later superciliousness, disposes of Presidents, Congressmen, party platforms, and such. Anon, it clears the stage of each and any mortal shred that thinks itself so potent to its day; and at and after which (with precious, golden exceptions

---

[6]For fear of mistake, I may as well distinctly specify, as cheerfully included in the model and standard of these Vistas, a practical, stirring, worldly, moneymaking, even materialistic character. It is undeniable that our farms, stores, offices, dry goods, coal and groceries, enginery, cash accounts, trades, earnings, markets, etc., should be attended to in earnest, and actively pursued, just as if they had a real and permanent existence. I perceive clearly that the extreme business energy, and this almost maniacal appetite for wealth prevalent in the United States, are parts of amelioration and progress, indispensably needed to prepare the very results I demand. My theory includes riches, and the getting of riches, and the amplest products, power, activity, inventions, movements, etc. Upon them, as upon sub-strata, I raise the edifice designed in these Vistas.

once or twice in a century), all that relates to sir potency is flung to molder in a burial-vault, and no one bothers himself the least bit about it afterwards. But the People ever remain, tendencies continue, and all the idiocratic transfers in unbroken chain go on.

In a few years the dominion-heart of America will be far inland, toward the West. Our future national capital may not be where the present one is. It is possible, nay likely that in less than fifty years, it will migrate a thousand or two miles, will be refounded, and everything belonging to it made on a different plan, original, far more superb. The main social, political, spine-character of the States will probably run along the Ohio, Missouri and Mississippi rivers, and west and north of them, including Canada. Those regions, with the group of powerful brothers toward the Pacific (destined to the mastership of that sea and its countless paradises of islands), will compact and settle the traits of America, with all the old retained, but more expanded, grafted on newer, hardier, purely native stock. A giant growth, composite from the rest, getting their contribution, absorbing it, to make it more illustrious. From the north, intellect, the sun of things, also the idea of unswayable justice, anchor amid the last, the wildest tempests. From the south the living soul, the animus of good and bad, haughtily admitting no demonstration but its own. While from the west itself comes solid personality, with blood and brawn, and the deep quality of all-accepting fusion.

Political democracy, as it exists and practically works in America, with all its threatening evils, supplies a training school for making first-class men. It is life's gymnasium, not of good only, but of all. We try often, though we fall back often. A brave delight, fit for freedom's athletes, fills these arenas, and fully satisfies, out of the action in them, irrespective of success. Whatever we do not attain, we at any rate attain the experiences of the fight, the hardening of the strong campaign, and throb with currents of attempt at least. Time is ample. Let the victors come after us. Not for nothing does evil play its part among us. Judging from the main portions of the history of the world, so far, justice is always in jeopardy, peace walks amid hourly pitfalls, and of slavery, misery, meanness, the craft of tyrants and the credulity of the populace, in some of the protean forms, no voice can at any time say, They are not. The clouds break a little, and the sun shines out—but soon and certain the lowering darkness falls again, as if to last forever. Yet is there an immortal courage and prophecy in every sane soul that cannot, must not, under any circumstances, capitulate. *Vive,* the attack—the perennial assault! *Vive,* the unpopular cause—the spirit that audaciously aims—the never-abandoned efforts, pursued the same amid opposing proofs and precedents.

Once, before the war (alas! I dare not say how many times the mood has come!) I, too, was filled with doubt and gloom. A foreigner, an acute and good man, had impressively said to me, that day—putting in form, indeed, my own observations: "I have traveled much in the United States, and watched their politicians, and listened to the speeches of the candidates, and read the journals, and gone into the public-houses, and heard the unguarded talk of men. And I have found your vaunted America honeycombed from top to toe with infidelism, even to itself and its own program. I have marked the brazen hell-faces of secession and slavery gazing defiantly from all the windows and doorways. I have everywhere found, primarily, thieves and scalliwags arranging the nominations to offices, and sometimes filling the offices themselves. I have found the north just as full of bad stuff as the south. Of the holders of public office in the Nation or the States or their municipalities, I have found that not one in a hundred has been chosen by any spontaneous selection of the outsiders, the people, but all have been nominated and put through by little or large caucuses of the politicians, and have got in by corrupt rings and electioneering, not capacity or desert. I have noticed how the millions of sturdy farmers and mechanics are thus the helpless supple-jacks of comparatively few politicians. And I have noticed more and more, the alarming spectacle of parties usurping the government, and openly and shamelessly wielding it for party purposes."

Sad, serious, deep truths. Yet are there other, still deeper, amply confronting, dominating truths. Over those politicians and great and little rings, and over all their insolence and wiles, and over the powerfullest parties, looms a power, too sluggish maybe, but ever holding decisions and decrees in hand, ready, with stern process, to execute them as soon as plainly needed—and at times, indeed, summarily crushing to atoms the mightiest parties, even in the hour of their pride.

In saner hours far different are the amounts of these things from what, at first sight, they appear. Though it is no doubt important who is elected governor, mayor, or legislator (and full of dismay when incompetent or vile ones get elected, as they sometimes do), there are other, quieter contingencies, infinitely more important. Shams, etc., will always be the show, like ocean's scum; enough, if waters deep and clear make up the rest. Enough, that while the piled embroidered shoddy gaud and fraud spreads to the superficial eye, the hidden warp and weft are genuine, and will wear forever. Enough, in short, that the race, the land which could raise such as the late rebellion, could also put it down.

The average man of a land at last only is important. He, in these States, remains immortal owner and boss, deriving good uses, somehow, out of any sort of servant in office, even the basest (certain universal requisites, and their settled regularity and protection, being first secured); a nation like ours, in a sort of geological formation state, trying continually new experiment, choosing new delegations, is not served by the best men only but sometimes more by those that provoke it—by the combats they arouse. Thus national rage, fury, discussion, etc., better than content. Thus, also, the warning signals, invaluable for after times.

What is more dramatic than the spectacle we have seen repeated, and doubtless long shall see—the popular judgment taking the successful candidates on trial in the offices—standing off, as it were, and observing them and their doings for a while, and always giving, finally, the fit, exactly due reward? I think, after all, the sublimest part of political history, and its culmination, is currently issuing from the American people. I know nothing grander, better exercise, better digestion, more positive proof of the past, the triumphant result of faith in human-kind, than a well-contested American national election.

Then still the thought returns (like the thread-passage in overtures), giving the key and echo to these pages. When I pass to and fro, different latitudes, different seasons, beholding the crowds of the great cities, New York, Boston, Philadelphia, Cincinnati, Chicago, St. Louis, San Francisco, New Orleans, Baltimore—when I mix with these interminable swarms of alert, turbulent, good-natured, independent citizens, mechanics, clerks, young persons—at the idea of this mass of men, so fresh and free, so loving and so proud, a singular awe falls upon me. I feel, with dejection and amazement, that among our geniuses and talented writers or speakers, few or none have yet really spoken to this people, created a single image-making work for them, or absorbed the central spirit and the idiosyncrasies which are theirs—and which, thus, in highest ranges, so far remain entirely uncelebrated, unexpressed.

Dominion strong is the body's; dominion stronger is the mind's. What has filled, and fills today our intellect, our fancy, furnishing the standards therein, is yet foreign. The great poems, Shakespeare included, are poisonous to the idea of the pride and dignity of the common people, the life-blood of democracy. The models of our literature, as we get it from other lands, ultramarine, have had their birth in courts, and basked and grown in castle sunshine; all smells of princes' favors. Of workers of a certain sort, we have, indeed, plenty, contributing after their kind; many elegant, many learned, all complacent. But touched by the national test, or tried by the standards of democratic personality, they wither to ashes. I say I have not seen a single writer, artist, lecturer, or what not, that has confronted the voiceless but ever erect and active, pervading, underlying will and typic aspiration of the land, in a spirit kindred to itself. Do you call those genteel little creatures American poets? Do you term that perpetual, pistareen, paste-pot work, American art, American drama, taste, verse? I think I hear, echoed as from some mountaintop afar in the west, the scornful laugh of the Genius of these States.

Democracy, in silence, biding its time, ponders its own ideals, not of literature and art only—not of men only, but of women. The idea of the women of America (extricated from this daze, this fossil and unhealthy air which hangs about the word *lady*) developed, raised to become the robust equals, workers, and, it may be, even practical and political deciders

with the men—greater than man, we may admit, through their
divine maternity, always their towering, emblematical attribute
—but great, at any rate, as man, in all departments; or, rather,
capable of being so, soon as they realize it, and can bring themselves to give up toys and fictions, and launch forth, as men
do, amid real, independent, stormy life.

Then, as toward our thought's finale (and, in that, over-
arching the true scholar's lesson), we have to say there can be
no complete or epical presentation of democracy in the aggregate, or anything like it, at this day, because its doctrines will
only be effectually incarnated in any one branch, when, in all,
their spirit is at the root and center. Far, far, indeed, stretch,
in distance, our Vistas! How much is still to be disentangled,
freed! How long it takes to make this American world see that
it is, in itself, the final authority and reliance.

Did you, too, O friend, suppose democracy was only for elections, for politics, and for a party name? I say democracy is
only of use there that it may pass on and come to its flower and
fruits in manners, in the highest forms of interaction between
men, and their beliefs—in religion, literature, colleges, and
schools—democracy in all public and private life, and in the
army and navy.[7] I have intimated that, as a paramount scheme,
it has yet few or no full realizers and believers. I do not see,
either, that it owes any serious thanks to noted propagandists
or champions, or has been essentially helped, though often
harmed, by them. It has been and is carried on by all the moral
forces, and by trade, finance, machinery, intercommunications,
and, in fact, by all the developments of history, and can no
more be stopped than the tides, or the earth in its orbit. Doubtless, also, it resides, crude and latent, well down in the hearts
of the fair average of the American-born people, mainly in the
agricultural regions. But it is not yet, there or anywhere, the
fully received, the fervid, the absolute faith.

I submit, therefore, that the fruition of democracy, on aught

---

[7]The whole present system of the officering and personnel of the
army and navy of these States, and the spirit and letter of their trebly
aristocratic rules and regulations, is a monstrous exotic, a nuisance and
revolt, and belong here just as much as orders of nobility, or the Pope's
council of cardinals. I say if the present theory of our army and navy
is sensible and true, then the rest of America is an unmitigated fraud.

like a grand scale, resides altogether in the future. As, under any profound and comprehensive view of the gorgeous-composite feudal world, we see in it, through the long ages and cycles of ages, the results of a deep, integral, human and divine principle, or fountain, from which issued laws, ecclesia, manners, institutes, costumes, personalities, poems (hitherto unequaled), faithfully partaking of their source, and indeed only arising either to betoken it, or to furnish parts of that varied-flowing display, whose center was one and absolute—so, long ages hence, shall the due historian or critic make at least an equal retrospect, an equal history for the democratic principle. It too must be adorned, credited with its results—then, when it, with imperial power, through amplest time, has dominated mankind—has been the source and test of all the moral, aesthetic, social, political, and religious expressions and institutes of the civilized world—has begotten them in spirit and in form, and has carried them to its own unprecedented heights—has had (it is possible) monastics and ascetics, more numerous, more devout than the monks and priests of all previous creeds —has swayed the ages with a breadth and rectitude tallying Nature's own—has fashioned, systematized, and triumphantly finished and carried out, in its own interest, and with unparalleled success, a new earth and a new man.

Thus we presume to write, as it were, upon things that exist not, and travel by maps yet unmade, and a blank. But the throes of birth are upon us; and we have something of this advantage in seasons of strong formations, doubts, suspense—for then the afflatus of such themes haply may fall upon us, more or less; and then, hot from surrounding war and revolution, our speech, though without polished coherence, and a failure by the standard called criticism, comes forth, real at least as the lightnings.

And maybe we, these days, have, too, our own reward— (for there are yet some, in all lands, worthy to be so encouraged). Though not for us the joy of entering at the last the conquered city—not ours the chance ever to see with our own eyes the peerless power and splendid *éclat* of the democratic principle, arrived at meridian, filling the world with effulgence and majesty far beyond those of past history's kings, or all dynastic sway—there is yet, to whoever is eligible among us,

the prophetic vision, the joy of being tossed in the brave tur
moil of these times—the promulgation and the path, obedient
lowly reverent to the voice, the gesture of the god, or holy
ghost, which others see not, hear not—with the proud consciousness that amid whatever clouds, seductions, or heart-
wearying postponements, we have never deserted, never des-
paired, never abandoned the faith.

So much contributed, to be conned well, to help prepare and
brace our edifice, our planned Idea—we still proceed to give
it in another of its aspects—perhaps the main, the high facade
of all. For to democracy, the leveler, the unyielding principle
of the average, surely joined another principle, equally unyielding, closely tracking the first, indispensable to it, opposite
(as the sexes are opposite), and whose existence, confronting
and ever modifying the other, often clashing, paradoxical, yet
neither of highest avail without the other, plainly supplies to
these grand cosmic politics of ours, and to the launched forth
mortal dangers of republicanism, to-day, or any day, the counterpart and offset whereby Nature restrains the deadly original
relentlessness of all her first-class laws. This second principle
is individuality, the pride and centripetal isolation of a human
being in himself—identity—personalism. Whatever the name,
its acceptance and thorough infusions through the organiza-
tions of political commonalty now shooting Aurora-like about
the world, are of utmost importance, as the principle itself is
needed for very life's sake. It forms, in a sort, or is to form,
the compensating balance-wheel of the successful working
machinery of aggregate America.

And, if we think of it, what does civilization itself rest upon
—and what object has it, what its religions, arts, schools, etc.,
but rich, luxuriant, varied personalism? to that, all bends; and
it is because toward such result democracy alone, on anything
like Nature's scale, breaks up the limitless fallows of human-
kind, and plants the seed, and gives fair play, that its claims
now precede the rest. The literature, songs, aesthetics, etc., of
a country are of importance principally because they furnish
the materials and suggestions of personality for the women
and men of that country, and enforce them in a thousand

effective ways.[8] As the topmost claim of a strong consolidating of the nationality of these States is, that only by such powerful compaction can the separate States secure that full and free swing within their spheres, which is becoming to them, each after its kind, so will individuality, and unimpeded branchings, flourish best under imperial republican forms.

Assuming Democracy to be at present in its embryo condition, and that the only large and satisfactory justification of it resides in the future, mainly through the copious production of perfect characters among the people, and through the advent of a sane and pervading religiousness, it is with regard to the atmosphere and spaciousness fit for such characters, and of certain nutriment and cartoon-draftings proper for them, and indicating them for New World purposes, that I continue the present statement—an exploration, as of new ground, wherein, like other primitive surveyors, I must do the best I can, leaving

---

[8]After the rest is satiated, all interest culminates in the field of persons, and never flags there. Accordingly in this field have the great poets and literatuses signally toiled. They too, in all ages, all lands, have been creators, fashioning, making types of men and women, as Adam and Eve are made in the divine fable. Behold, shaped, bred by orientalism, feudalism, through their long growth and culmination, and breeding back in return—(when shall we have an equal series, typical of democracy?)—behold, commencing in primal Asia (apparently formulated, in what beginning we know, in the gods of the mythologies, and coming down thence), a few samples out of the countless product, bequeathed to the moderns, bequeathed to America as studies. For the men, Yudishtura, Rama, Arjuna, Solomon, most of the Old and New Testament characters; Achilles, Ulysses, Theseus, Prometheus, Hercules, Aeneas, Plutarch's heroes; the Merlin of Celtic bards; the Cid, Arthur and his knights, Siegfried and Hagen in the Nibelungen; Roland and Oliver, Roustam in the Shah-Nemah; and so on to Milton's Satan, Cervantes' Don Quixote, Shakespeare's Hamlet, Richard II, Lear, Marc Antony, etc., and the modern Faust. These, I say, are models, combined, adjusted to other standards than America's, but of priceless value to her and hers.

Among women, the goddesses of the Egyptian, Indian, and Greek mythologies, certain Bible characters, especially the Holy Mother; Cleopatra, Penelope; the portraits of Brunhelde and Cheriemhilde in the Nibelungen; Oriana, Una, etc.; the modern Consuelo, Walter Scott's Jeanie and Effie Deans, etc., etc. (Yet woman portrayed or outlined at her best, or as perfect human mother, does not hitherto, it seems to me, fully appear in literature.)

it to those who come after me to do much better. (The service, in fact, if any, must be to break a sort of first path or track, no matter how rude and ungeometrical.)

We have frequently printed the word Democracy. Yet I cannot too often repeat that it is a word the real gist of which still sleeps, quite unawakened, notwithstanding the resonance and the many angry tempests out of which its syllables have come, from pen or tongue. It is a great word, whose history, I suppose, remains unwritten, because that history has yet to be enacted. It is, in some sort, younger brother of another great and often-used word, Nature, whose history also waits unwritten. As I perceive, the tendencies of our day, in the States (and I entirely respect them), are toward those vast and sweeping movements, influences, moral and physical, of humanity, now and always current over the planet, on the scale of the impulses of the elements. Then it is also good to reduce the whole matter to the consideration of a single self, a man, a woman, on permanent grounds. Even for the treatment of the universal, in politics, metaphysics, or anything, sooner or later we come down to one single, solitary soul.

There is, in sanest hours, a consciousness, a thought that rises, independent, lifted out from all else, calm, like the stars, shining eternal. This is the thought of identity—yours for you, whoever you are, as mine for me. Miracle of miracles, beyond statement, most spiritual and vaguest of earth's dreams, yet hardest basic fact, and only entrance to all facts. In such devout hours, in the midst of the significant wonders of heaven and earth (significant only because of the Me in the center), creeds, conventions, fall away and become of no account before this simple idea. Under the luminousness of real vision, it alone takes possession, takes value. Like the shadowy dwarf in the fable, once liberated and looked upon, it expands over the whole earth, and spreads to the roof of heaven.

The quality of Being, in the object's self, according to its own central idea and purpose, and of growing therefrom and thereto—not criticism by other standards, and adjustments thereto—is the lesson of Nature. True, the full man wisely gathers, culls, absorbs; but if, engaged disproportionately in that, he slights or overlays the precious idiocrasy and special nativity and intention that he is, the man's self, the main thing, is a failure, however wide his general cultivation. Thus, in our times refinement and delicatesse are not only attended to sufficiently, but threaten to eat us up, like a cancer. Already, the democratic genius watches, ill-pleased, these tendencies. Provision for a little healthy rudeness, savage virtue, justification of what one has in one's self, whatever it is, is demanded. Negative qualities, even deficiencies, would be a relief. Singleness and normal simplicity and separation, amid this more and more complex, more and more artificialized state of society—how pensively we yearn for them! how we would welcome their return!

In some such direction, then—at any rate enough to preserve the balance—we feel called upon to throw what weight we can, not for absolute reasons, but current ones. To prune, gather, trim, conform, and ever cram and stuff, and be genteel and proper, is the pressure of our days. While aware that much can be said even in behalf of all this, we perceive that we have not now to consider the question of what is demanded to serve a half-starved and barbarous nation, or set of nations, but what is most applicable, most pertinent, for numerous congeries of conventional, overcorpulent societies, already becoming stifled and rotten with flatulent, infidelistic literature, and polite conformity and art. In addition to established sciences, we suggest a science as it were of healthy average personalism, on original-universal grounds, the object of which should be to raise up and supply through the States a copious race of superb American men and women, cheerful, religious, ahead of any yet known.

America has yet morally and artistically originated nothing. She seems singularly unaware that the models of persons, books, manners, etc., appropriate for former conditions and for European lands, are but exiles and exotics here. No current of her life, as shown on the surfaces of what is authoritatively called her society, accepts or runs into social or aesthetic democracy; but all the currents set squarely against it. Never, in the Old World, was thoroughly upholstered exterior appearance and show, mental and other, built entirely on the idea of caste, and on the sufficiency of mere outside acquisition—never were glibness, verbal intellect more the test, the emulation—more loftily elevated as head and sample—than they are on the surface of our republican States this day. The writers of a time hint the mottoes of its gods. The word of the modern, say these voices, is the word Culture.

We find ourselves abruptly in close quarters with the enemy. This word Culture, or what it has come to represent, involves, by contrast, our whole theme, and has been, indeed, the spur, urging us to engagement. Certain questions arise. As now taught, accepted and carried out, are not the processes of culture rapidly creating a class of supercilious infidels, who believe in nothing? Shall a man lose himself in countless masses of adjustments, and be so shaped with reference to this, that, and the other, that the simply good and healthy and brave parts of him are reduced and clipped away, like the bordering of box in a garden? You can cultivate corn and roses and orchards —but who shall cultivate the mountain peaks, the ocean, and the tumbling gorgeousness of the clouds? Lastly—is the readily given reply that culture only seeks to help, systematize, and put in attitude, the elements of fertility and power, a conclusive reply?

I do not so much object to the name, or word, but I should certainly insist, for the purposes of these States, on a radical change of category, in the distribution of precedence. I should demand a program of culture, drawn out, not for a single class alone, or for the parlors or lecture rooms, but with an eye to practical life, the west, the workingmen, the facts of farms and jack-planes and engineers, and of the broad range of the women also of the middle and working strata, and with reference to the perfect equality of women, and of a grand and powerful motherhood. I should demand of this program or theory a scope generous enough to include the widest human area. It must have for its spinal meaning the formation of a typical personality of character, eligible to the uses of the high average of men—and *not* restricted by conditions ineligible to the masses. The best culture will always be that of the manly and courageous instincts, and loving perceptions, and of self-respect —aiming to form, over this continent, an idiocrasy of universalism, which, true child of America, will bring joy to its mother, returning to her in her own spirit, recruiting myriads of offspring, able, natural, perceptive, tolerant, devout believers in her, America, and with some definite instinct why and for what she has arisen, most vast, most formidable of historic births, and is, now and here, with wonderful step, journeying through Time.

The problem, as it seems to me, presented to the New World, is, under permanent law and order, and after preserving cohesion (ensemble-Individuality) at all hazards, to vitalize man's free play of special Personalism, recognizing in it something that calls ever more to be considered, fed, and adopted as the sub-stratum for the best that belongs to us (government indeed is for it), including the new aesthetic of our future.

To formulate beyond this present vagueness—to help line and put before us the species, or a specimen of the species, of the democratic ethnology of the future, is a work toward which the genius of our land, with peculiar encouragement, invites her well-wishers. Already certain limnings, more or less grotesque, more or less fading and watery, have appeared. We too (repressing doubts and qualms) will try our hand.

Attempting, then, however crudely, a basic model or portrait of personality for general use for the manliness of the States (and doubtless that is most useful which is most simple and comprehensive for all, and toned low enough), we should prepare the canvas well beforehand. Parentage must consider itself in advance. (Will the time hasten when fatherhood and motherhood shall become a science—and the noblest science?) To our model, a clear-blooded, strong-fibered physique is indispensable; the questions of food, drink, air, exercise, assimilation, digestion, can never be intermitted. Out of these we descry a well-begotten selfhood—in youth, fresh, ardent, emotional, aspiring, full of adventure; at maturity, brave, perceptive, under control, neither too talkative nor too reticent, neither flippant nor somber; of the bodily figure, the movements easy, the complexion showing the best blood, somewhat flushed, breast expanded, an erect attitude, a voice whose sound outvies music, eyes of calm and steady gaze, yet capable also of flashing —and a general presence that holds its own in the company of the highest. (For it is native personality, and that alone, that endows a man to stand before presidents or generals, or in any distinguished collection, with *aplomb*—and *not* culture, or any knowledge or intellect whatever.)

With regard to the mental-educational part of our model, enlargement of intellect, stores of cephalic knowledge, etc., the concentration thitherward of all the customs of our age, especially in America, is so overweening, and provides so fully for that part, that, important and necessary as it is, it really needs nothing from us here—except, indeed, a phrase of warning and restraint. Manners, costumes, too, though important, we need not dwell upon here. Like beauty, grace of motion, etc., they are results. Causes, original things, being attended to, the right manners unerringly follow. Much is said, among artists, of "the grand style," as if it were a thing by itself. When a man, artist or whoever, has health, pride, acuteness, noble aspirations, he has the motive-elements of the grandest style. The rest is but manipulation (yet that is no small matter).

Leaving still unspecified several sterling parts of any model fit for the future personality of America, I must not fail, again and ever, to pronounce myself on one, probably the least attended to in modern times—a hiatus, indeed, threatening its gloomiest consequences after us. I mean the simple, unsophisticated Conscience, the primary moral element. If I were asked to specify in what quarter lie the ground of darkest dread, respecting the America of our hopes, I should have to point to this particular. I should demand the invariable application to individuality, this day and any day, of that old, ever-true plumb-rule of persons, eras, nations. Our triumphant modern civilizee, with his all-schooling and his wondrous appliances, will still show himself but an amputation while this deficiency remains. Beyond (assuming a more hopeful tone), the vertebration of the manly and womanly personalism of our Western world, can only be, and is, indeed, to be (I hope), its all penetrating Religiousness.

The ripeness of Religion is doubtless to be looked for in this field of individuality, and is a result that no organization or church can ever achieve. As history is poorly retained by what the technists call history, and is not given out from their pages, except the learner has in himself the sense of the well-wrapt, never yet written, perhaps impossible to be written, history—so Religion, although casually arrested, and, after a fashion, preserved in the churches and creeds, does not depend at all upon them, but is a part of the identified soul, which, when greatest, knows not bibles in the old way, but in new ways—the identified soul, which can really confront Religion when it extricates itself entirely from the churches, and not before.

Personalism fuses this, and favors it. I should say, indeed, that only in the perfect uncontamination and solitariness of individuality may the spirituality of religion positively come forth at all. Only here, and on such terms, the meditation, the devout ecstasy, the soaring flight. Only here, communion with the mysteries, the eternal problems, whence? whither? Alone, and identity, and the mood—and the soul emerges, and all statements, churches, sermons, melt away like vapors. Alone, and silent thought and awe, and aspiration—and then the interior consciousness, like a hitherto unseen inscription, in magic ink, beams out its wondrous lines to the sense. Bibles may convey, and priests expound, but it is exclusively for the noiseless operation of one's isolated Self, to enter the pure ether of veneration, reach the divine levels, and commune with the unutterable.

To practically enter into politics is an important part of American personalism. To every young man, north and south, earnestly studying these things, I should here, as an offset to what I have said in former pages, now also say, that maybe to views of very large scope, after all, perhaps the political (perhaps the literary and sociological) America goes best about its development its own way—sometimes, to temporary sight, appalling enough. It is the fashion among dilettanti and fops (perhaps I myself am not guiltless), to decry the whole formulation of the active politics of America, as beyond redemption, and to be carefully kept away from. See you that you do not fall into this error. America, it may be, is doing very well upon the whole, notwithstanding these antics of the parties and their leaders, these half-brained nominees,

and many ignorant ballots, and many elected failures and
blatherers. It is the dilettanti, and all who shirk their duty,
who are not doing well. As for you, I advise you to enter
more strongly yet into politics. I advise every young man to
do so. Always inform yourself; always do the best you can;
always vote. Disengage yourself from parties. They have been
useful, and to some extent remain so; but the floating, un-
committed electors, farmers, clerks, mechanics, the masters of
parties—watching aloof, inclining victory this side or that side
—such are the ones most needed, present and future. For
America, if eligible at all to downfall and ruin, is eligible within
herself, not without; for I see clearly that the combined foreign
world could not beat her down. But these savage, wolfish
parties alarm me. Owning no law but their own will, more
and more combative, less and less tolerant of the idea of
ensemble and of equal brotherhood, the perfect equality of
the States, the ever-overarching American ideas, it behooves
you to convey yourself implicitly to no party, nor submit blindly
to their dictators, but steadily hold yourself judge and master
over all of them.

So much (hastily tossed together, and leaving far more unsaid), for an ideal, or intimations of an ideal, toward American
manhood. But the other sex, in our land, requires at least a
basis of suggestion.

I have seen a young American woman, one of a large family
of daughters, who, some years since, migrated from her meager
country home to one of the northern cities, to gain her own
support. She soon became an expert seamstress, but finding
the employment too confining for health and comfort, she went
boldly to work for others, to housekeep, cook, clean, etc. After
trying several places, she fell upon one where she was suited.
She has told me that she finds nothing degrading in her position; it is not inconsistent with personal dignity, self-respect,
and the respect of others. She confers benefits and receives
them. She has good health; her presence itself is healthy and
bracing; her character is unstained; she has made herself
understood, and preserves her independence, and has been
able to help her parents, and educate and get places for her
sisters, and her course of life is not without opportunities for

mental improvement, and of much quiet, uncosting happiness and love.

I have seen another woman who, from taste and necessity conjoined, has gone into practical affairs, carries on a mechanical business, partly works at it herself, dashes out more and more into real hardy life, is not abashed by the coarseness of the contact, knows how to be firm and silent at the same time, holds her own with unvarying coolness and decorum, and will compare, any day, with superior carpenters, farmers, and even boatmen and drivers. For all that, she has not lost the charm of the womanly nature, but preserves and bears it fully, though through such rugged presentation.

Then there is the wife of a mechanic, mother of two children, a woman of merely passable English education, but of fine wit, with all her sex's grace and intuitions, who exhibits, indeed, such a noble female personality, that I am fain to record it here. Never abnegating her own proper independence, but always genially preserving it, and what belongs to it—cooking, washing, child-nursing, house-tending—she beams sunshine out of all these duties, and makes them illustrious. Physiologically sweet and sound, loving work, practical, she yet knows that there are intervals, however few, devoted to recreation, music, leisure, hospitality—and affords such intervals. Whatever she does and wherever she is, that charm, that indescribable perfume of genuine womanhood attends her, goes with her, exhales from her, which belongs of right to all the sex, and is, or ought to be, the invariable atmosphere and common aureola of old as well as young.

My dear mother once described to me a resplendent person, down on Long Island, whom she knew in early days. She was known by the name of the Peacemaker. She was well toward eighty years old, of happy and sunny temperament, had always lived on a farm, and was very neighborly, sensible and discreet, an invariable and welcomed favorite, especially with young married women. She had numerous children and grandchildren. She was uneducated, but possessed a native dignity. She had come to be a tacitly agreed upon domestic regulator, judge, settler of difficulties, shepherdess, the reconciler in the land. She was a sight to draw near and look upon, with her large figure, her profuse snow-white hair (uncoifed by any head-dress or cap), dark eyes, clear complexion, sweet breath, and peculiar personal magnetism.

The foregoing portraits, I admit, are frightfully out of line from these imported models of womanly personality—the stock feminine characters of the current novelists, or of the foreign court poems (Ophelias, Enids, princesses, or ladies of one thing or another), which fill the envying dreams of so many poor girls, and are accepted by our men, too, as supreme ideals of feminine excellence to be sought after. But I present mine just for a change.

Then there are mutterings (we will not now stop to heed them here, but they must be heeded), of something more revolutionary. The day is coming when the deep questions of woman's entrance amid the arenas of practical life, politics, the suffrage, etc., will not only be argued all around us, but may be put to decision, and real experiment.

Of course, in these States, for both man and woman, we must entirely recast the types of highest personality from what the oriental, feudal, ecclesiastical worlds bequeath us, and which yet possess the imaginative and aesthetic fields of the United States, pictorial and melodramatic, not without use as studies, but making sad work, and forming a strange anachronism upon the scenes and exigencies around us. Of course, the old undying elements remain. The task is, to successfully adjust them to new combinations, our own days. Nor is this so incredible. I can conceive a community, today and here, in which, on a sufficient scale, the perfect personalities, without noise meet; say in some pleasant western settlement or town, where a couple of hundred best men and women, of ordinary worldly status, have by luck been drawn together, with nothing extra of genius or wealth, but virtuous, chaste, industrious, cheerful, resolute, friendly and devout. I can conceive such a community organized in running order, powers judiciously delegated—farming, building, trade, courts, mails, schools, elections, all attended to; and then the rest of life, the main thing, freely branching and blossoming in each individual, and bearing golden fruit. I can see there, in every young and old man, after his kind, and in every woman after hers, a true personality, developed, exercised proportionately in body, mind, and spirit. I can imagine this case as one not necessarily rare or difficult, but in buoyant accordance with the municipal and general requirements of our times. And I realize in it the culmination of something better than any stereotyped *éclat* of history or poems. Perhaps unsung, undramatized, unput in essays or biographies—perhaps even some such community already exists, in Ohio, Illinois, Missouri, or somewhere, practically fulfilling itself, and thus outvying, in cheapest vulgar life, all that has been hitherto shown in best ideal pictures.

In short, and to sum up, America, betaking herself to formative action (as it is about time for more solid achievement, and less windy promise), must, for her purposes, cease to recognize a theory of character grown of feudal aristocracies, or formed by merely literary standards, or from any ultramarine full-dress formulas of culture, polish, caste, etc., and must sternly promulgate her own new standard, yet old enough, and accepting the old, the perennial elements, and combining them into groups, unities, appropriate to the modern, the democratic, the west, and to the practical occasions and needs of our own cities, and of the agricultural regions. Ever the most precious in the common. Ever the fresh breeze of field, or hill or lake, is more than any palpitation of fans, though of ivory, and redolent with perfume; and the air is more than the costliest perfumes.

And now, for fear of mistake, we may not intermit to beg our absolution from all that genuinely is, or goes along with, even Culture. Pardon us, venerable shade! if we have seemed to speak lightly of your office. The whole civilization of the earth, we know, is yours, with all the glory and the light thereof. It is, indeed, in your own spirit, and seeking to tally the loftiest teachings of it, that we aim these poor utterances. For you, too, mighty minister! know that there is something greater than you, namely, the fresh, eternal qualities of Being. From them, and by them, as you, at your best, we too evoke the last, the needed help, to vitalize our country and our days. Thus we pronounce not so much against the principle of culture; we only supervise it, and promulgate along with it, as deep, perhaps a deeper, principle. As we have shown the New

World including in itself the all-leveling aggregate of democracy, we show it also including the all-varied, all-permitting, all-free theorem of individuality, and erecting therefor a lofty and hitherto unoccupied framework or platform, broad enough for all, eligible to every farmer and mechanic—to the female equally with the male—a towering selfhood, not physically perfect only—not satisfied with the mere mind's and learning's stores, but religious, possessing the idea of the infinite (rudder and compass sure amid this troublous voyage, o'er darkest, wildest wave, through stormiest wind, of man's or nation's progress)—realizing, above the rest, that known humanity, in deepest sense, is fair adhesion to itself, for purposes beyond— and that, finally, the personality of mortal life is most important with reference to the immortal, the unknown, the spiritual, the only permanently real, which as the ocean waits for and receives the rivers, waits for us each and all.

Much is there, yet, demanding line and outline in our Vistas, not only on these topics, but others quite unwritten. Indeed, we could talk the matter, and expand it, through lifetime. But it is necessary to return to our original premises. In view of them, we have again pointedly to confess that all the objective grandeurs of the world, for highest purposes, yield themselves up, and depend on mentality alone. Here, and here only, all balances, all rests. For the mind, which alone builds the permanent edifice, haughtily builds it to itself. By it, with what follows it, are conveyed to mortal sense the culminations of the materialistic, the known, and a prophecy of the unknown. To take expression, to incarnate, to endow a literature with grand and archetypal models—to fill with pride and love the utmost capacity, and to achieve spiritual meanings, and suggest the future—these, and these only, satisfy the soul. We must not say one word against real materials; but the wise know that they do not become real till touched by emotions, the mind. Did we call the latter imponderable? Ah, let us rather proclaim that the slightest song-tune, the countless ephemera of passions aroused by orators and tale-tellers, are more dense, more weighty than the engines there in the great factories, or the granite blocks in their foundations.

Approaching thus the momentous spaces, and considering

with reference to a new and greater personalism, the needs
and possibilities of American imaginative literature, through
the medium-light of what we have already broached, it will
at once be appreciated that a vast gulf of difference separates
the present accepted condition of these spaces, inclusive of
what is floating in them, from any condition adjusted to, or
fit for, the world, the America, there sought to be indicated,
and the copious races of complete men and women, along these
Vistas crudely outlined. It is, in some sort, no less a difference
than lies between that long-continued nebular state and vagueness of the astronomical worlds, compared with the subsequent
state, the definitely formed worlds themselves, duly compacted,
clustering in systems, hung up there, chandeliers of the universe, beholding and mutually lit by each other's lights, serving
for ground of all substantial foothold, all vulgar uses—yet
serving still more as an undying chain and echelon of spiritual
proofs and shows. A boundless field to fill! A new creation,
with needed orbic works launched forth, to revolve in free and
lawful circuits—to move, self-poised, through the ether, and
shine like heaven's own suns! With such, and nothing less, we
suggest that New World literature, fit to rise upon, cohere, and
signalize in time, these States.

What, however, do we more definitely mean by New World
literature? Are we not doing well enough here already? Are
not the United States this day busily using, working, more
printer's type, more presses, than any other country? uttering
and absorbing more publications than any other? Do not our
publishers fatten quicker and deeper (helping themselves,
under shelter of a delusive and sneaking law, or rather absence
of law, to most of their forage, poetical, pictorial, historical,
romantic, even comic, without money and without price—and
fiercely resisting the timidest proposal to pay for it). Many
will come under this delusion—but my purpose is to dispel
it. I say that a nation may hold and circulate rivers and oceans
of very readable print, journals, magazines, novels, library
books, "poetry," etc.—such as the States today possess and
circulate—of unquestionable aid and value—hundreds of new
volumes annually composed and brought out here, respectable
enough, indeed unsurpassed in smartness and erudition—with

further hundreds, or rather millions (as by free forage or theft aforementioned), also thrown into the market—and yet, all the while, the said nation, land, strictly speaking, may possess no literature at all.

Repeating our inquiry, what, then, do we mean by real literature? especially the democratic literature of the future? Hard questions to meet. The clues are inferential, and turn us to the past. At best, we can only offer suggestions, comparisons, circuits.

It must still be reiterated, as, for the purpose of these memoranda, the deep lesson of history and time, that all else in the contributions of a nation or age, through its politics, materials, heroic personalities, military *éclat,* etc., remains crude, and defers, in any close and thoroughgoing estimate, until vitalized by national, original archetypes in literature. They only put the nation in form, finally tell anything—prove, complete anything —perpetuate anything. Without doubt, some of the richest and most powerful and populous communities of the antique world, and some of the grandest personalities and events, have, to after and present times, left themselves entirely unbequeathed. Doubtless, greater than any that have come down to us, were among those lands, heroisms, persons, that have not come down to us at all, even by name, date, or location. Others have arrived safely, as from voyages over wide, century-stretching seas. The little ships, the miracles that have buoyed them, and by incredible chances safely conveyed them (or the best of them, their meaning and essence) over long wastes, darkness, lethargy, ignorance, etc., have been a few inscriptions—a few immortal compositions, small in size, yet compassing what measureless values of reminiscence, contemporary portraitures, manners, idioms and beliefs, with deepest inference, hint and thought, to tie and touch forever the old, new body, and the old, new soul! These! and still these! bearing the freight so dear —dearer than pride—dearer than love. All the best experience of humanity, folded, saved, freighted to us here. Some of these tiny ships we call Old and New Testament, Homer, Aeschylus, Plato, Juvenal, etc. Precious minims! I think, if we were forced to choose, rather than have you, and the likes of you, and what belongs to, and has grown of you, blotted out and gone, we could better afford, appalling as that would be, to lose all actual ships, this day fastened by wharf, or floating on wave, and see them, with all their cargoes, scuttled and sent to the bottom.

Gathered by geniuses of city, race or age, and put by them in highest of art's forms, namely, the literary form, the peculiar combinations and the outshows of that city, age, or race, its particular modes of the universal attributes and passions, its faiths, heroes, lovers and gods, wars, traditions, struggles, crimes, emotions, joys (for the subtle spirit of these), having been passed on to us to illumine our own selfhood, and its experiences—what they supply, indispensable and highest, if taken away, nothing else in all the world's boundless storehouses could make up to us, or ever again return.

For us, along the great highways of time, those monuments stand—those forms of majesty and beauty. For us those beacons burn through all the nights. Unknown Egyptians, graving hieroglyphs; Hindus, with hymn and apothegm and endless epic; Hebrew prophet, with spirituality, as in flashes of lightning, conscience like red-hot iron, plaintive songs and screams of vengeance for tyrannies and enslavement; Christ, with bent head, brooding love and peace, like a dove; Greek, creating eternal shapes of physical and aesthetic proportion! Roman, lord of satire, the sword, and the codex;—of the figures, some far off and veiled, others nearer and visible; Dante, stalking with lean form, nothing but fiber, not a grain of superfluous flesh: Angelo, and the great painters, architects, musicians; rich Shakespeare, luxuriant as the sun, artist and singer of feudalism in its sunset, with all the gorgeous colors, owner thereof, and using them at will; and so to such as German Kant and Hegel, where they, though near us, leaping over the ages, sit again, impassive, imperturbable, like the Egyptian gods. Of these, and the like of these, is it too much, indeed, to return to our favorite figure, and view them as orbs and systems of orbs, moving in free paths in the spaces of that other heaven, the cosmic intellect, the soul?

Ye powerful and resplendent ones! ye were, in your atmospheres, grown not for America, but rather for her foes, the feudal and the old—while our genius is democratic and modern. Yet could ye, indeed, but breathe your breath of life into our

New World's nostrils—not to enslave us, as now, but, for our needs, to breed a spirit like your own—perhaps (dare we to say it?) to dominate, even destroy, what you yourselves have left! On your plane, and no less, but even higher and wider, must we mete and measure for today and here. I demand races of orbic bards, with unconditional, uncompromising sway. Come forth, sweet democratic despots of the west!

By points like these we, in reflection, token what we mean by any land's or people's genuine literature. And thus compared and tested, judging amid the influence of loftiest products only, what do our current copious fields of print, covering in manifold forms, the United States, better, for an analogy, present, than, as in certain regions of the sea, those spreading, undulating masses of squid, through which the whale swimming, with head half out, feeds?

Not but that doubtless our current so-called literature (like an endless supply or small coin) performs a certain service, and maybe too, the service needed for the time, the preparation-service, as children learn to spell. Everybody reads, and truly nearly everybody writes, either books, or for the magazines or journals. The matter has magnitude, too, after a sort. But is it really advancing? or, has it advanced for a long while? There is something impressive about the huge editions of the dailies and weeklies, the mountain-stacks of white paper piled in the press-vaults, and the proud, crashing, ten-cylinder presses, which I can stand and watch any time by the half hour. Then (though the States in the field of imagination present not a single first-class work, not a single great literatus), the main objects, to amuse, to titillate, to pass away time, to circulate the news, and rumors of news, to rhyme, and read rhyme, are yet attained, and on a scale of infinity. Today, in books, in the rivalry of writers, especially novelists, success (so-called) is for him or her who strikes the mean flat average, the sensational appetite for stimulus, incident, persiflage, etc., and depicts, to the common caliber, sensual, exterior life. To such, or the luckiest of them, as we see, the audiences are limitless and profitable; but they cease presently. While this day, or any day, to workmen portraying interior or spiritual life, the audiences were limited, and often laggard—but they last forever.

Compared with the past, our modern science soars, and our journals serve—but ideal and even ordinary romantic literature, does not, I think, substantially advance. Behold the prolific brood of the contemporary novel, magazine tale, theatre play, etc. The same endless thread of tangled and superlative love story, inherited, apparently from the Amadises and Palmerins of the thirteenth, fourteenth and fifteenth centuries over there in Europe. The costumes and associations brought down to date, the seasoning hotter and more varied, the dragons and ogres left out —but the *thing*, I should say, has not advanced—is just as sensational, just as strained—remains about the same, nor more, nor less.

What is the reason our time, our lands, that we see no fresh local courage, sanity, of our own—the Mississippi, stalwart Western men, real mental and physical facts, Southerners, etc., in the body of our literature? especially the poetic part of it. But always, instead, a parcel of dandies and ennuyees, dapper little gentlemen from abroad, who flood us with their thin sentiment of parlors, parasols, piano songs, tinkling rhymes, the five-hundredth importation—or whimpering and crying about something, chasing one aborted conceit after another, and forever occupied in dyspeptic amours with dyspeptic women. While, current and novel, the grandest events and revolutions, and stormiest passions of history are crossing today with unparalleled rapidity and magnificence over the stages of our own and all the continents, offering new materials, opening new vistas, with largest needs, inviting the daring launching forth of conceptions in literature, inspired by them, soaring in highest regions, serving art in its highest (which is only the other name for serving God, and serving humanity), where is the man of letters, where is the book, with any nobler aim than to follow in the old track, repeat what has been said before—and, as its utmost triumph, sell well, and be erudite or elegant?

Mark the roads, the processes, through which these States have arrived, standing easy, henceforth ever-equal, ever-compact, in their range today. European adventures? the most antique? Asiatic or African? old history—miracles—romances? Rather, our own unquestioned facts. They hasten, incredible, blazing bright as fire. From the deeds and days of Columbus

down to the present, and including the present—and especially
the late Secession War—when I con them, I feel, every leaf,
like stopping to see if I have not made a mistake, and fallen on
the splendid figments of some dream. But it is no dream. We
stand, live, move in the huge flow of our age's materialism—
in its spirituality. We have founded for us the most positive of
lands. The founders have passed to other spheres—but what
are these terrible duties they have left us?

Their politics the United States have, in my opinion, with all
their faults, already substantially established, for good, on their
own native, sound, long-vistaed principles, never to be over-
turned, offering a sure basis for all the rest. With that, their
future religious forms, sociology, literature, teachers, schools,
costumes, etc., are of course to make a compact whole, uniform, on tallying principles. For how can we remain, divided,
contradicting ourselves, this way?[9] I say we can only attain
harmony and stability by consulting ensemble and the ethic
purports, and faithfully building upon them. For the New
World, indeed, after two grand stages of preparation-strata,
I perceive that now a third stage, being ready for (and without
which the other two were useless), with unmistakable signs
appears. The first stage was the planning and putting on record
the political foundation rights of immense masses of people—
indeed all people—in the organization of republican National,
State, and municipal governments, all constructed with reference to each, and each to all. This is the American program,
not for classes, but for universal man, and is embodied in the
compacts of the Declaration of Independence, and, as it began
and has now grown, with its amendments, the Federal Constitution—and in the State governments, with all their interiors,
and with general suffrage; those having the sense note only of

[9]Note, today, an instructive, curious spectacle and conflict. Science
(twin, in its fields, of Democracy in its)—Science, testing absolutely
all thoughts, all works, has already burst well upon the world—a sun,
mounting, most illuminating, most glorious—surely never again to
set. But against it, deeply entrenched, holding possession, yet remains
(not only through the churches and schools, but by imaginative
literature, and unregenerate poetry), the fossil theology of the mythic-
materialistic, superstitious, untaught and credulous fable-loving, primitive ages of humanity.

what is in themselves, but that their certain several things started, planted, hundreds of others in the same direction duly arise and follow. The Second stage relates to material prosperity, wealth, produce, laborsaving machines, iron, cotton, local, State, and continental railways, intercommunication and trade with all lands, steamships, mining, general employment, organization of great cities, cheap appliances for comfort, numberless technical schools, books, newspapers, a currency for money circulation, etc. The Third stage, rising out of the previous ones, to make them and all illustrious, I, now, for one, promulge, announcing a native expression-spirit, getting into form, adult, and through mentality, for these States, self-contained, different from others, more expansive, more rich and free, to be evidenced by original authors and poets to come, by American personalities, plenty of them, male and female, traversing the States, none excepted—and by native superber tableaux and growth of language, songs, operas, orations, lectures, architecture—and by a sublime and serious Religious Democracy sternly taking command, dissolving the old, sloughing off surfaces, and from its own interior and vital principles, reconstructing, democratizing society.

For America, type of progress, and of essential faith in man, above all his errors and wickedness—few suspect how deep, how deep it really strikes. The world evidently supposes, and we have evidently supposed so too, that the States are merely to achieve the equal franchise, an elective government—to inaugurate the respectability of labor, and become a nation of practical operatives, law-abiding, orderly, and well-off. Yes, those are indeed parts of the task of America; but they not only do not exhaust the progressive conception, but rather arise, teeming with it, as the mediums of deeper, higher progress. Daughter of a physical revolution—mother of the true revolutions, which are of the interior life, and of the arts. For so long as the spirit is not changed, any change of appearance is of no avail.

The old men, I remember as a boy, were always talking of American independence. What is independence? Freedom from all laws or bonds except those of one's own being, controlled by the universal ones. To lands, to man, to woman, what is there at last to each, but the inherent soul, nativity idiocrasy, free, highest poised, soaring its own flight, following out itself?

At present, these States, in their theology and social standards (of greater importance than their political institutions) are entirely held possession of by foreign lands. We see the sons and daughters of the New World, ignorant of its genius, not yet inaugurating the native, the universal, and the near still importing the distant, the partial, and the dead. We see London, Paris, Italy—not original, superb, as where they belong—but second-hand here, where they do not belong. We see the shreds of Hebrews, Romans, Greeks; but where, on her own soil, do we see, in any faithful, highest, proud expression, America, herself? I sometimes question whether she has a corner in her own house.

Not but that in one sense, and a very grand one, good theology, good art, or good literature, has certain features shared in common. The combination fraternizes, ties the races—is, in many particulars, under laws applicable indifferently to all, irrespective of climate or date, and, from whatever source, appeals to emotions, pride, love, spirituality, common to human-kind. Nevertheless, they touch a man closest (perhaps only actually touch him), even in these, in their expression through autochthonic lights and shades, flavors, fondnesses, aversions, specific incidents, illustrations, out of his own nationality, geography, surroundings, antecedents, etc. The spirit and the form are one, and depend far more on association, identity, and place, than is supposed. Subtly interwoven with the materiality and personality of a land, a race—Teuton, Turk, Californian, or what not—there is always something—I can hardly tell what it is—history but describes the results of it—it is the same as the untellable look of some human faces. Nature, too, in her stolid forms, is full of it—but to most it is there a secret. This something is rooted in the invisible roots, the profoundest meanings of that place, race, or nationality; and to absorb and again effuse it, uttering words and products as from its midst, and carrying it into highest regions, is the work, or a main part of the work, of any country's true author, poet, historian, lecturer, and perhaps even priest and philosoph. Here, and here only, are the foundations for our really valuable and permanent verse, drama, etc.

But at present (judged by any higher scale than that which finds the chief ends of existence to be to feverishly make money during one half of it, and by some "amusement," or perhaps foreign travel, flippantly kill time, the other half), and considered with reference to purposes of patriotism, health, a noble personality, religion, and the democratic adjustments, all these swarms of poems, literary magazines, dramatic plays, resultant so far from American intellect, and the formation of our best ideas, are useless and a mockery. They strengthen and nourish no one, express nothing characteristic, give decision and purpose to no one, and suffice only the lowest level of vacant minds.

Of what is called the drama, or dramatic presentation in the United States, as now put forth at the theatres, I should say it deserves to be treated with the same gravity, and on a par with the questions of ornamental confectionery at public dinners, or the arrangement of curtains and hangings in a ballroom—nor more, nor less. Of the other, I will not insult the reader's intelligence (once really entering into the atmosphere of these Vistas), by supposing it necessary to show, in detail, why the copious dribble, either of our little or well-known rhymesters, does not fulfill, in any respect, the needs and august occasions of this land. America demands a poetry that is bold, modern, and all-surrounding and cosmical, as she is herself. It must in no respect ignore science or the modern, but inspire itself with science and the modern. It must bend its vision toward the future, more than the past. Like America, it must extricate itself from even the greatest models of the past, and, while courteous to them, must have entire faith in itself, and the products of its own democratic spirit only. Like her, it must place in the van, and hold up at all hazards, the banner of the divine pride of man in himself (the radical foundation of the new religion). Long enough have the People been listening to poems in which common humanity, deferential, bends low, humiliated, acknowledging superiors. But America listens to no such poems. Erect, inflated, and fully self-esteeming be the chant; and then America will listen with pleased ears.

Nor may the genuine gold, the gems, when brought to light
at last, be probably usher'd forth from any of the quarters
currently counted on. Today, doubtless, the infant genius of
American poetic expression (eluding those highly refined imported and gilt-edged themes, and sentimental and butterfly
flights, pleasant to orthodox publishers—causing tender spasms
in the coteries, and warranted not to chafe the sensitive cuticle
of the most exquisitely artificial gossamer delicacy), lies sleeping far away, happily unrecognized and uninjured by the coteries, the art-writers, the talkers and critics of the saloons, or
the lecturers in the colleges—lies sleeping, aside, unrecking
itself, in some western idiom, or native Michigan or Tennessee
repartee, or stump speech—or in Kentucky or Georgia, or the
Carolinas—or in some slang or local song or allusion of the
Manhattan, Boston, Philadelphia, or Baltimore mechanic—or
up in the Maine woods—or off in the hut of the California
miner, or crossing the Rocky Mountains, or along the Pacific
railroad—or on the breasts of the young farmers of the northwest, or Canada, or boatmen of the lakes. Rude and coarse
nursing beds, these; but only from such beginnings and stocks,
indigenous here, may haply arrive, be grafted, and sprout in
time, flowers of genuine American aroma, and fruits truly and
fully our own.

I say it were a standing disgrace to these States—I say it were
a disgrace to any nation, distinguished above others by the
variety and vastness of its territories, its materials, its inventive
activity, and the splendid practicality of its people, not to rise
and soar above others, also in its original styles in literature
and art, and its own supply of intellectual and aesthetic masterpieces, archetypal, and consistent with itself. I know not a land
except ours that has not, to some extent, however small, made
its title clear. The Scotch have their born ballads, subtly expressing their past and present, and expressing character. The Irish
have theirs. England, Italy, France, Spain, theirs. What has
America? With exhaustless mines of the richest ore of epic,
lyric, tale, tune, picture, etc., in the Four Years' War; with
indeed, I sometimes think, the richest masses of material ever
afforded a nation, more variegated, and on a larger scale—
the first sign of proportionate, native, imaginative Soul, and

first-class works to match, is (I cannot too often repeat), so far wanting.

Long ere the second centennial arrives, there will be some forty to fifty great States, among them Canada and Cuba. When the present century closes, our population will be sixty or seventy millions. The Pacific will be ours, and the Atlantic mainly ours. There will be daily electric communication with every part of the globe. What an age! what a land! Where, elsewhere, one so great? The individuality of one nation must then, as always, lead the world. Can there be any doubt who the leader ought to be? Bear in mind, though, that nothing less than the mightiest original non-subordinated Soul has ever really, glorious led, or ever can lead. (This Soul—its other name, in these Vistas, is Literature.)

In fond fancy leaping those hundred years ahead let us survey America's works, poems, philosophies, fulfilling prophecies, and giving form and decision to best ideals. Much that is now undreamed of, we might then perhaps see established, luxuriantly cropping forth, richness, vigor of letters and of artistic expression, in whose products character will be a main requirement, and not merely erudition or elegance.

Intense and loving comradeship, the personal and passionate attachment of man to man—which, hard to define, underlies the lessons and ideals of the profound saviors of every land and age, and which seems to promise, when thoroughly developed, cultivated, and recognized in manners and literature, the most substantial hope and safety of the future of these States, will then be fully expressed.[10]

[10]It is to the development, identification, and general prevalence of that fervid comradeship (the adhesive love, at least rivaling the amative love hitherto possessing imaginative literature if not going beyond it), that I look for the counterbalance and offset of our materialistic and vulgar American democracy, and for the spiritualization thereof. Many will say it is a dream, and will not follow my inferences; but I confidently expect a time when there will be seen, running like a half-hid warp through all the myriad audible and visible worldy interests of America, threads of manly friendship, food and loving, pure and sweet, strong and life-long, carried to degrees hitherto unknown—not only giving tone to individual character, and making it unprecedently emotional, muscular, heroic, and refined, but having

A strong-fibered joyousness and faith, and the sense of health *al fresco*, may well enter into the preparation of future noble American authorship. Part of the test of a great literatus shall be the absence in him of the idea of the covert, the lurid, the maleficent, the devil, the grim estimates inherited from the Puritans, hell, natural depravity, and the like. The great literatus will be known, among the rest, by his cheerful simplicity, his adherence to natural standards, his limitless faith in God, his reverence, and by the absence in him of doubt, ennui, burlesque, persiflage, or any strained and temporary fashion.

Nor must I fail, again and yet again, to clinch, reiterate more plainly still (O that indeed such survey as we fancy may show in time this part completed also!) the lofty aim, surely the proudest and the purest, in whose service the future literatus of whatever field, may gladly labor. As we have intimated, offsetting the material civilization of our race, our nationality, its wealth, territories, factories, population, products, trade, and military and naval strength, and breathing breath of life into all these, and more, must be its moral civilization— the formulation, expression, aidancy whereof, is the very highest height of literature. The climax of this loftiest range of civilization, rising above all the gorgeous shows and results of wealth, intellect, power, and art, as such—above even theology and religious fervour—is to be its development, from the eternal bases, and the fit expression, of absolute Conscience, moral soundness, Justice. Even in religious fervor there is a touch of animal heat. But moral conscientiousness, crystalline, without flaw, not Godlike only, entirely human, awes and enchants forever. Great is emotional love, even in the order of the rational universe. But, if we must make gradations, I am clear there is something greater. Power, love, veneration, products, genius, aesthetics, tried by subtlest comparisons, analyses, and in serenest moods, somewhere fail, somehow become vain. Then noiseless, with flowing steps, the lord, the sun, the last ideal comes. By the names right, justice, truth, we suggest, but do not describe it. To the world of men it remains a dream, an

---

the deepest relations to general politics. I say democracy infers such loving comradeship, as its most inevitable twin or counterpart, without which it will be incomplete, in vain, and incapable of perpetuating itself.

idea as they call it. But no dream is it to the wise—but the proudest, almost only solid lasting thing of all. Its analogy in the material universe is what holds together this world, and every object upon it, and carries its dynamics on forever sure and safe. Its lack, and the persistent shirking of it, as in life, sociology, literature, politics, business, and even sermonizing, these times, or any times, still leaves the abysm, the mortal flaw and smutch, mocking civilization today, with all its un-questioned triumphs, and all the civilization so far known.[11]

Present literature, while magnificently fulfilling certain popu-lar demands, with plenteous knowledge and verbal smartness, is profoundly sophisticated, insane, and its very joy is morbid. It needs tally and express Nature, and the spirit of Nature, and to know and obey the standards. I say the question of Nature, largely considered, involves the questions of the aesthetic, the emotional, and the religious—and involves happiness. A fitly born and bred race, growing up in right conditions of outdoor as much as indoor harmony, activity and development, would probably, from and in those conditions, find it enough merely *to live*—and would, in their relations to the sky, air, water, trees, etc., and to the countless common shows, and in the fact of life itself, discover and achieve happiness—with Being suffused night and day by wholesome ecstasy, surpassing all

---

[11] I am reminded as I write that out of this very conscience, or idea of conscience, of intense moral right, and in its name and strained con-struction, the worst fanaticisms, wars, persecutions, murders, etc., have yet, in all lands, in the past, been broached, and have come to their devilish fruition. Much is to be said, but I may say here, and in re-sponse, that side by side with the unflagging stimulation of the elements of religion and conscience must henceforth move with equal sway, science, absolute reason, and the general proportionate development of the whole man. These scientific facts, deductions, are divine too—precious counted parts of moral civilization, and, with physical health, indispensable to it, to prevent fanaticism. For abstract religion, I per-ceive, is easily led astray, ever credulous, and is capable of devouring, remorseless, like fire and flame. Conscience, too, isolated from all else, and from the emotional nature, may attain the beauty and purity of glacial, snowy ice. We want, for these States, for the general character, a cheerful, religious fervor, endued with the ever-present modifications of the human emotions, friendship, benevolence, with a fair field for scientific inquiry, the right of individual judgment, and always the cooling influences of material Nature.

the pleasures that wealth, amusement, and even gratified intellect, erudition, or the sense of art, can give.

In the prophetic literature of these States (the reader of my speculations will miss their principal stress unless he allows well for the point that a new Literature, perhaps a new Metaphysics, certainly a new Poetry, are to be, in my opinion, the only sure and worthy supports and expressions of the American Democracy), Nature, true Nature, and the true idea of Nature, long absent, must, above all, become fully restored, enlarged, and must furnish the pervading atmosphere to poems, and the test of all high literary and aesthetic compositions. I do not mean the smooth walks, trimmed hedges, posys and nightingales of the English poets, but the whole orb, with its geologic history, the cosmos, carrying fire and snow, that rolls through the illimitable areas, light as a feather, though weighing billions of tons. Furthermore, as by what we now partially call Nature is intended, at most, only what is entertainable by the physical conscience, the sense of matter, and of good animal health—on these it must be distinctly accumulated, incorporated, that man, comprehending these, has, in towering superaddition, the moral and spiritual consciences, indicating his destination beyond the ostensible, the mortal.

To the heights of such estimate of Nature indeed ascending, we proceed to make observations for our Vistas, breathing rarest air. What is I believe called Idealism seems to me to suggest (guarding against extravagance, and ever modified even by its opposite) the course of inquiry and desert of favor for our New World metaphysics, their foundation of and in literature, giving hue to all.[12]

---

[12]The culmination and fruit of literary artistic expression, and its final fields of pleasure for the human soul, are in metaphysics, including the mysteries of the spiritual world, the soul itself, and the question of the immortal continuation of our identity. In all ages, the mind of man has brought up here—and always will. Here, at least, of whatever race or era, we stand on common ground. Applause, too, is unanimous, antique or modern. Those authors who work well in this field—though their reward, instead of a handsome percentage, or royalty, may be but simply the laurel crown of the victors in the great Olympic games—will be dearest to humanity, and their works, however aesthetically defective, will be treasured forever. The altitude of literature and poetry has always been religion—and always will be. The Indian Vedas, the

The elevating and etherealizing ideas of the unknown and of unreality must be brought forward with authority, as they are the legitimate heirs of the known, and of reality, and at least as great as their parents. Fearless of scoffing, and of the ostent, let us take our stand, our ground, and never desert it, to confront the growing excess and arrogance of realism. To the cry, now victorious—the cry of sense, science, flesh, incomes, farms, merchandise, logic, intellect, demonstrations, solid perpetuities, buildings of brick and iron, or even the facts of the shows of trees, earth, rocks, etc., fear not, my brethren, my sisters, to sound out with equally determined voice, that conviction brood-

---

Naçkas of Zoroaster, the Talmud of the Jews, the Old Testament, the Gospel of Christ and His disciples, Plato's works, the Koran of Mohammed, the Edda of Snorro, and so on toward our own day, to Swedenborg, and to the invaluable contributions of Leibnitz, Kant, and Hegel—these, with such poems only in which (while singing well of persons and events, of the passions of man, and the shows of the material universe), the religious tone, the consciousness of mystery, the recognition of the future, of the unknown, of Deity over and under all, and of the divine purpose, are never absent, but indirectly give tone to all—exhibit literature's real heights and elevations, towering up like the great mountains of the earth.

Standing on this ground—the last, the highest, only permanent ground—and sternly criticizing, from it, all works, either of the literary, or any art, we have peremptorily to dismiss every pretensive production, however fine its aesthetic or intellectual points, which violates or ignores, or even does not celebrate, the central divine idea of All, suffusing universe, of eternal trains of purpose, in the development, by however slow degrees, of the physical, moral, and spiritual cosmos. I say he has studied, meditated to no profit, whatever may be his mere erudition, who has not absorbed this simple consciousness and faith. It is not entirely new—but it is for Democracy to elaborate it, and look to build upon and expand from it, with uncompromising reliance. Above the doors of teaching the inscription is to appear, Though little or nothig can be absolutely known, perceived, except from a point of view which is evanescent, yet we know at least one permanency, that Time and Space, in the will of God, furnish successive chains, completions of material births and beginnings, solve all discrepancies, fears and doubts, and eventually fulfill happiness—and that the prophecy of those births, namely spiritual results, throws the true arch over all teaching, all science. The local considerations of sin, disease, deformity, ignorance, death, etc., and their measurement by the superficial mind, and ordinary legislation and theology, are to be met by science, boldly accepting, promulging this faith, and planting the seeds of superber laws—of the explication of the physical universe through the spiritual—and clearing the way for a religion, sweet and unimpugnable alike to little child or great savant.

ing within the recesses of every envisioned soul—illusions!
apparitions! figments all! True, we must not condemn the show,
neither absolutely deny it, for the indispensability of its meanings; but how clearly we see that, migrate in soul to what we
can already conceive of superior and spiritual points of view,
and palpable as it seems under present relations, it all and
several might, nay certainly would, fall apart and vanish.

I hail with joy the oceanic, variegated, intense practical
energy, the demand for facts, even the business materialism of
the current age, our States. But woe to the age and land in which
these things, movements, stopping at themselves, do not tend
to ideas. As fuel to flame, and flame to the heavens, so must
wealth, science, materialism—even this democracy of which we
make so much—unerringly feed the highest mind, the soul. In-
finitude the flight: fathomless the mystery. Man, so diminutive,
dilates beyond the sensible universe, competes with, outcopes
space and time, meditating even one great idea. Thus, and thus
only, does a human being, his spirit, ascend above, and justify,
objective Nature, which, probably nothing in itself, is incredibly
and divinely serviceable, indispensable, real, here. And as the
purport of objective Nature is doubtless folded, hidden, somewhere here—as somewhere here is what this globe and its manifold forms, and the light of day, and night's darkness, and life
itself, with all its experiences, are for—it is here the great literature, especially verse, must get its inspiration and throbbing
blood. Then may we attain to a poetry worthy the immortal
soul of man, and which, while absorbing materials, and, in their
own sense, the shows of Nature, will, above all, have, both
directly and indirectly, a freeing, fluidizing, expanding, religious
character, exulting with science, fructifying the moral elements,
and stimulating aspirations, and meditations on the unknown.

The process, so far, is indirect and peculiar, and though it
may be suggested, cannot be defined. Observing rapport, and
with intuition, the shows and forms presented by Nature, the
sensuous luxuriance, the beautiful in living men and women,
the actual play of passions, in history and life—and, above all,
from those developments either in Nature or human personality
in which power (dearest of all to the sense of the artist) trans-
acts itself—out of these, and seizing what is in them, the poet,

the aesthetic worker in any field, by the divine magic of his genius, projects them, their analogies, by curious removes, indirections, in literature and art. (No useless attempt to repeat the material creation, by daguerreotyping the exact likeness by mortal mental means.) This is the image-making faculty, coping with material creation, and rivaling, almost triumphing over it. This alone, when all the other parts of a specimen of literature or art are ready and waiting, can breathe into it the breath of life, and endow it with identity.

"The true question to ask," says the Librarian of Congress in a paper read before the Social Science Convention at New York, October 1869, "The true question to ask respecting a book, is, *has it helped any human soul?*" This is the hint, statement, not only of the great literatus, his book, but of every great artist. It may be that all works of art are to be first tried by their art qualities, their image-forming talent, and their dramatic, pictorial, plot-constructing, euphonious and other talents. Then, whenever claiming to be first-class works, they are to be strictly and sternly tried by their foundation in, and radiation, in the highest sense and always indirectly, of, the ethic principles, and eligibility to free, arouse, dilate.

As, within the purposes of the Cosmos, and vivifying all meteorology, and all the congeries of the mineral, vegetable and animal worlds—all the physical growth and development of man, and all the history of the race of politics, religions, wars, etc., there is a moral purpose, a visible or invisible intention, certainly underlying all—its results and proof needing to be patiently waited for—needing intuition, faith, idiosyncrasy, to its realization, which many, and especially the intellectual, do not have—so in the product, or congeries of the product, of the greatest literatus. This is the last, profoundest measure and test of a first-class literary or aesthetic achievement, and when understood and put in force must fain, I say, lead to works, books, nobler than any hitherto known. Lo! Nature (the only complete, actual poem), existing calmly in the divine scheme, containing all, content, careless of the criticisms of a day, or these endless and wordy chatterers. And lo! to the consciousness of the soul, the permanent identity, the thought, the something, before which the magnitude even of democracy, art, liter-

ature, etc., dwindles, becomes partial, measurable—something
that fully satisfies (which those do not). That something is the
All, and the idea of All, with the accompanying idea of eternity,
and of itself, the soul, buoyant, indestructible, sailing space
forever, visiting every region, as a ship the sea. And again lo!
the pulsations in all matter, all spirit, throbbing forever—the
eternal beats, eternal systole and diastole of life in things—
wherefrom I feel and know that death is not the ending, as was
thought, but rather the real beginning—and that nothing ever
is or can be lost, nor ever die, nor soul, nor matter.

In the future of these States must arise poets immenser far,
and make great poems of death. The poems of life are great,
but there must be the poems of the purports of life, not only in
itself, but beyond itself. I have eulogized Homer, the sacred
bards of Jewry, Aeschylus, Juvenal, Shakespeare, etc., and
acknowledged their inestimable value. But (with perhaps the
exception in some, not all respects, of the second-mentioned)
I say there must, for future and democratic purposes, appear
poets (dare I to say so?) of higher class even than any of those
—poets not only possessed of the religious fire and abandon
of Isaiah, luxuriant in the epic talent of Homer, or for proud
characters as in Shakespeare, but consistent with the Hegelian
formulas, and consistent with modern science. America needs,
and the world needs, a class of bards who will, now and ever,
so link and tally the rational physical being of man, with the
ensembles of time and space, and with this vast and multiform
show, Nature, surrounding him, ever tantalizing him, equally
a part, and yet not a part of him, as to essentially harmonize,
satisfy, and put at rest. Faith, very old, now scared away by
science, must be restored, brought back by the same power that
caused her departure—restored with new sway, deeper, wider,
higher than ever. Surely, this universal ennui, this coward fear,
this shuddering at death, these low, degrading views, are not
always to rule the spirit pervading future society, as it has the
past, and does the present. What the Roman Lucretius sought
most nobly, yet all too blindly, negatively to do for his age and
its successors, must be done positively by some great coming
literatus, especially poet, who, while remaining fully poet, will
absorb whatever science indicates, with spiritualism, and out of

them, and out of his own genius, will compose the great poem of death. Then will man indeed confront Nature, and confront time and space, both with science, and *con amore*, and take his right place, prepared for life, master of fortune and misfortune. And then that which was long wanted will be supplied, and the ship that had it not before in all her voyages, will have an anchor.

There are still other standards, suggestions, for products of high literatures. That which really balances and conserves the social and political world is not so much legislation, police, treaties, and dread of punishment, as the latent eternal intuitional sense, in humanity, of fairness, manliness, decorum, etc. Indeed, this perennial regulation, control, and oversight, by self-suppliance, is *sine qua non* to democracy; and a highest, widest aim of democratic literature may well be to bring forth, cultivate, brace, and strengthen this sense, in individuals and society. A strong mastership of the general inferior self by the superior self, is to be aided, secured, indirectly, but surely, by the literatus, in his works, shaping, for individual or aggregate democracy, a great passionate body, in and along with which goes a great masterful spirit.

And still, providing for contingencies, I fain confront the fact, the need of powerful native philosophs and orators and bards, these States, as rallying points to come, in times of danger, and to fend off ruin and defection. For history is long, long, long. Shift and turn the combinations of the statement as we may, the problem of the future of America is in certain respects as dark as it is vast. Pride, competition, segregation, vicious wilfulness, and license beyond example, brood already upon us. Unwieldly and immense, who shall hold in behemoth? who bridle leviathan? Flaunt it as we choose, athwart and over the roads of our progress loom huge uncertainty, and dreadful, threatening gloom. It is useless to deny it: Democracy grows rankly up the thickest, noxious, deadliest plants and fruits of all—brings worse and worse invaders—needs newer, larger, stronger, keener compensations and compellers.

Our lands, embracing so much (embracing indeed the whole, rejecting none), hold in their breast that flame also, capable of consuming themselves, consuming us all. Short as the span of our national life has been, already have death and downfall crowded close upon us—and will again crowd close, no doubt, even if warded off. Ages to come may never know, but I know, how narrowly during the late Secession War—and more than once, and more than twice or thrice—our Nationality (wherein bound up, as in a ship in a storm, depended, and yet depend, all our best life, all hope, all value), just grazed, just by a hair escaped destruction. Alas! to think of them! the agony and bloody sweat of certain of those hours! those cruel, sharp, suspended crises!

Even today, amid these whirls, incredible flippancy, and blind fury of parties, infidelity, entire lack of first-class captains and leaders, added to the plentiful meanness and vulgarity of the ostensible masses—that problem, the labor question, beginning to open like a yawning gulf, rapidly widening every year —what prospect have we? We sail a dangerous sea of seething currents, cross and undercurrents, vortices—all so dark, untried —and whither shall we turn? It seems as if the Almighty had spread before this nation charts of imperial destinies, dazzling as the sun, yet with many a deep intestine difficulty, and human aggregate of cankerous imperfection— saying, lo! the roads, the only plans of development, long and varied with all terrible balks and ebullitions. You said in your soul, I will be empire of empires, overshadowing all else, past and present, putting the history of Old-World dynasties, conquests behind me, as of no account—making a new history, a history of democracy, making old history a dwarf—I alone inaugurating largeness, culminating time. If these, O lands of America, are indeed the prizes, the determinations of your soul, be it so. But behold the cost, and already specimens of the cost. Thought you greatness was to ripen for you like a pear? If you would have greatness, know that you must conquer it through ages, centuries—must pay for it with a proportionate price. For you too, as for all lands, the struggle, the traitor, the wily person in office, scrofulous wealth, the surfeit of prosperity, the demonism of greed, the hell of passion, the decay of faith, the long postponement, the fossil-like lethargy, the ceaseless need of revolutions, prophets, thunderstorms, deaths, births, new projections and invigorations of ideas and men.

Yet I have dreamed, merged in that hidden-tangled problem of our fate, whose long unraveling stretches mysteriously through time—dreamed out, portrayed, hinted already—a little or a larger band—a band of brave and true, unprecedented yet—armed and equipped at every point—the members separated, it may be, by different dates and States, or south, or north, or east, or west—Pacific, Atlantic, Southern, Canadian —a year, a century here, and other centuries there—but always one, compact in soul, conscience-conserving, God-inculcating, inspired achievers, not only in literature, the greatest art, but achievers in all art—a new, undying order, dynasty, from age to age transmitted—a band, a class, at least as fit to cope with current years, our dangers, needs, as those who, for their times, so long, so well, in armor or in cowl, upheld and made illustrious, that far-back feudal, priestly world. To offset chivalry, indeed, those vanished countless knights, old altars, abbeys, priests, ages and strings of ages, a knightlier and more sacred cause today demands, and shall supply, in a New World, to larger, grander work, more than the counterpart and tally of them.

Arrived now, definitely, at an apex for these Vistas, I confess that the promulgation and belief in such a class or institution—a new and greater literatus order—its possibility (nay certainty), underlies these entire speculations—and that the rest, the other parts, as superstructures, are all founded upon it. It really seems to me the condition, not only of our future national and democratic development, but of our perpetuation. In the highly artificial and materialistic bases of modern civilization, with the corresponding arrangements and methods of living, the force-infusion of intellect alone, the depraving influences of riches just as much as poverty, the absence of all high ideals in character—with the long series of tendencies, shapings, which few are strong enough to resist, and which now seem, with steam-engine speed, to be everywhere turning out the generations of humanity like uniform iron castings—all of which, as compared with the feudal ages, we can yet do nothing better than accept, make the best of, and even welcome, upon the whole, for their oceanic practical grandeur, and their restless wholesale kneading of the masses—I say of all this tremendous and dominant play of solely materialistic bearings upon current life in the United States, with the results as already seen, accumulating, and reaching far into the future, that they must either be confronted and met by at least an equally subtle and tremendous force-infusion for purposes of spiritualization, for the pure conscience, for genuine aesthetics, and for absolute and primal manliness and womanliness—or else our modern civilization, with all its improvements, is in vain, and we are on the road to a destiny, a status, equivalent, in its real world, to that of the fabled damned.

Prospecting thus the coming unsped days, and that new order in them—marking the endless train of exercise, development, unwind, in nation as in man, which life is for—we see, foreindicated, amid these prospects and hopes, new law-forces of spoken and written language—not merely the pedagogue-forms, correct, regular, familiar with precedents, made for matters of outside propriety, fine words, thoughts definitely told out—but a language fanned by the breath of Nature, which leaps overhead, cares mostly for impetus and effects, and for what it plants and invigorates to grow—tallies life and character, and seldomer tells a thing than suggests or necessitates it. In fact, a new theory of literary composition for imaginative works of the very first class, and especially for higest poems, is the sole course open to these States. Books are to be called for, and supplied, on the assumption that the process of reading is not a half sleep, but, in highest sense, an exercise, a gymnast's struggle; that the reader is to do something for himself, must be on the alert, must himself or herself construct indeed the poem, argument, history, metaphysical essay—the text furnishing the hints, the clue, the start or framework. Not the book needs so much to be the complete thing, but the reader of the book does. That were to make a nation of supple and athletic minds, well trained, intuitive, used to depend on themselves, and not on a few coteries of writers.

Investigating here, we see, not that it is a little thing we have, in having the bequeathed libraries, countless shelves of volumes, records, etc.; yet how serious the danger, depending entirely on them, of the bloodless vein, the nerveless arm, the false application, at second or third hand. We see that the real interest of this people of ours in the theology, history, poetry, politics, and personal models of the past (the British islands, for instance, and indeed all the past), is not necessarily to mold ourselves or our literature upon them, but to attain fuller, more definite comparisons, warnings, and the insight to ourselves, our own present, and our own far grander, different, future history, religion, social customs, etc. We see that almost everything that has been written, sung, or stated, of old, with reference to humanity under the feudal and oriental institutes, religious, and for other lands, needs to be rewritten, resung, restated, in terms consistent with the institution of these States, and to come in range and obedient uniformity with them.

We see, as in the universes of the material cosmos, after meteorological, vegetable, and animal cycles, man at last arises, born through them, to prove them, concentrate them, to turn upon them with wonder and love—to command them, adorn them, and carry them upward into superior realms—so, out of the series of the preceding social and political universes, now arise these States. We see that while many were supposing things established and completed, really the grandest things always remain; and discover that the work of the New World is not ended, but only fairly begun.

We see our land, America, her literature, aesthetics, etc., as, substantially, the getting in form, or effusement and statement, of deepest basic elements and loftiest final meanings, of history and man—and the portrayal (under the eternal laws and conditions of beauty) of our own physiognomy, the subjective tie and expression of the objective, as from our own combination, continuation, and points of view—and the deposit and record of the national mentality, character, appeals, heroism, wars, and even liberties—where these, and all, culminate in native literary and artistic formulation, to be perpetuated; and not having which native, first-class formulation, she will flounder about, and her other, however imposing, eminent greatness, prove merely a passing gleam; but truly having which, she will understand herself, live nobly, nobly contribute, emanate, and, swinging, poised safely on herself, illumined and illuming, become a full-formed world, and divine Mother not only of material but spiritual worlds, in ceaseless succession through time—

the main thing being the average, the bodily, the concrete, the democratic, the popular, on which all the superstructures of the future are to permanently rest.

SPECIMEN DAYS

Specimen Days was published in 1882, but most of it had been
written well before that date, some of it twenty years before.
Whitman begins with a description of the process by which it
came into being, and makes full confession of the fact that it
is not so much a book as a collection of jottings and memoranda. Nevertheless it has unity because of the man who is
writing; and it has both power and charm. The powerful part
is concerned with Whitman's hospital experiences in Washington during the Civil War. There is nothing quite like these
pages elsewhere. Published separately in 1875 as *Memoranda
During the War*, they find their place in *Specimen Days*, other
pages of which are concerned with an opposite sort of experience, by virtue of the absolute sympathy which without any
effort or pose they know how to express. Whitman saw many
wounded and dying men, Union and Confederate; he describes
them with a clarity in which tenderness takes its right tone,
without sentiment or condescension. What he saw was terrible,
and so is what he says. But it is the fact that we get, not merely
his feeling, though we know very well what that is. The sections
about Lincoln are also unique for the very sharp and touching
picture they sketch of a President in wartime—above all this
President, who was to become the subject of Whitman's
greatest poem.

The charming part is that which Whitman took from the
diary he kept while loafing and inviting his soul along Timber
Creek, a stream which flows into the Delaware River near
Camden. Here, as a guest of the Stafford family, he luxuriated
in the simplest sights and sounds of nature, making the acquaintance of birds, trees, insects, clouds, and flowers, and
recording with a sensitive pen the subtle state of mind that resulted in him. This was the time of his convalescence after the
paralytic stroke which removed him from Washington. The

accent is not on that, however; it is on the serene world he suddenly discovers, and loves as Thoreau loved his in Concord, or John Burroughs his along the Hudson. Some pages were written while he was a guest of Burroughs, and since he would stop between times in New York, that city wins his love all over again. There are notes of other places too—the Far West, Canada, and Camden itself. But the bulk of the book—here reprinted complete from the text of the Deathbed Edition—deals with his days of terrible war and his days of total peace.

Specimen Days

A Happy Hour's Command

Down in the Woods, July 2d, 1882.—If I do it at all I must
delay no longer. Incongruous and full of skips and jumps as is
that huddle of diary-jottings, war-memoranda of 1862-'65,
Nature-notes of 1877-'81, with Western and Canadian observations afterwards, all bundled up and tied by a big string, the
resolution and indeed mandate comes to me this day, this hour,
—(and what a day! what an hour just passing! the luxury of
riant grass and blowing breeze, with all the shows of sun and
sky and perfect temperature, never before so filling me body
and soul)—to go home, untie the bundle, reel out diary-scraps
and memoranda, just as they are, large or small, one after
another, into print-pages,[1] and let the melange's lacking and

---

[1] The pages from [388 to 404] are nearly verbatim an off-hand letter of
mine in January, 1882, to an insisting friend. Following, I give some
gloomy experiences. The war of attempted secession has, of course,
been the distinguishing event of my time. I commenced at the close
of 1862, and continued steadily through '63, '64, and '65, to visit the
sick and wounded of the army, both on the field and in the hospitals
in and around Washington city. From the first I kept little note-books
for impromptu jottings in pencil to refresh my memory of names
and circumstances, and what was specially wanted, &c. In these I
brief'd cases, persons, sights, occurrences in camp, by the bedside,
and not seldom by the corpses of the dead. Some were scratch'd down
from narratives I heard and itemized while watching, or waiting, or
tending somebody amid those scenes. I have dozens of such little
note-books left, forming a special history of those years, for myself
alone, full of associations never to be possibly said or sung. I wish
I could convey to the reader the associations that attach to these soil'd
and creas'd livraisons, each composed of a sheet or two of paper,
folded small to carry in the pocket, and fasten'd with a pin. I leave
them just as I threw them by after the war, blotch'd here and there

wants of connection take care of themselves. It will illustrate one phase of humanity anyhow; how few of life's days and hours (and they not by relative value or proportion, but by chance) are ever noted. Probably another point too, how we give long preparations for some object, planning and delving and fashioning, and then, when the actual hour for doing arrives, find ourselves still quite unprepared, and tumble the thing together, letting hurry and crudeness tell the story better than fine work. At any rate I obey my happy hour's command, which seems curiously imperative. May-be, if I don't do anything else, I shall send out the most wayward, spontaneous, fragmentary book ever printed.

Answer to an Insisting Friend

You ask for items, details of my early life—of genealogy and parentage, particularly of the women of my ancestry, and of its far back Netherlands stock on the maternal side—of the region where I was born and raised, and my father and mother

---

with more than one blood-stain, hurriedly written, sometimes at the clinique, not seldom amid the excitement of uncertainty, or defeat, or of action, or getting ready for it, or a march. Most of the pages from [411 to 484] are verbatim copies of those lurid and blood-smutch'd little note-books.

Very different are most of the memoranda that follow. Some time after the war ended I had a paralytic stroke, which prostrated me for several years. In 1876 I began to get over the worst of it. From this date, portions of several seasons, especially summers, I spent at a secluded haunt down in Camden county, New Jersey—Timber creek, quite a little river (it enters from the great Delaware, twelve miles away)—with primitive solitudes, winding stream, recluse and woody banks, sweet-feeding springs, and all the charms that birds, grass, wild-flowers, rabbits and squirrels, old oaks, walnut trees, &c., can bring. Through these times, and on these spots, the diary from page [486] onward was mostly written.

I suppose I publish and leave the whole gathering, first, from that eternal tendency to perpetuate and preserve which is behind all Nature, authors included; second, to symbolize two or three specimen interiors, personal and other, out of the myriads of my time, the middle range of the Nineteenth century in the New World; a strange, unloosen'd, wondrous time. But the book is probably without any definite purpose that can be told in a statement.

before me, and theirs before them—with a word about Brooklyn and New York cities, the times I lived there as lad and young man. You say you want to get at these details mainly as the go-befores and embryons of "Leaves of Grass." Very good; you shall have at least some specimens of them all. I have often thought of the meaning of such things—that one can only encompass and complete matters of that kind by exploring behind, perhaps very far behind, themselves directly, and so into their genesis, antecedents, and cumulative stages. Then as luck would have it, I lately whiled away the tedium of a week's half-sickness and confinement, by collating these very items for another (yet unfulfill'd, probably abandon'd,) purpose; and if you will be satisfied with them, authentic in date-occurrence and fact simply, and told my own way, garrulous-like, here they are. I shall not hesitate to make extracts, for I catch at any thing to save labor; but those will be the best versions of what I want to convey.

Genealogy—Van Velsor and Whitman

The later years of the last century found the Van Velsor family, my mother's side, living on their own farm at Cold Spring, Long Island, New York State, near the eastern edge of Queens county, about a mile from the harbor.[2] My father's side—probably the fifth generation from the first English arrivals in New England—were at the same time farmers on their own land—(and a fine domain it was, 500 acres, all good soil, gently sloping east and south, about one-tenth woods, plenty of grand old trees,) two or three miles off, at West Hills, Suffolk county. The Whitman name in the Eastern States, and so branching West and South, starts undoubtedly from one John Whitman, born 1602, in Old England, where he grew up, married, and his eldest son was born in 1629. He came over in

---

[2]Long Island was settled first on the west end by the Dutch, from Holland, then on the east end by the English—the dividing line of the two nationalities being a little west of Huntington, where my father's folks lived, and where I was born.

the "True Love" in 1640 to America, and lived in Weymouth, Mass., which place became the mother-hive of the New-Englanders of the name: he died in 1692. His brother, Rev. Zechariah Whitman, also came over in the "True Love," either at that time or soon after, and lived at Milford, Conn. A son of this Zechariah, named Joseph, migrated to Huntington, Long Island, and permanently settled there. Savage's "Genealogical Dictionary" (vol. iv, p. 524) gets the Whitman family establish'd at Huntington, per this Joseph, before 1664. It is quite certain that from that beginning, and from Joseph, the West Hill Whitmans, and all others in Suffolk county, have since radiated, myself among the number. John and Zechariah both went to England and back again divers times; they had large families, and several of their children were born in the old country. We hear of the father of John and Zechariah, Abijah Whitman, who goes over into the 1500's, but we know little about him, except that he also was for some time in America.

These old pedigree-reminiscences come up to me vividly from a visit I made not long since (in my 63d year) to West Hills, and to the burial grounds of my ancestry, both sides. I extract from notes of that visit, written there and then:

The Old Whitman and Van Velsor Cemeteries

July 29, 1881.—After more than forty years' absence, (except a brief visit, to take my father there once more, two years before he died,) went down Long Island on a week's jaunt to the place where I was born, thirty miles from New York city. Rode around the old familiar spots, viewing and pondering and dwelling long upon them, everything coming back to me. Went to the old Whitman homestead on the upland and took a view eastward, inclining south, over the broad and beautiful farm lands of my grandfather (1780,) and my father. There was the new house (1810,) the big oak a hundred and fifty or two hundred years old; there the well, the sloping kitchen-garden, and a little way off even the well-kept remains of the dwelling of my great-grandfather (1750–'60) still standing, with its mighty timbers and low ceilings. Near by, a stately grove of tall, vigorous black-walnuts, beautiful, Apollo-like, the sons or grandsons, no doubt, of black-walnuts during or before 1776. On the other side of the road spread the famous apple orchard, over twenty acres, the trees planted by hands long mouldering in the grave (my uncle Jesse's,) but quite many of them evidently capable of throwing out their annual blossoms and fruit yet.

I now write these lines seated on an old grave (doubtless of a century since at least) on the burial hill of the Whitmans of many generations. Fifty and more graves are quite plainly traceable, and as many more decay'd out of all form—depress'd mounds, crumbled and broken stones, cover'd with moss—the gray and sterile hill, the clumps of chestnuts outside, the silence, just varied by the soughing wind. There is always the deepest eloquence of sermon or poem in any of these ancient graveyards of which Long Island has so many; so what must this one have been to me? My whole family history, with its succession of links, from the first settlement down to date, told here —three centuries concentrate on this sterile acre.

The next day, July 30, I devoted to the maternal locality, and if possible was still more penetrated and impress'd. I write this paragraph on the burial hill of the Van Velsors, near Cold Spring, the most significant depository of the dead that could be imagin'd, without the slightest help from art, but far ahead of it, soil sterile, a mostly bare plateau-flat of half an acre, the top of a hill, brush and well grown trees and dense woods bordering all around, very primitive, secluded, no visitors, no road (you cannot drive here, you have to bring the dead on foot, and follow on foot.) Two or three-score graves quite plain; as many more almost rubb'd out. My grandfather Cornelius and my grandmother Amy (Naomi) and numerous relatives nearer or remoter, on my mother's side, lie buried here. The scene as I stood or sat, the delicate and wild odor of the woods, a slightly drizzling rain, the emotional atmosphere of the place, and the inferr'd reminiscences, were fitting accompaniments.

The Maternal Homestead

I went down from this ancient grave place eighty or ninety rods
to the site of the Van Velsor homestead, where my mother was
born (1795,) and where every spot had been familiar to me
as a child and youth (1825–'40.) Then stood there a long rambling, dark-gray, shingle-sided house, with sheds, pens, a great
barn, and much open road-space. Now of all those not a
vestige left; all had been pull'd down, erased, and the plough
and harrow pass'd over foundations, road-spaces and everything, for many summers; fenced in at present, and grain and
clover growing like any other fine fields. Only a big hole from
the cellar, with some little heaps of broken stone, green with
grass and weeds, identified the place. Even the copious old
brook and spring seem'd to have mostly dwindled away. The
whole scene, with what it arous'd, memories of my young days
there half a century ago, the vast kitchen and ample fireplace
and the sitting-room adjoining, the plain furniture, the meals,
the house full of merry people, my grandmother Amy's sweet
old face in its Quaker cap, my grandfather "the Major," jovial,
red, stout, with sonorous voice and characteristic physiognomy, with the actual sights themselves, made the most pronounc'd half-day's experience of my whole jaunt.

For there with all those wooded, hilly, healthy surroundings,
my dearest mother, Louisa Van Velsor, grew up—(her mother,
Amy Williams, of the Friends' or Quakers' denomination—the
Williams family, seven sisters and one brother—the father and
brother sailors, both of whom met their deaths at sea.) The
Van Velsor people were noted for fine horses, which the men
bred and train'd from blooded stock. My mother, as a young
woman, was a daily and daring rider. As to the head of the
family himself, the old race of the Netherlands, so deeply grafted on Manhattan island and in Kings and Queens counties,
never yielded a more mark'd and full Americanized specimen
than Major Cornelius Van Velsor.

Two Old Family Interiors

Of the domestic and inside life of the middle of Long Island, at and just before that time, here are two samples:

"The Whitmans, at the beginning of the present century, lived in a long story-and-a-half farm-house, hugely timber'd, which is still standing. A great smoke-canopied kitchen, with vast hearth and chimney, form'd one end of the house. The existence of slavery in New York at that time, and the possession by the family of some twelve or fifteen slaves, house and field servants, gave things quite a patriarchal look. The very young darkies could be seen, a swarm of them, toward sundown, in this kitchen, squatted in a circle on the floor, eating their supper of Indian pudding and milk. In the house, and in food and furniture, all was rude, but substantial. No carpets or stoves were known, and no coffee, and tea or sugar only for the women. Rousing wood fires gave both warmth and light on winter nights. Pork, poultry, beef, and all the ordinary vegetables and grains were plentiful. Cider was the men's common drink, and used at meals. The clothes were mainly homespun. Journeys were made by both men and women on horseback. Both sexes labor'd with their own hands—the men on the farm—the women in the house and around it. Books were scarce. The annual copy of the almanac was a treat, and was pored over through the long winter evenings. I must not forget to mention that both these families were near enough to the sea to behold it from the high places, and to hear in still hours the roar of the surf; the latter, after a storm, giving a peculiar sound at night. Then all hands, male and female, went down frequently on beach and bathing parties, and the men on practical expeditions for cutting salt hay, and for clamming and fishing."— *John Burroughs's* NOTES.

"The ancestors of Walt Whitman, on both the paternal and maternal sides, kept a good table, sustain'd the hospitalities, decorums, and an excellent social reputation in the county, and they were often of mark'd individuality. If space permitted, I should consider some of the men worthy special description; and still more some of the women. His great-grandmother on the paternal side, for instance, was a large swarthy woman, who lived to a very old age. She smoked tobacco, rode on horseback like a man, managed the most vicious horse, and, becoming a widow in later life, went forth every day over her farm-lands, frequently in the saddle, directing the labor of her slaves, with language in which, on exciting occasions, oaths were not spared. The two immediate grandmothers were, in the best sense, superior women. The maternal one (Amy Williams before marriage) was a Friend, or Quakeress, of sweet, sensible character, housewifely proclivities, and deeply intuitive and spiritual. The other, (Hannah Brush,) was an equally noble, perhaps stronger character, lived to be very old, had quite a family of sons, was a natural lady, was in early life a school-mistress, and had great solidity of mind. W. W. himself makes much of the women of his ancestry."—*The same*.

Out from these arrieres of persons and scenes, I was born May 31, 1819. And now to dwell awhile on the locality itself— as the successive growth stages of my infancy, childhood, youth and manhood were all pass'd on Long Island, which I sometimes feel as if I had incorporated. I roam'd, as boy and man, and have lived in nearly all parts, from Brooklyn to Montauk point.

Paumanok, and My Life on It as Child and Young Man

Worth fully and particularly investigating indeed this Paumanok, (to give the spot its aboriginal name,[3]) stretching east through Kings, Queens and Suffolk counties, 120 miles altogether—on the north Long Island sound, a beautiful varied and picturesque series of inlets, "necks" and sea-like expan-

[3]"Paumanok, (or Paumanake, or Paumanack, the Indian name of Long Island,) over a hundred miles long; shaped like a fish—plenty of sea shore, sandy, stormy, uninviting, the horizon boundless, the air too strong for invalids, the bays a wonderful resort for aquatic birds, the south-side meadows cover'd with salt hay, the soil of the island generally tough, but good for the locust-tree, the apple orchard, and the blackberry, and with numberless springs of the sweetest water in the world. Years ago, among the bay-men—a strong, wild race, now extinct, or rather entirely changed—a native of Long Island was called a *Paumanacker*, or *Creole-Paumanacker*."—*John Burroughs*.

sions, for a hundred miles to Orient point. On the ocean side the great south bay dotted with countless hummocks, mostly small, some quite large, occasionally long bars of sand out two hundred rods to a mile-and-a-half from the shore. While now and then, as at Rockaway and far east along the Hamptons, the beach makes right on the island, the sea dashing up without intervention. Several light-houses on the shores east; a long history of wrecks tragedies, some even of late years. As a youngster, I was in the atmosphere and traditions of many of these wrecks—of one or two almost an observer. Off Hempstead beach for example, was the loss of the ship "Mexico" in 1840, (alluded to in "the Sleepers" in L. of G.) And at Hampton, some years later, the destruction of the brig "Elizabeth," a fearful affair, in one of the worst winter gales, where Margaret Fuller went down, with her husband and child.

Inside the outer bars or beach this south bay is everywhere comparatively shallow; of cold winters all thick ice on the surface. As a boy I often went forth with a chum or two, on those frozen fields, with hand-sled, axe and eel-spear, after messes of eels. We would cut holes in the ice, sometimes striking quite an eel-bonanza, and filling our baskets with great, fat, sweet, white-meated fellows. The scenes, the ice, drawing the hand-sled, cutting holes, spearing the eels, &c., were of course just such fun as is dearest to boyhood. The shores of this bay, winter and summer, and my doings there in early life, are woven all through L. of G. One sport I was very fond of was to go on a bay-party in summer to gather sea-gull's eggs. (The gulls lay two or three eggs, more than half the size of hen's egg, right on the sand, and leave the sun's heat to hatch them.)

The eastern end of Long Island, the Peconic bay region, I knew quite well too—sail'd more than once around Shelter island, and down to Montauk—spent many an hour on Turtle hill by the old light-house, on the extreme point, looking out over the ceaseless roll of the Atlantic. I used to like to go down there and fraternize with the blue-fishers, or the annual squads of sea-bass takers. Sometimes, along Montauk peninsula, (it is some 15 miles long, and good grazing,) met the strange, unkempt, half-barbarous herdsmen, at that time living there entirely aloof from society or civilization, in charge, on those rich pasturages, of vast droves of horses, kine or sheep, own'd by farmers of the eastern towns. Sometimes, too, the few remaining Indians, or half-breeds, at that period left on Montauk peninsula, but now I believe altogether extinct.

More in the middle of the island were the spreading Hempstead plains, then (1830–'40) quite prairie-like, open, uninhabited, rather sterile, cover'd with kill-calf and huckleberry bushes, yet plenty of fair pasture for the cattle, mostly milchcows, who fed there by hundreds, even thousands, and at evening, (the plains too were own'd by the towns, and this was the use of them in common,) might be seen taking their way home, branching off regularly in the right places. I have often been out on the edges of these plains toward sundown, and can yet recall in fancy the interminable cow processions, and hear the music of the tin or copper bells clanking far or near, and breathe the cool of the sweet and slightly aromatic evening air, and note the sunset.

Through the same region of the island, but further east, extended wide central tracts of pine and scrub-oak, (charcoal was largely made here,) monotonous and sterile. But many a good day or half-day did I have, wandering through those solitary cross-roads, inhaling the peculiar and wild aroma. Here, and all along the island and its shores, I spent intervals many years, all seasons, sometimes riding, sometimes boating, but generally afoot, (I was always then a good walker,) absorbing fields, shores, marine incidents, characters, the bay-men, farmers, pilots—always had a plentiful acquaintance with the latter, and with fishermen—went every summer on sailing trips —always liked the bare sea-beach, south side, and have some of my happiest hours on it to this day.

As I write, the whole experience comes back to me after the lapse of forty and more years—the soothing rustle of the waves, and the saline smell—boyhood's times, the clam-digging, barefoot, and with trowsers roll'd up—hauling down the creek— the perfume of the sedge-meadows—the hay-boat, and the chowder and fishing excursions;—or, of later years, little voyages down and out New York bay, in the pilot boats. Those same later years, also, while living in Brooklyn, (1836–'50) I went regularly every week in the mild seasons down to Coney island, at that time a long, bare unfrequented shore, which I had all to myself, and where I loved, after bathing, to race up and down the hard sand, and declaim Homer or Shakespere to the surf and sea-gulls by the hour. But I am getting ahead too rapidly, and must keep more in my traces.

My First Reading—Lafayette

From 1824 to '28 our family lived in Brooklyn in Front, Cranberry and Johnson streets. In the latter my father built a nice house for a home, and afterwards another in Tillary street. We occupied them, one after the other, but they were mortgaged, and we lost them. I yet remember Lafayette's visit.[4] Most of these years I went to the public schools. It must have been about 1829 or '30 that I went with my father and mother to hear Elias Hicks preach in a ball-room on Brooklyn heights. At about the same time employ'd as a boy in an office, lawyers', father and two sons, Clarke's, Fulton street, near Orange. I had a nice desk and window-nook to myself; Edward C. kindly help'd me at my handwriting and composition, and, (the signal event of my life up to that time,) subscribed for me to a big circulating library. For a time I now revel'd in romance-reading of all kinds; first, the "American Nights," all the volumes, an amazing treat. Then, with sorties in very many other directions, took in Walter Scott's novels, one after another, and his poetry, (and continue to enjoy novels and poetry to this day).

[4]"On the visit of General Lafayette to this country, in 1824, he came over to Brooklyn in state, and rode through the city. The children of the schools turn'd out to join in the welcome. An edifice for a free public library for youths was just then commencing, and Lafayette consented to stop on his way and lay the corner-stone. Numerous children arriving on the ground, where a huge irregular excavation for the building was already dug, surrounded with heaps of rough stone, several gentlemen assisted in lifting the children to safe or convenient spots to see the ceremony. Among the rest, Lafayette, also helping the children, took up the five-year-old Walt Whitman, and pressing the child a moment to his breast, and giving him a kiss, handed him down to a safe spot in the excavation." —John Burroughs.

Printing Office—Old Brooklyn

After about two years went to work in a weekly newspaper and printing office, to learn the trade. The paper was the "Long Island Patriot," owned by S. E. Clements, who was also post-master. An old printer in the office, William Hartshorne, a revolutionary character, who had seen Washington, was a special friend of mine, and I had many a talk with him about long past times. The apprentices, including myself, boarded with his grand-daughter. I used occasionally to go out riding with the boss, who was very kind to us boys; Sundays he took us all to a great old rough, fortress-looking stone church, on Joralemon street, near where the Brooklyn city hall now is —(at that time broad fields and country roads everywhere around.⁵) Afterward I work'd on the "Long Island Star," Alden Spooner's paper. My father all these years pursuing his trade as carpenter and builder, with varying fortune. There was a growing family of children—eight of us—my brother Jesse the oldest, myself the second, my dear sisters Mary and Hannah Louisa, my brothers Andrew, George, Thomas Jefferson, and then my youngest brother, Edward, born 1835, and always badly crippled, as I am myself of late years.

⁵Of the Brooklyn of that time (1830–40) hardly anything remains, except the lines of old streets. The population was then between ten and twelve thousand. For a mile Fulton street was lined with magnificent elm trees. The character of the place was thoroughly rural. As a sample of comparative values, it may be mention'd that twenty-five acres in what is now the most costly part of the city, bounded by Flatbush and Fulton avenues, were then bought by Mr. Parmentier, a French *emigré*, for $4,000. Who remembers the old places as they were? Who remembers the old citizens of that time? Among the former were Smith & Wood's, Coe Downing's and other public houses at the ferry, the old Ferry itself, Love lane, the Heights as then, the Wallabout with the wooden bridge, and the road out beyond Fulton street to the old toll-gate. Among the latter were the majestic and genial General Jeremiah Johnson, with others, Gabriel Furman, Rev. E. M. Johnson, Alden Spooner, Mr. Pierrepont, Mr. Joralemon, Samuel Willoughby, Jonathan Trotter, George Hall, Cyrus P. Smith N. B. Morse, John Dikeman, Adrian Hegeman, William Udall, and old Mr. Duflon, with his military garden.

Growth—Health—Work

I developed (1833-4-5) into a healthy, strong youth (grew too fast, though, was nearly as big as a man at 15 or 16.) Our family at this period moved back to the country, my dear mother very ill for a long time, but recover'd. All these years I was down Long Island more or less every summer, now east, now west, sometimes months at a stretch. At 16, 17, and so on, was fond of debating societies, and had an active membership with them, off and on, in Brooklyn and one or two country towns on the island. A most omnivorous novel-reader, these and later years, devour'd everything I could get. Fond of the theatre, also, in New York, went whenever I could—sometimes witnessing fine performances.

1836-7, work'd as compositor in printing offices in New York city. Then, when little more than eighteen, and for a while afterwards, went to teaching country schools down in Queens and Suffolk counties, Long Island, and "boarded round." (This latter I consider one of my best experiences and deepest lessons in human nature behind the scenes, and in the masses.) In '39, '40, I started and publish'd a weekly paper in my native town, Huntington. Then returning to New York city and Brooklyn, work'd on as printer and writer, mostly prose, but an occasional shy at "poetry."

My Passion for Ferries

Living in Brooklyn or New York city from this time forward, my life, then, and still more the following years, was curiously identified with Fulton ferry, already becoming the greatest of its sort in the world for general importance, volume, variety, rapidity, and picturesqueness. Almost daily, later, ('50 to '60,) I cross'd on the boats, often up in the pilot-houses where I could get a full sweep, absorbing shows, accompaniments, surroundings. What oceanic currents, eddies, underneath—the great tides of humanity also, with ever-shifting movements.

Indeed, I have always had a passion for ferries; to me they afford inimitable, streaming, never-failing, living poems. The river and bay scenery, all about New York island, any time of a fine day—the hurrying, splashing sea-tides—the changing panorama of steamers, all sizes, often a string of big ones outward bound to distant ports—the myriads of white-sail'd schooners, sloops, skiffs, and the marvellously beautiful yachts —the majestic sound boats as they rounded the Battery and came along towards 5, afternoon, eastward bound—the prospect off toward Staten island, or down the Narrows, or the other way up the Hudson—what refreshment of spirit such sights and experiences gave me years ago (and many a time since.) My old pilot friends, the Balsirs, Johnny Cole, Ira Smith, William White, and my young ferry friend, Tom Gere—how well I remember them all.

Broadway Sights

Besides Fulton ferry, off and on for years, I knew and frequented Broadway—that noted avenue of New York's crowded and mixed humanity, and of so many notables. Here I saw, during those times, Andrew Jackson, Webster, Clay, Seward, Martin Van Buren, filibuster Walker, Kossuth, Fitz Greene Halleck, Bryant, the Prince of Wales, Charles Dickens, the first Japanese ambassadors, and lots of other celebrities of the time. Always something novel or inspiriting; yet mostly to me the hurrying and vast amplitude of those never-ending human currents. I remember seeing James Fenimore Cooper in a court-room in Chambers street, back of the city hall, where he was carrying on a law case—(I think it was a charge of libel he had brought against some one.) I also remember seeing Edgar A. Poe, and having a short interview with him, (it must have been in 1845 or '6) in his office, second story of a corner building, (Duane or Pearl street.) He was editor and owner or part owner of "the Broadway Journal." The visit was about a piece of mine he had publish'd. Poe was very cordial, in a quiet way, appear'd well in person, dress, &c. I have a distinct and pleasing remembrance of his looks, voice, manner and matter; very kindly and human, but subdued, perhaps a little jaded. For another of my reminiscences, here on the west side, just below Houston street, I once saw (it must have been about 1832, of a sharp, bright January day) a bent, feeble but stout-built very old man, bearded, swathed in rich furs, with a great ermine cap on his head, led and assisted, almost carried, down the steps of his high front stoop (a dozen friends and servants, emulous, carefully holding, guiding him) and then lifted and tuck'd in a gorgeous sleigh, envelop'd in other furs, for a ride. The sleigh was drawn by as fine a team of horses as I ever saw. (You needn't think all the best animals are brought up nowadays; never was such horseflesh as fifty years ago on Long Island, or south, or in New York city; folks look'd for spirit and mettle in a nag, not tame speed merely.) Well, I, a boy of perhaps thirteen or fourteen, stopp'd and gazed long at the spectacle of that fur-swathed old man, surrounded by friends and servants, and the careful seating of him in the sleigh. I remember the spirited, champing horses, the driver with his whip, and a fellow-driver by his side, for extra prudence. The old man, the subject of so much attention, I can almost see now. It was John Jacob Astor.

The years 1846, '47, and there along, see me still in New York city, working as writer and printer, having my usual good health, and a good time generally.

Omnibus Jaunts and Drivers

One phase of those days must by no means go unrecorded— namely, the Broadway omnibuses, with their drivers. The vehicles still (I write this paragraph in 1881) give a portion of the character of Broadway—the Fifth avenue, Madison avenue, and Twenty-third street lines yet running. But the flush days of the old Broadway stages, characteristic and copious, are over. The Yellow-birds, the Red-birds, the original Broadway, the Fourth avenue, the Knickerbocker, and a dozen others of twenty or thirty years ago, are all gone. And the men specially

identified with them, and giving vitality and meaning to them
—the drivers—a strange, natural, quick-eyed and wondrous
race—(not only Rabelais and Cervantes would have gloated
upon them, but Homer and Shakespere would)—how well I
remember them, and must here give a word about them. How
many hours, forenoons and afternoons—how many exhilarating
night-times I have had—perhaps June or July, in cooler air—
riding the whole length of Broadway, listening to some yarn,
(and the most vivid yarns ever spun, and the rarest mimicry)
—or perhaps I declaiming some stormy passage from Julius
Cæsar or Richard, (you could roar as loudly as you chose in
that heavy, dense, uninterrupted street-bass.) Yes, I knew all
the drivers then, Broadway Jack, Dressmaker, Balky Bill,
George Storms, Old Elephant, his brother Young Elephant
(who came afterward,) Tippy, Pop Rice, Big Frank, Yellow
Joe, Pete Callahan, Patsy Dee, and dozens more; for there were
hundreds. They had immense qualities, largely animal—eating,
drinking, women—great personal pride, in their way—perhaps
a few slouches here and there, but I should have trusted the
general run of them, in their simple good-will and honor, under
all circumstances. Not only for comradeship, and sometimes
affection—great studies I found them also. (I suppose the critics
will laugh heartily, but the influence of those Broadway omnibus jaunts and drivers and declamations and escapades undoubtedly enter'd into the gestation of "Leaves of Grass.")

Plays and Operas Too

And certain actors and singers, had a good deal to do with
the business. All through these years, off and on, I frequented
the old Park, the Bowery, Broadway and Chatham-square
theatres, and the Italian operas at Chambers-street, Astor-place
or the Battery—many seasons was on the free list, writing for
papers even as quite a youth. The old Park theatre—what
names, reminiscences, the words bring back! Placide, Clarke,
Mrs. Vernon, Fisher, Clara F., Mrs. Wood, Mrs. Seguin, Ellen
Tree, Hackett, the younger Kean, Macready, Mrs. Richardson,

Rice—singers, tragedians, comedians. What perfect acting!
Henry Placide in "Napoleon's Old Guard" or "Grandfather
Whitehead,"—or "the Provoked Husband" of Cibber, with
Fanny Kemble as Lady Townley—or Sheridan Knowles in his
own "Virginius"—or inimitable Power in "Born to Good
Luck." These, and many more, the years of youth and onward.
Fanny Kemble—name to conjure up great mimic scenes withal
—perhaps the greatest. I remember well her rendering of Bianca
in "Fazio," and Marianna in "the Wife." Nothing finer did
ever stage exhibit—the veterans of all nations said so, and my
boyish heart and head felt it in every minute cell. The lady
was just matured, strong, better than merely beautiful, born
from the footlights, had had three years' practice in London
and through the British towns, and then she came to give
America that young maturity and roseate power in all their
noon, or rather forenoon, flush. It was my good luck to see her
nearly every night she play'd at the old Park—certainly in
all her principal characters.

I heard, these years, well render'd, all the Italian and other
operas in vogue, "Sonnambula," "the Puritans," "Der Frei-
schutz," "Huguenots," "Fille d'Regiment," "Faust," "Etoile du
Nord," "Poliuto," and others. Verdi's "Ernani," "Rigoletto,"
and, "Trovatore," with Donnizetti's "Lucia" or "Favorita" or
"Lucrezia," and Auber's "Massaniello," or Rossini's "William
Tell" and "Gazza Ladra," were among my special enjoyments.
I heard Alboni every time she sang in New York and vicinity—
also Grisi, the tenor Mario, and the baritone Badiali, the finest
in the world.

This musical passion follow'd my theatrical one. As boy or
young man I had seen, (reading them carefully the day beforehand), quite all Shakspere's acting dramas, play'd wonderfully
well. Even yet I cannot conceive anything finer than old Booth
in "Richard Third," or "Lear," (I don't know which was best,)
or Iago, (or Pescara, or Sir Giles Overreach, to go outside of
Shakspere)—or Tom Hamblin in "Macbeth"—or old Clarke,
either as the ghost in "Hamlet," or as Prospero in "the Tempest," with Mrs. Austin as Ariel, and Peter Richings as Caliban.
Then other dramas, and fine players in them, Forrest as
Metamora or Damon or Brutus—John R. Scott as Tom Cringle

or Rolla—or Charlotte Cushman's Lady Gay Spanker in "London Assurance." Then of some years later, at Castle Garden, Battery, I yet recall the splendid seasons of the Havana musical troupe under Maretzek—the fine band, the cool sea-breezes, the unsurpass'd vocalism—Steffanone, Bosio, Truffi, Marini in "Marino Faliero," "Don Pasquale," or "Favorita." No better playing or singing ever in New York. It was here too I afterward heard Jenny Lind. (The Battery—its past associations— what tales those old trees and walks and sea-walls could tell!)

Through Eight Years

In 1848, '49, I was occupied as editor of the "daily Eagle" newspaper, in Brooklyn. The latter year went off on a leisurely journey and working expedition (my brother Jeff with me) through all the middle States, and down the Ohio and Mississippi rivers. Lived awhile in New Orleans, and work'd there on the editorial staff of "daily Crescent," newspaper. After a time plodded back northward, up the Mississippi, and around to, and by way of the great lakes, Michigan, Huron, and Erie, to Niagara falls and lower Canada, finally returning through central New York and down the Hudson; traveling altogether probably 8000 miles this trip, to and fro. '51, '53, occupied in house-building in Brooklyn. (For a little of the first part of that time in printing a daily and weekly paper, "the Freeman.") '55, lost my dear father this year by death. Commenced putting "Leaves of Grass" to press for good, at the job printing office of my friends, the brothers Rome, in Brooklyn, after many MS. doings and undoings—(I had great trouble in leaving out the stock "poetical" touches, but succeeded at last.) I am now (1856–'7) passing through my 37th year.

Sources of Character—Results—1860

To sum up the foregoing from the outset (and, of course, far, far more unrecorded,) I estimate three leading sources and formative stamps to my own character, now solidified for good or bad, and its subsequent literary and other outgrowth—the maternal nativity-stock brought hither from far-away Netherlands, for one, (doubtless the best)—the subterranean tenacity and central bony structure (obstinacy, wilfulness) which I get from my paternal English elements, for another—and the combination of my Long Island birth-spot, seashores, childhood's scenes, absorptions, with teeming Brooklyn and New York—with, I suppose, my experiences afterward in the secession outbreak, for the third.

For, in 1862, startled by news that my brother George, an officer in the 51st New York volunteers, had been seriously wounded (first Fredericksburg battle, December 13th,) I hurriedly went down to the field of war in Virginia. But I must go back a little.

Opening of the Secession War

News of the attack on fort Sumter and *the flag* at Charleston harbor, S. C., was receiv'd in New York city late at night (13th April, 1861,) and was immediately sent out in extras of the newspapers. I had been to the opera in Fourteenth street that night, and after the performance was walking down Broadway toward twelve o'clock, on my way to Brooklyn, when I heard in the distance the loud cries of the newsboys, who came presently tearing and yelling up the street, rushing from side to side even more furiously than usual. I bought an extra and cross'd to the Metropolitan hotel (Niblo's) where the great lamps were still brightly blazing, and, with a crowd of others, who gather'd impromptu, read the news, which was evidently authentic. For the benefit of some who had no papers, one of us read the telegram aloud, while all listen'd silently and attentively. No remark was made by any of the crowd, which had increas'd to thirty or forty, but all stood a minute or two, I remember, before they dispers'd. I can almost see them there now, under the lamps at midnight again.

National Uprising and Volunteering

I have said somewhere that the three Presidentiads preceding 1861 show'd how the weakness and wickedness of rulers are just as eligible here in America under republican, as in Europe under dynastic influences. But what can I say of that prompt and splendid wrestling with secession slavery, the arch-enemy personified, the instant he unmistakably show'd his face? The volcanic upheaval of the nation, after that firing on the flag at Charleston, proved for certain something which had been previously in great doubt, and at once substantially settled the question of disunion. In my judgment it will remain as the grandest and most encouraging spectacle yet vouchsafed in any age, old or new, to political progress and democracy. It was not for what came to the surface merely—though that was important—but what it indicated below, which was of eternal importance. Down in the abysms of New World humanity there had form'd and harden'd a primal hard-pan of national Union will, determin'd and in the majority, refusing to be tamper'd with or argued against, confronting all emergencies, and capable at any time of bursting all surface bonds, and beaking out like an earthquake. It is, indeed, the best lesson of the century, or of America, and it is a mighty privilege to have been part of it. (Two great spectacles, immortal proofs of democracy, unequall'd in all the history of the past, are furnish'd by the secession war—one at the beginning, the other at its close. Those are, the general, voluntary, arm'd upheaval, and the peaceful and harmonious disbanding of the armies in the summer of 1865.)

Contemptuous Feeling

Even after the bombardment of Sumter, however, the gravity of the revolt, and the power and will of the slave States for a strong and continued military resistance to national authority, were not at all realized at the North, except by a few. Nine-tenths of the people of the free States look'd upon the rebellion, as started in South Carolina, from a feeling one-half of contempt, and the other half composed of anger and incredulity. It was not thought it would be join'd in by Virginia, North Carolina, or Georgia. A great and cautious national official predicted that it would blow over "in sixty days," and folks generally believ'd the prediction. I remember talking about it on a Fulton ferry-boat with the Brooklyn mayor, who said he only "hoped the Southern fire-eaters would commit some overt act of resistance, as they would then be at once so effectually squelch'd, we would never hear of secession again—but he was afraid they never would have the pluck to really do anything." I remember, too, that a couple of companies of the Thirteenth Brooklyn, who rendezvou'd at the city armory, and started thence as thirty days' men, were all provided with pieces of rope, conspicuously tied to their musket-barrels, with which to bring back each man a prisoner from the audacious South, to be led in a noose, on our men's early and triumphant return!

Battle of Bull Run, July, 1861

All this sort of feeling was destin'd to be arrested and revers'd by a terrible shock—the battle of first Bull Run—certainly, as we now know it, one of the most singular fights on record. (All battles, and their results, are far more matters of accident than is generally thought; but this was throughout a casualty, a chance. Each side supposed it had won, till the last moment. One had, in point of fact, just the same right to be routed as the other. By a fiction, or series of fictions, the national forces at the last moment exploded in a panic and fled from the field.) The defeated troops commenced pouring into Washington over the Long Bridge at daylight on Monday, 22d —day drizzling all through with rain. The Saturday and Sunday of the battle (20th, 21st,) had been parch'd and hot to an extreme—the dust, the grime and smoke, in layers, sweated in, follow'd by other layers again sweated in, absorb'd by those excited souls—their clothes all saturated with the clay-powder filling the air—stirr'd up everywhere on the dry roads and trodden fields by the regiments, swarming wagons, artillery, &c.—all the men with this coating of murk and sweat and rain, now recoiling back, pouring over the Long Bridge—a horrible march of twenty miles, returning to Washington baffled, humiliated, panic-struck. Where are the vaunts, and the proud boasts with which you went forth? Where are your banners, and your bands of music, and your ropes to bring back your prisoners? Well, there isn't a band playing—and there isn't a flag but clings ashamed and lank to its staff.

The sun rises, but shines not. The men appear, at first sparsely and shame-faced enough, then thicker, in the streets of Washington—appear in Pennsylvania avenue, and on the steps and basement entrances. They come along in disorderly mobs, some in squads, stragglers, companies. Occasionally, a rare regiment, in perfect order, with its officers (some gaps, dead, the true braves,) marching in silence, with lowering faces, stern, weary to sinking, all black and dirty, but every man with his musket, and stepping alive; but these are the exceptions. Sidewalks of Pennsylvania avenue, Fourteenth street, &c., crowded, jamm'd with citizens, darkies, clerks, everybody, lookers-on; women in the windows, curious expressions from faces, as those swarms of dirt-cover'd return'd soldiers there (will they never end?) move by; but nothing said, no comments; (half our lookers-on secesh of the most venomous kind— they say nothing; but the devil snickers in their faces.) During the forenoon Washington gets all over motley with these defeated soldiers—queer-looking objects, strange eyes and faces, drench'd (the steady rain drizzles on all day) and fearfully worn, hungry, haggard, blister'd in the feet. Good people (but not over-many of them either,) hurry up something for their grub. They put wash-kettles on the fire, for soup, for coffee. They set tables on the sidewalks—wagon-loads of bread are purchas'd, swiftly cut in stout chunks. Here are two aged ladies, beautiful, the first in the city for culture and charm, they stand with store of eating and drink at an improvis'd table of rough plank, and give food, and have the store replenish'd from their house every half-hour all that day; and there in the rain they stand, active, silent, white-hair'd, and give food, though the tears stream down their cheeks, almost without intermission, the whole time. Amid the deep excitement, crowds and motion, and desperate eagerness, it seems strange to see many, very many, of the soldiers sleeping—in the midst of all, sleeping sound. They drop down anywhere, on the steps of houses, up close by the basements or fences, on the sidewalk, aside on some vacant lot, and deeply sleep. A poor seventeen or eighteen year old boy lies there, on the stoop of a grand house; he sleeps so calmly, so profoundly. Some clutch their muskets firmly even in sleep. Some in squads; comrades, brothers, close together—and on them, as they lay, sulkily drips the rain.

As afternoon pass'd, and evening came, the streets, the bar-rooms, knots everywhere, listeners, questioners, terrible yarns, bugaboo, mask'd batteries, our regiment all cut up, &c.—stories and story-tellers, windy, bragging, vain centres of street-crowds. Resolution, manliness, seem to have abandon'd Washington. The principal hotel, Willard's, is full of shoulder-straps—thick, crush'd, creeping with shoulder-straps. (I see them, and must have a word with them. There you are, shoulder-straps!—but where are your companies? where are your men? Incompetents! never tell me of chances of battle, of getting stray'd, and the like. I think this is your work, this retreat, after all. Sneak, blow, put on airs there in Willard's sumptuous parlors and bar-rooms, or anywhere—no explanation shall save you. Bull Run is your work; had you been half or one-tenth worthy your men, this would never have happen'd.)

Meantime, in Washington, among the great persons and their entourage, a mixture of awful consternation, uncertainty, rage, shame, helplessness, and stupefying disappointment. The worst is not only imminent, but already here. In a few hours—

perhaps before the next meal—the secesh generals, with their victorious hordes, will be upon us. The dream of humanity, the vaunted Union we thought so strong, so impregnable—lo! it seems already smash'd like a china plate. One bitter, bitter hour—perhaps proud America will never again know such an hour. She must pack and fly—no time to spare. Those white palaces—the dome-crown'd capitol there on the hill, so stately over the trees—shall they be left—or destroy'd first? For it is certain that the talk among certain of the magnates and officers and clerks and officials everywhere, for twenty-four hours in and around Washington after Bull Run, was loud and un-disguised for yielding out and out, and substituting the southern rule, and Lincoln promptly abdicating and departing. If the secesh officers and forces had immediately follow'd, and by a bold Napoleonic movement had enter'd Washington the first day, (or even the second,) they could have had things their own way, and a powerful faction north to back them. One of our returning colonels express'd in public that night, amid a swarm of officers and gentlemen in a crowded room, the opinion that it was useless to fight, that the southerners had made their title clear, and that the best course for the national government to pursue was to desist from any further attempt at stopping them, and admit them again to the lead, on the best terms they were willing to grant. Not a voice was rais'd against this judgment, amid that large crowd of officers and gentlemen. (The fact is, the hour was one of the three or four of those crises we had then and afterward, during the fluctua-tions of four years, when human eyes appear'd at least just as likely to see the last breath of the Union as to see it continue.)

The Stupor Passes—Something Else Begins

But the hour, the day, the night pass'd, and whatever returns, an hour, a day, a night like that can never again return. The President, recovering himself, begins that very night—sternly, rapidly sets about the task of reorganizing his forces, and placing himself in positions for future and surer work. If there were nothing else of Abraham Lincoln for history to stamp him with, it is enough to send him with his wreath to the memory of all future time, that he endured that hour, that day, bitterer than gall—indeed a crucifixion day—that it did not conquer him—that he unflinchingly stemm'd it, and resolv'd to lift himself and the Union out of it.

Then the great New York papers at once appear'd (commencing that evening, and following it up the next morning, and incessantly through many days afterwards,) with leaders that rang out over the land with the loudest, most reverberating ring of clearest bugles, full of encouragement, hope, inspiration, unfaltering defiance. Those magnificent editorials! they never flagg'd for a fortnight. The "Herald" commenced them—I remember the articles well. The "Tribune" was equally cogent and inspiriting—and the "Times," "Evening Post," and other principal papers, were not a whit behind. They came in good time, for they were needed. For in the humiliation of Bull Run, the popular feeling north, from its extreme of superciliousness, recoil'd to the depth of gloom and apprehension.

(Of all the days of the war, there are two especially I can never forget. Those were the day following the news, in New York and Brooklyn, of that first Bull Run defeat, and the day of Abraham Lincoln's death. I was home in Brooklyn on both occasions. The day of the murder we heard the news very early in the morning. Mother prepared breakfast—and other meals afterwards—as usual; but not a mouthful was eaten all day by either of us. We each drank half a cup of coffee; that was all. Little was said. We got every newspaper morning and evening, and the frequent extras of that period, and pass'd them silently to each other.)

Down at the Front

Falmouth, Va., opposite Fredericksburgh, December 21, 1862.
—Begin my visits among the camp hospitals in the army of the Potomac. Spend a good part of the day in a large brick mansion on the banks of the Rappahannock, used as a hospital

since the battle—seems to have receiv'd only the worst cases. Out doors, at the foot of a tree, within ten yards of the front of the house, I notice a heap of amputated feet, legs, arms, hands, &c., a full load for a one-horse cart. Several dead bodies lie near, each cover'd with its brown woolen blanket. In the door-yard, towards the river, are fresh graves, mostly of officers, their names on pieces of barrel-staves or broken boards, stuck in the dirt. (Most of these bodies were subsequently taken up and transported north to their friends.) The large mansion is quite crowded upstairs and down, everything impromptu, no system, all bad enough, but I have no doubt the best that can be done; all the wounds pretty bad, some frightful, the men in their old clothes, unclean and bloody. Some of the wounded are rebel soldiers and officers, prisoners. One, a Mississippian, a captain, hit badly in leg, I talk'd with some time; he ask'd me for papers, which I gave him. (I saw him three months afterward in Washington, with his leg amputated, doing well.) I went through the rooms, downstairs and up. Some of the men were dying. I had nothing to give at that visit, but wrote a few letters to folks home, mothers, &c. Also talk'd to three or four, who seem'd most susceptible to it, and needing it.

After First Fredericksburg

December 23 to 31.—The results of the late battle are exhibited everywhere about here in thousands of cases, (hundreds die every day,) in the camp, brigade, and division hospitals. These are merely tents, and sometimes very poor ones, the wounded lying on the ground, lucky, if their blankets are spread on layers of pine or hemlock twigs, or small leaves. No cots; seldom even a mattress. It is pretty cold. The ground is frozen hard, and there is occasional snow. I go around from one case to another. I do not see that I do much good to these wounded and dying; but I cannot leave them. Once in a while some youngster holds on to me convulsively, and I do what I can for him; at any rate, stop with him and sit near him for hours, if he wishes it.

Besides the hospitals, I also go occasionally on long tours through the camps, talking with the men, &c. Sometimes at night among the groups around the fires, in their shebang enclosures of bushes. These are curious shows, full of characters and groups. I soon get acquainted anywhere in camp, with officers or men, and am always well used. Sometimes I go down on picket with the regiment I know best. As to rations, the army here at present seems to be tolerably well supplied, and the men have enough, such as it is, mainly salt pork and hard tack. Most of the regiments lodge in the flimsy little shelter-tents. A few have built themselves huts of logs and mud, with fire-places.

Back to Washington

January, '63.—Left camp at Falmouth, with some wounded, a few days since, and came here by Aquia creek railroad, and so on government steamer up the Potomac. Many wounded were with us on the cars and boat. The cars were just common platform ones. The railroad journey of ten or twelve miles was made mostly before sunrise. The soldiers guarding the road came out from their tents or shebangs of bushes with rumpled hair and half-awake look. Those on duty were walking their posts, some on banks over us, others down far below the level of the track. I saw large cavalry camps off the road. At Aquia creek landing were numbers of wounded going north. While I waited some three hours, I went around among them. Several wanted word sent home to parents, brothers, wives, &c., which I did for them, (by mail the next day from Washington.) On the boat I had my hands full. One poor fellow died going up.

I am now remaining in and around Washington, daily visiting the hospitals. Am much in Patent-office, English street, H street, Armory-square, and others. Am now able to do a little good, having money, (as almoner of others home,) and getting experience. To-day, Sunday afternoon and till nine in the evening, visited Campbell hospital; attended specially to one case in ward 1, very sick with pleurisy and typhoid fever, young man, farmer's son, D. F. Russell, company E, 60th New York, downhearted and feeble; a long time before he would take any interest; wrote a letter home to his mother, in Malone, Franklin county, N.Y., at his request; gave him some fruit and one or two other gifts; envelop'd and directed his letter, &c. Then went thoroughly through ward 6, observ'd every case in the ward, without, I think, missing one; gave perhaps from twenty to thirty persons, each one some little gift, such as oranges, apples, sweet crackers, figs, &c.

Thursday, Jan. 21.—Devoted the main part of the day to Armory-square hospital; went pretty thoroughly through wards F, G, H, and I; some fifty cases in each ward. In ward F supplied the men throughout with writing paper and stamp'd envelope each; distributed in small portions, to proper subjects, a large jar of first-rate preserv'd berries, which had been donated to me by a lady—her own cooking. Found several cases I thought good subject for small sums of money, which I furnish'd. (The wounded men often come up broke, and it helps their spirits to have even the small sum I give them.) My paper and envelopes all gone, but distributed a good lot of amusing reading matter; also, as I thought judicious, tobacco, oranges, apples, &c. Interesting cases in ward I; Charles Miller, bed 19, company D, 53d Pennsylvania, is only sixteen years of age, very bright, courageous boy, left leg amputated below the knee; next bed to him, another young lad very sick; gave each appropriate gifts. In the bed above, also, amputation of the left leg; gave him a little jar of raspberries; bed 1, this ward, gave a small sum; also to a soldier on crutches, sitting on his bed near.... (I am more and more surprised at the very great proportion of youngsters from fifteen to twenty-one in the army. I afterwards found a still greater proportion among the southerners.)

Evening, same day, went to see D. F. R., before alluded to; found him remarkably changed for the better; up and dress'd —quite a triumph; he afterwards got well, and went back to his regiment. Distributed in the wards a quantity of note-paper, and forty or fifty stamp'd envelopes, of which I had recruited my stock, and the men were much in need.

Fifty Hours Left Wounded on the Field

Here is a case of a soldier I found among the crowded cots in the Patent-office. He likes to have some one to talk to, and we will listen to him. He got badly hit in his leg and side at Fredericksburgh that eventful Saturday, 13th of December. He lay the succeeding two days and nights helpless on the field, between the city and those grim terraces of batteries; his company regiment had been compell'd to leave him to his fate. To make matters worse, it happen'd he lay with his head slightly down hill, and could not help himself. At the end of some fifty hours he was brought off, with other wounded, under a flag of truce. I ask him how the rebels treated him as he lay during those two days and nights within reach of them—whether they came to him—whether they abused him? He answers that several of the rebels, soldiers and others, came to him at one time and another. A couple of them, who were together, spoke roughly and sarcastically, but nothing worse. One middle-aged man, however, who seem'd to be moving around the field, among the dead and wounded, for benevolent purposes, came to him in a way he will never forget; treated our soldier kindly, bound up his wounds, cheer'd him, gave him a couple of biscuits and a drink of whiskey and water; asked him if he could eat some beef. This good secesh, however, did not change our soldier's position, for it might have caused the blood to burst from the wounds, clotted and stagnated. Our soldier is from Pennsylvania; has had a pretty severe time; the wounds proved to be bad ones. But he retains a good heart, and is at present on the gain. (It is not uncommon for the men to remain on the field this way, one, two or even four or five days.)

Hospital Scenes and Persons

Letter Writing.—When eligible, I encourage the men to write, and myself, when called upon, write all sorts of letters for them, (including love letters, very tender ones.) Almost as I reel off these memoranda, I write for a new patient to his wife. M. de

F., of the 17th Connecticut, company H, has just come up (February 17th) from Windmill point, and is received in ward H, Armory-square. He is an intelligent looking man, has a foreign accent, black-eyed and hair'd, a Hebraic appearance. Wants a telegraphic message sent to his wife, New Canaan, Conn. I agree to send the message—but to make things sure I also sit down and write the wife a letter, and despatch it to the post-office immediately, as he fears she will come on, and he does not wish her to, as he will surely get well.

Saturday, January 30th.—Afternoon, visited Campbell hospital. Scene of cleaning up the ward, and giving the men all clean clothes—through the ward (6) the patient dressing or being dress'd—the naked upper half of the bodies—the good-humor and fun—the shirts, drawers, sheets of beds, &c., and the general fixing up for Sunday. Gave J. L. 50 cents.

Wednesday, February 4th.—Visited Armory-square hospital, went pretty thoroughly through wards E and D. Supplied paper and envelopes to all who wish'd—as usual, found plenty of men who needed those articles. Wrote letters. Saw and talk'd with two or three members of the Brooklyn 14th regt. A poor fellow in ward D, with a fearful wound in a fearful condition, was having some loose splinters of bone taken from the neighborhood of the wound. The operation was long, and one of great pain—yet, after it was well commenced, the soldier bore it in silence. He sat up, propp'd—was much wasted—had lain a long time quiet in one position (not for days only but weeks,) a bloodless, brown-skinn'd face, with eyes full of determination—belong'd to a New York regiment. There was an unusual cluster of surgeons, medical cadets, nurses, &c., around his bed—I thought the whole thing was done with tenderness, and done well. In one case, the wife sat by the side of her husband, his sickness typhoid fever, pretty bad. In another, by the side of her son, a mother—she told me she had seven children, and this was the youngest. (A fine, kind, healthy, gentle mother, good-looking, not very old, with a cap on her head, and dress'd like home—what a charm it gave to the whole ward.) I liked the woman nurse in ward E—I noticed how she sat a long time by a poor fellow who just had, that morning, in addition to his other sickness, bad hemorrhage—she gently assisted him, reliev'd him of the blood, holding a cloth to his mouth, as he coughed it up—he was so weak he could only just turn his head over on the pillow.

One young New York man, with a bright, handsome face, had been lying several months from a most disagreeable wound, receiv'd at Bull Run. A bullet had shot him right through the bladder, hitting him front, low in the belly, and coming out back. He had suffer'd much—the water came out of the wound, by slow but steady quantities, for many weeks— so that he lay almost constantly in a sort of puddle—and there were other disagreeable circumstances. He was a good heart, however. At present comparatively comfortable, had a bad throat, was delighted with a stick of horehound candy I gave him, with one or two other trifles.

Patent-Office Hospital

February 23.—I must not let the great hospital at the Patent-office pass away without some mention. A few weeks ago the vast area of the second story of that noblest of Washington buildings was crowded close with rows of sick, badly wounded and dying soldiers. They were placed in three very large apartments. I went there many times. It was a strange, solemn, and, with all its features of suffering and death, a sort of fascinating sight. I go sometimes at night to soothe and relieve particular cases. Two of the immense apartments are fill'd with high and ponderous glass cases, crowded with models in miniature of every kind of utensil, machine or invention, it ever enter'd into the mind of man to conceive; and with curiosities and foreign presents. Between these cases are lateral openings, perhaps eight feet wide and quite deep, and in these were placed the sick, besides a great long double row of them up and down through the middle of the hall. Many of them were very bad cases, wounds and amputations. Then there was a gallery running above the hall in which there were beds also. It was, indeed, a curious scene, especially at night when lit up. The glass cases, the beds, the forms lying there, the gallery above, and the marble pavement under foot—the suffering, and the fortitude to bear it in various degrees—occasionally, from some, the groan that could not be repress'd—sometimes a poor fellow dying, with emaciated face and glassy eye, the nurse by his side, the doctor also there, but no friend, no relative—such were the sights but lately in the Patent-office. (The wounded have since been removed from there, and it is now vacant again.)

The White House by Moonlight

February 24th.—A spell of fine soft weather. I wander about a good deal, sometimes at night under the moon. To-night took a long look at the President's house. The white portico—the palace-like, tall, round columns, spotless as snow—the walls also—the tender and soft moonlight, flooding the pale marble, and making peculiar faint languishing shades, not shadows—everywhere a soft transparent hazy, thin, blue moon-lace, hanging in the air—the brilliant and extra-plentiful clusters of gas, on and around the façade, columns, portico, &c.—everything so white, so marbly pure and dazzling, yet soft—the White House of future poems, and of dreams and dramas, there in the soft and copious moon—the gorgeous front, in the trees, under the lustrous flooding moon, full of reality, full of illusion—the forms of the trees, leafless, silent, in trunk and myriad-angles of branches, under the stars and sky—the White House of the land, and of beauty and night—sentries at the gates, and by the portico, silent, pacing there in blue overcoats—stopping you not at all, but eyeing you with sharp eyes, whichever way you move.

An Army Hospital Ward

Let me specialize a visit I made to the collection of barrack-like one-story edifices, Campbell hospital, out on the flats, at the end of the then horse railway route, one Seventh street.

There is a long building appropriated to each ward. Let us go into ward 6. It contains to-day, I should judge, eighty or a hundred patients, half sick, half wounded. The edifice is nothing but boards, well whitewash'd inside, and the usual slender-framed iron bedsteads, narrow and plain. You walk down the central passage, with a row on either side, their feet towards you, and their heads to the wall. There are fires in large stoves, and the prevailing white of the walls is reliev'd by some ornaments, stars, circles, &c., made of evergreens. The view of the whole edifice and occupants can be taken at once, for there is no partition. You may hear groans or other sounds of un-endurable suffering from two or three of the cots, but in the main there is quiet—almost a painful absence of demonstra-tion; but the pallid face, the dull'd eye, and the moisture on the lip, are demonstration enough. Most of these sick or hurt are evidently young fellows from the country, farmers' sons, and such like. Look at the fine large frames, the bright and broad countenances, and the many yet lingering proofs of strong constitution and physique. Look at the patient and mute manner of our American wounded as they lie in such a sad collection; representatives from all New England, and from New York, and New Jersey, and Pennsylvania—indeed from all the States and all the cities—largely from the west. Most of them are entirely without friends or acquaintances here —no familiar face, and hardly a word of judicious sympathy or cheer, through their sometimes long and tedious sickness, or the pangs of aggravated wounds.

A Connecticut Case

This young man in bed 25 is H. D. B., of the 27th Connecti-cut, company B. His folks live at Northford, near New Ha-ven. Though not more than twenty-one, or thereabouts, he has knock'd much around the world, on sea and land, and has seen some fighting on both. When I first saw him he was very sick, with no appetite. He declined offers of money—said he did

not need anything. As I was quite anxious to do something, he
confess'd that he had a hankering for a good home-made rice
pudding—thought he could relish it better than anything. At
this time his stomach was very weak. (The doctor, whom I con-
sulted, said nourishment would do him more good than anything; but things in the hospital, though better than usual, revolted him.) I soon procured B. his rice-pudding. A Washington
lady, (Mrs. O'C.,) hearing his wish, made the pudding herself,
and I took it up to him the next day. He subsequently told
me he lived upon it for three or four days. This B. is a
good sample of the American eastern young man—the typical
Yankee. I took a fancy to him, and gave him a nice pipe, for
a keepsake. He receiv'd afterwards a box of things from home,
and nothing would do but I must take dinner with him, which
I did, and a very good one it was.

Two Brooklyn Boys

Here in this same ward are two young men from Brooklyn,
members of the 51st New York. I had known both the two
as young lads at home, so they seem near to me. One of them,
J. L., lies there with an amputated arm, the stump healing
pretty well. (I saw him lying on the ground at Fredericksburgh
last December, all bloody, just after the arm was taken off.
He was very phlegmatic about it, munching away at a cracker
in the remaining hand—made no fuss.) He will recover, and
thinks and talks yet of meeting the Johnny Rebs.

A Secesh Brave

The grand soldiers are not comprised in those of one side,
any more than the other. Here is a sample of an unknown
southerner, a lad of seventeen. At the War department, a few
days ago, I witness'd a presentation of captured flags to the
Secretary. Among others a soldier named Gant, of the 104th

Ohio volunteers, presented a rebel battle-flag, which one of the officers stated to me was borne to the mouth of our cannon and planted there by a boy but seventeen years of age, who actually endeavor'd to stop the muzzle of the gun with fence-rails. He was kill'd in the effort, and the flag-staff was sever'd by a shot from one of our men.

The Wounded from Chancellorsville

May, '63.—As I write this, the wounded have begun to arrive from Hooker's command from bloody Chancellorsville. I was down among the first arrivals. The men in charge told me the bad cases were yet to come. If that is so I pity them, for these are bad enough. You ought to see the scene of the wounded arriving at the landing here at the foot of Sixth street, at night. Two boat loads came about half-past seven last night. A little after eight it rain'd a long and violent shower. The pale, helpless soldiers had been debark'd, and lay around on the wharf and neighborhood anywhere. The rain was, probably, grateful to them; at any rate they were exposed to it. The few torches light up the spectacle. All around—on the wharf, on the ground, out on side places—the men are lying on blankets, old quilts, &c., with bloody rags bound round heads, arms, and legs. The attendants are few, and at night few outsiders also—only a few hard-work'd transportation men and drivers. (The wounded are getting to be common, and people grow callous.) The men, whatever their condition, lie there, and patiently wait till their turn comes to be taken up. Near by, the ambulances are now arriving in clusters, and one after another is call'd to back up and take its load. Extreme cases are sent off on stretchers. The men generally make little or no ado, whatever their sufferings. A few groans that cannot be suppress'd, and occasionally a scream of pain as they lift a man into the ambulance. To-day, as I write, hundreds more are expected, and to-morrow and the next day more, and so on for many days. Quite often they arrive at the rate of 1000 a day.

A Night Battle, over a Week Since

May 12.—There was part of the late battle at Chancellorsville,
(second Fredericksburgh,) a little over a week ago, Saturday,
Saturday night and Sunday, under Gen. Joe Hooker, I would
like to give just a glimpse of—(a moment's look in a terrible
storm at sea—of which a few suggestions are enough, and full
details impossible.) The fighting had been very hot during the
day, and after an intermission the latter part, was resumed at
night, and kept up with furious energy till 3 o'clock in the
morning. That afternoon (Saturday) an attack sudden and
strong by Stonewall Jackson had gain'd a great advantage to
the southern army, and broken our lines, entering us like a
wedge, and leaving things in that position at dark. But Hooker
at 11 at night made a desperate push, drove the secesh forces
back, restored his original lines, and resumed his plans. This
night scrimmage was very exciting, and afforded countless
strange and fearful pictures. The fighting had been general
both at Chancellorsville and northeast at Fredericksburgh. (We
hear of some poor fighting, episodes, skedaddling on our part.
I think not of it. I think of the fierce bravery, the general rule.)
One corps, the 6th, Sedgewick's, fights four dashing and bloody
battles in thirty-six hours, retreating in great jeopardy, losing
largely but maintaining itself, fighting with the sternest desperation under all circumstances, getting over the Rappahannock
only by the skin of its teeth, yet getting over. It lost many,
many brave men, yet it took vengeance, ample vengeance.

But it was the tug of Saturday evening, and through the
night and Sunday morning, I wanted to make a special note of.
It was largely in the woods, and quite a general engagement.
The night was very pleasant, at times the moon shining out full
and clear, all Nature so calm in itself, the early summer grass
so rich, and foliage of the trees—yet there the battle raging,
and many good fellows lying helpless, with new accessions to
them, and every minute amid the rattle of muskets and crash
of cannon, (for there was an artillery contest too,) the red
life-blood oozing out from heads or trunks or limbs upon that
green and dew-cool grass. Patches of the woods take fire, and

several of the wounded, unable to move, are consumed—quite large spaces are swept over, burning the dead also—some of the men have their hair and beards singed—some, burns on their faces and hands—others holes burnt in their clothing. The flashes of fire from the cannon, the quick flaring flames and smoke, and the immense roar—the musketry so general, the light nearly bright enough for each side to see the other—the crashing, tramping of men—the yelling—close quarters—we hear the secesh yells—our men cheer loudly back, especially if Hooker is in sight—hand to hand conflicts, each side stands up to it, brave, determin'd as demons, they often charge upon us—a thousand deeds are done worth to write newer greater poems on—and still the woods on fire—still many are not only scorch'd—too many, unable to move, are burn'd to death.

Then the camps of the wounded—O heavens, what scene is this?—is this indeed *humanity*—these butchers' shambles? There are several of them. There they lie, in the largest, in an open space in the woods, from 200 to 300 poor fellows—the groans and screams—the odor of blood, mixed with the fresh scent of the night, the grass, the trees—that slaughter-house! O well is it their mothers, their sisters cannot see them—cannot conceive, and never conceiv'd, these things. One man is shot by a shell, both in the arm and leg—both are amputated—there lie the rejected members. Some have their legs blown off—some bullets through the breast—some indescribably horrid wounds in the face or head, all mutilated, sickening, torn, gouged out—some in the abdomen—some mere boys—many rebels, badly hurt—they take their regular turns with the rest, just the same as any—the surgeons use them just the same. Such is the camp of the wounded—such a fragment, a reflection afar off of the bloody scene—while over all the clear, large moon comes out at times softly, quietly shining. Amid the woods, that scene of flitting souls—amid the crack and crash and yelling sounds—the impalpable perfume of the woods—and yet the pungent, stifling smoke—the radiance of the moon, looking from heaven at intervals so placid—the sky so heavenly—the clear-obscure up there, those buoyant upper oceans—a few large placid stars beyond, coming silently and languidly out, and then disappearing—the melancholy, draperied night above, around. And there, upon the roads, the fields, and in those woods, that contest, never one more desperate in any age or land—both parties now in force—masses—no fancy battle, no semi-play, but fierce and savage demons fighting there —courage and scorn of death the rule, exceptions almost none.

What history, I say, can ever give—for who can know—the mad, determin'd tussle of the armies, in all their separate large and little squads—as this—each steep'd from crown to toe in desperate, mortal purports? Who know the conflict, hand-to-hand—the many conflicts in the dark, those shadowy-tangled, flashing-moonbeam'd woods—the writhing groups and squads—the cries, the din, the cracking guns and pistols—the distant cannon—the cheers and calls and threats and awful music of the oaths—the indescribable mix—the officers' orders, persuasions, encouragements—the devils fully rous'd in human hearts—the strong shout, *Charge, men, charge*—the flash of the naked sword, and rolling flame and smoke? And still the broken, clear and clouded heaven—and still again the moon-light pouring silvery soft its radiant patches over all. Who paint the scene, the sudden partial panic of the afternoon, at dusk? Who paint the irrepressible advance of the second division of the Third corps, under Hooker himself, suddenly order'd up —those rapid-filing phantoms through the woods? Who show what moves there in the shadows, fluid and firm—to save, (and it did save,) the army's name, perhaps the nation? as there the veterans hold the field. (Brave Berry falls not yet—but death has mark'd him—soon he falls.)

Unnamed Remains the Bravest Soldier

Of scenes like these, I say, who writes—whoe'er can write the story? Of many a score—aye, thousands, north and south, of unwrit heroes, unknown heroisms, incredible, impromptu, first-class desperations—who tells? No history ever—no poem sings, no music sounds, those bravest men of all—those deeds. No formal general's report, nor book in the library, nor column in the paper, embalms the bravest, north or south, east or west. Unnamed, unknown, remain, and still remain, the bravest soldiers. Our manliest—our boys—our hardy darlings; no picture gives them. Likely, the typic one of them (standing, no doubt, for hundreds, thousands,) crawls aside to some bush-clump, or ferny tuft, on receiving his death-shot—there sheltering a little while, soaking roots, grass and soil, with red blood —the battle advances, retreats, flits from the scene, sweeps by —and there, haply with pain and suffering (yet less, far less, than is supposed,) the last lethargy winds like a serpent round him—the eyes glaze in death—none recks—perhaps the burial squads, in truce, a week afterwards, search not the secluded spot—and there, at last, the Bravest Soldier crumbles in mother earth, unburied and unknown.

Some Specimen Cases

June 18th.—In one of the hospitals I find Thomas Haley, company M, 4th New York cavalry—a regular Irish boy, a fine specimen of youthful physical manliness—shot through the lungs—inevitably dying—came over to this country from Ireland to enlist—has not a single friend or acquaintance here —is sleeping soundly at this moment, (but it is the sleep of death)—has a bullet-hole straight through the lung. I saw Tom when first brought here, three days since, and didn't suppose he could live twelve hours—(yet he looks well enough in the face to a casual observer.) He lies there with his frame exposed above the waist, all naked, for coolness, a fine built man, the tan not yet bleach'd from his cheeks and neck. It is useless to talk to him, as with his sad hurt, and the stimulants they give him, and the utter strangeness of every object, face, furniture, &c., the poor fellow, even when awake, is like some frighten'd, shy animal. Much of the time he sleeps, or half sleeps. (Sometimes I thought he knew more than he show'd.) I often come and sit by him in perfect silence; he will breathe for ten minutes as softly and evenly as a young babe asleep. Poor youth, so handsome, athletic, with profuse beautiful shining hair. One time as I sat looking at him while he lay asleep, he suddenly, without the least start, awaken'd, open'd his eyes, gave me a long steady look, turning his face very slightly to gaze easier —one long, clear, silent look—a slight sigh—then turn'd back and went into his doze again. Little he knew, poor death-stricken boy, the heart of the stranger that hover'd near.

W. H. E., Co. F., 2d N. J.—His disease is pneumonia. He lay sick at the wretched hospital below Aquia creek, for seven or eight days before brought here. He was detail'd from his regiment to go there and help as nurse, but was soon taken down himself. Is an elderly, sallow-faced, rather gaunt, gray-hair'd man, a widower, with children. He express'd a great desire for good, strong green tea. An excellent lady, Mrs. W., of Washington, soon sent him a package; also a small sum of money. The doctor said give him the tea at pleasure; it lay on the table by his side, and he used it every day. He slept a great deal; could not talk much, as he grew deaf. Occupied bed 15, ward I, Armory. (The same lady above, Mrs. W., sent the men a large package of tobacco.)

J. G. lies in bed 52, ward I; is of company B, 7th Pennsylvania. I gave him a small sum of money, some tobacco, and envelopes. To a man, adjoining also gave twenty-five cents; he flush'd in the face when I offer'd it—refused at first, but as I found he had not a cent, and was very fond of having the daily papers to read, I prest it on him. He was evidently very grateful, but said little.

J. T. L., of company F., 9th New Hampshire, lies in bed 37, ward I. Is very fond of tobacco. I furnish him some; also with a little money. Has gangrene of the feet; a pretty bad case; will surely have to lose three toes. Is a regular specimen of an old-fashion'd, rude, hearty, New England countryman, impressing me with his likeness to that celebrated singed cat, who was better than she look'd.

Bed 3, ward E, Armory, has a great hankering for pickles, something pungent. After consulting the doctor, I gave him a small bottle of horse-radish; also some apples; also a book. Some of the nurses are excellent. The woman-nurse in this ward I like very much. (Mrs. Wright—a year afterwards I found her in Mansion house hospital, Alexandria—she is a perfect nurse.)

In one bed a young man, Marcus Small, company K, 7th Maine—sick with dysentery and typhoid fever—pretty critical case—I talk with him often—he thinks he will die—looks like it indeed. I write a letter for him home to East Livermore, Maine—I let him talk to me a little, but not much; advise him to keep very quiet—do most of the talking myself—stay quite a while with him, as he holds on to my hand—talk to him in a cheering, but slow, low and measured manner—talk about his furlough, and going home as soon as he is able to travel.

Thomas Lindly, 1st Pennsylvania cavalry, shot very badly through the foot—poor young man, he suffers horribly, has to be constantly dosed with morphine, his face ashy and glazed, bright young eyes—I give him a large handsome apple, lay it in sight, tell him to have it roasted in the morning, as he generally feels easier then, and can eat a little breakfast. I write two letters for him.

Opposite, an old Quaker lady is sitting by the side of her son, Amer Moore, 2d U. S. artillery—shot in the head two weeks since, very low, quite rational—from hips down paralyzed—he will surely die. I speak a very few words to him every day and evening—he answers pleasantly—wants nothing—(he told me soon after he came about his home affairs, his mother had been an invalid, and he fear'd to let her know his condition.) He died soon after she came.

My Preparations for Visits

In my visits to the hospitals I found it was in the simple matter of personal presence, and emanating ordinary cheer and magnetism, that I succeeded and help'd more than by medical nursing, or delicacies, or gifts of money, or anything else. During the war I possess'd the perfection of physical health. My habit, when practicable, was to prepare for starting out on one of those daily or nightly tours of from a couple to four or five hours, by fortifying myself with previous rest, bath, clean clothes, a good meal, and as cheerful an appearance as possible.

Ambulance Processions

June 25, Sundown.—As I sit writing this paragraph I see a train of about thirty huge four-horse wagons, used as ambulances, fill'd with wounded, passing up Fourteenth street, on their way, probably, to Columbian, Carver, and Mount Pleasant hospitals. This is the way the men come in now, seldom in small numbers, but almost always in these long, sad processions. Through the past winter, while our army lay opposite Fredericksburgh, the like strings of ambulances were of frequent occurrence along Seventh street, passing slowly up from the steamboat wharf, with loads from Aquia creek.

Bad Wounds—the Young

The soldiers are nearly all young men, and far more American than is generally supposed—I should say nine-tenths are native-born. Among the arrivals from Chancellorsville I find a large proportion of Ohio, Indiana, and Illinois men. As usual, there are all sorts of wounds. Some of the men fearfully burnt from the explosions of artillery caissons. One ward has a long row of officers, some with ugly hurts. Yesterday was perhaps worse than usual. Amputations are going on—the attendants are dressing wounds. As you pass by, you must be on your guard where you look. I saw the other day a gentleman, a visitor apparently from curiosity, in one of the wards, stop and turn a moment to look at an awful wound they were probing. He turn'd pale, and in a moment more he had fainted away and fallen on the floor.

The Most Inspiriting of
All War's Shows

June 29.—Just before sundown this evening a very large cavalry force went by—a fine sight. The men evidently had seen service. First came a mounted band of sixteen bugles, drums and cymbals, playing wild martial tunes—made by heart jump. Then the principal officers, then company after company, with their officers at their heads, making of course the main part of the cavalcade; then a long train of men with led horses, lots of mounted negroes with special horses—and a long string of baggage-wagons, each drawn by four horses—and then a motley rear guard. It was a pronouncedly warlike and gay show; the sabres clank'd, the men look'd young and healthy and strong; the electric tramping of so many horses on the hard road, and the gallant bearing, fine seat, and bright faced appearance of a thousand and more handsome young American men, were so good to see. An hour later another troop went by, smaller in numbers, perhaps three hundred men. They too look'd like serviceable men, campaigners used to field and fight.

July 3.—This forenoon, for more than an hour, again long strings of cavalry, several regiments, very fine men and horses, four or five abreast. I saw them in Fourteenth street, coming in town from north. Several hundred extra horses, some of the mares with colts, trotting along. (Appear'd to be a number of prisoners too.) How inspiriting always the cavalry regiments. Our men are generally well mounted, feel good, are young, gay on the saddle, their blankets in a roll behind them, their sabres clanking at their sides. This noise and movement and the tramp of many horses' hoofs has a curious effect upon one. The bugles play—presently you hear them afar off, deaden'd, mix'd with other noises. Then just as they had all pass'd, a string of ambulances commenc'd from the other way, moving up Fourteenth street north, slowly wending along, bearing a large lot of wounded to the hospitals.

Battle of Gettysburg

July 4th.—The weather to-day, upon the whole, is very fine, warm, but from a smart rain last night, fresh enough, and no dust, which is a great relief for this city. I saw the parade about noon, Pennsylvania avenue, from Fifteenth street down toward the capitol. There were three regiments of infantry, (I suppose the ones doing patrol duty here,) two or three societies of Odd Fellows, a lot of children in barouches, and a squad of policemen. (A useless imposition upon the soldiers—they have work enough on their backs without piling the like of this.) As I went down the Avenue, saw a big flaring placard on the bulletin board of a newspaper office, announcing "Glorious Victory for the Union Army!" Meade had fought Lee at Gettysburg, Pennsylvania, yesterday and day before, and repuls'd him most signally, taken 3,000 prisoners, &c. (I afterwards saw Meade's despatch, very modest, and a sort of order of the day from the President himself, quite religious, giving thanks to the Supreme, and calling on the people to do the same.) I walk'd on to Armory hospital—took along with me several bottles of blackberry and cherry syrup, good and strong, but innocent. Went through several of the wards, announc'd to the soldiers the news from Meade, and gave them all a good drink of the syrups with ice water, quite refreshing—prepar'd it all myself, and serv'd it around. Meanwhile the Washington bells are ringing their sundown peals for Fourth of July, and the usual fusilades of boys' pistols, crackers, and guns.

A Cavalry Camp

I am writing this, nearly sundown, watching a cavalry company (acting Signal service,) just come in through a shower, making their night's camp ready on some broad, vacant ground, a sort of hill, in full view opposite my window. There are the men in their yellow-striped jackets. All are dismounted; the freed horses stand with drooping heads and wet sides; they are to be led off presently in groups, to water. The little wall-tents and shelter tents spring up quickly. I see the fires already blazing, and pots and kettles over them. Some among the men are driving in tent-poles, wielding their axes with strong, slow blows. I see great huddles of horses, bundles of hay, groups of men (some with unbuckled sabres yet on their sides,) a few officers, piles of wood, the flames of the fires, saddles, harness, &c. The smoke streams upward, additional men arrive and dismount—some drive in stakes, and tie their horses to them; some go with buckets for water, some are chopping wood, and so on.

July 6th.—A steady rain, dark and thick and warm. A train of six-mule wagons had just pass'd bearing pontoons, great square-end flat-boats, and the heavy planking for overlaying them. We hear that the Potomac above here is flooded, and are wondering whether Lee will be able to get back across again, or whether Meade will indeed break him to pieces. The cavalry camp on the hill is a ceaseless field of observation for me. This forenoon there stand the horses, tether'd together, dripping, steaming, chewing their hay. The men emerge from their tents, dripping also. The fires are half quench'd.

July 10th.—Still the camp opposite—perhaps fifty or sixty tents. Some of the men are cleaning their sabres (pleasant to-day,) some brushing boots, some laying off, reading, writing —some cooking, some sleeping. On long temporary cross-sticks back of the tents are cavalry accoutrements—blankets and overcoats are hung out to air—there are the squads of horses tether'd, feeding, continually stamping and whisking their tails to keep off flies. I sit long in my third-story window and look at the scene—a hundred little things going on—peculiar objects connected with the camp that could not be described, any one of them justly, without much minute drawing and coloring in words.

A New York Soldier

This afternoon, July 22d, I have spent a long time with Oscar F. Wilber, company G, 154th New York, low with chronic diarrhœa, and a bad wound also. He asked me to read him a chapter in the New Testament. I complied, and ask'd him what I should read. He said, "Make your own choice." I open'd at the close of one of the first books of the evangelists, and read the chapters describing the latter hours of Christ, and the scenes at the crucifixion. The poor, wasted young man ask'd me to read the following chapter also, how Christ rose again. I read very slowly, for Oscar was feeble. It pleased him very much, yet the tears were in his eyes. He ask'd me if I enjoy'd religion. I said, "Perhaps not, my dear, in the way you mean, and yet, may-be, it is the same thing." He said, "It is my chief reliance." He talk'd of death, and said he did not fear it. I said, "Why, Oscar, don't you think you will get well?" He said, "I may, but it is not probable." He spoke calmly of his condition. The wound was very bad, it discharg'd much. Then the diarrhœa had prostrated him, and I felt that he was even then the same as dying. He behaved very manly and affectionate. The kiss I gave him as I was about leaving he return'd fourfold. He gave me his mother's address, Mrs. Sally D. Wilber, Alleghany post-office, Cattaraugus county, N. Y. I had several such interviews with him. He died a few days after the one just described.

Home-Made Music

August 8th.—To-night, as I was trying to keep cool, sitting by a wounded soldier in Armory-square, I was attracted by some pleasant singing in an adjoining ward. As my soldier was asleep, I left him, and entering the ward where the music was, I walk'd half-way down and took a seat by the cot of a young Brooklyn friend, S. R., badly wounded in the hand at Chancellorsville, and who has suffer'd much, but at that moment in the evening was wide awake and comparatively easy. He had turn'd over on his left side to get a better view of the singers, but the mosquito-curtains of the adjoining cots obstructed the sight. I stept round and loop'd them all up, so that he had a clear show, and then sat down again by him, and look'd and listen'd. The principal singer was a young lady-nurse of one of the wards, accompanying on a melodeon, and join'd by the lady-nurses of other wards. They sat there, making a charming group, with their handsome, healthy faces, and standing up a little behind them were some ten or fifteen of the convalescent soldiers, young men, nurses, &c., with books in their hands, singing. Of course it was not such a performance as the great soloists at the New York opera house take a hand in, yet I am not sure but I receiv'd as much pleasure under the circumstances, sitting there, as I have had from the best Italian compositions, express'd by world-famous performers. The men lying up and down the hospital, in their cots, (some badly wounded—some never to rise thence,) the cots themselves, with their drapery of white curtains, and the shadows down the lower and upper parts of the ward; then the silence of the men, and the attitudes they took—the whole was a sight to look around upon again and again. And there sweetly rose those voices up to the high, whitewash'd wooden roof, and pleasantly the roof sent it all back again. They sang very well, mostly quaint old songs and declamatory hymns, to fitting tunes. Here, for instance:

> My days are swiftly gliding by, and I a pilgrim stranger,
> Would not detain them as they fly, those hours of toil and danger;
> For O we stand on Jordan's strand, our friends are passing over,
> And just before, the shining shore we may almost discover.
> We'll gird our loins my brethren dear, our distant home discerning,
> Our absent Lord has left us word, let every lamp be burning,
> For O we stand on Jordan's strand, our friends are passing over,
> And just before, the shining shore we may almost discover.

Abraham Lincoln

August 12th.—I see the President almost every day, as I happen to live where he passes to or from his lodgings out of town. He never sleeps at the White House during the hot season, but has quarters at a healthy location some three miles north of the city, the Soldiers' home, a United States military establishment. I saw him this morning about 8½ coming in to business, riding on Vermont avenue, near L street. He always has a company of twenty-five or thirty cavalry, with sabres drawn and held upright over their shoulders. They say this guard was against his personal wish, but he let his counselors have their way. The party makes no great show in uniform or horses. Mr. Lincoln on the saddle generally rides a good-sized, easy-going gray horse, is dress'd in plain black, somewhat rusty and dusty, wears a black stiff hat, and looks about as ordinary in attire, &c., as the commonest man. A lieutenant, with yellow straps, rides at his left, and following behind, two by two, come the cavalry men, in their yellow-striped jackets. They are generally going at a slow trot, as that is the pace set them by the one they wait upon. The sabres and accoutrements clank, and the entirely unornamental *cortège* as it trots toward Lafayette square arouses no sensation, only some curious stranger stops and gazes. I see very plainly ABRAHAM LINCOLN'S dark brown face, with the deep-cut lines, the eyes, always to me with a deep latent sadness in the expression. We have got so that we exchange bows, and very cordial ones. Sometimes the President goes and comes in an open barouche. The cavalry always accompany him, with drawn sabres. Often I notice as he goes out evenings—and sometimes in the morning, when he returns early—he turns off and halts at the large and handsome residence of the Secretary of War, on K street, and holds conference there. If in his barouche, I can see from my window he does not alight, but sits in his vehicle, and Mr. Stanton comes out to attend him. Sometimes one of his sons, a boy of ten or twelve, accompanies him, riding at his right on a pony. Earlier in the summer I occasionally saw the President and his wife, toward the latter part of the afternoon, out in a barouche, on a pleasure ride through the city. Mrs. Lincoln was dress'd in complete black, with a long crape veil. The equipage is of the plainest kind, only two horses, and they nothing extra. They pass'd me once very close, and I saw the President in the face fully, as they were moving slowly, and his look, though abstracted, happen'd to be directed steadily in my eye. He bow'd and smiled, but far beneath his smile I noticed well the expression I have alluded to. None of the artists or pictures has caught the deep, though subtle and indirect expression of this man's face. There is something else there. One of the great portrait painters of two or three centuries ago is needed.

Heated Term

There has lately been much suffering here from heat; we have had it upon us now eleven days. I go around with an umbrella and a fan. I saw two cases of sun-stroke yesterday, one in Pennsylvania avenue, and another in Seventh street. The City railroad company loses some horses every day. Yet Washington is having a livelier August, and is probably putting in a more energetic and satisfactory summer than ever before during its existence. There is probably more human electricity, more population to make it, more business, more light-heartedness, than ever before. The armies that swiftly circumambiated from Fredericksburgh—march'd, struggled, fought, had out their mighty clinch and hurl at Gettysburg—wheel'd, circumambiated again, return'd to their ways, touching us not, either at their going or coming. And Washington feels that she has pass'd the worst; perhaps feels that she is henceforth mistress. So here she sits with her surrounding hills spotted with guns, and is conscious of a character and identity different from what it was five or six short weeks ago, and very considerably pleasanter and prouder.

Soldiers and Talks

Soldiers, soldiers, soldiers, you meet everywhere about the city, often superb-looking men, though invalids dress'd in worn uniforms, and carrying canes or crutches. I often have talks with them, occasionally quite long and interesting. One, for instance, will have been all through the peninsula under Mc-Clellan—narrates to me the fights, the marches, the strange, quick changes of that eventful campaign, and gives glimpses of many things untold in any official reports or books or journals. These, indeed, are the things that are genuine and precious. The man was there, has been out two years, has been through a dozen fights, the superfluous flesh of talking is long work'd off him, and he gives me little but the hard meat and sinew. I find it refreshing, these hardy, bright, intuitive, American young men, (experienc'd soldiers with all their youth.) The vocal play and significance moves one more than books. Then there hangs something majestic about a man who has borne his part in battles, especially if he is very quiet regarding it when you desire him to unbosom. I am continually lost at the absence of blowing and blowers among these old-young American militaires. I have found some man or other who has been in every battle since the war began, and have talk'd with them about each one in every part of the United States, and many of the engagements on the rivers and harbors too. I find men here from every State in the Union, without exception. (There are more Southerners, especially border State men, in the Union army than is generally supposed.[6]) I now doubt whether one can get a fair idea of what this war practically is, or what genuine America is, and her character, without some such experience as this I am having.

[6]MR. GARFIELD (*In the House of Representatives, April 15, '79.*) "Do gentlemen know that (leaving out all the border States) there were fifty regiments and seven companies of white men in our army fighting for the Union from the States that went into rebellion? Do they know that from the single State of Kentucky more Union soldiers fought under our flag than Napoleon took into the battle of Waterloo? more than Wellington took with all the allied armies against Napoleon? Do they remember that 186,000 color'd men fought under our flag against the rebellion and for the Union, and that of that number 90,000 were from the States which went into rebellion?"

Death of a Wisconsin Officer

Another characteristic scene of that dark and bloody 1863, from notes of my visit to Armory-square hospital, one hot but pleasant summer day. In ward H we approach the cot of a young lieutenant of one of the Wisconsin regiments. Tread the bare board floor lightly here, for the pain and panting of death are in this cot. I saw the lieutenant when he was first brought here from Chancellorsville, and have been with him occasionally from day to day and night to night. He had been getting along pretty well till night before last, when a sudden hemorrhage that could not be stopt came upon him, and to-day it still continues at intervals. Notice that water-pail by the side of the bed, with a quantity of blood and bloody pieces of muslin, nearly full; that tells the story. The poor young man is struggling painfully for breath, his great dark eyes with a glaze already upon them, and the choking faint but audible in his throat. An attendant sits by him, and will not leave him till the last; yet little or nothing can be done. He will die here in an hour or two, without the presence of kith or kin. Meantime the ordinary chat and business of the ward a little way off goes on indifferently. Some of the inmates are laughing and joking, others are playing checkers or cards, others are reading, &c.

I have noticed through most of the hospitals that as long as there is any chance for a man, no matter how bad he may be, the surgeon and nurses work hard, sometimes with curious tenacity, for his life, doing everything, and keeping somebody by him to execute the doctor's orders, and minister to him every minute night and day. See that screen there. As you advance through the dusk of early candle-light, a nurse will step forth on tiptoe, and silently but imperiously forbid you to make any noise, or perhaps to come near at all. Some soldier's life is flickering there, suspended between recovery and death. Perhaps at this moment the exhausted frame has just fallen into a light sleep that a step might shake. You must retire. The neighboring patients must move in their stocking feet. I have been serveral times struck with such mark'd efforts—everything bent to save a life from the very grip of the destroyer. But when that grip is once firmly fix'd, leaving no hope or chance at all, the surgeon abandons the patient. If it is a case where stimulus is any relief, the nurse gives milk-punch or brandy, or whatever is wanted, *ad libitum*. There is no fuss made. Not a bit of sentimentalism or whining have I seen about a single death-bed in hospital or on the field, but generally impassive indifference. All is over, as far as any efforts can avail; it is useless to expend emotions or labors. While there is a prospect they strive hard —at least most surgeons do; but death certain and evident, they yield the field.

Hospitals Ensemble

Aug., Sep., and Oct., '63.—I am in the habit of going to all, and to Fairfax seminary, Alexandria, and over Long bridge to the great Convalescent camp. The journals publish a regular directory of them—a long list. As a specimen of almost any one of the larger of these hospitals, fancy to yourself a space of three to twenty acres of ground, on which are group'd ten or twelve very large wooden barracks, with, perhaps, a dozen or twenty, and sometimes more than that number, small buildings, capable altogether of accommodating from five hundred to a thousand or fifteen hundred persons. Sometimes these wooden barracks or wards, each of them perhaps from a hundred to a hundred and fifty feet long, are rang'd in a straight row, evenly fronting the street; others are plann'd so as to form an immense V; and others again are ranged around a hollow square. They make altogether a huge cluster, with the additional tents, extra wards for contagious diseases, guard-houses, sutler's stores, chaplain's house; in the middle will probably be an edifice devoted to the offices of the surgeon in charge and the ward surgeons, principal attaches, clerks, &c. The wards are either letter'd alphabetically, ward G, ward K, or else numerically, 1, 2, 3, &c. Each has its ward surgeon and corps of nurses. Of course, there is, in the aggregate, quite a muster of employés, and over all the surgeon in charge. Here in Washington, when these army hospitals are all fill'd, (as they have been already several times,) they contain a popula-

tion more numerous in itself than the whole of the Washington
of ten or fifteen years ago. Within sight of the capitol, as I
write, are some thirty or forty such collections, at times holding
from fifty to seventy thousand men. Looking from any eminence and studying the topography in my rambles, I use them
as landmarks. Through the rich August verdure of the trees,
see that white group of buildings off yonder in the outskirts;
then another cluster half a mile to the left of the first; then
another a mile to the right, and another a mile beyond, and
still another between us and the first. Indeed, we can hardly
look in any direction but these clusters are dotting the landscape and environs. That little town, as you might suppose it,
off there on the brow of a hill, is indeed a town, but of wounds,
sickness, and death. It is Finley hospital, northeast of the city,
on Kendall green, as it used to be call'd. That other is Campbell
hospital. Both are large establishments. I have known these
two alone to have from two thousand to twenty-five hundred
inmates. Then there is Carver hospital, larger still, a wall'd and
military city regularly laid out, and guarded by squads of
sentries. Again, off east, Lincoln hospital, a still larger one; and
half a mile further Emory hospital. Still sweeping the eye
around down the river toward Alexandria, we see, to the
right, and locality where the Convalescent camp stands, with
its five, eight, or sometimes ten thousand inmates. Even all
these are but a portion. The Harewood, Mount Pleasant,
Armory-square, Judiciary hospitals, are some of the rest, and
all large collections.

A Silent Night Ramble

October 20th.—To-night after leaving the hospital at 10 o'clock,
(I had been on self-imposed duty some five hours, pretty closely
confined,) I wander'd a long time around Washington. The
night was sweet, very clear, sufficiently cool, a voluptuous half-
moon, slightly golden, the space near it of a transparent blue-
gray tinge. I walk'd up Pennsylvania avenue, and then to
Seventh street, and a long while around the Patent-office. Some-

how it look'd rebukefully strong, majestic, there in the delicate moonlight. The sky, the planets, the constellations all so bright, so calm, so expressively silent, so soothing, after those hospital scenes. I wander'd to and fro till the moist moon set, long after midnight.

Spiritual Characters
among the Soldiers

Every now and then, in hospital or camp, there are beings I meet—specimens of unworldliness, disinterestedness, and animal purity and heroism—perhaps some unconscious Indianian, or from Ohio or Tennessee—on whose birth the calmness of heaven seems to have descended, and whose gradual growing up, whatever the circumstances of work-life or change, or hardship, or small or no education that attended it, the power of a strange spiritual sweetness, fibre and inward health, have also attended. Something veil'd and abstracted is often a part of the manners of these beings. I have met them, I say, not seldom in the army, in camp, and in the hospitals. The Western regiments contain many of them. They are often young men, obeying the events and occasions about them, marching, soldiering, fighting, foraging, cooking, working on farms or at some trade before the war—unaware of their own nature, (as to that, who is aware of his own nature?) their companions only understanding that they are different from the rest, more silent, "something odd about them," and apt to go off and meditate and muse in solitude.

Cattle Droves about Washington

Among other sights are immense droves of cattle with their drivers, passing through the streets of the city. Some of the men have a way of leading the cattle by a peculiar call, a wild, pensive hoot, quite musical, prolong'd, indescribable, sounding something between the cooing of a pigeon and the hoot of an owl. I like to stand and look at the sight of one of these immense droves—a little way off—(as the dust is great.) There are always men on horseback, cracking their whips and shouting—the cattle low—some obstinate ox or steer attempts to escape—then a lively scene—the mounted men, always excellent riders and on good horses, dash after the recusant, and wheel and turn—a dozen mounted drovers, their great slouch'd, broad-brim'd hats, very picturesque—another dozen on foot— everybody cover'd with dust—long goads in their hands—an immense drove of perhaps 1000 cattle—the shouting, hooting, movement, &c.

Hospital Perplexity

To add to other troubles, amid the confusion of this great army of sick, it is almost impossible for a stranger to find any friend or relative, unless he has the patient's specific address to start upon. Besides the directory printed in the newspapers here, there are one or two general directories of the hospitals kept at provost's headquarters, but they are nothing like complete; they are never up to date, and, as things are, with the daily streams of coming and going and changing, cannot be. I have known cases, for instance such as a farmer coming here from northern New York to find a wounded brother, faithfully hunting round for a week, and then compell'd to leave and go home without getting any trace of him. When he got home he found a letter from the brother giving the right address.

Down at the Front

Culpepper, Va., Feb. '64.—Here I am pretty well down toward the extreme front. Three or four days ago General S., who is now in chief command, (I believe Meade is absent, sick,) moved a strong force southward from camp as if intending business. They went to the Rapidan; there has since been some manœuvring and a little fighting, but nothing of consequence. The telegraphic accounts given Monday morning last, make entirely too much of it, I should say. What General S. intended we here know not, but we trust in that competent commander. We were somewhat excited, (but not so very much either,) on Sunday, during the day and night, as orders were sent out to pack up and harness, and be ready to evacuate, to fall back towards Washington. But I was very sleepy and went to bed. Some tremendous shouts arousing me during the night, I went forth and found it was from the men above mention'd, who were returning. I talk'd with some of the men; as usual I found them full of gayety, endurance, and many fine little outshows, the sings of the most excellent good manliness of the world. It was a curious sight to see those shadowy columns moving through the night. I stood unobserv'd in the darkness and watch'd them long. The mud was very deep. The men had their usual burdens, overcoats, knappsacks, guns and blankets. Along and along they filed by me, with often a laugh, a song, a cheerful word, but never once a murmur. It may have been odd, but I never before so realized the majesty and reality of the American people *en masse*. It fell upon me like a great awe. The strong ranks moved neither fast nor slow. They had march'd seven or eight miles already through the slipping unctuous mud. The brave First corps stopt here. The equally brave Third corps moved on to Brandy station. The famous Brooklyn 14th are here, guarding the town. You see their red legs actively moving everywhere. Then they have a theatre of their own here. They give musical performances, nearly everything done capitally. Of course the audience is a jam. It is good sport to attend one of these entertainments of the 14th. I like to look around at the soldiers, and the general collection in front of the curtain, more than the scene on the stage.

Paying the Bounties

One of the things to note here now is the arrival of the pay-master with his strong box, and the payment of bounties to veterans re-enlisting. Major H. is here to-day, with a small mountain of greenbacks, rejoicing the hearts of the 2d division of the First corps. In the midst of a rickety shanty, behind a little table, sit the major and clerk Eldrige, with the rolls before them, and much moneys. A re-enlisted man gets in cash about $200 down, (and heavy instalments following, as the pay-days arrive, one after another.) The show of the men crowding around is quite exhilarating; I like to stand and look. They feel elated, their pockets full, and the ensuing furlough, the visit home. It is a scene of sparkling eyes and flush'd cheeks. The soldier has many gloomy and harsh experiences, and this makes up for some of them. Major H. is order'd to pay first all the re-enlisted men of the First corps their bounties and back pay, and then the rest. You hear the peculiar sound of the rustling of the new and crisp greenbacks by the hour, through the nimble fingers of the major and my friend clerk E.

Rumors, Changes, &c.

About the excitement of Sunday, and the orders to be ready to start, I have heard since that the said orders came from some cautious minor commander, and that the high principalities knew not and thought not of any such move; which is likely. The rumor and fear here intimated a long circuit by Lee, and flank attack on our right. But I cast my eyes at the mud, which was then at its deepest and palmiest condition, and retired composedly to rest. Still it is about time for Culpepper to have a change. Authorities have chased each other here like clouds in a stormy sky. Before the first Bull Run this was the rendez-vous and camp of instruction of the secession troops. I am stopping at the house of a lady who was witness'd all the eventful changes of the war, along this route of contending armies. She is a widow, with a family of young children, and lives here with her sister in a large handsome house. A number of army officers board with them.

Virginia

Dilapidated, fenceless, and trodden with war as Virginia is, wherever I move across her surface, I find myself rous'd to surprise and admiration. What capacity for products, improvements, human life, nourishment and expansion. Everywhere that I have been in the Old Dominion, (the subtle mockery of that title now!) such thoughts have fill'd me. The soil is yet far above the average of any of the northern States. And how full of breadth the scenery, everywhere distant mountains, everywhere convenient rivers. Even yet prodigal in forest woods, and surely eligible for all the fruits, orchards, and flowers. The skies and atmosphere most luscious, as I feel certain, from more than a year's residence in the State, and movements hither and yon. I should say very healthy, as a general thing. Then a rich and elastic quality, by night and by day. The sun rejoices in his strength, dazzling and burning, and yet, to me, never unpleasantly weakening. It is not the panting tropical heat, but invigorates. The north tempers it. The nights are often unsurpassable. Last evening (Feb. 8,) I saw the first of the new moon, the outlined old moon clear along with it; the sky and air so clear, such transparent hues of color, it seem'd to me I had never really seen the new moon before. It was the thinnest cut crescent possible. It hung delicate just above the sulky shadow of the Blue mountains. Ah, if it might prove an omen and good prophecy for this unhappy State.

Summer of 1864

I am back again in Washington, on my regular daily and nightly rounds. Of course there are many specialties. Dotting a ward here and there are always cases of poor fellows, long-suffering under obstinate wounds, or weak and dishearten'd from typhoid fever, or the like; mark'd cases, needing special and sympathetic nourishment. These I sit down and either talk to, or silently cheer them up. They always like it hugely, (and so do I.) Each case has its peculiarities, and needs some new adaptation. I have learnt to thus conform—learnt a good deal of hospital wisdom. Some of the poor young chaps, away from home for the first time in their lives, hunger and thirst for affection; this is sometimes the only thing that will reach their condition. The men like to have a pencil, and something to write in. I have given them cheap pocket-diaries, and almanacs for 1864, interleav'd with blank paper. For reading I generally have some old pictorial magazines or story papers—they are always acceptable. Also the morning or evening papers of the day. The best books I do not give, but lend to read through the wards, and then take them to others, and so on; they are very punctual about returning the books. In these wards, or on the field, as I thus continue to go round, I have come to adapt myself to each emergency, after its kind or call, however trivial, however solemn, every one justified and made real under its circumstances—not only visits and cheering talk and little gifts —not only washing and dressing wounds, (I have some cases where the patient is unwilling any one should do this but me) —but passages from the Bible, expounding them, prayer at the bedside, explanations of doctrine, &c. (I think I see my friends smiling at this confession, but I was never more in earnest in my life.) In camp and everywhere, I was in the habit of reading or giving recitations to the men. They were very fond of it, and liked declamatory poetical pieces. We would gather in a large group by ourselves, after supper, and spend the time in such readings, or in talking, and occasionally by an amusing game called the game of twenty questions.

A New Army Organization
Fit for America

It is plain to me out of the events of the war, north and south, and out of all considerations, that the current military theory, practice, rules and organization, (adopted from Europe from the feudal institutes, with, of course, the "modern improvements," largely from the French,) though tacitly followed, and believ'd in by the officers generally, are not at all consonant with the United States, nor our people, nor our days. What it will be I know not—but I know that as entire an abnegation of the present military system, and the naval too, and a building up from radically different root-bases and centres appropriate to us, must eventually result, as that our political system has resulted and become establish'd, different from feudal Europe, and built up on itself from original, perennial, democratic premises. We have undoubtedly in the United States the greatest military power—an exhaustless, intelligent, brave and reliable rank and file—in the world, any land, perhaps all lands. The problem is to organize this in the manner fully appropriate to it, to the principles of the republic, and to get the best service out of it. In the present struggle, as already seen and review'd, probably three-fourths of the losses, men, lives, &c., have been sheer superfluity, extravagance, waste.

Death of a Hero

I wonder if I could ever convey to another—to you, for instance, reader dear—the tender and terrible realities of such cases, (many, many happen'd,) as the one I am now going to mention. Stewart C. Glover, company E, 5th Wisconsin—was wounded May 5, in one of those fierce tussles of the Wilderness—died May 21—aged about 20. He was a small and beardless young man—a splendid soldier—in fact almost an ideal American, of his age. He had serv'd nearly three years, and would have been entitled to his discharge in a few days. He was in Hancock's corps. The fighting had about ceas'd for the day, and the general commanding the brigade rode by and call'd for volunteers to bring in the wounded. Glover responded among the first—went out gayly—but while in the act of bearing in a wounded sergeant to our lines, was shot in the knee by a rebel sharpshooter; consequence, amputation and death. He had resided with his father, John Glover, an aged and feeble man, in Batavia, Genesee county, N. Y., but was at school in Wisconsin, after the war broke out, and there enlisted —soon took to soldier-life, liked it, was very manly, was belov'd by officers and comrades. He kept a little diary, like so many of the soldiers. On the day of his death he wrote the following in it, *to-day the doctor says I must die—all is over with me—ah, so young to die.* On another blank leaf he pencill'd to his brother, *dear brother Thomas, I have been brave but wicked—pray for me.*

Hospital Scenes—Incidents

It is Sunday afternoon, middle of summer, hot and oppressive, and very silent through the ward. I am taking care of a critical case, now lying in a half lethargy. Near where I sit is a suffering rebel, from the 8th Louisiana; his name is Irving. He has been here a long time, badly wounded, and lately had his leg amputated; it is not doing very well. Right opposite me is a sick soldier-boy, laid down with his clothes on, sleeping, looking much wasted, his pallid face on his arm. I see by the yellow trimming on his jacket that he is a cavalry boy. I step softly over and find by his card that he is named William Cone, of the 1st Maine cavalry, and his folks live in Skowhegan.

Ice Cream Treat.—One hot day toward the middle of June, I gave the inmates of Carver hospital a general ice cream treat, purchasing a large quantity, and, under convoy of the doctor or head nurse, going around personally through the wards to see to its distribution.

An Incident.—In one of the fights before Atlanta, a rebel soldier, of large size, evidently a young man, was mortally wounded top of the head, so that the brains partially exuded. He lived three days, lying on his back on the spot where he first dropt. He dug with his heel in the ground during that time a hole big enough to put in a couple of ordinary knapsacks. He just lay there in the open air, and with little intermission kept his heel going night and day. Some of our soldiers then moved him to a house, but he died in a few minutes.

Another.—After the battles at Columbia, Tennessee, where we repuls'd about a score of vehement rebel charges, they left a great many wounded on the ground, mostly within our range. Whenever any of these wounded attempted to move away by any means, generally by crawling off, our men without exception brought them down by a bullet. They let none crawl away, no matter what his condition.

A Yankee Soldier

As I turn'd off the Avenue one cool October evening into Thirteenth street, a soldier with knapsack and overcoat stood at the corner inquiring his way. I found he wanted to go part of the road in my direction, so we walk'd on together. We soon fell into conversation. He was small and not very young, and a tough little fellow, as I judged in the evening light, catching glimpses by the lamps we pass'd. His answers were short, but clear. His name was Charles Carroll; he belong'd to one of the Massachusetts regiments, and was born in or near Lynn. His parents were living, but were very old. There were four sons, and all had enlisted. Two had died of starvation and misery in the prison at Andersonville, and one had been kill'd in the west. He only was left. He was now going home, and by the way he talk'd I inferr'd that his time was nearly out. He made great calculations on being with his parents to comfort them the rest of their days.

Union Prisoners South

Michael Stansbury, 48 years of age, a sea-faring man, a southerner by birth and raising, formerly captain of U. S. light ship Long Shoal, station'd at Long Shoal point, Pamlico sound—though a southerner, a firm Union man—was captur'd Feb. 17, 1863, and has been nearly two years in the Confederate prisons; was at one time order'd releas'd by Governor Vance, but a rebel officer re-arrested him; then sent on to Richmond for exchange—but instead of being exchanged was sent down (as a southern citizen, not a soldier,) to Salisbury, N. C., where he remain'd until lately, when he escap'd among the exchang'd by assuming the name of a dead soldier, and coming up via Wilmington with the rest. Was about sixteen months in Salisbury. Subsequent to October, '64, there were about 11,000 Union prisoners in the stockade; about 100 of them southern unionists, 200 U. S. deserters. During the past winter 1500 of the prisoners, to save their lives, join'd the confederacy, on condition of being assign'd merely to guard duty. Out of the 11,000 not more than 2500 came out; 500 of these were pitiable, helpless wretches—the rest were in a condition to travel. There were often 60 dead bodies to be buried in the morning; the daily average would be about 40. The regular food was a meal of corn, the cob and husk ground together, and sometimes once a week a ration of sorghum molasses. A diminutive ration of meat might possibly come once a month, not oftener. In the stockade, containing the 11,000 men, there was a partial show of tents, not enough for 2000. A large proportion of the men lived in holes in the ground, in the utmost wretchedness. Some froze to death, others had their hands and feet frozen. The rebel guards would occasionally, and on the least pretence, fire into the prison from mere demonism and wantonness. All the horrors that can be named, starvation, lassitude, filth, vermin, despair, swift loss of self-respect, idiocy, insanity, and frequent murder, were there. Stansbury has a wife and child living in Newbern—has written to them from here—is in the U. S. light-house employ still—(had been home to Newbern to see his family, and on his return to the ship was captured in his boat.) Has seen men brought there to Salisbury as hearty as you ever see in your life—in a few weeks completely dead gone, much of it from thinking on their condition—hope all gone. Has himself a hard, sad, strangely deaden'd kind of look, as of one chill'd for years in the cold and dark, where his good manly nature had no room to exercise itself.

Deserters

Oct. 24.—Saw a large squad of our own deserters, (over 300) surrounded with a cordon of arm'd guards, marching along Pennsylvania avenue. The most motley collection I ever saw, all sorts of rig, all sorts of hats and caps, many fine-looking young fellows, some of them shame-faced, some sickly, most of them dirty, shirts very dirty and long worn, &c. They tramp'd along without order, a huge huddling mass, not in ranks. I saw some of the spectators laughing, but I felt like anything else but laughing. These deserters are far more numerous than would be thought. Almost every day I see squads of them, sometimes two or three at a time, with a small guard; sometimes ten or twelve, under a larger one. (I hear that desertions from the army now in the field have often averaged 10,000 a month. One of the commonest sights in Washington is a squad of deserters.)

A Glimpse of War's Hell-Scenes

In one of the late movements of our troops in the valley, (near Upperville, I think,) a strong force of Moseby's mounted guerillas attack'd a train of wounded, and the guard of cavalry convoying them. The ambulances contain'd about 60 wounded, quite a number of them officers of rank. The rebels were in strength, and the capture of the train and its partial guard after a short snap was effectually accomplish'd. No sooner had our men surrender'd, the rebels instantly commenced robbing the train and murdering their prisoners, even the wounded. Here is the scene or a sample of it, ten minutes after. Among the wounded officers in the ambulances were one, a lieutenant of regulars, and another of higher rank. These two were dragg'd out on the ground on their backs, and were now surrounded by the guerillas, a demoniac crowd, each member of which was stabbing them in different parts of their bodies. One of the officers had his feet pinn'd firmly to the ground by bayonets stuck through them and thrust into the ground. These two officers, as afterwards found on examination, had receiv'd about twenty such thrusts, some of them through the mouth, face, &c. The wounded had all been dragg'd (to give a better chance also for plunder,) out of their wagons; some had been effectually dispatch'd, and their bodies were lying there lifeless and bloody. Others, not yet dead, but horribly mutilated, were moaning or groaning. Of our men who surrender'd, most had been thus maim'd or slaughter'd.

At this instant a force of our cavalry, who had been following the train at some interval, charged suddenly upon the secesh captors, who proceeded at once to make the best escape they could. Most of them got away, but we gobbled two officers and seventeen men, in the very acts just described. The sight was one which admitted of little discussion, as may be imagined. The seventeen captur'd men and two officers were put under guard for the night, but it was decided there and then that they should die. The next morning the two officers were taken in the town, separate places, but in the centre of the street, and shot. The seventeen men were taken to an open ground, a little one side. They were placed in a hollow square, half-encompass'd by two of our cavalry regiments, one of which regiments had three days before found the bloody corpses of three of their men hamstrung and hung up by the heels to limbs of trees by Moseby's guerillas, and the other had not long before had twelve men, after surrendering, shot and then hung by the neck to limbs of trees, and jeering inscriptions pinn'd to the breast of one of the corpses, who had been a sergeant. Those three, and those twelve, had been found, I say, by these environing regiments. Now, with revolvers, they form'd the grim cordon of the seventeen prisoners. The latter were placed in the midst of the hollow square, unfasten'd, and the ironical remark made to them that they were now to be given "a chance for themselves." A few ran for it. But what use? From every side the deadly pills came. In a few minutes the seventeen corpses strew'd the hollow square. I was curious to know whether some of the Union soldiers, some few, (some one or two at least of the youngsters,) did not abstain from shooting on the helpless men. Not one. There was no exultation, very little said, almost nothing, yet every man there contributed his shot.

Multiply the above by scores, aye hundreds—verify it in all the forms that different circumstances, individuals, places, could afford—light it with every lurid passion, the wolf's, the lion's lapping thirst for blood—the passionate, boiling volcanoes of human revenge for comrades, brothers slain—with the light of burning farms, and heaps of smutting, smouldering black embers—and in the human heart everywhere black, worse embers—and you have an inkling of this war.

Gifts—Money—Discrimination

As a very large proportion of the wounded came up from the front without a cent of money in their pockets, I soon discover'd that it was about the best thing I could do to raise their spirits, and show them that somebody cared for them, and practically felt a fatherly or brotherly interest in them, to give them small sums in such cases, using tact and discretion about it. I am regularly supplied with funds for this purpose by good women and men in Boston, Salem, Providence, Brooklyn, and New York. I provide myself with a quantity of bright new ten-cent and five-cent bills, and, when I think it incumbent, I give 25 or 30 cents, or perhaps 50 cents, and occasionally a still larger sum to some particular case. As I have started this subject, I take opportunity to ventilate the financial question. My supplies, altogether voluntary, mostly confidential, often seeming quite Providential, were numerous and varied. For instance, there were two distant and wealthy ladies, sisters, who sent regularly, for two years, quite heavy sums, enjoining that their names should be kept secret. The same delicacy was indeed a frequent condition. From several I had *carte blanche*. Many were entire strangers. From these sources, during from two to three years, in the manner described, in the hospitals, I bestowed, as almoner for others, many, many thousands of dollars. I learn'd one thing conclusively—that beneath all the ostensible greed and heartlessness of our times there is no end to the generous benevolence of men and women in the United States, when once sure of their object. Another thing became clear to me—while *cash* is not amiss to bring up the rear, tact and magnetic sympathy and unction are, and ever will be, sovereign still.

Items from My Note Books

Some of the half-eras'd, and not over-legible when made, memoranda of things wanted by one patient or another, will convey quite a fair idea. D. S. G., bed 52, wants a good book; has a sore, weak throat; would like some horehound candy; is from New Jersey, 28th regiment. C. H. L., 145th Pennsylvania, lies in bed 6, with jaundice and erysipelas; also wounded; stomach easily nauseated; bring him some oranges, also a little tart jelly; hearty, full-blooded young fellow—(he got better in a few days, and is now home on a furlough.) J. H. G., bed 24, wants an undershirt, drawers, and socks; has not had a change for quite a while; is evidently a neat, clean boy from New England—(I supplied him; also with a comb, toothbrush, and some soap and towels; I noticed afterward he was the cleanest of the whole ward.) Mrs. G., lady-nurse, ward F, wants a bottle of brandy—has two patients imperatively requiring stimulus— low with wounds and exhaustion. (I supplied her with a bottle of first-rate brandy from the Christian commission rooms.)

A Case from Second Bull Run

Well, poor John Mahay is dead. He died yesterday. His was a painful and long-lingering case, (see p. 417 *ante*.) I have been with him at times for the past fifteen months. He belonged to company A, 101st New York, and was shot through the lower region of the abdomen at second Bull Run, August, '62. One scene at his bedside will suffice for the agonies of nearly two years. The bladder had been perforated by a bullet going entirely through him. Not long since I sat a good part of the morning by his bedside, ward E, Armory square. The water ran out of his eyes from the intense pain, and the muscles of his face were distorted, but he utter'd nothing except a low groan now and then. Hot moist cloths were applied, and reliev'd him somewhat. Poor Mahay, a mere boy in age, but old in misfortune. He never knew the love of parents, was placed in infancy in one of the New York charitable institutions, and subsequently bound out to a tyrannical master in Sullivan county, (the scars of whose cowhide and club remain'd yet on his back.) His wound here was a most disagreeable one, for he was a gentle, cleanly, and affectionate boy. He found friends in his hospital life, and, indeed, was a universal favorite. He had quite a funeral ceremony.

Army Surgeons—Aid Deficiencies

I must bear my most emphatic testimony to the zeal, manliness, and professional spirit and capacity, generally prevailing among the surgeons, many of them young men, in the hospitals and the army. I will not say much about the exceptions, for they are few; (but I have met some of those few, and very incompetent and airish they were.) I never ceas'd to find the best men, and the hardest and most disinterested workers, among the surgeons in the hospitals. They are full of genius, too. I have seen many hundreds of them and this is my testimony. There are, however, serious deficiencies, wastes, sad want of system, in the commissions, contributions, and in all the voluntary, and a great part of the governmental nursing, edibles, medicines, stores, &c. (I do not say surgical attendance, because the surgeons cannot do more than human endurance permits.) Whatever puffing accounts there may be in the papers of the North, this is the actual fact. No thorough previous preparation, no system, no foresight, no genius. Always plenty of stores, no doubt, but never where they are needed, and never the proper application. Of all harrowing experiences, none is greater than that of the days following a heavy battle.

Scores, hundreds of the noblest men on earth, uncomplaining, lie helpless, mangled, faint, alone, and so bleed to death, or die from exhaustion, either actually untouch'd at all, or merely the laying of them down and leaving them, when there ought to be means provided to save them.

The Blue Everywhere

This city, its suburbs, the capital, the front of the White House, the places of amusement, the Avenue, and all the main streets, swarm with soldiers this winter, more than ever before. Some are out from the hospitals, some from the neighboring camps, &c. One source or another, they pour plenteously, and make, I should say, the mark'd feature in the human movement and costume-appearance of our national city. Their blue pants and overcoats are everywhere. The clump of crutches is heard up the stairs of the paymasters' offices, and there are characteristic groups around the doors of the same, often waiting long and wearily in the cold. Toward the latter part of the afternoon, you see the furlough'd men, sometimes singly, sometimes in small squads, making their way to the Baltimore depot. At all times, except early in the morning, the patrol detachments are moving around, especially during the earlier hours of evening, examining passes, and arresting all soldiers without them. They do not question the one-legged, or men badly disabled or maim'd, but all others are stopt. They also go around evenings through the auditoriums of the theatres, and make officers and all show their passes, or other authority, for being there.

A Model Hospital

Sunday, January 29th, 1865.—Have been in Armory-square this afternoon. The wards are very comfortable, new floors and plaster walls, and models of neatness. I am not sure but this is a model hospital after all, in important respects. I found several sad cases of old lingering wounds. One Delaware soldier, William H. Millis, from Bridgeville, whom I had been with after the battles of the Wilderness, last May, where he receiv'd a very bad wound in the chest, with another in the left arm, and whose case was serious (pneumonia had set in) all last June and July, I now find well enough to do light duty. For three weeks at the time mention'd he just hovered between life and death.

Boys in the Army

As I walk'd home about sunset, I saw in Fourteenth street a very young soldier, thinly clad, standing near the house I was about to enter. I stopt a moment in front of the door and call'd him to me. I knew that an old Tennessee regiment, and also an Indiana regiment, were temporarily stopping in new barracks, near Fourteenth street. This boy I found belonged to the Tennessee regiment. But I could hardly believe he carried a musket. He was but 15 years old, yet had been twelve months a soldier, and had borne his part in several battles, even historic ones. I ask'd him if he did not suffer from the cold, and if he had no overcoat. No, he did not suffer from cold, and had no overcoat, but could draw one whenever he wish'd. His father was dead, and his mother living in some part of East Tennessee; all the men were from that part of the country. The next forenoon I saw the Tennessee and Indiana regiments marching down the Avenue. My boy was with the former, stepping along with the rest. There were many other boys no older. I stood and watch'd them as they tramp'd along with slow, strong, heavy, regular steps. There did not appear to be a man over 30 years of age, and a large proportion were from 15 to perhaps 22 or 23. They had all the look of veterans, worn, stain'd, impassive, and a certain unbent, lounging gait, carrying in addition to their regular arms and knapsacks, frequently a frying-pan, broom,

&c. They were all of pleasant physiognomy; no refinement, nor blanch'd with intellect, but as my eye pick'd them, moving along, rank by rank, there did not seem to be a single repulsive, brutal or markedly stupid face among them.

Burial of a Lady Nurse

Here is an incident just occurr'd in one of the hospitals. A lady named Miss or Mrs. Billings, who has long been a practical friend of soldiers, and nurse in the army, and had become attached to it in a way that no one can realize but him or her who has had experience, was taken sick, early this winter, linger'd some time, and finally died in the hospital. It was her request that she should be buried among the soldiers, and after the military method. This request was fully carried out. Her coffin was carried to the grave by soldiers, with the usual escort, buried, and a salute fired over the grave. This was at Annapolis a few days since.

Female Nurses for Soldiers

There are many women in one position or another, amongst the hospitals, mostly as nurses here in Washington, and among the military stations; quite a number of them young ladies acting as volunteers. They are a help in certain ways, and deserve to be mention'd with respect. Then it remains to be distinctly said that few or no young ladies, under the irresistible conventions of society, answer the practical requirements of nurses for soldiers. Middle-aged or healthy and good condition'd elderly women, mothers of children, are always best. Many of the wounded must be handled. A hundred things which cannot be gainsay'd, must occur and must be done. The presence of a good middle-aged or elderly woman, the magnetic touch of hands, the expressive features of the mother, the silent soothing

of her presence, her words, her knowledge and privileges arrived at only through having had children, are precious and
final qualifications. It is a natural faculty that is required; it is
not merely having a genteel young woman at a table in a ward.
One of the finest nurses I met was a red-faced illiterate old
Irish woman; I have seen her take the poor wasted naked
boys so tenderly up in her arms. There are plenty of excellent
clean old black women that would make tip-top nurses.

Southern Escapees

Feb. 23, '65.—I saw a large procession of young men from the
rebel army, (deserters they are call'd, but the usual meaning
of the word does not apply to them,) passing the Avenue to-
day. There were nearly 200, come up yesterday by boat from
James river. I stood and watch'd them as they shuffled along,
in a slow, tired, worn sort of way; a large proportion of light-
hair'd blonde, light gray-eyed young men among them. Their
costumes had a dirt-stain'd uniformity; most had been originally gray; some had articles of our uniform, pants on one,
vest or coat on another; I think they were mostly Georgia and
North Carolina boys. They excited little or no attention. As I
stood quite close to them, several good looking enough youths,
(but O what a tale of misery their appearance told,) nodded or
just spoke to me, without doubt divining pity and fatherliness
out of my face, for my heart was full enough of it. Several of
the couples trudg'd along with their arms about each other,
some probably brothers, as if they were afraid they might
somehow get separated. They nearly all look'd what one might
call simple, yet intelligent, too. Some had pieces of old carpet,
some blankets, and others old bags around their shoulders.
Some of them here and there had fine faces, still it was a
procession of misery. The two hundred had with them about
half a dozen arm'd guards. Along this week I saw some such
procession, more or less in numbers, every day, as they were
brought up by the boat. The government does what it can for
them, and sends them north and west.

Feb. 27.—Some three or four hundred more escapees from the confederate army came up on the boat. As the day has been very pleasant indeed, (after a long spell of bad weather,) I have been wandering around a good deal, without any other object than to be out-doors and enjoy it; have met these escaped men in all directions. Their apparel is the same ragged, long-worn motley as before described. I talk'd with a number of the men. Some are quite bright and stylish, for all their poor clothes— walking with an air, wearing their old head-coverings on one side, quite saucily. I find the old, unquestionable proofs, as all along the past four years, of the unscrupulous tyranny exercised by the secession government in conscripting the common people by absolute force everywhere, and paying no attention whatever to the men's time being up—keeping them in military service just the same. One gigantic young fellow, a Georgian, at least six feet three inches high, broad-sized in proportion, attired in the dirtiest, drab, well-smear'd rags, tied with strings, his trousers at the knees all strips and streamers, was complacently standing eating some bread and meat. He appear'd contented enough. Then a few minutes after I saw him slowly walking along. It was plain he did not take anything to heart.

Feb. 28.—As I pass'd the military headquarters of the city, not far from the President's house, I stopt to interview some of the crowd of escapees who were lounging there. In appearance they were the same as previously mention'd. Two of them, one about 17, and the other perhaps 25 or '6, I talk'd with some time. They were from North Carolina, born and rais'd there, and had folks there. The elder had been in the rebel service four years. He was first conscripted for two years. He was then kept arbitrarily in the ranks. This is the case with a large proportion of the secession army. There was nothing downcast in these young men's manners; the younger had been soldiering about a year; he was conscripted; there were six brothers (all the boys of the family) in the army, part of them as conscripts, part as volunteers; three had been kill'd; one had escaped about four months ago, and now this one had got away; he was a pleasant and well-talking lad, with the peculiar North Carolina idiom (not at all disagreeable to my ears.) He and the elder one were of the same company, and escaped together—and wish'd to remain together. They thought of getting transportation away to Missouri, and working there; but were not sure it was judicious. I advised them rather to go to some of the directly northern States, and get farm work for the present. The younger had made six dollars on the boat, with some tobacco he brought; he had three and a half left. The elder had nothing; I gave him a trifle. Soon after, met John Wormley, 9th Alabama, a West Tennessee rais'd boy, parents both dead —had the look of one for a long time on short allowance—said very little—chew'd tobacco at a fearful rate, spitting in proportion—large clear dark-brown eyes, very fine—didn't know what to make of me—told me at last he wanted much to get some clean underclothes, and a pair of decent pants. Didn't care about coat or hat fixings. Wanted a chance to wash himself well, and put on the underclothes. I had the very great pleasure of helping him to accomplish all those wholesome designs.

March 1st.—Plenty more butternut or clay-color'd escapees every day. About 160 came in to-day, a large portion South Carolinians. They generally take the oath of allegiance, and are sent north, west, or extreme south-west if they wish. Several of them told me that the desertions in their army, of men going home, leave or no leave, are far more numerous than their desertions to our side. I saw a very forlorn looking squad of about a hundred, late this afternoon, on their way to the Baltimore depot.

The Capitol by Gas-Light

To-night I have been wandering awhile in the capitol, which is all lit up. The illuminated rotunda looks fine. I like to stand aside and look a long, long while, up at the dome; it comforts me somehow. The House and Senate were both in session till very late. I look'd in upon them, but only a few moments; they were hard at work on tax and appropriation bills. I wander'd through the long and rich corridors and apartments under the Senate; an old habit of mine, former winters, and now more satisfaction than ever. Not many persons down there, occasionally a flitting figure in the distance.

The Inauguration

March 4.—The President very quietly rode down to the capitol in his own carriage, by himself, on a sharp trot, about noon, either because he wish'd to be on hand to sign bills, or to get rid of marching in line with the absurd procession, the muslin temple of liberty, and pasteboard monitor. I saw him on his return, at three o'clock, after the performance was over. He was in his plain two-horse barouche, and look'd very much worn and tired; the lines, indeed, of vast responsibilities, intricate questions, and demands of life and death, cut deeper than ever upon his dark brown face; yet all the old goodness, tenderness, sadness, and canny shrewdness, underneath the furrows. (I never see that man without feeling that he is one to become personally attach'd to, for his combination of purest, heartiest tenderness, and native western form of manliness.) By his side sat his little boy, of ten years. There were no soldiers, only a lot of civilians on horseback, with huge yellow scarfs over their shoulders, riding around the carriage. (At the inauguration four years ago, he rode down and back again surrounded by a dense mass of arm'd cavalrymen eight deep, with drawn sabres; and there were sharp-shooters station'd at every corner on the route.) I ought to make mention of the closing levee of Saturday night last. Never before was such a compact jam in front of the White House—all the grounds fill'd, and away out to the spacious sidewalks. I was there, as I took a notion to go—was in the rush inside with the crowd—surged along the passage-ways, the blue and other rooms, and through the great east room. Crowds of country people, some very funny. Fine music from the Marine band, off in a side place. I saw Mr. Lincoln, drest all in black, with white kid gloves and a claw-hammer coat, receiving, as in duty bound, shaking hands,

looking very disconsolate, and as if he would give anything to
be somewhere else.

Attitude of Foreign Governments
during the War

Looking over my scraps, I find I wrote the following during
1864. The happening to our America, abroad as well as at
home, these years, is indeed most strange. The democratic republic had paid her to-day the terrible and resplendent compliment of the united wish of all the nations of the world that her
union should be broken, her future cut off, and that she should
be compell'd to descend to the level of kingdoms and empires
ordinarily great. There is certainly not one government in
Europe but is now watching the war in this country, with the
ardent prayer that the United States may be effectually split,
crippled, and dismember'd by it. There is not one but would
help toward that dismemberment, if it dared. I say such is the
ardent wish to-day of England and of France, as governments,
and of all the nations of Europe, as governments. I think indeed
it is to-day the real, heartfelt wish of all the nations of the
world, with the single exception of Mexico—Mexico, the only
one to whom we have ever really done wrong, and now the
only one who prays for us and for our triumph, with genuine
prayer. Is it not indeed strange? America, made up of all,
cheerfully from the beginning opening her arms to all, the result
and justifier of all, of Britain, Germany, France and Spain—all
here—the accepter, the friend, hope, last resource and general
house of all—she who has harm'd none, but been bounteous
to so many, to millions, the mother of strangers and exiles, all
nations—should now I say be paid this dread compliment
of general governmental fear and hatred. Are we indignant?
alarm'd? Do we feel jeopardized? No; help'd, braced, concentrated, rather. We are all too prone to wander from ourselves,
to affect Europe, and watch her frowns and smiles. We need
this hot lesson of general hatred, and henceforth must never
forget it. Never again will we trust the moral sense nor abstract
friendliness of a single *government* of the old world.

The Weather—Does It Sympathize with These Times?

Whether the rains, the heat and cold, and what underlies them all, are affected with what affects man in masses, and follow his play of passionate action, strain'd stronger than usual, and on a larger scale than usual—whether this, or no, it is certain that there is now, and has been for twenty months or more, on this American continent north, many a remarkable, many an unprecedented expression of the subtle world of air above us and around us. There, since this war, and the wide and deep national agitation, strange analogies, different combinations, a different sunlight, or absence of it; different products even out of the ground. After every great battle, a great storm. Even civic events the same. On Saturday last, a forenoon like whirling demons, dark, with slanting rain, full of rage; and then the afternoon, so calm, so bathed with flooding splendor from heaven's most excellent sun, with atmosphere of sweetness; so clear, it show'd the stars, long, long before they were due. As the President came out on the capitol portico, a curious little white cloud, the only one in that part of the sky, appear'd like a hovering bird, right over him.

Indeed, the heavens, the elements, all the meteorological influences, have run riot for weeks past. Such caprices, abruptest alternation of frowns and beauty, I never knew. It is a common remark that (as last summer was different in its spells of intense heat from any preceding it,) the winter just completed has been without parallel. It has remain'd so down to the hour I am writing. Much of the daytime of the past month was sulky, with leaden heaviness, fog, interstices of bitter cold, and some insane storms. But there have been samples of another description. Nor earth nor sky ever knew spectacles of superber beauty than some of the nights lately here. The western star, Venus, in the earlier hours of evening, has never been so large, so clear; it seems as if it told something, as if it held rapport indulgent with humanity, with us Americans. Five or six nights since, it hung close by the moon, then a little past its first quarter. The star was wonderful, the moon like a young mother. The sky, dark blue, the transparent night, the planets, the moderate west wind, the elastic temperature, the miracle of that great star, and the young and swelling moon swimming in the west, suffused the soul. Then I heard, slow and clear, the deliberate notes of a bugle come up out of the silence sounding so good through the night's mystery, no hurry, but firm and faithful, floating along, rising, falling leisurely, with here and there a long-drawn note; the bugle well play'd, sounding tattoo, in one of the army hospitals near here, where the wounded (some of them personally so dear to me,) are lying in their cots, and many a sick boy come down to the war from Illinois, Michigan, Wisconsin, Iowa, and the rest.

Inauguration Ball

March 6.—I have been up to look at the dance and supper-rooms, for the inauguration ball at the Patent office; and I could not help thinking, what a different scene they presented to my view a while since, fill'd with a crowded mass of the worst wounded of the war, brought in from second Bull Run, Antietam, and Fredericksburgh. To-night, beautiful women, perfumes, the violins' sweetness, the polka and the waltz; then the amputation, the blue face, the groan, the glassy eye of the dying, the clotted rag, the odor of wounds and blood, and many a mother's son amid strangers, passing away untended there, (for the crowd of the badly hurt was great, and much for nurse to do, and much for surgeon.)

Scene at the Capitol

I must mention a strange scene at the capitol, the hall of Representatives, the morning of Saturday last, (March 4th.) The day just dawn'd but in half-darkness, everything dim, leaden, and soaking. In that dim light, the members nervous from long-drawn duty, exhausted, some asleep, and many half asleep. The gas-light, mix'd with the dingy day-break, produced an un-earthly effect. The poor little sleepy, stumbling pages, the smell of the hall, the members with heads leaning on their desks, the sounds of the voices speaking, with unusual intonations—the general moral atmosphere also of the close of this important session—the strong hope that the war is approaching its close —the tantalizing dread lest the hope may be a false one—the grandeur of the hall itself, with its effect of vast shadows up toward the panels and spaces over the galleries—all made a mark'd combination.

In the midst of this, with the suddenness of a thunderbolt, burst one of the most angry and crashing storms of rain and hail ever heard. It beat like a deluge on the heavy glass roof of the hall, and the wind literally howl'd and roar'd. For a moment, (and no wonder,) the nervous and sleeping Repre-sentatives were thrown into confusion. The slumberers awaked with fear, some started for the doors, some look'd up with blanch'd cheeks and lips to the roof, and the little pages began to cry; it was a scene. But it was over almost as soon as the drowsied men were actually awake. They recover'd themselves; the storm raged on, beating, dashing, and with loud noises at times. But the House went ahead with its business then, I think, as calmly and with as much deliberation as at any time in its career. Perhaps the shock did it good. (One is not without im-pression, after all, amid these members of Congress, of both the Houses, that if the flat routine of their duties should ever be broken in upon by some great emergency involving real danger, and calling for first-class personal qualities, those qual-ities would be found generally forthcoming, and from men not now credited with them.)

A Yankee Antique

March 27, 1865.—Sergeant Calvin F. Harlowe, company C, 29th Massachusetts, 3d brigade, 1st division, Ninth corps—a mark'd sample of heroism and death, (some may say bravado, but I say *heroism*, of grandest, oldest order)—in the late attack by the rebel troops, and temporary capture by them, of fort Steadman, at night. The fort was surprised at dead of night. Suddenly awaken'd from their sleep, and rushing from their tents, Harlowe, with others, found himself in the hands of the secesh—they demanded his surrender—he answer'd, *Never while I live.* (Of course it was useless. The others surrender'd; the odds were too great.) Again he was ask'd to yield, this time by a rebel captain. Though surrounded, and quite calm, he again refused, call'd sternly to his comrades to fight on, and himself attempted to do so. The rebel captain then shot him— but at the same instant he shot the captain. Both fell together mortally wounded. Harlowe died almost instantly. The rebels were driven out in a very short time. The body was buried next day, but soon taken up and sent home, (Plymouth county, Mass.) Harlowe was only 22 years of age—was a tall, slim, dark-hair'd, blue-eyed young man—had come out originally with the 29th; and that is the way he met his death, after four years' campaign. He was in the Seven Days fight before Richmond, in second Bull Run, Antietam, first Fredericksburgh, Vicksburgh, Jackson, Wilderness, and the campaigns following—was as good a soldier as ever wore the blue, and every old officer in the regiment will bear that testimony. Though so young, and in a common rank, he had a spirit as resolute and brave as any hero in the books, ancient or modern—It was too great to say the words "I surrender"—and so he died. (When I think of such things, knowing them well, all the vast and complicated events of the war, on which history dwells and makes its volumes, fall aside, and for the moment at any rate I see nothing but young Calvin Harlowe's figure in the night, disdaining to surrender.)

Wounds and Diseases

The war is over, but the hospitals are fuller than ever, from former and current cases. A large majority of the wounds are in the arms and legs. But there is every kind of wound, in every part of the body. I should say of the sick, from my observation, that the prevailing maladies are typhoid fever and the camp fevers generally, diarrhœa, catarrhal affections and bronchitis, rheumatism and pneumonia. These forms of sickness lead; all the rest follow. There are twice as many sick as there are wounded. The deaths range from seven to ten per cent. of those under treatment.[7]

Death of President Lincoln

April 16, '65.—I find in my notes of the time, this passage on the death of Abraham Lincoln: He leaves for America's history and biography, so far, not only its most dramatic reminiscence —he leaves, in my opinion, the greatest, best, most characteristic, artistic, moral personality. Not but that he had faults, and show'd them in the Presidency; but honesty, goodness, shrewdness, conscience, and (a new virtue, unknown to other lands, and hardly yet really known here, but the foundation and tie of all, as the future will grandly develop,) UNIONISM, in its truest and amplest sense, form'd the hard-pan of his character. These he seal'd with his life. The tragic splendor of his death, purging, illuminating all, throws round his form, his head, an aureole that will remain and will grow brighter through time, while history lives, and love of country lasts. By many has this Union been help'd; but if one name, one man, must be pick'd out, he, most of all, is the conservator of it, to the future. He was assassinated—but the Union is not assassinated—*ça ira!* One falls, and another falls. The soldier drops, sinks like a wave—but the ranks of the ocean eternally press on. Death does its work, obliterates a hundred, a thousand—President, general, captain, private—but the Nation is immortal.

[7] In the U. S. Surgeon-General's office since, there is a formal record and treatment of 253,142 cases of wounds by government surgeons. What must have been the number unofficial, indirect—to say nothing of the Southern armies?

Sherman's Army's Jubilation—
Its Sudden Stoppage

When Sherman's armies, (long after they left Atlanta,) were marching through South and North Carolina—after leaving Savannah, the news of Lee's capitulation having been receiv'd —the men never mov'd a mile without from some part of the line sending up continued, inspiriting shouts. At intervals all day long sounded out the wild music of those peculiar army cries. They would be commenc'd by one regiment or brigade, immediately taken up by others, and at length whole corps and armies would join in these wild triumphant choruses. It was one of the characteristic expressions of the western troops, and became a habit, serving as a relief and outlet to the men—a vent for their feelings of victory, returning peace, &c. Morning, noon, and afternoon, spontaneous, for occasion or without occasion, these huge, strange cries, differing from any other, echoing through the open air for many a mile, expressing youth, joy, wildness, irrepressible strength, and the ideas of advance and conquest, sounded along the swamps and uplands of the South, floating to the skies. ('There never were men that kept in better spirits in danger or defeat—what then could they do in victory?'—said one of the 15th corps to me, afterwards.) This exuberance continued till the armies arrived at Raleigh. There the news of the President's murder was receiv'd. Then no more shouts or yells, for a week. All the marching was comparatively muffled. It was very significant—hardly a loud word or laugh in many of the regiments. A hush and silence pervaded all.

No Good Portrait of Lincoln

Probably the reader has seen physiognomies (often old farmers, sea-captains, and such) that, behind their homeliness, or even ugliness, held superior points so subtle, yet so palpable, making the real life of their faces almost as impossible to depict as a wild perfume or fruit-taste, or a passionate tone of the living voice—and such was Lincoln's face, the peculiar color, the lines of it, the eyes, mouth, expression. Of technical beauty it had nothing—but to the eye of a great artist it furnished a rare study, a feast and fascination. The current portraits are all failures—most of them caricatures.

Releas'd Union Prisoners from South

The releas'd prisoners of war are now coming up from the southern prisons. I have seen a number of them. The sight is worse than any sight of battle-fields, or any collection of wounded, even the bloodiest. There was, (as a sample,) one large boat load, of several hundreds, brought about the 25th, to Annapolis; and out of the whole number only three individuals were able to walk from the boat. The rest were carried ashore and laid down in one place or another. Can those be *men*—those little livid brown, ash-streak'd, monkey-looking dwarfs?—are they really not mummied, dwindled corpses? They lay there, most of them, quite still, but with a horrible look in their eyes and skinny lips (often with not enough flesh on the lips to cover their teeth.) Probably no more appalling sight was ever seen on this earth. (There are deeds, crimes, that may be forgiven; but this is not among them. It steeps its perpetrators in blackest, escapeless, endless damnation. Over 50,000 have been compell'd to die the death of starvation— reader, did you ever try to realize what *starvation* actually is?— in those prisons—and in a land of plenty.) An indescribable meanness, tyranny, aggravating course of insults, almost incredible—was evidently the rule of treatment through all the southern military prisons. The dead there are not to be pitied as much as some of the living that come from there—if they can be call'd living—many of them are mentally imbecile, and will never recuperate.[8]

[8]*From a review of* "ANDERSONVILLE, A STORY OF SOUTHERN MILITARY PRISONS," *published serially in the* "Toledo Blade," *in 1879, and afterwards in book form.*

"There is a deep fascination in the subject of Andersonville—for

Death of a Pennsylvania Soldier

Frank H. Irwin, company E, 93d Pennsylvania—died May 1, '65—My letter to his mother.—Dear madam: No doubt you and Frank's friends have heard the sad fact of his death in hospital here, through his uncle, or the lady from Baltimore, who took his things. (I have not seen them, only heard of them visiting Frank.) I will write you a few lines—as a casual friend that sat by his death-bed. Your son, corporal Frank H. Irwin, was wounded near fort Fisher, Virginia, March 25th, 1865— the wound was in the left knee, pretty bad. He was sent up to Washington, was receiv'd in ward C, Armory-square hospital, March 28th—the wound became worse, and on the 4th of April the leg was amputated a little above the knee—the operation was perform'd by Dr. Bliss, one of the best surgeons in

that Golgotha, in which lie the whitening bones of 13,000 gallant young men, represents the dearest and costliest sacrifice of the war for the preservation of our national unity. It is a type, too, of its class. Its more than hundred hecatombs of dead represent several times that number of their brethren, for whom the prison gates of Belle Isle, Danville, Salisbury, Florence, Columbia, and Cahaba open'd only in eternity. There are few families in the North who have not at least one dear relative or friend among these 60,000 whose sad fortune it was to end their service for the Union by lying down and dying for it in a southern prison pen. The manner of their death, the horrors that cluster'd thickly around every moment of their existence, the loyal, unfaltering steadfastness with which they endured all that fate had brought them, has never been adequately told. It was not with them as with their comrades in the field, whose every act was per- form'd in the presence of those whose duty it was to observe such matters and report them to the world. Hidden from the view of their friends in the north by the impenetrable veil which the military opera- tions of the rebels drew around the so-called confederacy, the people knew next to nothing of their career or their sufferings. Thousands died there less heeded even than the hundreds who perish'd on the battle-field. Grant did not lose as many men kill'd outright, in the terrible campaign from the Wilderness to the James river—43 days of desperate fighting—as died in July and August at Andersonville. Nearly twice as many died in that prison as fell from the day that Grant cross'd the Rapidan, till he settled down in the trenches be- fore Petersburg. More than four times as many Union dead lie under the solemn soughing pines about that forlorn little village in southern Georgia, than mark the course of Sherman from Chattanooga to Atlanta. The nation stands aghast at the expenditure of life which attended the two bloody campaigns of 1864, which virtually crush'd the confederacy, but no one remembers that more Union soldiers died the army—he did the whole operation himself—there was a good deal of bad matter gather'd—the bullet was found in the knee. For a couple of weeks afterwards he was doing pretty well. I visited and sat by him frequently, as he was fond of having me. The last ten or twelve days of April I saw that his case was critical. He previously had some fever, with cold spells. The last week in April he was much of the time flighty—but always mild and gentle. He died first of May. The actual cause of death was pyæmia, (the absorption of the matter in the system instead of its discharge.) Frank, as far as I saw, had everything requisite in surgical treatment, nursing, &c. He had watches much of the time. He was so good and well-behaved and affectionate, I myself liked him very much. I was in the

---

in the rear of the rebel lines than were kill'd in the front of them. The great military events which stamp'd out the rebellion drew attention away from the sad drama which starvation and disease play'd in those gloomy pens in the far recesses of sombre southern forests."

From a letter of "Johnny Bouquet," in N. Y. Tribune, March 27, '81.

"I visited at Salisbury, N. C., the prison pen or the site of it, from which nearly 12,000 victims of southern politicians were buried, being confined in a pen without shelter, exposed to all the elements could do, to all the disease herding animals together could create, and to all the starvation and cruelty an incompetent and intense caitiff government could accomplish. From the conversation and almost from the recollection of the northern people this place has dropp'd, but not so in the gossip of the Salisbury people, nearly all of whom say that the half was never told; that such was the nature of habitual outrage here that when Federal prisoners escaped the townspeople harbor'd them in their barns, afraid the vengeance of God would fall on them, to deliver even their enemies back to such cruelty. Said one old man at the Boyden House, who join'd in the conversation one evening: 'There were often men buried out of that prison pen alive. I have the testimony of a surgeon that he has seen them pull'd out of the dead cart with their eyes open and taking notice, but too weak to lift a finger. There was not the least excuse for such treatment, as the confederate government had seized every sawmill in the region, and could just as well have put up shelter for these prisoners as not, wood being plentiful here. It will be hard to make any honest man in Salisbury say that there was the slightest necessity for those prisoners having to live in old tents, caves and holes half-full of water. Representations were made to the Davis government against the officers in charge of it, but no attention was paid to them. Promotion was the punishment for cruelty there. The inmates were skeletons. Hell could have no terrors for any man who died there, except the inhuman keepers.'"

habit of coming in afternoons and sitting by him, and soothing him, and he liked to have me—liked to put his arm out and lay his hand on my knee—would keep it so a long while. Toward the last he was more restless and flighty at night—often fancied himself with his regiment—by his talk sometimes seem'd as if his feelings were hurt by being blamed by his officers for something he was entirely innocent of—said, "I never in my life was thought capable of such a thing, and never was." At other times he would fancy himself talking as it seem'd to children or such like, his relatives I suppose, and giving them good advice; would talk to them a long while. All the time he was out of his head not one single bad word or idea escaped him. It was remark'd that many a man's conversation in his senses was not half as good as Frank's delirium. He seem'd quite willing to die—he had become very weak and had suffer'd a good deal, and was perfectly resign'd, poor boy. I do not know his past life, but I feel as if it must have been good. At any rate what I saw of him here, under the most trying circumstances, with a painful wound, and among strangers, I can say that he behaved so brave, so composed, and so sweet and affectionate, it could not be surpass'd. And now like many other noble and good men, after serving his country as a soldier, he has yielded up his young life at the very outset in her service. Such things are gloomy—yet there is a text, "God doeth all things well"—the meaning of which, after due time, appears to the soul.

I thought perhaps a few words, though from a stranger, about your son, from one who was with him at the last, might be worth while—for I loved the young man, though I but saw him immediately to lose him. I am merely a friend visiting the hospitals occasionally to cheer the wounded and sick.   W. W.

The Armies Returning

May 7.—Sunday.—To-day as I was walking a mile or two south of Alexandria, I fell in with several large squads of the returning Western army, *(Sherman's men* as they call'd themselves) about a thousand in all, the largest portion of them half sick, some convalescents, on their way to a hospital camp. These fragmentary excerpts, with the unmistakable Western physiognomy and idioms, crawling along slowly—after a great campaign, blown this way, as it were, out of their latitude—I mark'd with curiosity, and talk'd with off and on for over an hour. Here and there was one very sick; but all were able to walk, except some of the last, who had given out, and were seated on the ground, faint and despondent. These I tried to cheer, told them the camp they were to reach was only a little way further over the hill, and so got them up and started, accompanying some of the worst a little way, and helping them, or putting them under the support of stronger comrades.

May 21.—Saw General Sheridan and his cavalry to-day; a strong, attractive sight; the men were mostly young, (a few middle-aged,) superb-looking fellows, brown, spare, keen, with well-worn clothing, many with pieces of water-proof cloth around their shoulders, hanging down. They dash'd along pretty fast, in wide close ranks, all spatter'd with mud; no holiday soldiers; brigade after brigade. I could have watch'd for a week. Sheridan stood on a balcony, under a big tree, coolly smoking a cigar. His looks and manner impress'd me favorably.

May 22.—Have been taking a walk along Pennsylvania avenue and Seventh street north. The city is full of soldiers, running around loose. Officers everywhere, of all grades. All have the weather-beaten look of practical service. It is a sight I never tire of. All the armies are now here (or portions of them,) for to-morrow's review. You see them swarming like bees everywhere.

The Grand Review

For two days now the broad spaces of Pennsylvania avenue along to Treasury hill, and so by detour around to the President's house, and so up to Georgetown, and across the aqueduct bridge, have been alive with a magnificent sight, the

returning armies. In their wide ranks stretching clear across
the Avenue, I watch them march or ride along, at a brisk pace,
through two whole days—infantry, cavalry, artillery—some
200,000 men. Some days afterwards one or two other corps;
and then, still afterwards, a good part of Sherman's immense
army, brought up from Charleston, Savannah, &c.

Western Soldiers

May 26-7.—The streets, the public buildings and grounds of
Washington, still swarm with soldiers from Illinois, Indiana,
Ohio, Missouri, Iowa, and all the Western States. I am continually meeting and talking with them. They often speak to
me first, and always show great sociability, and glad to have
a good interchange of chat. These Western soldiers are more
slow in their movements, and in their intellectual quality also;
have no extreme alertness. They are larger in size, have a
more serious physiognomy, are continually looking at you as
they pass in the street. They are largely animal, and hand-
somely so. During the war I have been at times with the
Fourteenth, Fifteenth, Seventeenth, and Twentieth Corps. I
always feel drawn toward the men, and like their personal
contact when we are crowded close together, as frequently
these days in the street-cars. They all think the world of
General Sherman; call him "old Bill," or sometimes "uncle
Billy."

A Soldier on Lincoln

May 28.—As I sat by the bedside of a sick Michigan soldier
in hospital to-day, a convalescent from the adjoining bed rose
and came to me, and presently we began talking. He was a
middle-aged man, belonged to the 2d Virginia regiment, but
lived in Racine, Ohio, and had a family there. He spoke of

President Lincoln, and said: "The war is over, and many are lost. And now we have lost the best, the fairest, the truest man in America. Take him altogether, he was the best man this country ever produced. It was quite a while I thought very different; but some time before the murder, that's the way I have seen it." There was deep earnestness in the soldier. (I found upon further talk he had known Mr. Lincoln personally, and quite closely, years before.) He was a veteran; was now in the fifth year of his service; was a cavalry man, and had been in a good deal of hard fighting.

Two Brothers, One South, One North

May 28–9.—I staid to-night a long time by the bedside of a new patient, a young Baltimorean, aged about 19 years, W. S. P., (2d Maryland, southern,) very feeble, right leg amputated, can't sleep hardly at all—has taken a great deal of morphine, which, as usual, is costing more than it comes to. Evidently very intelligent and well bred—very affectionate— held on to my hand, and put it by his face, not willing to let me leave. As I was lingering, soothing him in his pain, he says to me suddenly, "I hardly think you know who I am—I don't wish to impose upon you—I am a rebel soldier." I said I did not know that, but it made no difference. Visiting him daily for about two weeks after that, while he lived, (death had mark'd him, and he was quite alone,) I loved him much, always kiss'd him, and he did me. In an adjoining ward I found his brother, an officer of rank, a Union soldier, a brave and religious man, (Col. Clifton K. Prentiss, sixth Maryland infantry, Sixth corps, wounded in one of the engagements at Petersburgh, April 2—linger'd, suffer'd much, died in Brooklyn, Aug. 20, '65.) It was in the same battle both were hit. One was a strong Unionist, the other Secesh; both fought on their respective sides, both badly wounded, and both brought together here after a separation of four years. Each died for his cause.

Some Sad Cases Yet

May 31.—James H. Williams, aged 21, 3d Virginia cavalry.—
About as mark'd a case of a strong man brought low by a
complication of diseases, (laryngitis, fever, debility and diarrhœa,) as I have ever seen—has superb physique, remains
swarthy yet, and flushed and red with fever—is altogether
flighty—flesh of his great breast and arms tremulous, and
pulse pounding away with treble quickness—lies a good deal
of the time in a partial sleep, but with low muttering and groans
—a sleep in which there is no rest. Powerful as he is, and so
young, he will not be able to stand many more days of the
strain and sapping heat of yesterday and to-day. His throat
is in a bad way, tongue and lips parch'd. When I ask him
how he feels, he is able just to articulate, "I feel pretty bad
yet, old man," and looks at me with his great bright eyes.
Father, John Williams, Millensport, Ohio.

June 9-10.—I have been sitting late to-night by the bedside
of a wounded captain, a special friend of mine, lying with a
painful fracture of left leg in one of the hospitals, in a large
ward partially vacant. The lights were put out, all but a little
candle, far from where I sat. The full moon shone in through
the windows, making long, slanting silvery patches on the floor.
All was still, my friend too was silent, but could not sleep; so
I sat there by him, slowly wafting the fan, and occupied with
the musings that arose out of the scene, the long shadowy
ward, the beautiful ghostly moonlight on the floor, the white
beds, here and there an occupant with huddled form, the bedclothes thrown off. The hospitals have a number of cases of
sun-stroke and exhaustion by heat, from the late reviews. There
are many such from the Sixth corps, from the hot parade of
day before yesterday. (Some of these shows cost the lives of
scores of men.)

Sunday, Sep. 10.—Visited Douglas and Stanton hospitals.
They are quite full. Many of the cases are bad ones. lingering
wounds, and old sickness. There is a more than usual look of
despair on the countenances of many of the men; hope has
left them. I went through the wards, talking as usual. There

are several here from the confederate army whom I had seen in other hospitals, and they recognized me. Two were in a dying condition.

Calhoun's Real Monument

In one of the hospital tents for special cases, as I sat to-day tending a new amputation, I heard a couple of neighboring soldiers talking to each other from their cots. One down with fever, but improving, had come up belated from Charleston not long before. The other was what we now call an "old veteran," (*i.e.*, he was a Connecticut youth, probably of less than the age of twenty-five years, the four last of which he had spent in active service in the war in all parts of the country.) The two were chatting of one thing and another. The fever soldier spoke of John C. Calhoun's monument, which he had seen, and was describing it. The veteran said: "I have seen Calhoun's monument. That you saw is not the real monument. But I have seen it. It is the desolated, ruined south; nearly the whole generation of young men between seventeen and thirty destroyed or maim'd; all the old families used up— the rich impoverish'd, the plantations cover'd with weeds, the slaves unloos'd and become the masters, and the name of southerner blacken'd with every shame—all that is Calhoun's real monument."

Hospitals Closing

October 3.—There are two army hospitals now remaining. I went to the largest of these (Douglas) and spent the afternoon and evening. There are many sad cases, old wounds, incurable sickness, and some of the wounded from the March and April battles before Richmond. Few realize how sharp and bloody those closing battles were. Our men exposed themselves more than usual; press'd ahead without urging. Then the southerners fought with extra desperation. Both sides knew that with the successful chasing of the rebel cabal from Richmond, and the occupation of that city by the national troops, the game was up. The dead and wounded were unusually many. Of the wounded the last lingering driblets have been brought to hospital here. I find many rebel wounded here, and have been extra busy to-day 'tending to the worst cases of them with the rest.

Oct., Nov. and Dec., '65—Sundays.—Every Sunday of these months visited Harewood hospital out in the woods, pleasant and recluse, some two and a half or three miles north of the capitol. The situation is healthy, with broken ground, grassy slopes and patches of oak woods, the trees large and fine. It was one of the most extensive of the hospitals, now reduced to four or five partially occupied wards, the numerous others being vacant. In November, this became the last military hospital kept up by the government, all the others being closed. Cases of the worst and most incurable wounds, obstinate illness, and of poor fellows who have no homes to go to, are found here.

Dec. 10—Sunday.—Again spending a good part of the day at Harewood. I write this about an hour before sundown. I have walk'd out for a few minutes to the edge of the woods to soothe myself with the hour and scene. It is a glorious, warm, golden-sunny, still afternoon. The only noise is from a crowd of cawing crows, on some trees three hundred yards distant. Clusters of gnats swimming and dancing in the air in all directions. The oak leaves are thick under the bare trees, and give a strong and delicious perfume. Inside the wards everything is gloomy. Death is there. As I enter'd, I was confronted by it the first thing; a corpse of a poor soldier, just dead, of typhoid fever. The attendants had just straighten'd the limbs, put coppers on the eyes, and were laying it out.

The roads.—A great recreation, the past three years, has been in taking long walks out from Washington, five, seven, perhaps ten miles and back; generally with my friend Peter Doyle, who is as fond of it as I am. Fine moonlight nights, over the perfect military roads, hard and smooth—or Sundays —we had these delightful walks, never to be forgotten. The roads connecting Washington and the numerous forts around the city, made one useful result, at any rate, out of the war.

Typical Soldiers

Even the typical soldiers I have been personally intimate with,
—it seems to me if I were to make a list of them it would
be like a city directory. Some few only have I mention'd in
the foregoing pages—most are dead—a few yet living. There
is Reuben Farwell, of Michigan, (little 'Mitch;') Benton
H. Wilson, color-bearer, 185th New York; Wm. Stansberry;
Manvill Winterstein, Ohio; Bethuel Smith; Capt. Simms, of
51st New York, (kill'd at Petersburgh mine explosion,)
Capt. Sam. Pooley and Lieut. Fred. McReady, same reg't.
Also, same reg't., my brother, George W. Whitman—in active
service all through, four years, re-enlisting twice—was pro-
moted, step by step, (several times immediately after battles,)
lieutenant, captain, major and lieut. colonel—was in the actions
at Roanoke, Newbern, 2d Bull Run, Chantilly, South Mountain, Antietam, Fredericksburgh, Vicksburgh, Jackson, the
bloody conflicts of the Wilderness, and at Spottsylvania, Cold
Harbor, and afterwards around Petersburgh; at one of these
latter was taken prisoner, and pass'd four or five months in
secesh military prisons, narrowly escaping with life, from a
severe fever, from starvation and half-nakedness in the winter.
(What a history that 51st New York had! Went out early—
march'd, fought everywhere—was in storms at sea, nearly
wreck'd—storm'd forts—tramp'd hither and yon in Virginia,
night and day, summer of '62—afterwards Kentucky and Mississippi—re-enlisted—was in all the engagements and campaigns, as above.) I strengthen and comfort myself much with
the certainty that the capacity for just such regiments, (hundreds, thousands of them) is inexhaustible in the United States,
and that there isn't a county nor a township in the republic
—nor a street in any city—but could turn out, and, on occasion,
would turn out, lots of just such typical soldiers, whenever
wanted.

"Convulsiveness"

As I have look'd over the proof-sheets of the preceding pages, I have once or twice fear'd that my diary would prove, at best, but a batch of convulsively written reminiscences. Well, be it so. They are but parts of the actual distraction, heat, smoke and excitement of those times. The war itself, with the temper of society preceding it, can indeed be best described by that very word *convulsiveness*.

Three Years Summ'd Up

During those three years in hospital, camp or field, I made over six hundred visits or tours, and went, as I estimate, counting all, among from eighty thousand to a hundred thousand of the wounded and sick, as sustainer of spirit and body in some degree, in time of need. These visits varied from an hour or two, to all day or night; for with dear or critical cases I generally watch'd all night. Sometimes I took up my quarters in the hospital, and slept or watch'd there several nights in succession. Those three years I consider the greatest privilege and satisfaction, (with all their feverish excitements and physical deprivations and lamentable sights,) and, of course, the most profound lesson of my life. I can say that in my ministerings I comprehended all, whoever came in my way, northern or southern, and slighted none. It arous'd and brought out and decided undream'd-of depths of emotion. It has given me my most fervent views of the true *ensemble* and extent of the States. While I was with wounded and sick in thousands of cases from the New England States, and from New York, New Jersey, and Pennsylvania, and from Michigan, Wisconsin, Ohio, Indiana, Illinois, and all the Western States, I was with more or less from all the States, North and South, without exception. I was with many from the border States, especially from Maryland and Virginia, and found, during those lurid years 1862–63, far more Union southerners, especially Tennesseans, than is supposed. I was with many rebel officers and men among our wounded, and gave them always what I had, and tried to cheer them the same as any. I was among the army teamsters considerably, and, indeed, always found myself drawn to them. Among the black soldiers, wounded or sick, and in the contraband camps, I also took my way whenever in their neighborhood, and did what I could for them.

The Million Dead, Too, Summ'd Up

The dead in this war—there they lie, strewing the fields and woods and valleys and battle-fields of the south—Virginia, the Peninsula—Malvern hill and Fair Oaks—the banks of the Chickahominy—the terraces of Fredericksburgh—Antietam bridge—the grisly ravines of Manassas—the bloody promenade of the Wilderness—the varieties of the *strayed* dead, (the estimate of the War department is 25,000 national soldiers kill'd in battle and never buried at all, 5,000 drown'd—15,000 inhumed by strangers, or on the march in haste, in hitherto unfound localities—2,000 graves cover'd by sand and mud by Mississippi freshets, 3,000 carried away by caving-in of banks, &c.,)—Gettysburgh, the West, Southwest—Vicksburgh —Chattanooga—the trenches of Petersburgh—the numberless battles, camps, hospitals everywhere—the crop reap'd by the mighty reapers, typhoid, dysentery, inflammations—and blackest and loathesomest of all, the dead and living burial-pits, the prison-pens of Andersonville, Salisbury, Belle-Isle, &c., (not Dante's pictured hell and all its woes, its degradations, filthy torments, excell'd those prisons)—the dead, the dead, the dead—*our* dead—or South or North, ours all, (all, all, all, finally dear to me)—or East or West—Atlantic coast or Mississippi valley—somewhere they crawl'd to die, alone, in bushes, low gullies, or on the sides of hills—(there, in secluded spots, their skeletons, bleach'd bones, tufts of hair, buttons, fragments of clothing, are occasionally found yet)— our young men once so handsome and so joyous, taken from us—the son from the mother, the husband from the wife, the dear friend from the dear friend—the clusters of camp graves, in Georgia, the Carolinas, and in Tennessee—the single graves left in the woods or by the road-side, (hundreds, thousands, obliterated)—the corpses floated down the rivers, and caught and lodged, (dozens, scores, floated down the upper Potomac, after the cavalry engagements, the pursuit of Lee, following Gettysburgh)—some lie at the bottom of the sea—the general million, and the special cemeteries in almost all the States—the infinite dead—(the land entire saturated, perfumed with their impalpable ashes' exhalation in Nature's chemistry distill'd, and shall be so forever, in every future grain of wheat and ear of corn, and every flower that grows, and every breath we draw)—not only Northern dead leavening Southern soil—thousands, aye tens of thousands, of Southerners, crumble to-day in Northern earth.

And everywhere among these countless graves—everywhere in the many soldiers Cemeteries of the Nation, (there are now, I believe, over seventy of them)—as at the time in the vast trenches, the depositories of slain, Northern and Southern, after the great battles—not only where the scathing trail passed those years, but radiating since in all the peaceful quarters of the land—we see, and ages yet may see, on monuments and gravestones, singly or in masses, to thousands or tens of thousands, the significant word UNKNOWN.

(In some of the cemeteries nearly *all* the dead are unknown. At Salisbury, N. C., for instance, the known are only 85, while the unknown are 12,027, and 11,700 of these are buried in trenches. A national monument has been put up here, by order of Congress, to mark the spot—but what visible, material monument can ever fittingly commemorate that spot?)

The Real War Will Never Get in the Books

And so good-bye to the war. I know not how it may have been, or may be, to others—to me the main interest I found, (and still, on recollection, find,) in the rank and file of the armies, both sides, and in those specimens amid the hospitals, and even the dead on the field. To me the points illustrating the latent personal character and eligibilities of these States, in the two or three millions of American young and middle-aged men, North and South, embodied in those armies—and especially the one-third or one-fourth of their number, stricken by wounds or disease at some time in the course of the contest —were of more significance even than the political interests involved. (As so much of a race depends on how it faces death, and how it stands personal anguish and sickness. As, in the glints of emotions under emergencies, and the indirect traits and asides in Plutarch, we get far profounder clues to the antique world than all its more formal history.)

Future years will never know the seething hell and the black infernal background of countless minor scenes and interiors, (not the official surface-courteousness of the Generals, not the few great battles of the Secession war; and it is best they should not—the real war will never get in the books. In the mushy influences of current times, too, the fervid atmosphere and typical events of those years are in danger of being totally forgotten. I have at night watch'd by the side of a sick man in the hospital, one who could not live many hours. I have seen his eyes flash and burn as he raised himself and recurr'd to the cruelties on his surrender'd brother, and mutilations of the corpse afterward. (See, in the preceding pages, the incident at Upperville—the seventeen kill'd as in the description, were left there on the ground. After they dropt dead, no one touch'd them—all were made sure of, however. The carcasses were left for the citizens to bury or not, as they chose.)

Such was the war. It was not a quadrille in a ball-room. Its interior history will not only never be written—its practicality, minutiæ of deeds and passions, will never be even suggested. The actual soldier of 1862-'65, North and South, with all his ways, his incredible dauntlessness, habits, practices, tastes, language, his fierce friendship, his appetite, rankness, his superb strength and animality, lawless gait, and a hundred unnamed lights and shades of camp, I say, will never be written—perhaps must not and should not be.

The preceding notes may furnish a few stray glimpses into that life, and into those lurid interiors, never to be fully convey'd to the future. The hospital part of the drama from '61 to

'65, deserves indeed to be recorded. Of that many-threaded drama, with its sudden and strange surprises, its confounding of prophecies, its moments of despair, the dread of foreign interference, the interminable campaigns, the bloody battles, the mighty and cumbrous and green armies, the drafts and bounties —the immense money expenditure, like a heavy-pouring constant rain—with, over the whole land, the last three years of the struggle, an unending, universal mourning-wail of women, parents, orphans—the marrow of the tragedy concentrated in those Army Hospitals—(it seem'd sometimes as if the whole interest of the land, North and South, was one vast central hospital, and all the rest of the affair but flanges)—those forming the untold and unwritten history of the war—infinitely greater (like life's) than the few scraps and distortions that are ever told or written. Think how much, and of importance, will be—how much, civic and military, has already been—buried in the grave, in eternal darkness.

An Interregnum Paragraph

Several years now elapse before I resume my diary. I continued at Washington working in the Attorney-General's department through '66 and '67, and some time afterward. In February '73 I was stricken down by paralysis, gave up my desk, and migrated to Camden, New Jersey, where I lived during '74 and '75, quite unwell—but after that began to grow better; commenc'd going for weeks at a time, even for months, down in the country, to a charmingly recluse and rural spot along Timber creek, twelve or thirteen miles from where it enters the Delaware river. Domicil'd at the farm-house of my friends, the Staffords, near by, I lived half the time along this creek and its adjacent fields and lanes. And it is to my life here that I, perhaps, owe partial recovery (a sort of second wind, or semi-renewal of the lease of life) from the prostration of 1874-'75. If the notes of that outdoor life could only prove as glowing to you, reader dear, as the experience itself was to me. Doubtless in the course of the following, the fact of invalidism will crop out, (I call myself a *half-Paralytic* these days, and reverently bless the Lord it is no worse,) between some of the lines —but I get my share of fun and healthy hours, and shall try to indicate them. (The trick is, I find, to tone your wants and tastes low down enough, and make much of negatives, and of mere daylight and the skies.)

New Themes Entered Upon

1876, '77.—I find the woods in mid-May and early June my best places for composition.[9] Seated on logs or stumps there, or resting on rails, nearly all the following memoranda have been jotted down. Wherever I go, indeed, winter or summer city or country, alone at home or traveling, I must take notes —(the ruling passion strong in age and disablement, and even the approach of—but I must not say it yet.) Then underneath the following excerpta—crossing the *t's* and dotting the *i's* of certain moderate movements of late years—I am fain to fancy the foundations of quite a lesson learn'd. After you have exhausted what there is in business, politics, conviviality, love, and so on—have found that none of these finally satisfy, or permanently wear—what remains? Nature remains; to bring out from their torpid recesses, the affinities of a man or woman with the open air, the trees, fields, the changes of seasons—the sun by day and the stars of heaven by night. We will begin from these convictions. Literature flies so high and is so hotly spiced, that our notes may seem hardly more than breaths of common air, or draughts of water to drink. But that is part of our lesson.

[9]Without apology for the abrupt change of field and atmosphere— after what I have put in the preceding fifty or sixty pages—temporary episodes, thank heaven!—I restore my book to the bracing and buoyant equilibrium of concrete outdoor Nature, the only permanent reliance for sanity of book or human life.

Who knows, (I have it in my fancy, my ambition,) but the pages now ensuing may carry ray of sun, or smell of grass or corn, or call of bird, or gleam of stars by night, or snow-flakes falling fresh and mystic, to denizen of heated city house, or tired workman or work-woman?—or may-be in sick-room or prison—to serve as cooling breeze, or Nature's aroma, to some fever'd mouth or latent pulse.

Dear, soothing, healthy, restoration-hours—after three confining years of paralysis—after the long strain of the war, and its wounds and death.

Entering a Long Farm-Lane

As every man has his hobby-liking, mine is for a real farm-lane fenced by old chestnut-rails gray-green with dabs of moss and lichen, copious weeds and briers growing in spots athwart the heaps of stray-pick'd stones at the fence bases—irregular paths worn between, and horse and cow tracks—all characteristic accompaniments marking and scenting the neighborhood in their seasons—apple-tree blossoms in forward April—pigs, poultry, a field of August buckwheat, and in another the long flapping tassels of maize—and so to the pond, the expansion of the creek, the secluded-beautiful, with young and old trees, and such recesses and vistas.

To the Spring and Brook

So, still sauntering on, to the spring under the willows—musical as soft clinking glasses—pouring a sizeable stream, thick as my neck, pure and clear, out from its vent where the bank arches over like a great brown shaggy eyebrow or mouth-roof—gurgling, gurgling ceaselessly—meaning, saying something, of course (if one could only translate it)—always gurgling there, the whole year through—never giving out—oceans of mint, blackberries in summer—choice of light and shade—just the place for my July sun-baths and water-baths too—but mainly the inimitable soft sound-gurgles of it, as I sit there hot afternoon. How they and all grow into me, day after day—everything in keeping—the wild, just-palpable perfume, and the dapple of leaf-shadows, and all the natural-medicinal, elemental-moral influences of the spot.

Babble on, O brook, with that utterance of thine! I too

will express what I have gather'd in my days and progress, native, subterranean, past—and now thee. Spin and wind thy way—I with thee, a little while, at any rate. As I haunt thee so often, season by season, thou knowest reckest not me, (yet why be so certain? who can tell?)—but I will learn from thee, and dwell on thee—receive, copy, print from thee.

An Early Summer Reveille

Away then to loosen, to unstring the divine bow, so tense, so long. Away, from curtain, carpet, sofa, book—from "society" —from city house, street, and modern improvements and luxuries—away to the primitive winding, aforementioned wooded creek, with its untrimm'd bushes and turfy banks—away from ligatures, tight boots, buttons, and the whole cast-iron civilized life—from entourage of artificial store, machine, studio, office, parlor—from tailordom and fashion's clothes—from any clothes, perhaps, for the nonce, the summer heats advancing, there in those watery, shaded solitudes. Away, thou soul, (let me pick thee out singly, reader dear, and talk in perfect freedom, negligently, confidentially,) for one day and night at least, returning to the naked source-life of us all—to the breast of the great silent savage all-acceptive Mother. Alas! how many of us are so sodden—how many have wander'd so far away, that return is almost impossible.

But to my jottings, taking them as they come, from the heap, without particular selection. There is little consecutiveness in dates. They run any time within nearly five or six years. Each was carelessly pencilled in the open air, at the time and place. The printers will learn this to some vexation perhaps, as much of their copy is from those hastily-written first notes.

Birds Migrating at Midnight

Did you ever chance to hear the midnight flight of birds passing through the air and darkness overhead, in countless armies, changing their early or late summer habitat? It is something not to be forgotten. A friend called me up just after 12 last night to mark the peculiar noise of unusually immense flocks migrating north (rather late this year.) In the silence, shadow and delicious odor of the hour, (the natural perfume belonging to the night alone,) I thought it rare music. You could *hear* the characteristic motion—once or twice "the rush of mighty wings," but oftener a velvety rustle, long drawn out—sometimes quite near—with continual calls and chirps, and some song-notes. It all lasted from 12 till after 3. Once in a while the species was plainly distinguishable; I could make out the bobolink, tanager, Wilson's thrush, white-crown'd sparrow, and occasionally from high in the air came the notes of the plover.

Bumble-Bees

May-month—month of swarming, singing, mating birds—the bumble-bee month—month of the flowering lilac—(and then my own birth-month.) As I jot this paragraph, I am out just after sunrise, and down towards the creek. The lights, perfumes, melodies—the blue birds, grass birds and robins, in every direction—the noisy, vocal, natural concert. For undertones, a neighboring wood-pecker tapping his tree, and the distant clarion of chanticleer. Then the fresh earth smells—the colors, the delicate drabs and thin blues of the perspective. The bright green of the grass has receiv'd an added tinge from the last two days' mildness and moisture. How the sun silently mounts in the broad clear sky, on his day's journey! How the warm beams bathe all, and come streaming kissingly and almost hot on my face.

A while since the croaking of the pond-frogs and the first white of the dog-wood blossoms. Now the golden dandelions in endless profusion, spotting the ground everywhere. The white cherry and pear-blows—the wild violets, with their blue eyes looking up and saluting my feet, as I saunter the wood-edge—the rosy blush of budding apple-trees—the light-clear emerald hue of the wheat-fields—the darker green of the rye

—a warm elasticity pervading the air—the cedar-bushes pro-
fusely deck'd with their little brown apples—the summer fully
awakening—the convocation of black birds, garrulous flocks of
them, gathering on some tree, and making the hour and place
noisy as I sit near.

Later.—Nature marches in procession, in sections, like the
corps of an army. All have done much for me, and still do. But
for the last two days it has been the great wild bee, the humble-
bee, or "bumble," as the children call him. As I walk, or
hobble, from the farm-house down to the creek, I traverse the
before-mention'd lane, fenced by old rails, with many splits,
splinters, breaks, holes, &c., the choice habitat of those croon-
ing, hairy insects. Up and down and by and between these rails,
they swarm and dart and fly in countless myriads. As I wend
slowly along, I am often accompanied with a moving cloud of
them. They play a leading part in my morning, midday or
sunset rambles, and often dominate the landscape in a way I
never before thought of—fill the long lane, not by scores or
hundreds only, but by thousands. Large and vivacious and
swift, with wonderful momentum and a loud swelling perpetual hum, varied now and then by something almost like a
shriek, they dart to and fro, in rapid flashes, chasing each other,
and (little things as they are,) conveying to me a new and
pronounc'd sense of strength, beauty, vitality and movement.
Are they in their mating season? or what is the meaning of this
plenitude, swiftness, eagerness, display? As I walk'd, I thought
I was follow'd by a particular swarm, but upon observation I
saw that it was a rapid succession of changing swarms, one
after another.

As I write, I am seated under a big wild-cherry tree—the
warm day temper'd by partial clouds and a fresh breeze, neither
too heavy nor light—and here I sit long and long, envelop'd in
the deep musical drone of these bees, flitting, balancing, darting
to and fro about me by hundreds—big fellows with light yellow
jackets, great glistening swelling bodies, stumpy heads and
gauzy wings—humming their perpetual rich mellow boom.
(Is there not a hint in it for a musical composition, of which
it should be the back-ground? some bumble-bee symphony?)
How it all nourishes, lulls me, in the way most needed; the open

air, the rye-fields, the apple orchards. The last two days have been faultless in sun, breeze, temperature and everything; never two more perfect days, and I have enjoy'd them wonderfully. My health is somewhat better, and my spirit at peace. (Yet the anniversary of the saddest loss and sorrow of my life is close at hand.)

Another jotting, another perfect day: forenoon, from 7 to 9, two hours envelop'd in sound of bumble-bees and bird-music. Down in the apple-trees and in a neighboring cedar were three or four russet-back'd thrushes, each singing his best, and roulading in ways I never heard surpass'd. Two hours I abandon myself to hearing them, and indolently absorbing the scene. Almost every bird I notice has a special time in the year— sometimes limited to a few days—when it sings its best; and now is the period of these russet-backs. Meanwhile, up and down the lane, the darting, droning, musical bumble-bees. A great swarm again for my entourage as I return home, moving along with me as before.

As I write this, two or three weeks later, I am sitting near the brook under a tulip tree, 70 feet high, thick with the fresh verdure of its young maturity—a beautiful object—every branch, every leaf perfect. From top to bottom, seeking the sweet juice in the blossoms, it swarms with myriads of these wild bees, whose loud and steady humming makes an undertone to the whole, and to my mood and the hour. All of which I will bring to a close by extracting the following verses from Henry A. Beers's little volume:

"As I lay yonder in tall grass
A drunken bumble-bee went past
Delirious with honey toddy.
The golden sash about his body
Scarce kept it in his swollen belly
Distent with honeysuckle jelly.
Rose liquor and the sweet-pea wine
Had fill'd his soul with song divine;
Deep had he drunk the warm night through,
His hairy thighs were wet with dew.
Full many an antic he had play'd
While the world went round through sleep and shade.

Oft had he lit with thirsty lip
Some flower-cup's nectar'd sweets to sip,
When on smooth petals he would slip,
Or over tangled stamens trip,
And headlong in the pollen roll'd,
Crawl out quite dusted o'er with gold;
Or else his heavy feet would stumble
Against some bud, and down he'd tumble
Amongst the grass; there lie and grumble
In low, soft bass—poor maudlin bumble!"

Cedar-Apples

As I journey'd to-day in a light wagon ten or twelve miles
through the country, nothing pleas'd me more, in their homely
beauty and novelty (I had either never seen the little things to
such advantage, or had never noticed them before) than that
peculiar fruit, with its profuse clear-yellow dangles of inch-long
silk or yarn, in boundless profusion spotting the dark-green
cedar bushes—contrasting well with their bronze tufts—the
flossy shreds covering the knobs all over, like a shock of wild
hair on elfin pates. On my ramble afterward down by the creek
I pluck'd one from its bush, and shall keep it. These cedar-
apples last only a little while however, and soon crumble
and fade.

Summer Sights and Indolences

June 10th.—As I write, 5½P.M., here by the creek, nothing can
exceed the quiet splendor and freshness around me. We had a
heavy shower, with brief thunder and lightning, in the middle
of the day; and since, overhead, one of those not uncommon yet
indescribable skies (in quality, not details or forms) of limpid
blue, with rolling silver-fringed clouds, and a pure-dazzling
sun. For underlay, trees in fulness of tender foliage—liquid,
reedy, long-drawn notes of birds—based by the fretful mewing

of a querulous cat-bird, and the pleasant chippering-shriek of two kingfishers. I have been watching the latter the last half hour, on their regular evening frolic over and in the stream; evidently a spree of the liveliest kind. They pursue each other, whirling and wheeling around, with many a jocund downward dip, splashing the spray in jets of diamonds—and then off they swoop, with slanting wings and graceful flight, sometimes so near me I can plainly see their dark-gray feather-bodies and milk-white necks.

Sundown Perfume—Quail-Notes— the Hermit-Thrush

June 19th, 4 to 6½, P.M.—Sitting alone by the creek—solitude here, but the scene bright and vivid enough—the sun shining, and quite a fresh wind blowing (some heavy showers last night,) the grass and trees looking their best—the clare-obscure of different greens, shadows, half-shadows, and the dappling glimpses of the water, through recesses—the wild flageolet-note of a quail near by—the just-heard fretting of some hylas down there in the pond—crows cawing in the distance—a drove of young hogs rooting in soft ground near the oak under which I sit—some come sniffing near me, and then scamper away, with grunts. And still the clear notes of the quail—the quiver of leaf-shadows over the paper as I write—the sky aloft, with white clouds, and the sun well declining to the west—the swift darting of many sand-swallows coming and going, their holes in a neighboring marl-bank—the odor of the cedar and oak, so palpable, as evening approaches—perfume, color, the bronze-and-gold of nearly ripen'd wheat—clover-fields, with honey-scent—the well-up maize, with long rustling leaves—the great patches of thriving potatoes, dusky green, fleck'd all over with white blossoms—the old, warty, venerable oak above me—and ever, mix'd with the dual notes of the quail, the soughing of the wind through some near-by pines.

As I rise for return, I linger long to a delicious song-epilogue (is it the hermit-thrush?) from some bushy recess off there in the swamp, repeated leisurely and pensively over and over again. This, to the circle-gambols of the swallows flying by dozens in concentric rings in the last rays of sunset, like flashes of some airy wheel.

A July Afternoon by the Pond

The fervent heat, but so much more endurable in this pure air —the white and pink pond-blossoms, with great heart-shaped leaves; the glassy waters of the creek, the banks, with dense bushery, and the picturesque beeches and shade and turf; the tremulous, reedy call of some bird from recesses, breaking the warm, indolent, half-voluptuous silence; an occasional wasp, hornet, honey-bee or bumble (they hover near my hands or face, yet annoy me not, nor I them, as they appear to examine, find nothing, and away they go)—the vast space of the sky overhead so clear, and the buzzard up there sailing his slow whirl in majestic spirals and discs; just over the surface of the pond, two large slate-color'd dragon-flies, with wings of lace, circling and darting and occasionally balancing themselves quite still, their wings quivering all the time, (are they not showing off for my amusement?)—the pond itself, with the sword-shaped calamus; the water snakes—occasionally a flitting blackbird, with red dabs on his shoulders, as he darts slantingly by—the sounds that bring out the solitude, warmth, light and shade—the quawk of some pond duck—(the crickets and grasshoppers are mute in the noon heat, but I hear the song of the first cicadas;)—then at some distance the rattle and whirr of a reaping machine as the horses draw it on a rapid walk through a rye field on the opposite side of the creek—(what was the yellow or light-brown bird, large as a young hen, with short neck and long-stretch'd legs I just saw, in flapping and awkward flight over there through the trees?) the prevailing delicate, yet palpable, spicy, grassy, clovery perfume to my nostrils; and over all, encircling all, to my sight and soul, the free space of the sky, transparent and blue—and hovering there in the west, a mass of white-gray fleecy clouds the sailors call "shoals of mackerel"—the sky, with silver swirls like locks of toss'd hair, spreading, expanding —a vast voiceless, formless simulacrum—yet may-be the most real reality and formulator of everything—who knows?

Locusts and Katydids

Aug. 22.—Reedy monotones of locust, or sounds of katydid— I hear the latter at night, and the other both day and night. I thought the morning and evening warble of birds delightful; but I find I can listen to these strange insects with just as much pleasure. A single locust is now heard near noon from a tree two hundred feet off, as I write—a long whirring, continued, quite loud noise graded in distinct whirls, or swinging circles, increasing in strength and rapidity up to a certain point, and then a fluttering, quietly tapering fall. Each strain is continued from one to two minutes. The locust-song is very appropriate to the scene—gushes, has meaning, is masculine, is like some fine old wine, not sweet, but far better than sweet.

But the katydid—how shall I describe its piquant utterances? One sings from a willow-tree just outside my open bedroom window, twenty yards distant; every clear night for a fortnight past has sooth'd me to sleep. I rode through a piece of woods for a hundred rods the other evening, and heard the katydids by myriads—very curious for once; but I like better my single neighbor on the tree.

Let me say more about the song of the locust, even to repetition; a long, chromatic, tremulous crescendo, like a brass disk whirling round and round, emitting wave after wave of notes, beginning with a certain moderate beat or measure, rapidly increasing in speed and emphasis, reaching a point of great energy and significance, and then quickly and gracefully dropping down and out. Not the melody of the singing-bird—far from it; the common musician might think without melody, but surely having to the finer ear a harmony of its own; monotonous—but what a swing there is in that brassy drone, round and round, cymbal-line—or like the whirling of brass quoits.

The Lesson of a Tree

Sept. 1.—I should not take either the biggest or the most picturesque tree to illustrate it. Here is one of my favorites now before me, a fine yellow poplar, quite straight, perhaps 90 feet high, and four thick at the butt. How strong, vital, enduring! how dumbly eloquent! What suggestions of imperturbability and *being*, as against the human trait of mere *seeming*. Then the qualities, almost emotional, palpably artistic, heroic, of a tree; so innocent and harmless, yet so savage. It *is*, yet says nothing. How it rebukes by its tough and equable serenity all weathers, this gusty-temper'd little whiffet, man, that runs indoors at a mite of rain or snow. Science (or rather half-way science) scoffs at reminiscence of dryad and hamadryad, and of trees speaking. But, if they don't, they do as well as most speaking, writing, poetry, sermons—or rather they do a great deal better. I should say indeed that those old dryad-reminiscences are quite as true as any, and profounder than most reminiscences we get. ("Cut this out," as the quack mediciners say, and keep by you.) Go and sit in a grove or woods, with one or more of those voiceless companions, and read the foregoing and think.

One lesson from affiliating a tree—perhaps the greatest moral lesson anyhow from earth, rocks, animals, is that same lesson of inherency, of *what is*, without the least regard to what the looker on (the critic) supposes or says, or whether he likes or dislikes. What worse—what more general malady pervades each and all of us, our literature, education, attitude toward each other, (even toward ourselves,) than a morbid trouble about *seems*, (generally temporarily seems too,) and no trouble at all, or hardly any, about the sane, slow-growing, perennial, real parts of character, books, friendship, marriage—humanity's invisible foundations and hold-together? (As the all-basis, the nerve, the great-sympathetic, the plenum within humanity, giving stamp to everything, is necessarily invisible.)

Aug. 4, 6 P.M.—Lights and shades and rare effects on tree-foliage and grass—transparent greens, grays, &c., all in sunset pomp and dazzle. The clear beams are now thrown in many new places, on the quilted, seam'd, bronze-drab, lower-trunks, shadow'd except at this hour—now flooding their young and old columnar ruggedness with strong light, unfolding to my sense new amazing features of silent, shaggy charm, the solid bark, the expression of harmless impassiveness, with many a bulge and gnarl unreck'd before. In the revealings of such light, such exceptional hour, such mood, one does not wonder at the old story fables, (indeed, why fables?) of people falling into love-sickness with trees, seiz'd extatic with the mystic realism of the resistless silent strength in them—*strength,* which after all is perhaps the last, completest, highest beauty.

Trees I am familiar with here

Oaks, (many kinds—one sturdy old fellow, vital, green, bushy, five feet thick at the butt, I sit under every day.)

Cedars, plenty.

Tulip trees, (*Liriodendron,* is of the magnolia family—I have seen it in Michigan and southern Illinois, 140 feet high and 8 feet thick at the butt[10]; does not transplant well; best rais'd from seeds—the lumbermen call it yellow poplar.)

Sycamores.

Gum-trees, both sweet and sour.

Beeches.

Black-walnuts.

Sassafras.

Willows.

Catalpas.

Persimmons.

Mountain-ash.

Hickories.

Maples, many kinds.

Locusts.

Birches.

Dogwood.

Pine.

the Elm.

Chestnut.

Linden.

Aspen.

Spruce.

Hornbeam.

Laurel.

Holly.

[10]There is a tulip poplar within sight of Woodstown, which is twenty feet around, three feet from the ground, four feet across about eighteen feet up the trunk, which is broken off about three or four feet higher up. On the south side an arm has shot out from which rise two stems, each to about ninety-one or ninety-two feet from the ground. Twenty-five (or more) years since the cavity in the butt was large enough for, and nine men at one time, ate dinner therein. It is supposed twelve to fifteen men could now, at one time, stand within its trunk. The severe winds of 1877 and 1878 did not seem to

Autumn Side-Bits

Sept. 20.—Under an old black oak, glossy and green, exhaling aroma—amid a grove the Albic druids might have chosen—envelop'd in the warmth and light of the noonday sun, and swarms of flitting insects—with the harsh cawing of many crows a hundred rods away—here I sit in solitude, absorbing, enjoying all. The corn, stack'd in its cone-shaped stacks, russet-color'd and sere—a large field spotted thick with scarlet-gold pumpkins—an adjoining one of cabbages, showing well in their green and pearl, mottled by much light and shade—melon patches, with their bulging ovals, and great silver-streak'd, ruffled, broad-edged leaves—and many an autumn sight and sound beside—the distant scream of a flock of guinea-hens—and pour'd over all the September breeze, with pensive cadence through the tree tops.

Another Day.—The ground in all directions strew'd with *debris* from a storm. Timber creek, as I slowly pace its banks, has ebb'd low, and shows reaction from the turbulent swell of the late equinoctial. As I look around, I take account of stock—weeds and shrubs, knolls, paths, occasional stumps, some with smooth'd tops, (several I use as seats of rest, from place to place, and from one I am now jotting these lines,)—frequent wild-flowers, little white, star-shaped things, or the cardinal red of the lobelia, or the cherry-ball seeds of the perennial rose, or the many-threaded vines winding up and around trunks of trees.

Oct. 1, 2 and 3.—Down every day in the solitude of the creek. A serene autumn sun and westerly breeze to-day (3d) as I sit here, the water surface prettily moving in wind-ripples before me. On a stout old beech at the edge, decayed and slanting, almost fallen to the stream, yet with life and leaves in its mossy limbs, a gray squirrel, exploring, runs up and down, flirts his tail, leaps to the ground, sits on his haunches upright as he sees me, (a Darwinian hint?) and then races up the tree again.

---

damage it, and the two stems send out yearly many blossoms, scenting the air immediately about it with their sweet perfume. It is entirely unprotected by other trees, on a hill.—*Woodstown, N. J., "Register," April 15, '79.*

Oct. 4.—Cloudy and coolish; signs of incipient winter. Yet pleasant here, the leaves thick-falling, the ground brown with them already; rich coloring, yellows of all hues, pale and dark-green, shades from lightest to richest red—all set in and toned down by the prevailing brown of the earth and gray of the sky. So, winter is coming; and I yet in my sickness. I sit here amid all these fair sights and vital influences, and abandon myself to that thought, with its wandering trains of speculation.

The Sky—Days and Nights—Happiness

Oct. 20.—A clear, crispy day—dry and breezy air, full of oxygen. Out of the sane, silent, beauteous miracles that envelope and fuse me—trees, water, grass, sunlight, and early frost—the one I am looking at most to-day is the sky. It has that delicate, transparent blue, peculiar to autumn, and the only clouds are little or larger white ones, giving their still and spiritual motion to the great concave. All through the earlier day (say from 7 to 11) it keeps a pure, yet vivid blue. But as noon approaches the color gets lighter, quite gray for two or three hours—then still paler for a spell, till sun-down—which last I watch dazzling through the interstices of a knoll of big trees—darts of fire and a gorgeous show of light-yellow, liver-color and red, with a vast silver glaze askant on the water—the transparent shadows, shafts, sparkle, and vivid colors beyond all the paintings ever made.

I don't know what or how, but it seems to me mostly owing to these skies, (every now and then I think, while I have of course seen them every day of my life, I never really saw the skies before,) I have had this autumn some wondrously contented hours—may I not say perfectly happy ones? As I've read, Byron just before his death told a friend that he had known but three happy hours during his whole existence. Then there is the old German legend of the king's bell, to the same point. While I was out there by the wood, that beautiful sunset through the trees, I thought of Byron's and the bell story, and the notion started in me that I was having a happy hour. (Though perhaps my best moments I never jot down; when they come I cannot afford to break the charm by inditing memoranda. I just abandon myself to the mood, and let it float on, carrying me in its placid extasy.)

What is happiness, anyhow? Is this one of its hours, or the like of it?—so impalpable—a mere breath, an evanescent tinge? I am not sure—so let me give myself the benefit of the doubt. Hast Thou, pellucid, in Thy azure depths, medicine for case like mine? (Ah, the physical shatter and troubled spirit of me the last three years.) And dost Thou subtly mystically now drip it through the air invisibly upon me?

Night of Oct. 28.—The heavens unusually transparent—the stars out by myriads—the great path of the Milky Way, with its branch, only seen of very clear nights—Jupiter, setting in the west, looks like a huge hap-hazard splash, and has a little star for companion.

> Clothed in his white garments,
> Into the round and clear arena slowly entered the
> brahmin,
> Holding a little child by the hand,
> Like the moon with the planet Jupiter in a cloudless
> night-sky.
>
> Old Hindu Poem.

Early in November.—At its farther end the lane already described opens into a broad grassy upland field of over twenty acres, slightly sloping to the south. Here I am accustom'd to walk for sky views and effects, either morning or sundown. To-day from this field my soul is calm'd and expanded beyond description, the whole forenoon by the clear blue arching over all, cloudless, nothing particular, only sky and daylight. Their soothing accompaniments, autumn leaves, the cool dry air, the faint aroma—crows cawing in the distance—two great buzzards wheeling gracefully and slowly far up there—the occasional murmur of the wind, sometimes quite gently, then threatening through the trees—a gang of farm-laborers loading corn-stalks in a field in sight, and the patient horses waiting.

Colors—a Contrast

Such a play of colors and lights, different seasons, different hours of the day—the lines of the far horizon where the faint-tinged edge of the landscape loses itself in the sky. As I slowly hobble up the lane toward day-close, an incomparable sunset shooting in molten sapphire and gold, shaft after shaft, through the ranks of the long-leaved corn, between me and the west.

Another day.—The rich dark green of the tulip-trees and the oaks, the gray of the swamp-willows, the dull hues of the sycamores and black-walnuts, the emerald of the cedars (after rain,) and the light yellow of the beeches.

November 8, '76

The forenoon leaden and cloudy, not cold or wet, but indicating both. As I hobble down here and sit by the silent pond, how different from the excitement amid which, in the cities, millions of people are now waiting news of yesterday's Presidential election, or receiving and discussing the result—in this secluded place uncared-for, unknown.

Crows and Crows

Nov. 14.—As I sit here by the creek, resting after my walk, a warm languor bathes me from the sun. No sound but a cawing of crows, and no motion but their black flying figures from overhead, reflected in the mirror of the pond below. Indeed a principal feature of the scene to-day is these crows, their incessant cawing, far or near, and their countless flocks and processions moving from place to place, and at times almost darkening the air with their myriads. As I sit a moment writing this by the bank, I see the black, clear-cut reflection of them far below, flying through the watery looking-glass, by ones, twos, or long strings. All last night I heard the noises from their great roost in a neighboring wood.

A Winter Day on the Sea-Beach

One bright December mid-day lately I spent down on the New Jersey sea-shore, reaching it by a little more than an hour's railroad trip over the old Camden and Atlantic. I had started betimes, fortified by nice strong coffee and a good breakfast (cook'd by the hands I love, my dear sister Lou's—how much better it makes the victuals taste, and then assimilate, strengthen you, perhaps make the whole day comfortable afterwards.) Five or six miles at the last, our track enter'd a broad region of salt grass meadows, intersected by lagoons, and cut up everywhere by watery runs. The sedgy perfume, delightful to my nostrils, reminded me of "the mash" and south bay of my native island. I could have journey'd contentedly till night through these flat and odorous sea-prairies. From half-past 11 till 2 I was nearly all the time along the beach, or in sight of the ocean, listening to its hoarse murmur, and inhaling the bracing and welcome breezes. First, a rapid five-mile drive over the hard sand—our carriage wheels hardly made dents in it. Then after dinner (as there were nearly two hours to spare) I walk'd off in another direction, (hardly met or saw a person,) and taking possession of what appear'd to have been the reception-room of an old bath-house range, had a broad expanse of view all to myself—quaint, refreshing, unimpeded—a dry area of sedge and Indian grass immediately before and around me—space, simple, unornamented space. Distant vessels, and the far-off, just visible trailing smoke of an inward bound steamer; more plainly, ships, brigs, schooners, in sight, most of them with every sail set to the firm and steady wind.

The attractions, fascinations there are in sea and shore! How one dwells on their simplicity, even vacuity! What is it in us, arous'd by those indirections and directions? That spread of waves and gray-white beach, salt, monotonous, senseless—such an entire absence of art, books, talk, elegance—so indescribably

comforting, even this winter day—grim, yet so delicate-look-
ing, so spiritual—striking emotional, impalpable depths, subtler
than all the poems, paintings, music, I have ever read, seen,
heard. (Yet let me be fair, perhaps it is because I have read
those poems and heard that music.)

Sea-Shore Fancies

Even as a boy, I had the fancy, the wish, to write a piece, perhaps a poem, about the sea-shore—that suggesting, dividing
line, contact, junction, the solid marrying the liquid—that
curious, lurking something, (as doubtless every objective form
finally becomes to the subjective spirit,) which means far more
than its mere first sight, grand as that is—blending the real and
ideal, and each made portion of the other. Hours, days, in my
Long Island youth and early manhood, I haunted the shores
of Rockaway or Coney island, or away east to the Hamptons
or Montauk. Once, at the latter place, (by the old light-house,
nothing but sea-tossings in sight in every direction as far as the
eye could reach,) I remember well, I felt that I must one day
write a book expressing this liquid, mystic theme. Afterward,
I recollect, how it came to me that instead of any special lyrical
or epical or literary attempt, the sea-shore should be an invisible *influence*, a pervading gauge and tally for me, in my composition. (Let me give a hint here to young writers. I am not
sure but I have unwittingly follow'd out the same rule with
other powers besides sea and shores—avoiding them, in the
way of any dead set at poetizing them, as too big for formal
handling—quite satisfied if I could indirectly show that we
have met and fused, even if only once, but enough—that we
have really absorb'd each other and understand each other.)

There is a dream, a picture, that for years at intervals, (sometimes quite long ones, but surely again, in time,) has come
noiselessly up before me, and I really believe, fiction as it is, has
enter'd largely into my practical life—certainly into my writings, and shaped and color'd them. It is nothing more or less

than a stretch of interminable white-brown sand, hard and smooth and broad, with the ocean perpetually, grandly, rolling in upon it, with slow-measured sweep, with rustle and hiss and foam, and many a thump as of low bass drums. This scene, this picture, I say, has risen before me at times for years. Sometimes I wake at night and can hear and see it plainly.

In Memory of Thomas Paine

Spoken at Lincoln Hall, Philadelphia, Sunday, Jan. 28, '77, for 140th anniversary of T.P.'s birth-day

Some thirty-five years ago, in New York city, at Tammany hall, of which place I was then a frequenter, I happen'd to become quite well acquainted with Thomas Paine's perhaps most intimate chum, and certainly his later years' very frequent companion, a remarkably fine old man, Col. Fellows, who may yet be remember'd by some stray relics of that period and spot. If you will allow me, I will first give a description of the Colonel himself. He was tall, of military bearing, aged about 78 I should think, hair white as snow, clean-shaved on the face, dress'd very neatly, a tail-coat of blue cloth with metal buttons, buff vest, pantaloons of drab color, and his neck, breast and wrists showing the whitest of linen. Under all circumstances, fine manners; a good but not profuse talker, his wits still fully about him, balanced and live and undimm'd as ever. He kept pretty fair health, though so old. For employment—for he was poor—he had a post as constable of some of the upper courts. I used to think him very picturesque on the fringe of a crowd holding a tall staff, with his erect form, and his superb, bare, thick-hair'd, closely-cropt white head. The judges and young lawyers, with whom he was ever a favorite, and the subject of respect, used to call him Aristides. It was the general opinion among them that if manly rectitude and the instincts of absolute justice remain'd vital anywhere about New York City Hall, or Tammany, they were to be found in Col. Fellows. He liked young men, and enjoy'd to leisurely talk with them over a social glass of toddy, after his day's work, (he on these occasions never drank but one glass,) and it was at reiterated meetings of this kind in old Tammany's back parlor of those days, that he told me much about Thomas Paine. At one of our interviews he gave me a minute account of Paine's sickness and death. In short, from those talks, I was and am satisfied that my old friend, with his mark's advantages, had mentally, morally and emotionally gauged the author of "Common Sense," and besides giving me a good portrait of his appearance and manners, had taken the true measure of his interior character.

Paine's practical demeanor, and much of his theoretical belief, was a mixture of the French and English schools of a century ago, and the best of both. Like most old-fashion'd people, he drank a glass or two every day, but was no tippler, nor intemperate, let alone being a drunkard. He lived simply and economically, but quite well—was always cheery and courteous, perhaps occasionally a little blunt, having very positive opinions upon politics, religion, and so forth. That he labor'd well and wisely for the States in the trying period of their parturition, and in the seeds of their character, there seems to me no question. I dare not say how much of what our Union is owning and enjoying to-day—its independence— its ardent belief in, and substantial practice of, radical human rights—and the severance of its government from all ecclesiastical and superstitious dominion—I dare not say how much of all this is owing to Thomas Paine, but I am inclined to think a good portion of it decidedly is.

But I was not going either into an analysis or eulogium of the man. I wanted to carry you back a generation or two, and give you by indirection a moment's glance—and also to ventilate a very earnest and I believe authentic opinion, nay conviction, of that time, the fruit of the interviews I have mention'd, and of questioning and cross-questioning, clench'd by my best information since, that Thomas Paine had a noble personality, as exhibited in presence, face, voice, dress, manner, and what may be call'd his atmosphere and magnetism, especially the later years of his life. I am sure of it. Of the foul and foolish fictions yet told about the circumstances of his decease, the absolute fact is that as he lived a good life, after its kind, he died calmly and philosophically, as became him. He served the embryo Union with most precious service—a service that every man, woman and child in our thirty-eight States is to some extent receiving the benefit of to-day—and I for one here cheerfully, reverently throw my pebble on the cairn of his memory. As we all know, the season demands—or rather, will it ever be out of season?—that America learn to better dwell on her choicest possession, the legacy of her good and faithful men—that she well preserve their fame, if unquestion'd—or, if need be, that she fail not to dissipate what clouds have intruded on that fame, and burnish it newer, truer and brighter, continually.

A Two Hours' Ice-Sail

Feb. 3, '77.—From 4 to 6 P.M. crossing the Delaware, (back again at my Camden home,) unable to make our landing, through the ice; our boat stanch and strong and skilfully piloted, but old and sulky, and poorly minding her helm. (*Power*, so important in poetry and war, is also first point of all in a winter steam-boat, with long stretches of ice-packs to tackle.) For over two hours we bump'd and beat about, the invisible ebb, sluggish but irresistible, often carrying us long distances against our will. In the first tinge of dusk, as I look'd around, I thought there could not be presented a more chilling, arctic, grim-extended, depressing scene. Everything was yet plainly visible; for miles north and south, ice, ice, ice, mostly broken, but some big cakes, and no clear water in sight. The shores, piers, surfaces, roofs, shipping, mantled with snow. A faint winter vapor hung a fitting accompaniment around and over the endless whitish spread, and gave it just a tinge of steel and brown.

Feb. 6.—As I cross home in the 6 P.M. boat again, the transparent shadows are filled everywhere with leisurely falling, slightly slanting, curiously sparse but very large, flakes of snow. On the shores, near and far, the glow of just-lit gas-clusters at intervals. The ice, sometimes in hummocks, sometime floating fields, through which our boat goes crunching. The light permeated by that peculiar evening haze, right after sunset, which sometimes renders quite distant objects so distinctly.

Spring Overtures—Recreations

Feb. 10.—The first chirping, almost singing, of a bird to-day. Then I noticed a couple of honey-bees spirting and humming about the open window in the sun.

Feb. 11.—In the soft rose and pale gold of the declining light, this beautiful evening, I heard the first hum and preparation of awakening spring—very faint—whether in the earth or roots, or starting of insects, I know not—but it was audible, as I lean'd on a rail (I am down in my country quarters awhile,) and look'd long at the western horizon. Turning to the east, Sirius, as the shadows deepen'd, came forth in dazzling splendor. And great Orion; and a little to the north-east the big Dipper, standing on end.

Feb. 20.—A solitary and pleasant sundown hour at the pond, exercising arms, chest, my whole body, by a tough oak sapling thick as my wrist, twelve feet high—pulling and pushing, inspiring the good air. After I wrestle with the tree awhile, I can feel its young sap and virtue welling up out of the ground and tingling through me from crown to toe, like health's wine. Then for addition and variety I launch forth in my vocalism; shout declamatory pieces, sentiments, sorrow, anger, &c., from the stock poets or plays—or inflate my lungs and sing the wild tunes and refrains I heard of the blacks down south, or patriotic songs I learn'd in the army. I make the echoes ring, I tell you! As the twilight fell, in a pause of these ebullitions, an owl somewhere the other side of the creek sounded *too-oo-oo-oo-oo*, soft and pensive (and I fancied a little sarcastic) repeated four or five times. Either to applaud the negro songs—or perhaps an ironical comment on the sorrow, anger, or style of the stock poets.

One of the Human Kinks

How is it that in all the serenity and lonesomeness of solitude, away off here amid the hush of the forest, alone, or as I have found in prairie wilds, or mountain stillness, one is never entirely without the instinct of looking around, (I never am, and others tell me the same of themselves, confidentially,) for somebody to appear, or start up out of the earth, or from behind some tree or rock? Is it a lingering, inherited remains of man's primitive wariness, from the wild animals? or from his savage ancestry far back? It is not at all nervousness or fear. Seems as if something unknown were possibly lurking in those bushes, or solitary places. Nay, it is quite certain there is—some vital unseen presence.

An Afternoon Scene

Feb. 22.—Last night and to-day rainy and thick, till mid-afternoon, when the wind chopp'd round, the clouds swiftly drew off like curtains, the clear appear'd, and with it the fairest, grandest, most wondrous rainbow I ever saw, all complete, very vivid at its earth-ends, spreading vast effusions of illuminated haze, violet, yellow, drab-green, in all directions overhead, through which the sun beam'd—an indescribable utterance of color and light, so gorgeous yet so soft, such as I had never witness'd before. Then its continuance: a full hour pass'd before the last of those earth-ends disappear'd. The sky behind was all spread in translucent blue, with many little white clouds and edges. To these a sunset, filling, dominating the esthetic and soul senses, sumptuously, tenderly, full. I end this note by the pond, just light enough to see, through the evening shadows, the western reflections in its water-mirror surface, with inverted figures of trees. I hear now and then the *flup* of a pike leaping out, and rippling the water.

The Gates Opening

April 6.—Palpable spring indeed, or the indications of it. I am sitting in bright sunshine, at the edge of the creek, the surface just rippled by the wind. All is solitude, morning freshness, negligence. For companions my two kingfishers sailing, winding, darting, dipping, sometimes capriciously separate, then flying together. I hear their guttural twittering again and again; for awhile nothing but that peculiar sound. As soon approaches other birds warm up. The reedy notes of the robin, and a musical passage of two parts, one a clear delicious gurgle, with several other birds I cannot place. To which is join'd, (yes, I just hear it,) one low purr at intervals from some impatient hylas at the pond-edge. The sibilant murmur of a pretty stiff breeze now and then through the trees. Then a poor little dead leaf, long frost-bound, whirls from somewhere up aloft in one wild escaped freedom-spree in space and sunlight, and then dashes down to the waters, which hold it closely and soon drown it out of sight. The bushes and trees are yet bare, but the beeches have their wrinkled yellow leaves of last season's foliage largely left, frequent cedars and pines yet green, and the grass not without proofs of coming fulness. And over all a wonderfully fine dome of clear blue, the play of light coming and going, and great fleeces of white clouds swimming so silently.

The Common Earth, the Soil

The soil, too—let others pen-and-ink the sea, the air, (as I sometimes try)—but now I feel to choose the common soil for theme—naught else. The brown soil here, (just between winter-close and opening spring and vegetation)—the rain-shower at night, and the fresh smell next morning—the red worms wriggling out of the ground—the dead leaves, the incipient grass, and the latent life underneath—the effort to start something—already in shelter'd spots some little flowers—the distant emerald show of winter wheat and the rye-fields—the yet naked trees, with clear interstices, giving prospects hidden in summer—the tough fallow and the plow-team, and the stout boy whistling to his horses for encouragement—and there the dark fat earth in long slanting stripes upturn'd.

Birds and Birds and Birds

A little later—bright weather.—An unusual melodiousness, these days, (last of April and first of May) from the black-birds; indeed all sorts of birds, darting, whistling, hopping or perch'd on trees. Never before have I seen, heard, or been in the midst of, and got so flooded and saturated with them and their performances, as this current month. Such oceans, such successions of them. Let me make a list of those I find here:

Black birds (plenty,)
Ring doves,
Owls,
Woodpeckers,
King-birds,
Crows (plenty,)
Wrens,
Kingfishers,
Quails,
Turkey-buzzards,
Hen-hawks,
Yellow birds,
Thrushes,
Reed birds,

Meadow-larks (plenty,)
Cat-birds (plenty,)
Cuckoos,
Pond snipes (plenty,)
Cheewinks,
Quawks,
Ground robins,
Ravens,
Gray snipes,
Eagles,
High-holes,
Herons,
Tits,
Woodpigeons.

Early came the

Blue birds,
Killdeer,
Plover,
Robin,
Woodcock,

Meadow lark,
White-bellied swallow,
Sandpiper,
Wilson's thrush,
Flicker.

Full-Starr'd Nights

May 21.—Back in Camden. Again commencing one of those unusually transparent, full-starr'd, blue-black nights, as if to show that however lush and pompous the day may be, there is something left in the not-day that can outvie it. The rarest, finest sample of long-drawn-out clear-obscure, from sundown to 9 o'clock. I went down to the Delaware, and cross'd and cross'd. Venus like blazing silver well up in the west. The large pale thin crescent of the new moon, half an hour high, sinking languidly under a bar-sinister of cloud, and then emerging. Arcturus right overhead. A faint fragrant sea-odor wafted up from the south. The gloaming, the temper'd coolness, with every feature of the scene, indescribably soothing and tonic—one of those hours that give hints to the soul, impossible to put in a statement. (Ah, where would be any food for spirituality without night and the stars?) The vacant spaciousness of the air, and the veil'd blue of the heavens, seem'd miracles enough.

As the night advanc'd it changed its spirit and garments to ampler stateliness. I was almost conscious of a definite presence, Nature silently near. The great constellation of the Water-Serpent stretch'd its coils over more than half the heavens. The Swan with outspread wings was flying down the Milky Way. The northern Crown, the Eagle, Lyra, all up there in their places. From the whole dome shot down points of light, rapport with me, through the clear blue-black. All the usual sense of motion, all animal life, seem'd discarded, seem'd a fiction; a curious power, like the placid rest of Egyptian gods, took possession, none the less potent for being impalpable. Earlier I had seen many bats, balancing in the luminous twilight, darting their black forms hither and yon over the river; but now they altogether disappear'd. The evening star and the moon had gone. Alertness and peace lay calmly couching together through the fluid universal shadows.

Aug. 26.—Bright has the day been, and my spirits an equal *forzando*. Then comes the night, different, inexpressibly pensive, with its own tender and temper'd splendor. Venus lingers in the west with a voluptuous dazzle unshown hitherto this summer. Mars rises early, and the red sulky moon, two days past her full; Jupiter at night's meridian, and the long curling-slanted Scorpion stretching full view in the south, Antares-neck'd. Mars walks the heavens lord-paramount now; all through this month I go out after supper and watch for him; sometimes getting up at midnight to take another look at his unparallel'd lustre. (I see lately an astronomer has made out through the new Washington telescope that Mars has certainly one moon, perhaps two.) Pale and distant, but near in the heavens, Saturn precedes him.

Mulleins and Mulleins

Large, placid mulleins, as summer advances, velvety in texture, of a light greenish-drab color, growing everywhere in the fields —at first earth's big rosettes in their broad-leav'd low cluster-plants, eight, ten, twenty leaves to a plant—plentiful on the fallow twenty-acre lot, at the end of the lane, and especially by the ridge-sides of the fences—then close to the ground, but soon springing up—leaves as broad as my hand, and the lower ones twice as long—so fresh and dewy in the morning—stalks now four or five, even seven or eight feet high. The farmers, I find, think the mullein a mean unworthy weed, but I have grown to a fondness for it. Every object has its lesson, enclosing the suggestion of everything else—and lately I sometimes think all is concentrated for me in these hardy, yellow-flower'd weeds. As I come down the lane early in the morning, I pause before their soft wool-like fleece and stem and broad leaves, glittering with countless diamonds. Annually for three summers now, they and I have silently return'd together; at such long intervals I stand or sit among them, musing—and woven with the rest, of so many hours and moods of partial rehabilitation —of my sane or sick spirit, here as near at peace as it can be.

Distant Sounds

The axe of the wood-cutter, the measured thud of a single threshing-flail, the crowing of chanticleer in the barn-yard, (with invariable responses from other barn-yards,) and the lowing of cattle—but most of all, or far or near, the wind—through the high tree-tops, or through low bushes, laving one's face and hands so gently, this balmy-bright noon, the coolest for a ling time, (Sept. 2)—I will not call it *sighing*, for to me it is always a firm, sane, cheery expression, though a monotone, giving many varieties, or swift or slow, or dense or delicate. The wind in the patch of pine woods off there—how sibilant. Or at sea, I can imagine it this moment, tossing the waves, with spirts of foam flying far, and the free whistle, and the scent of the salt—and that vast paradox somehow with all its action and restlessness conveying a sense of eternal rest.

Other adjuncts.—But the sun and moon here and these times. As never more wonderful by day, the gorgeous orb imperial, so vast, so ardently, lovingly hot—so never a more glorious moon of nights, especially the last three or four. The great planets too—Mars never before so flaming bright, so flashing-large, with slight yellow tinge, (the astronomers say —is it true?—nearer to us than any time the past century) —and well up, lord Jupiter, (a little while since close by the moon)—and in the west, after the sun sinks, voluptuous Venus, now languid and shorn of her beams, as if from some divine excess.

A Sun-Bath—Nakedness

Sunday, Aug. 27.—Another day quite free from mark'd prostration and pain. It seems indeed as if peace and nutriment from heaven subtly filter into me as I slowly hobble down these country lanes and across fields, in the good air—as I sit here in solitude with Nature—open, voiceless, mystic, far removed, yet palpable, eloquent Nature. I merge myself in the scene, in the perfect day. Hovering over the clear brook-water, I am sooth'd by its soft gurgle in one place, and the hoarser murmurs of its three-foot fall in another. Come, ye disconsolate, in whom any latent eligibility is left—come get the sure virtues of creek-shore, and wood and field. Two months (July and August, '77), have I absorb'd them, and they begin to make a new man of me. Every day, seclusion—every day at least two or three hours of freedom, bathing, no talk, no bonds, no dress, no books, no *manners*.

Shall I tell you reader, to what I attribute my already much-restored health? That I have been almost two years, off and on, without drugs and medicines, and daily in the open air. Last summer I found a particularly secluded little dell off one side by my creek, originally a large dug-out marl-pit, now abandon'd, fill'd with bushes, trees, grass, a group of willows, a straggling bank, and a spring of delicious water running right through the middle of it, with two or three little cascades. Here I retreated every hot day, and follow it up this summer. Here I realize the meaning of that old fellow who said he was seldom less alone than when alone. Never before did I get so close to Nature; never before did she come so close to me. By old habit, I pencill'd down from time to time, almost automatically, moods, sights, hours, tints and outlines, on the spot. Let me specially record the satisfaction of this current forenoon, so serene and primitive, so conventionally exceptional, natural.

An hour or so after breakfast I wended my way down to the recesses of the aforesaid dell, which I and certain thrushes, catbirds, &c., had all to ourselves. A light south-west wind was blowing through the tree-tops. It was just the place and time for my Adamic air-bath and flesh-brushing from head to foot. So hanging clothes on a rail near by, keeping old broadbrim straw on head and easy shoes on feet, haven't I had a good time the last two hours! First with the stiff-elastic bristles rasping arms, breast, sides, till they turn'd scarlet—then partially bathing in the clear waters of the running brook—taking everything very leisurely, with many rests and pauses—stepping about bare-footed every few minutes now and then in some neighboring black ooze, for unctuous mud-bath to

my feet—a brief second and third rinsing in the crystal running waters—rubbing with the fragrant towel—slow negligent
promenades on the turf up and down in the sun, varied with
occasional rests, and further frictions of the bristle-brush—
sometimes carrying my portable chair with me from place
to place, as my range is quite extensive here, nearly a hundred rods, feeling quite secure from intrusion, (and that indeed
I am not at all nervous about, if it accidentally happens.)

As I walk'd slowly over the grass, the sun shone out enough
to show the shadow moving with me. Somehow I seem'd to get
identity with each and every thing around me, in its condition.
Nature was naked, and I was also. It was too lazy, soothing, and joyous-equable to speculate about. Yet I might have
thought somehow in this vein: Perhaps the inner never lost
rapport we hold with earth, light, air, trees, &c., is not to be
realized through eyes and mind only, but through the whole
corporeal body, which I will not have blinded or bandaged
any more than the eyes. Sweet, sane, still Nakedness in Nature!
—ah if poor, sick, prurient humanity in cities might really
know you once more! Is not nakedness then indecent? No,
not inherently. It is your thought, your sophistication, your
fear, your respectability, that is indecent. There come moods
when these clothes of ours are not only too irksome to wear,
but are themselves indecent. Perhaps indeed he or she to whom
the free exhilarating extasy of nakedness in Nature has never
been eligible (and how many thousands there are!) has not
really known what purity is—nor what faith or art or health
really is. (Probably the whole curriculum of first-class philosophy, beauty, heroism, form, illustrated by the old Hellenic
race—the highest height and deepest depth known to civilization in those departments—came from their natural and religious idea of Nakedness.)

Many such hours, from time to time, the last two summers
—I attribute my partial rehabilitation largely to them. Some
good people may think it a feeble or half-crack'd way of
spending one's time and thinking. May-be it is.

The Oaks and I

Sept. 5, '77.—I write this, 11 A.M., shelter'd under a dense oak by the bank, where I have taken refuge from a sudden rain. I came down here, (we had sulky drizzles all the morning, but an hour ago a lull,) for the before-mention'd daily and simple exercise I am fond of—to pull on that young hickory sapling out there—to sway and yield to its tough-limber upright stem—haply to get into my old sinews some of its elastic fibre and clear sap. I stand on the turf and take these health-pulls moderately and at intervals for nearly an hour, inhaling great draughts of fresh air. Wandering by the creek, I have three or four naturally favorable spots where I rest—besides a chair I lug with me and use for more deliberate occasions. At other spots convenient I have selected, besides the hickory just named, strong and limber boughs of beech or holly, in easy-reaching distance, for my natural gymnasia, for arms, chest, trunk-muscles. I can soon feel the sap and sinew rising through me, like mercury to heat. I hold on boughs or slender trees caressingly there in the sun and shade, wrestle with their innocent stalwartness—and *know* the virtue thereof passes from them into me. (Or may-be we interchange—may-be the trees are more aware of it all then I ever thought.)

But now pleasantly imprison'd here under the big oak—the rain dripping, and the sky cover'd with leaden clouds—nothing but the pond on one side, and the other a spread of grass, spotted with the milky blossoms of the wild carrot—the sound of an axe wielded at some distant wood-pile—yet in this dull scene, (as most folks would call it,) why am I so (almost) happy here and alone? Why would any intrusion, even from people I like, spoil the charm? But am I alone? Doubtless there comes a time—perhaps it has come to me—when one feels through his whole being, and pronouncedly the emotional part, that identity between himself subjectively and Nature objectively which Schelling and Fichte are so fond of pressing. How it is I know not, but I often realize a presence here—in clear moods I am certain of it, and neither chemistry nor reasoning nor aesthetics will give the least explanation. All the past two summers it has been strengthening and nourishing my sick body and soul, as never before. Thanks, invisible physician, for thy silent delicious medicine, the day and night, thy waters and thy airs, the banks, the grass, the trees, and e'en the weeds!

A Quintette

While I have been kept by the rain under the shelter of my great oak, (perfectly dry and comfortable, to the rattle of the drops all around,) I have pencill'd off the mood of the hour in a little quintette, which I will give you:

> At vacancy with Nature,
> Acceptive and at ease,
> Distilling the present hour,
> Whatever, wherever it is,
> And over the past, oblivion.

Can you get hold of it, reader dear? and how do you like it anyhow?

The First Frost—Mems

Where I was stopping I saw the first palpable frost, on my sunrise walk, October 6; all over the yet-green spread a light blue-gray veil, giving a new show to the entire landscape. I had but little time to notice it, for the sun rose cloudless and mellow-warm, and as I returned along the lane it had turn'd to glittering patches of wet. As I walk I notice the bursting pods of wild-cotton, (Indian hemp they call it here,) with flossy-silky contents, and dark red-brown seeds—a startled rabbit—I pull a handful of the balsamic life-everlasting and stuff it down in my trowsers-pocket for scent.

Three Young Men's Deaths

December 20.—Somehow I got thinking to-day of young men's deaths—not at all sadly or sentimentally, but gravely, realistically, perhaps a little artistically. Let me give the following three cases from budgets of personal memoranda, which I have been turning over, alone in my room, and resuming and dwelling on, this rainy afternoon. Who is there to whom the theme does not come home? Then I don't know how it may be to others, but to me not only is there nothing gloomy or depressing in such cases—on the contrary, as reminiscences, I find them soothing, bracing, tonic.

ERASTUS HASKELL.—[I just transcribe verbatim from a letter written by myself in one of the army hospitals, 16 years ago, during the secession war.] *Washington, July 28, 1863.*—Dear M.,—I am writing this in the hospital, sitting by the side of a soldier, I do not expect to last many hours. His fate has been a hard one—he seems to be only about 19 or 20—Erastus Haskell, company K, 141st N. Y.—has been out about a year, and sick or half-sick more than half that time—has been down on the peninsula—was detail'd to go in the band as fifer-boy. While sick, the surgeon told him to keep up with the rest—(probably work'd and march'd too long.) He is a shy, and seems to me a very sensible boy—has fine manners—never complains—was sick down on the peninsula in an old storehouse—typhoid fever. The first week this July was brought up here—journey very bad, no accommodations, no nourishment, nothing but hard jolting, and exposure enough to make a well man sick; (these fearful journeys do the job for many)— arrived here July 11th—a silent dark-skinn'd Spanish-looking youth, with large very dark blue eyes, peculiar looking. Doctor F. here made light of his sickness—said he would recover soon, &c.; but I thought very different, and told F. so repeatedly; (I came near quarreling with him about it from the first)—but he laugh'd, and would not listen to me. About four days ago, I told Doctor he would in my opinion lose the boy without doubt—but F. again laugh'd at me. The next day he changed his opinion—I brought the head surgeon of the post—he said the boy would probably die, but they would make a hard fight for him.

The last two days he has been lying panting for breath—a pitiful sight. I have been with him some every day or night since he arrived. He suffers a great deal with the heat—says little or nothing—is flighty the last three days, at times—knows me always, however,—calls me "Walter"—(sometimes calls the name over and over and over again, musingly, abstractedly, to himself.) His father lives at Breesport, Chemung county, N.Y., is a mechanic with large family—is a steady, religious man; his mother too is living. I have written to them, and shall write again today—Erastus has not receiv'd a word from home for months.

As I sit here writing to you, M., I wish you could see the whole scene. This young man lies within reach of me, flat on his back, his hands clasp'd across his breast, his thick black hair cut close; he is dozing, breathing hard, every breath a spasm—it looks so cruel. He is a noble youngster,—I consider him past all hope. Often there is no one with him for a long while. I am here as much as possible.

WILLIAM ALCOTT, fireman. *Camden, Nov., 1874.*—Last Monday afternoon his widow, mother, relatives, mates of the fire department, and his other friends, (I was one, only lately it is true, but our love grew fast and close, the days and nights of those eight weeks by the chair of rapid decline, and the bed of death,) gather'd to the funeral of this young man, who had grown up, and was well-known here. With nothing special, perhaps, to record, I would give a word or two to his memory. He seem'd to me not an inappropriate specimen in character and elements, of that bulk of the average good American race that ebbs and flows perennially beneath this scum of eructations on the surface. Always very quiet in manner, neat in person and dress, good temper'd—punctual and industrious at his work, till he could work no longer—he just lived his steady, square, unobtrusive life, in its own humble sphere, doubtless unconscious of itself. (Though I think there were currents of emotion and intellect underdevelop'd beneath, far deeper than his acquaintances ever suspected—or than he himself ever did.)

He was no talker. His troubles, when he had any, he kept to himself. As there was nothing querulous about him in life, he made no complaints during his last sickness. He was one of those persons that while his associates never thought of attributing any particular talent or grace to him, yet all insensibly, really, liked Billy Alcott.

I, too, loved him. At last, after being with him quite a good deal—after hours and days of panting for breath, much of the time unconscious, (for though the consumption that had been lurking in his system, once thoroughly started, made rapid progress, there was still great vitality in him, and indeed for four or five days he lay dying, before the close,) late on Wednesday night, Nov. 4th, where we surrounded his bed in silence, there came a lull—a longer drawn breath, a pause, a faint sigh —another—a weaker breath, another sigh—a pause again and just a tremble—and the face of the poor wasted young man (he was just 26), fell gently over, in death, on my hand, on the pillow.

CHARLES CASWELL.—[I extract the following, verbatim, from a letter to me dated September 29, from my friend John Burroughs, at Esopus-on-Hudson, New York State.] S. was away when your picture came, attending his sick brother, Charles—who has since died—an event that has sadden'd me much. Charlie was younger than S., and a most attractive young fellow. He work'd at my father's and had done so for two years. He was about the best specimen of a young country farm-hand I ever knew. You would have loved him. He was like one of your poems. With his great strength, his blond hair, his cheerfulness and contentment, his universal good will, and his silent manly ways, he was a youth hard to match. He was murder'd by an old doctor. He had typhoid fever, and the old fool bled him twice. He lived to wear out the fever, but had not strength to rally. He was out of his head nearly all the time. In the morning, as he died in the afternoon. S. was standing over him, when Charlie put up his arms around S.'s neck, and pull'd his face down and kiss'd him. S. said he knew then the end was near. (S. stuck to him day and night to the last.) When I was home in August, Charlie was cradling on the hill, and it was a picture to see him walk through the grain. All work seem'd play to him. He had no vices, any more than Nature has, and was belov'd by all who knew him.

I have written thus to you about him, for such young men belong to you; he was of your kind. I wish you could have known him. He had the sweetness of a child, and the strength and courage and readiness of a young Viking. His mother and father are poor; they have a rough, hard farm. His mother works in the field with her husband when the work presses. She has had twelve children.

February Days

February 7, 1878.—Glistening sun to-day, with slight haze, warm enough, and yet tart, as I sit here in the open air, down in my country retreat, under an old cedar. For two hours I have been idly wandering around the woods and pond, lugging my chair, picking out choice spots to sit awhile—then up and slowly on again. All is peace here. Of course, none of the summer noises or vitality; to-day hardly even the winter ones. I amuse myself by exercising my voice in recitations, and in ringing the changes on all the vocal and alphabetical sounds. Not even an echo; only the cawing of a solitary crow, flying at some distance. The pond is one bright, flat spread, without a ripple—a vast Claude Lorraine glass, in which I study the sky, the light, the leafless trees, and an occasional crow, with flapping wings, flying overhead. The brown fields have a few white patches of snow left.

Feb. 9.—After an hour's ramble, now retreating, resting, sitting close by the pond, in a warm nook, writing this, shelter'd from the breeze, just before noon. The *emotional* aspects and influences of Nature! I, too, like the rest, feel these modern tendencies (from all the prevailing intellections, literature and poems,) to turn everything to pathos, ennui, morbidity, dissatisfaction, death. Yet how clear it is to me that those are not the born results, influences of Nature at all, but of one's own distorted, sick or silly soul. Here, amid this wild, free scene, how healthy, how joyous, how clean and vigorous and sweet!

Mid-afternoon.—One of my nooks is south of the barn, and here I am sitting now, on a log, still basking in the sun, shielded from the wind. Near me are the cattle, feeding on corn-stalks. Occasionally a cow or the young bull (how handsome and bold he is!) scratches and munches the far end of the log on which I sit. The fresh milky odor is quite perceptible, also the perfume of hay from the barn. The perpetual rustle of dry corn-stalks, the low sough of the wind round the barn gables, the grunting of pigs, the distant whistle of a locomotive, and occasional crowing of chanticleers, are the sounds.

Feb. 19.—Cold and sharp last night—clear and not much wind—the full moon shining, and a fine spread of constellations and little and big stars—Sirius very bright, rising early, preceded by many-orb'd Orion, glittering, vast, sworded, and chasing with his dog. The earth hard frozen, and a stiff glare of ice over the pond. Attracted by the calm splendor of the night, I attempted a short walk, but was driven back by the cold. Too severe for me also at 9 o'clock, when I came out this morning, so I turn'd back again. But now, near noon, I have walk'd down the lane, basking all the way in the sun (this farm has a pleasant southerly exposure,) and here I am, seated under the lee of a bank, close by the water. There are bluebirds already flying about, and I hear much chirping and twittering and two or three real songs, sustain'd quite awhile, in the mid-day brilliance and warmth. (There! that is a true carol, coming out boldly and repeatedly, as if the singer meant it.) Then as the noon strengthens, the reedy trill of the robin—to my ear the most cheering of bird-notes. At intervals, like bars and breaks (out of the low murmur that in any scene, however quiet, is never entirely absent to a delicate ear,) the occasional crunch and cracking of the ice-glare congeal'd over the creek, as it gives way to the sunbeams—sometimes with low sigh—sometimes with indignant, obstinate tug and snort.

(Robert Burns says in one of his letters: "There is scarcely any earthly object gives me more—I do not know if I should call it pleasure—but something which exalts me—something which enraptures me—than to walk in the shelter'd side of a wood in a cloudy winter day, and hear the stormy wind howling among the trees, and raving over the plain. It is my best season of devotion." Some of his most characteristic poems were composed in such scenes and seasons.)

A Meadow Lark

March 16.—Fine, clear dazzling morning, the sun an hour high, the air just tart enough. What a stamp in advance my whole day receives from the song of that meadow lark perch'd on a fence-stake twenty rods distant! Two or three liquid-simple notes, repeated at intervals, full of careless happiness and hope. With its peculiar shimmering-slow progress and rapid-noiseless action of the wings, it flies on a ways, lights on another stake, and so on to another, shimmering and singing many minutes.

Sundown Lights

May 6, 5 P.M.—This is the hour for strange effects in light and shade—enough to make a colorist go delirious—long spokes of molten silver sent horizontally through the trees (now in their brightest tenderest green,) each leaf and branch of endless foliage a lit-up miracle, then lying all prone on the youthful-ripe, interminable grass, and giving the blades not only aggregate but individual splendor, in ways unknown to any other hour. I have particular spots where I get these effects in their perfection. One broad splash lies on the water, with many a rippling twinkle, offset by the rapidly deepening black-green murky-transparent shadows behind, and at intervals all along the banks. These, with great shafts of horizontal fire thrown among the trees and along the grass as the sun lowers, give effects more and more peculiar, more and more superb, unearthly, rich and dazzling.

Thoughts under an Oak—a Dream

June 2.—This is the fourth day of a dark northeast storm, wind and rain. Day before yesterday was my birthday. I have now enter'd on my 60th year. Every day of the storm, protected by overshoes and a waterproof blanket, I regularly come down to the pond, and ensconce myself under the lee of the great oak; I am here now writing these lines. The dark smoke-color'd clouds roll in furious silence athwart the sky; the soft green leaves dangle all round me; the wind steadily keeps up its hoarse, soothing music over my head—Nature's mighty whisper. Seated here in solitude I have been musing over my life—connecting events, dates, as links of a chain, neither sadly nor cheerily, but somehow, to-day here under the oak, in the rain, in an unusually matter-of-fact spirit.

But my great oak—sturdy, vital, green—five feet thick at the butt. I sit a great deal near or under him. Then the tulip tree near by—the Apollo of the woods—tall and graceful, yet robust and sinewy, inimitable in hang of foliage and throwing-out of limb; as if the beauteous, vital, leafy creature could walk, if it only would. (I had a sort of dream-trance the other day, in which I saw my favorite trees step out and promenade up, down and around, very curiously—with a whisper from one, leaning down as he pass'd me, *We do all this on the present occasion, exceptionally, just for you.*)

Clover and Hay Perfume

July 3d, 4th, 5th.—Clear, hot, favorable weather—has been a good summer—the growth of clover and grass now generally mow'd. The familiar delicious perfume fills the barns and lanes. As you go along you see the fields of grayish white slightly tinged with yellow, the loosely stack'd grain, the slow-moving wagons passing, and farmers in the fields with stout boys pitching and loading the sheaves. The corn is about beginning to tassel. All over the middle and southern states the spear-shaped battalia, multitudinous, curving, flaunting—long, glossy, dark-green plumes for the great horseman, earth. I hear the cheery notes of my old acquaintance Tommy quail; but too late for the whip-poor-will, (though I heard one solitary lingered night before last.) I watch the broad majestic flight of a turkey-buzzard, sometimes high up, sometimes low enough to see the lines of his form, even his spread quills, in relief against the sky. Once or twice lately I have seen an eagle here at early candle-light flying low.

An Unknown

June 15.—To-day I noticed a new large bird, size of a nearly grown hen—a haughty, white-bodied dark-wing'd hawk—I suppose a hawk from his bill and general look—only he had a clear, loud, quite musical, sort of bell-like call, which he repeated again and again, at intervals, from a lofty dead tree-top, overhanging the water. Sat there a long time, and I on the opposite bank watching him. Then he darted down, skimming pretty close to the stream—rose slowly, a magnificent sight, and sail'd with steady wide-spread wings, no flapping at all, up and down the pond two or three times, near me, in circles in clear sight, as if for my delectation. Once he came quite close over my head; I saw plainly his hook'd bill and hard restless eyes.

Bird-Whistling

How much music (wild, simple, savage, doubtless, but so tart-sweet,) there is in mere whistling. It is four-fifths of the utterance of birds. There are all sorts and styles. For the last half-hour, now, while I have been sitting here, some feather'd fellow away off in the bushes has been repeating over and over again what I may call a kind of throbbing whistle. And now a bird about the robin size has just appear'd, all mulberry red, flitting among the bushes—head, wings, body, deep red, not very bright—no song, as I have heard. *4 o'clock:* There is a real concert going on around me—a dozen different birds pitching in with a will. There have been occasional rains, and the growths all show its vivifying influences. As I finish this, seated on a log close by the pond-edge, much chirping and trilling in the distance, and a feather'd recluse in the woods near by is singing deliciously—not many notes, but full of music of almost human sympathy—continuing for a long, long while.

Horse-Mint

Aug. 22.—Not a human being, and hardly the evidence of one, in sight. After my brief semi-daily bath, I sit here for a bit, the brook musically brawling, to the chromatic tones of a fretful cat-bird somewhere off in the bushes. On my walk hither two hours since, through fields on the old lane, I stopt to view, now the sky, now the mile-off woods on the hill, and now the apple orchards. What a contrast from New York's or Philadelphia's streets! Everywhere great patches of dingy-blossom'd horse-mint wafting a spicy odor through the air, (especially evenings.) Everywhere the flowering boneset, and the rose-bloom of the wild bean.

Three of Us

July 14.—My two kingfishers still haunt the pond. In the bright sun and breeze and perfect temperature of to-day, noon, I am sitting here by one of the gurgling brooks, dipping a French water-pen in the limpid crystal, and using it to write these lines, again watching the feather'd twain, as they fly and sport athwart the water, so close, almost touching into its surface. Indeed there seem to be three of us. For nearly an hour I indolently look and join them while they dart and turn and take their airy gambols, sometimes far up the creek disappearing for a few moments, and then surely returning again, and performing most of their flight within sight of me, as if they knew I appreciated and absorb'd their vitality, spirituality, faithfulness, and the rapid, vanishing, delicate lines of moving yet quiet electricity they draw for me across the spread of the grass, the trees, and the blue sky. While the brook babbles, babbles, and the shadows of the boughs dapple in the sunshine around me, and the cool west by-nor'-west wind faintly soughs in the thick bushes and tree tops.

Among the objects of beauty and interest now beginning to appear quite plentifully in this secluded spot, I notice the humming-bird, the dragon-fly with its wings of slate-color'd gauze, and many varieties of beautiful and plain butterflies, idly flapping among the plants and wild posies. The mullein has shot up out of its nest of broad leaves, to a tall stalk towering some-blossoms. The milk-weed, (I see a great gorgeous creature of gamboge and black lighting on one as I write,) is in flower, with its delicate red fringe; and there are profuse clusters of a feathery blossom waving in the wind on taper stems. I see lots of these and much else in every direction, as I saunter or sit. For the last half hour a bird has persistently kept up a simple, sweet, melodious song, from the bushes. (I have a positive conviction that some of these birds sing, and others fly and flirt above here, for my especial benefit.)

Death of William Cullen Bryant

New York City.—Came on from West Philadelphia, June 13, in the 2 P.M. train to Jersey city, and so across and to my friends. Mr. and Mrs. J. H. J., and their large house, large family (and large hearts,) amid which I feel at home, at peace —away up on Fifth avenue, near Eighty-sixth street, quiet, breezy, overlooking the dense woody fringe of the park—plenty of space and sky, birds chirping, and air comparatively fresh and odorless. Two hours before starting, saw the announcement of William Cullen Bryant's funeral, and felt a strong desire to attend. I had known Mr. Bryant over thirty years ago, and he had been markedly kind to me. Off and on, along that time for years as they pass'd, we met and chatted together. I thought him very sociable in his way, and a man to become attach'd to. We were both walkers, and when I work'd in Brooklyn he several times came over, middle of afternoons, and we took rambles miles long, till dark, out towards Bedford or Flatbush, in company. On these occasions he gave me clear accounts of scenes in Europe—the cities, looks, architecture, art, especially Italy—where he had travel'd a good deal.

June 14.—The Funeral.—And so the good, stainless, noble old citizen and poet lies in the closed coffin there—and this is his funeral. A solemn, impressive, simple scene, to spirit and senses. The remarkable gathering of gray heads, celebrities— the finely render'd anthem, and other music—the church, dim even now at approaching noon, in its light from the mellow- stain'd windows—the pronounc'd eulogy on the bard who loved Nature so fondly, and sung so well her shows and seasons —ending with these appropriate well-known lines:

> I gazed upon the glorious sky,
>   And the green mountains round,
> And thought that when I came to lie
>   At rest within the ground,
> 'Twere pleasant that in flowery June,
> When brooks send up a joyous tune,
>   And groves a cheerful sound,
> The sexton's hand, my grave to make,
> The rich green mountain turf should break.

Jaunt up the Hudson

June 20th.—On the "Mary Powell," enjoy'd everything beyond precedent. The delicious tender summer day, just warm enough —the constantly changing but ever beautiful panorama on both sides of the river—(went up near a hundred miles)—the high straight walls of the stony Palisades—beautiful Yonkers, and beautiful Irvington—the never-ending hills, mostly in rounded lines, swathed with verdure,—the distant turns, like great shoulders in blue veils—the frequent gray and brown of the tall-rising rocks—the river itself, now narrowing, now expanding—the white sails of the many sloops, yachts, &c., some near, some in the distance—the rapid succession of handsome villages and cities, (our boat is a swift traveler, and makes few stops)—the Race—picturesque West Point, and indeed all along—the costly and often turreted mansions forever showing in some cheery light color, through the woods—make up the scene.

Happiness and Raspberries

June 21.—Here I am, on the west bank of the Hudson, 80 miles north of New York, near Esopus, at the handsome, roomy, honeysuckle-and-rose-embower'd cottage of John Burroughs. The place, the perfect June days and nights, (leaning toward crisp and cool,) the hospitality of J. and Mrs. B., the air, the fruit, (especially my favorite dish, currants and raspberries, mixed, sugar'd, fresh and ripe from the bushes— I pick 'em myself)—the room I occupy at night, the perfect bed, the window giving an ample view of the Hudson and the opposite shores, so wonderful toward sunset, and the rolling music of the RR. trains, far over there—the peaceful rest—the early Venus-heralded dawn—the noiseless splash of sunrise, the light and warmth indescribably glorious, in which, (soon as the sun is well up,) I have a capital rubbing and rasping with the flesh-brush—with an extra scour on the back by Al. J., who is here with us—all inspiriting my invalid frame with new life, for the day. Then, after some whiffs of morning air, the delicious coffee of Mrs. B., with the cream, strawberries, and many substantials, for breakfast.

A Specimen Tramp Family

June 22.—This afternoon we went out (J. B., Al. and I) on quite a drive around the country. The scenery, the perpetual stone fences, (some venerable old fellows, dark-spotted with lichens)—the many fine locust-trees—the runs of brawling water, often over descents of rock—these, and lots else. It is lucky the roads are first-rate here, (as they are,) for it is up or down hill everywhere, and sometimes steep enough. B. has a tip-top horse, strong, young, and both gentle and fast. There is a great deal of waste land and hills on the river edge of Ulster county, with a wonderful luxuriance of wild flowers and bushes—and it seems to me I never saw more vitality of trees—eloquent hemlocks, plenty of locusts and fine maples, and the balm of Gilead, giving out aroma. In the fields and along the road-sides unusual crops of the tall-stemm'd wild daisy, white as milk and yellow as gold.

We pass'd quite a number of tramps, singly or in couples—one squad, a family in a rickety one-horse wagon, with some baskets evidently their work and trade—the man seated on a low board, in front, driving—the gauntish woman by his side, with a baby well bundled in her arms, its little red feet and lower legs sticking out right towards us as we pass'd—and in the wagon behind, we saw two (or three) crouching little children. It was a queer, taking, rather sad picture. If I had been alone and on foot, I should have stopp'd and held confab. But on our return nearly two hours afterward, we found them a ways further along the same road, in a lonesome open spot, haul'd aside, unhitch'd, and evidently going to camp for the night. The freed horse was not far off, quietly cropping the grass. The man was busy at the wagon, the boy had gather'd some dry wood, and was making a fire—and as we went a little further we met the woman afoot. I could not see her face, in its great sun-bonnet, but somehow her figure and gait told misery, terror, destitution. She had the rag-bundled, half-starv'd infant still in her arms, and in her hands held two or three baskets, which she had evidently taken to the next house for sale. A little barefoot five-year-old girl-child, with fine eyes, trotted behind her, clutching her gown. We stopp'd, asking about the baskets, which we bought. As we paid the money, she kept her face hidden in the recesses of her bonnet. Then as we started, and stopp'd again, Al., (whose sympathies were evidently arous'd,) went back to the camping group to get another basket. He caught a look of her face, and talk'd with her a little. Eyes, voice and manner were those of a corpse, animated by electricity. She was quite young—the man she was traveling with, middle-aged. Poor woman—what story was it, out of her fortunes, to account for that inexpressibly scared way, those glassy eyes, and that hollow voice?

Manhattan from the Bay

June 25.—Returned to New York last night. Out to-day on the water for a sail in the wide bay, southeast of Staten island—a rough, tossing ride, and a free sight—the long stretch of Sandy Hook, the highlands of Navesink, and the many vessels outward and inward bound. We came up through the midst of all, in the full sun. I especially enjoy'd the last hour or two. A moderate sea-breeze had set in; yet over the city, and the waters adjacent, was a thin haze, concealing nothing, only adding to the beauty. From my point of view, as I write amid the soft breeze, with a sea-temperature, surely nothing on earth of its kind can go beyond this show. To the left the North river with its far vista —nearer, three or four war-ships, anchor'd peacefully—the Jersey side, the banks of Weehawken, the Palisades, and the gradually receding blue, lost in the distance—to the right the East river—the mast-hemm'd shores—the grand obelisk-like towers of the bridge, one on either side, in haze, yet plainly defin'd, giant brothers twain, throwing free graceful interlinking loops high across the tumbled tumultuous current below—(the tide is just changing to its ebb)—the broad water-spread everywhere crowded—no, not crowded, but thick as stars in the sky —with all sorts and sizes of sail and steam vessels, plying ferry-boats, arriving and departing coasters, great ocean Dons, iron-black, modern, magnificent in size and power, fill'd with their incalculable value of human life and precious merchandise—

with here and there, above all, those daring, careening things of grace and wonder, those white and shaded swift-darting fish-birds, (I wonder if shore or sea elsewhere can outvie them,) ever with their slanting spars, and fierce, pure, hawk-like beauty and motion—first-class New York sloop or schooner yachts, sailing, this fine day, the free sea in a good wind. And rising out of the midst, tall-topt, ship-hemm'd, modern, American, yet strangely oriental, V-shaped Manhattan, with its compact mass, its spires, its cloud-touching edifices, group'd at the centre—the green of the trees, and all the white, brown and gray of the architecture well blended, as I see it, under a miracle of limpid sky, delicious light of heaven above, and June haze on the surface below.

Human and Heroic New York

The general subjective view of New York and Brooklyn—(will not the time hasten when the two shall be municipally united in one, and named Manhattan?)—what I may call the human interior and exterior of these great seething oceanic populations, as I get it in this visit, is to me best of all. After an absence of many years, (I went away at the outbreak of the secession war, and have never been back to stay since,) again I resume with curiosity the crowds, the streets I knew so well, Broadway, the ferries, the west side of the city, democratic Bowery—human appearances and manners as seen in all these, and along the wharves, and in the perpetual travel of the horse-cars, or the crowded excursion steamers, or in Wall and Nassau streets by day—in the places of amusement at night—bubbling and whirling and moving like its own environment of waters—endless humanity in all phases—Brooklyn also—taken in for the last three weeks. No need to specify minutely—enough to say that (making all allowances for the shadows and side-streaks of a million-headed-city) the brief total of the impressions, the human qualities, of these vast cities, is to me comforting, even heroic, beyond statement. Alertness, generally fine physique, clear eyes that look straight at you, a singular combination of reticence and self-possession, with good nature and friendliness—a prevailing range of according manners, taste and intellect, surely beyond any elsewhere upon earth—and a palpable outcropping of that personal comradeship I look forward to as the subtlest, strongest future hold of this many-item'd Union—are not only constantly visible here in these mighty channels of men, but they form the rule and average. To-day, I should say—defiant of cynics and pessimists, and with a full knowledge of all their exceptions—an appreciative and perceptive study of the current humanity of New York gives the directest proof yet of successful Democracy, and of the solution of that paradox, the eligibility of the free and fully developed individual with the paramount aggregate. In old age, lame and sick, pondering for years on many a doubt and danger for this republic of ours—fully aware of all that can be said on the other side— I find in this visit to New York, and the daily contact and rapport with its myriad people, on the scale of the oceans and tides, the best, most effective medicine my soul has yet partaken—the grandest physical habitat and surroundings of land and water the globe affords—namely, Manhattan island and Brooklyn, which the future shall join in one city—city of superb democracy, amid superb surroundings.

Hours for the Soul

July 22d, 1878.—Living down in the country again. A wonderful conjunction of all that goes to make those sometime miracle-hours after sunset—so near and yet so far. Perfect, or nearly perfect days, I notice, are not so very uncommon; but the combinations that make perfect nights are few, even in a life time. We have one of those perfections to-night. Sunset left things pretty clear; the larger stars were visible soon as the shades allow'd. A while after 8, three or four great black clouds suddenly rose, seemingly from different points, and sweeping with broad swirls of wind but no thunder, underspread the orbs from view everywhere, and indicated a violent heat-storm. But without storm, clouds, blackness and all, sped and vanish'd

as suddenly as they had risen; and from a little after 9 till 11
the atmosphere and the whole show above were in that state of
exceptional clearness and glory just alluded to. In the northwest turned the Great Dipper with its pointers round the
Cynosure. A little south of east the constellation of the Scorpion
was fully up, with red Antares glowing in its neck; while dominating, majestic Jupiter swam, an hour and a half risen, in
the east—(no moon till after 11.) A large part of the sky
seem'd just laid in great splashes of phosphorus. You could look
deeper in, farther through, than usual; the orbs thick as heads
of wheat in a field. Not that there was any special brilliancy
either—nothing near as sharp as I have seen of keen winter
nights, but a curious general luminousness throughout to sight,
sense, and soul. The latter had much to do with it. (I am con-
vinced there are hours of Nature, especially of the atmosphere,
mornings and evenings, address'd to the soul. Night transcends,
for that purpose, what the proudest day can do.) Now, indeed,
if never before, the heavens declared the glory of God. It was
to the full the sky of the Bible, of Arabia, of the prophets, and
of the oldest poems. There, in abstraction and stillness, (I had
gone off by myself to absorb the scene, to have the spell unbroken,) the copiousness, the removedness, vitality, loose-clear-
crowdedness, of that stellar concave spreading overhead, softly
absorb'd into me, rising so free, interminably high, stretching
east, west, north, south—and I, though but a point in the centre
below, embodying all.

As if for the first time, indeed, creation noiseless sank into
and through me its placid and untellable lesson, beyond—O, so
infinitely beyond!—anything from art, books, sermons, or from
science, old or new. The spirit's hour—religion's hour—the
visible suggestion of God in space and time—now once definitely indicated, if never again. The untold pointed at—the
heavens all paved with it. The Milky Way, as if some super-
human symphony, some ode of universal vagueness, disdaining
syllable and sound—a flashing glance of Deity, address'd to the
soul. All silently—the indescribable night and stars—far off
and silently.

THE DAWN.—*July 23.*—This morning, between one and
two hours before sunrise, a spectacle wrought on the same

background, yet of quite different beauty and meaning. The moon well up in the heavens, and past her half, is shining brightly—the air and sky of that cynical-clear, Minerva-like quality, virgin cool—not the weight of sentiment or mystery, or passion's ecstasy indefinable—not the religious sense, the varied All, distill'd and sublimated into one, of the night just described. Every star now clear-cut, showing for just what it is, there in the colorless ether. The character of the heralded morning, ineffably sweet and fresh and limpid, but for the aesthetic sense alone, and for purity without sentiment. I have itemized the night—but dare I attempt the cloudless dawn? (What subtle tie is this between one's soul and the break of day? Alike, and yet no two nights or morning shows ever exactly alike.) Preceded by an immense star, almost unearthly in its effusion of white splendor, with two or three long unequal spoke-rays of diamond radiance, shedding down through the fresh morning air below—an hour of this, and then the sunrise.

THE EAST.—What a subject for a poem! Indeed, where else a more pregnant, more splendid one? Where one more ideal-istic-real, more subtle, more sensuous-delicate? The East, answering all lands, all ages, peoples; touching all senses, here, immediate, now—and yet so indescribably far off—such retro-spect! The East—long-stretching—so losing itself—the orient, the gardens of Asia, the womb of history and song—forth-issuing all those strange, dim cavalcades—

> Florid with blood, pensive, rapt with musings, hot with passion,
> Sultry with perfume, with ample and flowing garments,
> With sunburnt visage, intense soul and glittering eyes.

Always the East—old, how incalculably old! And yet here the same—ours yet, fresh as a rose, to every morning, every life, to-day—and always will be.

Sept. 17.—Another presentation—same theme—just before sunrise again, (a favorite hour with me.) The clear gray sky, a faint glow in the dull liver-color of the east, the cool fresh odor and the moisture—the cattle and horses off there grazing in the fields—the star Venus again, two hours high. For sounds, the chirping of crickets in the grass, the clarion of chanticleer, and the distant crawing of an early crow. Quietly over the dense fringe of cedars and pines rises that dazzling, red, transparent disk of flame, and the low sheets of white vapor roll and roll into dissolution.

THE MOON.—*May 18.*—I went to bed early last night, but found myself waked shortly after 12, and, turning awhile sleepless and mentally feverish, I rose, dress'd myself, sallied forth and walk'd down the lane. The full moon, some three or four hours up—a sprinkle of light and less-light clouds just lazily moving—Jupiter an hour high in the east, and here and there throughout the heavens a random star appearing and disappearing. So, beautifully veil'd and varied—the air, with that early-summer perfume, not at all damp or raw—at times Luna languidly emerging in richest brightness for minutes, and then partially envelop'd again. Far off a whip-poor-will plied his notes incessantly. It was that silent time between 1 and 3.

The rare nocturnal scene, how soon it sooth'd and pacified me! Is there not something about the moon, some relation or reminder, which no poem or literature has yet caught? (In very old and primitive ballads I have come across lines or asides that suggest it.) After a while the clouds mostly clear'd, and as the moon swam on, she carried, shimmering and shifting, delicate color-effects of pellucid green and tawny vapor. Let me conclude this part with an extract, (some writer in the "Tribune," May 16, 1878:)

No one ever gets tired of the moon. Goddess that she is by dower of her eternal beauty, she is a true woman by her tact —knows the charm of being seldom seen, of coming by surprise and staying but a little while; never wears the same dress two nights running, nor all night the same way; commends herself to the matter-of-fact people by her usefulness, and makes her uselessness adored by poets, artists, and all lovers in all lands; lends herself to every symbolism and to every emblem; is Diana's bow and Venus's mirror and Mary's throne; is a sickle, a scarf, an eyebrow, his face or her face, as look'd at by her or by him: is the madman's hell, the poet's heaven, the baby's toy, the philosopher's study; and while her admirers follow her footsteps, and hang on her lovely looks, she knows how to keep her woman's secret—her other side—unguess'd and unguessable.

Furthermore.—February 19, 1880.—Just before 10 P.M. cold and entirely clear again, the show overhead, bearing south-west, of wonderful and crowded magnificence. The moon in her third quarter—the clusters of the Hyades and Pleiades, with the planet Mars between—in full crossing sprawl in the sky the great Egyptian X, (Sirius, Procyon, and the main stars in the constellations of the Ship, the Dove, and of Orion;) just north of east Bootes, and in his knee Arcturus, an hour high, mounting the heaven, ambitiously large and sparkling, as if he meant to challenge with Sirius the stellar supremacy.

With the sentiment of the stars and moon such nights I get all the free margins and indefiniteness of music or poetry, fused in geometry's utmost exactness.

Straw-Color'd and Other Psyches

Aug. 4.—A pretty sight! Where I sit in the shade—a warm day, the sun shining from cloudless skies, the forenoon well advanc'd —I look over a ten-acre field of luxuriant clover-hay, (the second crop)—the livid-ripe red blossoms and dabs of August brown thickly spotting the prevailing dark-green. Over all flutter myriads of light-yellow butterflies, mostly skimming along the surface, dipping and oscillating, giving a curious animation to the scene. The beautiful, spiritual insects! straw-color'd Psyches! Occasionally one of them leaves his mates, and mounts, perhaps spirally, perhaps in a straight line in the air, fluttering up, up, till literally out of sight. In the lane as I came along just now I noticed one spot, ten feet square or so, where more than a hundred had collected, holding a revel, a gyration-dance, or butterfly good-time, winding and circling, down and across, but always keeping within the limits. The little creatures have come out all of a sudden the last few days, and are now very plentiful. As I sit outdoors, or walk, I hardly look around without somewhere seeing two (always two) fluttering through the air in amorous dalliance. Then their inimitable color, their fragility, peculiar motion—and that strange, frequent way of one leaving the crowd and mounting up, up in the free ether, and apparently never returning. As I look over the field, these yellow-wings everywhere mildly sparkling, many snowy blossoms of the wild carrot gracefuly blending on their tall and taper stems—while for sounds, the distant guttural screech of a flock of guinea-hens comes shrilly yet somehow musically to my ears. And now a faint growl of heat-thunder in the north —and ever the low rising and falling wind-purr from the tops of the maples and willows.

Aug. 20.—Butterflies and butterflies, (taking the place of the bumble-bees of three months since, who have quite disappear'd,) continue to flit to and fro, all sorts, white, yellow, brown, purple—now and then some gorgeous fellow flashing lazily by on wings like artists' palettes dabb'd with every color. Over the breast of the pond I notice many white ones, crossing, pursuing their idle capricious flight. Near where I sit grows a tall-stemm'd weed topt with a profusion of rich scarlet blossoms, on which the snowy insects alight and dally, sometimes four or five of them at a time. By-and-by a humming-bird visits the same, and I watch him coming and going, daintily balancing and shimmering about. These white butterflies give new beautiful contrasts to the pure greens of the August foliage, (we have had some copious rains lately,) and over the glistening bronze of the pond-surface. You can tame even such insects; I have one big and handsome moth down here, knows and comes to me, likes me to hold him up on my extended hand.

Another Day, later.—A grand twelve-acre field of ripe cabbages with their prevailing hue of malachite green, and floating-flying over and among them in all directions myriads of these same white butterflies. As I came up the lane to-day I saw a living globe of the same, two to three feet in diameter, many scores cluster'd together and rolling along in the air, adhering to their ball-shape, six or eight feet above the ground.

A Night Remembrance

Aug. 25, 9–10 a.m.—I sit by the edge of the pond, everything quiet, the broad polish'd surface spread before me—the blue of the heavens and the white clouds reflected from it—and flitting across, now and then, the reflection of some flying bird. Last night I was down here with a friend till after midnight; everything a miracle of splendor—the glory of the stars, and the completely rounded moon—the passing clouds, silver and luminous-tawny—now and then masses of vapory illuminated scud—and silently by my side my dear friend. The shades of the trees, and patches of moonlight on the grass—the softly blowing breeze, and just-palpable odor of the neighboring ripening corn—the indolent and spiritual night, inexpressibly rich, tender, suggestive—something altogether to filter through one's soul, and nourish and feed and soothe the memory long afterwards.

Wild Flowers

This has been and is yet a great season for wild flowers; oceans of them line the roads through the woods, border the edges of the water-runlets, grow all along the old fences, and are scatter'd in profusion over the fields. An eight-petal'd blossom of gold-yellow, clear and bright, with a brown tuft in the middle, nearly as large as a silver half-dollar, is very common; yesterday on a long drive I noticed it thickly lining the borders of the brooks everywhere. Then there is a beautiful weed cover'd with blue flowers, (the blue of the old Chinese teacups treasur'd by our grand-aunts,) I am continually stopping to admire—a little larger than a dime, and very plentiful. White, however, is the prevailing color. The wild carrot I have spoken of; also the fragrant life-everlasting. But there are all hues and beauties, especially on the frequent tracts of half-open scrub-oak and dwarf-cedar hereabout—wild asters of all colors. Notwithstanding the frost-touch the hardy little chaps maintain themselves in all their bloom. The tree-leaves, too, some of them are beginning to turn yellow or drab or dull green. The deep wine-color of the sumachs and gum-trees is already visible, and the straw-color of the dog-wood and beech. Let me give the names of some of these perennial blossoms and friendly weeds I have made acquaintance with hereabout one season or another in my walks :

wild azalea,	dandelions,
wild honeysuckle,	yarrow,
wild roses,	coreopsis,
golden rod,	wild pea,
larkspur,	woodbine,
early crocus,	elderberry,
sweet flag, (great patches of it,)	poke-weed,
	sun-flower,
creeper, trumpet-flower,	chamomile,
scented marjoram,	violets,
snakeroot,	clematis,
Solomon's seal,	bloodroot,
sweet balm,	swamp magnolia,
mint, (great plenty,)	milk-weed,
wild geranium,	wild daisy, (plenty,)
wild heliotrope,	wild chrysanthemum.
burdock,	

A Civility Too Long Neglected

The foregoing reminds me of something. As the individualities I would mainly portray have certainly been slighted by folks who make pictures, volumes, poems, out of them—as a faint testimonial of my own gratitude for many hours of peace and comfort in half-sickness, (and not by any means sure but they will somehow get wind of the compliment,) I hereby dedicate the last half of these Specimen Days to the

bees,	water-snakes,
black-birds,	crows,
dragon-flies,	millers,

pond-turtles,
mulleins, tansy,
    peppermint,
moths (great and little,
    some splendid fellows,)
glow-worms, (swarming
    millions of them in-
    describably strange and
    beautiful at night over
    the pond and creek,)

mosquitoes,
    butterflies,
    wasps and hornets,
    cat birds (and all other
    birds,)
    cedars,
    tulip-trees (and all other
    trees,)
    and to the spots and
    memories of those days,
    and of the creek.

Delaware River—Days and Nights

April 5, 1879.—With the return of spring to the skies, airs,
waters of the Delaware, return the sea-gulls. I never tire of
watching their broad and easy flight, in spirals, or as they oscil-
late with slow unflapping wings, or look down with curved
beak, or dipping to the water after food. The crows, plenty
enough all through the winter, have vanish'd with the ice. Not
one of them now to be seen. The steamboats have again come
forth—bustling up, handsome, freshly painted, for summer
work—the Columbia, the Edwin Forrest, (the Republic not
yet out,) the Reybold, the Nelly White, the Twilight, the Ariel,
the Warner, the Perry, the Taggart, the Jersey Blue—even the
hulky old Trenton—not forgetting those saucy little bull-pups
of the current, the steamtugs.

But let me bunch and catalogue the affair—the river itself,
all the way from the sea—cape Island on one side and Hen-
lopen light on the other—up the broad bay north, and so to
Philadelphia, and on further to Trenton;—the sights I am most
familiar with, (as I live a good part of the time in Camden, I
view matters from that outlook)—the great arrogant, black,
full-freighted ocean steamers, inward or outward bound—the
ample width here between the two cities, intersected by Windmill island—an occasional man-of-war, sometimes a foreigner,
at anchor, with her guns and port-holes, and the boats, and
the brown-faced sailors, and the regular oar-strokes, and the

gay crowds of "visiting day"—the frequent large and handsome three-masted schooners, (a favorite style of marine build, hereabout of late years,) some of them new and very jaunty, with their white-gray sails and yellow pine spars—the sloops dashing along in a fair wind—(I see one now, coming up, under broad canvas, her gaff-topsail shining in the sun, high and picturesque—what a thing of beauty amid the sky and waters!) —the crowded wharf-slips along the city—the flags of different nationalities, the sturdy English cross on its ground of blood, the French tricolor, the banner of the great North German empire, and the Italian and the Spanish colors—sometimes, of an afternoon, the whole scene enliven'd by a fleet of yachts, in a half calm, lazily returning from a race down at Gloucester;— the neat, rakish, revenue steamer "Hamilton" in mid-stream, with her perpendicular stripes flaunting at—and, turning the eyes north, the long ribands of fleecy-white steam, or dingy-black smoke, stretching far, fan-shaped, slanting diagonally across from the Kensington or Richmond shores, in the west-by-south-west wind.

Scenes on Ferry and River—Last Winter's Nights

Then the Camden ferry. What exhilaration, change, people, business, by day. What soothing, silent, wondrous hours, at night, crossing on the boat, most all to myself—pacing the deck, alone, forward or aft. What communion with the waters, the air, the exquisite *chiaroscuro*—the sky and stars, that speak no word, nothing to the intellect, yet so eloquent, so communicative to the soul. And the ferry men—little they know how much they have been to me, day and night—how many spells of listlessness, ennui, debility, they and their hardy ways have dispell'd. And the pilots—captains Hand, Walton, and Giberson by day, and captain Olive at night; Eugene Crosby, with his strong young arm so often supporting, circling, convoying me over the gaps of the bridge, through impediments, safely aboard. Indeed all my ferry friends—captain Frazee the superintendent, Lindell, Hiskey, Fred Rauch, Price, Watson, and a dozen more. And the ferry itself, with its queer scenes—sometimes children suddenly born in the waiting-houses (an actual fact—and more than once)—sometimes a masquerade party, going over at night, with a band of music, dancing and whirling like mad on the broad deck, in their fantastic dresses; sometimes the astronomer, Mr. Whitall, (who posts me up in points about the stars by a living lesson there and then, and answering every question)—sometimes a prolific family group, eight, nine, ten, even twelve! (Yesterday, as I cross'd, a mother, father, and eight children, waiting in the ferry-house, bound westward somewhere.)

I have mention'd the crows. I always watch them from the boats. They play quite a part in the winter scenes on the river, by day. Their black splatches are seen in relief against the snow and ice everywhere at that season—sometimes flying and flapping—sometimes on little or larger cakes, sailing up or down the stream. One day the river was mostly clear—only a single long ridge of broken ice making a narrow stripe by itself, running along down the current for over a mile, quite rapidly. On this white stripe the crows were congregated, hundreds of them—a funny procession—("half mourning" was the comment of some one.)

Then the reception room, for passengers waiting—life illustrated thoroughly. Take a March picture I jotted there two or three weeks since. Afternoon, about $3\frac{1}{2}$ o'clock, it begins to snow. There has been a matinee performance at the theatre— from $4\frac{1}{4}$ to 5 comes a stream of homeward bound ladies. I never knew the spacious room to present a gayer, more lively scene—handsome, well-drest Jersey women and girls, scores of them, streaming in for nearly an hour—the bright eyes and glowing faces, coming in from the air—a sprinkling of snow on bonnets or dresses as they enter—the five or ten minutes' waiting—the chatting and laughing—(women can have capital times among themselves, with plenty of wit, lunches, jovial abandon)—Lizzie, the pleasant-manner'd waiting-room woman —for sound, the bell-taps and steam-signals of the departing boats with their rhythmic break and undertone—the domestic pictures, mothers with bevies of daughters, (a charming sight)

—children, countrymen—the railroad men in their blue clothes and caps—all the various characters of city and country represented or suggested. Then outside some belated passenger frantically running, jumping after the boat. Towards six o'clock the human stream gradually thickening—now a pressure of vehicles, drays, piled railroad crates—now a drove of cattle, making quite an excitement, the drovers with heavy sticks, belaboring the steaming sides of the frighten'd brutes. Inside the reception room, business bargains, flirting, love-making, *eclaircissements*, proposals—pleasant, sober-faced Phil coming in with his burden of afternoon papers—or Jo, or Charley (who jump'd in the dock last week, and saved a stout lady from drowning,) to replenish the stove, after clearing it with long crow-bar poker.

Besides all this "comedy human," the river affords nutriment of a higher order. Here are some of my memoranda of the past winter, just as pencill'd down on the spot.

A January Night.—Fine trips across the wide Delaware tonight. Tide pretty high, and a strong ebb. River, a little after 8, full of ice, mostly broken, but some large cakes making our strong-timber'd steamboat hum and quiver as she strikes them. In the clear moonlight they spread, strange, unearthly, silvery, faintly glistening, as far as I can see. Bumping, trembling, sometimes hissing like a thousand snakes, the tide-procession, as we wend with or through it, affording a grand undertone, in keeping with the scene. Overhead, the splendor indescribable; yet something haughty, almost supercilious, in the night. Never did I realize more latent sentiment, almost *passion,* in those silent interminable stars up there. One can understand, such a night, why, from the days of the Pharaohs or Job, the dome of heaven, sprinkled with planets, has supplied the subtlest, deepest criticism on human pride, glory, ambition.

Another Winter Night.—I don't know anything more *filling* than to be on the wide firm deck of a powerful boat, a clear, cool, extra-moonlight night, crushing proudly and resistlessly through this thick, marbly, glistening ice. The whole river is now spread with it—some immense cakes. There is such weirdness about the scene—partly the quality of the light, with its tinge of blue, the lunar twilight—only the large stars holding their own in the radiance of the moon. Temperature sharp, comfortable for motion, dry, full of oxygen. But the sense of power—the steady, scornful, imperious urge of our strong new engine, as she ploughs her way through the big and little cakes.

Another.—For two hours I cross'd and recross'd, merely for pleasure—for a still excitement. Both sky and river went through several changes. The first for awhile held two vast fan-shaped echelons of light clouds, through which the moon waded now radiating, carrying with her an aureole of tawny transparent brown, and now flooding the whole vast with clear vapory light-green, through which, as through an illuminated veil, she moved with measur'd womanly motion. Then, another trip, the heavens would be absolutely clear, and Luna in all her effulgence. The big Dipper in the north, with the double star in the handle much plainer than common. Then the sheeny track of light in the water, dancing and rippling. Such transformations; such pictures and poems, inimitable.

Another.—I am studying the stars, under advantages, as I cross to-night. (It is late in February, and again extra clear.) High toward the west, the Pleiades, tremulous with delicate sparkle, in the soft heavens. Aldebaran, leading the V-shaped Hyades—and overhead Capella and her kids. Most majestic of all, in full display in the high south, Orion, vast-spread, roomy, chief histrion of the stage, with his shiny yellow rosette on his shoulder, and his three Kings—and a little to the east, Sirius, calmly arrogant, most wondrous single star. Going late ashore, (I couldn't give up the beauty and soothingness of the night,) as I staid around, or slowly wander'd, I heard the echoing calls of the railroad men in the West Jersey depot yard, shifting and switching trains, engines, &c.; amid the general silence otherways, and something in the acoustic quality of the air, musical, emotional effects, never thought of before. I linger'd long and long, listening to them.

Night of March 18, '79.—One of the calm, pleasantly cool, exquisitely clear and cloudless, early spring nights—the atmosphere again that rare vitreous blue-black, welcom'd by astronomers. Just at 8, evening, the scene overhead of certainly solemnest beauty, never surpass'd. Venus nearly down in the west, of a size and lustre as if trying to outshow herself, before departing. Teeming, maternal orb—I take you again to myself. I am reminded of that spring preceding Abraham Lincoln's murder, when I, restlessly haunting the Potomac banks, around Washington city, watch'd you, off there, aloof, moody as myself:

> As we walk'd up and down in the dark blue so mystic,
> As we walk'd in silence the transparent shadowy night,
> As I saw you had something to tell, as you bent to
>   me night after night,
> As you droop from the sky low down, as if to my side,
>   (while the other stars all look'd on,)
> As we wander'd together the solemn night.

With departing Venus, large to the last, and shining even to the edge of the horizon, the vast dome presents at this moment, such a spectacle! Mercury was visible just after sunset—a rare sight. Arcturus is now risen, just north of east. In calm glory all the stars of Orion hold the place of honor, in meridian, to the south—with the Dog-star a little to the left. And now, just rising, Spica, late, low, and slightly veil'd. Castor, Regulus and the rest, all shining unusually clear, (no Mars or Jupiter or moon till morning.) On the edges of the river, many lamps twinkling—with two or three huge chimneys, a couple of miles up, belching forth molten, steady flames, volcano-like, illuminating all around—and sometimes an electric or calcium, its Dante-Inferno gleams, in far shafts, terrible, ghastly-powerful. Of later May nights, crossing, I like to watch the fishermen's little buoy-lights—so pretty, so dreamy—like corpse candles—undulating delicate and lonesome on the surface of the shadowy waters, floating with the current.

The First Spring Day on Chestnut Street

Winter relaxing its hold, has already allow'd us a foretaste of spring. As I write, yesterday afternoon's softness and brightness, (after the morning fog, which gave it a better setting, by contrast,) show'd Chestnut street—say between Broad and

Fourth—to more advantage in its various asides, and all its stores, and gay-dress'd crowds generally, than for three months past. I took a walk there between one and two. Doubtless, there were plenty of hard-up folks along the pavements, but nine-tenths of the myriad-moving human panorama to all appearance seem'd flush, well-fed, and fully-provided. At all events it was good to be on Chestnut street yesterday. The peddlers on the sidewalk—("sleeve-buttons, three for five cents")—the handsome little fellow with canary-bird whistles—the cane men, toy men, toothpick men—the old woman squatted in a heap on the cold stone flags, with her basket of matches, pins and tape—the young negro mother, sitting, begging, with her two little coffee-color'd twins on her lap—the beauty of the cramm'd conservatory of rare flowers, flaunting reds, yellows, snowy lilies, incredible orchids, at the Baldwin mansion near Twelfth street—the show of fine poultry, beef, fish, at the restaurants—the china stores, with glass and statuettes—the luscious tropical fruits—the street cars plodding along, with their tintinnabulating bells—the fat, cab-looking, rapidly driven one-horse vehicles of the post-office, squeez'd full of coming or going letter-carriers, so healthy and handsome and manly-looking, in their gray uniforms—the costly books, pictures, curiosities, in the windows—the gigantic policemen at most of the corners—will all be readily remember'd and recognized as features of this principal avenue of Philadelphia. Chestnut street, I have discover'd, is not without individuality, and its own points, even when compared with the great promenade-streets of other cities. I have never been in Europe, but acquired years' familiar experience with New York's, (perhaps the world's,) great thoroughfare, Broadway, and possess to some extent a personal and saunterer's knowledge of St. Charles street in New Orleans, Tremont street in Boston, and the broad trottoirs of Pennsylvania avenue in Washington. Of course it is a pity that Chestnut were not two or three times wider; but the street, any fine day, shows vividness, motion, variety, not easily to be surpass'd. (Sparkling eyes, human faces, magnetism, well-dress'd women, ambulating to and fro—with lots of fine things in the windows—are they not about the same, the civilized world over?)

How fast the flitting figures come!
    The mild, the fierce, the stony face;
Some bright with thoughtless smiles—and some
    Where secret tears have left their trace.

A few days ago one of the six-story clothing stores along here had the space inside its plate-glass show-window partition'd into a little corral, and litter'd deeply with rich clover and hay, (I could smell the odor outside,) on which reposed two magnificent fat sheep, full-sized but young—the handsomest creatures of the kind I ever saw. I stopp'd long and long, with the crowd, to view them—one lying down chewing the cud, and one standing up, looking out, with dense-fringed patient eyes. Their wool, of a clear tawny color, with streaks of glistening black—altogether a queer sight amidst that crowded promenade of dandies, dollars and drygoods.

Up the Hudson to Ulster County

April 23.—Off to New York on a little tour and visit. Leaving the hospitable, home-like quarters of my valued friends, Mr. and Mrs. J. H. Johnston—took the 4 P.M. boat, bound up the Hudson, 100 miles or so. Sunset and evening fine. Especially enjoy'd the hour after we passed Cozzens's landing—the night lit by the crescent moon and Venus, now swimming in tender glory, and now hid by the high rocks and hills of the western shore, which we hugg'd close. (Where I spend the next ten days is in Ulster county and its neighborhood, with frequent morning and evening drives, observations of the river, and short rambles.)

April 24—Noon.—A little more and the sun would be oppressive. The bees are out gathering their bread from willows and other trees. I watch them returning, darting through the air or lighting on the hives, their thighs covered with the yellow forage. A solitary robin sings near. I sit in my shirt sleeves and gaze from an open bay-window on the indolent scene—the thin haze, the Fishkill hills in the distance—off on the river, a sloop with slanting mainsail, and two or three little shad-boats. Over on the railroad opposite, long freight trains, sometimes weighted by cylinder-tanks of petroleum, thirty, forty, fifty cars in a string, panting and rumbling along in full view, but the sound soften'd by distance.

Days at J. B.'s—Turf Fires—
Spring Songs

April 26.—At sunrise, the pure clear sound of the meadow lark. An hour later, some notes, few and simple, yet delicious and perfect, from the bush-sparrow—towards noon the reedy trill of the robin. To-day is the fairest, sweetest yet—penetrating warmth—a lovely veil in the air, partly heat-vapor and partly from the turf-fires everywhere in patches on the farms. A group of soft maples near by silently bursts out in crimson tips, buzzing all day with busy bees. The white sails of sloops and schooners glide up or down the river; and long trains of cars, with ponderous roll, or faint bell notes, almost constantly on the opposite shore. The earliest wild flowers in the woods and fields, spicy arbutus, blue liverwort, frail anemone, and the pretty white blossoms of the bloodroot. I launch out in slow rambles, discovering them. As I go along the roads I like to see the farmers' fires in patches, burning the dry brush, turf, debris. How the smoke crawls along, flat to the ground, slanting, slowly rising, reaching away, and at last dissipating. I like its acrid smell—whiffs just reaching me—welcomer than French perfume.

The birds are plenty; of any sort, or of two or three sorts, curiously, not a sign, till suddenly some warm, gushing, sunny April (or even March) day—lo! there they are, from twig to twig or fence to fence, flirting, singing, some mating, preparing to build. But most of them *en passant*—a fortnight, a month in these parts, and then away. As in all phases, Nature keeps up her vital, copious, eternal procession. Still, plenty of the birds hang around all or most of the season—now their love-time, and era of nest-building. I find flying over the river, crows, gulls and hawks. I hear the afternoon shriek of the latter, darting about, preparing to nest. The oriole will soon be heard here, and the twanging *meoeow* of the cat-bird; also the king-bird, cuckoo and the warblers. All along, there are three peculiarly characteristic spring songs—the meadow-lark's, so sweet, so alert and remonstrating (as if he said, "don't you see?" or, "can't you understand?")—the cheery, mellow, human tones of the robin—(I have been trying for years to get a brief term, or phrase, that would identify and describe that robin-call)—and the amorous whistle of the high-hole. Insects are out plentifully at midday.

April 29.—As we drove lingering along the road we heard, just after sundown, the song of the wood-thrush. We stopp'd without a word, and listen'd long. The delicious notes—a sweet, artless, voluntary, simple anthem, as from the flute-stops of some organ, watted through the twilight—echoing well to us from the perpendicular high rock, where, in some thick young trees' recesses at the base, sat the bird—fill'd our senses, our souls.

Meeting a Hermit

I found in one of my rambles up the hills a real hermit, living in a lonesome spot, hard to get at, rocky, the view fine, with a little patch of land two rods square. A man of youngish middle age, city born and raised, had been to school, had travel'd in Europe and California. I first met him once or twice on the road, and pass'd the time of day, with some small talk; then, the third time, he ask'd me to go along a bit and rest in his hut (an almost unprecedented compliment, as I heard from others afterwards.) He was of Quaker stock, I think; talk'd with ease and moderate freedom, but did not unbosom his life, or story, or tragedy, or whatever it was.

An Ulster County Waterfall

I jot this mem. in a wild scene of woods and hills, where we have come to visit a waterfall. I never saw finer or more copious hemlocks, many of them large, some old and hoary. Such a sentiment to them, secretive, shaggy—what I call weather-beaten and let-alone—a rich underlay of ferns, yew sprouts and mosses, beginning to be spotted with the early summer wild-flowers. Enveloping all, the monotone and liquid gurgle from the hoarse impetuous copious fall—the greenish-tawny, darkly transparent waters, plunging with velocity down the rocks, with patches of milk-white foam—a stream of hurrying amber, thirty feet wide, risen far back in the hills and woods, now rushing with volume—every hundred rods a fall, and sometimes three or four in that distance. A primitive forest, druidical, solitary and savage—not ten visitors a year—broken rocks everywhere—shade overhead, thick underfoot with leaves —a just palpable wild and delicate aroma.

Walter Dumont and His Medal

As I saunter'd along the high road yesterday, I stopp'd to watch a man near by, ploughing a rough stony field with a yoke of oxen. Usually there is much geeing and hawing, excitement, and continual noise and expletives, about a job of this kind. But I noticed how different, how easy and wordless, yet firm and sufficient, the work of this young ploughman. His name was Walter Dumont, a farmer, and son of a farmer, working for their living. Three years ago, when the steamer "Sunny-side" was wreck'd of a bitter icy night on the west bank here, Walter went out in his boat—was the first man on hand with assistance—made a way through the ice to shore, connected a line, perform'd work of first-class readiness, daring, danger, and saved numerous lives. Some weeks after, one evening when he was up at Esopus, among the usual loafing crowd at the country store and post-office, there arrived the gift of an unexpected official gold medal for the quiet hero. The impromptu presentation was made to him on the spot, but he blush'd, hesitated as he took it, and had nothing to say.

Hudson River Sights

It was a happy thought to build the Hudson river railroad right along the shore. The grade is already made by nature; you are sure of ventilation one side—and you are in nobody's way. I see, hear, the locomotives and cars, rumbling, roaring, flaming, smoking, constantly, away off there, night and day—less than a mile distant, and in full view by day. I like both sight and sound. Express trains thunder and lighten along; of freight trains, most of them very long, there cannot be less than a hundred a day. At night far down you see the headlight approaching, coming steadily on like a meteor. The river at night has its special character-beauties. The shad fishermen go forth in their boats and pay out their nets—one sitting forward, rowing, and one standing up aft dropping it properly—marking the line with little floats bearing candles, conveying, as they glide over the water, an indescribable sentiment and doubled brightness. I like to watch the tows at night, too, with their twinkling lamps, and hear the husky panting of the steamers; or catch the sloops' and schooners' shadowy forms, like phantoms, white, silent, indefinite, out there. Then the Hudson of a clear moonlight night.

But there is one sight the very grandest. Sometimes in the fiercest driving storm of wind, rain, hail or snow, a great eagle will appear over the river, now soaring with steady and now overhended wings—always confronting the gale, or perhaps cleaving into, or at times literally *sitting* upon it. It is like reading some first-class natural tragedy or epic, or hearing martial trumpets. The splendid bird enjoys the hubbub—is adjusted and equal to it—finishes it so artistically. His pinions just oscillating—the position of his head and neck—his resistless, occasionally varied flight—now a swirl, now an upward movement—the black clouds driving—the angry wash below —the hiss of rain, the wind's piping (perhaps the ice colliding, grunting)—he tacking or jibing—now, as it were, for a change, abandoning himself to the gale, moving with it with such velocity—and now, resuming control, he comes up against it, lord of the situation and the storm—lord, amid it, of power and savage joy.

Sometimes (as at present writing,) middle of sunny afternoon, the old "Vanderbilt" steamer stalking ahead—I plainly hear her rhythmic, slushing paddles—drawing by long hawsers an immense and varied following string, ("an old sow and pigs," the river folks call it.) First comes a big barge, with a house built on it, and spars towering over the roof; then canal boats, a lengthen'd, clustering train, fasten'd and link'd together —the one in the middle, with high staff, flaunting a broad and gaudy flag—others with the almost invariable lines of new-wash'd clothes, drying; two sloops and a schooner aside the tow—little wind, and that adverse—with three long, dark, empty barges bringing up the rear. People are on the boats: men lounging, women in sun-bonnets, children, stovepipes with streaming smoke.

Two City Areas, Certain Hours

New York, May 24, '79.—Perhaps no quarters of this city (I have return'd again for awhile,) make more brilliant, animated, crowded, spectacular human presentations these fine May afternoons than the two I am now going to describe from personal observation. First: that area comprising Fourteenth street (especially the short range between Broadway and Fifth avenue) with Union square, its adjacencies, and so retrostretching down Broadway for half a mile. All the walks here are wide, and the spaces ample and free—now flooded with liquid gold from the last two hours of powerful sunshine. The whole area at 5 o'clock, the days of my observations, must have contain'd from thirty to forty thousand finely-dress'd people, all in motion, plenty of them good-looking, many beautiful women, often youths and children, the latter in groups with their nurses—the trottoirs everywhere close-spread, thick-tangled, (yet no collision, no trouble,) with masses of bright color, action, and tasty toilets; (surely the women dress better than ever before, and the men do too.) As if New York would show these afternoons what it can do in its humanity, it choicest physique and physiognomy, and its countless prodigality of locomotion, dry goods, glitter, magnetism, and happiness.

Second: also from 5 to 7 P.M. the stretch of Fifth avenue, all the way from the Central Park exits at Fifty-ninth street, down to Fourteenth, especially along the high grade by Forti-eth street, and down the hill. A Mississippi of horses and rich vehicles, not by dozens and scores, but hundreds and thousands —the broad avenue filled and cramm'd with them—a moving, sparkling, hurrying crush, for more than two miles. (I wonder they don't get block'd, but I believe they never do.) Altogether it is to me the marvel sight of New York. I like to get in one of the Fifth avenue stages and ride up, stemming the swift-moving procession. I doubt if London or Paris or any city in the world can show such a carriage carnival as I have seen here five or six times these beautiful May afternoons.

Central Park Walks and Talks

May 16 to 22.—I visit Central Park now almost every day, sitting, or slowly rambling, or riding around. The whole place presents its very best appearance this current month—the full flush of the trees, the plentiful white and pink of the flowering shrubs, the emerald green of the grass spreading everywhere, yellow dotted still with dandelions—the specialty of the plen-tiful gray rocks, peculiar to these grounds, cropping out, miles and miles—and over all the beauty and purity, three days out of four, of our summer skies. As I sit, placidly, early after-noon, off against Ninetieth street, the policeman, C. C., a well-form'd sandy-complexion'd young fellow, comes over and stands near me. We grow quite friendly and chatty forthwith. He is a New Yorker born and raised, and in answer to my questions tells me about the life of a New York Park police-man, (while he talks keeping his eyes and ears vigilantly open, occasionally pausing and moving where he can get full views of the vistas of the road, up and down, and the spaces around.) The pay is $2.40 a day (seven days to a week)—the men come on and work eight hours straight ahead, which is all that is required of them out of the twenty-four. The position has more risks than one might suppose—for instance if a team or horse runs away (which happens daily) each man is expected not only to be prompt, but to waive safety and stop wildest nag or nags—(*do it*, and don't be thinking of your bones or face) —give the alarm-whistle too, so that other guards may repeat, and the vehicles up and down the tracks be warn'd. Injuries to the men are continually happening. There is much alertness and quiet strength. (Few appreciate, I have often thought, the Ulyssean capacity, derring do, quick readiness in emergencies, practically, unwitting devotion and heroism, among our American young men and working-people—the firemen, the railroad employés, the steamer and ferry men, the police, the conductors and drivers—the whole splendid average of native stock, city and country.) It is good work, though; and upon the whole, the Park force members like it. They see life, and the excitement keeps them up. There is not so much difficulty as might be supposed from tramps, roughs, or in keeping people "off the grass." The worst trouble of the regular Park employé is from malarial fever, chills, and the like.

A Fine Afternoon, 4 to 6

Ten thousand vehicles careering through the Park this perfect afternoon. Such a show! and I have seen all—watch'd it narrowly, and at my leisure. Private barouches, cabs and coupés, some fine horseflesh—lapdogs, footmen, fashions, foreigners, cockades on hats, crests on panels—the full oceanic tide of New York's wealth and "gentility." It was an impressive, rich interminable circus on a grand scale, full of action and color in the beauty of the day, under the clear sun and moderate breeze. Family groups, couples, single drivers—of course dresses generally elegant—much "style," (yet perhaps little or nothing, even in that direction, that fully justified itself.) Through the windows of two or three of the richest carriages I saw faces almost corpse-like, so ashy and listless. Indeed the whole affair exhibited less of sterling America, either in spirit or countenance, than I had counted on from such a select mass-spectacle. I suppose, as a proof of limitless wealth, leisure, and the aforesaid "gentility," it was tremendous. Yet what I saw those hours (I took two other occasions, two other afternoons to watch the same scene,) confirms a thought that haunts me every additional glimpse I get of our top-loftical general or rather exceptional phases of wealth and fashion in this country —namely, that they are ill at ease, much too conscious, cased in too many cerements, and far from happy—that there is nothing in them which we who are poor and plain need at all envy, and that instead of the perennial smell of the grass and woods and shores, their typical redolence is of soaps and essences, very rare may be, but suggesting the barber shop— something that turns stale and musty in a few hours anyhow.

Perhaps the show on the horseback road was prettiest. Many groups (threes a favorite number,) some couples, some singly —many ladies—frequently horses or parties dashing along on a full run—fine riding the rule—a few really first-class animals. As the afternoon waned, the wheel'd carriages grew less, but the saddle-riders seemed to increase. They linger'd long—and I saw some charming forms and faces.

Departing of the Big Steamers

May 15.—A three hours' bay-trip from 12 to 3 this afternoon, accompanying "the City of Brussels" down as far as the Narrows, in behoof of some Europe-bound friends, to give them a good send off. Our spirited little tug, the "Seth Low," kept close to the great black "Brussels," sometimes one side, sometimes the other, always up to her, or even pressing ahead, (like the blooded pony accompanying the royal elephant.) The whole affair, from the first, was an animated, quick-passing, characteristic New York scene; the large, good-looking, well-dress'd crowd on the wharf-end—men and women come to see their friends depart, and bid them God-speed—the ship's sides swarming with passengers—groups of bronze-faced sailors, with uniform'd officers at their posts—the quiet directions, as she quickly unfastens and moves out, prompt to a minute —the emotional faces, adieus and fluttering handkerchiefs, and many smiles and some tears on the wharf—the answering faces, smiles, tears and fluttering handkerchiefs, from the ship— (what can be subtler and finer than this play of faces on such occasions in these responding crowds?—what go more to one's heart?)—the proud, steady, noiseless cleaving of the grand oceaner down the bay—we speeding by her side a few miles, and then turning, wheeling, amid a babel of wild hurrahs, shouted partings, ear-splitting steam whistles, kissing of hands and waving of handkerchiefs.

This departing of the big steamers, noons or afternoons— there is no better medicine when one is listless or vapory. I am fond of going down Wednesdays and Saturdays—their more special days—to watch them and the crowds on the wharves, the arriving passengers, the general bustle and activity, the eager looks from the faces, the clear-toned voices, (a travel'd foreigner, a musician, told me the other day she thinks an American crowd has the finest voices in the world,) the whole look of the great, shapely black ships themselves, and their groups and lined sides—in the setting of our bay with the blue sky overhead. Two days after the above I saw the "Britannic," the "Donau," the "Helvetia" and the "Schiedam" steam out, all off for Europe—a magnificent sight.

Two Hours on the Minnesota

From 7 to 9, aboard the United States school-ship Minnesota, lying up the North river. Captain Luce sent his gig for us about sundown, to the foot of Twenty-third street, and receiv'd us aboard with officer-like hospitality and sailor heartiness. There are several hundred youths on the Minnesota to be train'd for efficiently manning the government navy. I like the

idea much; and, so far as I have seen to-night, I like the way
it is carried out on this huge vessel. Below, on the gun-deck,
were gather'd nearly a hundred of the boys, to give us some
of their singing exercises, with a melodeon accompaniment,
play'd by one of their number. They sang with a will. The
best part, however, was the sight of the young fellows themselves. I went over among them before the singing began, and
talk'd a few minutes informally. They are from all the States;
I asked for the Southerners, but could only find one, a lad
from Baltimore. In age, apparently, they range from about
fourteen years to nineteen or twenty. They are all of American
birth, and have to pass a rigid medical examination; wellgrown youths, good flesh, bright eyes, looking straight at you,
healthy, intelligent, not a slouch among them, nor a menial—
in every one the promise of a man. I have been to many public
aggregations of young and old, and of schools and colleges,
in my day, but I confess I have never been so near satisfied,
so comforted, (both from the fact of the school itself, and
the splendid proof of our country, our composite race, and
the sample-promises of its good average capacities, its future,)
as in the collection from all parts of the United States on this
navy training ship. ("Are there going to be *any men* there?"
was the dry and pregnant reply of Emerson to one who had
been crowding him with the rich material statistics and possibilities of some western or Pacific region.)

May 26.—Aboard the Minnesota again. Lieut. Murphy kindly came for me in his boat. Enjoy'd specially those brief trips
to and fro—the sailors, tann'd, strong, so bright and able-
looking, pulling their oars in long side-swing, man-of-war
style, as they row'd me across. I saw the boys in companies
drilling with small arms; had a talk with Chaplain Rawson.
At 11 o'clock all of us gathered to breakfast around a long
table in the great ward room—I among the rest—a genial,
plentiful, hospitable affair every way—plenty to eat, and of
the best; became acquainted with several new officers. This
second visit, with its observations, talks, (two or three at
random with the boys,) confirm'd my first impressions.

Mature Summer Days and Nights

Aug. 4.—Forenoon—as I sit under the willow shade, (have retreated down in the country again,) a little bird is leisurely dousing and flirting himself amid the brook almost within reach of me. He evidently fears me not— takes me for some concomitant of the neighboring earthy banks, free bushery and wild weeds. *6 p. m.*—The last three days have been perfect ones for the season, (four nights ago copious rains, with vehement thunder and lightning.) I write this sitting by the creek watching my two kingfishers at their sundown sport. The strong, beautiful, joyous creatures! Their wings glisten in the slanted sunbeams as they circle and circle around, occasionally dipping and dashing the water, and making long stretches up and down the creek. Wherever I go over fields, through lanes, in byplaces, blooms the white-flowering wild-carrot, its delicate pat of snow-flakes crowning its slender stem, gracefully oscillating in the breeze.

Exposition Building— New City Hall—River Trip

Philadelphia, Aug. 26.—Last night and to-night of unsurpass'd clearness, after two days' rain; moon splendor and star splendor. Being out toward the great Exposition building, West Philadelphia, I saw it lit up, and thought I would go in. There was a ball, democratic but nice; plenty of young couples waltzing and quadrilling—music by a good string-band. To the sight and hearing of these—to moderate strolls up and down the roomy spaces—to getting off aside, resting in an armchair and looking up a long while at the grand high roof with its graceful and multitudinous work of iron rods, angles, gray colors, plays of light and shade, receding into dim outlines— to absorbing (in the intervals of the string band,) some capital voluntaries and rolling caprices from the big organ at the other end of the building—to sighting a shadow'd figure or group or couple of lovers every now and then passing some near or farther aisle—I abandon'd myself for over an hour.

Returning home, riding down Market street in an open summer car, something detain'd us between Fifteenth and Broad, and I got out to view better the new, three-fifths-built marble edifice, the City Hall, of magnificent proportions—a majestic and lovely show there in the moonlight—flooded all over, façades, myriad silver-white lines and carv'd heads and mouldings, with the soft dazzle—silent, weird, beautiful—well, I know that never when finish'd will that magnificent pile impress one as it impress'd me those fifteen minutes.

To-night, since, I have been long on the river. I watch the C-shaped Northern Crown, (with the star Alshacca that blazed out so suddenly, alarmingly, one night a few years ago.) The moon in her third quarter, and up nearly all night. And there, as I look eastward, my long-absent Pleiades, welcome again to sight. For an hour I enjoy the soothing and vital scene to the low splash of waves—new stars steadily, noiselessly rising in the east.

As I cross the Delaware, one of the deck-hands, F. R., tells me how a woman jump'd overboard and was drown'd a couple of hours since. It happen'd in mid-channel—she leap'd from the forward part of the boat, which went over her. He saw her rise on the other side in the swift running water, throw her arms and closed hands high up, (white hands and bare forearms in the moonlight like a flash,) and then she sank. (I found out afterwards that this young fellow had promptly jump'd in, swam after the poor creature, and made, though unsuccessfully, the bravest efforts to rescue her; but he didn't mention that part at all in telling me the story.)

Swallows on the River

Sept. 3.—Cloudy and wet, and wind due east; air without palpable fog, but very heavy with moisture—welcome for a change. Forenoon, crossing the Delaware, I noticed unusual numbers of swallows in flight, circling, darting, graceful beyond description, close to the water. Thick, around the bows of the ferry-boat as she lay tied in her slip, they flew; and as we went out I watch'd beyond the pier-heads, and across the broad stream, their swift-winding loop-ribands of motion, down close to it, cutting and intersecting. Though I had seen swallows all my life, seem'd as though I never before realized their peculiar beauty and character in the landscape. (Some time ago, for an hour, in a huge old country barn, watching these birds flying, recall'd the 22d book of the Odyssey, where Ulysses slays the suitors, bringing things to *eclaircissement*, and Minerva, swallow-bodied, darts up through the spaces of the hall, sits high on a beam, looks complacently on the show of slaughter, and feels in her element, exulting, joyous.)

Begin a Long Jaunt West

The following three or four months (Sept. to Dec. '79) I made quite a western journey, fetching up at Denver, Colorado, and penetrating the Rocky Mountain region enough to get a good notion of it all. Left West Philadelphia after 9 o'clock one night, middle of September, in a comfortable sleeper. Oblivious of the two or three hundred miles across Pennsylvania; at Pittsburgh in the morning to breakfast. Pretty good view of the city and Birmingham—fog and damp, smoke, coke-furnaces, flames, discolor'd wooden houses, and vast collections of coal-barges. Presently a bit of fine region, West Virginia, the Panhandle, and crossing the river, the Ohio. By day through the latter State—then Indiana—and so rock'd to slumber for a second night, flying like lightning through Illinois.

In the Sleeper

What a fierce weird pleasure to lie in my berth at night in the luxurious palace-car, drawn by the mighty Baldwin—embodying, and filling me, too, full of the swiftest motion, and most resistless strength! It is late, perhaps midnight or after—

distances join'd like magic—as we speed through Harrisburg, Columbus, Indianapolis. The element of danger adds zest to it all. On we go, rumbling and flashing, with our loud whinnies thrown out from time to time, or trumpet-blasts, into the darkness. Passing the homes of men, the farms, barns, cattle—the silent villages. And the car itself, the sleeper, with curtains drawn and lights turn'd down—in the berths the slumberers, many of them women and children—as on, on, on, we fly like lightning through the night—how strangely sound and sweet they sleep! (They say the French Voltaire in his time designated the grand opera and a ship of war the most signal illustrations of the growth of humanity's and art's advance beyond primitive barbarism. Perhaps if the witty philosopher were here these days, and went in the same car with perfect bedding and feed from New York to San Francisco, he would shift his type and sample to one of our American sleepers.)

Missouri State

We should have made the run of 960 miles from Philadelphia to St. Louis in thirty-six hours, but we had a collision and bad locomotive smash about two-thirds of the way, which set us back. So merely stopping over night that time in St. Louis, I sped on westward. As I cross'd Missouri State the whole distance by the St. Louis and Kansas City Northern Railroad, a fine early autumn day, I thought my eyes had never looked on scenes of greater pastoral beauty. For over two hundred miles successive rolling prairies, agriculturally perfect view'd by Pennsylvania and New Jersey eyes, and dotted here and there with fine timber. Yet fine as the land is, it isn't the finest portion; (there is a bed of impervious clay and hardpan beneath this section that holds water too firmly, "drowns the land in wet weather, and bakes it in dry," as a cynical farmer told me.) South are some richer tracts, though perhaps the beauty-spots of the State are the northwestern counties. Altogether, I am clear, (now, and from what I have seen and learn'd since,) that Missouri, in climate, soil, relative situation, wheat, grass, mines, railroads, and every important materialistic respect, stands in the front rank of the Union. Of Missouri averaged politically and socially I have heard all sorts of talk, some pretty severe—but I should have no fear myself of getting along safely and comfortably anywhere among the Missourians. They raise a good deal of tobacco. You see at this time quantities of the light greenish-gray leaves pulled and hanging out to dry on temporary frameworks or rows of sticks. Looks much like the mullein familiar to eastern eyes.

Lawrence and Topeka, Kansas

We thought of stopping in Kansas City, but when we got there we found a train ready and a crowd of hospitable Kansians to take us on to Lawrence, to which I proceeded. I shall not soon forget my good days in L., in company with Judge Usher and his sons, (especially John and Linton,) true westerners of the noblest type. Nor the similar days in Topeka. Nor the brotherly kindness of my RR. friends there, and the city and State officials. Lawrence and Topeka are large, bustling, half-rural, handsome cities. I took two or three long drives about the latter, drawn by a spirited team over smooth roads.

The Prairies

And an Undelivered Speech

At a large popular meeting at Topeka—the Kansas State Silver Wedding, fifteen or twenty thousand people—I had been erroneously bill'd to deliver a poem. As I seem'd to be made much of, and wanted to be good-natured, I hastily pencill'd out the following little speech. Unfortunately, (or fortunately,) I had such a good time and rest, and talk and dinner, with the U. boys, that I let the hours slip away and didn't drive over to the meeting and speak my piece. But here it is just the same:

"My friends, your bills announce me as giving a poem; but I have no poem—have composed none for this occasion. And I can honestly say I am now glad of it. Under these skies resplendent in September beauty—amid the peculiar landscape you are used to, but which is new to me—these interminable and stately prairies—in the freedom and vigor and sane enthusiasm of this perfect western air and autumn sunshine—it seems to me a poem would be almost an impertinence. But if you care to have a word from me, I should speak it about these very prairies; they impress me most, of all the objective shows I see or have seen on this, my first real visit to the West. As I have roll'd rapidly hither for more than a thousand miles, through fair Ohio, through bread-raising Indiana and Illinois—through ample Missouri, that contains and raises everything; as I have partially explor'd your charming city during the last two days, and, standing on Oread hill, by the university, have launch'd my view across broad expanses of living green, in every direction—I have again been most impress'd, I say, and shall remain for the rest of my life most impress'd, with that feature of the topography of your western central world —that vast Something, stretching out on its own unbounded scale, unconfined, which there is in these prairies, combining the real and ideal, and beautiful as dreams.

"I wonder indeed if the people of this continental inland West know how much of first-class *art* they have in these prairies—how original and all your own—how much of the influences of a character for your future humanity, broad, patriotic, heroic and new? how entirely they tally on land the grandeur and superb monotony of the skies of heaven, and the ocean with its waters? how freeing, soothing, nourishing they are to the soul?

"Then is it not subtly they who have given us our leading modern Americans, Lincoln and Grant?—vast-spread, average men—their foregrounds of character altogether practical and real, yet (to those who have eyes to see) with finest backgrounds of the ideal, towering high as any. And do we not see, in them, foreshadowings of the future races that shall fill these prairies?

"Not but what the Yankee and Atlantic States, and every

other part—Texas, and the States flanking the south-east and the Gulf of Mexico—the Pacific shore empire—the Territories and Lakes, and the Canada line (the day is not yet, but it will come, including Canada entire)—are equally and integrally and indissolubly this Nation, the *sine qua non* of the human, political and commercial New World. But this favor'd central area of (in round numbers) two thousand miles square seems fated to be the home both of what I would call America's distinctive ideas and distinctive realities."

On to Denver—a Frontier Incident

The jaunt of five or six hundred miles from Topeka to Denver took me through a variety of country, but all unmistakably prolific, western, American, and on the largest scale. For a long distance we follow the line of the Kansas river, (I like better the old name, Kaw,) a stretch of very rich, dark soil, famed for its wheat, and call'd the Golden Belt—then plains and plains, hour after hour—Ellsworth county, the centre of the State—where I must stop a moment to tell a characteristic story of early days—scene the very spot where I am passing—time 1868. In a scrimmage at some public gathering in the town, A. had shot B. quite badly, but had not kill'd him. The sober men of Ellsworth conferr'd with one another and decided that A. deserv'd punishment. As they wished to set a good example and establish their reputation the reverse of a Lynching town, they open an informal court and bring both men before them for deliberate trial. Soon as this trial begins the wounded man is led forward to give his testimony. Seeing his enemy in durance and unarm'd, B. walks suddenly up in a fury and shoots A. through the head—shoots him dead. The court is instantly adjourn'd, and its unanimous members, without a word of debate, walk the murderer B. out, wounded as he is, and hang him.

In due time we reach Denver, which city I fall in love with from the first, and have that feeling confirm'd, the longer I stay there. One of my pleasantest days was a jaunt, via Platte cañon, to Leadville.

An Hour on Kenosha Summit

Jottings from the Rocky Mountains, mostly pencill'd during a day's trip over the South Park RR., returning from Leadville, and especially the hour we were detain'd, (much to my satisfaction,) at Kenosha summit. As afternoon advances, novelties, far-reaching splendors, accumulate under the bright sun in this pure air. But I had better commence with the day.

The confronting of Platte cañon just at dawn, after a ten miles' ride in early darkness on the rail from Denver—the seasonable stoppage at the entrance of the cañon, and good breakfast of eggs, trout, and nice griddle-cakes—then as we travel on, and get well in the gorge, all the wonders, beauty, savage power of the scene—the wild stream of water, from sources of snows, brawling continually in sight one side—the dazzling sun, and the morning lights on the rocks—such turns and grades in the track, squirming around corners, or up and down hills—far glimpses of a hundred peaks, titanic necklaces, stretching north and south—the huge rightly-named Domerock—and as we dash along, others similar, simple, monolithic, elephantine.

An Egotistical "Find"

"I have found the law of my own poems," was the unspoken but more-and-more decided feeling that came to me as I pass'd, hour after hour, amid all this grim yet joyous elemental abandon—this plenitude of material, entire absence of art, untrammel'd play of primitive Nature—the chasm, the gorge, the crystal mountain stream, repeated scores, hundreds of miles —the broad handling and absolute uncrampedness—the fantastic forms, bathed in transparent browns, faint reds and grays, towering sometimes a thousand, sometimes two or three thousand feet high—at their tops now and then huge masses pois'd, and mixing with the clouds, with only their outlines, hazed in misty lilac, visible. ("In Nature's grandest shows," says an old Dutch writer, an ecclesiastic, "amid the ocean's depth, if so might be, or countless worlds rolling above at night, a man thinks of them, weighs all, not for themselves or the abstract, but with reference to his own personality, and how they may affect him or color his destinies.")

New Senses—New Joys

We follow the stream of amber and bronze brawling along its bed, with its frequent cascades and snow-white foam. Through the cañon we fly—mountains not only each side, but seemingly, till we get near right in front of us—every rood a new view flashing, and each flash defying description—on the almost perpendicular sides, clinging pines, cedars, spruces, crimson sumach bushes, spots of wild grass—but dominating all, those towering rocks, rocks, rocks, bathed in delicate vari-colors, with the clear sky of autumn overhead. New senses, new joys, seem develop'd. Talk as you like, a typical Rocky Mountain cañon, or a limitless sea-like stretch of the great Kansas or Colorado plains, under favoring circumstances, tallies, per-haps expresses, certainly awakes, those grandest and subtlest element-emotions in the human soul, that all the marble temples and sculptures from Phidias to Thorwaldsen—all paintings, poems, reminiscences, or even music, probably never can.

Steam-Power, Telegraphs, &c.

I get out on a ten minutes' stoppage at Deer creek, to enjoy the unequal'd combination of hill, stone and wood. As we speed again, the yellow granite in the sunshine, with natural spires, minarets, castellated perches far aloft—then long stretches of straight-upright palisades, rhinoceros color—then gamboge and tinted chromos. Ever the best of my pleasures the cool-fresh Colorado atmosphere, yet sufficiently warm. Signs of man's restless advent and pioneerage, hard as Nature's face is—deserted dug-outs by dozens in the sidehills—the scantlinghut, the telegraph-pole, the smoke of some impromptu chimney or outdoor fire—at intervals little settlements of log-houses, or parties of surveyors or telegraph builders, with their comfortable tents. Once, a canvas office where you could send a message by electricity anywhere around the world! Yes, pronounc'd signs of the man of latest dates, dauntless grappling with these grisliest shows of the old kosmos. At several places steam saw-mills, with their piles of logs and boards, and the pipes puffing. Occasionally Platte cañon expanding into a grassy flat of a few acres. At one such place, toward the end, where we stop, and I get out to stretch my legs, as I look skyward, or rather mountain-top-ward, a huge hawk or eagle (a rare sight here) is idly soaring, balancing along the ether, now sinking low and coming quite near, and then up again in stately-languid circles—then higher, higher, slanting to the north, and gradually out of sight.

America's Back-Bone

I jot these lines literally at Kenosha summit, where we return, afternoon, and take a long rest, 10,000 feet above sea-level. At this immense height the South Park stretches fifty miles before me. Mountainous chains and peaks in every variety of perspective, every hue of vista, fringe the view, in nearer, or middle, or far-dim distance, or fade on the horizon. We have now reach'd, penetrated the Rockies, (Hayden calls it the Front Range,) for a hundred miles or so; and though these chains spread away in every direction, specially north and south, thousands and thousands farther, I have seen specimens of the utmost of them, and know henceforth at least what they are, and what they look like. Not themselves alone, for they typify stretches and areas of half the globe—are, in fact, the vertebræ or back-bone of our hemisphere. As the anatomists say a man is only a spine, topp'd, footed, breasted and radiated, so the whole Western world is, in a sense, but an expansion of these mountains. In South America they are the Andes, in Central America and Mexico the Cordilleras, and in our States they go under different names—in California the Coast and Cascade ranges—thence more eastwardly the Sierra Nevadas—but mainly and more centrally here the Rocky Mountains proper, with many an elevation such as Lincoln's, Grey's, Harvard's, Yale's, Long's and Pike's peaks, all over 14,000 feet high. (East, the highest peaks of the Alleghanies, the Adirondacks, the Catskills, and the White Mountains, range from 2000 to 5500 feet—only Mount Washington, in the latter, 6300 feet.)

The Parks

In the middle of all here, lie such beautiful contrasts as the sunken basins of the North, Middle, and South Parks, (the latter I am now on one side of, and overlooking,) each the size of a large, level, almost quadrangular, grassy, western county, wall'd in by walls of hills, and each park the source of a river. The ones I specify are the largest in Colorado, but the whole of that State, and of Wyoming, Utah, Nevada and western California, though their sierras and ravines, are copiously mark'd by similar spreads and openings, many of the small ones of paradisiac loveliness and perfection, with their offsets of mountains, streams, atmosphere and hues beyond compare.

Art Features

Talk, I say again, of going to Europe, of visiting the ruins of feudal castles, or Coliseum remains, or kings' palaces—when you can come *here*. The alternations one gets, too; after the Illinois and Kansas prairies of a thousand miles—smooth and easy areas of the corn and wheat of ten million democratic farms in the future—here start up in every conceivable presentation of shape, these non-utilitarian piles, coping the skies, emanating a beauty, terror, power, more than Dante or Angelo ever knew. Yes, I think the chyle of not only poetry and painting, but oratory, and even the metaphysics and music fit for the New World, before being finally assimilated, need first and feeding visits here.

Mountain streams.—The spiritual contrast and etheriality of the whole region consist largely to me in its never-absent peculiar streams—the snows of inaccessible upper areas melting and running down through the gorges continually. Nothing like the water of pastoral plains, or creeks with wooded banks and turf, or anything of the kind elsewhere. The shapes that element takes in the shows of the globe cannot be fully understood by an artist until he has studied these unique rivulets.

Aerial effects.—But perhaps as I gaze around me the rarest sight of all is in atmospheric hues. The prairies—as I cross'd them in my journey hither—and these mountains and parks, seem to me to afford new lights and shades. Everywhere the aerial gradations and sky-effects inimitable; nowhere else such perspectives, such transparent lilacs and grays. I can conceive of some superior landscape painter, some fine colorist, after sketching awhile out here, discarding all his previous work, delightful to stock exhibition amateurs, as muddy, raw and artificial. Near one's eye ranges an infinite variety; high up, the bare whitey-brown, above timber line; in certain spots afar patches of snow any time of year; (no trees, no flowers, no birds, at those chilling altitudes.) As I write I see the Snowy Range through the blue mist, beautiful and far off. I plainly see the patches of snow.

Denver Impressions

Through the long-lingering half-light of the most superb of evenings we return'd to Denver, where I staid several days leisurely exploring, receiving impressions, with which I may as well taper off this memorandum, itemizing what I saw there. The best was the men, three-fourths of them large, able, calm, alert, American. And cash! why they create it here. Out in the smelting works, (the biggest and most improv'd ones, for the precious metals, in the world,) I saw long rows of vats, pans, cover'd by bubbling-boiling water, and fill'd with pure silver, four or five inches thick, many thousand dollars' worth in pan. The foreman who was showing me shovel'd it carelessly up with a little wooden shovel, as one might toss beans. Then large silver bricks, worth $2000 a brick, dozens of piles, twenty in a pile. In one place in the mountains, at a mining camp, I had a few days before seen rough bullion on the ground in the open air, like the confectioner's pyramids at some swell dinner in New York. (Such a sweet morsel to roll over with a poor author's pen and ink—and appropriate to slip in here—that the silver product of Colorado and Utah, with the gold product of California, New Mexico, Nevada and Dakota, foots up an addition to the world's coin of considerably over a hundred millions every year.)

A city, this Denver, well-laid out—Laramie street, and 15th and 16th and Champa streets, with others, particularly fine— some with tall storehouses of stone or iron, and windows of plate-glass—all the streets with little canals of mountain water running along the sides—plenty of people, "business," modern-ness—yet not without a certain racy wild smack, all its own. A place of fast horses, (many mares with their colts,) and I saw lots of big greyhounds for antelope hunting. Now and then groups of miners, some just come in, some starting out, very picturesque.

One of the papers here interview'd me, and reported me as saying off-hand: "I have lived in or visited all the great cities on the Atlantic third of the republic—Boston, Brooklyn with its hills, New Orleans, Baltimore, stately Washington, broad Philadelphia, teeming Cincinnati and Chicago, and for thirty years in that wonder, wash'd by hurried and glittering tides, my own New York, not only the New World's but the world's city —but, newcomer to Denver as I am, and threading its streets, breathing its air, warm'd by its sunshine, and having what there is of its human as well as aerial ozone flash'd upon me now for only three or four days, I am very much like a man feels some-times toward certain people he meets with, and warms to, and hardly knows why. I, too, can hardly tell why, but as I enter'd the city in the slight haze of a late September afternoon, and have breath'd its air, and slept well o' nights, and have roam'd or rode leisurely, and watch'd the comers and goers at the hotels, and absorb'd the climatic magnetism of this curiously attractive region, there has steadily grown upon me a feeling of affection for the spot, which, sudden as it is, has become so definite and strong that I must put it on record."

So much for my feeling toward the Queen city of the plains and peaks, where she sits in her delicious rare atmosphere, over 5000 feet above sea-level, irrigated by mountain streams, one way looking east over the prairies for a thousand miles, and having the other, westward, in constant view by day, draped in their voilet haze, mountain tops innumerable. Yes, I fell in love with Denver, and even felt a wish to spend my declining and dying days there.

I Turn South—and Then East Again

Leave Denver at 8 A.M. by the Rio Grande RR. going south. Mountains constantly in sight in the apparently near distance, veil'd slightly, but still clear and very grand—their cones, colors, sides, distinct against the sky—hundreds, it seem'd thousands, interminable necklaces of them, their tops and slopes hazed more or less slightly in that blue-gray, under the autumn sun, for over a hundred miles—the most spiritual show of objective Nature I ever beheld, or even thought possible. Occasionally the light strengthens, making a contrast of yellow-tinged silver on one side, with dark and shaded gray on the other. I took a long look at Pike's peak, and was a little disappointed. (I suppose I had expected something stunning.) Our view over plains to the left stretches amply, with corrals here and there, the frequent cactus and wild sage, and herds of cattle feeding. Thus about 120 miles to Pueblo. At that town we board the comfortable and well-equipt Atchinson, Topeka and Santa Fe RR., now striking east.

Unfulfill'd Wants—the Arkansas River

I had wanted to go to the Yellowstone river region—wanted specially to see the National Park, and the geysers and the "hoodoo" or goblin land of that country; indeed, hesitated a little at Pueblo, the turning point—wanted to thread the Veta pass—wanted to go over the Santa Fe trail away southwestward to New Mexico—but turn'd and set my face eastward—leaving behind me whetting glimpse-tastes of southeastern Colorado, Pueblo, Bald mountain, the Spanish peaks, Sangre de Christos, Mile-Shoe-curve (which my veteran friend on the locomotive told me was "the boss railroad curve of the universe,") fort Garland on the plains, Veta, and the three great peaks of the Sierra Blancas.

The Arkansas river plays quite a part in the whole of this region—I see it, or its high-cut rocky northern shore, for miles, and cross and recross it frequently, as it winds and squirms like a snake. The plains vary here even more than usual—sometimes a long sterile stretch of scores of miles—then green, fertile and grassy, an equal length. Some very large herds of sheep. (One wants new words in writing about these plains, and all the inland American West—the terms, *far, large, vast,* &c., are insufficient.)

A Silent Little Follower—the Coreopsis

Here I must a say a word about a little follower, present even now before my eyes. I have been accompanied on my whole journey from Barnegat to Pike's Peak by a pleasant floricultural friend, or rather millions of friends—nothing more or less than a hardy little yellow five-petal'd September and October wild-flower, growing I think everywhere in the middle and northern United States. I had seen it on the Hudson and over Long Island, and along the banks of the Delaware and through New Jersey, (as years ago up the Connecticut, and one fall by Lake Champlain.) This trip it follow'd me regularly, with its slender stem and eyes of gold, from Cape May to the Kaw valley, and so through the cañons and to these plains. In Missouri I saw immense fields all bright with it. Toward western Illinois I woke up one morning in the sleeper and the first thing when I drew the curtain of my berth and look'd out was its pretty countenance and bending neck.

Sept. 25th.—Early morning—still going east after we leave Sterling, Kansas, where I stopp'd a day and night. The sun up about half an hour; nothing can be fresher or more beautiful than this time, this region. I see quite a field of my yellow flower in full bloom. At intervals dots of nice two-story houses, as we ride swiftly by. Over the immense area, flat as a floor, visible for twenty miles in every direction in the clear air, a prevalence of autumn-drab and reddish-tawny herbage—sparse stacks of hay and enclosures, breaking the landscape—as we rumble by, flocks of prairie-hens starting up. Between Sterling and Florence a fine country. (Remembrances to E. L., my old-young soldier friend of war times, and his wife and boy at S.)

The Prairies and Great Plains in Poetry

(After traveling Illinois, Missouri, Kansas and Colorado)

Grand as the thought that doubtless the child is already born who will see a hundred millions of people, the most prosperous and advanc'd of the world, inhabiting these Prairies, the great Plains, and the valley of the Mississippi, I could not help thinking it would be grander still to see all those inimitable American areas fused in the alembic of a perfect poem, or other esthetic work, entirely western, fresh and limitless—altogether our own, without a trace or taste of Europe's soil, reminiscence, technical letter or spirit. My days and nights, as I travel here—what an exhilaration!—not the air alone, and the sense of vastness, but every local sight and feature. Everywhere something characteristic—the cactuses, pinks, buffalo grass, wild sage—the receding perspective, and the far circle-line of the horizon all times of day, especially forenoon—the clear, pure, cool, rarefied nutriment for the lungs, previously quite unknown—the black patches and streaks left by surface-conflagrations—the deep-plough'd furrow of the "fire-guard"—the slanting snow-racks built all along to shield the railroad from winter drifts—the prairie-dogs and the herds of antelope—the curious "dry rivers" —occasionally a "dug-out" or corral—Fort Riley and Fort Wallace—those towns of the northern plains, (like ships on the sea,) Eagle-Tail, Coyotè, Cheyenne, Agate, Monotony, Kit Carson—with ever the ant-hill and the buffalo-wallow—ever the herds of cattle and the cow-boys ("cow-punchers") to me a strangely interesting class, bright-eyed as hawks, with their swarthy complexions and their broad-brimm'd hats—apparently always on horseback, with loose arms slightly raised and swinging as they ride.

The Spanish Peaks—Evening
on the Plains

Between Pueblo and Bent's fort, southward, in a clear afternoon sun-spell I catch exceptionally good glimpses of the Spanish peaks. We are in southeastern Colorado—pass immense herds of cattle as our first-class locomotive rushes us along—two or three times crossing the Arkansas, which we follow many miles, and of which river I get fine views, sometimes for quite a distance, its stony, upright, not very high, palisade banks, and then its muddy flats. We pass Fort Lyon—lots of adobie houses —limitless pasturage, appropriately fleck'd with those herds of cattle—in due time the declining sun in the west—a sky of limpid pearl over all—and so evening on the great plains. A calm, pensive, boundless landscape—the perpendicular rocks of the north Arkansas, hued in twilight—a thin line of violet on the southwestern horizon—the palpable coolness and slight aroma—a belated cow-boy with some unruly member of his herd—an emigrant wagon toiling yet a little further, the horses slow and tired—two men, apparently father and son, jogging along on foot—and around all the indescribable *chiaroscuro*

and sentiment, (profounder than anything at sea,) athwart
these endless wilds.

America's Characteristic Landscape

Speaking generally as to the capacity and sure future destiny
of that plain and prairie area (larger than any European king-
dom) it is the inexhaustible land of wheat, maize, wool, flax,
coal, iron, beef and pork, butter and cheese, apples and grapes
—land of ten million virgin farms—to the eye at present wild
and unproductive—yet experts say that upon it when irrigated
may easily be grown enough wheat to feed the world. Then
as to scenery (giving my own thought and feeling,) which I
know the standard claim is that Yosemite, Niagara falls, the
upper Yellowstone and the like, afford the greatest natural
shows, I am not so sure but the Prairies and Plains, while less
stunning at first sight, last longer, fill the esthetic sense fuller,
precede all the rest, and make North America's characteristic landscape.

Indeed through the whole of this journey, with all its shows
and varieties, what most impress'd me, and will longest remain
with me, are these same prairies. Day after day, and night after
night, to my eyes, to all my senses—the esthetic one most of
all—they silently and broadly unfolded. Even their simplest
statistics are sublime.

Earth's Most Important Stream

The valley of the Mississippi river and its tributaries, (this
stream and its adjuncts involve a big part of the question,)
comprehends more than twelve hundred thousand square miles,
the greater part prairies. It is by far the most important stream
on the globe, and would seem to have been marked out by
design, slow-flowing from north to south, through a dozen

climates, all fitted for man's healthy occupancy, its outlet un-
frozen all the year, and its line forming a safe, cheap continental avenue for commerce and passage from the north
temperate to the torrid zone. Not even the mighty Amazon
(though larger in volume) on its line of east and west—not the
Nile in Africa, nor the Danube in Europe, nor the three great
rivers of China, compare with it. Only the Mediterranean sea
has play'd some such part in history, and all through the past,
as the Mississippi is destined to play in the future. By its demesnes, water'd and welded by its branches, the Missouri, the
Ohio, the Arkansas, the Red, the Yazoo, the St. Francis and
others, it already compacts twenty-five millions of people, not
merely the most peaceful and money-making, but the most
restless and warlike on earth. Its valley, or reach, is rapidly
concentrating the political power of the American Union. One
almost thinks it *is* the Union—or soon will be. Take it out,
with its radiations, and what would be left? From the car windows through Indiana, Illinois, Missouri, or stopping some
days along the Topeka and Santa Fe road, in southern Kansas,
and indeed wherever I went, hundreds and thousands of miles
through this region, my eyes feasted on primitive and rich
meadows, some of them partially inhabited, but far, immensely
far more untouch'd, unbroken—and much of it more lovely
and fertile in its unplough'd innocence than the fair and valuable fields of New York's, Pennsylvania's, Maryland's or
Virginia's richest farms.

Prairie Analogies— the Tree Question

The word Prairie is French, and means literally meadow. The
cosmical analogies of our North American plains are the
Steppes of Asia, the Pampas and Llanos of South America,
and perhaps the Saharas of Africa. Some think the plains have
been originally lake-beds; others attribute the absence of forests
to the fires that almost annually sweep over them—(the cause,
in vulgar estimation, of Indian summer.) The tree question will

soon become a grave one. Although the Atlantic slope, the Rocky mountain region, and the southern portion of the Mississippi valley, are well wooded, there are here stretches of hundreds and thousands of miles where either not a tree grows, or often useless destruction has prevail'd; and the matter of the cultivation and spread of forests may well be press'd upon thinkers who look to the coming generations of the prairie States.

Mississippi Valley Literature

Lying by one rainy day in Missouri to rest after quite a long exploration—first trying a big volume I found there of "Milton, Young, Gray, Beattie and Collins," but giving it up for a bad job—enjoying however for awhile, as often before, the reading of Walter Scott's poems, "Lay of the Last Minstrel," "Marmion," and so on—I stopp'd and laid down the book, and ponder'd the thought of a poetry that should in due time express and supply the teeming region I was in the midst of, and have briefly touch'd upon. One's mind needs but a moment's deliberation anywhere in the United States to see clearly enough that all the prevalent book and library poets, either as imported from Great Britain, or follow'd and *doppel-gang'd* here, are foreign to our States, copiously as they are read by us all. But to fully understand not only how absolutely in opposition to our times and lands, and how little and cramp'd, and what anachronisms and absurdities many of their pages are, for American purposes, one must dwell or travel awhile in Missouri, Kansas and Colorado, and get rapport with their people and country.

Will the day ever come—no matter how long deferr'd—when those models and lay-figures from the British islands—and even the precious traditions of the classics—will be reminiscences, studies only? The pure breath, primitiveness, boundless prodigality and amplitude, strange mixture of delicacy and power, of continence, of real and ideal, and of all original and first-class elements, of these prairies, the Rocky mountains,

and of the Mississippi and Missouri rivers—will they ever
appear in, and in some sort form a standard for our poetry
and art? (I sometimes think that even the ambition of my
friend Joaquin Miller to put them in, and illustrate them, places
him ahead of the whole crowd.)

Not long ago I was down New York bay, on a steamer,
watching the sunset over the dark green heights of Navesink,
and viewing all that inimitable spread of shore, shipping and
sea, around Sandy hook. But an intervening week or two, and
my eyes catch the shadowy outlines of the Spanish peaks. In
the more than two thousand miles between, though of infinite
and paradoxical variety, a curious and absolute fusion is doubtless steadily annealing, compacting, identifying all. But subtler
and wider and more solid, (to produce such compaction,) than
the laws of the States, or the common ground of Congress or
the Supreme Court, or the grim welding of our national wars,
or the steel ties of railroads, or all the kneading and fusing
processes of our material and business history, past or present,
would in my opinion be a great throbbing, vital, imaginative
work, or series of works, or literature, in constructing which
the Plains, the Prairies, and the Mississippi river, with the
demesnes of its varied and ample valley, should be the concrete background, and America's humanity, passions, struggles,
hopes, there and now—an *eclaircissement* as it is and is to be
on the stage of the New World, of all Time's hitherto drama
of war, romance and evolution—should furnish the lambent
fire, the ideal.

An Interviewer's Item

Oct. 17, '79.—To-day one of the newspapers of St. Louis prints
the following informal remarks of mine on American, especially
Western literature: "We called on Mr. Whitman yesterday and
after a somewhat desultory conversation abruptly asked him:
'Do you think we are to have a distinctively American literature?' 'It seems to me,' said he, 'that our work at present is to
lay the foundations of a great nation in products, in agricul-

ture, in commerce, in networks of intercommunication, and in all that relates to the comforts of vast masses of men and families, with freedom of speech, ecclesiasticism, &c. These we have founded and are carrying out on a grander scale than ever hitherto, and Ohio, Illinois, Indiana, Missouri, Kansas and Colorado, seem to me to be the seat and field of these very facts and ideas. Materialistic prosperity in all its varied forms, with those other points that I mentioned, intercommunication and freedom, are first to be attended to. When those have their results and get settled, then a literature worthy of us will begin to be defined. Our American superiority and vitality are in the bulk of our people, not in a gentry like the old world. The greatness of our army during the secession war, was in the rank and file, and so with the nation. Other lands have their vitality in a few, a class, but we have it in the bulk of the people. Our leading men are not of much account and never have been, but the average of the people is immense, beyond all history. Sometimes I think in all departments, literature and art included, that will be the way our superiority will exhibit itself. We will not have great individuals or great leaders, but a great average bulk, unprecedentedly great.' "

The Women of the West

Kansas City.—I am not so well satisfied with what I see of the women of the prairie cities. I am writing this where I sit leisurely in a store in Main street, Kansas city, a streaming crowd on the sidewalks flowing by. The ladies (and the same in Denver) are all fashionably drest, and have the look of "gentility" in face, manner and action, but they do *not* have, either in physique or the mentality appropriate to them, any high native originality of spirit or body, (as the men certainly have, appropriate to them.) They are "intellectual" and fashionable, but dyspeptic-looking and generally doll-like; their ambition evidently is to copy their eastern sisters. Something far different and in advance must appear, to tally and complete the superb masculinity of the West, and maintain and continue it.

The Silent General

Sept. 28, '79.—So General Grant, after circumambiating the world, has arrived home again—landed in San Francisco yesterday, from the ship City of Tokio from Japan. What a man he is! what a history! what an illustration—his life—of the capacities of that American individuality common to us all. Cynical critics are wondering "what the people can see in Grant" to make such a hubbub about. They aver (and it is no doubt true) that he has hardly the average of our day's literary and scholastic culture, and absolutely no pronounc'd genius or conventional eminence of any sort. Correct: but he proves how an average western farmer, mechanic, boatman, carried by tides of circumstances, perhaps caprices, into a position of incredible military or civic responsibilities, (history has presented none more trying, no born monarch's, no mark more shining for attack or envy,) may steer his way fitly and steadily through them all, carrying the country and himself with credit year after year—command over a million armed men—fight more than fifty pitch'd battles—rule for eight years a land larger than all the kingdoms of Europe combined—and then, retiring, quietly (with a cigar in his mouth) make the promenade of the whole world, through its courts and coteries, and kings and czars and mikados, and splendidest glitters and etiquettes, as phlegmatically as he ever walk'd the portico of a Missouri hotel after dinner. I say all this is what people like —and I am sure I like it. Seems to me it transcends Plutarch. How those old Greeks, indeed, would have seized on him! A mere plain man—no art, no poetry—only practical sense, ability to do, or try his best to do, what devolv'd upon him. A common trade, moneymaker, tanner, farmer of Illinois— general for the republic, in its terrific struggle with itself, in the war of attempted secession—President following, (a task of peace, more difficult than the war itself)—nothing heroic, as the authorities put it—and yet the greatest hero. The gods, the destinies, seem to have concentrated upon him.

President Hayes's Speeches

Sept. 30.—I see President Hayes has come out West, passing quite informally from point to point, with his wife and a small cortege of big officers, receiving ovations, and making daily and sometimes double-daily addresses to the people. To these addresses—all impromptu, and some would call them ephemeral—I feel to devote a memorandum. They are shrewd, good-natur'd, face-to-face speeches, on easy topics not too deep; but they give me some revised ideas of oratory—of a new, opportune theory and practice of that art, quite changed from the classic rules, and adapted to our days, our occasions, to American democracy, and to the swarming populations of the West. I hear them criticised as wanting in dignity, but to me they are just what they should be, considering all the circumstances, who they come from, and who they are address'd to. Underneath, his objects are to compact and fraternize the States, encourage their materialistic and industrial development, soothe and expand their self-poise, and tie all and each with resistless double ties not only of inter-trade barter, but human comradeship.

From Kansas city I went on to St. Louis, where I remain'd nearly three months, with my brother T. J. W., and my dear nieces.

St. Louis Memoranda

Oct., Nov., and Dec., '79.—The points of St. Louis are its position, its absolute wealth, (the long accumulations of time and trade, solid riches, probably a higher average thereof than any city,) the unrivall'd amplitude of its well-laid out environage of broad plateaus, for future expansion—and the great State of which it is the head. It fuses northern and southern qualities, perhaps native and foreign ones, to perfection, rendezvous the whole stretch of the Mississippi and Missouri rivers, and its American electricity goes well with its German phlegm. Fourth, Fifth and Third streets are store-streets, showy, modern, metropolitan, with hurrying crowds, vehicles, horse-cars, hubbub, plenty of people, rich goods, plate-glass windows, iron fronts often five or six stories high. You can purchase anything in St. Louis (in most of the big western cities for the matter of that) just as readily and cheaply as in the Atlantic marts. Often in going about the town you see reminders of old, even decay'd civilization. The water of the west, in some places, is not good, but they make it up here by plenty of very fair wine, and inexhaustible quantities of the best beer in the world. There are immense establishments for slaughtering beef and pork—and I saw flocks of sheep, 5000 in a flock. (In Kansas city I had visited a packing establishment that kills and packs an average of 2500 hogs a day the whole year round, for export. Another in Atchison, Kansas, same extent; others nearly equal elsewhere. And just as big ones here.)

Nights on the Mississippi

Oct. 29th, 30th, and 31st.—Wonderfully fine, with the full harvest moon, dazzling and silvery. I have haunted the river every night lately, where I could get a look at the bridge by moonlight. It is indeed a structure of perfection and beauty unsurpassable, and I never tire of it. The river at present is very low; I noticed to-day it had much more of a blue-clear look than usual. I hear the slight ripples, the air is fresh and cool, and the view, up or down, wonderfully clear, in the moonlight. I am out pretty late: it is so fascinating, dreamy. The cool night-air, all the influences, the silence, with those far-off eternal stars, do me good. I have been quite ill of late. And so, well-near the centre of our national demesne, these night views of the Mississippi.

Upon Our Own Land

"Always, after supper, take a walk half a mile long," says an old proverb, dryly adding, "and if convenient let it be upon your own land." I wonder does any other nation but ours afford opportunity for such a jaunt as this? Indeed has any previous period afforded it? No one, I discover, begins to know the real geographic, democratic, indissoluble American Union in the present, or suspect it in the future, until he explores these Central States, and dwells awhile observantly on their prairies, or amid their busy towns, and the mighty father of waters. A ride of two or three thousand miles, "on one's own land," with hardly a disconnection, could certainly be had in no other place than the United States, and at no period before this. If you want to see what the railroad is, and how civilization and progress date from it—how it is the conqueror of crude nature, which it turns to man's use, both on small scales and on the largest—come hither to inland America.

I return'd home, east, Jan. 5, 1880, having travers'd, to and fro and across, 10,000 miles and more. I soon resumed my seclusions down in the woods, or by the creek, or gaddings about cities, and an occasional disquisition, as will be seen following.

Edgar Poe's Significance

Jan. 1, '80.—In diagnosing this disease called humanity—to assume for the nonce what seems a chief mood of the personality and writings of my subject—I have thought that poets, somewhere or other on the list, present the most mark'd indications. Comprehending artists in a mass, musicians, painters, actors, and so on, and considering each and all of them as radiations or flanges of that furious whirling wheel, poetry, the centre and axis of the whole, where else indeed may we so well investigate the causes, growth, tally-marks of the time —the age's matter and malady?

By comon consent there is nothing better for man or woman than a perfect and noble life, morally without flaw, happily balanced in activity, physically sound and pure, giving its due proportion, and no more, to the sympathetic, the human emotional element—a life, in all these, unhasting, unresting, untiring to the end. And yet there is another shape of personality dearer far to the artist-sense, (which likes the play of strongest lights and shades,) where the perfect character, the good, the heroic, although never attain'd, is never lost sight of, but through failures, sorrows, temporary downfalls, is return'd to again and again, and while often violated, is passionately adhered to as long as mind, muscles, voice, obey the power we call volition. This sort of personality we see more or less in Burns, Byron, Schiller, and George Sand. But we do not see it in Edgar Poe. (All this is the result of reading at intervals the last three days a new volume of his poems—I took it on my rambles down by the pond, and by degrees read it all through there.) While to the character first outlined the service Poe renders is certainly that entire contrast and contradiction which is next best to fully exemplifying it.

Almost without the first sign of moral principle, or of the concrete or its heroisms, or the simpler affections of the heart, Poe's verses illustrate an intense faculty for technical and abstract beauty, with the rhyming art to excess, an incorrigible propensity toward nocturnal themes, a demoniac undertone behind every page—and, by final judgment, probably belong among the electric lights of imaginative literature, brilliant and dazzling, but with no heat. There is an indescribable magnetism about the poet's life and reminiscences as well as the poems. To one who could work out their subtle retracing and retrospect, the latter would make a close tally no doubt between the author's birth and antecedents, his childhood and youth, his physique, his so-call'd education, his studies and associates, the literary and social Baltimore, Richmond, Philadelphia and New York, of those times—not only the places and circumstances in themselves, but often, very often, in a strange spurning of, and reaction from them all.

The following from a report in the Washington "Star" of November 16, 1875, may afford those who care for it something further of my point of view toward this interesting figure and influence of our era. There occurr'd about that date in Baltimore a public reburial of Poe's remains, and dedication of a monument over the grave:

"Being in Washington on a visit at the time, 'the old gray' went over to Baltimore, and though ill from paralysis, consented to hobble up and silently take a seat on the platform, but refused to make any speech, saying, 'I have felt a strong impulse to come over and be here to-day myself in memory of Poe, which I have obey'd, but not the slightest impulse to make a speech, which, my dear friends, must also be obeyed.' In an informal circle, however, in conversation after the ceremonies, Whitman said; 'For a long while, and until lately, I had a distaste for Poe's writings. I wanted, and still want for poetry, the clear sun shining, and fresh air blowing —the strength and power of health, not of delirium, even amid the stormiest passions—with always the background of the eternal moralities. Non-complying with these requirements, Poe's genius has yet conquer'd a special recognition for itself, and I too have come to fully admit it, and appreciate it and him.

" 'In a dream I once had, I saw a vessel on the sea, at midnight, in a storm. It was no great full-rigg'd ship, nor majestic steamer, steering firmly through the gale, but seem'd one of those superb little schooner yachts I had often seen lying anchor'd, rocking so jauntily, in the waters around New York, or up Long Island sound—now flying uncontroll'd with torn sails and broken spars through the wild sleet and winds and waves of the night. On the deck was a slender, slight, beautiful figure, a dim man, apparently enjoying all the terror, the murk and the dislocation of which he was the centre and the victim. That figure of my lurid dream might stand for Edgar Poe, his spirit, his fortunes, and his poems—themselves all lurid dreams.' "

Much more may be said, but I most desired to exploit the idea put at the beginning. By its popular poets the calibres of an age, the weak spots of its embankments, its sub-currents, (often more significant than the biggest surface ones,) are unerringly indicated. The lush and the weird that have taken such extraordinary possession of Nineteenth-century verse-lovers—what mean they? The inevitable tendency of poetic culture to morbidity, abnormal beauty—the sickliness of all technical thought or refinement in itself—the abnegation of the perennial and democratic concretes at first hand, the body, the earth and sea, sex and the like—and the substitution of something for them at second or third hand—what bearings have they on current pathological study?

Beethoven's Septette

Feb. 11, '80.—At a good concert to-night in the foyer of the opera house, Philadelphia—the band a small but first-rate one. Never did music more sink into and soothe and fill me—never so prove its soul-rousing power, its impossibility of statement. Especially in the rendering of one of Beethoven's master septettes by the well-chosen and perfectly-combined instruments (violins, viola, clarionet, horn, 'cello and contrabass,) was I carried away, seeing, absorbing many wonders. Dainty abandon, sometimes as if Nature laughing on a hillside in the sunshine; serious and firm monotonies, as of winds; a horn sounding through the tangle of the forest, and the dying echoes; soothing floating of waves, but presently rising in surges, angrily lashing, muttering, heavy, piercing peals of laughter, for interstices; now and then weird, as Nature herself is in certain moods—but mainly spontaneous, easy, careless—often the sentiment of the postures of naked children playing or sleeping. It did me good even to watch the violinists drawing their bows so masterly—every motion a study. I allow'd myself, as I sometimes do, to wander out of myself. The conceit came to me of a copious grove of singing birds, and in their midst a simple harmonic duo, two human souls, steadily asserting their own pensiveness, joyousness.

A Hint of Wild Nature

Feb. 13.—As I was crossing the Delaware to-day, saw a large flock of wild geese, right overhead, not very high up, ranged in V-shape, in relief against the noon clouds of light smoke-color. Had a capital though momentary view of them, and then of their course on and on southeast, till gradually fading—(my eyesight yet first rate for the open air and its distances, but I use glasses for reading.) Queer thoughts melted into me the two or three minutes, or less, seeing these creatures cleaving the sky—the spacious, airy realm—even the prevailing smoke-gray color everywhere, (no sun shining)—the waters below—the rapid flight of the birds, appearing just for a minute—flashing to me such a hint of the whole spread of Nature, with her eternal unsophisticated freshness, her never-visited recesses of sea, sky, shore—and then disappearing in the distance.

Loafing in the Woods

March 8.—I write this down in the country again, but in a new spot, seated on a log in the woods, warm, sunny, mid-day. Have been loafing here deep among the trees, shafts of tall pines, oak, hickory, with a thick undergrowth of laurels and grapevines—the ground cover'd everywhere by debris, dead leaves, breakage, moss—everything solitary, ancient, grim. Paths (such as they are) leading hither and yon—(how made I know not, for nobody seems to come here, nor man nor cattle-kind.) Temperature to-day about 60, the wind through the pine-tops; I sit and listen to its hoarse sighing above (and to the *stillness*) long and long, varied by aimless rambles in the old roads and paths, and by exercise-pulls at the young saplings, to keep my joints from getting stiff. Blue-birds, robins, meadow-larks begin to appear.

Next day, 9th.—A snowstorm in the morning, and continuing most of the day. But I took a walk over two hours, the same woods and paths, amid the falling flakes. No wind, yet the musical low murmur through the pines, quite pronounced, curious, like waterfalls, now still'd, now pouring again. All the senses, sight, sound, smell, delicately gratified. Every snow-flake lay where it fell on the evergreens, holly-trees, laurels, &c., the multitudinous leaves and branches piled, bulging-white, defined by edge-lines of emerald—the tall straight columns of the plentiful bronze-topt pines—a slight resinous odor blending with that of the snow. (For there is a scent to everything, even the snow, if you can only detect it—no two places, hardly any two hours, anywhere, exactly alike. How different the odor of noon from midnight, or winter from summer, or a windy spell from a still one.)

A Contralto Voice

May 9, Sunday.—Visit this evening to my friends the J.'s—good supper, to which I did justice—lively chat with Mrs. J. and I. and J. As I sat out front on the walk afterward, in the evening air, the church-choir and organ on the corner opposite gave Luther's hymn, *Eine feste Burg,* very finely. The air was borne by a rich contralto. For nearly half an hour there in the dark, (there was a good string of English stanzas,) came the music, firm and unhurried, with long pauses. The full silver star-beams of Lyra rose silently over the church's dim roof-ridge. Vari-color'd lights from the stain'd glass windows broke through the tree-shadows. And under all—under the Northern Crown up there, and in the fresh breeze below, and the *chiaroscuro* of the night, that liquid-full contralto.

Seeing Niagara to Advantage

June 4, '80.—For really seizing a great picture or book, or piece of music, or architecture, or grand scenery—or perhaps for the first time even the common sunshine, or landscape, or may-be even the mystery of identity, most curious mystery of all—there comes some lucky five minutes of a man's life, set amid a fortuitous concurrence of circumstances, and bringing in a brief flash the culmination of years of reading and travel and thought. The present case about two o'clock this afternoon, gave me Niagara, its superb severity of action and color and majestic grouping, in one short, indescribable show. We were very slowly crossing the Suspension bridge—not a full stop anywhere, but next to it—the day clear, sunny, still—and I out on the platform. The falls were in plain view about a mile off, but very distinct, and no roar—hardly a murmur. The river tumbling green and white, far below me; the dark high banks, the plentiful umbrage, many bronze cedars, in shadow; and tempering and arching all the immense materiality, a clear sky overhead, with a few white clouds, limpid, spiritual, silent. Brief, and as quiet as brief, that picture—a remembrance always afterwards. Such are the things, indeed, I lay away with my life's rare and blessed bits of hours, reminiscent, past—the wild sea-storm I once saw one winter day—off Fire island—the elder Booth in Richard, that famous night forty years ago in the old Bowery—or Alboni in the children's scene in Norma—or night-views, I remember, on the field, after battles in Virginia—or the peculiar sentiment of moonlight and stars over the great Plains, western Kansas —or scooting up New York bay, with a stiff breeze and a good yacht, off Navesink. With these, I say, I henceforth place that view, that afternoon, that combination complete, that five minutes' perfect absorption of Niagara—not the great majestic gem alone by itself, but set complete in all its varied, full, indispensable surroundings.

Jaunting to Canada

To go back a little, I left Philadelphia, 9th and Green streets, at 8 o'clock P.M., June 3, on a first-class sleeper, by the Lehigh Valley (North Pennsylvania) route, through Bethlehem, Wilkesbarre, Waverly, and so (by Erie) on through Corning to Hornellsville, where we arrived at 8, morning, and had a bounteous breakfast. I must say I never put in such a good night on any railroad track—smooth, firm, the minimum of jolting, and all the swiftness compatible with safety. So without change to Buffalo, and thence to Clifton, where we arrived early afternoon; then on to London, Ontario, Canada, in four more—less than twenty-two hours altogether. I am domiciled at the hospitable house of my friends Dr. and Mrs. Bucke, in the ample and charming garden and lawns of the asylum.

Sunday with the Insane

June 6.—Went over to the religious services (Episcopal) main Insane asylum, held in a lofty, good-sized hall, third story. Plain boards, whitewash, plenty of cheap chairs, no ornament or color, yet all scrupulously clean and sweet. Some three hundred persons present, mostly patients. Everything, the prayers, a short sermon, the firm, orotund voice of the minister, and most of all, beyond any portraying or suggesting, *that audience*, deeply impress'd me. I was furnish'd with an arm-chair near the pulpit, and sat facing the motley, yet perfectly well-behaved and orderly congregation. The quaint dresses and bonnets of some of the women, several very old and gray, here and there like the heads in old pictures. O the looks that came from those faces! There were two or three I shall probably never forget. Nothing at all markedly repulsive or hideous—strange enough I did not see one such. Our common humanity, mine and yours, everywhere:

> *"The same old blood—the same red, running blood;"*

yet behind most, an inferr'd arriere of such storms, such wrecks, such mysteries, fires, love, wrong, greed for wealth, religious problems, crosses—mirror'd from those crazed faces (yet now temporarily so calm, like still waters,) all the woes and sad happenings of life and death—now from every one the devotional element radiating—was it not, indeed, *the peace of God that passeth all understanding,* strange as it may sound? I can only say that I took long and searching eye-sweeps as I sat there, and it seem'd so, rousing unprecedented thoughts, problems unanswerable. A very fair choir, and melodeon accompaniment. They sang "Lead, kindly light," after the sermon. Many join'd in the beautiful hymn, to which the minister read the introductory text, *"In the daytime also He led them with a cloud, and all the night with a light of fire."* Then the words:

Lead, kindly light, amid the encircling gloom,
  Lead thou me on.
The night is dark, and I am far from home;
  Lead thou me on.
Keep thou my feet; I do not ask to see
The distant scene; one step enough for me.

I was not ever thus, nor pray'd that thou
  Should'st lead me on;
I lov'd to choose and see my path; but now
  Lead thou me on.
I loved the garish day, and spite of fears
Pride ruled my will; remember not past years.

A couple of days after, I went to the "Refractory building," under special charge of Dr. Beemer, and through the wards pretty thoroughly, both the men's and women's. I have since made many other visits of the kind through the asylum, and around among the detach'd cottages. As far as I could see, this is among the most advanced, perfected, and kindly and rationally carried on, of all its kind in America. It is a town in itself, with many buildings and a thousand inhabitants.

I learn that Canada, and especially this ample and populous province, Ontario, has the very best and plentiest benevolent institutions in all departments.

Reminiscence of Elias Hicks

June 8.—To-day a letter from Mrs. E. S. I., Detroit, accompanied in a little post-office roll by a rare old engraved head of Elias Hicks, (from a portrait in oil by Henry Inman, painted for J. V. S., must have been 60 years or more ago, in New York)—among the rest the following excerpt about E. H. in the letter:

"I have listen'd to his preaching so often when a child, and sat with my mother at social gatherings where he was the centre, and every one so pleas'd and stirr'd by his conversation. I hear that you contemplate writing or speaking about him, and I wonder'd whether you had a picture of him. As I am the owner of two, I send you one."

Grand Native Growth

In a few days I go to lake Huron, and may have something to say of that region and people. From what I already see, I should say the young native population of Canada was growing up, forming a hardy, democratic, intelligent, radically sound, and just as American, good-natured and *individualistic* race, as the average range of best specimens among us. As among us, too, I please myself by considering that this element, though it may not be the majority, promises to be the leaven which must eventually leaven the whole lump.

A Zollverein between the U.S. and Canada

Some of the more liberal of the presses here are discussing the question of a zollverein between the United States and Canada. It is proposed to form a union for commercial purposes—to altogether abolish the frontier tariff line, with its double sets of custom house officials now existing between the two countries, and to agree upon one tariff for both, the proceeds of this tariff to be divided between the two governments on the basis of population. It is said that a large proportion of the merchants of Canada are in favor of this step, as they believe it would materially add to the business of the country, by removing the restrictions that now exist on trade between Canada and the States. Those persons who are opposed to the measure believe that it would increase the material welfare of the country, but it would loosen the bonds between Canada and England; and this sentiment overrides the desire for commercial prosperity. Whether the sentiment can continue to bear the strain put upon it is a question. It is thought by many that commercial considerations must in the end prevail. It seems also to be generally agreed that such a zollverein, or common customs union, would bring practically more benefits to the Canadian provinces than to the United States. (It seems to me a certainty of time, sooner or later, that Canada shall form two or three grand States, equal and independent, with the rest of the American Union. The St. Lawrence and lakes are not for a frontier line, but a grand interior or mid-channel.)

The St. Lawrence Line

August 20.—Premising that my three or four months in Canada were intended, among the rest, as an exploration of the line of the St. Lawrence, from lake Superior to the sea, (the engineers here insist upon considering it as one stream, over 2000 miles long, including lakes and Niagara and all)—that I have only partially carried out my programme; but for the seven or eight hundred miles so far fulfill'd, I find that the *Canada question* is absolutely control'd by this vast water line, with its first-class features and points of trade, humanity, and many more—here I am writing this nearly a thousand miles north of my Philadelphia starting-point (by way of Montreal and Quebec) in the midst of regions that go to further extreme of grimness, wildness of beauty, and a sort of still and pagan *sacredness*, while yet Christian, inhabitable, and partially fertile, than perhaps any other on earth. The weather remains perfect; some might call it a little cool, but I wear my old gray overcoat and find it just right. The days are full of sunbeams and oxygen. Most of the forenoons and afternoons I am on the forward deck of the steamer.

The Savage Saguenay

Up these black waters, over a hundred miles—always strong, deep, (hundreds of feet, sometimes thousands,) ever with high, rocky hills for banks, green and gray—at times a little like some parts of the Hudson, but much more pronounc'd and defiant. The hills rise higher—keep their ranks more unbroken. The river is straighter and of more resolute flow, and its hue, though dark as ink, exquisitely polish'd and sheeny under the August sun. Different, indeed, this Saguenay from all other rivers—different effects—a bolder, more vehement play of lights and shades. Of a rare charm of singleness and simplicity. (Like the organ-chant at midnight from the old Spanish convent, in "Favorita"—one strain only, simple and monotonous and unornamented—but indescribably penetrating and grand and masterful.) Great place for echoes: while our steamer was tied at the wharf at Tadousac (taj-oo-sac) waiting, the escape-pipe letting off steam, I was sure I heard a band at the hotel up in the rocks—could even make out some of the tunes. Only when our pipe stopp'd, I knew what caused it. Then at cape Eternity and Trinity rock, the pilot with his whistle producing similar marvellous results, echoes indescribably weird, as we lay off in the still bay under their shadows.

Capes Eternity and Trinity

But the great, haughty, silent capes themselves; I doubt if any crack points, or hills, or historic places of note, or anything of the kind elsewhere in the world, outvies these objects—(I write while I am before them face to face.) They are very simple, they do not startle—at least they did not me—but they linger in one's memory forever. They are placed very near each other, side by side, each a mountain rising flush out of the Saguenay. A good thrower could throw a stone on each in passing—at least it seems so. Then they are as distinct in form as a perfect physical man or a perfect physical woman. Cape Eternity is bare, rising, as just said, sheer out of the water, rugged and grim (yet with an indescribable beauty) nearly two thousand feet high. Trinity rock, even a little higher, also rising flush, top-rounded like a great head with close-cut verdure of hair. I consider myself well repaid for coming my thousand miles to get the sight and memory of the unrivall'd duo. They have stirr'd me more profoundly than anything of the kind I have yet seen. If Europe or Asia had them, we should certainly hear of them in all sorts of sent-back poems, rhapsodies, &c., a dozen times a year through our papers and magazines.

Chicoutimi and Ha-Ha Bay

No indeed—life and travel and memory have offer'd and will preserve to me no deeper-cut incidents, panorama, or sights to cheer my soul, than these at Chicoutimi and Ha-ha bay, and my days and nights up and down this fascinating savage river— the rounded mountains, some bare and gray, some dull red, some draped close all over with matted green verdure or vines —the ample, calm, eternal rocks everywhere—the long streaks of motley foam, a milk-white curd on the glistening breast of the steam—the little two-masted schooner, dingy yellow, with patch'd sails, set wing-and-wing, nearing us, coming saucily up the water with a couple of swarthy, black-hair'd men aboard —the strong shades falling on the light gray or yellow outlines of the hills all through the forenoon, as we steam within gun- shot of them—while ever the pure and delicate sky spreads over all. And the splendid sunsets, and the sights of evening —the same old stars, (relatively a little different, I see, so far north) Arcturus and Lyra, and the Eagle, and great Jupiter like a silver globe, and the constellation of the Scorpion. Then northern lights nearly every night.

The Inhabitants—Good Living

Grim and rocky and black-water'd as the demesne hereabout is, however, you must not think genial humanity, and comfort, and good-living are not to be met. Before I began this memo- randum I made a first-rate breakfast of sea-trout, finishing off with wild raspberries. I find smiles and courtesy everywhere— physiognomies in general curiously like those in the United States—(I was astonish'd to find the same resemblance all through the province of Quebec.) In general the inhabitants of this rugged country (Charlevoix, Chicoutimi and Tadousac counties, and lake St. John region) a simple, hardy population, lumbering, trapping furs, boating, fishing, berry-picking and a little farming. I was watching a group of young boatmen eating their early dinner—nothing but an immense loaf of bread, had apparently been the size of a bushel measure, from which they cut chunks with a jack-knife. Must be a tremendous winter country this, when the solid frost and ice fully set in.

Cedar-Plums Like—Names

(Back again in Camden and down in Jersey)

One time I thought of naming this collection "Cedar-Plums Like" (which I still fancy wouldn't have been a bad name, nor inappropriate.) A melange of loafing, looking, hobbling, sitting, traveling—a little thinking thrown in for salt, but very little—not only summer but all seasons—not only days but nights—some literary meditations—books, authors examined, Carlyle, Poe, Emerson tried, (always under my cedar-tree, in the open air, and never in the library)—mostly the scenes everybody sees, but some of my own caprices, meditations, egotism—truly an open air and mainly summer formation—singly, or in clusters—wild and free and somewhat acrid—indeed more like cedar-plums than you might guess at first glance.

But do you know what they are? (To city man, or some sweet parlor lady, I now talk.) As you go along roads, or barrens, or across country, anywhere through these States, middle, eastern, western, or southern, you will see, certain seasons of the year, the thick woolly tufts of the cedar mottled with bunches of china-blue berries, about as big as fox-grapes. But first a special word for the tree itself: everybody knows that the cedar is a healthy, cheap, democratic wood, streak'd red and white—an evergreen—that it is not a *cultivated* tree—that it keeps away moths—that it grows inland or seaboard all climates, hot or cold, any soil—in fact rather prefers sand

and bleak side spots—content if the plough, the fertilizer and the trimming-axe, will but keep away and let it alone. After a long rain, when everything looks bright, often have I stopt in my wood-saunters, south or north, or far west, to take in its dusky green, wash'd clean and sweet, and speck'd copiously with its fruit of clear, hardy blue. The wood of the cedar is of use—but what profit on earth are those sprigs of acrid plums? A question impossible to answer satisfactorily. True, some of the herb doctors give them for stomachic affections, but the remedy is as bad as the disease. Then in my rambles down in Camden county I once found an old crazy woman gathering the clusters with zeal and joy. She show'd, as I was told afterwards, a sort of infatuation for them, and every year placed and kept profuse bunches high and low about her room.They had a strange charm on her uneasy head, and effected docility and peace. (She was harmless, and lived near by with her well-off married daughter.) Whether there is any connection between those bunches, and being out of one's wits, I cannot say, but I myself entertain a weakness for them. Indeed, I love the cedar, anyhow—its naked ruggedness, its just palpable odor, (so different from the perfumer's best,) its silence, its equable acceptance of winter's cold and summer's heat, of rain or drouth—its shelter to me from those, at times—its associations —(well, I never could explain *why* I love anybody, or anything). The service I now specially owe to the cedar is, while I cast around for a name for my proposed collection, hesitating, puzzled—after rejecting a long, long string, I lift my eyes, and lo! the very term I want. At any rate, I go no further— I tire in the search. I take what some invisible kind spirit has put before me. Besides, who shall say there is not affinity enough between (at least the bundle of sticks that produced) many of these pieces, or granulations, and those blue berries? their uselessness growing wild—a certain aroma of Nature I would so like to have in my pages—the thin soil whence they come—their content in being let alone—their stolid and deaf repugnance to answering questions, (this latter the nearest, dearest trait affinity of all.)

Then reader dear, in conclusion, as to the point of the name for the present collection, let us be satisfied to *have* a name

—something to identify and bind it together, to concrete all its vegetable, mineral, personal memoranda, abrupt raids of criticism, crude gossip of philosophy, varied sands, and clumps —without bothering ourselves because certain pages do not present themselves to you or me as coming under their own name with entire fitness or amiability. (It is a profound, vexatious, never-explicable matter—this of names. I have been exercised deeply about it my whole life.)

After all of which the name "Cedar-Plums Like" got its nose put out of joint; but I cannot afford to throw away what I pencill'd down the lane there, under the shelter of my old friend, one warm October noon. Besides, it wouldn't be civil to the cedar tree.

Death of Thomas Carlyle

Feb. 10, '81.—And so the flame of the lamp, after long wasting and flickering, has gone out entirely.

[11] In the pocket of my receptacle-book I find a list of suggested and rejected names for this volume, or parts of it—such as the following:

As the wild bee hums in May,
& August mulleins grow,
& Winter snow-flakes fall,
& stars in the sky roll round.

Away from Books—away from Art,
Now for the Day and Night—the lesson done,
Now for the Sun and Stars.

Notes of a half-Paralytic,
Week in and Week out,
Embers of Ending Days,
Ducks and Drakes,
Flood Tide and Ebb,
Gossip at Early Candle-light,
Echoes and Escapades,
Such as I.....Evening Dews,
Notes after Writing a Book,
Far and Near at 63,
Drifts and Cumulus,
Maize-Tassels.....Kindlings,
Fore and Aft.....Vestibules,
Scintilla at 60 and after,
Sands on the Shores of 64,

As Voices in the Dusk, from
  Speakers far or hid,
Autochthons.....Embryons,
Wing-and-Wing,
Notes and Recallés,
Only Mulleins and Bumble-Bees,
Pond-Babble.....Tête-à-Têtes,
Echoes of a Life in the 19th
  Century in the New World,
Flanges of Fifty Years,
Abandons.....Hurry Notes,
A Life-Mosaic.....Native Moments,
Types and Semi-Tones,
Oddments.....Sand-Drifts,
Again and Again.

As a representative author, a literary figure, no man else will bequeath to the future more significant hints of our stormy era, its fierce paradoxes, its din, and its struggling parturition periods, than Carlyle. He belongs to our own branch of the stock too; neither Latin nor Greek, but altogether Gothic. Rugged, mountainous, volcanic, he was himself more a French revolution than any of his volumes. In some respects, so far in the Nineteenth century, the best equipt, keenest mind, even from the college point of view, of all Britain; only he had an ailing body. Dyspepsia is to be traced in every page, and now and then fills the page. One may include among the lessons of his life—even though that life stretch'd to amazing length— how behind the tally of genius and morals stands the stomach, and gives a sort of casting vote.

Two conflicting agonistic elements seem to have contended in the man, sometimes pulling him different ways like wild horses. He was a cautious, conservative Scotchman, fully aware what a fœtid gas-bag much of modern radicalism is; but then his great heart demanded reform, demanded change—often terribly at odds with his scornful brain. No author ever put so much wailing and despair into his books, sometimes palpable, oftener latent. He reminds me of that passage in Young's poems where as death presses closer and closer for his prey, the soul rushes hither and thither, appealing, shrieking, berating, to escape the general doom.

Of short-comings, even positive blur-spots, from an American point of view, he had serious share.

Not for his merely literary merit, (though that was great) —not as "maker of books," but as launching into the self-complacent atmosphere of our days a rasping, questioning, dislocating agitation and shock, is Carlyle's final value. It is time the English-speaking peoples had some true idea about the verteber of genius, namely power. As if they must always have it cut and bias'd to the fashion, like a lady's cloak! What a needed service he performs! How he shakes our comfortable reading circles with a touch of the old Hebraic anger and prophecy—and indeed it is just the same. Not Isaiah himself more scornful, more threatening: "The crown of pride, the drunkards of Ephraim, shall be trodden under feet: And the glorious beauty which is on the head of the fat valley shall be a fading flower." (The word prophecy is much misused; it seems narrow'd to prediction merely. That is not the main sense of the Hebrew word translated "prophet"; it means one whose mind bubbles up and pours forth as a fountain, from inner, divine spontaneities revealing God. Prediction is a very minor part of prophecy. The great matter is to reveal and outpour the God-like suggestions pressing for birth in the soul. This is briefly the doctrine of the Friends or Quakers.)

Then the simplicity and amid ostensible frailty the towering strength of this man—a hardy oak knot, you could never wear out—an old farmer dress'd in brown clothes, and not hand-some—his very foibles fascinating. Who cares that he wrote about Dr. Francia, and "Shooting Niagara"—and "the Nigger Question,"—and didn't at all admire our United States? (I doubt if he ever thought or said half as bad words about us as we deserve.) How he splashes like leviathan in the seas of modern literature and politics! Doubtless, respecting the latter, one needs first to realize, from actual observation, the squalor, vice and doggedness ingrain'd in the bulk-population of the British Islands, with the red tape, the fatuity, the flunkeyism everywhere, to understand the last meaning in his pages. Accordingly, though he was no chartist or radical, I consider Carlyle's by far the most indignant comment or protest anent the fruits of feudalism to-day in Great Britain—the increasing poverty and degradation of the homeless, landless twenty millions, while a few thousands, or rather a few hundreds, possess the entire soil, the money, and the fat berths. Trade and shipping, and clubs and culture, and prestige, and guns, and a fine select class of gentry and aristocracy, with every modern improvement, cannot begin to salve or defend such stupendous hoggishness.

The way to test how much he has left his country were to consider, or try to consider, for a moment, the array of British thought, the resultant *ensemble* of the last fifty years, as existing to-day, *but with Carlyle left out*. It would be like an army with no artillery. The show were still a gay and rich one— Byron, Scott, Tennyson, and many more—horsemen and rapid infantry, and banners flying—but the last heavy roar so dear to the ear of the train'd soldier, and that settles fate and victory, would be lacking.

For the last three years we in America have had transmitted glimpses of a thin-bodied, lonesome, wifeless, childless, very old man, lying on a sofa, kept out of bed by indomitable will, but, of late, never well enough to take the open air. I have noted this news from time to time in brief descriptions in the papers. A week ago I read such an item just before I started out for my customary evening stroll between eight and nine. In the fine cold night, unusually clear, (Feb. 5, '81,) as I walk'd some open grounds adjacent, the condition of Carlyle, and his approaching—perhaps even then actual—death, filled me with thoughts eluding statement, and curiously blending with the scene. The planet Venus, an hour high in the west, with all her volume and lustre recover'd, (she has been shorn and languid for nearly a year,) including an additional sentiment I never noticed before—not merely voluptuous, Paphian, steeping, fascinating—now with calm commanding seriousness and hauteur—the Milo Venus now. Upward to the zenith, Jupiter, Saturn, and the moon past her quarter, trailing in procession, with the Pleiades following, and the constellation Taurus, and red Aldebaran. Not a cloud in heaven. Orion strode through the southeast, with his glittering belt—and a trifle below hung the sun of the night, Sirius. Every star dilated, more vitreous, nearer than usual. Not as in some clear nights when the larger stars entirely outshine the rest. Every little star or cluster just as distinctly visible, and just as nigh. Berenice's hair showing every gem, and new ones. To the northeast and north the Sickle, the Goat and kids, Cassiopea, Castor and Pollux, and the two Dippers. While through the whole of this silent indescribable show, inclosing and bathing my whole receptivity, ran the thought of Carlyle dying. (To soothe and spiritualize, and, as far as may be, solve the mysteries of death and genius, consider them under the stars at midnight.)

And now that he has gone hence, can it be that Thomas Carlyle, soon to chemically dissolve in ashes and by winds, remains an identity still? In ways perhaps eluding all the statements, lore and speculations of ten thousand years—eluding all possible statements to moral sense—does he yet exist, a

definite, vital being, a spirit, an individual—perhaps now wafted in space among those stellar systems, which, suggestive and
limitless as they are, merely edge more limitless, far more
suggestive systems? I have no doubt of it. In silence, of a
fine night, such questions are answer'd to the soul, the best
answers that can be given. With me, too, when depress'd by
some specially sad event, or tearing problem, I wait till I go
out under the stars for the last voiceless satisfaction.

Later Thoughts and Jottings

Carlyle from American Points of View

There is surely at present an inexplicable *rapport* (all the
more piquant from its contradictoriness) between that deceas'd
author and our United States of America—no matter whether
it lasts or not.[12] As we Westerners assume definite shape, and
result in formations and fruitage unknown before, it is curious
with what a new sense our eyes turn to representative out-
growths of crises and personages in the Old World. Beyond
question, since Carlyle's death, and the publication of Froude's
memoirs, not only the interest in his books, but every personal
bit regarding the famous Scotchman—his dyspepsia, his buffetings, his parentage, his paragon of a wife, his career in
Edinburgh, in the lonesome nest on Craigenputtock moor, and
then so many years in London—is probably wider and livelier
to-day in this country than in his own land. Whether I succeed

---

[12]It will be difficult for the future—judging by his books, personal
dis-sympathies, &c.,—to account for the deep hold this author has taken
on the present age, and the way he has color'd its method and thought.
I am certainly at a loss to account for it all as affecting myself. But
there could be no view, or even partial picture, of the middle and
latter part of our Nineteenth century, that did not markedly include
Thomas Carlyle. In his case (as so many others, literary productions,
works of art, personal identities, events,) there has been an impalpable
something more effective than the palpable. Then I find no better text,
(it is always important to have a definite, special, even oppositional,
living man to start from,) for sending out certain speculations and
comparisons for home use. Let us see what they amount to—those
reactionary doctrines, fears, scornful analyses of democracy—even
from the most erudite and sincere mind of Europe.

or no, I, too, reaching across the Atlantic and taking the man's dark fortune-telling of humanity and politics, would offset it all, (such is the fancy that comes to me,) by a far more profound horoscope-casting of those themes—G. F. Hegel's.[13]

First, about a chance, a never-fulfill'd vacuity of this pale cast of thought—this British Hamlet from Cheyne row, more puzzling than the Danish one, with his contrivances for settling the broken and spavin'd joints of the world's government, especially its democratic dislocation. Carlyle's grim fate was cast to live and dwell in, and largely embody, the parturition agony and qualms of the old order, amid crowded accumulations of ghastly morbidity, giving birth to the new. But conceive of him (or his parents before him) coming to America, recuperated by the cheering realities and activity of our people and country—growing up and delving face-to-face resolutely among us here, especially at the West—inhaling and exhaling our limitless air and eligibilities—devoting his mind to the theories and developments of this Republic amid its practical facts as exemplified in Kansas, Missouri, Illinois, Tennessee, or Louisiana. I say *facts*, and face-to-face confrontings—so different from books, and all those quiddities and mere reports in the libraries, upon which the man (it was wittily said of him at the age of thirty, that there was no one in Scotland who had glean'd so much and seen so little,) almost wholly fed, and which even his sturdy and vital mind but reflected at best.

Something of the sort narrowly escaped happening. In 1835, after more than a dozen years of trial and non-success, the author of "Sartor Resartus" removing to London, very poor, a confirmed hypochondriac, "Sartor" universally scoffed at, no

[13]Not the least mentionable part of the case, (a streak, it may be, of that humor with which history and fate love to contrast their gravity,) is that although neither of my great authorities during their lives consider'd the United States worthy of serious mention, all the principal works of both might not inappropriately be this day collected and bound up under the conspicuous title: *"Speculations for the use of North America, and Democracy there, with the relations of the same to Metaphysics, including Lessons and Warnings (encouragements too, and of the vastest,) from the Old World to the New."*

literary prospects ahead, deliberately settled on one last cast-ing-throw of the literary dice—resolv'd to compose and launch forth a book on the subject of *the French Revolution*—and if that won no higher guerdon or prize than hitherto, to sternly abandon the trade of author forever, and emigrate for good to America. But the venture turn'd out a lucky one, and there was no emigration.

Carlyle's work in the sphere of literature as he commenced and carried it out, is the same in one or two leading respects that Immanuel Kant's was in speculative philosophy. But the Scotchman had none of the stomachic phlegm and never-perturb'd placidity of the Konigsberg sage, and did not, like the latter, understand his own limits, and stop when he got to the end of them. He clears away jungle and poison-vines and underbrush—at any rate hacks valiantly at them, smiting hip and thigh. Kant did the like in his sphere, and it was all he profess'd to do; his labors have left the ground fully prepared ever since—and greater service was probably never perform'd by mortal man. But the pang and hiatus of Carlyle seem to me to consist in the evidence everywhere that amid a whirl of fog and fury and cross-purposes, he firmly believ'd he had a clue to the medication of the world's ills, and that his bounden mission was to exploit it.[14]

There were two anchors, or sheet-anchors, for steadying, as a last resort, the Carlylean ship. One will be specified presently. The other, perhaps the main, was only to be found in some mark'd form of personal force, an extreme degree of competent urge and will, a man or men "born to command." Probably there ran through every vein and current of the Scotchman's blood something that warm'd up to this kind of trait and character above aught else in the world, and which makes him in my opinion the chief celebrator and promulger

[14]I hope I shall not myself fall into the error I charge upon him, of prescribing a specific for indispensable evils. My utmost pretension is probably but to offset that old claim of the exclusively curative power of first-class individual men, as leaders and rulers, by the claims, and general movement and result, of ideas. Something of the latter kind seems to me the distinctive theory of America, of democracy, and of the modern—or rather, I should say, it *is* democracy, and *is* the modern.

of it in literature—more than Plutarch, more than Shakspere. The great masses of humanity stand for nothing—at least nothing but nebulous raw material; only the big planets and shining suns for him. To ideas almost invariably languid or cold, a number-one forceful personality was sure to rouse his eulogistic passion and savage joy. In such case, even the standard of duty hereinafter rais'd, was to be instantly lower'd and vail'd. All that is comprehended under the terms republicanism and democracy were distasteful to him from the first, and as he grew older they became hateful and contemptible. For an undoubtedly candid and penetrating faculty such as his, the bearings he persistently ignored were marvellous. For instance, the promise, nay certainty of the democratic principle, to each and every State of the current world, not so much of helping it to perfect legislators and executives, but as the only effectual method for surely, however slowly, training people on a large scale toward voluntarily ruling and managing themselves (the ultimate aim of political and all other development)—to gradually reduce the fact of *governing* to its minimum, and to subject all its staffs and their doings to the telescopes and microscopes of committees and parties—and greatest of all, to afford (not stagnation and obedient content, which went well enough with the feudalism and ecclesiasticism of the antique and medieval world, but) a vast and sane and recurrent ebb and tide action for those floods of the great deep that have henceforth palpably burst forever their old bounds—seem never to have enter'd Carlyle's thought. It was splendid how he refus'd any compromise to the last. He was curiously antique. In that harsh, picturesque, most potent voice and figure, one seems to be carried back from the present of the British islands more than two thousand years, to the range between Jerusalem and Tarsus. His fullest best biographer justly says of him:

"He was a teacher and a prophet, in the Jewish sense of the word. The prophecies of Isaiah and Jeremiah have become a part of the permanent spiritual inheritance of mankind, because events proved that they had interpreted correctly the signs of their own times, and their prophecies were fulfill'd. Carlyle, like them, believ'd that he had a special message to deliver to the present age. Whether he was correct in that belief, and whether his message was a true message, remains to be seen. He has told us that our most cherish'd ideas of political liberty, with their corollaries, are mere illusions, and that the progress which has seem'd to go along with them is a progress towards anarchy and social dissolution. If he was wrong, he has misused his powers. The principles of his teachings are false. He has offer'd himself as a guide upon a road of which he had no knowledge; and his own desire for himself would be the speediest oblivion both of his person and his works. If, on the other hand, he has been right; if, like his great predecessors, he has read truly the tendencies of this modern age of ours, and his teaching is authenticated by facts, then Carlyle, too, will take his place among the inspired seers."

To which I add an amendment that under no circumstances, and no matter how completely time and events disprove his lurid vaticinations, should the English-speaking world forget this man, nor fail to hold in honor his unsurpass'd conscience, his unique method, and his honest fame. Never were convictions more earnest and genuine. Never was there less of a flunkey or temporizer. Never had political progressivism a foe it could more heartily respect.

The second main point of Carlyle's utterance was the idea of *duty being done*. (It is simply a new codicil—if it be particularly new, which is by no means certain—on the time-honor'd bequest of dynasticism, the mould-eaten rules of legitimacy and kings.) He seems to have been impatient sometimes to madness when reminded by persons who thought at least as deeply as himself, that this formula, though precious, is rather a vague one, and that there are many other considerations to a philosophical estimate of each and every department either in general history or individual affairs.

Altogether, I don't know anything more amazing than these persistent strides and throbbings so far through our Nineteenth century of perhaps its biggest, sharpest, and most erudite brain, in defiance and discontent with everything; contemptuously ignoring, (either from constitutional inaptitude, ignorance itself, or more likely because he demanded a definite cure-all here and now,) the only solace and solvent to be had.

There is, apart from mere intellect, in the make-up of every superior human identity, (in its moral completeness, considered as *ensemble*, not for that moral alone, but for the whole being, including physique,) a wondrous something that realizes without argument, frequently without what is called education, (though I think it the goal and apex of all education deserving the name)—an intuition of the absolute balance, in time and space, of the whole of this multifarious, mad chaos of fraud, frivolity, hoggishness—this revel of fools, and incredible make-believe and general unsettledness, we call *the world;* a soul-sight of that divine clue and unseen thread which holds the whole congeries of things, all history and time, and all events, however trivial, however momentous, like a leash'd dog in the hand of the hunter. Such soul-sight and root-centre for the mind—mere optimism explains only the surface or fringe of it—Carlyle was mostly, perhaps entirely without. He seems instead to have been haunted in the play of his mental action by a spectre, never entirely laid from first to last, (Greek scholars, I believe, find the same mocking and fantastic apparition attending Aristophanes, his comedies,)—the spectre of world-destruction.

How largest triumph or failure in human life, in war or peace, may depend on some little hidden centrality, hardly more than a drop of blood, a pulse-beat, or a breath of air! It is certain that all these weighty matters, democracy in America, Carlyleism, and the temperament for deepest political or literary exploration, turn on a simple point in speculative philosophy.

The most profound theme that can occupy the mind of man—the problem on whose solution science, art, the bases and pursuits of nations, and everything else, including intelligent human happiness, (here to-day, 1882, New York, Texas, California, the same as all times, all lands,) subtly and finally resting, depends for competent outset and argument, is doubtless involved in the query: What is the fusing explanation and tie—what the relation between the (radical, democratic) Me, the human identity of understanding, emotions, spirit, &c., on the one side, of and with the (conservative) Not Me, the whole of the material objective universe and laws, with what is behind them in time and space, on the other side? Immanuel Kant, though he explain'd, or partially explain'd, as may be said, the laws of the human understanding, left this question an open one. Schelling's answer, or suggestion of answer, is (and very valuable and important, as far as it goes,) that the same general and particular intelligence, passion, even the standards of right and wrong, which exist in a conscious and formulated state in man, exist in an unconscious state, or in perceptible analogies, throughout the entire universe of external Nature, in all its objects large or small, and all its movements and processes—thus making the impalpable human mind, and concrete Nature, notwithstanding their duality and separation, convertible, and in centrality and essence one. But G. F. Hegel's fuller statement of the matter probably remains the last best word that has been said upon it, up to date. Substantially adopting the scheme just epitomized, he so carries it out and fortifies it and merges everything in it, with certain serious gaps now for the first time fill'd, that it becomes a coherent metaphysical system, and substantial answer (as far as there can be any answer) to the foregoing question—a system which, while I distinctly admit that the brain of the future may add to, revise, and even entirely reconstruct, at any rate beams forth to-day, in its entirety, illuminating the thought of the universe, and satisfying the mystery thereof to the human mind, with a more consoling scientific assurance than any yet.

According to Hegel the whole earth, (an old nucleus-thought, as in the Vedas, and no doubt before, but never hitherto brought so absolutely to the front, fully surcharged with modern scientism and facts, and made the sole entrance to each and all,) with its infinite variety, the past, the surroundings of to-day, or what may happen in the future, the contrarieties of material with spiritual, and of natural with artificial, are all, to the eye of the *ensemblist,* but necessary sides and unfoldings, different steps or links, in the endless process of Creative thought, which amid numberless apparent failures and contradictions, is held together by central and never-broken unity—not contradictions or failures at all, but radiations of one consistent and eternal purpose; the whole mass of everything steadily, unerringly tending and flowing toward the permanent *utile* and *morale,* as rivers to oceans. As life is the whole law and incessant effort of the visible universe, and death only the other or invisible side of the same, so the *utile,* so truth, so health, are the continuous-immutable laws of the moral universe, and vice and disease, with all their perturbations, are but transient, even if ever so prevalent expressions.

To politics throughout, Hegel applies the like catholic standard and faith. Not any one party, or any one form of government, is absolutely and exclusively true. Truth consists in the just relations of objects to each other. A majority or democracy may rule as outrageously and do as great harm as an oligarchy or despotism—though far less likely to do so. But the great evil is either a violation of the relations just referr'd to, or of the moral law. The specious, the unjust, the cruel, and what is called the unnatural, though not only permitted but in a certain sense, (like shade to light,) inevitable in the divine scheme, are by the whole constitution of that scheme, partial, inconsistent, temporary, and though having ever so great an ostensible majority, are certainly destin'd to failure, after causing great suffering.

Theology, Hegel translates into science.[15] All apparent contradictions in the statement of the Deific nature by different ages, nations, churches, points of view, are but fractional and imperfect expression of one essential unity, from which they all proceed—crude endeavors or distorted parts, to be regarded both as distinct and united. In short (to put it in our own form, or summing up,) that thinker or analyzer or overlooker who by an inscrutable combination of train'd wisdom and natural intuition most fully accepts in perfect faith the moral unity and sanity of the creative scheme, in history, science, and all life and time, present and future, is both the truest cosmical devotee or religioso, and the profoundest philosopher. While he who, by the spell of himself and his circumstance, sees darkness and despair in the sum of the workings of God's providence, and who, in that, denies or prevaricates, is, no matter how much piety plays on his lips, the most radical sinner and infidel.

[15] I am much indebted to J. Gostick's abstract.

I am the more assured in recounting Hegel a little freely here,[16] not only for offsetting the Carlylean letter and spirit—cutting it out all and several from the very roots, and below the roots—but to counterpoise, since the late death and deserv'd apotheosis of Darwin, the tenets of the evolutionists. Unspeakably precious as those are to biology, and henceforth indispensable to a right aim and estimate in study, they neither comprise or explain everything—and the last word or whisper still remains to be breathed, after the utmost of those claims, floating high and forever above them all, and above technical metaphysics. While the contributions which German Kant and Fichte and Schelling and Hegel have bequeath'd to humanity —and which English Darwin has also in his field—are indispensable to the erudition of America's future, I should say that in all of them, and the best of them, when compared with the lightning flashes and flights of the old prophets and *exaltés*, the spiritual poets and poetry of all lands, (as in the Hebrew Bible,) there seems to be, nay certainly is, something lacking —something cold, a failure to satisfy the deepest emotions of the soul—a want of living glow, fondness, warmth, which the old *exaltés* and poets supply, and which the keenest modern philosophers so far do not.

Upon the whole, and for our purposes, this man's name certainly belongs on the list with the just-specified, first-class moral physicians of our current era—and with Emerson and two or three others—though his prescription is drastic, and perhaps destructive, while theirs is assimilating, normal and tonic. Feudal at the core, and mental offspring and radiation of feudalism as are his books, they afford ever-valuable lessons and affinities to democratic America. Nations or individuals,

---

[16] I have deliberately repeated it all, not only in offset to Carlyle's ever-lurking pessimism and world-decadence, but as presenting the most thoroughly *American points of view* I know. In my opinion the above formulas of Hegel are an essential and crowning justification of New World democracy in the creative realms of time and space. There is that about them which only the vastness, the multiplicity and the vitality of America would seem able to comprehend, to give scope and illustration to, or to be fit for, or even originate. It is strange to me that they were born in Germany, or in the old world at all. While a Carlyle, I should say, is quite the legitimate European product to be expected.

we surely learn deepest from unlikeness, from a sincere oppo-
nent, from the light thrown even scornfully on dangerous spots
and liabilities. (Michel Angelo invoked heaven's special protection against his friends and affectionate flatterers; palpable
foes he could manage for himself.) In many particulars Carlyle
was indeed, as Froude terms him, one of those far-off Hebraic
utterers, a new Micah or Habbakuk. His words at times bubble
forth with abysmic inspiration. Always precious, such men;
as precious now as any time. His rude, rasping, taunting, contradictory tones—what ones are more wanted amid the supple,
polish'd, money-worshipping, Jesus-and-Judas-equalizing, suffrage-sovereignty echoes of current America? He has lit up our
Nineteenth century with the light of a powerful, penetrating,
and perfectly honest intellect of the first-class, turn'd on British
and European politics, social life, literature, and representative
personages—thoroughly dissatisfied with all, and mercilessly
exposing the illness of all. But while he announces the malady,
and scolds and raves about it, he himself, born and bred in
the same atmosphere, is a mark'd illustration of it.

A Couple of Old Friends—
a Coleridge Bit

Latter April.—Have run down in my country haunt for a
couple of days, and am spending them by the pond. I had
already discover'd my kingfisher here (but only one—the mate
not here yet.) This fine bright morning, down by the creek, he
has come out for a spree, circling, flirting, chirping at a round
rate. While I am writing these lines he is disporting himself in
scoots and rings over the wider parts of the pond, into whose
surface he dashes, once or twice making a loud *souse*—the
spray flying in the sun—beautiful! I see his white and dark-gray
plumage and peculiar shape plainly, as he has deign'd to come
very near me. The noble, graceful bird! Now he is sitting on
the limb of an old tree, high up, bending over the water—seems
to be looking at me while I memorandize. I almost fancy he
knows me. *Three days later.*—My second kingfisher is here

with his (or her) mate. I saw the two together flying and whirling around. I had heard, in the distance, what I thought was the clear rasping staccato of the birds several times already— but I couldn't be sure the notes came from both until I saw them together. To-day, at noon they appear'd, but apparently either on business, or for a little limited exercise only. No wild frolic now, full of free fun and motion, up and down for an hour. Doubtless, now they have cares, duties, incubation responsibilities. The frolics are deferr'd till summer-close.

I don't know as I can finish to-day's memorandum better than with Coleridge's lines, curiously appropriate in more ways than one:

"All Nature seems at work—slugs leave their lair,
The bees are stirring—birds are on the wing,
And winter, slumbering in the open air,
Wears on his smiling face a dream of spring;
And I, the while, the sole unbusy thing,
Nor honey make, nor pair, nor build, nor sing."

A Week's Visit to Boston

May 1, '81.—Seems as if all the ways and means of American travel to-day had been settled, not only with reference to speed and directness, but for the comfort of women, children, invalids, and old fellows like me. I went on by a through train that runs daily from Washington to the Yankee metropolis without change. You get in a sleeping-car soon after dark in Philadelphia, and after ruminating an hour or two, have your bed made up if you like, draw the curtains, and go to sleep in it—fly on through Jersey to New York—hear in your half-slumbers a dull jolting and bumping sound or two—are unconsciously toted from Jersey city by a midnight steamer around the Battery and under the big bridge to the track of the New Haven road—resume your flight eastward, and early the next morning you wake up in Boston. All of which was my experience. I wanted to go to the Revere house. A tall unknown gentleman, (a fellow-passenger on his way to Newport he told me, I had just chatted a few moments before with him,) assisted me out through the depot crowd, procured a hack, put me in it with my traveling bag, saying smilingly and quietly, "Now I want you to let this be *my* ride," paid the driver, and before I could remonstrate bow'd himself off.

The occasion of my jaunt, I suppose I had better say here, was for a public reading of "the death of Abraham Lincoln" essay, on the sixteenth anniversary of that tragedy; which reading duly came off, night of April 15. Then I linger'd a week in Boston—felt pretty well (the mood propitious, my paralysis lull'd)—went around everywhere, and saw all that was to be seen, especially human beings. Boston's immense material growth—commerce, finance, commission stores, the plethora of goods, the crowded streets and sidewalks—made of course the first surprising show. In my trip out West, last year, I thought the wand of future prosperity, future empire, must soon surely be wielded by St. Louis, Chicago, beautiful Denver, perhaps San Francisco; but I see the said wand stretch'd out just as decidedly in Boston, with just as much certainty of staying; evidences of copious capital—indeed no centre of the New World ahead of it, (half the big railroads in the West are built with Yankees' money, and they take the dividends.) Old Boston with its zigzag streets and multitudinous angles, (crush up a sheet of letter-paper in your hand, throw it down, stamp it flat, and that is a map of old Boston)—new Boston with its miles upon miles of large and costly houses—Beacon street, Commonwealth avenue, and a hundred others. But the best new departures and expansions of Boston, and of all the cities of New England, are in another direction.

The Boston of To-day

In the letters we get from Dr. Schliemann (interesting but fishy) about his excavations there in the far-off Homeric area, I notice cities, ruins, &c., as he digs them out of their graves, are certain to be in layers—that is to say, upon the foundation of an old concern, very far down indeed, is always another city or set of ruins, and upon that another superadded—and sometimes upon that still another—each representing either a long or rapid stage of growth and development, different from its predecessor, but unerringly growing out of and resting on it. In the moral, emotional, heroic, and human growths, (the main of a race in my opinion,) something of this kind has certainly taken place in Boston. The New England metropolis of to-day may be described as sunny, (there is something else that makes warmth, mastering even winds and meteorologies, though those are not to be sneez'd at,) joyous, receptive, full of ardor, sparkle, a certain element of yearning, magnificently tolerant, yet not to be fool'd; fond of good eating and drinking—costly in costume as its purse can buy; and all through its best average of houses, streets, people, that subtle something (generally thought to be climate, but it is not—it is something indefinable in the *race*, the turn of its development) which effuses behind the whirl of animation, study, business, a happy and joyous public spirit, as distinguish'd from a sluggish and saturnine one. Makes me think of the glints we get (as in Symond's books) of the jolly old Greek cities. Indeed there is a good deal of the Hellenic in B., and the people are getting handsomer too— padded out, with freer motions, and with color in their faces. I never saw (although this is not Greek) so many *fine-looking gray hair'd women*. At my lecture I caught myself pausing more than once to look at them, plentiful everywhere through the audience—healthy and wifely and motherly, and wonderfully charming and beautiful—I think such as no time or land but ours could show.

My Tribute to Four Poets

April 16.—A short but pleasant visit to Longfellow. I am not one of the calling kind, but as the author of "Evangeline" kindly took the trouble to come and see me three years ago in Camden, where I was ill, I felt not only the impulse of my own pleasure on that occasion, but a duty. He was the only particular eminence I called on in Boston, and I shall not soon forget his lit-up face and glowing warmth and courtesy, in the modes of what is called the old school.

And now just here I feel the impulse to interpolate something about the mighty four who stamp this first American century with its birthmarks of poetic literature. In a late magazine one of my reviewers, who ought to know better, speaks of my "attitude of contempt and scorn and intolerance" toward the leading poets—of my "deriding" them, and preaching their "uselessness." If anybody cares to know what I think—and have long thought and avow'd—about them, I am entirely willing to propound. I can't imagine any better luck befalling these States for a poetical beginning and initiation than has come from Emerson, Longfellow, Bryant, and Whittier. Emerson, to me, stands unmistakably at the head, but for the others I am at a loss where to give any precedence. Each illustrious, each rounded, each distinctive. Emerson for his sweet, vital-tasting melody, rhym'd philosophy, and poems as amber-clear as the honey of the wild bee he loves to sing. Longfellow for rich color, graceful forms and incidents—all that makes life beautiful and love refined—competing with the singers of Europe on their own ground, and, with one exception, better and finer work than that of any of them. Bryant pulsing the first interior verse-throbs of a mighty world—bard of the river and the wood, ever conveying a taste of open air, with scents as from hayfields, grapes, birch-borders—always lurkingly fond of threnodies—beginning and ending his long career with chants of death, with here and there through all, poems, or passages of poems, touching the highest universal truths, enthusiasms, duties—morals as grim and eternal, if not as stormy and fateful, as anything in Eschylus. While in Whittier, with his special themes—(his outcropping love of heroism and war, for all his Quakerdom, his verses at times like the measur'd step of Cromwell's old veterans)—in Whittier lives the zeal, the moral energy, that founded New England—the splendid rectitude and ardor of Luther, Milton, George Fox—I must not, dare not, say the wilfulness and narrowness—though doubtless the world needs now, and always will need, almost above all, just such narrowness and wilfulness.

Millet's Pictures—Last Items

April 18.—Went out three or four miles to the house of Quincy Shaw, to see a collection of J. F. Millet's pictures. Two rapt hours. Never before have I been so penetrated by this kind of expression. I stood long and long before "the Sower." I believe what the picture-men designate "the first Sower," as the artist executed a second copy, and a third, and, some think, improved in each. But I doubt it. There is something in this that could hardly be caught again—a sublime murkiness and original pent fury. Besides this masterpiece, there were many others, (I shall never forget the simple evening scene, "Watering the Cow,") all inimitable, all perfect as pictures, works of mere art; and then it seem'd to me, with that last impalpable ethic purpose from the artist (most likely unconscious to himself) which I am always looking for. To me all of them told the full story of what went before and necessitated the great French revolution —the long precedent crushing of the masses of a heroic people into the earth, in abject poverty, hunger—every right denied, humanity attempted to be put back for generations—yet Nature's force, titanic here, the stronger and hardier for that repression—waiting terribly to break forth, revengeful—the pressure on the dykes, and the bursting at last—the storming of the Bastille—the execution of the king and queen—the tempest of massacres and blood. Yet who can wonder?

Could we wish humanity different?
Could we wish the people made of wood or stone?
Or that there be no justice in destiny or time?

The true France, base of all the rest, is certainly in these pictures. I comprehend "Field-People Reposing," "the Diggers," and "the Angelus" in this opinion. Some folks always think of the French as a small race, five or five and a half feet high, and ever frivolous and smirking. Nothing of the sort. The bulk of the personnel of France, before the revolution, was large-sized, serious, industrious as now, and simple. The revolution and Napoleon's wars dwarf'd the standard of human size, but it will come up again. If for nothing else, I should dwell on my brief Boston visit for opening to me the new world of Millet's pictures. Will America ever have such an artist out of her own gestation, body, soul?

Sunday, April 17.—An hour and a half, late this afternoon, in silence and half light, in the great nave of Memorial hall, Cambridge, the walls thickly cover'd with mural tablets, bearing the names of students and graduates of the university who fell in the secession war.

April 23.—It was well I got away in fair order, for if I had staid another week I should have been killed with kindness, and with eating and drinking.

Birds—and a Caution

May 14.—Home again; down temporarily in the Jersey woods. Between 8 and 9 A.M. a full concert of birds, from different quarters, in keeping with the fresh scent, the peace, the naturalness all around me. I am lately noticing the russet-back, size of the robin or a trifle less, light breast and shoulders, with irregular dark stripes—tail long—sits hunch'd up by the hour these days, top of a tall bush, or some tree, singing blithely. I often get near and listen, as he seems tame; I like to watch the working of his bill and throat, the quaint sidle of his body, and flex of his long tail. I hear the woodpecker, and night and early morning the shuttle of the whip-poor-will—noons, the gurgle of thrush delicious, and *meo-o-ow* of the cat-bird. Many I cannot name; but I do not very particularly seek information. (You must not know too much, or be too precise or scientific about birds and trees and flowers and water-craft; a certain free margin, and even vagueness—perhaps ignorance, credulity —helps your enjoyment of these things, and of the sentiment of feather'd, wooded, river, or marine Nature generally. I repeat it—don't want to know too exactly, or the reasons why. My own notes have been written off-hand in the latitude of middle New Jersey. Though they describe what I saw—what appear'd to me—I dare say the expert ornithologist, botanist or entomologist will detect more than one slip in them.)

Samples of My Common-Place Book

I ought not to offer a record of these days, interests, recuperations, without including a certain old, well-thumb'd common-place book,[17] filled with favorite excerpts, I carried in my pocket for three summers, and absorb'd over and over again, when the mood invited. I find so much in having a poem or fine suggestion sink into me (a little then goes a great ways) prepar'd by these vacant-sane and natural influences.

[17]*Samples of my common-place book down at the creek :*
I have—says old Pindar—many swift arrows in my quiver which speak to the wise, though they need an interpreter to the thoughtless.
Such a man as it takes ages to make, and ages to understand.
—H. D. Thoreau.
If you hate a man, don't kill him, but let him live.—*Buddhistic.*
Famous swords are made of refuse scraps, thought worthless.
Poetry is the only verity—the expression of a sound mind speaking after the ideal—and not after the apparent.—*Emerson.*
The form of oath among the Shoshone Indians is, "The earth hears me. The sun hears me. Shall I lie?"
The true test of civilization is not the census, nor the size of cities, nor the crops—no, but the kind of a man the country turns out.
—Emerson.

> The whole wide ether is the eagle's sway:
> The whole earth is a brave man's fatherland.—*Euripides.*

> Spices crush'd, their pungence yield,
>   Trodden scents their sweets respire;
> Would you have its strength reveal'd?
>   Cast the incense in the fire.

Matthew Arnold speaks of "the huge Mississippi of falsehood called History."

> The wind blows north, the wind blows south,
>   The wind blows east and west;
> No matter how the free wind blows,
>   Some ship will find it best.

Preach not to others what they should eat, but eat as becomes you, and be silent.—*Epictetus.*
Victor Hugo makes a donkey meditate and apostrophize thus:

> My brother, man, if you would know the truth,
> We both are by the same dull walls shut in;
> The gate is massive and the dungeon strong.
> But you look through the key-hole out beyond,
> And call this knowledge; yet have not at hand
> The key wherein to turn the fatal lock.

"William Cullen Bryant surprised me once," relates a writer in a New York paper, "by saying that prose was the natural language of composition, and he wonder'd how anybody came to write poetry."

> Farewell ! I did not know thy worth;
>   But thou art gone, and now 'tis prized:
> So angels walk'd unknown on earth,
>   But when they flew were recognized.—*Hood.*

John Burroughs, writing of Thoreau, says: "He improves with age—in fact requires age to take off a little of his asperity, and fully ripen him. The world likes a good hater and refuser almost as well as it likes a good lover and accepter—only it likes him farther off."

Louise Michel at the burial of Blanqui, (1881)
Blanqui drill'd his body to subjection to his grand conscience and his noble passions, and commencing as a young man, broke with all that is sybaritish in modern civilization. Without the power to sacrifice self, great ideas will never bear fruit.

> Out of the leaping furnace flame
> A mass of molten silver came;
> Then, beaten into pieces three,
> Went forth to meet its destiny.
> The first a crucifix was made,
> Within a soldier's knapsack laid;
> The second was a locket fair,
> Where a mother kept her dead child's hair;
> The third—a bangle, bright and warm,
> Around a faithless woman's arm.

> A mighty pain to love it is,
> And 'tis a pain that pain to miss;

My Native Sand and Salt Once More

July 25, '81.—Far Rockaway, L. I.—A good day here, on a
jaunt, amid the sand and salt, a steady breeze setting in from
the sea, the sun shining, the sedge-odor, the noise of the surf,

---

> But of all pain the greatest pain,
> It is to love, but love in vain.

Maurice F. Egan on De Guérin

> A pagan heart, a Christian soul had he,
>   He follow'd Christ, yet for dead Pan he sigh'd,
>   Till earth and heaven met within his breast:
> As if Theocritus in Sicily
>   Had come upon the Figure crucified,
>   And lost his gods in deep, Christ-given rest.

> And if I pray, the only prayer
>   That moves my lips for me,
> Is, leave the mind that now I bear,
>   And give me Liberty.—*Emily Brontë.*

> I travel on not knowing,
>   I would not if I might;
> I would rather walk with God in the dark,
>   Then go alone in the light;
> I would rather walk with Him by faith
>   Than pick my way by sight.

Prof. Huxley in a late lecture

I myself agree with the sentiment of Thomas Hobbes, of Malmes-
bury, that "the scope of all speculation is the performance of some
action or thing to be done." I have not any very great respect for,
or interest in, mere "knowing," as such.

Prince Metternich

Napoleon was of all men in the world the one who most profoundly
despised the race. He had a marvellous insight into the weaker sides
of human nature, (and all our passions are either foibles themselves,
or the cause of foibles.) He was a very small man of imposing
character. He was ignorant, as a sub-lieutenant generally is: a remarkable instinct supplied the lack of knowledge. From his mean opinion
of men, he never had any anxiety lest he should go wrong. He
ventur'd everything, and gain'd thereby an immense step toward
success. Throwing himself upon a prodigious arena, he amaz'd the
world, and made himself master of it, while others cannot even get
so far as being masters of their own hearth. Then he went on and
on, until he broke his neck.

a mixture of hissing and booming, the milk-white crests curling over. I had a leisurely bath and naked ramble as of old, on the warm-gray shore-sands, my companions off in a boat in deeper water—(I shouting to them Jupiter's menaces against the gods, from Pope's Homer.)

July 28—to Long Branch.—8½ A.M., on the steamer "Plymouth Rock," foot of 23d Street, New York, for Long Branch. Another fine day, fine sights, the shores, the shipping and bay —everything comforting to the body and spirit of me. (I find the human and objective atmosphere of New York city and Brooklyn more affiliative to me than any other.) *An hour later* —Still on the steamer, now sniffing the salt very plainly—the long pulsating *swash* as our boat steams seaward—the hills of Navesink and many passing vessels—the air the best part of all. At Long Branch the bulk of the day, stopt at a good hotel, took all very leisurely, had an excellent dinner, and then drove for over two hours about the place, especially Ocean avenue, the finest drive one can imagine, seven or eight miles right along the beach. In all directions costly villas, palaces, millionaires— (but few among them I opine like my friend George W. Childs, whose personal integrity, generosity, unaffected simplicity, go beyond all worldly wealth.)

Hot Weather New York

August.—In the big city awhile. Even the height of the dog-days, there is a good deal of fun about New York, if you only a-void fluster, and take all the buoyant wholesomeness that offers. More comfort, too, than most folks think. A middle-aged man, with plenty of money in his pocket, tells me that he has been off for a month to all the swell places, has disburs'd a small fortune, has been hot and out of kilter everywhere, and has return'd home and lived in New York city the last two weeks quite contented and happy. People forget when it is hot here, it is generally hotter still in other places. New York is so situated, with the great ozonic brine on both sides, it comprises the most favorable health-chances in the world. (If only the suffocating crowding of some of its tenement houses could be broken up.) I find I never sufficiently realized how beautiful are the upper two-thirds of Manhattan island. I am stopping at Mott Haven, and have been familiar now for ten days with the region above One-hundredth street, and along the Harlem river and Washington heights. Am dwelling a few days with my friends, Mr. and Mrs. J. H. J., and a merry housefull of young ladies. Am putting the last touches on the printer's copy of my new volume of "Leaves of Grass"—the completed book at last. Work at it two or three hours, and then go down and loaf along the Harlem river; have just had a good spell of this recreation. The sun sufficiently veil'd, a soft south breeze, the river full of small or large shells (light taper boats) darting up and down, some singly, now and then long ones with six or eight young fellows practicing—very inspiriting sights. Two fine yachts lie anchor'd off the shore. I linger long, enjoying the sundown, the glow, the streak'd sky, the heights, distances, shadows.

Aug. 10.—As I haltingly ramble an hour or two this forenoon by the more secluded parts of the shore, or sit under an old cedar half way up the hill, the city near in view, many young parties gather to bathe or swim, squads of boys, generally twos or threes, some larger ones, along the sand-bottom, or off an old pier close by. A peculiar and pretty carnival—at its height a hundred lads or young men, very democratic, but all decent behaving. The laughter, voices, calls, responses—the springing and diving of the bathers from the great string-piece of the decay'd pier, where climb or stand long ranks of them, naked, rose-color'd with movements, postures ahead of any sculpture. To all this, the sun, so bright, the dark-green shadow of the hills the other side, the amber-rolling waves, changing as the tide comes into a transparent tea-color—the frequent splash of the playful boys, sousing—the glittering drops sparkling, and the good western breeze blowing.

"Custer's Last Rally"

Went to-day to see this just-finish'd painting by John Mulvany, who has been out in far Dakota, on the spot, at the forts, and among the frontiersmen, soldiers and Indians, for the last two years, on purpose to sketch it in from reality, or the best that could be got of it. Sat for over an hour before the picture, completely absorb'd in the first view. A vast canvas, I should say twenty or twenty-two feet by twelve, all crowded, and yet not crowded, conveying such a vivid play of color, it takes a little time to get used to it. There are no tricks; there is no throwing of shades in masses; it is all at first painfully real, overwhelming, needs good nerves to look at it. Forty or fifty figures, perhaps more, in full finish and detail in the mid-ground, with three times that number, or more, through the rest—swarms upon swarms of savage Sioux, in their war-bonnets, frantic, mostly on ponies, driving through the back-ground, through the smoke, like a hurricane of demons. A dozen of the figures are wonderful. Altogether a western, autochthonic phase of America, the frontiers, culminating, typical, deadly, heroic to the uttermost—nothing in the books like it, nothing in Homer, nothing in Shakespere; more grim and sublime than either, all native, all our own, and all a fact. A great lot of muscular, tan-faced men, brought to bay under terrible circumstances—death ahold of them, yet every man undaunted, not one losing his head, wringing out every cent of the pay before they sell their lives. Custer (his hair cut short) stands in the middle, with dilated eye and extended arm, aiming a huge cavalry pistol. Captain Cook is there, partially wounded, blood on the white handkerchief around his head, aiming his carbine coolly, half kneeling—(his body was after-wards found close by Custer's.) The slaughter'd or half-slaughter'd horses, for breastworks, make a peculiar feature. Two dead Indians, herculean, lie in the foreground, clutching their Winchester rifles, very characteristic. The many soldiers, their faces and attitudes, the carbines, the broad-brimm'd hats, the powder-smoke in puffs, the dying horses with their rolling eyes almost human in their agony, the clouds of war-bonneted Sioux in the background, the figures of Custer and Cook—with indeed the whole scene, dreadful, yet with an attraction and beauty that will remain in my memory. With all its color and fierce action, a certain Greek continence pervades it. A sunny sky and clear light envelop all. There is an almost entire absence of the stock traits of European war pictures. The physiognomy of the work is realistic and Western. I only saw it for an hour or so; but it needs to be seen many times—needs to be studied over and over again. I could look on such a work at brief intervals all my life without tiring; it is very tonic to me; then it has an ethic purpose below all, as all great art must have. The artist said the sending of the picture abroad, probably to London, had been talk'd of. I advised him if it went abroad to take it to Paris. I think they might appreciate it there—nay, they certainly would. Then I would like to show Messieur Crapeau that some things can be done in America as well as others.

Some Old Acquaintances—Memories

Aug. 16.—"Chalk a big mark for to-day," was one of the sayings of an old sportsman-friend of mine, when he had had unusually good luck—come home thoroughly tired, but with satisfactory results of fish or birds. Well, to-day might warrant such a mark for me. Everything propitious from the start. An hour's fresh stimulation, coming down ten miles of Manhattan island by railroad and 8 o'clock stage. Then an excellent breakfast at Pfaff's restaurant, 24th street. Our host himself, an old friend of mine, quickly appear'd on the scene to welcome me and bring up the news, and, first opening a big fat bottle of the best wine in the cellar, talk about ante-bellum times, '59 and '60, and the jovial suppers at his then Broadway place, near Bleecker street. Ah, the friends and names and frequenters, those times, that place. Most are dead—Ada Clare, Wilkins, Daisy Sheppard, O'Brien, Henry Clapp, Stanley, Mullin, Wood, Brougham, Arnold—all gone. And there Pfaff and I, sitting opposite each other at the little table, gave a remembrance to them in a style they would have themselves fully confirm'd,

namely, big, brimming, fill'd-up champagne-glasses, drain'd
in abstracted silence, very leisurely, to the last drop. (Pfaff is
a generous German *restaurateur*, silent, stout, jolly, and I
should say the best selector of champagne in America.)

A Discovery of Old Age

Perhaps the best is always cumulative. One's eating and drinking one wants fresh, and for the nonce, right off, and have done
with it—but I would not give a straw for that person or poem,
or friend, or city, or work of art, that was not more grateful
the second time than the first—and more still the third. Nay,
I do not believe any grandest eligibility ever comes forth at
first. In my own experience, (persons, poems, places, characters,) I discover the best hardly ever at first, (no absolute rule
about it, however,) sometimes suddenly bursting forth, or
stealthily opening to me, perhaps after years of unwitting famil-
iarity, unappreciation, usage.

A Visit, at the Last, to R. W. Emerson

Concord, Mass.—Out here on a visit—elastic, mellow, Indian-
summery weather. Came to-day from Boston, (a pleasant ride
of 40 minutes by steam, through Somerville, Belmont, Waltham,
Stony Brook, and other lively towns,) convoy'd by my friend
F. B. Sanborn, and to his ample house, and the kindness and
hospitality of Mrs. S. and their fine family. Am writing this
under the shade of some old hickories and elms, just after
4 P.M., on the porch, within a stone's throw of the Concord
river. Off against me, across stream, on a meadow and side-
hill, haymakers are gathering and wagoning-in probably their
second or third crop. The spread of emerald-green and brown,
the knolls, the score or two of little haycocks dotting the meadow, the loaded-up wagons, the patient horses, the slow-strong
action of the men and pitchforks—all in the just-waning after-

noon, with patches of yellow sun-sheen, mottled by long shadows—a cricket shrilly chirping, herald of the dusk—a boat with two figures noiselessly gliding along the little river, passing under the stone bridge-arch—the slight settling haze of aerial moisture, the sky and the peacefulness expanding in all directions and overhead—fill and soothe me.

Same evening.—Never had I a better piece of luck befall me: a long and blessed evening with Emerson, in a way I couldn't have wish'd better or different. For nearly two hours he has been placidly sitting where I could see his face in the best light, near me. Mrs. S.'s back-parlor well fill'd with people, neighbors, many fresh and charming faces, women, mostly young, but some old. My friend A. B. Alcott and his daughter Louisa were there early. A good deal of talk, the subject Henry Thoreau—some new glints of his life and fortunes, with letters to and from him—one of the best by Margaret Fuller, others by Horace Greeley, Channing, &c.—one from Thoreau himself, most quaint and interesting. (No doubt I seem'd very stupid to the room-full of company, taking hardly any part in the conversation; but I had "my own pail to milk in," as the Swiss proverb puts it.) My seat and the relative arrangement were such that, without being rude, or anything of the kind, I could just look squarely at E., which I did a good part of the two hours. On entering, he had spoken very briefly and politely to several of the company, then settled himself in his chair, a trifle push'd back, and, though a listener and apparently an alert one, remain'd silent through the whole talk and discussion. A lady friend quietly took a seat next him, to give special attention. A good color in his face, eyes clear, with the well-known expression of sweetness, and the old clear-peering aspect quite the same.

Next Day.—Several hours at E.'s house, and dinner there. An old familiar house, (he has been in it thirty-five years,) with surroundings, furnishment, roominess, and plain elegance and fullness, signifying democratic ease, sufficient opulence, and an admirable old-fashioned simplicity—modern luxury, with its mere sumptuousness and affectation either touch'd lightly upon or ignored altogether. Dinner the same. Of course the best of the occasion (Sunday, September 18, '81) was the sight of E. himself. As just said, a healthy color in the cheeks, and good light in the eyes, cheery expression, and just the amount of talking that best suited, namely, a word or short phrase only where needed, and almost always with a smile. Besides Emerson himself, Mrs. E., with their daughter Ellen, the son Edward and his wife, with my friend F. S. and Mrs. S., and others, relatives and intimates. Mrs. Emerson, resuming the subject of the evening before, (I sat next to her,) gave me further and fuller information about Thoreau, who, years ago, during Mr. E.'s absence in Europe, had lived for some time in the family, by invitation.

Other Concord Notations

Though the evening at Mr. and Mrs. Sanborn's, and the memorable family dinner at Mr. and Mrs. Emerson's, have most pleasantly and permanently fill'd my memory, I must not slight other notations of Concord. I went to the old Manse, walk'd through the ancient garden, enter'd the rooms, noted the quaintness, the unkempt grass and bushes, the little panes in the windows, the low ceilings, the spicy smell, the creepers embowering the light. Went to the Concord battle ground, which is close by, scann'd French's statue, "the Minute Man," read Emerson's poetic inscription on the base, linger'd a long while on the bridge, and stopp'd by the grave of the unnamed British soldiers buried there the day after the fight in April '75. Then riding on, (thanks to my friend Miss M. and her spirited white ponies, she driving them,) a half hour at Hawthorne's and Thoreau's graves. I got out and went up of course on foot, and stood a long while and ponder'd. They lie close together in a pleasant wooded spot well up the cemetery hill, "Sleepy Hollow." The flat surface of the first was densely cover'd by myrtle, with a border of arbor-vitæ, and the other had a brown headstone, moderately elaborate, with inscriptions. By Henry's side lies his brother John, of whom much was expected, but he died young. Then to Walden pond, that beautifully embower'd sheet of water, and spent over an hour there. On the spot in the woods where Thoreau had his solitary house is now quite a cairn of stones, to mark the place; I too carried one and deposited on the heap. As we drove back, saw the "School of Philosophy;" but it was shut up, and I would not have it open'd for me. Near by stopp'd at the house of W. T. Harris, the Hegelian, who came out, and we had a pleasant chat while I sat in the wagon. I shall not soon forget those Concord drives, and especially that charming Sunday forenoon one with my friend Miss M., and the white ponies.

Boston Common—More of Emerson

Oct. 10–13.—I spend a good deal of time on the Common, these delicious days and nights—every mid-day from 11.30 to about 1—and almost every sunset another hour. I know all the big trees, especially the old elms along Tremont and Beacon streets, and have come to a sociable-silent understanding with most of them, in the sunlit air, (yet crispy-cool enough,) as I saunter along the wide unpaved walks. Up and down this breadth by Beacon street, between these same old elms, I walk'd for two hours, of a bright sharp February mid-day twenty-one years ago, with Emerson, then in his prime, keen, physically and morally magnetic, arm'd at every point, and when he chose, wielding the emotional just as well as the intellectual. During those two hours he was the talker and I the listener. It was an argument-statement, reconnoitring, review, attack, and pressing home, (like an army corps in order, artillery, cavalry, infantry,) of all that could be said against that part (and a main part) in the construction of my poems, "Children of Adam." More precious than gold to me that dissertation—it afforded me, ever after, this strange and paradoxical lesson; each point of E.'s statement was unanswerable, no judge's charge ever more complete or convincing, I could never hear the points better put—and then I felt down in my soul the clear and unmistakable conviction to disobey all, and pursue my own way. "What have you to say then to such things?" said E., pausing in conclusion. "Only that while I can't answer them at all, I feel more settled than ever to adhere to my own theory, and exemplify it," was my candid response. Whereupon we went and had a good dinner at the American House. And thenceforward I never waver'd or was touch'd with qualms, (as I confess I had been two or three times before).

An Ossianic Night—Dearest Friends

Nov. '81.—Again back in Camden. As I cross the Delaware in long trips to-night, between 9 and 11, the scene overhead is a peculiar one—swift sheets of flitting vapor-gauze, follow'd by dense clouds throwing an inky pall on everything. Then a spell of that transparent steel-gray black sky I have noticed under similar circumstances, on which the moon would beam for a few moments with calm lustre, throwing down a broad dazzle of highway on the waters; then the mists careering again. All silently, yet driven as if by the furies they sweep along, sometimes quite thin, sometimes thicker—a real Ossianic night—amid the whirl, absent or dead friends, the old, the past, somehow tenderly suggested—while the Gael-strains chant themselves from the mists—["Be thy soul blest, O Carril! in the midst of thy eddying winds. O that thou would'st come to my hall when I am alone by night! And thou dost come, my friend. I hear often thy light hand on my harp, when it hangs on the distant wall, and the feeble sound touches my ear. Why dost thou not speak to me in my grief, and tell me when I shall behold my friends? But thou passest away in thy murmuring blast; the wind whistles through the gray hairs of Ossian."]

But most of all, those changes of moon and sheets of hurrying vapor and black clouds, with the sense of rapid action in weird silence, recall the far-back Erse belief that such above were the preparations for receiving the wraiths of just-slain warriors—["We sat that night in Selma, round the strength of the shell. The wind was abroad in the oaks. The spirit of the mountain roar'd. The blast came rustling through the hall, and gently touch'd my harp. The sound was mournful and low, like the song of the tomb. Fingal heard it the first. The crowded sighs of his bosom rose. Some of my heroes are low, said the gray-hair'd king of Morven. I hear the sound of death on the harp. Ossian, touch the trembling string. Bid the sorrow rise, that their spirits may fly with joy to Morven's woody hills. I touch'd the harp before the king; the sound was mournful and low. Bend forward from your clouds, I said, ghosts of my fathers! bend. Lay by the red terror of your course. Receive the falling chief; whether he comes from a distant land, or rises from the rolling sea. Let his robe of mist be near; his spear that is form'd of a cloud. Place a half-extinguish'd meteor by his side, in the form of a hero's sword. And oh! let his countenance be lovely, that his friends may delight in his presence. Bend from your clouds, I said, ghosts of my fathers, bend. Such was my song in Selma, to the lightly trembling harp."]

How or why I know not, just at the moment, but I too muse and think of my best friends in their distant homes—of William O'Connor, of Maurice Bucke, of John Burroughs, and of Mrs. Gilchrist—friends of my soul—stanchest friends of my other soul, my poems.

Only a New Ferry Boat

Jan. 12, '82.—Such a show as the Delaware presented an hour before sundown yesterday evening, all along between Philadelphia and Camden, is worth weaving into an item. It was full tide, a fair breeze from the southwest, the water of a pale tawny color, and just enough motion to make things frolicsome and lively. Add to these an approaching sunset of unusual splendor, a broad tumble of clouds, with much golden haze and profusion of beaming shaft and dazzle. In the midst of all, in the clear drab of afternoon light, there steam'd up the river the large, new boat, "the Wenonah," as pretty an object as you could wish to see, lightly and swiftly skimming along, all trim and white, cover'd with flags, transparent red and blue, streaming out in the breeze. Only a new ferry-boat, and yet in its fitness comparable with the prettiest product of Nature's cunning, and rivaling it. High up in the transparent ether gracefully balanced and circled four or five great sea hawks, while here below, amid the pomp and picturesqueness of sky and river, swam this creation of artificial beauty and motion and power, in its way no less perfect.

Death of Longfellow

Camden, April 3, '82.—I have just return'd from an old forest haunt, where I love to go occasionally away from parlors, pavements, and the newspapers and magazines—and where, of a clear forenoon, deep in the shade of pines and cedars and a tangle of old laurel-trees and vines, the news of Longfellow's death first reach'd me. For want of anything better, let me lightly twine a sprig of the sweet ground-ivy trailing so plentifully through the dead leaves at my feet, with reflections of that half hour alone, there in the silence, and lay it as my contribution on the dead bard's grave.

Longfellow in his voluminous works seems to me not only to be eminent in the style and forms of poetical expression that mark the present age, (an idiosyncrasy, almost a sickness, of verbal melody,) but to bring what is always dearest as poetry to the general human heart and taste, and probably must be so in the nature of things. He is certainly the sort of bard and counteractant most needed for our materialistic, self-assertive, money-worshipping, Anglo-Saxon races, and especially for the present age in America—an age tyrannically regulated with reference to the manufacturer, the merchant, the financier, the politician and the day workman—for whom and among whom he comes as the poet of melody, courtesy, deference—poet of the mellow twilight of the past in Italy, Germany, Spain, and in Northern Europe—poet of all sympathetic gentleness—and universal poet of women and young people. I should have to think long if I were ask'd to name the man who has done more, and in more valuable directions, for America.

I doubt if there ever was before such a fine intuitive judge and selecter of poems. His translations of many German and Scandinavian pieces are said to be better than the vernaculars.

He does not urge or lash. His influence is like good drink or air. He is not tepid either, but always vital, with flavor, motion, grace. He strikes a splendid average, and does not sing exceptional passions, or humanity's jagged escapades. He is not revolutionary, brings nothing offensive or new, does not deal hard blows. On the contrary, his songs soothe and heal, or if they excite, it is a healthy and agreeable excitement. His very anger is gentle, is at second hand, (as in the "Quadroon Girl" and the "Witnesses.")

There is no undue element of pensiveness in Longfellow's strains. Even in the early translation, the Manrique, the movement is as of strong and steady wind or tide, holding up and buoying. Death is not avoided through his many themes, but there is something almost winning in his original verses and rendering on that dread subject—as, closing "the Happiest Land" dispute,

> And then the landlord's daughter
> Up to heaven rais'd her hand,
> And said, "Ye may no more contend,
> There lies the happiest land."

To the ungracious complaint-charge of his want of racy nativity and special originality, I shall only say that America and the world may well be reverently thankful—can never be thankful enough—for any such singing-bird vouchsafed out of the centuries, without asking that the notes be different from those of other songsters; adding what I have heard Longfellow himself say, that ere the New World can be worthily original, and announce herself and her own heroes, she must be well saturated with the originality of others, and respectfully consider the heroes that lived before Agamemnon.

Starting Newspapers

Reminiscences—(From the "Camden Courier.")—As I sat taking my evening sail across the Delaware in the staunch ferryboat "Beverly," a night or two ago, I was join'd by two young reporter friends. "I have a message for you," said one of them; "the C. folks told me to say they would like a piece sign'd by your name, to go in their first number. Can you do it for them?" "I guess so," said I; "what might it be about?" "Well, anything on newspapers, or perhaps what you've done yourself, starting them." And off the boys went, for we had reach'd the Philadelphia side. The hour was fine and mild, the bright half-moon shining; Venus, with excess of splendor, just setting in the west, and the great Scorpion rearing its length more than half up in the southeast. As I cross'd leisurely for an hour in the pleasant night-scene, my young friend's words brought up quite a string of reminiscences.

I commenced when I was but a boy of eleven or twelve writing sentimental bits for the old "Long Island Patriot," in Brooklyn; this was about 1832. Soon after, I had a piece or two in George P. Morris's then celebrated and fashionable "Mirror," of New York city. I remember with what half-suppress'd excitement I used to watch for the big, fat, red-faced, slow-moving, very old English carrier who distributed the "Mirror" in Frooklyn; and when I got one, opening and cutting the leaves with trembling figures. How it made my heart double-beat to see *my piece* on the pretty white paper, in nice type.

My first real venture was the "Long Islander," in my own beautiful town of Huntington, in 1839. I was about twenty years old. I had been teaching country school for two or three years in various parts of Suffolk and Queens counties, but liked printing; had been at it while a lad, learn'd the trade of compositor, and was encouraged to start a paper in the region where I was born. I went to New York, bought a press and types, hired some little help, but did most of the work myself, including the press-work. Everything seem'd turning out well; (only my own restlessness prevented me gradually establishing a permanent property there.) I bought a good horse, and every week went all round the country serving my papers, devoting one day and night to it. I never had happier jaunts—going over to south side, to Babylon, down the south road, across to Smithtown and Comac, and back home. The experiences of those jaunts, the dear old-fashion'd farmers and their wives, the stops by the hay-fields, the hospitality, nice dinners, occasional evenings, the girls, the rides through the brush, come up in my memory to this day.

I next went to the "Aurora" daily in New York city—a sort of free lance. Also wrote regularly for the "Tattler," an evening paper. With these and a little outside work I was occupied off and on, until I went to edit the "Brooklyn Eagle," where for two years I had one of the pleasantest sits of my life—a good owner, good pay, and easy work and hours. The troubles in the Democratic party broke forth about those times (1848–'49) and I split off with the radicals, which led to rows with the boss and "the party," and I lost my place.

Being now out of a job, I was offer'd impromptu, (it happen'd between the acts one night in the lobby of the old Broadway theatre near Pearl street, New York city,) a good chance to go down to New Orleans on the staff of the "Crescent," a daily to be started there with plenty of capital behind it. One of the owners, who was north buying material, met me walking in the lobby, and though that was our first acquaintance, after fifteen minutes' talk (and a drink) we made a formal bargain, and he paid me two hundred dollars down to bind the contract and bear my expenses to New Orleans. I started two days afterwards; had a good leisurely time, as the paper wasn't to be out in three weeks. I enjoy'd my journey and Louisiana life much. Returning to Brooklyn a year or two afterward I started the "Freeman," first as a weekly, then daily. Pretty soon the secession war broke out, and I, too, got drawn in the current southward, and spent the following three years there, (as memorandized preceding.)

Besides starting them as aforementioned, I have had to do, one time or another, during my life, with a long list of papers, at divers places, sometimes under queer circumstances. During the war, the hospitals at Washington, among other means of amusement, printed a little sheet among themselves, surrounded by wounds and death, the "Armory Square Gazette," to which I contributed. The same long afterward, casually, to a paper —I think it was call'd the "Jimplecute"—out in Colorado where I stopp'd at the time. When I was in Quebec province, in Canada, in 1880, I went into the queerest little old French printing office near Tadousac. It was far more primitive and ancient than my Camden friend William Kurtz's place up on Federal street. I remember, as a youngster, several characteristic old printers of a kind hard to be seen these days.

The Great Unrest of Which We Are Part

My thoughts went floating on vast and mystic currents as I sat to-day in solitude and half-shade by the creek—returning mainly to two principal centres. One of my cherish'd themes for a never-achiev'd poem has been the two impetuses of man and the universe—in the latter, creation's incessant unrest,[18] exfoliation. (Darwin's evolution, I suppose.) Indeed what is Nature but change, in all its visible, and still more its invisible processes? Or what is humanity in its faith, love, heroism, poetry, even morals, but *emotion?*

By Emerson's Grave

May 6, '82.—We stand by Emerson's new-made grave without sadness—indeed a solemn joy and faith, almost hauteur—our soul-benison no mere

> "Warrior, rest, thy task is done,"

for one beyond the warriors of the world lies surely symboll'd

---

[18]"Fifty thousand years ago the constellation of the Great Bear or Dipper was a starry cross; a hundred thousand years hence the imaginary Dipper will be upside down, and the stars which form the bowl and handle will have changed places. The misty nebulæ are moving, and besides are whirling around in great spirals, some one way, some another. Every molecule of matter in the whole universe is swinging to and fro; every particle of ether which fills space is in jelly-like vibration. Light is one kind of motion, heat another, electricity another, magnetism another, sound another. Every human sense is the result of motion; every perception, every thought is but motion of the molecules of the brain translated by that incomprehensible thing we call mind. The processes of growth, of existence, of decay, whether in worlds, or in the minutest organisms, are but motion."

here. A just man, poised on himself, all-loving, all-inclosing, and sane and clear as the sun. Nor does it seem so much Emerson himself we are here to honor—it is conscience, simplicity, culture, humanity's attributes at their best, yet applicable if need be to average affairs, and eligible to all. So used are we to suppose a heroic death can only come from out of battle or storm, or mighty personal contest, or amid dramatic incidents or danger, (have we not been taught so for ages by all the plays and poems?) that few even of those who most sympathizingly mourn Emerson's late departure will fully appreciate the ripen'd grandeur of that event, with its play of calm and fitness, like evening light on the sea.

How I shall henceforth dwell on the blessed hours when, not long since, I saw that benignant face, the clear eyes, the silently smiling mouth, the form yet upright in its great age—to the very last, with so much spring and cheeriness, and such an absence of decrepitude, that even the term *venerable* hardly seem'd fitting.

Perhaps the life now rounded and completed in its mortal development, and which nothing can change or harm more, has its most illustrious halo, not in its splendid intellectual or esthetic products, but as forming in its entirety one of the few, (alas! how few!) perfect and flawless excuses for being, of the entire literary class.

We can say, as Abraham Lincoln at Gettysburg, It is not we who come to consecrate the dead—we reverently come to receive, if so it may be, some consecration to ourselves and daily work from him.

At Present Writing—Personal

A letter to a German friend—extract

May 31, '82.—"From to-day I enter upon my 64th year. The paralysis that first affected me nearly ten years ago, has since remain'd, with varying course—seems to have settled quietly down, and will probably continue. I easily tire, am very clumsy, cannot walk far; but my spirits are first-rate. I go around in public almost every day—now and then take long trips, by railroad or boat, hundreds of miles—live largely in the open air—am sun-burnt and stout, (weigh 190)—keep up my activity and interest in life, people, progress, and the questions of the day. About two-thirds of the time I am quite comfortable. What mentality I ever had remains entirely unaffected; though physically I am a half-paralytic, and likely to be so, long as I live. But the principal object of my life seems to have been accomplish'd—I have the most devoted and ardent of friends, and affectionate relatives—and of enemies I really make no account."

After Trying a Certain Book

I tried to read a beautifully printed and scholarly volume on "the Theory of Poetry," received by mail this morning from England—but gave it up at last for a bad job. Here are some capricious pencillings that follow'd, as I find them in my notes:

In youth and maturity Poems are charged with sunshine and varied pomp of day; but as the soul more and more takes precedence, (the sensuous still included,) the Dusk becomes the poet's atmosphere. I too have sought, and ever seek, the brilliant sun, and make my songs according. But as I grow old, the half-lights of evening are far more to me.

The play of Imagination, with the sensuous objects of Nature for symbols, and Faith—with Love and Pride as the unseen impetus and moving-power of all, make up the curious chess-game of a poem.

Common teachers or critics are always asking "What does it mean?" Symphony of fine musician, or sunset, or sea-waves rolling up the beach—what do they mean? Undoubtedly in the most subtle-elusive sense they mean something—as love does, and religion does, and the best poems;—but who shall fathom and define those meanings? (I do not intend this as a warrant for wildness and frantic escapades—but to justify the soul's frequent joy in what cannot be defined to the intellectual part, or to calculation.)

At its best, poetic lore is like what may be heard of conversation in the dusk, from speakers far or hid, of which we get only a few broken murmurs. What is not gather'd is far more—perhaps the main thing.

Grandest poetic passages are only to be taken at free removes, as we sometimes look for stars at night, not by gazing directly toward them, but off one side.

(*To a poetic student and friend.*)—I only seek to put you in rapport. Your own brain, heart, evolution, must not only understand the matter, but largely supply it.

Final Confessions—Literary Tests

So draw near their end these garrulous notes. There have doubtless occurr'd some repetitions, technical errors in the consecutiveness of dates, in the minutiæ of botanical, astronomical, &c., exactness, and perhaps elsewhere;—for in gathering up, writing, peremptorily dispatching copy, this hot weather, (last of July and through August, '82,) and delaying not the printers, I have had to hurry along, no time to spare. But in the deepest veracity of all—in reflections of objects, scenes, Nature's outpourings, to my senses and receptivity, as they seem'd to me —in the work of giving those who care for it, some authentic glints, specimen-days of my life—and in the *bona fide* spirit and relations, from author to reader, on all the subjects design'd, and as far as they go, I feel to make unmitigated claims.

The synopsis of my early life, Long Island, New York city, and so forth, and the diary-jottings in the Secession war, tell their own story. My plan in starting what constitutes most of the middle of the book, was originally for hints and data of a Nature-poem that should carry one's experiences a few hours, commencing at noon-flush, and so through the after-part of the day—I suppose led to such idea by my own life-afternoon now arrived. But I soon found I could move at more ease, by giving the narrative at first hand. (Then there is a humiliating lesson one learns, in serene hours, of a fine day or night. Nature seems to look on all fixed-up poetry and art as something almost impertinent.)

Thus I went on, years following, various seasons and areas, spinning forth my thought beneath the night and stars, (or as I was confined to my room by half-sickness,) or at midday looking out upon the sea, or far north steaming over the Saguenay's black breast, jotting all down in the loosest sort of chronological order, and here printing from my impromptu notes, hardly even the seasons group'd together, or anything corrected—so afraid of dropping what smack of outdoors or sun or starlight might cling to the lines, I dared not try to meddle with or smooth them. Every now and then, (not often, but for a foil,) I carried a book in my pocket—or perhaps tore out from some broken or cheap edition a bunch of loose leaves; most always had something of the sort ready, but only took it out when the mood demanded. In that way, utterly out of reach of literary conventions, I re-read many authors.

I cannot divest my appetite of literature, yet I find myself eventually trying it all by Nature—*first premises* many call it, but really the crowning results of all, laws, tallies and proofs. (Has it never occurr'd to any one how the last deciding tests applicable to a book are entirely outside of technical and grammatical ones, and that any truly first-class production has little or nothing to do with the rules and calibres of ordinary critics? or the bloodless chalk of Allibone's Dictionary? I have fancied the ocean and the daylight, the mountain and the forest, putting their spirit in a judgment on our books. I have fancied some disembodied human soul giving its verdict.)

Nature and Democracy—Morality

Democracy most of all affiliates with the open air, is sunny and hardy and sane only with Nature—just as much as Art is. Something is required to temper both—to check them, restrain them from excess, morbidity. I have wanted, before departure, to bear special testimony to a very old lesson and requisite. American Democracy, in its myriad personalities, in factories, work-shops, stores, offices—through the dense streets and houses of cities, and all their manifold sophisticated life—must either be fibred, vitalized, by regular contact with out-door light and air and growths, farm-scenes, animals, fields, trees, birds, sun-warmth and free skies, or it will certainly dwindle and pale. We cannot have grand races of mechanics, work people, and commonalty, (the only specific purpose of America,) on any less terms. I conceive of no flourishing and heroic elements of Democracy in the United States, or of Democracy maintaining itself at all, without the Nature-element forming a main part—to be its health-element and beauty-element—to really underlie the whole politics, sanity, religion and art of the New World.

Finally, the morality: "Virtue," said Marcus Aurelius, "what is it, only a living and enthusiastic sympathy with Nature?" Perhaps indeed the efforts of the true poets, founders, religions, literatures, all ages, have been, and ever will be, our time and times to come, essentially the same—to bring people back from their persistent strayings and sickly abstractions, to the costless average, divine, original concrete.

Bibliographical Check List

BY GAY WILSON ALLEN

Editions

Leaves of Grass. [First edition.] Brooklyn, N.Y. 1855. 95 pp.

Leaves of Grass. [Second edition.] Brooklyn, N.Y. 1856. 384 pp.

Leaves of Grass. [Third edition.] Boston: Thayer and Eldridge, 1860–61. 456 pp.

Drum-Taps. New York. 1865. 72 pp. *Drum-Taps and Sequel.* 1865. 72 + 24 pp.

Leaves of Grass. [Fourth edition.] New York. 1867. 338 pp.

Democratic Vistas. Washington, D.C. 1871. 84 pp.

Leaves of Grass. [Fifth edition.] Washington, D.C. 1871. 384 pp. *With Passage to India.* 1872. 120 pp.

Leaves of Grass. [Sixth edition.] Camden, N.J. 1876. (Vol. I of Author's Edition of *Complete Works.*)

Two Rivulets. Including *Democratic Vistas, Centennial Songs,* and *Passage to India.* Camden, N.J. 1876. (Vol. II of Author's Edition of *Complete Works.*)

Leaves of Grass. [Seventh edition.] Boston: James R. Osgood and Co., 1881–82. 382 pp. (Reprinted in Philadelphia by Rees Welsh and Co. in 1882 and by David McKay.)

Specimen Days and Collect. Philadelphia: Rees Welsh and Co., 1882–83. 374 pp. (Volume of *Complete Works* as companion to *Leaves of Grass* reprinted by Rees Welsh and Co. in 1882.)

November Boughs. Philadelphia: David McKay, 1888. 140 pp.

Complete Poems and Prose of Walt Whitman, 1855–1888. [Eighth edition of poems, third of *Complete Works.*] Philadelphia: published by the author, 1888. 382 + 374 pp.

Leaves of Grass, with *Sands at Seventy* and *A Backward Glance O'er Travel'd Roads*. [Eighth separate edition of poems.] Philadelphia, 1889. 404 + 18 pp.

Good-Bye, My Fancy. [Second Annex to *Leaves of Grass;* first was "Sands at Seventy" in eighth edition of poems.] Philadelphia: David McKay, 1891. 66 pp.

Leaves of Grass. [Ninth edition.] Philadelphia: David McKay, 1891–92. 438 pp. (Also bound as Vol. I of the fourth edition of *Complete Works* to p. 383, reprint of 1881 edition; new poems annexed pp. 383–422.)

Complete Prose Works. Philadelphia: David McKay, 1892. 522 pp. (Also bound as Vol. II of *Complete Works;* later redated 1894 and 1897.)

Leaves of Grass. [Tenth edition.] Boston: Small, Maynard and Co., 1897. 455 pp. (Includes posthumous poems, "Old Age Echoes.")

The Complete Writings of Walt Whitman. Issued under the editorial supervision of the Literary Executors. New York and London: G. P. Putnam's Sons, 1902. 10 vols.

The Collected Writings of Walt Whitman, under the General Editorship of Gay Wilson Allen and Sculley Bradley, in process of publication by New York University Press. Published to date:

The Correspondence, edited by Edwin Haviland Miller. Vols. I–V (complete). 1961–69.

The Early Poems and the Fiction, edited by Thomas L. Brasher, 1963.

Prose Works 1892, edited by Floyd Stovall: Vol. I: *Specimen Days*, 1963; Vol. II: *Collect and Other Prose*, 1964.

Leaves of Grass: Comprehensive Reader's Edition, edited by Harold W. Blodgett and Sculley Bradley, 1965.
[Future volumes will include a Variorum *Leaves of Grass*, Diaries and Notebooks, Journalistic Writings, and a Bibliography.]

Uncollected Writings (in Order of Publication)

Calamus. A Series of Letters Written during the Years 1868–1880. By Walt Whitman to a Young Friend (Peter Doyle). Ed. by Richard Maurice Bucke, M.D. Boston: Laurens Maynard. 1897. viii, 172 pp.

The Wound Dresser. A Series of Letters Written from the Hospitals in Washington during the War of the Rebellion by Walt Whitman. Ed. by Richard Maurice Bucke, M.D. Boston: Small, Maynard and Co. 1898. viii, 201 pp.

Notes and Fragments. Ed. by Dr. Richard Maurice Bucke. (Printed for private distribution.) London, Ontario, Canada. 1899. 211 pp.

Letters Written by Walt Whitman to His Mother from 1866 to 1872. Ed. by Thomas B. Harned. New York and London: G. P. Putnam's Sons. 1902. 132 pp.

Walt Whitman's Diary in Canada. Ed. by William Sloane Kennedy. Boston: Small, Maynard and Co. 1904. 73 pp.

An American Primer. [Notes on language and style.] Ed. by Horace Traubel. Boston: Small, Maynard and Co. 1904. 35 pp.

The Letters of Anne Gilchrist and Walt Whitman. Ed. by Thomas B. Harned. New York: Doubleday, Page and Co. 1918. 242 pp.

The Gathering of the Forces. [Mainly editorials in the Brooklyn *Daily Eagle* in 1846–47.] Ed. by Cleveland Rodgers and John Black. New York and London: G. P. Putnam's Sons. 1920. 2 vols.

The Uncollected Poetry and Prose of Walt Whitman. [Poems published before *Leaves of Grass* and prose from stories, editorials, reviews, diaries, manuscript notes, etc.] Ed. by Emory Holloway. New York: Doubleday, Page and Co. 1921. 2 vols.

Pictures. An Unpublished Poem by Walt Whitman. Ed. by Emory Holloway. New York: The June House. 1927. London: Faber and Gwyer. 1927. 37 pp.

The Half-Breed and Other Stories. Ed. by Thomas Ollive Mabbott. New York: Columbia University Press. 1927. 129 pp.

Walt Whitman's Workshop. [Speeches, unpublished prefaces, and other fragments in Library of Congress.] Ed. by Clifton J. Furness. Cambridge: Harvard University Press. 1928. 265 pp.

The Eighteenth Presidency. Voice of Walt Whitman to Each Young Man in the Nation, North, South, East and West. Note by Jean Catel. Montpellier, France: Causse, Graille and Castelnau. 1928. 31 pp. (See 1956 edition below.)

A Child's Reminiscence. Ed. by Thomas O. Mabbott and Rollo G. Silver. [First published text and self-written review of the poem "Out of the Cradle . . ."] Seattle: University of Washington Book Store. 1930. 44 pp.

I Sit and Look Out. Editorials from the Brooklyn *Daily Times.* Ed. by Emory Holloway and Vernolian Schwarz. New York: Columbia University Press. 1932. 248 pp.

Walt Whitman and the Civil War. A Collection of Original Articles and Manuscripts. Ed. by Charles I. Glicksberg. Philadelphia: University of Pennsylvania Press. 1933. 201 pp.

New York Dissected. [Newspaper articles of the 1850's.] Ed. by Emory Holloway and Ralph Adimari. New York: Rufus Rockwell Wilson. 1936. 257 pp.

Walt Whitman's Backward Glances . . . [Origin and early versions of the essay.] Ed. by Sculley Bradley and John A. Stevenson. Philadelphia: University of Pennsylvania Press. 1947. 51 pp.

Faint Clews & Indirections: Manuscripts of Walt Whitman and His Family. Ed. by Clarence Gohdes and Rollo G. Silver. Durham: Duke University Press. 1949. 250 pp.

Walt Whitman Looks at the Schools. [Editorials and articles of the 1840's.] Ed. by Florence Bernstein Freedman. New York: King's Crown Press. 1950. 278 pp.

Walt Whitman of the New York Aurora: Editor at Twenty-Two. Ed. by Joseph Jay Rubin and Charles H. Brown. State College, Pennsylvania: Bald Eagle Press. 1950. 148 pp.

Whitman's Manuscripts: Leaves of Grass (1860): A Parallel Text. Ed. by Fredson Bowers. Chicago: University of Chicago Press. 1955. lxxiv, 264 pp.

The Eighteenth Presidency: A Critical Text. Ed. by Edward F. Grier. Lawrence: University of Kansas Press. 1956. 47 pp.

An 1855–56 Notebook: Toward the Second Edition of Leaves of Grass. Introduction and Notes by Harold W. Blodgett. With Foreword by Charles E. Feinberg. Additional Notes by William White. Carbondale: Southern Illinois University Press. 1959. 41 pp.

The Early Poems and the Fiction. Ed. by Thomas L. Brasher. New York: The New York University Press. 1963.

Reprints and Selections

Walt Whitman's Leaves of Grass: The First (1855) Edition. Ed. with an Introduction by Malcolm Cowley. New York: Viking. 1959. 145 pp.

Leaves of Grass. Facsimile Edition of the 1860 Text. With an Introduction by Roy Harvey Pearce. Cornell University Press. 1961. 467 pp.

Walt Whitman's Blue Book: The 1860–61 Leaves of Grass. Containing His Manuscript Additions and Revisions. Ed. by Arthur Golden. Vol. I: Facsimile. Vol. II: Textual Analysis. New York Public Library. 1968.

Walt Whitman's Poems. Selections with Critical Aids. Ed. by Gay Wilson Allen and Charles T. Davis. New York University Press. 1955. 1968.

Whitman. The Laurel Poetry Series. Selected, with an Introduction and Notes, by Leslie A. Fiedler. New York: Dell. 1959.

Books about Whitman

Allen, Gay Wilson. *The Solitary Singer: A Critical Biography of Walt Whitman.* New York: Macmillan. 1955. Grove. 1959. Rev. Ed.: New York University Press. 1967. 616 pp.

———. *Walt Whitman as Man, Poet, and Legend.* With a

Check List of Whitman Publications 1945–60, by Evie Allison Allen. Southern Illinois University Press. 1961. 260 pp.

———. "Walt Whitman: The Man," in *Walt Whitman, Man, Poet, Philosopher: Three Lectures*....Library of Congress. 1955. Pp. 1–14.

Asselineau, Roger. *L'Evolution de Walt Whitman: Après la première édition des Feuilles d'herbe*. Paris: Didier. 1954. 567 pp. *The Evolution of Walt Whitman: The Creation of a Poet*. Harvard University Press. 1960. 376 pp. *The Evolution of Walt Whitman: The Creation of a Book*. Harvard University Press. 1962. 392 pp.

Balzagette, Léon. *Le "Poème-Evangile" de Walt Whitman*. Paris: Mercure de France. 1921. 357 pp.

Beaver, Joseph. *Walt Whitman, Poet of Science*. New York: King's Crown Press. 1951. 178 pp.

Binns, Henry B. *A Life of Walt Whitman*. London: Methuen. 1905. xxviii, 369 pp.

Blodgett, Harold W. *Walt Whitman in England*. Cornell University Press. 1934. 244 pp.

Bucke, Richard M. *Walt Whitman*. Philadelphia: David McKay. 1883. 236 pp.

Burroughs, John. *Notes on Walt Whitman, as Poet and Person*. New York: American News Co. 1867. 108 pp. New York: J. S. Redfield. 1871. 126 pp.

Canby, Henry S. *Walt Whitman, an American: A Study in Biography*. Boston: Houghton Mifflin Co. 1943. 381 pp.

Carpenter, Edward. *Days with Walt Whitman*. New York: Macmillan. 1906. 187 pp.

Catel, Jean. *Walt Whitman: La Naissance du Poète*. Paris: Rieder. 1929. 483 pp.

Chukovskii, Kornei. *Moii Uhtmen* [My Whitman, long biographical-critical Introduction, selected translations, bibliographical notes]. Moscow: State Publishing Co. "Progress." 1966. 271 pp.

Daiches, David. "Walt Whitman: The Philosopher," in *Walt Whitman, Man, Poet, Philosopher: Three Lectures*.... Library of Congress. 1955. Pp. 35–53.

De Selincourt, Basil. *Walt Whitman: A Critical Study.* London: M. Secker. 1914. 250 pp.

Dutton, Geoffrey. *Whitman.* Edinburgh: Oliver and Boyd Ltd. 1961. New York: Grove Press. 1961.

Faner, Robert D. *Walt Whitman & Opera.* University of Pennsylvania Press. 1951. 249 pp.

Holloway, Emory. *Whitman: An Interpretation in Narrative.* New York: Alfred A. Knopf. 1926. 330 pp.

Kennedy, William Sloane. *The Fight of a Book for the World* West Yarmouth, Mass.: Stonecroft Press. 1926. 304 pp.

————. *Reminiscences of Walt Whitman.* London: A. Gardner. 1896. 190 pp.

Miller, James E., Jr. *A Critical Guide to Leaves of Grass.* University of Chicago Press. 1957. 268 pp.

————, Shapiro, Karl, and Slote, Bernice. *Start with the Sun: Studies in Cosmic Poetry.* University of Nebraska Press. 1960.

O'Connor, William D. *The Good Gray Poet: A Vindication.* New York: Bunce & Harrington. 1866. 46 pp.

Perry, Bliss. *Walt Whitman: His Life and Work.* Boston: Houghton Mifflin and Co. 1906. 318 pp.

Schyberg, Frederik. *Walt Whitman.* Copenhagen: Gyldendal. 1933. 349 pp. Translated into English by Evie Allison Allen. Columbia University Press. 1951. 387 pp.

Symonds, John A. *Walt Whitman: A Study.* London: J. C. Nimmo. 1893. xxxv, 160 pp.

Traubel, Horace, ed. *In Re Walt Whitman.* Ed. by Literary Executors. Philadelphia: David McKay. 1893. 452 pp.

————. *With Walt Whitman in Camden.* Vol. I, Boston: Small Maynard. 1906. Vol. II, New York: D. Appleton and Co. 1908. Vol. III, New York: Mitchell Kennerly. 1904. Vol. IV, Philadelphia: University of Pennsylvania Press. 1953. Vol. IV, second issue, Carbondale, Illinois: Southern Illinois University Press. 1959. [Other volumes in process of being edited.]

Van Doren, Mark. "Walt Whitman: The Poet," in *Walt Whitman, Man, Poet, Philosopher: Three Lectures* .... Library of Congress. 1955. Pp. 15–33. Reprinted in *The Happy*

Critic and Other Essays, by Mark Van Doren. New York: Hill and Wang. 1961. Also in *Studies in Leaves of Grass,* ed. by Gay Wilson Allen. Columbus, Ohio: Charles E. Merrill Publishing Co. 1972.

The Walt Whitman Review, Wayne State University Press, Detroit, Michigan, prints scholarly and critical articles on Whitman and lists current publications.

Collections of Criticism

Leaves of Grass: One Hundred Years After. Ed. with introduction by Milton Hindus. Stanford, Cal.: Stanford University Press. 1955. 149 pp.

Studies in Leaves of Grass. Compiled by Gay Wilson Allen. Columbus, Ohio: Charles E. Merrill Publishing Co. 1972. 118 pp.

Walt Whitman. Ed. by Francis Murphy. Harmondsworth, Middlesex, England: Penguin Books Ltd. 1969. 482 pp. (Penguin Critical Anthology series.)

Walt Whitman: The Critical Heritage. Ed. by Milton Hindus. London: Routledge & Kegan Paul. 1971. 292 pp. (Critical Heritage series.)

Walt Whitman in Europe Today. Ed. by Roger Asselineau and William White. Detroit: Wayne State University Press. 1972. 42 pp.

Whitman: A Collection of Critical Essays. Ed. by Roy Harvey Pearce. Englewood Cliffs, N. J.: Prentice-Hall Inc. 1962. 185 pp.